AN
ENCYCLOPEDIA OF
Naval History

AN

ENCYCLOPEDIA OF

Naval History

Anthony Bruce and William Cogar

Checkmark Books™

An imprint of Facts On File, Inc.

An Encyclopedia of Naval History

First paperback printing 1999

Copyright © 1998 by Anthony Bruce

Checkmark Books
An imprint of Facts On File, Inc.
11 Penn Plaza
New York NY 10001

Library of Congress Cataloging-in-Publication Data

Bruce, A. P. C. (Anthony Peter Charles)
    An encyclopedia of naval history / Anthony Bruce and William
Cogar.
        p.   cm.
    Includes bibliographical references and index.
    ISBN 0-8160-2697-1 (HC)
    ISBN 0-8160-4068-0 (pbk)
    1. Naval art and science—History—Encyclopedias. I. Cogar.
William B., 1949– . II. Title.
    V27.B86   1997
    359′.003—dc21   97-7243

Text design by Grace M. Ferrara
Cover design by Nora Wertz

Printed in the United States of America

VB BVC 10 9 8 7 6 5 4 3 2 1
  (pbk) 10 9 8 7 6 5 4 3 2 1

This book is printed on acid-free paper.

CONTENTS

PREFACE

An Encyclopedia of Naval History provides a comprehensive account of world naval history from the beginning of the 16th century to the present day. It aims to make the subject accessible to a wide readership and has as its starting point the period when national navies were being created in Europe at the end of the Middle Ages. The galleon and the broadside gun also emerged at this time and provided the basic equipment of the sailing navies that was to survive for some 300 years until their demise in the mid-19th century. During the last 100 years the pace of change in naval technology has accelerated rapidly. The ironclad ended the long reign of the wooden warship but was itself superseded by the battleship within a few years.

The battleship went through several stages of development within a short period until the all-big-gun dreadnought had become the essential basis of naval power in the period before World War I. The development of air power had a revolutionary impact on naval warfare and soon brought about the demise of the battleship. In World War II the aircraft carrier was the capital ship of the world's navies, but its reign was even shorter. While the carrier remains an important component of major navies, the nuclear-powered submarine is firmly established as the capital ship of contemporary fleets.

Although it dates back to the American War of Independence, the submarine did not come of age until the two world wars. The Axis powers almost succeeded in bringing Britain to its knees using the submarine as a weapon of economic warfare, although in the end they were undermined by effective countermeasures. In the postwar period, the submarine-launched ballistic missile has been responsible for maintaining the nuclear balance of terror between the two superpowers. The contemporary submarine also has assumbed a full range of conventional roles but with increased powers of endurance.

This encyclopedia provides a full account of the far-reaching changes that have occurred in naval warfare over the past 500 years, although changing technology is only one dimension of the book. Other major themes include the key battles, wars, commanders, navies and ships that have shaped the course of naval history across the globe. Although the book contains more than 1,000 A-to-Z entries, its coverage of people and events has necessarily been selective. The aim has been to provide entries for all the major topics under each of these headings. Specific battles and people have been set in the context of the major wars of the period, which provide an overview of the use of naval power and its impact. For reasons of space, the naval role in exploration, scientific research and other noncombatant activity has not been covered in depth, although individual achievements in these areas often are mentioned in the biographies of leading naval commanders.

Many of the topics covered in this encyclopedia are linked by an extensive system of cross-references that indicate where other relevant material may be found. They are identified by small capital letters. A synoptic index groups related entries under broad subject headings, including, for example, ships, navies, battles and wars. Most of the major entries include a guide to further reading on their subject.

Many of these specialist studies, together with a wide range of more general authorities produced by leading naval writers from Alfred Thayer Mahan onward, have been consulted in the course of compiling this encyclopedia. Tribute must also be paid to several pioneering reference works, including H. Pempsel's *Atlas of Naval Warfare*, London, 1977, and *The Oxford Companion to Ships and the Sea*, London, 1979, which have appeared in recent years. Without them this encyclopedia could not have been produced.

Abe, Hiroaki
1890–1949

Japanese vice admiral who led the bombardment groups during the assault on Wake Island, December 8–23, 1941, and at the Battle of MIDWAY, June 1942, in the Pacific during WORLD WAR II, 1939–45. During the opening stages of the naval battle of GUADALCANAL, November 12–13, 1942, he was instructed to bombard Henderson Airfield, the U.S. air base on Guadalcanal, that provided the Americans with local air superiority. As he approached Guadalcanal his force was intercepted by a UNITED STATES NAVY task force under the command of Rear Admiral Daniel CALLAGHAN.

In the night action that followed, two Japanese battleships, a cruiser and 15 destroyers were ranged against a weaker force of four American cruisers and eight destroyers. Abe lost his flagship, the *Hiei* (which was the first Japanese battleship to be sunk in World War II), and two destroyers, while American losses—two cruisers and four destroyers—were less severe. In these circumstances Abe was unable to complete his mission against Guadalcanal and, as a result, was dismissed from his post.

S. E. Morison, *History of United States Naval Operations in World War II*, vol. 5, Boston, 1950.

Aboukir, H.M.S.

The destruction of three British armored CRUISERS—the *Aboukir*, the *Cressy* and the *Hogue*—during the opening stages of WORLD WAR I, 1914–18, was a major blow to British naval prestige. They were all Cressy-class cruisers, built in 1901–3, with a displacement of 12,000 tons and a maximum speed of 21 knots.

The *Aboukir* was torpedoed by the German submarine *U-9* on September 22, 1914, as she patrolled without cruiser protection off the Dutch coast. Suspecting a mine rather than a submarine because there was no indication of any enemy activity, the *Cressy* and the *Hogue* came to the aid of the survivors, but they too were torpedoed by the same U-boat almost immediately. All three ships sank within minutes. As many as 1,459 men were lost, with just over 800 being saved.

The destruction of three elderly ships had little strategic significance in itself, but the incident was damaging to British morale and increased German interest in the development of submarine warfare. It also confirmed the need to fit older ships with a bulge—an additional width at the waterline—to give improved protection against mines and torpedoes, and modifications were carried out as a result.

Achilles, H.M.S.

A British light CRUISER of the successful Leander class, built 1930–35, the *Achilles* fought with distinction in the Battle of the RIVER PLATE, December 13, 1939, at the beginning of World War II, 1939–45. She had a displacement of some 6,500 tons and her main armament consisted of eight 6-inch guns, which were to be used to great effect.

Operated by the Royal New Zealand Navy, 1936–43, the *Achilles* and her sister ship *AJAX* drew the fire of the *ADMIRAL GRAF SPEE*, a German POCKET-BATTLESHIP, as she attempted to sink the British heavy cruiser *EXETER* in the South Atlantic. Their successful action allowed the *Exeter* to escape destruction. It also led directly to the scuttling of the *Graf Spee*, which had been responsible for heavy Allied merchant shipping losses in the first three months of the war. The *Achilles* saw much action in the Pacific later in the war. Together with the *Leander*, she formed part of the Anzac force operating with U.S. naval forces against the Japanese. She saw action at GUADALCANAL in 1942 and took part in the assault on OKINAWA, 1945. In 1948 the *Achilles* was transferred to the Indian navy as she was surplus to British postwar requirements.

An earlier *Achilles*, built in 1794, was a British 74-gun

The pursuit of the German pocket-battleship *Admiral Graf Spee* off the River Plate, December 13, 1939   *(Copyright © National Maritime Museum, Greenwich, London)*

ship that took part in the Battle of TRAFALGAR, 1805, and forced the surrender of a French and a Spanish warship.

Admiral Graf Spee

*N*amed after the German admiral of WORLD WAR I, 1914–18, who died during the Battle of the FALKLAND ISLANDS, 1914, the *Admiral Graf Spee* was a POCKET-BATTLE-SHIP of 11,900 tons. She was designed as a commerce raider and was launched in 1934; her armament consisted of six 11-inch (28 cm) and eight 5.9-inch (15 cm) guns. Operated by a crew of 1,124, she was 616 feet 9 inches (187.9 m) in length and had a maximum speed of 26 knots. Shortly before the beginning of WORLD WAR II, 1939–45, she left German waters for an operational career that lasted for less than three months in the Indian Ocean and the South Atlantic. During that time her one activity resulted in the loss of nine British merchantmen with a combined

displacement of over 50,000 tons. But her success was short-lived and her performance in the Battle of the RIVER PLATE, December 13, 1939, was to cast doubt on the whole pocket-battleship concept.

There was a rapid response from the ROYAL NAVY. On December 13, 1939, the *Admiral Graf Spee* was intercepted by three British cruisers—the *AJAX, ACHILLES* and *EXETER*—in the waters off the mouth of the River Plate, between Argentina and Uruguay. Although the British were out-gunned, they fought gallantly: The *Exeter* was crippled but the *Graf Spee* was also damaged. The German ship was too slow to evade the three cruisers, and her large-caliber guns could not respond quickly enough. Her captain, Hans Langsdorff, handled the engagement badly and was unable to pursue his opponents. He withdrew as quickly as possible, entering Montevideo harbor in neutral Uruguay to carry out emergency repairs.

False information supplied by British intelligence convinced Langsdorff that when he returned to sea he faced certain destruction from a newly arrived British force. The German government wished to avoid at all costs the humiliation of surrendering the *Admiral Graf Spee* to the British and, following discussions with the naval high command, Langsdorff decided that there was only one course of action open to him. On December 17, 1939, the German ship was scuttled in the River Plate and Langsdorff, unable to bear the shame of his action, committed suicide shortly afterward. Before these final acts, the majority of the crew, together with the prisoners taken from ships sunk by the *Admiral Graf Spee*, had been landed in Uruguay.

Michael Powell, *The Last Voyage of the Graf Spee*, London, 1976.

Admiral Popov

A unique circular warship, named after its designer, Vice Admiral Andrei Popov, built for the RUSSIAN NAVY at Nicolaev on the Black Sea. Launched in 1875, her revolutionary shape was explained by the need to produce a stable gun platform that would not pitch or role regardless of the condition of the sea. The *Admiral Popov* was 101 feet (30.8 m) in diameter and had a displacement of 3,533 tons. Two huge funnels were needed for the ship's eight engines, which powered six propellers. She was armed with two revolving 11.8-inch (30 cm) weapons mounted amidships in a BARBETTE, a semicircular gun platform.

A critical flaw in the design quickly appeared. On a river the *Admiral Popov* was found to be completely uncontrollable when going downstream; in rough seas it suffered from pounding and was soon awash because of its low freeboard. In spite of these problems a second ship, the *Novgorod*, was built shortly afterward to the same design, but neither ship was ever used in action by the Russian navy.

Admiral Scheer

O ne of three Deutschland-class POCKET-BATTLESHIPS built for the GERMAN NAVY in the interwar period. Launched in 1933, the *Admiral Scheer* had a displacement of 12,200 tons, was 616 feet. 9 inches (187.99 m) in length and had a beam of 71 feet 3 inches (21.72 m). She had improved armor compared with the *Deutschland*, the first ship of this class to be completed, a maximum speed of 26 knots and could carry two aircraft. Operated by a crew of 1,150, her main armament included six 11-inch (28 cm) and eight 5.9-inch (15 cm) guns. The ADMIRAL GRAF SPEE was the third member of the Deutschland class.

The *Admiral Scheer* operated as a commerce raider for much of WORLD WAR II, 1939–45, and during a five-month period in the Atlantic and Indian oceans (October 23, 1940 to April 1, 1941), she sank or captured 17 merchant ships totaling 113,233 tons while successfully eluding the Royal Navy. A further victim was the British ARMED MERCHANT CRUISER *JERVIS BAY*, which, acting to protect an Allied convoy, made a suicide attack on the *Admiral Scheer* on November 5, 1940. The *Admiral Scheer* never managed to repeat this remarkable run of success, but from 1942 played a valuable role operating from Norway against the ARCTIC CONVOYS. In the latter part of the war she was relegated to a support role in the Baltic Sea before her destruction at Kiel by Royal Air Force bombers in April 1945.

Admiralty

A term used to describe the government department that was formerly responsible for naval matters in the United Kingdom and in some other countries. In the United States there is a Department of the Navy, a branch of the Defense Department, while in Britain navy affairs are now the responsibility of a unified Ministry of Defence. In some other countries the term "Ministry of Marine" might be used. The origins of the Admiralty in England, date back to the late thirteenth century. The Crown appointed the Lord High Admiral as the executive head of the navy, and his headquarters became known as the Admiralty. The officials responsible for running this office were known as Lords Commissioners of the Admiralty, and they met collectively as the Board of Admiralty. This basic structure continued until 1964, when the three services were brought together under a single Ministry of Defence.

The word "admiralty" also means "sovereignty at sea," a concept that often has been exercised by special maritime courts dealing with a wide range of civil and criminal matters. In Britain prior to 1875, the High Court of Admiralty were responsible for considering such maritime cases for more than 500 years. In many other countries the civil courts apply maritime codes.

N. A. M. Rodger, *The Admiralty*, Lavenham, 1979.

Adventure, H.M.S.

T he British ship H.M.S. *Adventure* was one of the two converted Whitby colliers used by Captain James COOK on his second voyage of discovery, 1772–75. Acquired by the ADMIRALTY for some £2,000, the *Rayleigh*, as she was first known in the service of the ROYAL NAVY, had a displacement of 336 tons, was armed with 10 carriage guns and 10 swivels and carried a crew of 83.

The *Adventure* and her sister ship, the ENDEAVOUR, were the first vessels to cross the Antarctic in their search for the great southern continent, Terra Australis Incognita, that eighteenth-century geographers believed existed. During the second year of the voyage the two ships lost contact with each other, and the *Adventure*, commanded by Tobias

Furneaux, was forced to return to England prematurely. As a result, the *Adventure* became the first ship to complete a circumnavigation of the globe in an easterly direction.

Advice Boat

A small ship used by the world's navies during the age of sail for transmitting orders and dispatches as well as for reconnaissance and patrol duties. It also provided a means of communication between ships and between the fleet and the home command. Usually similar in appearance to a yacht, the advice boat, which was also known by its Spanish name, *aviso*, was a fast and maneuverable sailing ship. Speed was in fact its most important characteristic, but the advice boat was not a single, standard design. Rather, advice boats came in different sizes with a variety of rigs. As the age of the sailing warship came to an end during the nineteenth century, the advice boat survived for a while in a modified form. While retaining its full rig, some were fitted with paddle wheels or later with propellers.

Agadir Crisis
1911

*T*he arrival of the *Panther*, a German gunboat, in the small Moroccan port of Agadir on July 1, 1911 produced a crisis in Anglo-German relations that was to continue until November of that year. The gunboat had been dispatched to protect German commercial interests that were under threat from increased French activity in Morocco. The Germans believed that the French were in breach of an international agreement made in 1906 to respect Moroccan independence.

However, it was Britain rather than France that was concerned about the *Panther*'s arrival. Britain feared that Germany planned to establish a naval base at Agadir, which was strategically located on the Atlantic, far too close to Gibraltar and Britain's principal trade routes for comfort. There was also a general British concern about the rapid growth of German naval power, which had led to an arms race between the two countries. France and Germany negotiated over Morocco's future during the summer, and, early in November, an agreement was reached that averted open hostilities for the time being. Nevertheless, the Agadir crisis was symptomatic of the growing international tensions that eventually led to WORLD WAR I, 1914–18.

Agamemnon, H.M.S.

*N*otable as the first warship that featured an engine and propeller as part of the original design, H.M.S.

Agamemnon was built for the ROYAL NAVY and launched at Woolwich, southeast London, in 1852. Despite this novel feature, her engine, which was positioned well aft to reduce the strain on her structure, was regarded as no more than a supplementary means of power; the vessel was still fully rigged. Equipped with 91 guns, she was heavily employed during the CRIMEAN WAR, 1853–56, and saw action during the bombardment of Sevastopol, October 1854–September 1855. Her peacetime duties included helping to lay the first cable across the Atlantic in 1858.

An earlier British *Agamemnon* was a famous 64-gun ship launched in 1781. Commanded personally by Admiral Lord NELSON during operations against the French in the Mediterranean in 1793–94, she had an eventful career, and Nelson regarded her as the best ship of her type in the Royal Navy. During the latter phase of the FRENCH REVOLUTIONARY AND NAPOLEONIC WARS, 1792–1815, she was in action at the Battle of COPENHAGEN, 1801, and the Battle of TRAFALGAR, 1805, before going aground in the Plate River between Uruguay and Argentina and meeting her end in 1809.

Agincourt, H.M.S.

*T*his British-built DREADNOUGHT, which was originally ordered by Brazil, was purchased by Turkey during construction but was never delivered to that country. The *Agincourt*'s completion, however, coincided with the outbreak of the WORLD WAR I, 1914–18, and she was taken over by the ROYAL NAVY. She was then the longest BATTLESHIP in the world but not the best protected, her limited armor protection falling short of normal British standards.

On the other hand, she had the largest number of main guns (14 12-inch (30 cm) guns in twin turrets) and the heaviest secondary armament of any warship of the time. She was capable of producing an impressive volume of fire. Operated by a crew of 1,115, the *Agincourt* had a maximum speed of over 22 knots, a displacement of 27,500 tons and was 671 feet 6 inches (204.5 m) in length. She served with the British GRAND FLEET throughout the war and fought at the Battle of JUTLAND, 1916, without sustaining any damage. She was finally scrapped in 1922.

Richard Hough, *The Big Battleship, or the Curious Career of HMS Agincourt*, London, 1966.

Aircraft Carrier

A warship with a flight deck from which aircraft take off and land. Aircraft were operated from the decks of warships fitted with temporary platforms not long after the first powered flights were made. The first takeoff occurred from an American ship—the cruiser U.S.S. *Birmingham*—in November 1910 and the first landing—on the cruiser U.S.S. *PENNSYLVANIA*—in January 1911. In Britain a take-off from a ship under way did not occur until May 1912. These early experiments persuaded the British Admiralty to convert the *HERMES,* an old cruiser, to carry three seaplanes, which was a timely decision in view of the imminent outbreak of WORLD WAR I, 1914–18. In December 1914 she was followed by the *ARK ROYAL,* often described as an aircraft carrier but more accurately as the first specially designed seaplane carrier. The British Admiralty gradually realized the potential of ship-based aircraft, and, in 1915, the *Campania,* a converted seaplane carrier, was fitted with a taking-off deck. The need for these aircraft to return directly to their ships rather than to land in the sea and be hoisted on board rapidly became obvious.

As a result the British ordered the first aircraft carrier with a full-length landing deck that was unobstructed by a bridge or funnel. The *ARGUS,* which was commissioned in 1916, was not ready until the last weeks of the war, but she provided the solution to the problem of landing aircraft on moving ships. For the remainder of the war the Royal Navy was compelled to convert existing warships to provide an adequate carrier capability. These included the *FURIOUS* originally a light battle cruiser, which became the world's first fully operational aircraft carrier when it was completed in 1918. Other countries, including the United States, followed a similar path, with the first American carrier, the converted collier *LANGLEY,* entering service in 1922. By 1918 the results of wartime experimentation were evident; the first British ship to be designed as an aircraft carrier—the *HERMES*—began construction, although it was not to be completed until 1923. The Japanese had launched the first true aircraft carrier, the *HOSHO,* a year earlier. The *Hosho,* like the *Hermes,* was a custom-built ship that had a flush flight deck, funnels to one side and arresting gear to halt aircraft as they landed. Aircraft were stored below-decks; because space was limited they were equipped with folding wings.

During the interwar period the United States, Japan and, to a lesser extent, Britain developed significant carrier forces that were to play a key role in naval operations in WORLD WAR II, 1939–45. This investment reflected a growing belief in the importance of air power in naval warfare and the vulnerability of conventional warships without air cover. The newly developed carrier forces included converted capital ships, as agreed at the WASHINGTON CONFERENCE, 1922, and later custom-built carriers. The latter featured island superstructures (the bridge and funnels were located to one side to give an unobstructed flight deck) and armor protection as standard features. By the beginning of World War II the large fleet carrier, which could operate up to 100 aircraft, had largely displaced the BATTLESHIP, which was increasingly vulnerable to air attack, as the capital ship of the world's navies. This change

was evident from the early stages of the war when British carriers played a significant role in the Battle for Norway, in carrier operations in the Mediterranean and in the sinking of the German battleship *BISMARCK.* The Japanese attack on PEARL HARBOR, December 7, 1941, by carrier-based aircraft followed although, ironically, the absent U.S. carrier force escaped destruction. The Pacific War, 1941–45, was dominated by the fights between opposing American and Japanese carrier squadrons. Japan was never able to recover from the loss of six of its original ten carriers at the Battles of MIDWAY and the CORAL SEA in 1942.

Light fleet carriers and escort carriers, which could accommodate significantly fewer aircraft, also played an important role during the war. Apart from convoy protection duties, the escort carrier was used extensively during the Battle of the ATLANTIC 1939–45, to bring aircraft into service against the U-boat.

The aircraft carrier underwent further development in the immediate postwar period, stimulated by a series of British inventions, including the steam catapult, the angled flight deck and an improved landing device. Despite these important British contributions, the Americans have subsequently led carrier development, and they launched the first nuclear carrier, the U.S.S. *ENTERPRISE,* in 1960. It was the U.S. Navy's second nuclear carrier, the *NIMITZ,* launched in 1962, that provided the model for subsequent carrier development. She could accommodate 100 aircraft and was operated by a crew of 5,700. The escalating cost of building new fleet carriers—and their potential vulnerability to missile attack—has encouraged medium-size powers such as Britain and France to produce light carriers that may only accommodate helicopters or vertical takeoff aircraft such as the Sea Harrier. Similar ships are in service in the Russian navy. In their various forms, carriers have been fully involved in every major postwar conflict from the KOREAN WAR, 1950–53, to the GULF WAR, 1991, and Bosnia. Their often critical role in these conventional wars has confirmed the aircraft carrier's place alongside the nuclear submarine as one of the two principal ships of the modern navy.

David Brown, *Carrier Operations in World War 2,* 2 vols. London, 1974; N. Friedman, *U.S. Aircraft Carriers,* Annapolis, 1983; John Winton, *Air Power at Sea,* London, 1987.

Ajax, H.M.S.

A British light cruiser of the successful Leander class, built 1930–35, H.M.S. *Ajax* fought with distinction in the Battle of the RIVER PLATE, December 13, 1939, at the beginning of the WORLD WAR II, 1939–45. She had a displacement of some 6,800 tons, and her main armament consisted of eight 6-inch (15 cm) guns, which would be used to great effect. Operated by a crew of 570, she had a

North American B25 Mitchells take off from the aircraft carrier USS *Hornet* in 1942   *(Copyright © National Maritime Museum, Greenwich, London)*

length of 554 ft. 6 in. (169 m) and a beam of 55 ft. 9 in. (17 m).

Together with H.M.S. ACHILLES, her sister ship, the AJAX drew the fire of the ADMIRAL GRAF SPEE, a German POCKET-BATTLESHIP, as the German vessel attempted to sink the British heavy cruiser EXETER in the South Atlantic. Their successful action allowed the *Exeter* to escape destruction and eventually led to the scuttling of the *Graf Spee*, which had been responsible for heavy Allied shipping losses in the three months before the battle.

Other famous ships named *Ajax* in British service have included a 74-gun ship, completed in 1798, that fought at the Battle of TRAFALGAR, 1805, and was destroyed in an explosion in 1807. A Victorian *Ajax*, launched in 1846, was the first BATTLESHIP to be fitted with a propeller, following the completion of successful trials with the FRIGATE RATTLER.

Akagi

*J*apanese aircraft carrier of the World War II, 1939–45, that served as Vice Admiral Chuichi NAGUMO's flagship during the attack on the American fleet at PEARL HARBOR, December 7, 1941. Completed in 1927, the *Akagi* was based on a battle cruiser hull, had a displacement of 36,500 tons and was 855 feet 4 inches (260.6 m) in length. She had a crew of 1,340 and carried 63 aircraft of three different types: the Mitsubishi A6M2 Zero fighter; the Aichi D3A1 dive-bomber; and the Nakajima B5N2 torpedo-bomber.

After Pearl Harbor and subsequent operations, she was involved in the sinking of the British aircraft carrier HERMES in the Indian Ocean in 1942. The *Akagi* met her end during the Battle of MIDWAY, June 1942, when she was twice hit by dive-bombers from the American carrier ENTERPRISE. The bombs started fires that could not be controlled, and Nagumo and his crew were forced to abandon the *Akagi*. She finally was torpedoed and sunk by one of her own escort ships.

Alabama

A three-masted British-built Confederate *schooner* of 1,016 tons, the *Alabama* was the most successful commerce raider of the AMERICAN CIVIL WAR, 1861–65. She was equipped with an auxiliary steam engine that was capable of up to 13 knots. When the war began she was under construction in Laird's Yard in Birkenhead, northwest England, and was completed to the Confederate navy's specifications in 1862. As a neutral power, Britain issued a detention order; but before it could be enforced the *Alabama* slipped away during sea trials, with her new Confederate crew successfully eluding a Union frigate. Under the command of Captain Raphael SEMMES, she made for the Azores, where she was fitted out and armed with guns brought from Liverpool in British ships.

Her active service began in August 1862. During nearly two years of cruising she destroyed some 70 Union ships, causing losses amounting to about $6 million. The end finally came off Cherbourg in the English Channel when she challenged the *KEARSARGE*, one of her Union pursuers, on June 19, 1864. A steamer of 1,031 tons, the *Kearsarge* used her 11-inch shells to deadly effect: After 20 minutes the veteran Confederate raider was badly damaged, and she sank quickly.

The Union government held the British responsible for the losses caused by the *Alabama* and two other British-built Confederate cruisers. An acrimonious period in Anglo-American relations followed, and it was not until 1872 that the *Alabama* claims were finally settled by arbitration. As a result, the British paid substantial damages ($15.5 million) to the American government.

Alaska, U.S.S.

T he U.S.S. *Alaska* and her sister ship, the *U.S.S. Guam*, were notable as the last BATTLE CRUISERS to be built. They were constructed for the U.S. NAVY in reply to intelligence reports that the Japanese were building a major new class of surface warships. These reports proved to be false, and this perceived Japanese threat never materialized during WORLD WAR II, 1939–45. The *Alaska* had a displacement of 27,500 tons and dimensions of 808 feet 6 inches (246.4 m) and a beam of 91 feet (27.7 m). With a maximum speed of 33 knots, she was equipped with 9-inch armor protection to the main belt and with the following guns: nine 12-inch (30 cm), 12 5-inch (13 cm), 56 40-mm (1.57 in) antiaircraft and 34 20-mm antiaircraft. She had

a crew of 2,200 and could operate two aircraft. The *Alaska* was not launched until 1944 but was used, with the *Guam*, in the closing stages of the Pacific War, 1941–45, in operations against OKINAWA in 1945. Both ships were decommissioned soon after the end of the war although the navy did not finally scrap them until 1960.

Albemarle

A Confederate IRONCLAD RAM, built on the Roanoke River, North Carolina. Made partly from scrap materials because of supply difficulties during the AMERICAN CIVIL WAR, 1861–65, she entered service in April 1864. The *Albemarle* had a shallow draft, which increased her ability to evade enemy warships. The Albemarle was 152 feet (46.3 m) in length, 34 feet (10.4 m) in the beam and was equipped with two 6.4-inch (16 cm) Brooke guns, which were cast-iron rifled weapons. Her contribution to the naval side of the war was to be notable but short-lived. She was soon involved in a successful Confederate combined operation against the Union naval base at Plymouth, North Carolina, on April 19, 1864. The *Albemarle* sank the U.S.S. *Southfield* and forced several other Union warships to leave the area. On May 5 she attacked and dispersed a squadron of eight Union gunboats, suffering slight damage herself. The end came dramatically on October 28, 1864, during the hours of darkness, when a modified launch, commanded by Lieutenant William B. CUSHING, attacked the *Albemarle* at Plymouth with a SPAR TORPEDO and sank her quickly.

Albuquerque, Alfonso de
1453–1515

P ortuguese naval commander who used sea power to create a colonial empire in Asia. Often described as the "father of naval strategy," he was Governor General of the Portuguese Indies, 1508–15. In a series of expeditions beginning in 1503, he seized key points on the sea route from Portugal to India. These included several Arab towns on the East African coast, which were taken in 1506. Goa fell in 1510, adding to his earlier conquests on the west coast of India in 1505. Albuquerque subsequently moved eastward, capturing Malacca on the Malay peninsula—a victory that put Portugal in a position to establish a monopoly in the spice trade. He was then instructed to turn his attention to Aden and the Red Sea, but his expedition there in 1513 met strong opposition and was unsuccessful, although he did manage to establish a hold on the Persian Gulf with the recapture of Hormuz in 1515.

On his return to India in 1515, Albuquerque learned that he had fallen from power as a result of court intrigues and had been replaced by one of his enemies. Albuquerque died soon afterward, before his achievements in the East had been recognized at home. He was one of the first commanders to appreciate that naval forces could operate independently and were more than simply an adjunct to land warfare. He used sea power as an instrument to support key national political and economic objectives—imperial expansion and the creation of trade monopolies.

Prestage, Edgar, *Alfonso de Albuquerque*, London, 1929.

Alecto, H.M.S.

H.M.S. *Alecto* was notable as the British warship that was set against her sister ship, the H.M.S. RATTLER, in a famous competition between screw and paddle in 1845. The *Alecto* was a paddle-wheel propelled frigate of 880 tons whose method of propulsion was destined to become obsolete when an alternative was developed. The invention of the screw propeller in the 1830s, and the first successful experiments with this propeller in Britain, encouraged the Royal Navy to convert the *Rattler*, which had begun life as a paddle SLOOP, to screw propulsion.

The *Rattler*'s trials included a 100-mile (161-km) race and a decisive tug-of-war with the *Alecto*. Both ships had similar 220-horsepower engines, but the *Rattler* emerged as the clear victor from the trials, which proved conclusively that the screw propeller was more powerful than the paddle wheel and persuaded the authorities that it should be adopted by the Royal Navy. As well as providing less speed, paddles had other disadvantages in naval use: They reduced the number of guns that could be accommodated on board and were vulnerable to damage by enemy action. The Admiralty had correctly anticipated the outcome of these trials, because orders for several screw warships, including the AJAX, the first SHIP OF THE LINE to be so equipped, had already been placed.

Aleutian Islands Campaign
1942–43

The Aleutians, an archipelago of several dozen small, barren and inhospitable islands, extend for nearly 1,200 miles (1,930 km) in a westerly direction from the Alaska peninsula, across the northern edge of the Pacific Ocean. Former Russian possessions (now part of the State of Alaska), a number of these islands were occupied by the Japanese during WORLD WAR II, 1939–45. On June 7, 1942, largely as a diversionary action in support of the MIDWAY campaign, two Japanese light carriers successfully landed Japanese ground forces on Attu and Kiska, the two largest of the westerly islands in the group. Although the Aleutians had little strategic significance in themselves, the Japanese occupying forces were perceived to represent a potential threat to Alaska. As a result, Americans devoted considerable resources to expelling them, delaying other operations in the central Pacific as a result. At the same time, the action did not affect the outcome at Midway, as the Japanese had hoped.

Based on Umnak in the central Aleutians, Americans' year-long operations against the enemy occupying forces began in August 1942 with the bombardment of Kiska. At the end of the same month the Americans established an air base at Adak. On May 11, 1943, an amphibious task force, commanded by Rear Admiral Francis Rockwell, landed the U.S. 7th Infantry at Holtz and Massacre Bay on Attu, the westernmost island in the chain. During a campaign lasting 18 days the Japanese offered strong resistance, and only 29 members of the 2,500-strong garrison were to survive. The 11,000 Americans suffered almost 1,700 casualties. The recovery of Kiska was much less problematic. When a joint American-Canadian force of 34,000 men landed on August 15, 1943, it found the island deserted. The remaining Japanese garrison of some 6,000 men had left under cover of darkness some two weeks earlier and the islands were back under American control.

S. E. Morison, *History of United States Naval Operations in World War II*, 15 vols., Boston, 1948–64.

Algeciras, Battle of
July 6, 1801

An action during the FRENCH REVOLUTIONARY AND NAPOLEONIC WARS, 1792–1815, when a British squadron, commanded by Rear Admiral Sir James SAUMAREZ (Baron de Saumarez), attacked French warships anchored in Algeciras Bay, near the British colony of Gibraltar. On July 6, 1801 Saumarez, whose squadron consisted of six ships of the line, attacked a French force under the command of Admiral Durand Linois. Although the French were forced to run their ships ashore during the action, the British sustained significant damage, and one warship, the 74-gun *Hannibal*, ran aground and was forced to surrender. Saumarez was compelled to retire to Gibraltar, but he completed essential repairs quickly and was ready to seek his revenge only six days later.

In a second engagement, on July 12–13, often known as the action of the Straits of Gibraltar, Saumarez, who was heavily outnumbered, fought French and Spanish ships under the command of Admiral Linois and Admiral Moreno, respectively. This action, which began at dusk on July 12, continued through the night. The loss of two Spanish first-rate ships at midnight marked a turning point in the battle. The *San Hermenegildo* had been hit by the British and in the confusion that followed engaged the *San Carlos*, which she mistook for an enemy warship. Both soon caught fire and sank. This was quickly followed by the capture of the French 74-gun ship *St. Anthoine*. The victorious British squadron also sustained heavy damage, but every ship managed to return to Gibraltar, whose security had been enhanced by this outcome.

Allemand, Zacharie Jacques Théodore
1762–1826

*F*rench naval commander, born at Port Louis, Brittany. He entered the navy at an early age but made relatively slow progress in his career, reaching the rank of lieutenant at the time of the French Revolution, 1789.

The outbreak of the FRENCH REVOLUTIONARY AND NAPOLEONIC WARS, 1792–1815, provided him with an opportunity to make more rapid progress. After a period as a commerce raider in the Atlantic, operating against British merchant shipping, he was promoted to rear admiral. Early in 1805 he was appointed to the command of the Rochefort squadron, whose main responsibility was to operate against British naval and maritime interests in the western approaches. He accomplished this objective with great skill while always eluding a significant engagement with the enemy.

In 1809 he was appointed to the command of the French Mediterranean Fleet with the rank of vice admiral and during the following year was created a Count of the Empire. This honor reflected Allemand's high professional standing and his long service to France, even though his name is not associated with any major battle.

Alliance

*L*aunched in 1778, this American-built FRIGATE served until the conclusion of the AMERICAN WAR OF INDEPENDENCE, 1775–83. In 1779 she sailed to France, where she joined the squadron commanded by John Paul JONES. She was one of four ships that accompanied the *BONHOMME RICHARD*, Jones's flagship, on a privateering expedition around the coasts of Britain. The *Alliance* was present at the famous action off Flamborough Head, England, September 23, 1779, when the *Bonhomme Richard* fought and captured the British warship *Serapis*. As well as serving regularly as an escort ship, the *Alliance* carried a member of President George Washington's staff across the Atlantic in 1781. He was on a mission to secure French naval support in operations against the British off the eastern coast of America. The *Alliance* was not decommissioned until 1785, by which time she was the last warship of the War of Independence still operated by the UNITED STATES NAVY.

Allin, Sir Thomas
1612–85

*B*ritish naval commander, originally a Lowestoft merchant and shipowner, who went to sea on the Royalist side during the English Civil War, 1642–49. In reward for his services to the Crown he gained rapid advancement after 1660 in the Restoration navy and reached the rank of admiral. He proved to be an able and resourceful officer. As commander in chief in the Mediterranean, he captured part of a Dutch convoy from Smyrna in 1663.

During the Second ANGLO-DUTCH WAR, 1665–67, Allin distinguished himself at the Battles of *LOWESTOFT*, 1665, and ORFORDNESS, 1666. In 1689 Allin returned to the Mediterranean, where he operated against the Barbary pirates. His latter years were spent as comptroller of the navy, although he was called back to sea briefly during the Third Dutch War, 1672–74.

Altmark

A German naval tanker of 8,053 tons that acted as an auxiliary to the POCKET BATTLESHIP *ADMIRAL GRAF SPEE* in the opening stages of the WORLD WAR II, 1939–45. During the *Graf Spee*'s commerce-raiding activities in the South Atlantic, in which nine Allied merchant ships were sunk, the *Altmark* rescued 299 British survivors. These prisoners of war remained on the tanker as she hid in the South Atlantic following the Battle of the RIVER PLATE and the scuttling of the *Graf Spee* on December 17, 1939.

With her larger protector sunk, the *Altmark*'s captain decided to return to Germany. During the final stages of the *Altmark*'s journey home, she entered Norwegian waters in an unsuccessful attempt to evade the British. Her action was to no avail: British aircraft soon spotted her. Forced to take refuge in Jossing Fjord, on February 16, 1940 she was intercepted there by the British DESTROYER *Cossack*, commanded by Captain (later Admiral) Sir Philip VIAN. Well aware that British prisoners were being held on the *Altmark*, Vian had his men rapidly board the German vessel. After some fierce hand-to-hand fighting the British boarding party gained the advantage and the prisoners were released. Having achieved her main objective, the *Cossack* withdrew rapidly amid protests from the Norwegian government about British violation of its neutrality. Because she was not a warship, the *Altmark* was permitted to return to Germany, and she continued to work as a supply ship until she was destroyed in an accident in November 1942.

The *Altmark* incident increased German fears that Britain might soon occupy Norway, and, as a result, Adolf Hitler brought forward his own plans to seize that country.

Richard Hough, *The Longest Battle. The War at Sea, 1939–45*, London, 1986.

America

Built in New York in 1851 as a racing yacht, the 150-ton *America* served as a Confederate BLOCKADE runner during the AMERICAN CIVIL WAR, 1861–65. Before the war she competed successfully in England; her racing victories included a celebrated triumph in a yacht race around the Isle of Wight in 1851. In recognition of this achievement the Royal Yacht Squadron presented her crew with a trophy that has been known ever since as the America's Cup.

During the Civil War the CONFEDERATE NAVY requisitioned the *America* and prepared her for combat. Based at Savannah, she was used on a variety of missions including blockade running. Her wartime career seemed to have ended when she was scuttled in Florida to avoid capture, but she was later raised and commissioned into the Union navy. Her operational service in the latter part of the war included support for the siege of Charleston in 1863. After the war the U.S. Navy retained her for a period as a training vessel. Eventually, however, the *America* reverted to civilian use as a cruising and racing yacht. She survived until 1942 when she was accidentally destroyed.

American Civil War
1861–65

The American Civil War began with the Confederate attack on Fort Sumter on April 12, 1861. The North's immediate response included the imposition of a naval blockade on the South, with the aim of undermining its ability to wage war, engage in international and intercoastal trade, and of destroying its economy. At first the blockade posed little threat to the South, as the Northern navy did not have the resources to make it effective. The U.S. Navy had about ninety wooden ships, of which slightly less than half were in commission when the war broke out. However, within months the construction of new blockading ships was well under way, and within a year several Southern harbors were completely cut off from the outside world. At first the confederacy had no warships of its own, but soon a few merchant ships were requisitioned and armed. In a dramatic but unsuccessful attempt to break the blockade, the Confederacy converted the former Northern steam-powered FRIGATE MERRIMACK, which had been seized at Norfolk Navy Yard, into an armored ship. Renamed the *Virginia*, she attacked and sank two Northern warships in HAMPTON ROADS on March 8. The following day she was attacked by the *MONITOR* in the first battle ever between opposing armored ships. After several hours' fighting the engagement ended in a draw.

The *Merrimack* was not the only innovation associated with the CONFEDERATE NAVY, which also pioneered the use of torpedoes, mines and submersible vessels. However, the Confederacy was never able to create a substantial navy, although it acquired sufficient ships to conduct an effective commerce-raiding campaign in the Atlantic. Its most successful raider was the *ALABAMA*, which captured 71 Union ships in some twenty months before she was finally sunk off Cherbourg on June 19, 1864. Apart from its conduct of the war on the open seas, the Union navy developed a significant river fleet that operated in close cooperation with Northern ground forces. A notable example is this operation to seize control of the Mississippi and capture New Orleans. These objectives were largely achieved following a successful attack on the Mississippi forts by a force under Commodore David FARRAGUT on April 24, 1862. These gains were extended as the North's river fleet, equipped with specially designed TINCLADS, forced the Confederates to relinquish control of other waterways. In July 1864 a combined operation led by General Ulysses S. Grant captured Vicksburg. Unionist gunboats had played an important role in operations on the central Mississippi preceding the siege of Vicksburg, and its ironclads had bombarded the city. As a result of this operation, the Confederacy was split in two.

By 1864, as the Confederacy's overall military position deteriorated further, the Union navy sought to close the remaining gaps in its blockade. At the Battle of MOBILE BAY, August 5, 1864, it succeeded in closing Mobile to Confederate blockade runners, although not without significant cost to itself. The growing difficulties of resupplying Confederate ground forces because of the ever-tightening blockade was a significant factor in General Lee's decision to surrender on April 9, 1865.

Chronological List of Naval Events

1861

April 12	The war begins when Confederate forces attack Fort Sumter
August	The North imposes an increasingly effective blockade of the Confederate coast. The South replies with a commerce-raiding campaign that continues throughout the war
1862	
March 8–9	Action in Chesapeake Bay
April 24	Union assault on the Confederate Mississippi forts of Jackson and St. Philip leads to the capture of New Orleans and most of the Mississippi
December 12	The *Cairo*, a Northern gunboat, is sunk by a Confederate mine in a tributary of the Mississippi and becomes the first victim of mine warfare

1863	
July 4	Vicksburg falls to General Grant and cuts the Confederacy in two following a combined operation in which gunboats commanded by Admiral FARRAGUT play a key role
1864	
February 17	The Confederate submersible *H. L. HUNLEY* becomes the first of its kind to sink an enemy ship
August 5	Battle of Mobile Bay results in a Confederate defeat, and the port can no longer be used by Confederate blockade runners
1865	
April 9	General Lee's surrender to General Grant at Appomatox, Virginia brings the war to an end

Tony Gibbons, *Warships and Naval Battles of the U.S. Civil War*, London, 1989.

American War of Independence
1775–83

The first armed conflict between British troops and American militia occurred at Lexington on April 19, 1775 following a long period of tension between the 13 colonies and the mother country. During the first phase of the war, when 13 frigates authorized by Congress were under construction, the eastern seaboard of America was dominated by the Royal Navy. Its most important function during this period was to bring troop reinforcements from England and land them in support of a planned offensive to defeat the revolution.

In June 1776 Admiral Sir Peter PARKER, who landed a British contingent under the command of General Sir Henry Clinton at Charleston, South Carolina, exchanged fire with shore batteries and sustained heavy damage to his squadron. Early in July a British fleet commanded by Admiral Richard HOWE landed some 32,000 troops on Staten Island, New York, with the aim of launching an offensive in New Jersey. An early but ineffective challenge to British naval forces came on September 6–7 when a primitive one-man submarine, made by David BUSHNELL, tried to attack the British fleet in New York harbor. During this period the only significant engagements on water took place on the rivers and lakes of the Canadian border, where both sides built makeshift flotillas. As Benedict Arnold's American forces retreated from Canada, opposing ships fought on LAKE CHAMPLAIN in October 1776. Although the Americans lost the battle, they delayed the British advance south.

The character of the naval war changed significantly after the French entered the war on the American side in 1778. American successes against the British army, notably

The *Monitor* engages the *Merrimack* on March 9, 1862   *(Copyright © National Maritime Museum, Greenwich, London)*

the victory at Saratoga, 1777, had persuaded the French to recognize the independence of the colonies and to declare war on Britain. The French fleet consisted of some 80 ships, compared with 130 available to the Royal Navy. They were reinforced by the Spanish fleet, which joined the war in 1779, and by the Dutch, who were drawn into the conflict in 1780 when Britain declared war on the Netherlands for trading with the colonies. The struggle for the command of the seas, which took place in the Atlantic, the Caribbean and the East Indies, was critically important in determining the outcome of the war. The fledgling American navy, commanded by Esek HOPKINS, played very little part in this struggle, although the exploits of John Paul JONES off the coast of Britain in 1778 were a notable exception. (See also UNITED STATES NAVY.)

The first French naval forces arrived off the American coast early in July 1778. Commanded by the Admiral the Comte d'ESTAING, they consisted of twelve ships of the line and made contact with George Washington's headquarters before seeking to bring Admiral Howe's fleet to battle off Newport, Rhode Island in August. D'Estaing did not succeed in doing so and later left for the West Indies, where British and French naval forces were to struggle for supremacy for more than three years. The French made some initial gains, while Britain built up its naval strength in the area. Later actions at GRENADA, July 1779, and MARTINIQUE, 1780, were more evenly balanced.

During this period the French navy was less energetic in European waters and failed to exploit Britain's relative naval weakness in the Channel and adjoining areas. At the Battle of USHANT, July 27, 1778, the French failed to exploit British disorder, and the battle ended indecisively. When Spain entered the war the focus of activity in Europe shifted to Gibraltar; Spain wished to recapture the fortress there, which was besieged from 1779 to 1783. At the Battle of CAPE ST. VINCENT, January 8, 1780, the British defeated the Spanish blockading force and Gibraltar was resupplied.

By 1781 land operations in America had entered a critical phase, with the British forces under General Cornwallis at Yorktown, Virginia, almost completely surrounded. The British needed to retain control of Chesapeake Bay and the offshore waters of the Atlantic but faced a powerful challenge from the French. Early in September 1781 Admiral the Comte de GRASSE, who had brought troop reinforcements from the West Indies, arrived off the entrance to Chesapeake Bay. British naval forces under Rear Admiral Thomas Graves met the French at the Battle of CHESAPEAKE Bay, September 5, 1781, but were unable to defeat them. The sea blockade remained in place and the British army at Yorktown was forced to surrender to General George Washington on October 19. The war for independence had now been won, and the focus of the naval war shifted back to the West Indies, although there were parallel operations in Europe and the East Indies.

During this final phase of the war, the Royal Navy reestablished its command of the seas in a series of successful engagements in Europe and the West Indies. At the Battle of the DOGGER BANK, August 5, 1781, the British gained the upper hand in a fierce engagement with the Dutch, while the French were defeated at the second Battle of USHANT, December 1781. The French suffered the same fate in the West Indies, where they were heavily defeated by stronger British naval forces commanded by Admiral George RODNEY at the Battle of the SAINTS, April 1782. This marked the end of the war in the West Indies for the British, although the victory had come too late to influence the outcome of the struggle for independence. The French fight against the British was also carried to India, where Admiral Pierre de SUFFREN fought a series of actions in 1782–83 against a British squadron commanded by Sir Edward HUGHES. The French, who fought the campaign without a land base, gained a local advantage without making any real impact on the overall course of events.

The final naval operation took place in Europe when a squadron under Admiral Richard HOWE succeeded in resupplying Gibraltar in October 1782. Soon afterward, on November 30, the Treaty of Paris, recognizing the independence of the United States, was concluded. It was to become effective when hostilities among Britain, France and Spain had come to an end. This was achieved shortly afterward, when the Peace of Versailles was concluded on January 20, 1783.

Chronological List of Naval Events

General

1775

April 19	British soldiers and American militia clash at Lexington

1776

July 4	Declaration of Independence

1778

June 17	France declares war on Britain

1779

June 21	Spain declares war on Britain

1780

February 28	Russia forms League of Armed Neutrality to protect its trade from interference by the belligerents
December 20	England declares war on the Netherlands

North America and the West Indies

1776	The Royal Navy's blockade of the eastern seaboard of America begins

The construction of 13 American frigates, authorized by Congress, begins

1778

July 11–22 The French fleet, commanded by Count d'Estaing, arrives off New York

December 15 Battle of St. Lucia

1779

July 6 Battle of Grenada: Byron vs d'Estaing; France gains the initiative in the West Indies

December 3 Siege of Savannah begins as the French fleet, with 4,000 troops on board, arrives

1780

March 20 Action off MONTE CHRISTI, Santo Domingo, between English and French naval force

April 17 Battle of DOMINICA

June 20 Second action off Monte Christi

September Admiral George Rodney foils Franco-American assault on New York

1781

March 16 Action off Chesapeake Bay (also known as the action off Cape Henry)

April 29 Action off Martinique

September 5 Battle of Chesapeake Bay: In a decisive engagement, Admiral de Grasse cuts the British army's sea links

October 19 The British capitulate at Yorktown

1782

January 25/26 Battle of St. Kitts

April 9 British and French fleets meet off Dominica

April 12 Battle of the Saints: The British defeat the French off Dominica

Europe

1778

April–May John Paul Jones, American naval commander, attacks British shipping in the Irish Sea and lands briefly at Whitehaven on the British mainland

July 27 Battle of Ushant: The British and French fleets meet off the Brittany coast but the result is inconclusive

1779

September 23 John Paul Jones captures the British frigate *Serapis* off Flamborough Head

1780

January 16 Battle of Cape St. Vincent (also known as the Moonlight Battle)

1781

August 5 Battle of the Dogger Bank

December 12 Second Battle of Ushant

1782

February 5 Spain captures Port Mahon, Minorca

September 13–14 Gibraltar, blockaded by land since July 1779, is attacked by a powerful Franco-Spanish naval force

October Large supply convoy reaches Gibraltar, which was still besieged

East Indies

1781

April 16 Battle of Porto Praya: Admiral Suffren attacks a British squadron en route to the Cape of Good Hope and India

1782

February 17 Action off Sadras; the first of five inconclusive Anglo-French actions (listed below) fought in the Indian Ocean, 1782–83

April 12 Battle of Providien

July 6 Action off Negapatam

September 3 Action off Trincomalee

1783

April 20 Action off Cuddalore

Peace

1782

November 30 Treaty of Paris recognizes the independence of the United States of America

1783

January 20 Peace of Versailles between England and the Franco-Spanish alliance

W. M. James, *The British Navy in Adversity*, London, 1926; P. Mackesy, *The War for America, 1775–83*, London, 1964; D. Syrett, *The Royal Navy in American Waters, 1775–1783*. Aldershot, England, 1989.

The British fleet defeats the Spanish during the "Moonlight Battle" (the Battle of Cape St. Vincent), January 16, 1780 *(Copyright © National Maritime Museum, Greenwich, London)*

Amethyst, H.M.S.

During the Chinese Civil War, 1946–49, on April 30, 1949, the British frigate *Amethyst* was attacked by Communist forces as she headed up the Yangtse-Kiang River. She was carrying much-needed supplies for the British community in Nanking. Communist gunfire badly damaged the ship and caused the death of 17 crew and wounded 30 more before she was trapped off an island in the Yangtse. The reason for the attack has never been satisfactorily explained and may reflect no more than the assertion of Communist control over a major waterway. The British warships *London, Black Swan,* and *Consort* attempted to rescue the *Amethyst* but failed. Some 70 further casualties resulted.

The *Amethyst* was forced to remain immobile for some fourteen weeks while unsuccessful negotiations to secure her safe passage were held. During this period of waiting the crew of the *Amethyst* carried out temporary repairs. In the absence of any progress the captain, Lieutenant-Commander J. S. Kerans, eventually decided to make a dash for the open sea under cover of darkness on July 30–31. He sailed the 140 miles (225 km) downriver to the sea at maximum speed and successfully avoided gunfire from

forts lining the river. This courageous action boosted Britain's national morale and was without doubt a superb feat of pilotage.

Amphibious Vehicles

Wheeled and tracked vehicles capable of operating on land and water. First used during WORLD WAR II, 1939–45, they have been particularly used in amphibious operations to ferry in personnel and material from ships directly onto the beach without the need for harbor installations. One of the best known was the American 2.5-ton DUKW, usually known as the "Duck," while the British produced the eight-wheeled Terrapin, which saw limited service in World War II.

The DUKW was a U.S. army amphibious truck, first introduced in 1943, that was used extensively in the latter stages of World War II when combined operations were a major operational feature. Allied naval forces could land men and supplies direct from ships offshore onto beaches without the need for conventional harbor installations. Capable of carrying 5,000 lbs. (2,268 kg) of cargo or 30 men, the DUKW managed 6 knots in the water and up to

50 miles per hour (80 km per hour) on land. The Americans also developed tracked landing vessels that saw service in World War II and after. (See also LANDING CRAFT.) In the postwar period, the development of the HOVERCRAFT and the helicopter have increased the flexibility of amphibious forces. (See also AMPHIBIOUS WARFARE.)

Amphibious Warfare

*A*mphibious or combined operations involving two or more armed services have been a feature of naval warfare since ancient times. They include a wide variety of different actions, from commando raids to full-scale invasions, but have important features in common. An amphibious operation often begins with a naval bombardment against enemy-held positions on land. Naval units bring ground troops close to the shore, but often they are conveyed to the landing beach in specialist landing craft. A successful large-scale amphibious operation depends on an element of surprise as well as on local air and sea superiority and lightly defended beaches.

The development of amphibious warfare accelerated beginning in the 16th century with the establishment of standing navies and the adoption of the naval gun. Small-scale amphibious operations were a feature of the Elizabethan period, when English raids against Spanish possessions across the world were commonplace. The major European wars of the 17th and 18th centuries—which were often global in scope—produced a need for large-scale amphibious operations. The SEVEN YEARS' WAR, 1756–63, which saw the development of the first specially designed landing craft, produced several major combined operations, including the capture of QUEBEC in 1759, when the ROYAL NAVY brought thousands of British troops up the St. Lawrence River. Smaller-scale amphibious raids were also an important feature of the naval warfare of the period. During periodic wars with France, England launched regular attacks on the enemy coast with the aim of tying down large numbers of French troops in defensive positions.

Amphibious operations played a part in many of the major wars of the 19th century including the CRIMEAN WAR, 1853–56, and the AMERICAN CIVIL WAR, 1861–65, although techniques had changed very little since the previous century. The use of specialist craft was largely unknown, and a typical amphibious vessel might be simply a barge or rowing boat. This continued to be the case during WORLD WAR I, 1914–18, although, with the exception of Gallipoli, 1915, and ZEEBRUGGE, 1918, such operations were few and far between. It was not until WORLD WAR II, 1939–45, that the major naval powers gave serious attention to the techniques and equipment of amphibious warfare. An important early example was the German occupation of Norway in 1940 and the amphibious Allied

counterattack. Combined operations were central to the Japanese conquest of Southeast Asia, the American counteroffensive (when amphibious craft were used on a massive scale during successive "island-hopping" operations) and the opening of a second front in Europe. Smaller commando raids, including the failed British attack on DIEPPE in 1942, were important in refining landing techniques that would subsequently be used on a wider scale.

Specialist LANDING CRAFT were developed with the objective of ensuring that the first wave of troops, tanks and other equipment reached the landing beach quickly. To ensure that reinforcements and supplies were landed, artificial harbors and portable pipelines were developed. Landing beaches were selected with care, and great efforts were taken to deceive the enemy about their location. For example, the Germans were led to believe that the NORMANDY landings, June 1944, were merely the precursor to the main invasion farther up the coast to the northeast.

Combined operations also have been a feature of the postwar period and those at INCHON, Korea, 1950, and SUEZ, 1956, closely resembled the amphibious landings of the latter part of World War II. They were also an important feature of a more recent example, the FALKLANDS WAR, 1982, in which modern equipment, including the HELICOPTER and short takeoff aircraft, was combined with the traditional techniques of amphibious warfare.

M. Bartlett, ed., *Assault from the Sea: Essays in the History of Amphibious Warfare*, Annapolis, 1983. J. D. Ladd, *Assault from the Sea, 1939–45*, Newton Abbot, Devon, 1976.

Anglo-Dutch Wars
1652–54; 1665–67; 1672–74

*T*he three Anglo-Dutch naval wars of the 17th century were largely the product of commercial rivalries, with each side trying to increase its trade at the expense of the other. The English Navigation Act, 1651, required English imports to be carried in English ships and was a specifically anti-Dutch measure; it led to increasing tensions that soon broke into open hostilities between the two nations.

First Anglo-Dutch War, 1652–54

The first Anglo-Dutch War, 1652–54, was triggered by the Battle of DOVER, May 19, 1652, following Dutch Admiral Marten TROMP's refusal to salute the English flag. It was followed by a series of individual engagements and an English blockade of Holland, which proved to be effective in disrupting its international trade. Following its defeat at the Battle of SCHEVENINGEN, July 31, 1653, Holland initiated peace talks that led to the Treaty of Westminster, April 1654.

Chronological List of Naval Events

1651	The Navigation Act, aimed against Dutch shipping, becomes law in England
1652	
May 19	Battle of DOVER (or Goodwin Sands)
July	The English and Dutch declare war
August 16	Action off Plymouth
August 28	The Dutch defeat a British squadron off ELBA
September 28	Battle of KENTISH KNOCK
November 30	Battle of DUNGENESS
1653	
February 18–20	Battle of PORTLAND
March 4	The Dutch defeat a British squadron that had been lured from LEGHORN
June 2–3	Battle of the GABBARD (or the first Battle of North Foreland)
June–July	British blockade of Holland
July 31	Battle of SCHEVENINGEN (or the first Battle of the Texel) ends in the defeat of the Dutch fleet
1654	
April 5	Treaty of Westminster concludes the war

Second Anglo-Dutch War, 1665–67

The Treaty of Westminster, 1654, did nothing to resolve the underlying tensions between England and Holland, and it is not surprising that English attempts to disrupt the Dutch slave trade were among the factors that led to a second naval war. English naval forces defeated the Dutch at the opening Battle of LOWESTOFT, but the tide later turned against them. The FOUR DAYS' BATTLE, June 1–4, 1666—one of the longest in naval history—ended in heavy defeat for the English fleet under George MONCK, Duke of Albemarle. Admiral Michiel de RUYTER, the victor of this battle, led a Dutch raid into the Thames that caused significant damage to shipping in the CHATHAM area and created great embarrassment in London. The English were finally persuaded to negotiate an end to the war in the Treaty of Breda, 1667, which was favorable to Dutch trading interests.

Chronological List of Naval Events

1663–64	English seize Dutch possessions in the West Indies and North America

1665	
May	England declares war on the Dutch
June 3	Battle of Lowestoft
August	Battle of Bergen
1666	
January	France enters the war against England
June 1–4	Four Days' Battle
June 25	Battle of ORFORDNESS (also known as St. James's Day Fight or the Second Battle of North Foreland)
August	Peace negotiations begin but make little progress
1657	
May	Franco-Dutch squadron attacks British possessions in the West Indies
June	Dutch fleet, commanded by Admiral de Ruyter, makes a surprise raid into the Thames estuary and up the Medway to CHATHAM, forcing England to make peace
July 21	Treaty of Breda

Third Dutch War, 1672–74

In 1672, when Louis XIV of France invaded Holland, his English ally rapidly joined the war. Naval operations began with an unprovoked attack on the Dutch Smyrna convoy, March 13, 1672, which ended in failure. In later engagements at Solebay, May 28, 1672, SCHOONEVELDT, May 28, 1673, and the TEXEL, August 11, 1673, the Dutch under Admiral de Ruyter proved to be a difficult adversary. At the Texel he won a decisive victory over Anglo-French naval forces, and the English government, which was aware of the unpopularity of a war of aggression in alliance with France, sued for peace. England's involvement in the war ended with the Treaty of Westminster, 1674, although the conflict between France and Holland continued.

Chronological List of Naval Events

1672	
March 13	Unprovoked English attack on a Dutch convoy in the English Channel
May 28	Battle of Solebay (or Southwold Bay)
1673	
May 28	First Battle of Schooneveldt
June 4	Second Battle of Schooneveldt
July	Admiral de Ruyter cruises off the Thames

August 21	Battle of the Texel; de Ruyter gains a victory against his British and French opponents
1674	
February 19	Treaty of Westminster

C. R. Boxer, *The Anglo-Dutch Wars of the Seventeenth Century, 1652–74,* London, 1974.

Anglo-German Naval Treaty
1935

The Treaty of Versailles, 1919, which imposed terms on Germany after World War I, had prevented Germany from building its own submarines or aircraft carriers. Versailles also had imposed many other restrictions on naval construction. Following Hitler's denunciation of the Versailles treaty, Britain negotiated a new naval treaty with Germany.

The main provision of this new treaty, the Anglo-German Naval Treaty of 1935, allowed the GERMAN NAVY to build up to 35% of the total tonnage of the ROYAL NAVY. This was expressed in terms of overall strength and meant that the Germans could exceed the British in specific classes of ship. A further clause limited German submarine construction to 45% of the British total unless there was evidence of building by a potentially hostile third power.

Although the new treaty was the subject of severe international criticism on the grounds that it was appeasement of Hitler, at least it brought Germany within the scope of international naval agreements. It also reflected a revised British government view that the Treaty of Versailles was unnecessarily harsh. In a second agreement with Hitler, signed in 1937, Germany was formally tied more closely to existing international agreements. However, these constraints proved to be short-lived. By April 1939 Hitler had denounced the terms of the 1935 treaty, having invoked an escape clause some two years earlier. This allowed him to build in excess of permitted levels on the grounds of potentially hostile Soviet naval construction activity, but his real objective was to build a new German navy that could dominate British trade routes.

Annapolis

Located on the southern bank of the Severn River, near Chesapeake Bay in the United States, the city of Annapolis, Maryland has had long associations with the U.S. Navy. Originally settled by Puritans from Virginia in 1649 as the town of Providence, it served briefly as the capital of the United States in 1783–84. The UNITED STATES NAVAL ACADEMY has been based in Annapolis since its foundation in 1845 by George BANCROFT, the then Secretary of the Navy, except for a short period during the AMERICAN CIVIL WAR, 1861–65. The Academy is an undergraduate college that educates men and women who wish to be commissioned officers in the navy or marine corps. Some 1,200 candidates are admitted to the college every year and spend four years studying for a bachelor of science degree. They then become commissioned officers in the UNITED STATES NAVY and must serve for at least six years. Annapolis also has provided the land-based headquarters of the U.S. Atlantic Fleet.

Anson, George, First Baron Anson
1697–1762

English naval commander, born at Shugborough Park, Staffordshire. Anson entered the ROYAL NAVY in 1712 and became a captain in 1724, but it was not until the War of JENKINS' EAR, 1739–43, that he first achieved prominence as the last of the great CORSAIRS. When war against Spain and France broke out, he was appointed, as a commodore, to command a squadron of six ships to operate against Spanish naval and commercial interests in the Pacific.

George Anson's greatest success was his attack, off the Philippines in June 1742, on the *Nuestra Señora de Covadonga,* one of the Spanish treasure galleons that plied between Mexico and Manila. It raised the total booty seized during the voyage to more than £500,000. After a circumnavigation of the globe that lasted some three years and nine months, he returned to England, arriving at Spithead in June 1744. However, the weather and disease had taken their toll; by that time Anson was reduced to a single ship, the *Centurion,* and 200 men (out of a total of over 1,300 at the beginning of his voyage). Some four years later he published *Voyage Round the World,* the story of his circumnavigation. He returned to sea as a flag officer during the latter stages of the War of the AUSTRIAN SUCCESSION, 1740–48, defeating the French at CAPE FINISTERRE, 1747, and capturing treasure valued at £300,000.

Anson spent the final years of his naval career as First Lord of the Admiralty during the Pelham and Pitt administrations. During his two separate periods of office, he was responsible for a number of long-overdue reforms, including the reorganization of the inefficient and corrupt naval dockyards, which helped to prepare the Royal Navy for action in the SEVEN YEARS' WAR, 1756–63. He also laid the foundations of the naval profession by improving professional training and introducing a standard uniform for naval officers. In 1761, shortly before his death, he was appointed Admiral of the Fleet in recognition of his achievements.

S. W. C. Pack, *Admiral Lord Anson,* London, 1960.

Antiaircraft Guns

*A*mong the earliest antiaircraft guns were the pre–WORLD WAR I, 1914–18, naval guns that were specially adapted for this purpose. Like all weapons of this kind, the gun needed to elevate to a high angle and have a high rate of fire. A key example was the Krupp 88 mm naval gun, which had a range of up to 17,000 feet (5,182 m) and a rate of fire of up to 15 rounds a minute. However, the chances of any one gun hitting its target were relatively low because the gunner had no information about the speed or altitude of the intended target.

During WORLD WAR II, 1939–45, the introduction of ranging radar sets and then the radio proximity fuse heralded the arrival of improved fire control and greatly increased the chances that a heavy gun would hit its target. Warships also made full use of light machine guns of up to 20 mm, which were often grouped together. ROCKETS also were sometimes deployed and often were effective against low-flying aircraft.

In the postwar period, the big gun has been replaced by the surface-to-air MISSILE, which has proved to be a much more effective defense against enemy aircraft. Modern aircraft now fly at too high a cruising altitude to fall within the range of the big guns. Missiles often are used in conjunction with light antiaircraft guns and rapid-firing machine guns when attacking targets at lower altitudes.

Antisubmarine Warfare

*I*n 1917, during WORLD WAR I, 1914–18, when the menace of the German submarine fleet had reached a critical stage, the British and French established the Allied Submarine Detection Investigation Committee (ASDIC). The committee concluded that there were three methods of detecting submerged submarines: echo-sounding, monitoring their noise and measuring their magnetic displacement. The same three methods, although far more sophisticated, are still employed in antisubmarine warfare (ASW) today.

Today ASDIC is known by the American term SONAR (Sound Navigation and Ranging) and is similar to commercial echo sounders. A transducer, using a quartz crystal vibrator, emits a high-frequency sound wave that passes through the water and is reflected back by any solid object it encounters. Because sound travels at a known, steady speed through water, the depth of an object (or the seabed) can be calculated from the time it takes the sound pulse to travel from the ship's transmitter back to the receiver. If the submarine is moving, a bearing can be obtained by measuring the change of pulse, or what is known as the Doppler effect.

Early ASDIC sets projected a narrow beam ahead of the attacking ship, but the signal was lost when the ship passed over its target and the DEPTH CHARGE was released from the sides or starn. The first attempt to solve this problem was to devise ahead-firing weapons, like the SQUID and HEDGEHOG, that could be programmed while ASDIC was still in contact. However, more advanced ASDIC units were later devised that entirely overcame this difficulty. Today buoys containing sonar (Sonobuoys) are dropped into the water above the suspected target and relay their findings back to an ASW aircraft or HELICOPTER. A second method relies on detecting the noise that all submerged submarines make as they pass through the water. Generally speaking, the larger a submarine, the more noise it makes. Monitoring a submarine's noise is carried out passively with underwater microphones (hydrophones).

Submarines also can be detected by measuring the difference they cause to the earth's magnetic field because they are made of a large mass of metal. This is known as magnetic anomaly detection (MAD) and has been used commercially for many years to find deposits of minerals and oil from MAD-equipped aircraft. A more recent method of detection is by analyzing the air and water samples in areas where enemy submarines are believed to be operating. Although modern nuclear submarines do not have to surface for extended periods, they discharge large quantities of cooling water, which, because it is hot and mildly radioactive, can be detected by infrared detectors. Once detected, submarines will be attacked by a modern version of the depth charge.

William Hackmann, *Seek and Strike: Sonar, Anti-submarine Warfare and the Royal Navy, 1914–34*, London, 1984.

Apraksin, Fedor, Count
1661–1728

*R*ussian admiral who played a major role in the creation of the RUSSIAN NAVY in the early years of the 18th century. Apraksin, who was a close friend of Tsar PETER THE GREAT, was appointed governor of the fort of Azov on the Black Sea following its capture from the Turks. He implemented Peter's plans for a new fleet, which was built in the Azov dockyards. In 1707 Apraksin was appointed admiral with responsibility for developing the new Baltic fleet, which was to protect Russia's lines of communication and defend St. Petersburg from attack.

He commanded this fleet during the Great Northern War, 1700–21, when Russia fought Charles XII of Sweden in a struggle for supremacy in the Baltic. Apraksin saved St. Petersburg from a Swedish invasion force in 1708, but his most notable victory was achieved at GANGUT in 1714. The Russian Baltic fleet, which consisted of 30 sailing ships and 180 galleys, decisively defeated the Swedes and ended their domination of the Baltic. As a result of Apraksin's victory, the Russians gained control of the Gulf of Finland and proceeded with the invasion of Finland.

Apraksin extended these gains in 1719–20 when raids against Sweden were organized and Stockholm was attacked. Apraksin's territorial gains were confirmed by the Treaty of Nystad, 1721, and Russia's position in the Baltic was secure. Apraksin, the "father of the Russian navy," was promoted to the highest naval rank in recognition of his services.

R. C. Anderson, *Naval Wars in the Baltic in the Sailing Ship Epoch,* London, 1910.

Arbuthnot, Marriot
1711–84

*B*ritish admiral and commander in chief of the North American station during the AMERICAN WAR OF INDEPENDENCE, 1775–83, Arbuthnot had spent much of his active naval career in North American and Caribbean waters. During the SEVEN YEARS' WAR, 1756–63, he served at the Battle of QUIBERON BAY, November 1759, where he commanded the *Portland,* a fourth-rate ship. (See RATING OF SHIPS.) He was later involved in the capture of Havana in 1762 as part of the squadron commanded by Admiral Sir George Pocock. During the American War of Independence, Arbuthnot received wide acclaim for his part in the siege and capture of the port of Charleston, South Carolina,

1779, which also involved army units commanded by General Sir Henry Clinton.

Vice Admiral Arbuthnot was less fortunate on March 16, 1781, when he fought the First Battle of the CHESAPEAKE with a French squadron commanded by Commodore Sochet Destouches. The result was inconclusive, but if Arbuthnot had not followed the officially prescribed tactics—the *FIGHTING INSTRUCTIONS*—so closely, the outcome almost certainly would have been a British victory. This marked the end of Arbuthnot's career; he was recalled to England soon afterward and received no further naval appointments.

Arctic Convoys
1941–45

*T*he full horror of modern naval warfare was demonstrated vividly in the Arctic CONVOYS of WORLD WAR II, 1939–45. Following the German invasion of the Soviet Union in June 1941, Joseph Stalin, the Soviet leader, turned to the Allies to replace his battered war machine. The only Soviet ports accessible from the Atlantic were Murmansk and Archangel, and British convoys (which included some American merchantmen) started arriving there in August 1941. They continued until December 1944, with 36 convoys making the outward journey, al-

A British Arctic convoy arrives at Murmansk, northern Russia, in 1941   *(Copyright © National Maritime Museum, Greenwich, London)*

though fewer survived to return home. The Royal Navy provided covering forces from the home fleet and elsewhere. They were supplemented by a squadron of the UNITED STATES NAVY, including the battleship *Washington*. The Arctic convoys were subject to several major threats, including appalling weather conditions. Extreme cold and ice made the journey a hazardous one. The convoys were also constantly threatened by the U-BOATS operating on these routes. German surface ships and aircraft operating from occupied Norway presented considerable dangers; the convoys required the full protection of the British home fleet.

The effect of this formidable concentration of power was demonstrated in the successful German attack on CONVOY PQ-17, July 1942, which resulted in the loss of 24 of its 32 ships. In total, British losses were heavy, although later convoys had a greater chance of success as the balance of naval power gradually shifted in Britain's favor. The British merchant fleet lost 87 ships and over 800 men; the ROYAL NAVY lost 18 warships and over 2,000 men. The GERMAN NAVY also suffered major setbacks in its encounters with the British home fleet as it attacked the convoys. It was defeated at the Battle of the BARENTS SEA, December 1942, and a year later the battleship *BISMARCK* was sunk following its attempt to destroy an Arctic convoy. The Germans also lost 38 U-boats, the *SCHARNHORST* and a destroyer.

The real effect of this costly operation is difficult to assess. Some 4 million tons of supplies, including 5,000 tanks and 7,000 aircraft, were shipped to Russia by this route. Although the Soviets received more plentiful Allied supplies by other means, the Arctic convoys provided a lifeline at a critical point in 1941. They demonstrated Britain's clear commitment to its Soviet ally despite Stalin's belief that the Allies were not giving him sufficient support.

Richard Woodman, *Arctic Convoys*, London, 1994.

Arethusa, H.M.S.

Seven British ships named *Arethusa* have served in the ROYAL NAVY. The most historically significant of these was a fourth-rate of 50 guns. (See RATING OF SHIPS.) Built at Pembroke, Wales in 1849, she served in the CRIMEAN WAR, 1853–56, and was involved in the bombardment of Sevastopol (October 1854–September 1855), where she played a major role.

She was notable as the last British ship to fight an engagement entirely under sail. Like many of her sister ships, she sustained some damage from Russian shore fire, confirming once more that the wooden sailing warship offered no real protection against the modern shell. The Crimean War demonstrated beyond doubt that the *Arethusa* and her contemporaries were obsolete. The world's

navies rapidly replaced the wooden sailing ship with the IRONCLAD, the forerunner of the modern warship. In 1873 the *Arethusa* began a new career as a naval training ship, serving in this role for another 60 years.

Argus, H.M.S.

The British ship *Argus* was notable as the first proper AIRCRAFT CARRIER, establishing the basic design followed by all subsequent ships of this type. She was laid down in 1914 as a passenger liner for an Italian company but was commandeered by the British Admiralty during WORLD WAR I, 1914–18. Completed as an aircraft carrier, the *Argus* was the first ship with a full-size flush flight deck of 550 feet (167.6 m) in length. Two electrically powered lifts served the hangar below. The *Argus* had a displacement of 21,000 tons, a maximum speed of 24 knots and a complement of 748 men. She could carry 20 Sopwith Cuckoo aircraft.

The *Argus* was completed too late to participate in World War I but saw peacetime service in the Grand Fleet and in the Atlantic Fleet. In 1930 she was placed in the reserve but was later converted to operate Queen Bee target aircraft. Her WORLD WAR II, 1939–45, service included periods with the Mediterranean Fleet, 1939–40, and with FORCE H in 1942. Again placed in reserve in 1944, the *Argus* was finally scrapped in 1947.

Arima, Masafumi
1895–1944

A specialist in naval air power, Rear Admiral Arima commanded the Japanese 26th Naval Air Flotilla during WORLD WAR II, 1939–45. He met his end as the Japanese navy's first KAMIKAZE pilot, during an attack on the American aircraft carrier *Franklin* in October 1944; the *Franklin* was part of a force bombarding the island of Formosa prior to the Luzon landings. Just before the Japanese air attack on the American forces, in which 86 aircraft were deployed, Arima announced that he was planning to fly into the *Franklin* without regard for his own personal safety. He underlined his intention not to return by tearing off his own badges of rank. Arima was one of 20 pilots lost in the attack, which damaged but did not sink the American carrier.

Arizona, U.S.S.

A WORLD WAR I, 1914–18, American battleship of the Pennsylvania class, commissioned in October 1916 and sunk by the Japanese during the attack on PEARL

HARBOR, December 1941. With a displacement of 31,400 tons, the *Arizona* was armed with 12 14-inch (36 cm) guns and 22 5-inch (13 cm) guns (which were later reduced to 15). She was operated by a crew of 915, was 608 feet (185.32 m) in length and had a beam of 97 feet (29.56 m). During rebuilding and modernization in 1928–31, facilities for three aircraft and two catapults were provided. On December 7, 1941 the *Arizona* was one of eight battleships of the U.S. Pacific Fleet lying in Pearl Harbor's "Battleship Row" when she was hit by bombs and torpedoes from the Japanese carrier-based aircraft during the surprise attack on the American base. The resulting fires caused her magazines to explode, and she quickly sank to the bottom of the harbor, where she remains to this day. More than 1,000 officers and men are entombed in the ship. The *Arizona* is an official memorial to all the American servicemen who died during the Japanese attack on Pearl Harbor.

Arkansas, U.S.S.

Notable as the oldest American battleship to serve in WORLD WAR II, 1939–45, the U.S.S. *Arkansas* was commissioned in 1912. She had a displacement of 26,100 tons, main armament of 12 12-inch (30 cm) guns and a crew of up to 1,650. She was 562 feet 6 inches (170.45 m) in length and had a beam of 106 feet 3 inches (32.39m). The *Arkansas* served with an American crew as a member of the Sixth Battle Cruiser Squadron of the British GRAND FLEET in the final stages of WORLD WAR I, 1914–18, and was present at the surrender of the German High Seas Fleet in the Fifth of Forth, Scotland, on November 20, 1918.

Modified during the interwar period, the *Arkansas* played a useful second-line role during World War II. For much of the war she served in the Atlantic but also went briefly to the Pacific theater in 1945. During the NORMANDY landings, June 1944, she returned to front-line action as part of the bombardment force. The *Arkansas* survived World War II only to be sunk deliberately during an atomic bomb test at Bikini Atoll in July 1946.

Ark Royal, H.M.S.

Three British AIRCRAFT CARRIERS and a Tudor warship have all shared the name *Ark Royal*. The first *Ark Royal* was a GALLEON of 800 tons built at Deptford, London, in 1587. She was originally produced for Sir Walter RALEIGH and was known as *Ark Ralegh*; when the Crown acquired her shortly before the SPANISH ARMADA, 1588, she was renamed the *Ark Royal*. Armed with 55 guns, she served as Lord HOWARD of Effingham's flagship in the battle against Spain. The *Ark Royal* was a "lofty-built" ship but she could sail well. Howard himself said "we can see no

sail, great nor small but how so ever they be off, we fetch them and speak with them."

The name then fell into disuse in the British service until WORLD WAR I, 1914–18, when it was revived by the ROYAL NAVY for a seaplane carrier that was a converted freighter. The second British aircraft carrier to be called *Ark Royal*, completed in 1938, achieved distinction in a brief WORLD WAR II, 1939–45, career, spent largely in the Mediterranean. She was also involved in the destruction of the BISMARCK in 1941, her torpedo-bombers causing the vital damage that reduced the German ship's speed. This *Ark Royal* was known as the ship that the enemy could not sink. The Germans had published a succession of false propaganda stories about her destruction, but they could not sink her until 1941, when she was torpedoed in the Mediterranean.

The name was again revived by the British later that year when an aircraft carrier of 36,800 tons was launched. Together with the *Eagle*, her sister ship, she formed the nucleus of Britain's carrier force in the postwar period. With the aid of an expensive refit she remained in service until 1978. The fourth *Ark Royal* in British service was also an aircraft carrier, launched in June 1981.

Michael Apps, *The Four Ark Royals*, London, 1976.

Armada   *See* SPANISH ARMADA.

Armed Merchant Cruiser

During WORLD WAR I, 1914–18, merchant ships were commandeered in large numbers, mainly by the British and German navies, for use as naval auxiliaries, with many of the faster vessels being used as armed merchant cruisers (AMCs). Passenger liners and other merchant ships were converted for this purpose and were equipped with medium-size naval guns. They relieved regular cruisers in carrying out patrol duties; the GERMAN NAVY in particular used them to attack merchant ships and troop convoys. Actions between opposing AMCs were relatively rare, but one notable example occurred at the beginning of the war, in September 1914, when the British AMC *CARMANIA* sank the German *Cap Trafalgar* after a hard-fought battle in the South Atlantic. Despite their successes, AMCs suffered from a number of weaknesses, including the absence of armor protection and relatively poor armament—weaknesses that became more evident as the war progressed. In the latter stages of the war, as submarine operations intensified, they were reassigned to other work.

The Germans in particular used disguised AMCs or decoy ships. These were the equivalent of the ROYAL NAVY's Q-SHIP's. Unlike their British counterparts, merchant ships rather than submarines were their target, and they also had mine-laying duties—indeed, the German navy insisted that they lay their mines before initiating raiding activities. Operations began when the *Moewe*, the most successful of these ships, left on the first of her sorties late in 1915. She was followed by a number of others, including the *GREIF*, *WOLF*, *Leopard* and *SEEADLER*. The latter was a fully rigged sailing ship rather than a conventional tramp steamer. Apart from their immediate toll of Allied ships, the German commerce raiders caused considerable disruption to shipping and troop movements during their widely scattered operations in 1915–17.

AMCs were also employed on similar missions during WORLD WAR II, 1939–45. The Royal Navy used some 60 former passenger liners as AMCs; they were normally equipped with up to eight 8-inch (20 cm) guns and a variety of antiaircraft guns. Results were mixed, but potentially these ships were all highly vulnerable. Particularly heavy losses were sustained when they were used as convoy escorts. As a result, the British withdrew all their AMCs by early 1944. The German navy had decommissioned all its AMCs a year earlier for similar reasons, having lost over half its small fleet of nine AMCs while they were engaged in commerce-raiding activities.

Armor

The development of the high-explosive shell led to the first use of metal armor for naval purposes during the CRIMEAN WAR, 1854–56. The French pioneered the wartime use of armor to protect their floating batteries and later, in 1859, built *LA GLOIRE*, the world's first IRONCLAD warship. It was protected with wrought-iron armor up to 4.7 inches (12 cm) thick. In 1861 the British responded with the *WARRIOR*, their own ironclad warship, and in the AMERICAN CIVIL WAR, 1861–65, ironclads appeared soon afterward. (See MONITOR and MERRIMACK.) During this period the process of producing armor changed rapidly. It soon became evident that wrought-iron armor was not strong enough to resist shell fire; to increase its effectiveness, it was combined with steel. The process of producing steel for this purpose was itself refined, partly in response to changes in weapons technology.

In the 1880s the appearance of armor-piercing shells led to the application of carbon to harden the face of the steel, while the steel itself was strengthened by the use of a nickel-steel alloy. From this period armor could be used to protect the sides of a warship, the deck (to safeguard the engines and magazines), the bridge and the gun turrets. In practice, the extent to which armor was used and its thickness would depend on whether protection or speed was the critical factor in a particular warship design. The BATTLE CRUISER is an example of a warship where armor protection was reduced to give greater speed. During the two world wars, these developments led to the general use of rolled homogeneous steel armor as the standard protection for most armored warships. Recent improvements in armor-piercing shells have stimulated further developments, leading to the replacement of rolled homogeneous steel armor by lamination. Various materials, including titanium, glass fiber and ceramics, are combined to dissipate the force of an enemy shell or missile and in some circumstances have proved to be more effective than conventional armor.

Arnauld de la Perière, Lothar von
1886–1941

Lothar von Arnauld de la Perière, an experienced German naval officer, was the most successful submarine commander of WORLD WAR I, 1914–18. He was appointed to the command of *U-35* in November 1915 and served for more than two years. He sank as many as 189 Allied merchant ships (totaling 446,708 tons), mainly by gunfire, during the period to March 1918, when he relinquished his command.

Awarded the *Ordre pour la Mérite* for his achievements, this ace of aces commanded *U-139*, a cruiser submarine, during the last six months of the war. After an extended period with the Turkish navy during the interwar years, Arnauld de la Perière returned to the GERMAN NAVY during the WORLD WAR II, 1939–45, rising to the rank of vice admiral before dying in an air crash early in 1941. (See also U-BOAT.)

Arnold, Benedict
1741–1801

American military leader and traitor. Arnold served with distinction in land operations during the early stages of the AMERICAN WAR OF INDEPENDENCE, 1775–83, but was later to betray his country to the British. During the course of the fighting Arnold also demonstrated his abilities as a naval commander. An apothecary by profession, Arnold first saw military service in the colonial militia during the French and Indian War, 1754–63.

As a militia colonel, Arnold was involved in the capture of Fort Ticonderoga at the beginning of the American Revolution. At the end of the same year he was badly wounded in an unsuccessful attack on British-held Quebec. By mid-1776 he was forced to retreat to LAKE CHAMPLAIN, where a small flotilla had been assembled on Washington's instructions. Arnold spent the next four months constructing additional vessels. Despite these efforts, his force of 15 boats did not compare favorably with a British flotilla of 25 vessels. On October 11 Arnold was severely defeated off Valcour Island and was forced to withdraw southward, with the British in close pursuit. Two days later he suffered further heavy losses and was forced to beach his flagship, the *Congress*. However, Arnold's strategic objective—to delay a British invasion from Canada toward New York—had been achieved; it was now too late in the year for the enemy to proceed south. Arnold then returned to land service, distinguishing himself in the Saratoga campaign, 1777, and later holding the command of Philadelphia. In 1780 he was appointed to the command of West Point. He soon defected following the discovery of his secret negotiations with General Clinton to hand over West Point to the British for a large sum of money. He is regarded as the most notorious traitor in American history. After a short period of service in the British army, he left for England, where he spent most of the rest of his life.

Flexner, James T., *The Traitor and the Spy*, New York, 1953.

Asan Incident
July 25, 1894

An engagement between Chinese and Japanese naval squadrons that occurred shortly before the SINO-JAPANESE WAR, 1894–95, was formally declared on August 1, 1894. The conflict between the two countries had arisen over their rival claims to predominance in Korea. In June 1894 Chinese troops disembarked at Asan, some 40 miles southwest of Seoul. A Japanese squadron, commanded by Rear Admiral Tsuboi, was dispatched to disrupt the operation. On July 25 it intercepted the Chinese cruiser *Tsi-Yuen* and the sloop *Kwang-Yi* near Phung-Tao on the west coast of Korea. They were on their return journey from Asan after delivering a cargo of Chinese ground troops. The cruiser managed to escape to the port of Wei-hai-wei but the *Kwang-Yi* was lost.

Later the same day the Japanese intercepted the British merchant steamer *Kowshing*, which was carrying more Chinese troops to Asan and was escorted by Chinese naval forces. The *Kowshing* was ordered to follow the Japanese squadron, but the Chinese escort threatened the British captain and prevented him from moving. After some hours of negotiation the Japanese commander decided on more direct action. The armored cruiser *Naniwa* opened fire and sank the *Kowshing* and damaged the Chinese escorts. The Japanese had achieved their immediate objective, but at the cost of alienating the international community and making war with China inevitable.

ASDIC

The term "ASDIC," which originally was used to describe SONAR, took its name from the initials of the Allied Submarine Detection Investigation Committee. This committee had been established jointly by the British and French shortly before the end of WORLD WAR I, 1914–18, with the aim of developing reliable ANTISUBMARINE WARFARE techniques. The committee oversaw the development of this underwater device, in which the French were to play a leading role during the interwar years. The ASDIC device used ultrasonic waves to detect the position and range of submerged submarines and was to come into general operational use during WORLD WAR II, 1939–45.

Associations, H.M.S.

A British second-rate SHIP OF THE LINE (see RATING OF SHIPS), the *Association* served as Sir Clowdisley SHOVELL's flagship during the War of the SPANISH SUCCESSION, 1701–14. Built at Portsmouth, England, in 1697, it was armed with 90 guns.

In October 1707 Shovell, who was commander in chief of the British fleet in the Mediterranean, was returning home for the winter months. Weather conditions were poor and the *Association*'s crew had little idea of her real position as she approached the west coast of the British Isles. Because of strong currents she was much farther north than had been estimated. As a result of this navigational error, the *Association* and four accompanying warships were wrecked off the Scilly Isles. Some 2,000 sailors were drowned; Shovell himself managed to struggle ashore, only to be murdered by a local woman who stole his valuables.

As a direct result of these losses, work to establish a more accurate method of determining longitude was officially commissioned. Significant improvements in the art of navigation ultimately resulted from this project, including the development of an accurate chronometer.

Athenia

The first British ship to be sunk in WORLD WAR II, 1939–45, the *Athenia* was a passenger liner of 13,581 tons. She was traveling across the Atlantic from Liverpool to the United States when she was torpedoed by the German submarine *U-30* without any warning. The incident occurred south of Rockall Bank during the evening of the first day of the war, September 3, 1939. Some 1,300 survivors were picked up, but 112 passengers and crew lost their lives in the attack.

Germany justified this action on the spurious grounds that the U-BOAT commander had believed that the *Athenia* was an ARMED MERCHANT CRUISER and therefore a legitimate wartime target. The attack provided the British with a timely warning that the GERMAN NAVY was likely to adopt a policy of unrestricted submarine warfare and that CONVOY protection would be a major task of the Allied navies in the Atlantic and elsewhere.

Atlantic, Battle of the
1915–17

During the WORLD WAR I, 1914–18, the main surface fleets of Britain and Germany were used cautiously, acting primarily as blockading forces. They met in battle only at JUTLAND, 1916, and on four other occasions. The British surface fleet had quickly established domination of the seas and German merchant ships were forced to seek refuge in neutral ports. This eventually led to severe shortages in supplies and raw materials in Germany. In these circumstances the GERMAN NAVY, at the instigation of Admiral Alfred von TIRPITZ and other naval leaders, turned to the submarine to increase economic pressure on Britain, which depended for its survival on supplies brought by sea. It waged a three-year war—with some interruptions—against merchant ships in the Atlantic Ocean and elsewhere. The U-BOAT BLOCKADE of Britain began on February 18, 1915; as of that date, Allied shipping of all kinds that entered the "war zone"—defined loosely as all the approaches to the British Isles—was to be torpedoed without warning. Among the victims of this first campaign were an American tanker and a number of American citizens who were passengers on two British liners, the LUSITANIA (sunk May 7, 1915) and the *Arabic*, that were sunk by the Germans. These incidents outraged American opinion, although it was nearly two years before the United States entered the war.

Following the destruction of the second passenger ship on August 19, 1915, the Germans were compelled to announce, on September 1, an end to unrestricted submarine warfare. The German government said that in the future, no liners would be attacked without warning and the safety of noncombatants would be assured as long as no resistance was offered. The destruction of Allied merchant vessels, which were unaffected by this policy change, continued to rise. A million tons of shipping were lost in 1915–16. Following the sinking of the *Sussex*, a cross-Channel steamer, in the spring of 1916, U.S. President Woodrow Wilson secured a promise from Germany that it would not attack any more merchantmen without warning and would do its "utmost to confine the operations of war for the rest of its duration to the fighting forces of the belligerents." However, pressure from the German navy to reintroduce unrestricted submarine warfare grew during 1916 as it became clear that Germany could not hope to win the war by the efforts of its army alone.

After considerable internal debate, Germany resumed full U-boat attacks on February 1, 1917, on the assumption that Britain would be starved out within six months, well before any American intervention could become effective. With 127 U-boats in service, Allied shipping losses did begin to rise at an alarming rate: 259 ships were destroyed in February, 325 in March and 423 in April, when losses reached a peak. This was well in excess of the rate of

replacement, and Britain was in danger of being cut off. The Royal Navy introduced countermeasures, but the use of improved mines, hydrophones and depth charges was not sufficient to provide the protection required. The Royal Navy had long opposed the introduction of the CONVOY system, but this system proved to be the only way of winning the battle against the U-boat in the Atlantic.

Following the intervention of the British prime minister David Lloyd George, convoys were introduced on May 10, 1917. Shipping losses gradually diminished during the remainder of the year as the system was extended, eventually to cover neutral as well as Allied ships. By the last quarter of 1917 the destruction of Allied shipping tonnage was running at a little more than half that of six months earlier. In total, 2,566 ships (5,750,000 tons) were sunk by U-boats in 1917. Allied losses continued to fall in the following year. By May 1918 the Allies were building more shipping than was being destroyed by U-boats. The first Battle of the Atlantic had been won and the threat to Britain's supply lifeline was virtually over.

John Terraine, *Business in Great Waters: The U-boat Wars, 1916–45*, London, 1989.

Atlantic, Battle of the
1939–45

The battle for control of the Atlantic was a key determinant of the outcome of both world wars and offered Germany perhaps the best prospects of defeating her opponents. As in WORLD WAR I, 1914–18, Britain's survival depended on the preservation of the North American supply route, while the defeat of Germany would entail transporting large numbers of U.S. troops across the Atlantic. Neither the British nor the German navies were fully prepared for the longest battle of the war when fighting began in 1939. A U-BOAT construction program was well under way and 98 submarines had been built (compared with Britain's 70). However, this was not a sufficient number of boats for the task of disrupting the Atlantic supply routes. Nonetheless, under the energetic direction of Admiral Karl DÖNITZ, Germany was well advanced in training crews and developing the WOLF PACK tactics that were to prove so effective at first.

The ROYAL NAVY was better prepared to combat the U-boat threat in 1939 than it had been during World War I. Its extensive experience of the CONVOY system was soon put to full use, and it was confident that it had the technology to locate and destroy enemy submarines. (See

ASDIC.) However, at least initially, the British Admiralty overlooked the importance of air power in defeating the U-boat. Unconstrained submarine warfare on the part of Germany quickly became the pattern in World War II as the U-boat war intensified. Losses of Allied shipping mounted as more U-boats entered service; auxiliary cruisers and long-range aircraft (particularly the Focke-Wulf Condor) also played an important role in the German offensive in the Atlantic. With the German occupation of France and Norway in 1940, U-boats could be based much closer to the North Atlantic shipping lanes, their main intended area of operations. Other weaknesses in the British position quickly became evident. In the early stages of the war Britain had insufficient convoy escort vessels, and air protection was virtually nonexistent. The British were also ill-equipped to respond effectively to German wolf pack tactics. Allied shipping losses rapidly mounted, and a three-year struggle for control of the Atlantic ensued. British efforts were underpinned by growing American support and direct involvement in convoy escort duties from May 1941 onward. Convoy escort techniques improved with experience, and more escort vessels, increasingly equipped with RADAR, appeared. Moreover, the British had access to information from enemy signals traffic, but this advantage was neutralized by the fact that the Germans also could intercept Allied signals. Air protection gradually increased, although a shortage of long-range aircraft meant that there was greater vulnerability to U-boat attack in the mid-Atlantic.

These improvements laid the foundation for the decisive struggle in the winter of 1942–43, when the balance gradually tipped in the Allies' favor. By mid-1943 U-boat losses had reached unsustainable levels and the Germans were forced to abandon the fight in the Atlantic. There is no single explanation for this gradual reversal of fortunes. The Allies' greater provision of long-range air cover and the introduction of the escort AIRCRAFT CARRIER, which provided immediate air support for each protected convoy, were key factors in shifting the balance of power. Other major contributory factors were a substantial increase in the number of escort vessels and improvements in the methods of detecting and attacking enemy submarines. The Germans also lost their Atlantic U-boat bases when the Allies invaded France in 1944. U-boats continued to operate against Allied shipping for the duration of the war, but they were never again able to mount a serious challenge. The introduction of new U-boats with longer range and higher speed might have changed the balance of advantage, but the war ended before many were built. The Battle of the Atlantic produced some 50,000 Allied and 32,000 German casualties. The Germans had sunk 2,575 Allied and neutral ships for the loss of 781 U-boats.

John Costello and Terry Hughes, *The Battle of the Atlantic*, London, 1977; John Terraine, *Business in Great Waters: The U-boat Wars, 1916–45*, London, 1989.

A British Short Sunderland flying boat attacks a German wolf pack during the Battle of the Atlantic, 1939–45 *(Copyright © National Maritime Museum, Greenwich, London)*

Atlantic Conveyer

A British container ship of 14,950 tons, owned by Cunard. It was one of several vessels requisitioned by the British government during the FALKLANDS WAR, 1982. The *Atlantic Conveyer* was used to transport aircraft and equipment from Britain to the Falklands. She was hit by an Argentinian EXOCET off the Falklands on May 25, 1982; 12 lives, including the captain's, were lost as a result. The crew was forced to abandon the ship, which quickly sank with one Lynx, three Chinook and ten Wessex HELICOPTERS aboard.

Atlantis

L aunched in 1937 as a German passenger ship—the *Goldenfels* of the Hansa Line—this vessel was converted, equipped and employed by the German Navy as an ARMED MERCHANT CRUISER during WORLD WAR II, 1939–45. She had a displacement of 7,860 tons and, on the outbreak of war, was equipped with six 5.9-inch (15-cm) guns. The *Atlantis* left Germany at the end of March 1940, covering 102,000 miles (164,150 km) in 600 days during a cruise through the Atlantic, Indian and Pacific Oceans in which she altered her appearance several times. Operating with Japanese assistance, she destroyed 22 Allied ships with a total displacement of more than 145,697 tons before the end came. Eventually she was sunk by the British cruiser *Devonshire* off Ascension Island in the South Atlantic in November 1941. The *Atlantis* was the most successful armed merchant cruiser employed during World War II or any other war.

Audacity, H.M.S.

A British ship notable as the world's first escort carrier. Although her operational life was only three months, she had a great influence on ship design (see AIRCRAFT CARRIER). The *Audacity* began life as the 5,537-ton German merchant ship *Hannover* and was captured by the British in 1940. She was converted as an escort carrier to meet a pressing wartime need, evident from the early days of the WORLD WAR II, 1939–45, to provide greater protection for British convoys. Allied shipping losses in the Atlantic and elsewhere were mounting at the hands of German U-BOATS and the Focke-Wulf Condor bomber. The *Audacity's* superstructure was removed and a wooden flight deck, 460 feet (140.2 m) in length, was installed. She operated six American-made Grumman Martlet fighters, which had to be parked on the flight deck because there was no hangar to accommodate them. For self-defense she was equipped with a 4-inch (10-cm) gun aft and six 20-mm Oerlikons.

The *Audacity's* operational service began in September 1941, and she rapidly proved herself, with her aircraft scoring a number of victories against the Condor. In December 1941, however, she was sunk west of Portugal by a U-boat while escorting a convoy from Gibraltar to Britain—but not before she had claimed two more Condors. As a result of these short-lived but striking successes, the *Audacity* became the model for similar escort carriers that were constructed in the United States during the war. The first examples appeared toward the end of 1942 and were known as carrier vessel escorts. In the meantime, the Allied navies had to rely on conversions like the *Audacity*, which were known as merchant aircraft carriers. See also ATLANTIC, BATTLE OF THE, 1939–45.

Augusta, Battle of
April 22, 1676

*W*hen the British made peace with the Dutch in 1674 at the end of the third ANGLO-DUTCH WAR, 1672–74, fighting between the French and the Dutch navies continued. The opposing fleets met on three occasions in 1676 as they intervened in a dispute over Sicily, which was then under Spanish rule. During an uprising against Spain, the people of the island appealed for French help, while the Spanish government asked the Dutch for help. The first action, the Battle of Stromboli on January 8, 1676, had been indecisive, but Dutch Admiral Michiel de RUYTER had prevented the French fleet, commanded by Admiral the Marquis DUQUESNE, from reaching Sicily. The two fleets met again off Augusta on the east coast of Sicily on April 22. The combined Spanish-Dutch fleet was slightly smaller (27 warships compared to 29) than the French and also suffered from a divided command: De Ruyter had been joined by Spanish Admiral Don Francisco de la Cerda.

De Ruyter led the van division and was heavily involved in the action while the Spanish fought at a distance. The Dutch rear could join the fighting only in the evening, by which time the French had decided to withdraw. The most notable consequence of the battle was the fact that Holland's greatest admiral, De Ruyter, was fatally wounded and died within a week. This loss severely weakened the Dutch fleet, which was defeated by the French at the Battle of Palermo on June 12, 1676. As a result of this battle, the French navy established itself as the dominant naval power in the Mediterranean.

Aurora

*L*ate 19th-century Russian CRUISER that signaled the beginning of the Bolshevik revolution in October 1917 by firing the opening shot that marked the assault on official buildings in Petrograd (later Leningrad). The *Aurora* was laid down in 1896, launched in 1900 and completed in 1902. She was the name ship of a class of three medium-size cruisers and had a displacement of 6,731 tons. Equipped with eight medium-caliber (6-inch) guns, she had a length of 416 feet 9 inches (127 m) and a beam of 55 feet 3 inches (16.8 m). Her deck was protected by 2.5-inch (64-mm) armor, and she was operated by a crew of up to 578. The *Aurora* served with the Baltic Fleet and survived the Battle of TSUSHIMA, 1905, during the RUSSO-JAPANESE WAR, 1904–5. She was interned in a neutral port after the battle but eventually rejoined the Baltic Fleet.

The *Aurora* had a relatively uneventful WORLD WAR I, 1914–18, until the final days immediately preceding the October Revolution. With support for the Bolsheviks under Lenin growing rapidly in the RUSSIAN NAVY, the *Aurora* was moved up the Neva River into the heart of Petrograd, where she could dominate the city and encourage other naval units to join the revolution. Her firing of a blank shell was the signal that triggered the Bolshevik attack on the Winter Palace and brought the unstable Kerensky government to an end.

The *Aurora* has survived as an important symbol of the Bolshevik victory. Used for many years as a training ship moored on the Neva, she returned to action during WORLD WAR II, 1939–45. In the postwar period, she was repaired and restored and has since had a dual role as a museum and training ship at a permanent berth in Leningrad (now St. Petersburg) on the Nevska, a tributary of the Neva, near the scene of her most famous exploit in 1917.

Austrian Succession, War of the
1740–48

A general European war in which Frederick the Great of Prussia sought to dismember the Austrian Empire following the death of Holy Roman Emperor Charles VI in 1740. Frederick opposed Charles's nomination of his daughter, Maria Theresa, as his successor and revived old Prussian claims to the Austrian province of Silesia. Frederick was supported by France, Spain, Bavaria and Saxony. Maria Theresa enjoyed the support of England, which was then fighting Spain in the Americas in the War of JENKINS' EAR, 1739–43. The major battles of the war took place on land in central Europe, southern Germany, the Netherlands and Italy.

Except for the War of Jenkins' Ear, naval operations did not play a critical role in determining the outcome of the wider conflict, although there were some important individual actions. For example, when British Commodore George ANSON circumnavigated the globe, 1740–44, he successfully raided Spanish possessions before capturing an enemy treasure galleon. The English fought the Spanish again on February 11, 1744 when, in company with the French, they sought to break the Royal Navy's blockade of Toulon, which had been imposed since 1742. Later in 1744 the Royal Navy was forced to maintain a fleet in the English Channel to prevent an expected French invasion attempt that never materialized. The British secured another success at the First Battle of CAPE FINISTERRE, May 3, 1747, when they captured an entire French convoy. At the second Battle of CAPE FINISTERRE, October 1747, the Royal Navy was unable to repeat this success and the French convoy escaped.

There was also a naval dimension to Anglo-French colonial rivalry in North America and India, where action at sea complemented land battles. In a remarkably successful combined operation, the British seized control of Louisbourg, Nova Scotia, Canada, from the French in 1745. In a final operation of the war the British defeated the Spanish fleet at the Battle of Havana, October 1748. The war did nothing to resolve these colonial conflicts, although the Treaty of Aix-la-Chapelle, October 18, 1748, produced a settlement of the territorial conflicts in Europe.

Chronological List of Naval Events

1739–43	War of Jenkins' Ear; Anglo-Spanish conflict in the West Indies is soon subsumed in the wider war among Spain, France, Prussia and Bavaria on the one hand and Austria, Britain and Holland on the other
1740	Anson's circumnavigation of the globe begins. During the voyage he raids Spanish possessions on the west coast of the Americas
1742–44	British blockade of Toulon, France, where a joint French and Spanish fleet is based.
1744	
February 11	Battle of Toulon
March–April	French plan to invade England foiled by the Royal Navy and poor weather
1745	
April–June	Combined British operation leads to the Battle of Louisbourg, Nova Scotia, Canada, on June 16
1746	
July 25	Battle of Negapatam; the French drive the British away and take Madras soon afterward
1747	
May 3	First Battle of Cape Finisterre
October 14	Second Battle of Cape Finisterre results in the loss of the last effective French escort squadron
1748	
October 1	Battle of Havana
October 18	Treaty of Aix-la-Chappelle.

Reed Browning, *The War of the Austrian Succession*, London, 1994; Michael Morpurgo, *The War of Jenkins' Ear*, London, 1993.

Austro-Hungarian Navy

*E*stablished in 1719 following Austria-Hungary's acquisition of territory in Italy (which gave the empire control of several Adriatic Sea ports), the Austro-Hungarian navy survived until the final collapse of the empire at the the end of WORLD WAR I, 1914–18. The navy's first Adriatic base was established at Trieste; following the annexation of Venice in 1797, a major port facility was established there. Following the loss of Venice in 1866, it was later replaced by a dockyard at Pola (Pula). The Adriatic was the Austro-Hungarian navy's normal sphere of operations, and the navy's role was largely defensive. However, during the Schleswig-Holstein War, 1864, when the empire was an ally of Prussia, a small Austrian naval squadron, commanded by Admiral Wilhelm von TEGETTHOFF, broke a Danish blockade of the Elbe and Weser rivers. During the Austro-Italian War of 1866, the Austrian and Italian navies fought at the Battle of LISSA, which was notable as the first encounter between IRONCLADS in the open sea. The Italians were defeated in a battle in which Austrian ramming tactics were an important determinant of the outcome.

During World War I the activities of Austria's naval forces were severely restricted because these forces were effectively bottled up by the Allies, who maintained control of the Otranto Straits. Austria's capital ships were, therefore, largely inactive at Pola, with routine wartime activity being carried out by destroyers and torpedo boats seeking to deny the Allies access to the area. Their efforts were supplemented by the navy's air arm, which was relatively well developed and successful. At the end of the war, the Austrian fleet formed the nucleus of the navy of the new Yugoslav nation, but following Allied objections many of its ships were reallocated to Italy and France. The Hapsburgs also created a separate flotilla that operated on the Danube River and had a varied and eventful history from its creation in 1440.

Lawrence Sondhaus, *The Hapsburg Empire and the Sea: Austrian Naval Policy, 1797–1866*, London, 1989.

Ayscue, Sir George
fl. 1646–71

*B*ritish admiral whose career spanned the Commonwealth and early Restoration periods. Ayscue's earlier career during the Commonwealth period initially prospered, particularly after his success, in 1648, in preserving part of the fleet's loyalty to Parliament's side. However, doubts about his performance in the First ANGLO-DUTCH WAR, 1652–54, brought his career to a temporary halt. Just before the Restoration, 1660, when there was still no demand for his services in England, he became an adviser to the SWEDISH NAVY. Returning to England after the Restoration, he served in the Royal Navy of King Charles II. His service in the Second Anglo-Dutch War, 1665–67, ended with the capture and destruction of his flagship, the *Prince Royal*, during the FOUR DAYS' BATTLE, 1666. He was taken to Holland, where he was imprisoned until the war ended in 1667.

Azores, Battle of the
August 31, 1591

*P*olitical and commercial rivalry between Britain and Spain continued after the defeat of the SPANISH ARMADA, 1588. This rivalry led to a naval battle off the Azores, a group of Atlantic islands some 900 miles west of Lisbon, in August 1591. A British squadron of seven ships—the *Defiance*, REVENGE, *Nonpareil, Bonaventure, Lion, Foresight* and *Crane*—under the command of Lord Thomas Howard, had been ordered to the Azores to intercept the Spanish treasure fleet. The squadron waited at the island of Flores for some weeks, but the opportunity never arose. Unknown to Howard, a much larger force of 53 ships, under Don Alonso de Bazan, had been sent from Spain to provide an escort for the treasure fleet. On August 31, as the enemy approached the Azores, the English commander was forced to weigh anchor; all but one of his ships made good their escape after a running battle that lasted until nightfall.

One member of the English squadron was not, however, quite so fortunate. The *Revenge*, the flagship of Sir Richard GRENVILLE, the second in command, had delayed its departure for too long in order to bring on board several ill crew members. It was soon surrounded by several Spanish warships, but Grenville was determined to fight. In an epic 15-hour battle, commemorated in Lord Tennyson's poem "The last fight of the *Revenge*," the British vessel held off 15 Spanish GALLEONS, sinking one and badly damaging another. At the end the *Revenge* was severely damaged and was captured by the Spanish. Grenville himself was mortally wounded, and he died on board the Spanish flagship *San Pablo* three days later. The *Revenge*, taken under Spanish command, was lost in a storm almost at once.

A. L. Rowse, *Sir Richard Grenville of the Revenge: An Elizabethan hero*, London, 1937.

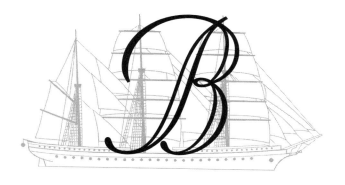

Bachmann, Gustav
1860–1943

German admiral who was head of the Baltic naval station, Kiel, at the beginning of WORLD WAR I, 1914–18. Bachmann, who enjoyed a short-lived tenure as chief of the Admiralty Staff (February–September 1915), was a strong advocate of the key role of the submarine in German naval strategy (see ATLANTIC, BATTLE OF THE, 1915–17). He held office while the first unrestricted U-BOAT campaign was under way. However, following the sinking of two passenger liners, American protests forced the Germans to revert, in September 1915, to submarine warfare conducted according to the prize rules. This international code was intended to give some measure of protection to noncombatants on the high seas in wartime. Bachmann did not long survive the collapse of the first U-boat campaign and was replaced by Admiral Henning van HOLTZENDORFF in September 1915. He returned to the command of the naval station at Kiel, where he remained until his retirement in October 1918, just before the end of the war. See also GERMAN NAVY.

Bacon, Sir Reginald
1863–1947

British admiral who commanded the Dover Patrol, the naval force whose role was to protect the English Channel and hunt German submarines, during WORLD WAR I, 1914–18. Appointed to the command in April 1915, Bacon was responsible for the security of British military transport crossing the English Channel and for the shipping passing through it. He had been brought out of retirement early in 1915 to command the Royal Marine Siege Brigade in France and had been moved to the Dover Patrol at the request of Winston CHURCHILL, First Lord of the Admiralty. An experienced naval officer, Bacon had been closely involved in Admiral Lord FISHER's naval reforms. He had also commanded the DREADNOUGHT and had been involved in the introduction of the SUBMARINE into the ROYAL NAVY.

During 1917 concern was expressed in Whitehall about the effectiveness of the Dover Patrol's response to the unrestricted warfare then being waged by German U-boats. As public concern at the level of shipping losses mounted, the Admiralty eventually relieved Bacon of his command. He made way for Sir Roger KEYES, who was to implement a plan for the blocking of ZEEBRUGGE and Ostend early in 1918. Bacon's skills were, however, too valuable to lose, and for the rest of the war he served as naval controller of munitions and inventions.

Sir Reginald Bacon, *The Concise Story of the Dover Patrol*, London, 1932.

Bainbridge, William
1774–1833

American naval officer whose career was marked by influence and triumph on the one hand and by misfortune and humiliation on the other. William Bainbridge was born in 1774 into a privileged New Jersey family and was commissioned in the U.S. Navy in 1798. He was a controversial figure who would lose his command three times. The first was the schooner *Retaliation*, which fell to superior French forces during America's QUASI-WAR, 1798–1800. The second episode centered around the American policy of paying tribute to the Barbary states rather than having a naval force in the Mediterranean to ensure respect and protection for neutral trade. While commanding the *George Washington* in 1800, Bainbridge delivered the tribute to the Dey of Algiers, who then forced him to hoist the Algerine flag and sail to Constantinople to deliver presents to the Sultan of Turkey.

Bainbridge's final and greatest humiliation came in 1803, when he ran the *Philadelphia* aground in Tripoli harbor. Surrendering his ship and crew, he was imprisoned, only to see his ship burned in the daring cutting-out operation (the act of entering a harbor and making a surprise attack on enemy ships) by young Stephen DECATUR. Exonerated for the loss of his ship, Bainbridge would eventually regain honor in the WAR OF 1812 commanding the *CONSTITUTION* in its victory over the British frigate *Java*, an action in which he was twice wounded. This engagement contributed greatly to American naval honor and tradition. His later years were spent commanding navy yards. He also found himself was embroiled in matters of personal honor, including acting as second to Commodore James BARRON, who killed Stephen Decatur in a famous duel in 1820.

David F. Long, *Ready to Hazard: A Biography of Commodore William Bainbridge, 1774–1833*, Hanover, N.H., 1981.

Balchen, Sir John
1670–1744

Distinguished British admiral who was tried twice by court-martial during the War of the SPANISH SUCCESSION, 1702–13, because he had lost his ship on two separate occasions, in 1707 and 1709, to the same French admiral, René DUGUAY-TROUIN. However, Balchen had fought well during these engagements, and both trials ended with his acquittal by the court. His naval career subsequently prospered, and he received periodic promotions; he was appointed admiral in 1743 and was knighted in 1744.

In July 1744, during the War of the AUSTRIAN SUCCESSION, 1740–48, Balchen was ordered to relieve a convoy of supply ships that was blockaded in the Tagus River by a powerful French squadron. Balchen forced the enemy to withdraw and escorted the rescued ships to Gibraltar. On the voyage home his ship was caught in a storm and sank in circumstances that remain obscure. All 1,100 men on board, including Admiral Balchen, were lost.

Ball, Sir Alexander
1757–1809

One of the "band of brothers," the group of senior officers who served under Admiral Horatio NELSON in the Mediterranean in 1798–99, Rear Admiral Ball was a veteran of the British effort to subdue the rebellious colonies in the AMERICAN WAR OF INDEPENDENCE, 1775–83. As captain of the *Alexander*, a 74-gun SHIP OF THE LINE, he saved the *Vanguard*, Nelson's flagship, from destruction after it had been dismasted in a storm off Sardinia in May 1798. This incident marked the beginning of Ball's close association with Nelson. During the Battle of the NILE, August 1, 1798, Ball engaged and helped to destroy *L'ORIENT*, the French flagship. Ball was then ordered to Malta, where he organized a blockade of the island. The action continued for two years before the French surrendered. He then effectively retired from the navy, returning

to Malta shortly afterward as the first British governor, a post he held until his death.

Baltimore Clipper

A fast American sailing vessel type of up to 200 tons, developed in Baltimore and in the surrounding Chesapeake Bay area during the second half of the 18th century. More accurately described as a schooner, the Baltimore clipper was up to 90 ft. (27.4 m) long and had two raked masts and two jibs. It had a v-shape underwater section instead of the standard rounded form, a flush deck and an overhanging bow and stern. Although it had been conceived as a fast trading vessel, the UNITED STATES NAVY also regularly employed the Baltimore clipper as a small warship. During the WAR OF 1812, for example, Baltimore clippers regularly attacked British convoys and had little difficulty in eluding the much slower ROYAL NAVY escorts.

Bancroft, George
1800–91

Historian, educator, secretary of the navy and one of the great intellectual leaders of nineteenth-century America, Bancroft was born in Worcester, Massachusetts in October 1800. He was educated at Harvard and then at Göttingen and Berlin, receiving the doctor of philosophy degree before his twentieth birthday. Returning to America in 1822, he founded the preparatory Round Hill School, Massachusetts, based on the German system of education. Bancroft then embarked on writing the first scholarly *History of the United States*, a project begun in 1834 and completed in ten volumes in 1874. While fiercely anti-British and extremely patriotic in its interpretation of events, the *History* was valuable owing to its extensive use of resource materials, and it established Bancroft's reputation as a great historian. He also rose in stature as a leader in the Democratic party, being appointed secretary of the navy by President James K. Polk in 1845. Industrious and energetic, despite considerable opposition he established the U.S. NAVAL ACADEMY. (See also ANNAPOLIS.) The official eulogizer at the funerals of Presidents Andrew Jackson and Abraham Lincoln, he served as American ambassador to Britain from 1846 to 1849 and to Prussia from 1867 to 1874.

Lilian Handlin, *George Bancroft: The Intellectual as Democrat*, New York, 1984.

Bantry Bay, Battle of
May 1, 1689

During the opening phase of the War of the GRAND ALLIANCE, 1688–97, the French mounted a major operation in support of the exiled English monarch King JAMES II. This began some two months after the Roman Catholic James had landed in Ireland in March 1689 in an attempt to regain the English throne from his Protestant daughter Mary and her husband William, Prince of Orange. A powerful naval force of 34 units, including 24 ships of the line, was dispatched from Brest under the command of Admiral the Marquis de CHÂTEAU-RENAULT. It carried troop reinforcements and supplies for James. Château-Renault arrived off Bantry Bay, a small seaport on the southwest coast of Ireland, at the end of April. Shortly afterward, on May 1, he was discovered by an English naval force commanded by Arthur HERBERT, later the Earl of Torrington, which had been dispatched from Portsmouth in search of the enemy. The English fleet consisted of 17 ships of the line, including Herbert's flagship, the *Elizabeth*, and three BOMB VESSELS.

The French fleet left its anchorage and moved toward the English fleet as it entered Bantry Bay. It soon became evident that the English, who were substantially outnumbered, were in serious difficulty. Fighting continued from 10:30 A.M. until 5:00 P.M., with Herbert unable to make his escape because the wind was against him. Despite his advantage, the French commander broke of the engagement and returned the fleet to its anchorage, following a dispute between Château-Renault and his two immediate subordinates. It was also fortunate for the English, who were now able to withdraw, that the ten French fireships accompanying the fleet had been landing supplies and were thus unable to play any part in the battle. Once Château-Renault had achieved his objectives, the fleet departed for France on May 6.

Barbarossa (Khair-ed-Din)

c. 1483–1546

*O*riginally a Barbary pirate, Khair-ed-Din served with the Turks and rose to become admiral of the Ottoman empire's navy—and one of the last, and certainly among the greatest, of the GALLEY admirals. Known as *Barbarossa* because of his red hair, he came from a Greek family of CORSAIRS who operated in the eastern Mediterranean. He proved to be a highly successful pirate, and the scope of his operations was soon extended: In 1518, he and his brother, Aruj, led a group of corsairs that expelled the Spanish from Algiers.

However, the threat from Spain remained and Barbarossa, who became Dey of Algiers, entered into an alliance with Selim I, the Ottoman Sultan, in 1519. He offered a fleet to the empire in return for support in his struggle against Spain. Under Barbarossa's rule Algiers became the main center of corsair activity and its influence extended along much of the North African coast. He organized and controlled the Barbary pirates and developed a significant

Khair-ed Din (right), known as Barbarossa, and his brother, Aruj, were leading Barbary pirates during the first half of the sixteenth century *(Copyright © National Maritime Museum, Greenwich, London)*.

battle fleet. Barbarossa also created an army, using it to capture Tunis in 1534, although it was retaken when Emperor Charles V dispatched a fleet shortly afterward.

With his base at Algiers secure, Barbarossa could accept a call from Sultan Suleiman the Magnificent in 1533 to serve as chief admiral of the Turkish fleet. The sultan needed an able naval commander if he was finally to win the protracted struggle between the Muslim Turks and the Christians for control of the eastern Mediterranean. Barbarossa reorganized the Turkish fleet, which subsequently pursued successful operations against the Venetian empire, 1537–39, causing Venice territorial losses in the Aegean. In 1541 he saved Algiers from the navy of Emperor Charles V, and he subsequently extended his operations into the western Mediterranean. In alliance with the French, Barbarossa ravaged the coasts of Catalonia and Italy, but his operations were halted by the Peace of Crépy, 1544.

By this time the Turks had established their presence throughout the Mediterranean. With his work effectively completed, Barbarossa retired to his palace at Constantinople—built with the fortune he had acquired as a corsair—where he died two years later. His success in developing and operating the Ottoman fleet reflected his great seamanship as well as his tactical and administrative skills.

E. Bradford, *The Sultan's Admiral: The Life of Barbarossa*, London, 1973.

Barbary Pirates   *See* CORSAIR.

Barbette

$\mathcal{T}$he fixed platform or mounting, normally a semicircle, on which a revolving gun was mounted on an IRONCLAD warship. Developed and refined during the second half of the nineteenth century, it was the precursor of the turret. Shells were supplied by means of a lift through the floor of the barbette. Customarily the barbette was heavily armored, but until it was fitted with a hood it offered no protection to gun crews in the event of an enemy attack. The barbette hood was widely used from the 1880s onward, and, as the power of weapons increased, it was reinforced. The modern turret resulted when both the hood and the barbette had equal armor protection. By the end of the 19th century, the turret had superseded the barbette on contemporary warships.

Barents Sea, Battle of the
December 31, 1942

$\mathcal{A}$ battle between British and German surface units in the Barents Sea during WORLD WAR II, 1939–45, as the Allies battled to maintain a supply route to their Soviet ally. The onset of winter provided the best possible conditions—lack of daylight and poor weather conditions—for the passage of Arctic convoys between Britain and the Soviet Union during the war. On December 25, 1942, the first half of a British convoy, which had been designated JW 51A, reached Murmansk after an uneventful journey from Loch Ewe, Scotland. The second half of the convoy, known as JW 51B, had left Britain on December 22. Fourteen merchantmen were escorted by six destroyers and five smaller warships. Two days after its departure the convoy, which was commanded by Captain R. Sherbrooke, was scattered by a severe gale. The warships that had escorted the first half of the convoy turned back in order to provide additional support for the remainder, but had to abandon the attempt due to poor weather conditions.

By December 30 the second British convoy had been spotted by a U-BOAT, and a German squadron operating from Alten fjord in northern Norway was dispatched to intercept it. Commanded by Admiral Oscar Kummetz in the heavy cruiser ADMIRAL HIPPER, the squadron also in-cluded the POCKET-BATTLESHIP *Lützow* and six destroyers. Kummetz divided his forces as he approached the British convoy, with the aim of attacking it on both flanks. The course of the battle was confused and consisted of a series of small engagements. The *Hipper* scored early successes against the *Onslow*, the *Bramble* and, later, the *Achates*. However, the tide turned as the *Hipper* was confronted by the sudden appearance of the British cruisers *Sheffield* and *Jamaica*. She sustained some damage at the hands of the cruisers but avoided the fate of the destroyer *Friedrich Eckholdt*, which was sunk. Kummetz decided to withdraw to his base, and the British convoy completed its journey to Murmansk without further incident. The British had achieved a notable success against a much stronger enemy squadron. The disastrous performance by the German navy led directly to the resignation of Grand Admiral Erich RAEDER as naval commander in chief and his replacement by Grand Admiral DÖNITZ. Hitler also imposed severe restrictions on the use of the German navy's heavy surface ships—for much of the rest of the war, they were largely confined to a training role—and placed increasing reliance on the U-boat as his main instrument of naval strategy. See also ARCTIC CONVOYS, 1941–45.

Richard Woodman, *Arctic Convoys*, London, 1994.

Barfleur, Battle of
May 19, 1692

$\mathcal{A}$fter the French victory over the Anglo-Dutch fleet at the Battle of BEACHY HEAD, June 30, 1690, almost two years elapsed before the next major naval engagement of the War of the GRAND ALLIANCE, 1688–97. During this period the French retained their superiority in the English Channel, but this superiority did not survive the Battle of Barfleur or the Battle of LA HOGUE, May 22–24, that followed it. The origins of the battle lay in the preparations being made at the French naval base at Cherbourg to sail the deposed King James and his supporters to England in a bid to regain the crown. A French escort in the form of 44 SHIPS OF THE LINE under the command of Admiral Comte de TOURVILLE had left Brest and moved into the Channel on May 17. The French were not at full strength because expected reinforcements under the command of Admiral Jean d'Estrées had not arrived from Toulon.

The English were fully aware of these movements and, on May 18, Admiral Edward RUSSELL (later the Earl of Orford) and his much more powerful Anglo-Dutch fleet of 96 ships of the line left Portsmouth for the Normandy coast. The French were sighted off Cap Barfleur, the northeast point of the Cotentin Peninsula, early the following day. The French engaged the English at about 10:30 A.M., completely unaware of the enemy's numerical superiority, but the wind soon dropped. Weather conditions were poor and by midafternoon heavy fog had closed in. This enabled the French fleet, under considerable pressure due to the size of the enemy's fleet, to withdraw from the battle without the loss of a single ship. The French anchored for the night but the next day continued their retreat westward toward the Channel Islands. With the Anglo-Dutch fleet in pursuit, the decisive Battle of La Hogue, when the French navy was defeated, quickly followed. As a result, James and his supporters had to abandon their plan to return to England.

John Ehrman, *The Navy in the War of William III, 1689–1697*, Cambridge, England, 1953.

Barney, Joshua
1759–1818

American naval officer, born in Baltimore County, Maryland, on July 6, 1759, who entered merchant service at the age of thirteen and assumed his first command at fifteen. In the AMERICAN WAR OF INDEPENDENCE, 1775–83, he first saw naval service on the *Hornet* in 1775, participating in the capture of New Providence (Nassau), Bahamas, by Commodore Esek HOPKIN's squadron. Twice captured and twice exchanged by the British in 1776 and 1777, he was captured for a third time while first lieutenant of the *Intrepid*, spending a year in prison in England before escaping and reaching Boston via France in 1781. Commanding the State of Pennsylvania's converted merchantman *Hyder-Ally*, he engaged in one of the most famous actions of the war when he defeated and seized as a prize the more powerful British warship *General Monk*.

When the United States created a permanent navy in 1794, Barney was selected to command one of the new frigates being built to combat the excesses of the Barbary CORSAIRS. Reflecting the period's exaggerated sensitivity to honor and pride, Barney refused the appointment because he would have to serve under an officer who had been junior to him in rank during the War of Independence. He commanded a French ship and squadron from 1796 until 1802. On the outbreak of the WAR OF 1812, Barney engaged in privateering activities, taking several large British ships. Asked in the summer of 1814 to advise on the defense of Washington, then threatened by British land and sea forces, Barney commanded a flotilla that delayed the enemy assault. With his sailors and marines, he joined the militia forces at the Battle of Bladensburg, during which he was injured and captured by the British. However, Barney and his command's heroic action was the only bright spot for the Americans in the otherwise disastrous defense of the capital. After the war, he was honored by the City of Washington.

Hulbert Footner, *Sailor of Fortune: The Life and Adventures of Commodore Barney*, New York, 1940.

Barron, James
1769–1851

James Barron saw service with his father and brother in the Continental Navy in the latter part of the AMERICAN WAR OF INDEPENDENCE, 1775–83. Entering the U.S. Navy as a lieutenant in 1798, he served on the *UNITED STATES* and so distinguished himself that he was promoted to captain in 1799, commanding the frigate *President* as part of the Mediterranean Squadron. In 1807 he was appointed to the command of a force with orders to relieve vessels in the Mediterranean Squadron. He embarked on the hastily outfitted and improperly crewed *Chesapeake*, only to be stopped off the Virginia coast by the British frigate *Leopard*, which demanded the return of alleged deserters from the ROYAL NAVY. Barron refused and a sharp fight ensued. Because it was ill-prepared, the American vessel sustained all the damage and was forced to strike her colors. One of the wounded was Barron himself. The alleged deserters were removed and the *Chesapeake* returned to Hampton Roads. Court-martialed on charges of surrendering his ship, Barron was acquitted of cowardice but found guilty of the lesser charge of negligence and sentenced to five years' suspension from the service. Seeking service at sea during the WAR OF 1812, Barron was given only shore duty. Angered by what he considered a cabal that persecuted him, he challenged the popular hero Commodore Stephen DECATUR to a duel, which occurred in 1820. It resulted in Decatur's death and Barron being seriously wounded. Barron spent the rest of his life anticipating further sea service, which never materialized.

Paul B. Watson, *The Tragic Career of Commodore James Barron, U.S. Navy (1769–1851)*, New York, 1942.

Barrow, Sir John
1764–1848

Distinguished British naval administrator who served as second secretary of the Admiralty for 40 years. During his earlier career Barrow worked in China for Lord Macartney, who was the British ambassador, and had later published an account of his travels there. In 1797, when Macartney was sent to southern Africa to advise on the government of the new British colony of the Cape of Good Hope, Barrow accompanied him as his private secretary.

In 1804, not long after he arrived back in England, Barrow was appointed to the Admiralty as second secretary. In this post he was responsible for the civilian administration of the Admiralty and was the principal adviser to the political head of the navy.

He served successive First Lords of the Admiralty during the NAPOLEONIC WARS, 1803–15, and in the long period of peace that followed, when retrenchment was the dominant influence on naval policy. Barrow's long tenure at the Admiralty is attributable to his ability to secure the confidence of his various political masters, which in turn depended on his skills as a senior administrator and on the high quality of his advice.

The Admiralty second secretary was also noted as an author. Apart from his accounts of his travels in China and South Africa, he wrote several naval biographies and a history of Arctic exploration. Barrow had himself sponsored several voyages of exploration during his tenure at the Admiralty. He finally retired in 1845, having been made a baronet and awarded other honors in recognition of his long service to the Royal Navy.

C. C. Lloyd, *Mr. Barrow of the Admiralty. A Life of Sir John Barrow, 1764–1848*, London, 1970.

Barry, John
c. 1745–1803

A native of Ireland who immigrated to Pennsylvania, Barry was appointed a captain in the Continental Navy at the outset of the AMERICAN WAR OF INDEPENDENCE, 1775–83. While commanding the frigate *LEXINGTON,* he captured a British tender, thus becoming the first American captain to take a prize in the war. After commanding several other vessels that engaged in various forays and minor actions, he was given command of the FRIGATE *Alliance* and captured several more British vessels. In March 1783 this vessel saw the last naval action of the war when it fought the British frigate *Sybil* in the West Indies. With the permanent establishment of the UNITED STATES NAVY in 1794, Barry was given command of the new frigate *United States,* subsequently seeing action in the West Indies during the QUASI-WAR, 1798–1800, against France. Too ill to command the Mediterranean Squadron against Tripoli in 1803, he died that year as the U.S. Navy's most senior officer.

William B. Clark, *Gallant John Barry, 1745–1803: The Story of a Naval Hero of Two Wars,* New York, 1938.

Bart, Jean
1650–1702

F rench privateer and naval officer. The son of a fisherman, Bart served in the Dutch navy during the opening stages of his career. He returned to French service when war broke out with Holland in 1672. He fought for France in the Mediterranean, but at first he was denied a regular commission because of his low social origins. Bart's outstanding performance marked him out, however, and he was made a lieutenant in 1679. He gained rapid promotion to captain and then to admiral. During the War of the GRAND ALLIANCE, 1688–97, he commanded a small squadron in the North Sea and was responsible for the destruction of several English warships. Bart eventually was captured by the English and held at Plymouth, but he soon escaped and on his arrival in France was given the command of a squadron. He was later awarded the status of a noble. Bart's naval career came to an end when peace was made at the Treaty of Ryswick, 1697.

J. S. Bromley, *Corsairs and Navies, 1660–1760,* London, 1987.

Basque and Aix Roads, Battle of
April 11–12, 1809

A British naval operation to remove a potential French threat to its line of communications to Spain and Portugal during the Napoleonic Wars, 1803–15, was ordered when a French squadron assembled in the Basque and Aix roads off Rochefort in February 1809. Ten French SHIPS OF THE LINE, commanded by Rear Admiral Jean-Baptiste Willaumez, had left Brest in Brittany to proceed south to the Rochefort anchorage, where they were to join a small French squadron already anchored there. In response the British, who were concerned about the potential damage this powerful squadron could do in the Bay of Biscay, reacted immediately. The Channel Fleet, commanded by Admiral Lord GAMBIER, followed the French squadron from Brest and blockaded them in the Basque and Aix roads.

Early in April, Gambier was reinforced from England by a force of fireships and explosion vessels commanded by Captain Lord COCHRANE, who had been ordered to destroy the French fleet. During the night of April 11–12, Cochrane launched his attack in favorable wind conditions. The fireships caused as much panic as actual damage among the French ships, several of which ran aground in the confusion and had to be refloated the following morning. During this first phase of the operation, however, Gambier's Channel Fleet failed to respond to repeated to calls for assistance from Lord Cochrane, and it was not until the next afternoon that Gambier finally brought his force into action. During these later operations the Channel Fleet removed three French ships of the line. The action continued sporadically over the following two days but a decisive outcome was not achieved because the French were better prepared than the British had expected. The Admiralty later acceded to Cochrane's demand that Gambier be court-martialed for his failure to give adequate support during the battle. The court martial had little effect on Gambier's career and reputation, however: He was acquitted by a court whose members had been carefully selected in his favor.

Battle Cruiser

Largely the personal creation of Admiral Jackie FISHER, First Sea Lord, 1904–10, the battle cruiser was closely related to the DREADNOUGHT BATTLESHIP, another British invention. The first battle cruiser, originally known as a fast armored CRUISER, was introduced in the ROYAL NAVY in 1908. The battle cruiser was a more powerful and better armed cruiser that was capable, if necessary, of engaging a battleship in direct naval combat. Its main armament was of the same caliber as the DREADNOUGHT, but it had a higher maximum speed of 25 knots; improved performance was achieved by reducing its armor protection. Battle cruisers were assigned the traditional cruiser roles of protecting trade routes and conducting reconnaissance, acting in the latter case as the advanced scouts of a battle fleet. They also were expected to attack the enemy's scouting cruisers and deal with stragglers.

The British Invincibles, the first battle-cruiser class to appear, had eight 12-inch (30 cm) guns, a displacement of over 17,000 tons and a maximum speed of 25.5 knots. This class was propelled by the most powerful engines used in warships at that time. The first German battle cruiser was the VON DER TANN, which was completed in 1910 and had a displacement of 19,400 tons.

In practice, during WORLD WAR I, 1914–18, their role was to be extended well beyond their designers' original conceptions. As a result of its armament and size, the battle cruiser was considered fit to fight in the line of battle, even though its armor was relatively weak. The new role had already been indicated when its name was officially changed from fast armored cruiser to battle cruiser in 1912. As the spearhead of the British GRAND FLEET, these warships were engaged in much of the heavy naval fighting of the war. They proved to be ideal in situations such as the Battle of the FALKLAND ISLANDS, 1914, where their superior speed and long-range guns allowed them to engage the enemy's ships in battle with little risk to themselves. In the earlier Battle of HELIGOLAND BIGHT, 1914, for example, British battle cruisers had sunk two German cruisers.

Their limitations first became evident during the Battle of the DOGGER BANK, 1915, but their vulnerability to heavy gunfire was particularly obvious at the Battle of JUTLAND, 1916, when three British battle cruisers were sunk. Their German counterparts were better protected while losing little in terms of speed. The DERFFLINGER and Lützow, for example, each had eight 12-inch (30 cm) guns, a maximum speed of 28 knots and 12-inch (30 cm) armor. The best British battle cruiser of World War I was the Tiger, which had a displacement of over 28,000 tons and was armed with eight 13.5-inch (34 cm) guns; it was capable of 29 knots.

Although battle cruiser production continued in the immediate postwar period, the ship's remaining life was limited. The development of aerial reconnaissance in the interwar years meant that battle cruisers were no longer relevant to the needs of naval warfare. The fate of the HOOD, the last British battle cruiser to be built, which was sunk in 1941 during WORLD WAR II, 1939–45, was a final reminder of the limitations of this type of warship. It was clear that its reconnaissance duties could be carried out much more cost-effectively by aircraft.

Tony Gibbons, *The Complete Encyclopedia of Battleships and Battlecruisers. A Technical Directory of All the World's Capital Ships from 1860 to the Present Day*, London, 1983.

Battleship

First used in the 1860s to describe a SHIP OF THE LINE, the term "battleship" was soon applied to the first armored warships. In its different forms, the battleship dominated naval warfare for nearly a century. In their early stages of development, battleships were still of timber

A British battle cruiser in the Firth of Forth, Scotland *(Copyright © National Maritime Museum, Greenwich, London)*

construction but their hulls were covered with iron armor to protect them from shell-firing cannon. The French IRONCLAD LA GLOIRE and the British WARRIOR were the first examples, but battleship design underwent rapid change and they soon were superseded by designs with iron hulls.

Armor protection, artillery and methods of propulsion were all under active development. The rotating gun turret, which had been invented in the 1850s, was more widely used during the following decade when it first made its appearance on the U.S.S. MONITOR. (See BARBETTE.) The turret could not be used successfully on a ship with masts, and, in 1871, the 9,300-ton DEVASTATION, the first battleship without sails, was launched. The main features of the sailing ship of the line did not disappear immediately, although she now had an iron hull. It took some time for the modern battleship to emerge, but by the last years of 19th century, this process had been completed. Developments in the size and power of naval guns, improvements in armor protection and more efficient methods of propulsion as well as better production methods all contributed to this process.

By the time of the RUSSO-JAPANESE WAR, 1904–5, a typical battleship might have a displacement of about 15,000 tons, main armament of four 12-inch (30.5 cm) guns in turrets and a maximum speed of about 18 knots. It would normally be built as a class rather than as an individual type. Battleship design was revolutionized by the British in 1906 when H.M.S. DREADNOUGHT, the first "all-big-gun" ship, was launched. With a displacement of 21,250 metric tons, it was equipped with ten 12-inch guns in five twin turrets and had a maximum speed of 21 knots. It had greater firepower over longer distances and rendered every existing battleship obsolete.

The appearance of this radically new design intensified the naval race between Britain and Germany before WORLD WAR I, 1914–18. By introducing the *Dreadnought*, Britain ironically undercut its enormous lead in capital ships by rendering all previous warships obsolete. There was a race to achieve a lead in producing the new design. With the advantage of an earlier start, Britain had 20 dreadnoughts in service, compared with Germany's 15 at the beginning of the war; both navies each had two others nearing completion. The Germans were cautious about risking their modern warships, and not until 1916 did the HIGH SEAS FLEET adopt a more aggressive strategy. As a result of this new approach, British capital ships were lured out and engaged by the enemy at the Battle of JUTLAND, 1916, the only occasion during the war in which dreadnoughts fought each other. Predreadnought battleships were employed more adventurously—most notably in the DARDANELLES, where early in 1915 the Allies unsuccessfully attempted to force a passage through to Constantinople. The operation revealed their vulnerability to mines and torpedoes, and

they were withdrawn from the area after three capital ships had been lost. Thirty-six capital ships were lost during the war.

The Washington Naval Treaty, 1922, imposed restrictions on battleship tonnages, and all construction was virtually halted for several years. (See WASHINGTON CONFERENCE.) In the 1930s these restrictions were evaded by the Axis powers, which had several battleships under construction. These battleships included those of the YAMATO class, which had 18-inch guns and were the largest battleships ever built. The growing cost, size and complexity of battleships meant that there were no more than 56 in service at the beginning of WORLD WAR II, 1939–45, compared with 148 of all types at the start of World War I. Evidence was soon available at TARANTO, 1940, PEARL HARBOR, 1941, MIDWAY, 1942, and elsewhere of their extreme vulnerability to air and submarine attack.

Superseded by the AIRCRAFT CARRIER as the capital ship of the world's navies, battleships disappeared quite rapidly from navies in the postwar period, with only the United States retaining the four ships of the Iowa class during the 1980s and early 1990s. These ships were mothballed for a period but were sometimes taken out of storage in a crisis, and they have played a useful role. During the GULF WAR, 1991, for example, they were equipped with CRUISE MISSILES which were used against land-based targets in Baghdad and elsewhere.

Robert Gardiner ed., *The Eclipse of the Big Gun: The Warship, 1906–45*, London, 1992; A. D. Lambert, *Battleships in Transition: The Creation of the Steam Battlefleet, 1850–1860*, London: 1984; Anthony Preston, *Battleships*, London, 1989.

Bayern

*T*he last German BATTLESHIPS to be laid down before the beginning of the WORLD WAR I, 1914–18, the *Bayern* and her sister ship, the *Baden*, attempted to match the firepower of contemporary British warships with the adoption of eight 15-inch Krupp guns as the main armament. These eight guns were located in twin superfiring turrets (i.e., superimposed on the centerline) mounted fore and aft. The hull, which was a larger version of the KÖNIG design, had excellent protection against underwater damage. The *Bayern*'s maximum speed was 22.25 knots, she had a displacement of 28,000 tons and was operated by a crew of 1,171. She was 598 feet 5 inches (182.4 m) in length and had a beam of 99 feet 1 inch (30.2 m). Both ships served with the HIGH SEAS FLEET, the *Bayern* being commissioned in 1916 and the *Baden* early in the following year. Interned by the British at SCAPA FLOW at the end of the war, the *Bayern* was scuttled and the *Baden* was beached before sinking on June 21, 1919 as a result of protest action by their German crews.

The battleship U.S.S. *Alabama* joins the U.S. fleet in the Pacific, 1942   *(Copyright © Imperial War Museum, London)*

Bay of Pigs
April 17, 1961

A failed exiles' invasion of Cuba, backed by the United States, that sought to bring Fidel Castro's rule to an end. Castro's seizure of power in 1959 originally was welcomed by the United States, but relations between the two countries quickly deteriorated when Cuba was proclaimed a Communist state with developing links with the Soviet Union. Some 250,000 Cubans had fled abroad— mainly to the United States—as a result of these changes, and leading exiles made plans to remove Castro by force. The American government actively supported the planned invasion, even though President John Kennedy was on record as saying that he would not seek to remove Castro by force of arms. A group of 1,500 exiles were trained and equipped in the United States and the Central Intelligence Agency (CIA) provided six freighters to transport them to Cuba. The U.S. Navy was to cover the landing, and the aircraft carrier *Essex* and five destroyers were made available.

The landing on the Bay of Pigs, on the southern coast of Cuba, was a disaster, and the exiles were defeated within three days. Castro's forces killed or captured the entire invasion force, which was doomed to failure when an expected uprising failed to occur. Practical difficulties associated with the landing, including equipment failures, also made the exiles' task much more difficult. Although this was a CIA-inspired operation, its failure was a considerable embarrassment to all those involved, including the U.S. Navy. In practical terms, the failed operation encouraged Castro to develop closer military links with the Soviet Union, setting in train the events that were to lead to the CUBAN MISSILE CRISIS in October 1962.

Bazan, Alvaro de, Marquis of Santa Cruz
1526–1588

T he son of a leading Spanish naval commander, the Marquis of Santa Cruz planned and organized the SPAN-

ISH ARMADA, 1588, but died shortly before he was due to lead it to action. He first went to sea at an early age, and his first battle experience was in the Mediterranean, where he became an accomplished GALLEY captain. In 1568, King Philip II of Spain appointed him to the command of the galleys at Naples. Forming a close connection with Don JUAN of Austria, he commanded the reserve division of the Allied fleet at the Battle of LEPANTO, 1571. Bazan's intervention at a decisive stage in the battle, when the Turks advanced through the force commanded by Andrea DORIA, contributed substantially to the final victory. Bazan served again with Don Juan in 1572, participating in the capture of Tunis. He was appointed the Marquis of Santa Cruz by the Spanish crown in recognition of his contribution to this successful operation.

Santa Cruz's next campaign was in the Atlantic, where he operated in support of the Duke of Alva's conquest of Portugal and the Azores, 1580–83. His victories against the French fleet off Terceira in the Azores, in 1582–83, brought the islands under Spanish control and consolidated Spain's position in the Atlantic. The victorious admiral, soon to be appointed Captain General of the Ocean Sea, now turned to the operation—the proposed invasion of England—that was to dominate the rest of his life. Philip II supported the plan in principle although Santa Cruz later would argue with the king over finance and other issues. Preparations proceeded slowly and were disrupted further by an English naval attack on Cadiz in 1587 led by Sir Francis DRAKE. Part of the Spanish invasion force was seriously damaged in this attack. Santa Cruz's unexpected death in February 1588 was another major setback to the invasion plans as his successor, the Duke of MEDINA SIDONIA, was a far from adequate replacement for Spain's greatest admiral of the 16th century.

Beachy Head, Battle of
June 30, 1690

Following the inconclusive Battle of BANTRY BAY, May 1, 1689, the opening naval battle of the War of the GRAND ALLIANCE, 1688–97, the English and French fleets did not meet again until 1690. The Battle of Beachy Head had its origins in a French plan to blockade the Thames River as a prelude to a possible invasion of England. A French fleet of 72 ships under the command of the Vice Admiral Comte de TOURVILLE was first sighted off the Lizard, Cornwall, on June 21. Opposing the French was an Anglo-French fleet of 56 ships under the command of Arthur HERBERT, Earl of Torrington. The Dutch van, which contributed 22 ships to the total, was commanded by Admiral Cornelis EVERTSEN (1642–1706).

The opposing fleets made contact off the Isle of Wight on June 25, but Torrington's weaker force was compelled to withdraw as the French advanced through the English Channel toward its goal. After four days of retreat the English commanded was ordered, on June 29, to engage the enemy off Beachy Head on the Sussex coast. The battle began on the following day with the Dutch van leading the attack with great courage. Fierce fighting ensued with the French van under the Marquis de CHÂTEAU-RENAULT and the center under de Tourville. The English ships were not deployed properly and did not fully engage the enemy. The action ended at about 3 P.M. when the wind dropped. Losses during the battle itself were small—one Dutch ship and some fireships—but several other ships were badly damaged. Of these, one English warship and four Dutch were beached and destroyed to prevent them from falling into enemy hands. The French escaped with no losses.

The Anglo-Dutch fleet withdrew to the Nore, a naval anchorage in the Thames estuary, where Torrington was removed from his command. He was tried by court-martial and, through acquitted, never went to sea again. Fortunately for the English, the Comte de Tourville, who did not lose a single ship in the battle, failed to exploit his advantage. He reached Dover before turning back, with concerns over crew sickness and low supplies influencing his decision. Apart from burning the coastal town of Teignmouth, Devon, he left English waters without further incident.

G. Symcox, *The Crisis of French Seapower, 1688–97*, The Hague, 1974.

Beagle, H.M.S.

A Royal Navy ten-gun brig of 235 tons built at Woolwich in 1823, the *Beagle* will always be associated with Charles Darwin's memorable voyage. In 1825 the *Beagle* entered the surveying service and was used in a survey of the Straits of Magellan. In 1831, under the command of Captain Robert Fitzroy, the *Beagle* left on a scientific voyage around the world with Charles Darwin, a young naturalist, on board. The *Beagle* traveled westward from England, passing through the Magellan Straits and across the Pacific to New Zealand and Australia before returning home via the Cape of Good Hope. During her five-year circumnavigation of the globe, Darwin collected much evidence on the fauna and geology of areas the ship visited. As a result of the material collected on this voyage, particularly in the Galapagos Islands in the Pacific, Darwin, who published details of his observations in *The Voyage of the Beagle*, 1839, began to develop his theory of the origin of species. The *Beagle* spent her latter days on survey work in Australia.

Charles Darwin, *The Voyage of the Beagle*, London, 1839.

Beatty, David, First Earl
1871–1936

*B*ritish admiral who commanded the British GRAND FLEET during the latter part of WORLD WAR I, 1916–18. Beatty had been marked out for early promotion because of his qualities of leadership, energy and courage. His first ten years of naval service were uneventful, but in 1896 he took part in Lord Kitchener's reconquest of the Sudan. He commanded the gunboats that acted in support of the army as it advanced up the Nile. As a result he was awarded the Distinguished Service Order (DSO), and rapid promotion followed. In recognition of his contribution during the Boxer Rebellion, 1900, when he led naval landing parties in north China, he was promoted captain at the young age of 29. His career maintained its momentum, and, in 1910 he was appointed rear admiral before his thirty-ninth birthday, making him the youngest British officer to achieve that rank in over 100 years.

In 1912 Winston CHURCHILL, then First Lord of the ADMIRALTY, selected Beatty as his naval secretary. Two years later Beatty was appointed—over the heads of many of his colleagues—to the command of the BATTLE CRUISER squadron, raising his flag in *LION*. He commanded it with considerable flair during the war, taking the opportunity for offensive action whenever it arose. Beatty's intervention in the HELIGOLAND BIGHT on August 28, 1914 resulted in a decisive British victory and the loss of three German light cruisers. At the Battle of the DOGGER BANK, January 24, 1915, he destroyed the *BLÜCHER* and seriously damaged the battle cruiser *SEYDLITZ*, but signaling errors enabled the rest of Admiral Franz HIPPER's squadron to escape.

At the Battle of JUTLAND, May 1916, Beatty's decisive contribution was to draw the German HIGH SEAS FLEET toward the approaching Grand Fleet, maneuvering successfully to prevent the enemy from sighting it. His initiative, however, was achieved at the cost of three British battle cruisers, and Beatty has been criticized for acting prematurely without the support of his associated squadron of super-dreadnoughts. He also was ultimately responsible for several signaling and reporting failures arising from the operation of his force at Jutland. In spite of these weaknesses, the drawn battle did no damage to his reputation. In fact, there was speculation that if Beatty rather than Admiral John JELLICOE had been in overall command of the British fleet, the outcome might have been rather different.

Beatty did in fact succeed Jellicoe as commander of the Grand Fleet a few months after Jutland, in December 1916, when the latter was appointed First Sea Lord. Beatty was responsible for refitting the fleet after Jutland, rectifying the weaknesses in ship and shell design that the battle had revealed. Until this work was completed Beatty followed the same cautious strategy as his predecessor and maintained the distant BLOCKADE of Germany. The Germans

Beatty's naturally offensive spirit was constrained during his wartime command of the British Grand Fleet, 1916–18 *(Copyright © National Maritime Museum, Greenwich, London)*

were even more unwilling than the British to risk their main battle fleet, and the opportunity for a decisive encounter never materialized again. Beatty did, however, have the pleasure of accepting the surrender of the High Seas Fleet on November 21, 1918, giving the famous signal: "The German Flag will be hauled down at sunset, and will not be hoisted again without permission."

At the end of the war Beatty was created an earl and received other honors in recognition of his service with the Grand Fleet. As First Sea Lord, 1919–27, he was successful in preserving the capacity of the fleet in unfavorable circumstances.

Stephen Roskill, *Admiral of the Fleet Earl Beatty: The Last Naval Hero. An Intimate Portrait*, London, 1980.

Beaufort, Sir Francis
1774–1857

*B*ritish rear admiral and hydrographer (marine surveyor) who created the Beaufort Wind Scale, a numerical (0–12) scale used to assess and record the force of the wind. Beaufort, who was born in Navan, County

Neath, Ireland, entered the ROYAL NAVY in 1787 at the age of 13. He saw active service during the FRENCH REVOLUTIONARY AND NAPOLEONIC WARS, 1792–1815, but his main interests were increasingly scientific rather than operational. In 1808 he devised the wind scale on which his reputation now rests, and, from 1812, his work focused on coastal surveys and meteorology. By 1829 his growing scientific eminence was acknowledged with his appointment as hydrographer to the navy. During his long tenure Beaufort developed the navy's scientific branch, adding new areas (e.g., the compass department) as the need arose. Surveying was another area to which Beaufort devoted additional resources, and many important surveys across the world were completed during his tenure. He was promoted to the rank of rear admiral in 1846 and remained the navy's hydrographer until 1855. The Beaufort scale remains in use and is especially familiar to listeners of the BBC Radio's shipping forecast in Britain.

Alfred Friendly, *Beaufort of the Admiralty: The Life of Sir Francis Beaufort,* London, 1977.

Belcher, Sir Edward
1799–1877

*B*ritish naval commander and hydrographer who devoted much of his career to the development of surveying in the ROYAL NAVY. He also secured a wider recognition of its role in wartime operations. Entering the service in 1812, he saw action against Algiers in 1816 and later against the slave trade in West Africa. During the 1820s his scientific interests developed, and, in 1824, he joined a survey expedition to the Pacific. Other expeditions followed, including a major survey of the African coast. In 1835 he published a textbook on nautical surveying that became a standard work. Belcher's final expedition was to the Arctic, in 1852–54, when he went in search of Sir John Franklin, who had earlier traveled through the Bering Strait into the Arctic Sea. Starting from opposite points, the two expeditions eventually made contact and finally provided firm information about the link between the Pacific and Atlantic oceans. Belcher was appointed rear admiral in 1872.

Belfast, H.M.S.

*L*aunched in Belfast, Northern Ireland, in 1938, this British light CRUISER had a displacement of 11,500 tons. She was armed with 12 6-inch (15 cm) guns in triple turrets and several 40-mm antiaircraft guns. *Belfast*'s service in WORLD WAR II, 1939–45, almost came to a premature end when she detonated a German magnetic mine in the Firth of Forth in November 1939. It caused major structural damage to her hull, and she did not return to active service until major repairs were completed late in 1942.

Among the highlights of her subsequent wartime career was the Battle of NORTH CAPE, 1943, when the German battleship *SCHARNHORST* was destroyed. During the NORMANDY LANDINGS, in June 1944, she led the naval bombardment that supported Allied operations at Juno Beach. She was flagship in the Far East at the time of the *AMETHYST* incident in 1949 and served throughout the KOREAN WAR, 1950–53. The ROYAL NAVY finally decommissioned the *Belfast* in 1971, but she has been preserved ever since as a floating museum on the Thames River near Tower Bridge, London.

Belle Isle, Battle of
June 17, 1795

*A*n engagement between British and French naval forces during the FRENCH REVOLUTIONARY AND NAPOLEONIC WARS, 1792–1815; the British called it "Cornwallis's retreat." Vice Admiral William CORNWALLIS commanded a small squadron that was cruising off Brest to the north of Belle Isle on the French coast when it sighted a much more powerful French force commanded by Admiral Louis VILLARET DE JOYEUSE. Opposing the five British SHIPS OF THE LINE, including the 100-gun *Royal Sovereign*, and two frigates were 12 French ships of the line and 11 lesser warships. In view of the marked British inferiority, Cornwallis had little choice but to withdraw. He moved south but circumstances turned against him. The wind moved in the enemy's favor, and the slow-moving British ships of the line were forced to scuttle some of their equipment in order to improve their speed.

However, the French continued to gain ground, and by dawn on June 17 they had caught up with their opponents. Soon after the battle began the *Mars*, a British 74-gun ship, was badly damaged; she seemed in danger of capture until she was rescued by the *Royal Sovereign*. Deception eventually saved the day for the British: False signals by Cornwallis' leading frigate, the *Phantom*, convinced the French commander that his opponents were in touch with the main British fleet. Admiral Villaret-Joyeuse decided to abandon the pursuit, and the British completed their skillful withdrawal without loss.

Bellerophon, H.M.S.

*U*niversally known as "Billy Ruffian" by her crew, this 18th-century SHIP OF THE LINE was the most notable of the ROYAL NAVY's vessels of this name. The *Bellerophon*, which was armed with 74 guns, was launched on the Medway in 1786 and first commissioned four years later.

She is perhaps best remembered as the ship on which Napoleon formally surrendered on July 15, 1815 in Basque Roads (in the estuary of the Charente River) following his defeat at Waterloo. The *Bellerophon* then brought him to the shores of England before he was transferred to the *Northumberland* for the journey into exile on the island of St. Helena. During the previous 25 years the *Bellerophon* had seen action regularly. At the Battle of TRAFALGAR, 1805, for example, she was in the lee line and her crew suffered heavy casualties after a determined fight. The *Bellerophon*'s postwar service—as the convict ship *Captivity*—did little to preserve the memory of her glorious past.

Another famous *Bellerophon* was the WORLD WAR I, 1914–18 British battleship, which was almost identical to the original DREADNOUGHT design. She shared most of the *Dreadnought*'s strengths and weaknesses, although her armor protection was improved, as was her secondary armament, which consisted of 16 4-inch (10-cm) guns. Her main armament was ten 12-inch (30-cm) guns. She had a displacement of 18,800 tons. Like her sister ships the *Superb* and the *Temeraire*, the *Bellerophon* served throughout the war with the British GRAND FLEET, and all three saw action at the Battle of JUTLAND, 1916.

Benbow, John
1653–1702

*B*ritish naval commander of humble origins who rose through the ranks to become an admiral—a very unusual career progression in the 17th century. John Benbow's early service as a master's mate had been cut short when he was court-martialed in 1681 for criticizing his captain. Regarded as difficult and tough, he was forced to make his own way, and acquired a ship that he operated as a trader. In 1689 powerful connections helped him to return to the Royal Navy as a captain, and he advanced rapidly, serving as master of the fleet at the Battles of BEACHY HEAD, 1690, and LA HOGUE, 1692, during the War of the GRAND ALLIANCE, 1688–97.

Apart from leading an attack on St. Malo in 1693 and subsequent operations against the French coast, Benbow did not see active service again until the War of the SPANISH SUCCESSION, 1701–14, when he was appointed commander in chief in the West Indies. In 1702, in an unsuccessful action against the French in the Caribbean off Santa Marta, Benbow was mortally wounded. He was forced to withdraw to Jamaica, where he died. It was apparent that during this last action Benbow had not been properly supported by his captains, who had become disaffected because of his harsh manner toward them; two eventually were hanged as a result. Although Benbow came to be regarded as a hero in popular legend, there remains a doubt about his place in British naval history and whether his high reputation was well deserved.

Benson, William Shepherd
1855–1932

*A*merican naval officer, born in Macon, Georgia, on September 25, 1855. He entered the navy in 1872. Besides tours at sea, William Benson saw service at the United States Naval Academy in ANNAPOLIS, Maryland, including a period as Commandant of Midshipmen, 1907–8. In May 1915 he was appointed the first Chief of Naval Operations, a new position that had long been advocated by reformers. He held this post—the highest-ranking position in the U.S. Navy, designed to advise the civilian secretary of the navy—initially as a rear admiral, but he was promoted to admiral in 1916. As Chief of Naval Operations, Benson organized and thus centralized the navy's administration in time for America's entry into WORLD WAR I, 1914–18. He subsequently became a principal adviser at Versailles, helping to conclude the naval side of the treaty in 1919. Recipient of numerous medals, both foreign and American, he retired in 1919. He died on May 20, 1932 in Washington, D.C.

Mary Klachko with David F. Trask, *Admiral William Shepherd Benson: First Chief of Naval Operations*, Annapolis, 1987.

Bentham, Sir Samuel
1757–1832

*E*nglish naval architect, born in London, who spent his early career in the service of the RUSSIAN NAVY, a refuge for English seamen who were unable to obtain employment in the ROYAL NAVY. The brother of the utilitarian philosopher Jeremy Bentham, 1748–1832, Samuel Bentham had been unable to obtain suitable employment at home after training as a shipwright but soon had the opportunity to display great creativity and inventiveness in the service of his adopted country. The heavy naval armaments he designed for the Russian navy provided the foundations of its victory against the Turkish fleet in 1788. He had equipped a flotilla of gunboats with non-recoil guns that destroyed a much larger enemy fleet at the mouth of the Azov River. It was the first naval victory achieved by the use of shellfire. All previous guns had been CANNON that fired an iron ball rather than an explosive shell.

Returning to England in 1794, Bentham finally was employed in the service of the Royal Navy. He produced a wide range of innovations in the fields of naval architecture, shipbuilding and gunnery. Bentham made a real contribution to eventual victory against France in the Napoleonic Wars, 1803–15. He resigned in 1812 after becoming involved in an acrimonious dispute with the Admiralty about corruption and malpractice in the Royal Navy's dockyards.

Beresford, Charles, First Baron Beresford
1846–1919

*B*ritish admiral. Known in the ROYAL NAVY as "Charlie B," Beresford was a colorful aristocrat who became involved in an acrimonious and long-running dispute with Lord FISHER, First Sea Lord, in the years before WORLD WAR I, 1914–18. Beresford entered the navy in 1859 and first came to prominence in Egypt in 1882. As commander of the gunboat H.M.S. *Condor*, he played a leading role in the bombardment of Alexandria. Beresford silenced the guns of Fort Marabout and landed troops who restored peace to the town. In 1884–85 he commanded the naval brigade in General Garnet Wolseley's expedition to relieve General Charles "Chinese" Gordon, who was besieged by the forces of the Mahdi at Khartoum. During a period at the Admiralty, 1886–88, Beresford contributed to the creation of a naval intelligence arm and was influential in his advocacy of heavy investment in a powerful British battle fleet.

Promoted to rear admiral in 1899, Beresford served as commander in chief of the British Mediterranean and second in command overall under Admiral Jackie Fisher (later Lord Fisher). Although Beresford, like Fisher, was a reformer, the two men were personally incompatible, and a period of intense personal rivalry followed. Relations between them deteriorated to such an extent that by 1907, when Beresford was appointed to the command of the Channel Fleet, Fisher, who was then First Sea Lord, transferred many of his ships to a new Home Fleet. By 1909, as the feud intensified, Beresford was ordered to resign from the navy. At the same time, an official inquiry was held into various charges that Beresford had made against Fisher, including his failure to establish a naval war staff. The outcome did not entirely vindicate the conduct of either man, and Fisher resigned in 1910. Unlike Fisher, Beresford never served in the navy again, although he was to use his position as a long-serving Conservative Member of Parliament to voice his concerns at the direction of naval policy under Lord Fisher during World War I.

Geoffrey Bennett, *Charlie B*, London, 1968.

Berry, Sir Edward
1768–1831

*B*ritish rear admiral—one of Lord Nelson's "band of brothers" who served in eight major battles during the FRENCH REVOLUTIONARY AND NAPOLEONIC WARS, 1792–1815. His personal courage was soon evident when, in 1794, he led a boarding party to capture a French man-of-war. He first served with Nelson some two years later, and at the Battle of the NILE, 1798, he was captain of Nelson's flagship, the *Vanguard*. (Nelson later said that the "support

and assistance I have received from Captain Berry cannot be sufficiently expressed.") After the battle Berry was sent off with dispatches in the *Leander* but was captured by the French, who released him before the end of the year. He was present at the blockade of Malta in 1800 and, as commander of the AGAMEMNON, served with Nelson again at the Battle of TRAFALGAR, 1805. Ill health brought his career to a premature close, but by this time Berry had been awarded three gold medals for commanding a ship in three general actions—at the Nile, Trafalgar and San Domingo. It was a record of service that none of his contemporaries, except Admiral Lord COLLINGWOOD, could match.

Biddle, James
1783–1848

*A*merican naval officer, born in Philadelphia. Biddle entered the UNITED STATES NAVY in 1800, serving in the Mediterranean in operations against Tripoli, 1802–3. He was aboard the *Philadelphia* under the command of William BAINBRIDGE when the ship was grounded near Tripoli and captured by Barbary pirates in October 1803; Biddle, together with the rest of the crew, was imprisoned for 19 months. Later he obtained his first independent command and put his experience to good use in the WAR OF 1812. Biddle played a leading part in the capture of the British brig *Frolic*, although shortly afterward the prize was recaptured and he spent some time as a prisoner in Bermuda. After his return to the United States, he was appointed to the command of the *Hornet* and, in this vessel, fought the last regular naval engagement of the War of 1812. Following his capture of the British brig *Penguin* in the South Atlantic, he narrowly escaped attack by a British SHIP OF THE LINE. A prolonged chase ensued, and Biddle escaped only by throwing his stores and almost all of his guns overboard. He returned to New York in July 1815, after the peace had been signed. Biddle continued his career in the postwar navy and died in Philadelphia in 1848.

Biddle, Nicholas
1750–78

*A*merican naval officer who served as a midshipman in the British navy and joined a polar expedition before returning home in 1775. As the AMERICAN WAR OF INDE-PENDENCE, 1775–83, began, he joined the Pennsylvania State Navy and was appointed to the command of the brig *Andrea Doria* with the rank of captain. He soon was ordered to serve with the new Continental Navy in the same capacity. Biddle initially served in a squadron commanded by Esek HOPKINS, but because he was fifth on the seniority list he was soon appointed to the command of the newly launched frigate *Randolph*. In March 1778 he engaged the British 64-gun ship *Yarmouth* near Barbados. During this action the *Randolph* was hit by cannon fire and exploded. Biddle, who was sitting on deck at the time, was killed. The Continental Navy lost an experienced officer who almost certainly would have made a major contribution during the war against England.

Bireme

A GALLEY equipped with two banks of oars (rather than one), arranged on two different levels, one above the other. Each oar was powered by three or four rowers and the oars differed in length according to the level on which they were mounted. The bireme normally was equipped with a metal ram attached to the bow that was used to attack the enemy. It had the advantage of speed over the conventional galley, with its single bank of oars, but could not match the trireme, which had three banks. The bireme, which originated in ancient Rome, was widely used as a warship by the Turks, Venetians and other Mediterranean naval powers until it was replaced by the sailing ship during the 17th century. See also the Battle of LEPANTO, 1571.

Birkenhead, H.M.S.

N otable as the ROYAL NAVY's first iron-hulled warship, the *Birkenhead* was designed as a second-class steam frigate with a displacement of 1,400 tons. However, before she could be launched in 1845, the Admiralty decided to convert her into a TROOPSHIP because gun trials using a test hull of similar construction had produced disappointing results: Solid shot pierced the hull's iron plates with no real difficulty.

The *Birkenhead* entered service in 1851, but her working life was brought to a premature end early the next year. En route from Simonstown to Cape Town, on February

The destruction of the German battleship *Bismarck* on May 27, 1941   *(Copyright © National Maritime Museum, Greenwich, London)*

26, 1852, she struck an uncharted rock off Danger Point in Walker Bay, was badly holed and sank quickly, taking some 445 officers and men (from a total of 638) with her. Her loss proved to be one of the greatest maritime disasters of the Victorian period.

Bismarck

A famous German BATTLESHIP of 50,153 tons, launched in 1939, that was sunk by the British during WORLD WAR II, 1939–45. Equipped with main armament of eight 15-inch (38 cm) guns, she was 823 feet (251 m) in length and had a beam of 118 feet (36 m). She had a maximum speed of 29 knots and was operated by a crew of 2,192 men. Following her completion at Kiel at the beginning of 1941, the *Bismarck* departed from Glydia on May 20, flying the flag of Vice Admiral Gunther Lütjens. Accompanied by the heavy cruiser PRINZ EUGEN, her objective was to break out into the North Atlantic and attack allied shipping.

Two British cruisers—the *Suffolk* and the *Norfolk*—soon became aware of her movements, and she was first sighted on May 21 in Korsfjord, south of Bergen. As soon as she was discovered to have left this anchorage, the battleship *King George V*, the aircraft carrier *Victorious* and the battle cruiser *Repulse*, together with accompanying cruisers and destroyers, left SCAPA FLOW with the principal aim of protecting Allied convoys in the area. These ships formed part of the British home fleet commanded by Admiral John Tovey. He was also in overall command of the battle cruiser *Hood* and the battleship *Prince of Wales*, which were positioned south of Iceland, some 220 miles away.

They were ordered to intercept the *Bismarck*, but during an engagement with the German battleship south of Denmark Strait, between Iceland and Greenland, early on the following day, the *Prince of Wales* was damaged and the *Hood* blew up and sank. Only three members of the *Hood*'s crew of 1,400 survived and the loss of this warship caused great anguish in Britain. The *Bismarck*, which had been hit twice, lost some 1,000 tons of fuel, reducing her effective range significantly. As a result, Lütjens abandoned his plans to strike out into the North Atlantic and instead decided to move southeast to a French port. The *Bismarck* was shadowed by the *Prince of Wales*, the *Suffolk* and the *Norfolk*. Moving toward her from the south were the three ships of FORCE H—the aircraft carrier ARK ROYAL, the *Renown* and the *Sheffield*.

The British lost contact with the *Bismarck* during the morning of May 25 and did not regain it for a full day. Reconnaissance aircraft then sighted her still far out in the Atlantic. Later that same day Fairey Swordfish aircraft from the *Ark Royal* attacked her with torpedoes. Her rudders hit, she was forced to slow down. Other British naval units in the area also were involved in the fighting, but by May

27 Tovey's main force had gained ground and was able to engage her. The *King George V* and the *Rodney* attacked her with their heavy guns and caused massive damage. The *Bismarck* finally was sunk by torpedoes from the cruiser *Dorsetshire* with heavy loss of life. Only 110 German survivors were rescued. The loss of the *Bismarck* increased Hitler's concerns about the performance of his surface fleet and increased the prospects of the U-BOAT arm playing an enhanced role. The action provided a much-needed boost to British morale in this difficult period in the BATTLE OF THE ATLANTIC, 1939–45.

Ludovic Kennedy, *Pursuit: The Chase and Sinking of the Bismarck*, London, 1974.

Bismarck Sea, Battle of the
March 2–5, 1943

*S*ea and air battle between Japanese and Allied forces in the Pacific during WORLD WAR II, 1939–45. The Allies attacked a Japanese troop convoy of 16 ships (eight transports and eight destroyers) that had left Rabaul, New Britain, bound for northeast New Guinea with essential troop reinforcements (some 7,000 men) for the occupying forces. On March 2, 1943, as the convoy crossed the Bismarck Sea, it came under attack from American B-17 Flying Fortress bombers, and one transport was sunk. The escorting destroyers rescued some 850 survivors who were delivered to New Guinea. These were the only troops carried by the convoy to reach their intended destination.

Over the next two days, this attack was followed by sorties by B25s and other American aircraft as well as by Australian Bristol Beauforts and Beaufighters. Helped by new low-level bombing techniques, the Allied aircraft sank seven Japanese transport ships and four accompanying destroyers, and some 3,000 Japanese died. Allied losses amounted to no more than five aircraft. The surviving ships, with some 3,000 troops on board, were forced to return to Rabaul. This successful operation confirmed Allied air superiority over the Bismarck Sea and proved that the Japanese on New Guinea could now be supplied only by submarine.

Richard Hough, *The Longest Battle. The War at Sea, 1939–45*, London, 1986.

Blackwood, Sir Henry
1770–1832

*E*ntering the Royal Navy as a volunteer in 1781, Blackwood became one of lord NELSON's most successful captains. After a period as a frigate captain on the Newfoundland station, in 1799 he was sent to the Mediterranean, where he joined the blockade of Malta, during the French Revolutionary Wars, 1792–1802. As captain of the frigate *Penelope* he established his reputation during the pursuit of the *Guillaume Tell,* a French SHIP OF THE LINE that was attempting to escape from the island. The *Penelope* caused considerable damage to the enemy ship and enabled other British frigates to complete her destruction.

Nelson, then at Palermo, sent his congratulations to Blackwood, but the two men did not meet until the Battle of TRAFALGAR, 1805. Blackwood, in the *Euryalus,* was commander of the inshore squadron during the battle. He was responsible for keeping Nelson informed of the departure of the Franco-Spanish fleet from Cadiz and of its subsequent progress. Once the battle began, the role of the *Euryalus* was confined to conveying signals; Blackwood himself spent some time on board Admiral Nelson's flagship VICTORY. There he received Nelson's final instructions and was given wide powers in the final stages of the battle. Blackwood remained at sea until the end of 1812. He subsequently served in the West Indies and as commander in chief at the Nore, the naval anchorage in the Thames estuary.

Blake, Robert
1599–1657

*E*nglish naval commander who spent the first three-quarters of his life as a country gentleman before embarking on an eight-year career at sea, during which he won several brilliant victories. There is no doubt that Blake, who also was responsible for major improvements in naval tactics that were embodied in the *FIGHTING INSTRUCTIONS,* was one of England's greatest naval commanders.

A native of the west country, he became involved in national politics in 1640, at the age of 40, when he was returned to the Short Parliament as the member for Bridgwater. During the English Civil War, 1642–48, he fought for the Parliamentarians—first on land and then at sea. Blake first made his name as an army commander and was involved in the defense of Bristol, 1643, and Lyme Regis, 1644. His defense of Taunton, 1644–45, against superior royalist forces proved to be a turning point in the Civil War.

In 1649 he was appointed admiral or, more accurately, "general at sea" and was charged with the destruction of Prince Rupert's fleet. Blake drove the royalist enemy away from English shores and captured the Scilly Isles and Jersey. In the First ANGLO-DUTCH WAR, 1652–54, he fought a series of battles against Admiral Marten TROMP and Admiral Michiel de RUYTER. The final battle of the war in which Blake fought, at the GABBARD, June 1653, ended in a Dutch withdrawal. He next turned his attention to the Barbary Coast pirates, whom he defeated at the Battle of Porto Farina, off Tunis, in 1655. In 1657, during the war against Spain, he destroyed a Spanish treasure fleet at

Santa Cruz off Teneriffe. Forced to return home because of ill health, he died as his ship entered Plymouth Harbor.

John R. Powell, *Robert Blake,* New York, 1972.

Blane, Sir Gilbert
1749–1834

*S*cottish physician, born in Blanefield, Ayrshire, who served in the Royal Navy during the AMERICAN WAR OF INDEPENDENCE, 1775–83. In 1779 he sailed with Admiral Lord RODNEY, commander in chief in the West Indies, serving as Rodney's personal medical adviser. Blane later had a much wider influence on the development of British naval medicine than this first post might have implied. He developed a distinguished London practice and in 1795 was appointed commissioner of the Sick and Wounded Board of the Royal Navy. In this capacity he was active in promoting the results of the work James LIND had conducted on scurvy earlier in the century. Blane played a major role in securing the adoption of Lind's main recommendation—the compulsory use of lemon juice on board ship to prevent scurvy. This long-overdue but much-needed improvement in naval medicine had great salutory effects. Blane, whose service as a commissioner ended in 1802, also was responsible for the first collection of statistics in naval medicine.

Bligh, William
1754–1817

*B*ritish naval officer who was captain of the *BOUNTY* at the time of the famous mutiny in the South Seas in April 1789. Bligh entered the ROYAL NAVY in 1762 and established his reputation as master of the *Resolution* during Captain COOK's last voyage, 1776–79.

In 1787 Bligh was appointed to the command of the *Bounty,* an armed transport that was ordered to take breadfruit seedlings from Tahiti to the West Indies, where they were to be cultivated as food for plantation slaves. Having loaded her cargo, the *Bounty* left Tahiti for the Caribbean. Shortly afterward, on April 28, 1789, mutiny broke out as she passed the Friendly Islands on the first stage of her long westward journey. Under the leadership of Fletcher Christian, the second mate, the revolt was supported by the majority of the crew, who had been alienated by Bligh's allegedly tough methods and also were reluctant to leave the new, relaxed way of life they had experienced in Tahiti. Bligh and 18 loyal subordinates were set adrift in the ship's boat with nothing more than a compass to guide them. Courage and good fortune brought them to Timor, 3,600 miles away, after 48 days at sea, and eventually they returned to England. Ten mutineers eventually were captured and returned to England, where they stood trial, and three were hanged. However, the court martial failed to establish whether Bligh's methods or the attractions of life in the Pacific were the primary cause of the mutiny.

Bligh served during the FRENCH REVOLUTIONARY AND NAPOLEONIC WARS, 1792–1815, playing a valuable role at the Battle of CAMPERDOWN, 1797, and under Lord Nelson at the Battle of COPENHAGEN, 1801. His moment of glory quickly passed and the unfortunate Bligh was soon to be confronted with mutiny again. The Rum Rebellion, 1808, occurred during his time in Australia as governor of New South Wales, 1805–8, when he argued with his deputy about the rum trade and was arrested by mutinous soldiers. This act ended his term of office and he was imprisoned unlawfully for two years before he could return to England. Although he was no longer actively employed by the Royal Navy, his advancement continued and by 1814 he was a vice admiral. Bligh was an officer of considerable ability whose effectiveness was limited by his unpredictable temperament and by his inability to work productively with his colleagues.

Richard Hough, *Captain Bligh and Mr Christian: The Men and the Mutiny*, London, 1979.

Blockade

A naval tactic designed to disrupt the movement of enemy warships or merchant ships. During the age of sail the blockading of enemy ports and naval bases was an essential feature of naval warfare. It was designed in part to reduce or end an enemy's ability to wage war at sea by preventing the arrival or departure of his fleet. Blockades also were intended to disrupt an enemy's trade relations and supply routes. This disruption might be achieved by maintaining a naval presence outside an enemy port, but it also could mean patrolling his coastline or intercepting merchant ships at sea. The right to declare a blockade, to intercept merchant shipping and to seize cargo destined for an enemy have been recognized in international law since the 17th century. In the early 20th century detailed rules of blockade were acknowledged by the principal naval powers and embodied in international law.

Blockades were imposed regularly during 17th- and 18th-century wars, although their limitations quickly became apparent. Maintaining an effective blockade normally required more ships than were typically available, and evasion was widespread. Sailing ships could conduct an effective blockade only in the right weather conditions, and their impact depended on the available intelligence, which usually was limited, and on their coordination with other ships. However, a blockade could have a real impact if sufficient resources were invested in it. The British naval blockade of France during the FRENCH REVOLUTIONARY

AND NAPOLEONIC WARS, 1792–1815, is one example of an effective operation; the North's blockade of the Confederacy in the American Civil War, 1861–65, is another. Blockade runners tried to undermine this barrier in both wars, but the dominant naval power prevailed, despite their opponents' ingenuity. During the American Civil War, blockade runners used specially built ships and concealed weapons in disguised containers as they attempted to maintain supplies to the South.

As new weapons were developed, particularly the mine and the torpedo, the distant blockade became the norm. In the two world wars, participants on both sides sought to blockade the other from long range. The use of submarines and aircraft to intercept or destroy merchant shipping increased the effectiveness of the distant blockade. For example, U-boat attacks on British convoys in the Atlantic reached unsustainable levels in 1917 and again in 1942–43; without the introduction of effective countermeasures in both situations, Great Britain almost certainly would have collapsed. The Allied blockade of Germany in World War I was a significant factor in Germany's defeat. It was less effective in World War II because of Germany's policy of autarky and its ability to exploit the occupied countries. In the postwar period the blockade continues to be employed in various circumstances, although traditional techniques have been supplemented by the use of financial instruments and arms embargoes. Examples of conventional blockades include the American blockade of Soviet ships during the CUBAN MISSILE CRISIS, 1962, the mining of Haiphong harbor in 1972 during the VIETNAM WAR, and the 200-mile exclusion zone imposed during the FALKLANDS WAR, 1982.

R. Barker, *The Blockade Busters*, London, 1976.

Blockship

A blockship is a scuttled vessel used to obstruct a harbor entrance, an anchorage or a strategic waterway. Its function can be primarily defensive—to provide additional protection for the fleet lying at anchor—or it can provide a means to obstruct enemy movements. A blockship is typically a decommissioned ship weighted with heavy material, often concrete, and sunk at a predetermined location. A notable example of the use of blockships in the postwar period occurred during the SUEZ CRISIS, 1956, when the Egyptians successfully blocked the Suez Canal with nearly 50 such vessels for six months.

Blockships also were used during the two world wars, but without the same degree of success. In April 1918, during the latter stages of WORLD WAR I, 1914–18, the British used blockships in an attempt to obstruct the harbor entrances at Zeebrugge and Ostend (see ZEEBRUGGE RAID), which were used by U-boats based inland at Bruges and connected to the sea by canal. The Zeebrugge operation revealed the difficulties of positioning blockships under heavy enemy fire, and the canal was blocked only partially. At the beginning of World War II, 1939–45, the Royal Navy planned to strengthen the defenses of the naval base at SCAPA FLOW by obstructing a channel with a blockship. However, the blockship arrived too late to prevent the destruction of the battleship ROYAL OAK by a German U-boat.

Blücher

A German armored cruiser of WORLD WAR I, 1914–18, named after the Prussian field marshal of the Napoleonic Wars, sunk by the British during the Battle of DOGGER BANK in January 1915. A development of the Scharnhorst class, the *Blücher*, which was completed in 1911, had a displacement of 15,500 tons, a maximum speed of about 24 knots and was operated by a crew of 880. Armament consisted of 12 8.2-inch (21-cm) and eight 5.9-inch (15-cm) guns. As a result of a signaling error during the Dogger Bank action, the British concentrated their fire on the *Blücher*, hitting her with some 50 shells and two torpedoes while allowing the rest of the German force to escape. Only 260 members of her crew were saved as she went down.

Blücher was also the name of a German heavy cruiser commissioned within days of the beginning of the WORLD WAR II, 1939–45. This later *Blücher* was the second ship of the Hipper class and had a displacement of 14,000 tons. She was armed with eight 8-inch guns and had a maximum speed of 32 knots. On April 9, 1940 she was sunk by torpedoes fired from Norwegian shore batteries as she transported troops up Oslo Fjord during the invasion of Norway. Her sister ship, the *Admiral Hipper*, remained on active service until after the Battle of the BARENTS SEA, December 1942, when she was transferred to training duties. She survived until May 1945 when she was scuttled in Kiel Harbour.

Boisot, Louis

d. 1576

Dutch naval commander and admiral, based in Zeeland, who led the SEA BEGGARS during the early stages of the Dutch war of independence against Spain, 1568–1609. The SEA BEGGARS were Dutch privateers commissioned by William of Orange to attack Spanish merchant ships, to interrupt communications with Spain and, ultimately, to launch direct assaults on coastal positions occupied by the enemy. The highlights of Boisot's highly effective campaign against Spain included the destruction of a Spanish fleet in the Scheldt River off Walcheren in January 1574 that fatally weakened the position of enemy forces on the island. The relief of Leiden in October 1574 was another major example. The timely arrival of Boisot's fleet, which sailed across the flooded countryside, saved the occupants of the besieged city from starvation. During the next few months the Dutch revolt gained momentum, and there seemed little that the Spanish could do to reverse the tide. One exception to the string of Spanish defeats was their success in recapturing the island of Zierikzee, off Zeeland in 1576. Boisot, who was in command of the

British preoccupation with the *Blücher*, a German armored cruiser, at the Battle of the Dogger Bank, 1915, allowed other enemy ships to escape   (*Copyright © Imperial War Museum, London*)

island at the time, was killed as he attempted to stop the enemy crossing the water that separated the island from the mainland. Although Boisot did not live to witness the final emancipation of the Netherlands from the Spanish rule, his leadership and seamanship had made a significant contribution to the final victory.

Bomb Vessel

A small sailing vessel armed with heavy mortars that was used to attack enemy shore positions. A French invention of the 1670s, the bomb vessel was probably first used in action by Admiral Abraham DUQUESNE during the bombardment of Algiers in 1682. It was to remain a part of the armory of the sailing navies for nearly 200 years. During the 19th century, improvements in naval gunnery rendered it obsolete, and it gradually disappeared from operational service. The bomb vessel was equipped with one or two heavy mortars, which, on their introduction, were larger than any other gun then carried at sea. Mortars were short, wide-barreled guns that could fire projectiles of 200 pounds (90 kg) at a high angle. The shot from the gun of a SHIP OF THE LINE would be less than a quarter of that size. The mortar was well suited to its main purpose of shore bombardment.

One drawback of the heavy mortar was its recoil, which was so powerful that the bomb vessel's structure had to be substantially strengthened. Therefore bomb vessels were always heavily built, and the decks in particular had to be reinforced by substantial beam bridges. The ketch proved to be particularly adaptable for this purpose. A two-masted vessel with a displacement of up to 400 tons, it had a large open space forward of the mainmast. From this position, with the ketch properly anchored, the mortar could be fired over the bow, thus avoiding the need to expose the ship's side to the shore during a bombardment. Besides ketches, a variety of other ships were used as bomb vessels. These included the galiot, a flat-bottomed two-masted ship of shallow draft that could operate close to the shore. A French variant was the mortar prahm, an armed barge towed by a sailing ship.

Bonhomme Richard

*T*he frigate in which the American naval commander John Paul JONES defeated the British warship *Serapis* during the AMERICAN WAR OF INDEPENDENCE, 1775–83. This famous engagement, which resulted in the sinking of the victorious ship, took place on September 23, 1779 in the North Sea off Flamborough Head, northeast England. Originally, a French EAST INDIAMAN, known as the *Duc de Duras*, she was built in 1766 and had a displacement of 998 tons. She was 152 feet (46.2 m) in length and had a

beam of 40 feet (12 m). The French acquired her on Jones' behalf and refitted her, changing her name to *Bonhomme Richard* as a tribute to Benjamin Franklin. (The new name was a reference to Franklin's *Poor Richard's Almanac*.) She was armed with 40 guns and operated by a crew of 380.

On August 14, 1779 Jones sailed from the port of L'ORIENT in Brittany accompanied by four other ships (three French and one American) on a privateering expedition around the British coast. As he approached Flamborough Head on September 23, Jones met the *Serapis* which was escorting a convoy of merchantmen. The British convoy escaped to the north and the supporting ships on both sides soon dispersed, leaving the *Bonhomme Richard* and the *Serapis* to fight a fierce and costly three-hour battle at close quarters in the moonlight. When a fire broke out on the *Serapis*, it was forced to surrender, but the *Bonhomme Richard*, which had lost almost all of its guns, also was severely damaged. She sank two days later but not before Jones and his crew had transferred to the captured British ship. John Paul Jones sailed the *Serapis* east to neutral Holland, arriving at the Dutch North Sea island of Texel, where he was welcomed as a hero.

Borough, William
1536–99

*B*ritish naval commander whose early seagoing experience was largely gained on the voyages of exploration to Russia undertaken by his brother Stephen, 1525–84. He also carried out surveys of the Russian coast before returning to England, where he eventually took up the appointment of comptroller of the navy. In the latter part of his career Borough (or Burrough, as his name was sometimes spelled) served his country in the war against Spain. In 1587 he was appointed vice admiral in Sir Francis DRAKE's expedition to CADIZ and commanded the 500-ton *Golden Lion*. Relations between the two commanders deteriorated rapidly when Borough objected to Drake's planned attack on Lagos, Portugal. Borough disliked Drake's methods, particularly the absence of consultation with his subordinates, and his flamboyant style. Although Borough was arrested and threatened with severe punishment for alleged cowardice and other crimes, Drake was unable to sustain the charges when they were considered by Lord HOWARD of Effingham, the Lord High Admiral. At the time of the SPANISH ARMADA, 1588, William Borough commanded the *Bonavolia* in his final service at sea.

Boscawen, Edward
1711–61

*B*ritish naval commander who served with distinction in the War of the AUSTRIAN SUCCESSION, 1740–48, and in the SEVEN YEARS' WAR, 1756–63. Much of his early career was spent in the West Indies, where he distinguished himself in operations against the Spanish at Porto Bello, 1739, and Cartagena, 1741. Returning to England in 1742, he was appointed to the command of the 60-gun *Dreadnought*. His attempt to engage two French warships in the Bay of Biscay earned him the nickname "Old Dreadnought." Boscawen later commanded the 74-gun *Namur*, and it was in this ship that he fought the French at the Battle of CAPE FINISTERRE in October 1747, making a major contribution to the British victory. After the battle, in which he sustained serious neck injuries, he was promoted to rear admiral.

In the years of peace that followed, Boscawen was appointed a lord commissioner of the ADMIRALTY. By 1755 he had returned to the sea as commander of a squadron ordered to prevent French reinforcements reaching Canada. He accomplished this mission with some success and thereby helped to precipitate the Seven Years' War. In that war he operated in the seas off the French coast before being sent, as admiral of the blue (one of the three squadrons into which 18th-century navies were organized), to North America in 1758. He commanded the fleet that conveyed British land forces under Jeffrey Amherst and James Wolfe to Canada; these forces subsequently captured LOUISBURG and QUEBEC from the French. On his return he was appointed to the command of the Mediterranean fleet. Boscawen won a notable victory over the French Toulon fleet commanded by Admiral de la CLUE in the Battle of LAGOS, August 18–19, 1759—a fitting end to a distinguished career.

Edward Boscawen, *Boscawen's Letters to His Wife, 1755–56*, edited from the Falmouth papers by Peter K. Kemp, London, 1952.

Boston

*A*n American heavy CRUISER of the Baltimore class, the *Boston* was completed in 1943 and saw service in the Pacific in the latter part of WORLD WAR II, 1939–45. She had a displacement of 13,600 tons and was armed with nine 8-inch guns in three triple turrets as well as heavy ANTIAIRCRAFT armament. The *Boston* had high freeboard (the distance from the waterline to the upper deck) and a substantial superstructure that was divided in two. Her armor protection was also heavy for a ship of this type and included a 6-inch (15.24cm) belt extending between the turrets.

In 1955 the *Boston* and the *Canberra*, another Baltimore-class ship, were converted as the world's first guided MISSILE cruisers. They were also the first operational combat ships capable of firing supersonic antiaircraft weapons. Some of their original guns were removed, and the superstructure was partially remodeled. At the after end an 8-inch gun turret was replaced by two sets of launchers for the Terrier RIM-2 missile. The missiles had a range of 20 miles (32.5 km) and were radar-guided. The *Boston* was recommissioned as CAG.1 in 1955, and her service finally ended in 1970.

Bougainville, Louis Antoine, Comte de
1729–1811

*F*rench admiral, soldier and navigator who at an early age distinguished himself as a mathematician. He served in the French Army during the SEVEN YEARS' WAR, 1756–63, which included a period in Canada as General the Marquis de Montcalm's aide de camp. In 1761 Bougainville served in the campaign in Germany, and some two years later he entered the FRENCH NAVY and was sent to the Falkland Islands, with responsibility for their colonization. Only three years later, however, he evacuated them in favor of Spain.

Once the evacuation had been completed, he continued his journey westward across the Pacific. In command of the frigate *La Boudeuse* and the support vessel *L'Etoile*, Bougainville became the first Frenchman to circumnavigate the world. He failed to find Australia but had one of the Solomon Islands named after him. He returned home early in 1769. As a vice admiral during the AMERICAN WAR OF INDEPENDENCE, 1775–83, he commanded a division in the French fleet under Admiral the Marquis de GRASSE. His operational career concluded unhappily at the Battle of the SAINTS, 1782; he was accorded part of the blame for the French defeat. Despite this setback, Bougainville was later to be made a senator and received other honors from Napoleon I. He also produced a *Description of a Voyage Around the World* (2 vols. 1771–72), which popularized the theories of Rousseau, and had the bougainvillea plant named after him.

Bounty

A bounty—a reward or premium—was a widely used inducement to ensure that the world's navies had a sufficient flow of recruits in time of war. The state would make a payment, normally in cash, to those who agreed to serve. Occasionally, particularly in colonial America, payment was in the form of a grant of land. In England, cash payments had a long history, and by the end of the 18th century a bounty of up to five guineas was typically payable. Because this sum might not be sufficient to attract enough recruits in a particular area, local civic leaders sometimes offered a supplementary bounty as an inducement.

The availability of relatively large cash sums opened the door to corruption: Recruits who had received a bounty in one area would desert their new ship and join up again elsewhere in order to collect a second payment. Bounties

The *Bounty* mutineers cast William Bligh and his loyal crew adrift in the ship's launch, 1789 (*Copyright © National Maritime Museum, Greenwich, London*)

also were paid as a wartime performance bonus in some European navies and in the U.S. Navy, where crews received a payout when an enemy ship was sunk. With the introduction of conscription during the 19th century, the payment of recruitment bounties generally disappeared.

Bounty, H.M.S.

A British armed transport operated by the ROYAL NAVY, H.M.S. *Bounty* was the scene of a famous MUTINY in the South Seas on April 28, 1789. The *Bounty* episode remains vivid in the popular consciousness and has been the subject of three motion pictures. *Bounty* was a three-masted, full-rigged ship of 200 tons, built in Hull in 1784. She was operated by a crew of 44 and was armed with four large and ten small cannon. Launched as a merchantman in 1784, she was subsequently rebuilt for naval use.

Late in 1787 she was dispatched to Tahiti under the command of Lieutenant William BLIGH. He was ordered to obtain breadfruit seedlings from Tahiti and take them to the West Indies where they were to be grown as food for the slaves working in the sugar plantations. During the long and difficult 11-month voyage to Tahiti, Bligh's tough methods of command caused growing tensions on board ship. These problems came to a head shortly after the *Bounty*, now fully laden, had left the island. The majority of the crew, led by the second mate, Fletcher Christian, mutinied and quickly seized control. Although Bligh's brutal conduct was a major cause of the mutiny, the attractions of life on Tahiti were another important influence.

The deposed captain and 18 men who remained loyal to him were cast adrift in the ship's boat and faced an uncertain future, while the mutineers returned to Tahiti in the *Bounty*. Against all odds, with just a single compass to guide him, Bligh reached Timor, 3,600 miles (5,794 km) away, after a 48-day voyage; he eventually made his way back to England. In 1790 Christian and eight mutineers fell out with their companions. Accompanied by 18 islanders, they left Tahiti for the greater safety of the remote Pitcairn Islands, where the *Bounty* was beached and destroyed. They founded a permanent settlement on Pitcairn, and their descendants still live on the islands today.

The mutineers who chose to remain on Tahiti eventually were tracked down by a British frigate, the *Pandora*, that was sent as soon as news of Bligh's fate had reached England. Fourteen men were taken prisoner, but four were lost during the return journey when the *Pandora* was wrecked on the Great Barrier Reef. The surviving ten mutineers were court-martialed when they finally reached England and three were hanged.

Hough, Richard, *The Bounty*, London, 1984.

Bouvet

*N*amed after Admiral François BOUVET, this French battleship participated in the Allied attack on the Dardanelles during the WORLD WAR I, 1914–18. Launched in 1896, the *Bouvet* had a displacement of 12,007 tons and two 12-inch (30-cm) and two 10.8-inch (27-cm) guns. The last variant of the Charles Martel class, she had triple screws and could operate at speeds up to 17 knots.

The *Bouvet* was one of three pre-dreadnoughts lost during the bomabardment of Turkish forts on the peninsula on March 18, 1915. She hit a Turkish mine armed with 176 pounds (80 kg) of TNT, capsized and sank within two minutes; her rapid destruction was partly explained by the corrosion of her bulkheads. Some 660 men lost their lives.

Bouvet, François

*F*rench naval commander who served during in the AMERICAN WAR OF INDEPENDENCE, 1775–83, and FRENCH REVOLUTIONARY AND NAPOLEONIC WARS, 1792–1815, before his career was brought to a premature end in 1796. Bouvet gained his initial experience at sea as a civilian officer in the French East India Company, but he soon transferred to the naval forces of the crown. He remained in the East Indies and served under Admiral Pierre de SUFFREN during the latter's remarkable campaign against the British, 1781–83. He survived the politically inspired thinning of the officer corps during the French Revolution, 1789, and by the time the French Revolutionary Wars began in 1792 Bouvet was a rear admiral.

Bouvet was a divisional commander at the Battle of the GLORIOUS FIRST OF JUNE, 1794, and again in an expedition to land French troops in Ireland in December 1796, in support of the Irish rebellion against British rule. Poor weather badly affected the entire operation, and when Bouvet's ship was forced out to sea following an abortive attempt to land troops in Bantry Bay, he decided to return to France. However, other ships under his command had managed to retain their position in the bay, and Bouvet

was removed from his command for leaving them unprotected. His failure also undermined the uprising, which soon was crushed. Although Bouvet returned briefly to active service at the end of the war, this incident effectively marked the end of his naval career.

Brest

*P*ort city and French naval base in Brittany, northwestern France, situated on the Bay of Brest. The fine sheltered harbor makes it an obvious site for a naval base, and it has been used by the FRENCH NAVY since the 1630s. Developed initially by Cardinal Richelieu and then by Jean COLBERT, in 1680–88 the city was first fortified by Sébastien de Vauban, the celebrated French military engineer. The naval facilities at Brest gradually expanded to include shipbuilding, the École Navale and naval barracks. During WORLD WAR I, 1914–18, Brest served as a major entry port for American troops arriving to fight on the Western Front. In 1940, during WORLD WAR II, 1939–45, it was occupied by the Germans, who made it an important base for submarines engaged in the BATTLE OF THE ATLANTIC, 1939–45. It also served as the base for the German navy's Atlantic squadron, which consisted of the battle cruisers *SCHARNHORST* and *GNEISENAU* and the heavy cruiser *PRINZ EUGEN*. As a result of heavy Allied bombing raids, these ships, which sustained serious damage, were never used operationally and were all withdrawn to Germany during the "CHANNEL DASH" early in 1942. Liberated by American troops in 1944, Brest was rebuilt and once more has become an important French naval center.

Bretagne

*F*rench battleship that gives its name to a class consisting of three ships—the *Bretagne*, the *Lorraine* and the *Provence*, all launched in 1913. The *Bretagne* had a displacement of 21,300 tons, was 544 feet 6 inches (653 m) in length and had a beam of 88 feet 6 inches (106 m). Her armament included ten 340-mm (13.38-in) guns in five twin turrets and 14 138-mm (5.43-in) guns. Capable of a maximum speed of 20 knots, she was operated by a crew of 1,133. All the *Bretagnes* served in the Mediterranean during WORLD WAR I, 1914–18, acting in support of the Italian fleet, but they saw little action. All three ships were refitted in 1932–35. At the beginning of WORLD WAR II, 1939–45, both the *Bretagne* and the *Provence* were based at MERS-EL-KEBIR, Algeria. There, on July 3, 1940, they came under attack from British naval forces anxious to prevent any French warships from falling into German hands. The *Bretagne* blew up and capsized with the loss of 977 crew, while the *Provence* was badly damaged and beached during the attack. In November 1940 the *Provence* was refloated and moved to Toulon, where she was scuttled by the French in 1942 to prevent her capture by the Germans. The *Lorraine* was at Alexandria, Egypt, at the time of the French armistice in 1940 and was partially disarmed by the British. She later served on the Allied side and was involved in the invasion of the south of France in 1944. The *Lorraine* survived the war and was scrapped in 1953.

Brett, Sir Percy
1709–81

*E*nglish naval commander who helped to undermine the Jacobite Rebellion of 1745. During a regular patrol in the English Channel in 1745, Brett, who was commander of the 60-gun *Lion,* intercepted the 64-gun *Elizabeth,* a French warship on escort duty. In its charge was a small schooner carrying the Young Pretender, Prince Charles Edward Stuart, back to Scotland. After a four-hour battle both the *Lion* and the *Elizabeth* were severely damaged and forced to withdraw. Prince Charles Edward continued his voyage, but the *Elizabeth*'s cargo of arms and money for the rebellion was lost to him, and he arrived in Scotland at a considerable disadvantage.

Brett was rewarded with regular promotion following this success and reached the rank of admiral in 1778. His earlier career had not, however, progressed so smoothly. As a young lieutenant he had joined Admiral George ANSON on his circumnavigation of the globe, 1740–44, and was promoted as captain of the *Centurion* during the voyage. On their return the Admiralty refused to recognize the advancement because Anson was not a commander in chief and had, therefore, exceeded his powers in making a promotion at sea. Once Anson himself was appointed to the Admiralty a few months later, the authorities were persuaded to change their minds.

Brig

A two-masted sailing vessel of the 18th and 19th centuries. The word "brig" was originally an abbreviation for the BRIGANTINE, but evolved as a distinct type with square rigging on both her fore and mainmasts; she also carried on her main mast a lower fore and aft sail with a gaff and boom. With a displacement of between 140 and 500 tons, this relatively small design normally permitted only one deck, one battery of guns and a minimal crew. A brig with a displacement at the upper end of the scale might be over 100 feet (30.4 m) in length and have a beam of 30 feet (9.1 m). The brig was able to serve a dual purpose: In the merchant service it was used for cargo-carrying as well as whaling, while in the main navies of the period it was employed as a small warship. Equipped with up to 20 guns, the brig provided fast connections between a fleet and its bases and was also used in maritime patrol operations. In war, brigs were employed to transmit orders between the ships of a battle fleet. The brig also was widely used as a naval training ship and in this form survived well into the 20th century.

Brigantine

*T*he term "brigantine" originally referred to a small, half-decked sailing warship with oars that was deployed in the Mediterranean during the 16th century. Rigged with lateen sails, it had from eight to 12 banks of oars on each side and was highly maneuverable. In contrast to the GALLEY, its bow and stern were raised to offer greater protection from attack. It was widely used by pirates: Its name derives from the same root as the word "brigand."

More recently and familiarly, the term "brigantine" describes the two-masted, square-rigged sailing ship introduced in the late 17th century. Frequently used by pirates from northern Europe, principally from France, England and the Netherlands, the new type of brigantine was very different from the earlier Mediterranean one, but its close association with piracy meant that the name was still appropriate. The square rigging soon disappeared from the mainmast, which was simply equipped with fore-and-aft canvas. Except for its rigging, the brigantine was similar to the BRIG and used by the principal naval powers for much the same purposes—patrolling and communications—during the 18th and 19th centuries.

Brin, Benedetto
1833–98

*I*talian naval engineer and administrator who played a leading role in the creation of a national navy after the unification of Italy in 1870. He first served as a civil servant in the Ministry of Marine, where he was personally responsible for the design of the large battleships *Duilio* and *Dandolo* that formed the core strength of the early ITALIAN NAVY. Brin monitored the construction of these ships, which were notable because their 100-ton, 17.7-inch (45-cm) Armstrong muzzle-loaders were the largest guns then mounted in any ship. In 1876 he became Minister of Marine and, during an 11-year term, continued to oversee the development of the fleet and the construction industries that supported it. Brin concluded his political career as Minister for Foreign Affairs, but it is in his role as "father of the Italian navy" that he deserves to be remembered.

Britannia

*T*he name *Britannia* has been given to several British naval vessels, the earliest of which dates back to 1682.

Among ships of this name was the 100-gun SHIP OF THE LINE that served at the Battle of TRAFALGAR, October 1805, during the Napoleonic Wars, 1803–15. Built at Portsmouth in 1762, it was the flagship of Admiral William CARNEGIE, Earl of Northesk, who was third in command. *Britannia* was also the name of the notable British training ship that began its work in 1859. It preceded the formation of the Royal Navy College at Dartmouth, in Devon, and was eventually based in the River Dart. The name *Britannia* is also associated with a number of yachts used by the royal family, including the present vessel, which is due to be taken out of service in 1997.

Broadside

A term used in the age of the sailing navies to describe the simultaneous firing of all the guns on one side of a warship. The target ship would draw alongside or on a parallel course and then both vessels could open fire. A broadside could have a devastating effect on an enemy crew; its impact on the ship itself might be more uncertain. The effective range of guns was limited and increased only slowly up to the mid-19th century. To maximize the effect of a broadside, gunners delayed opening fire until an enemy ship was within 100 yards (91m). At point-blank range a broadside had a good chance of causing major structural damage to the opposing warship, but sinking a vessel by gunfire alone was always difficult because the damage generally was inflicted above the waterline. See also CROSSING THE T.

Broke, H.M.S.

*I*n a notable WORLD WAR I action on the night of April 20–21, 1917, two ships of the ROYAL NAVY's Dover Patrol engaged six German destroyers in the Straits of Dover. The British destroyers *Broke* and *Swift* were on regular patrol in the area of the South Goodwins, off the east coast of Kent, when they intercepted an enemy flotilla. Twelve German destroyers in two flotillas had left their base at Zeebrugge with the aim of attacking the Royal Navy at both ends of the South Goodwins net barrage.

The action began in the early hours of April 21, when the *Swift* torpedoed one German warship and gave chase to a second. The *Broke* also hit an enemy boat with a torpedo and then rammed another. Commander Edward EVANS of the *Broke* graphically described how they had carried the German destroyer "bodily along on our ram, pouring a deadly fire into her terrorised crew. Many clambered on to our forecastle, only to meet with instant death from our well-armed seamen and stokers. When we eventually broke clear, we left G42 a sinking, blazing wreck." The *Broke*, which herself was by now badly damaged and had 57 casualties, tried unsuccessfully to ram

another enemy ship before returning to base. As a result of this engagement, in which two German ships were sunk, there were no further German raids in this part of the English Channel until the final months of the war.

Broke, Sir Philip
1776–1841

*B*ritish rear admiral who commanded the 52-gun frigate *SHANNON* during its famous engagement with the American frigate *Chesapeake* during the WAR OF 1812. Broke, who had served widely during the FRENCH REVOLUTIONARY AND NAPOLEONIC WARS, 1792–1815, was appointed to the command of the Shannon in 1806. A noted gunnery officer, he gave priority to the training of his crew.

The effectiveness of Broke's training methods, which were widely emulated in the Royal Navy, was evident when he engaged the CHESAPEAKE off Boston on June 1, 1813. After an intense struggle lasting no more than 15 minutes, Broke and some of his men boarded and captured the American frigate, which eventually was taken to Britain. It was a rare British success in this war, and Broke's reputation rose accordingly. However, it proved to be his final moment of glory: He was wounded during the fight and was unable to serve at sea again.

Peter Padfield, *Broke and the* Shannon, London, 1968.

Brueys D'Aigailliers, François
1753–98

*F*rench naval commander whose service began as a lieutenant in the ROYAL NAVAL during the AMERICAN WAR OF INDEPENDENCE, 1775–83. Brueys continued in the FRENCH NAVY after the Revolution, but in 1793 he was condemned as a royalist and dismissed from his post. In 1795, after Napoleon came to power, he was employed with the rank of rear admiral.

Three years later Brueys, now a vice admiral, commanded the French Mediterranean fleet that escorted Napoleon's army to Egypt. In June 1798, as he sailed east, the French force captured Malta. Following the landing of the expeditionary force near Alexandria, Brueys moved his 13 warships in Aboukir Bay, at the mouth of the Nile River. Although he regarded this as a secure anchorage, events were soon to prove him wrong. On August 1 Admiral Horatio NELSON, with 14 SHIPS OF THE LINE under his command, discovered the enemy's berth after a long search.

The Battle of the NILE was about to begin. Brueys was completely unprepared for the British onslaught, and many of his men were on shore as Nelson attacked. The British closed in on the enemy from both sides, and only four of

Admiral Brueys d'Aigailliers, French naval commander, was fatally wounded at the Battle of the Nile, 1798 *(Copyright © National Maritime Museum, Greenwich, London)*

Brueys' ships managed to escape. The French commander himself was not so fortunate: He was killed on his flagship *L'ORIENT* in the first phase of the action.

Buccaneers

A buccaneer was a member of one of the groups of lawless seamen who plundered ships in the SPANISH MAIN and the Pacific during the 17th century. The term derives from the French word *boucan*, referring to smoke-dried meat and hides; those who traded in these items in the Caribbean were known as *boucaniers*. These French traders later turned to the often more rewarding activity of attacking Spanish merchant ships. Other nationalities, notably the British, soon enlarged the ranks of the buccaneers, and their activities spread throughout the Caribbean and beyond.

Among notable British buccaneers were Sir Henry MORGAN, who captured Panama in 1671, and William DAMPIER, who made a remarkable journey round the world in the 1680s. The buccaneer may be distinguished from the pirate by the fact that he did not normally attack ships of his own country. Governments sometimes used buccaneers in support of policy objectives, but few buccaneers received the official commissions that privateers had enjoyed in the previous century. However, during the War of the GRAND ALLIANCE, 1688–97, buccaneers were drawn into the conflict by their respective governments, and independent buccaneering disappeared for good.

Buchanan, Franklin
1800–74

A merican naval officer who became the first superintendent of the UNITED STATES NAVAL ACADEMY at ANNAPOLIS and one who epitomized divided loyalties caused by the AMERICAN CIVIL WAR, 1861–65. Born on September 17, 1800 in Baltimore, Maryland, Buchanan was commissioned a midshipman in 1815, rising to the rank of commander in 1841. An imaginative advocate of better officer education, he helped propose the plan for a permanent shore-based facility to educate and train naval officers. On the creation of the naval school at Annapolis in 1845, he served (until 1847) as its first superintendent, instilling a strong sense of discipline. After commanding a sloop during the war with Mexico, 1846–48, he captained the steam frigate *Susquehanna*, flagship of Commodore Matthew PERRY, who negotiated the first trade agreement with Japan.

With the outbreak of the Civil War, Buchanan resigned his commission, believing that his native Maryland would secede. When it did not, his request to remain with the Union was denied, and he joined the CONFEDERATE NAVY as a captain. Commanding the Chesapeake Bay Squadron on board the *Virginia* (the raised and reconstructed U.S.S. MERRIMACK), he did considerable damage to the Union squadron at Hampton Roads, Virginia, sinking the *Congress* and the *Cumberland*. A wound forced him to relinquish command the day before the *Virginia*'s famous encounter with the Union IRONCLAD *MONITOR*. He became the Confederacy's highest ranking naval officer, commanding the squadron defending MOBILE BAY in the C.S.S. *Tennessee*. He was defeated by the Union fleet under David FARRAGUT on August 5, 1864. He later served as president of Maryland Agricultural College, the future University of Maryland.

Charles Todorich, "Franklin Buchanan: Symbol for Two Navies," in *Captains of the Old Steam Navy: Makers of the American Naval Tradition, 1840–1880*, ed. James C. Bradford, Annapolis, 1986.

Bugia, Battle of
May 8, 1671

A successful British operation against Algerine COR-SAIRS based at Bugia Bay (now Bejaïa) on the north coast of Algeria. Under the command of Admiral Sir Edward SPRAGGE, the British Mediterranean squadron, consisting of six vessels, used FIRESHIPS in the first assault on May 2, which ended in complete failure. Spragge waited six days before making a second attempt. Following a two-hour bombardment, Spragge used three vessels to cut through a boom that the pirates had placed across the entrance to the harbor. In a devastating attack, the fireship *Little Victory* destroyed seven pirate ships and took three prizes. The Algerine corsairs also suffered heavy casualties, while English losses were relatively light. The defeated corsairs were forced to make peace with the ROYAL NAVY soon afterward, and their raids on British merchant shipping in the Mediterranean ceased.

Bulwark

A British pre-dreadnought BATTLESHIP of 15,000 tons, launched in 1902, the *Bulwark* was lost in a disastrous accident during the opening stages of WORLD WAR I, 1914–18. In November 1914 she was docked at Sheerness, Kent, when a massive explosion tore her apart as she was being loaded with ammunition. An official court of inquiry later ruled that the cause of the explosion was the instability of the ammunition; there was no evidence of sabotage. Whatever the cause, the cost in human life—738 deaths and only 12 survivors among her crew—was one of the highest in British naval history.

Burke, Arleigh Albert
1901–1996

American naval officer, born in Boulder, Colorado, on October 19, 1901. Burke was commissioned in 1923 and embarked upon a career that would lead him to become a famous destroyer squadron commander in WORLD WAR II, 1939–45, as well as the youngest chief of naval operations (during the 1950s). Because he was a specialist in ordnance, he was stationed in shore and sea billets dealing with this work well into World War II, although he requested combat duty. In March 1943 he was given command of successive DESTROYER divisions that engaged the Japanese while escorting cruiser forces in the SOLOMON ISLANDS. In October 1943 he commanded Destroyer Squadron 23, known as the "Little Beavers," displaying exceptional battle tactics and bravery in sinking various Japanese vessels during actions in the South Pacific.

He then became chief of staff to Admiral Marc MITSCHER, participating in actions such as the battles of the Philippine Sea, the LEYTE GULF, IWO JIMA and OKINAWA. Following the war he headed the controversial section of the Navy Department, Op-23, that campaigned to ensure for the navy a role in America's nuclear arsenal. Further commands followed, including that of a cruiser division during the KOREAN WAR, 1950–53, and service as a United Nations delegate at the Panmunjom peace talks. Raised over the 87 officers above him by President Eisenhower, Admiral Burke became chief of naval operations in 1955. He held the post successfully for an unprecedented six years, running the navy during many critical phases of the COLD WAR, before retiring in 1961.

E. B. Potter, *Admiral Arleigh Burke*, New York, 1990.

Bushnell, David
c. 1742–1824

American inventor, educated at Yale, who created the world's first operational SUBMARINE in 1776. A year earlier he had established that dynamite would explode under water, but it was as the inventor of the TURTLE during the AMERICAN WAR OF INDEPENDENCE, 1775–83, that he made his main contribution to the development of naval warfare. A small, hand-powered submarine, the *Turtle* floated upright in the water and could be partially submerged when two internal water tanks were filled. Power was provided by a hand-cranked propeller. She was armed with a detachable explosive charge that could be attached to the hull of an enemy warship secretly.

The first ever submarine attack against an enemy surface vessel took place on September 6–7, 1776 when Admiral Richard HOWE's flagship, the *Eagle*, which was blockading the Hudson River, was selected as the *Turtle*'s intended victim. However, the attack failed because the *Turtle*'s explosive charge could not be attached to the *Eagle*'s copper hull. Bushnell experimented with two other submarine prototypes but neither was a success. Although he abandoned his career as a naval architect at the end of the war, his contribution to the early history of the submarine was firmly established.

Byng, George, First Viscount Torrington
1663–1733

British admiral who was raised to the peerage as Viscount Torrington following his decisive victory over the Spanish at the Battle of CAPE PASSARO, August 1718, during the War of the Quadruple Alliance, 1718–20. His naval service had begun some 40 years earlier, in 1678, but was interrupted by a brief period in the army. Byng rose rapidly in the ROYAL NAVY largely because of his loyalty to William III (Prince William of Orange), whom he actively had helped during the Glorious Revolution, 1688. He served as a rear admiral during the War of the SPANISH SUCCESSION, 1701–14, and was involved in the capture of GIBRALTAR, 1704. The Battle of Cape Passaro, which secured Byng's reputation as a distinguished naval commander, was his last operational engagement. In 1727 he was appointed First Lord of the Admiralty, a post he held until his death. He was the father of John BYNG, who became the first and only British admiral to be executed following a court martial.

W. C. Brian Tunstall, ed., *The Byng Papers. Selected from the Letters and Papers of Admiral Sir George Byng, First Viscount Torrington, and of His Son Admiral the Hon John Byng*, 3 vols., London, 1930–32.

Byng, John
1704–1757

The only British admiral ever to have been sentenced to death by a court martial and executed for alleged shortcomings in battle, Byng was the fourth son of George BYNG, Viscount Torrington, 1663–1733, an admiral of the fleet. With the help of his father Byng had risen quickly to flag rank, despite his virtual lack of command experience. Some 38 uneventful years' service were brought to an abrupt end when the SEVEN YEARS' WAR, 1756–63, began.

Early in 1756, Byng was given the command of a naval expedition to the island of Minorca, where occupying British forces were besieged by the French. By the time Byng arrived French troops had already landed and occupied most of the island, with the exception of Port Mahon, where the British garrison was still holding out. Byng's action against the French fleet, which was protecting the invading forces, went wrong almost from the start. Six British ships were in short order damaged; Byng was unable to reassemble his original battle formation quickly; and the French were able to sail away. The British made no further attempt to give any assistance to the island, which was abandoned to its fate as Byng's fleet sailed back to its base at Gibraltar.

When Byng arrived at Spithead in July 1756 he was arrested and tried by court-martial. The various charges against him alleged that he had failed to do his utmost to save Minorca. Found guilty, he was sentenced to death—the only prescribed punishment for his crimes. The court's pleas urging King George III to show mercy were ignored, and Byng was executed on the quarter deck of the MONARCH on March 14, 1757.

In the face of the great public outcry over the loss

British admiral John Byng was shot for his failure to save Minorca during the Seven Years' War, 1756–63, "pour encourager les autres"   (*Copyright © National Maritime Museum, Greenwich, London*)

of Minorca, Byng was a convenient scapegoat, but his weaknesses as a commander did not justify the supreme penalty. His fate prompted Voltaire to write that in England, it is sometimes necessary to shoot an admiral from time to time "*pour encourager les autres*" (to encourage the others).

D. Pope, *At 12 Mr Byng Was Shot*, New York, 1962; W. C. Brian Tunstall, ed., *The Byng Papers. Selected from the Letters and Papers of Admiral Sir George Byng, First Viscount Torrington, and of His Son Admiral the Hon John Byng*, 3 vols., London, 1930–32.

Byrd, Richard Evelyn
1888–1957

American naval officer, aviator and explorer. Born on October 25, 1888, in Winchester, Virginia, into that state's famous Byrd family, he became America's foremost polar explorer. He commanded the first joint American-Canadian naval air station in Halifax, Nova Scotia in

1918. An inventor of several navigational instruments used in the U.S. Navy's Curtiss planes that made the first flight across the Atlantic in 1919, he also was involved in dirigible construction. With Floyd Bennett he made the first flight over the North Pole, leaving from and returning to their base at Kings Bay, Spitzbergen, Greenland, on May 9, 1926—a flight that covered the 1,360-mile distance in 15½ hours. Byrd subsequently received the Congressional Medal of Honor.

On November 29, 1929, on his first expedition to Antarctica, Byrd also became the first aviator to fly over the South Pole. Four other expeditions followed, producing many scientific and geographical discoveries. In 1933 he lived alone near the South Pole for several months; he recorded this feat in his books *Discovery*, 1935, and *Alone*, 1938. During WORLD WAR II, 1939–45, he served on various missions and assignments in the Atlantic and Pacific. In 1946 he commanded the U.S. Navy Antarctic Expedition—the largest expedition ever sent to that frozen continent, comprising some 13 vessels and 4,000 men. Extensive scientific and geographical tests and surveys were conducted, as well as training for navy personnel in cold-weather conditions. Byrd also advised the Department of Defense in matters of polar defense and strategy. During his lifetime he received many awards, foreign and domestic, as well as honorary degrees and academic prizes. He died in Boston on March 11, 1957.

Edwin P. Hoyt, *The Last Explorer: The Adventures of Admiral Byrd*, New York, 1968.

Byron, Admiral John
1723–86

British admiral who was given the nickname "Foul Weather Jack" because he endured more than his fair share of misfortune and poor weather during his naval career. As a young midshipman Byron served under Admiral Lord ANSON during his circumnavigation of the globe, 1740–44. On this voyage Byron's ship, the *Wager*, was wrecked off the coast of Chile in 1741, and he did not return to England for some five years. His account of his shipwreck was later used by his grandson George Gordon, Lord Byron, the poet, in *Don Juan*. John Byron commanded his own voyage around the world, in 1764–66, in search of Terra Australis Incognita, the nonexistent continent in the southern Pacific. He was later Governor of Newfoundland, 1769–72, but returned to sea during the AMERICAN WAR OF INDEPENDENCE, 1775–83.

In 1779 he was appointed, as a vice admiral, to the command of the Leeward Islands station in the Caribbean, where there was a very real French naval threat. On July 6, 1779, Byron fought a French squadron commanded by Admiral the Comte d'ESTAING in order to save the island of GRENADA. Good luck deserted him once more as he faced a superior enemy force. Without sufficient practical experience of naval tactics, Byron unwisely ordered the British squadron into action and sustained serious damage. However, because the French commander did not pursue his advantage, even greater losses were avoided. The Battle of Grenada marked the end of Byron's operational career; he returned to England shortly afterward.

Cadiz, Attack on
April 29, 1587

*E*arly in 1587, the British government learned of Spanish plans for an invasion of England and immediately took counteraction. Sir Francis DRAKE was commissioned to attack the enemy ships that were gathering at three main ports—Lisbon, Seville and Cadiz—in readiness for the invasion. Drake's fleet of 23 ships made for Cadiz, having abandoned a plan to attack Lisbon first. Cadiz was notable as the final destination of the Spanish treasure fleets sailing from America.

The British fleet arrived there on April 29 and entered the harbor covertly under French and Dutch flags. The Spaniards were completely unprepared for the attack and offered little resistance. Up to 37 Spanish ships and a vast quantity of stores were destroyed in the famous operation that "singed the King of Spain's beard." It delayed preparations for the SPANISH ARMADA, 1588, by several months. Following his success at Cadiz, Drake made other raids on the Spanish and Portuguese coasts and captured a treasure ship off the Azores. The Spanish fleet commander, Alvaro de BAZAN, Marquis of Santa Cruz, spent three unproductive months searching for Drake's fleet after the debacle at Cadiz before returning to his invasion plans.

Cadiz was to suffer another British naval attack some nine years later, in June 1596, when Lord HOWARD of Effingham sacked the town. The Spanish fleet, which was trapped by the raid, was destroyed on the orders of the Duke of MEDINA SIDONIA to avoid it falling into enemy hands. There were further English incursions in 1626 and 1702, but it was not until the Napoleonic Wars, 1803–15, that Cadiz was again badly affected by Anglo-Spanish naval conflict, with both sides attacking it at different times. It was also notable as the base from which the Franco-Spanish fleet went to meet the English at the Battle of TRAFALGAR, 1805.

Calabria, Battle of
July 9, 1940

*T*he first BATTLESHIP action between the British and Italian navies during WORLD WAR II, 1939–45. The British Mediterranean fleet, commanded by Admiral Andrew CUNNINGHAM, was escorting a troop convoy on its way from Malta to Egypt when it met the enemy off Calabria on July 9, 1940. Cunningham had at his disposal three battleships—the *WARSPITE, Royal Sovereign* and *Malaya*—the aircraft carrier *EAGLE* and supporting cruisers and destroyers. The Italian fleet of two battleships and 16 cruisers, commanded by Squadron-Admiral Angelo Campioni, was also on escort duty for a convoy bound for North Africa.

As contact was established, British torpedo-bombers from the *Eagle* attacked the enemy without success. Later, during the afternoon, the two fleets fired at each other from long distances for nearly two hours. The Italian battleship *Giulio Cesare* and the heavy cruiser *Bolzano* were both damaged by shells from the *Warspite*. At this point the Italians withdrew under cover of a smoke screen. Cunningham pursued them close to the Calabrian coast but did not make contact with them again. The inconclusive action, which cost the British little, revealed the Italian navy's lack of enthusiasm for a sustained fight.

Calder, Sir Robert
1745–1818

*B*ritish admiral whose career was ended by a court-martial shortly before the Battle of TRAFALGAR, 1805. Calder's earlier career, by contrast, had been highly successful. In 1762 he was involved in the capture of a Spanish treasure ship; his share of the prize money was £13,000. At the Battle of CAPE ST. VINCENT, February 14, 1797, he was captain of the fleet and was later knighted for his services there.

Sir Robert Calder had joined the Royal Navy's blockade of BREST in 1804, but was later detached to intercept the Comte de VILLENEUVE's Franco-Spanish fleet as it returned from the West Indies.

On July 22, 1805 Calder attacked Villeneuve off CAPE FINISTERRE in poor conditions; during the Battle of Ferrol (also known as the Battle of Vigo), he managed to destroy two enemy ships, but the rest of the enemy fleet eluded him. He did not continue the pursuit but returned to Brest in case the French went north. The French admiral in fact went south to Cadiz, but by the time Calder had been dispatched again it was too late to intercept him. It was not until the Battle of TRAFALGAR in October that a decisive engagement with the French occurred. As a result of his failure to continue operations against Villeneuve, Calder was sent back to England to face a court-martial. Found guilty of an error of judgment, he was severely reprimanded and his naval career came to a premature end.

California, U.S.S.

An American nuclear-powered guided missile CRUISER of 10,150 tons. Together with her sister ship the *South Carolina*, the *California* was the first vessel of its type. The main function of these cruisers, which were completed in 1974–75, is to act as escorts to the new generation of nuclear-powered aircraft carriers. Because they are able to maintain full speed virtually indefinitely, they are well equipped for this task. The *California*'s nuclear steam generator power plant has two screws and produces a maximum speed in excess of 30 knots. Operated by a crew of 540, the *California* is 596 ft. (181.7 m) in length and has a beam of 61 ft. (18.6 m). Both ships are armed for antisubmarine and antiaircraft work. On completion, the *California* was equipped with two single Tartar SAM launchers, one ASROC launcher, two 5-inch (13-cm) antiaircraft guns and two triple antisubmarine torpedo tubes. The ship also has a HELICOPTER landing pad aft.

An earlier *California*, completed in 1919 as a member of the Tennessee class, served in the UNITED STATES NAVY during the interwar period and beyond. A BATTLESHIP with a displacement of 32,600 tons, she was operated by a crew of 2,200 and was notable for her two cage masts. Her main armament consisted of 12 14-inch (36-cm) guns in four triple turrets and she also carried three aircraft. During modernization, in 1929–30, she was fitted with two catapults. The *California* was sunk by the Japanese at PEARL HARBOR, 1941, but was raised and rebuilt. Following her recommissioning in 1944, she spent the last year of WORLD WAR II, 1939–45, in the Pacific. Her sister ship, the *Tennessee*, was also seriously damaged at Pearl Harbor and was extensively modernized before returning to the Pacific theater, where she remained for the rest of the war.

Callaghan, Daniel Judson
1890–1942

American naval officer, born in 1890 in San Francisco, California, and commissioned in 1911. Until the early 1930s, Callaghan's career was tied to battleships; he served as gunnery officer to the commander in chief of the U.S. Fleet. From 1938 to mid-1941 he was naval aide to President Franklin Roosevelt. With America's entry into WORLD WAR II, 1939–45, Callaghan participated in the carrier strikes against Japanese-held islands in the Pacific in the spring of 1942. As chief of staff to Admiral Robert Lee GHORMLEY, commander, South Pacific Force, he was heavily involved in developing the plans to land American forces on GUADALCANAL, and in October 1942 he became commander of the task group designed to provide fire protection for the beachhead. On November 18, 1942 he was killed while commanding his squadron of cruisers and destroyers during the naval Battle of Guadalcanal.

Francis X. Murphy, *Fighting Admiral: The Story of Dan Callaghan*, New York, 1952.

Camouflage

The purpose of camouflage—also known as "dazzle-painting"—in a naval context is to confuse the enemy about a ship's identity, size, course and speed by painting her hull and superstructure to a specified pattern. The word is derived from the French *camoufler*—"to disguise." A variety of different colors, including blue, black, white and gray, have been used to create an irregular and contrasting pattern. The invention of a British marine artist, the marine camouflage technique was developed and perfected during WORLD WAR I, 1914–18. Quickly adopted by other countries, it was used extensively by every major naval participant in both world wars. There is no doubt that a camouflaged ship is a much more difficult target to hit, and many potential victims have been saved as a result.

Chris Ellis, *United States Navy Camouflage, 1939–45*, Henley on Thames, 1975.

Camperdown, Battle of
October 11, 1797

A major engagement of the FRENCH REVOLUTIONARY AND NAPOLEONIC WARS, 1792–1815, in which the Dutch were decisively defeated by the English fleet. Since 1795 Holland had been an unwilling ally of the French, and as a consequence her fleet had been blockaded by a British force under the command of Admiral Adam DUNCAN. On October 1, 1797, after a long period on duty, Duncan left his station to return to Yarmouth for a refit, leaving only five ships to keep watch on the Dutch. Eight days later a British lugger followed the fleet back to England with the news that the Dutch fleet, commanded by Vice Admiral Jan de WINTER, had departed the Netherlands port of Texel.

Duncan returned to the Dutch coast immediately in the *Venerable*, his 74-gun flagship. His opponents were sighted at about 9:00 A.M. on October 11 and the battle began shortly after noon some three miles northwest of Camperdown. Both sides had 16 SHIPS OF THE LINE at their disposal, but the Royal navy was equipped with more powerful guns. The English moved forward against the Dutch line in two columns headed by Duncan and Vice Admiral Richard Onslow, the second in command, respectively. At about 12:30 Onslow, in the *Monarch*, broke through the rear of the Dutch line; at the same time Duncan's column struck the Dutch van and the *Venerable* engaged the *Vrijheid*, Admiral de Winter's flagship. Just under three hours' heavy fighting at close quarters followed, and heavy casualties resulted on both sides.

In the end, with his flagship virtually destroyed, the Dutch commander was forced to surrender. Some of de Winter's ships were able to escape, but the British captured seven enemy ships of the line and four other vessels that were all too badly damaged to serve at sea again.

C. C. Lloyd, *St. Vincent and Camperdown*, London, 1963.

Camperdown, H.M.S.

A collision between the British warships *Camperdown* and *Victoria* in the Mediterranean resulted in the ROYAL NAVY's most costly peacetime disaster. The *Camperdown*, a twin-screw battleship of 10,600 tons, which was launched in 1885, rammed and sank the fleet flagship *Victoria*, a battleship of 10,470 tons, during the Mediterranean fleet's maneuvers off Tripoli in 1893.

These ships headed the two divisions of the fleet that had been moving ahead in parallel until they were ordered to turn inward in a practice maneuver. However, at this moment the two columns of ships were only 400 ft. (122 m) apart and the order to turn, which had been issued by Vice Admiral Sir George TRYON, commander in chief of the Mediterranean Fleet, was clearly incorrect. It was impossible for the leading ships to complete the maneuver without colliding, but corrective action was not taken.

The *Victoria* sank after the *Camperdown* hit her and 360 officers and men, including the unfortunate commander in chief, were lost. An inquiry was held into the disaster, but

no satisfactory explanation has ever been found for Admiral Tryon's bizarre conduct in issuing an order that he must have known would result in a collision.

Richard Hough, *Admirals in Collision*, London, 1959.

Camship

British merchantmen of WORLD WAR II, 1939–45, camships were fitted with a catapult that was capable of launching a fighter aircraft. Beginning in 1940, British CONVOYS crossing the Atlantic had suffered heavy losses during attacks by the Focke-Wulf FW 200 Condor, a long-range German bomber, and the catapult aircraft merchant ship was introduced in response. Equipped with obsolete Hawker Hurricane fighters, which nonetheless outperformed the Condors, the camship provided a measure of antiaircraft protection to the otherwise vulnerable merchant shipping that it accompanied.

The camship's one fundamental weakness was that, because it had no landing deck, the aircraft it had launched could not return to it and almost certainly would have to be ditched in the sea. The Hurricane's pilot would be at risk unless he was picked up from the sea very quickly. The MACSHIP, a merchant ship fitted with a temporary landing deck, was a more effective improvisation because aircraft were able to return to her after completing their missions.

Canaris, Wilhelm
1887–1945

German naval commander of Greek descent, born in Aplerbeck near Dortmund, who joined the Imperial German navy in 1905. During WORLD WAR I, 1914–18, Canaris served in the light cruiser *Dresden* and was present at the battles of CORONEL and the FALKLANDS in 1914. When his ship was sunk in March 1915 he was interned in Chile, but he later escaped and managed to make his way back to Germany. He subsequently served as a U-BOAT commander operating in the Mediterranean. In the postwar period he specialized in intelligence issues before his retirement with the rank of rear admiral in 1934. The next year Adolf Hitler appointed him chief of the Abwehr, the counterintelligence service of the German high command.

Canaris was a loyal German rather than a Nazi, and he grew increasingly hostile to the new regime. Although he joined the resistance movement there is no evidence that he leaked information to the Allies during WORLD WAR II, 1939–45; it is possible, however, that some of his colleagues did. At the same time, there is no doubt that he participated in a variety of anti-Nazi activities within the military and that this continued until his dismissal as chief of the Abwehr in February 1944. Soon after the July 1944 bomb plot against Hitler, he was arrested and imprisoned at Flossenberg concentration camp. He was hanged in April 1945, shortly before the Soviet army captured Berlin, but his professional and personal reputation remained intact.

H. Höhne, *Canaris*, London, 1976.

Canberra

*B*ritish passenger ship, operated as a cruise liner by the P & O Company. Completed in 1961, she had an overall length of 819 feet (250 m) and a displacement of 43,975 tons and embarked on a successful career as a popular cruise ship. During the FALKLANDS WAR, 1982, between Great Britain and Argentina, she was one of several merchant ships, including the passenger liner *QE2*, requisitioned by the British government. Conversion of the *Canberra* for service as a troopship took place within no more than two days and included the provision of a temporary HELICOPTER deck. On April 9, 1982 the *Canberra* left Southampton with 2,400 men of the Third Commando

Brigade and 30 nurses on board; she disembarked her complement in San Carlos Water, East Falkland, nearly six weeks later. Apart from other troop transport duties, she served as a hospital ship for much of the rest of the war and survived several Argentine attempts to sink her. She returned to commercial service after the war, but was scheduled to be decommissioned in 1997.

Cannon

*F*irst used at sea in the first half of the 14th century, the cannon was the principal mounted naval gun during the era of the sailing navies. Its design remained essentially unchanged throughout this long period. Cannon were large, muzzle-loading, smooth-bore ordnance that used a gunpowder charge to fire a solid ball. Early examples were constructed from bronze or wrought iron, but cost and the need to manufacture them in large quantities forced a change to cast iron. They were mounted on small wooden carriages that were fitted with wheels; when the cannon was fired the carriage would roll backward to absorb the recoil.

The *Canberra*, a P & O passenger liner, in service as a British troopship during the Falklands War, 1982 *(Copyright © Imperial War Museum, London)*

"Cannon" is a general term covering a wide variety of gun types and sizes. Although all cannon operated on the same basis, they differed in length, weight and caliber as well as the size of the shot they could fire and their effective range. At one extreme, the canon-royal weighed some 8,000 pounds (3,629 kg) and fired a 66-pound (30-kg) shot. The whole cannon and the demicannon were also large guns. The latter, which was widely used in the Royal Navy, had a length of 11 feet (3.4 m) and fired a 32-pound (14.5-kg) shot. Smaller-caliber cannon included the culverin and the perier. A typical culverin would fire a 17-pound (7.7-kg) shot and had a caliber of 5 inches (12.7 cm).

Although the basic principles of the cannon remained unchanged throughout its history, design changes were made from time to time. Improvements in the quality of gunpowder were one stimulus, allowing larger-caliber weapons to be introduced without increasing their overall weight. By the end of the 17th century, cannon production in England focused on two models: the 24-pounder (for use on the upper decks) and the 42-pounder (on the lower). Except for the carronade, a light carriage gun of the late 18th and 19th centuries, by this time cannon were designated by the weight of their shot, and their original 16th-century designations disappeared. Cannon were mounted in rows along the sides of the warships of the sailing navies and were fired simultaneously in a BROADSIDE whose effect was sometimes more apparent than real.

During the 18th century the extreme range of a whole cannon might be about a mile, although its effective range—the distance it would travel straight to its target before falling—was only some 280 yards (256 m). Gradually the effective range of cannon increased, and by the early 19th century it had been extended to some 400 yards (356 m). In practice, however, gunners tended to wait until the enemy target was much closer, typically 100 yards (91 m), before opening fire. At this distance there was much greater chance of causing major structural damage, although sinking a warship by cannon fire alone was always a difficult task, because most cannon damage occurred above the waterline. It was always much easier to disable the enemy by damaging masts or rigging.

Major developments in naval gunnery accompanied the introduction of the iron warship in the mid-19th century. Foremost among these changes was the replacement of the traditional cannon by rifled breech-loading ordnance that fired an explosive shell. In its contemporary form the cannon is a large-caliber, rapid-firing machine gun that is used at sea for low-level antiaircraft defense. Today, the traditional cannon is used for ceremonial purposes and historical displays.

Ian Hogg and John Batchelor, *Naval Gun*, Poole, 1978; Peter Padfield, *Guns at Sea*, London, Evelyn, 1973.

Canopus, H.M.S.

Based on the Majestic class, the *Canopus* and her sister ships were British BATTLESHIPS of 13,000 tons that were completed in 1900–02. They were built specifically for service in the Far East, although they saw action elsewhere. The Canopus-class ships were smaller and lighter than their predecessors, using stronger but thinner Krupp ARMOR for the first time. Operated by a crew of 680, *Canopus* was 421 ft. 6 in. (128.5 m) in length and had a beam of 74 ft. (22.6 m). Her main armament consisted of four 12-inch (30-cm) guns mounted in fore and aft pairs; there were also 12 6-inch (15-cm) guns and four 18-inch (46-cm) torpedo tubes. The first battleships to be fitted with the more efficient water tube boilers, the *Canopus* and the other ships in her class had a maximum speed of just over 18 knots.

The *Canopus* and her sisters—*Albion*, *Glory*, *Goliath*, *Ocean* and *Vengeance*—were used extensively during the WORLD WAR I, 1914–18. The *Canopus* herself was part of Rear Admiral Sir Christopher CRADOCK's force in the South Atlantic, but she did not participate in the Battle of CORONEL, 1914. She did, however, fire the opening shots in the subsequent Battle of the FALKLAND ISLANDS, 1914, as guardship at Port Stanley, although she was unable to join in the pursuit. All the Canopus-class ships except for the *Glory* were present in the DARDANELLES in 1915 and formed a significant part of the British battleship force in action there. The *Ocean* and the *Goliath* were lost during the operation, but the others survived and remained in service until the Armistice in November 1918. They were scrapped in 1919–22.

Cape Bon, Battle of
December 13, 1941

A battle between British and Italian naval forces off the coast of Libya during WORLD WAR II, 1939–45. By late 1941, as the British stepped up naval activity in the Mediterranean, the task of resupplying German and Italian land forces in North Africa had become much more difficult for the Italians. The destruction of the DUISBURG CONVOY, November 9, 1941, had been a notable British victory that was to be matched by England's success during the Battle of Cape Bon. In this later action a British aircraft action spotted three Italian warships—two cruisers and a torpedo boat—on a resupply mission off the North African coast. A Royal Navy destroyer squadron, headed by Commander G. H. Stokes, which was traveling through the area, was ordered to intercept them. In the early hours of December 13, the British force attacked the Italians and took them completely by surprise. The two Italian destroyers were sunk, with only the torpedo boat managing to escape. The action represented a further significant blow against German and Italian operations in the Mediterranean.

Cape Esperance, Battle of
October 11, 1942

*A*n engagement between American and Japanese naval units to the northwest of Cape Esperance on GUADALCANAL in the Pacific during WORLD WAR II. It was part of the continuing struggle for control of the SOLOMON ISLANDS in 1942–43. An American strike force consisting of the heavy cruisers *San Francisco* and *Salt Lake City*, the light cruisers *Boise* and *Helena* and five destroyers commanded by Rear Admiral Norman Scott was sent to intercept and destroy enemy ships in the channel between the eastern and western Solomons.

Shortly before midnight, the *Helena*'s radar identified a Japanese squadron commanded by Rear Admiral A. Goto some 14 nautical miles away. Consisting of the heavy cruisers *Aoba*, *Kinugasa* and *Furutaka* and two destroyers, it was under orders to bombard Guadalcanal airfield. Some minutes before he was notified of the radar information, Rear Admiral Scott had ordered his squadron to reverse course as result of information received from his spotter planes about Japanese movements. By this time the two naval forces were only four miles apart. Although the American commander was unsure of the location of some of his destroyers for a while, he went ahead with the attack. The Japanese were taken completely by surprise when the *Helena* and a destroyer opened fire. Rear Admiral Goto was killed, the *Aoba* and the *Furutaka* were damaged and a destroyer was sunk. The Japanese cruiser *Kinugasa* and the destroyer *Hatsuyuki* returned fire and hit the destroyer *Duncan*, which had also been struck by American shells during a confused action fought in darkness.

As the Japanese withdrew they suffered the loss of the cruiser *Furutaka* and the destroyer *Fubuki*, but the cruiser U.S.S. *Boise* and two American destroyers were also crippled during the final phase of the action. The engagement was a modest success for the Americans, who had successfully attacked the Japanese at sea for the first time and prevented the bombardment of Guadalcanal. Exaggerated American claims of Japanese losses were made at the time, but in fact the Japanese lost no more than a cruiser and a destroyer.

Cape Finisterre, First Battle of
May 3, 1747

*A*n engagement fought between the English and French fleets off the northwest coast of Spain during the War of the AUSTRIAN SUCCESSION, 1740–48. On April 29, 1747 two French convoys left Rochefort together on their way to India and North America respectively. They were escorted by two squadrons under the command of Admiral

de la Jonquière de la Pommarède and Admiral St. Georges. The Royal Navy responded to these movements by dispatching Admiral George ANSON and 13 ships of the line from Spithead. On May 3 Anson intercepted the two French convoys, which had not yet separated, some 25 miles northwest of Finisterre. The French commander Jonquière responded by ordering his convoy to escape to the west and by forming his warships in line of battle ahead. The running battle lasted for three hours and resulted in complete defeat for the French, who lost their squadron to the enemy. Anson completed his victory by capturing seven French merchantmen, although the remaining 20 managed to elude him in the hours of darkness. He was raised to the peerage for this victory, which brought him a generous allocation of PRIZE MONEY.

Cape Finisterre, Second Battle of
October 14, 1747

*W*hen British and French naval forces fought off Cape Finisterre (also known as the Battle of Ushant), on the northwestern corner of Spain, for a second time during the War of the AUSTRIAN SUCCESSION, 1740–48, the outcome was similar to that of the first. In August 1747, when the Royal Navy learned of French plans to dispatch a convoy to the West Indies, Rear Admiral Edward HAWKE and his Western Squadron of 14 ships of the line were sent to find them in the area between Ushant and Finisterre. However, British reports of enemy movements were premature, and it was not until October 14 that the French convoy, which had not left the Île d'Aix until October 6, was intercepted.

The French escort consisted of eight ships of the line under the command of Admiral the Marquis de l'Etenduère. Clearly outnumbered, it was in an unfavorable position in terms of relative strength, although its ship design was superior to that of the British. This fact may have helped the French to hold on for nine hours as they struggled against Hawke, who engaged the enemy after a general chase. However, by the end of the battle the French had lost six warships, with the surviving two badly damaged. At the same time the stubborn French resistance had enabled all the merchantmen to make good their escape from the area, and Hawke's damaged ships were not in a position to pursue them. However, Hawke dispatched a squadron to warn the British West Indies fleet of the expected arrival of a French convoy. Most of the convoy was later captured in the Leeward Islands.

Cape Finisterre, Battle of
July 22, 1805

*A*n inconclusive engagement between British and Franco-Spanish naval forces during the Napoleonic

Wars, 1803–15; also known as "Calder's Action." Vice Admiral Sir Robert CALDER commanded a squadron of 15 ships of the line that was ordered to intercept Admiral Comte de VILLENEUVE, who was returning to France after an abortive mission in the West Indies. The French already had managed to elude another British squadron under Lord NELSON. Calder was ordered to cruise off Cape Finisterre, on the northwestern corner of Spain, to intercept Villeneuve and thus prevent him from linking with a Spanish squadron in Ferrol, a nearby port.

On July 22, three days after Calder arrived in the designated area, he met the French in thick fog. The weather conditions delayed the engagement, which did not begin until 5 P.M., and limited its scope. The British seized two Spanish ships and prevented Villeneuve from reaching the Spanish ships at Ferrol. At the same time, however, Admiral Calder failed to bring the enemy to battle on that day or on either of the two following days. On his return home Calder was court-martialed for his failure to continue to engage the French. He was found guilty of this charge and was severely reprimanded. One of the explanations for his conduct, which cost him his career, was his greater concern for the safety of his prizes than for defeating the French.

Cape François, Battle of
October 21, 1757

*B*attle fought between French and English squadrons in the West Indies during the SEVEN YEARS' WAR, 1756–63. A small British squadron of three warships, under the command of Captain Arthur Forrest, had been positioned near the French naval base at Cape François on the northern coast of San Domingo (now Haiti) in the Caribbean. It was waiting to intercept a large convoy bound for France, but an enemy squadron of three ships of the line and four other warships, under the command of Admiral the Comte de KERSAINT, came out to engage it on October 21. During a battle of well over two hours, the British squadron fought effectively against the stronger French force. The ships on both sides suffered badly but the British were forced to withdraw to Port Royal, Jamaica, for repairs. This enabled the French convoy to leave Cape François and make its way back to France without further difficulty.

Cape Matapan, Battle of
March 28/29, 1941

A naval battle of WORLD WAR II, 1939–45, between the Italian navy and the British Mediterranean Fleet. Britain had taken advantage of Italian naval weakness following the successful attack at TARANTO, November 1940, to reinforce its army in Greece. On March 26, 1941,

an Italian naval force consisting of the battleship *Vittorio Veneto*, eight cruisers and nine destroyers, commanded by Admiral Angelo Iachino, left its home base to search for British convoys on the supply route from Alexandria, Egypt to Greece. Admiral Sir Andrew CUNNINGHAM, commander in chief of the British Mediterranean fleet, first became aware of Italian intentions on March 27, when he learned of the sighting of three enemy cruisers 320 miles (512 km) west of Crete. They were moving in a southeasterly direction. Cunningham ordered Rear Admiral Henry Pridham-Wippel to move four cruisers and four destroyers some 30 miles (48 km) west of Gavdos Island, south of Crete.

Later that day Cunningham left Alexandria for the same destination with the main British fleet, consisting of the battleships *Barham*, WARSPITE and *Valiant*, the new aircraft carrier FORMIDABLE and nine destroyers. He was determined to bring the Italians to action. The next morning the British cruisers made contact with the enemy and then withdrew under fire; their objective was to lure the enemy toward the British battleships that were some 80 miles (128 km) behind. However, following an attack by aircraft from the *Formidable*, Admiral Iachino decided to avoid a general engagement with the British if he could and reversed course. When the British pursuit began, the Italians were some 65 miles ahead. Cunningham would need to rely on a successful aerial attack on the Italian battleship *Vittorio Veneto* if he were to have any chance of catching the enemy. A second air strike at 3:30 P.M. scored a hit on the battleship's stern and temporarily reduced her speed.

During a third strike the cruiser *Pola* was severely damaged; Iachino detached her two sister ships, *Zara* and *Fitume*, plus four destroyers to tow her back to base. Later that evening the cruisers *Zara* and *Fitume* were sunk by fire from the British battleships' 15-inch (38-cm) guns as they prepared to salvage the *Pola*. Two Italian destroyers were also sunk. The *Pola* was found later that night and was destroyed after her crew had been evacuated. Iachino, in the meantime, continued his withdrawal and reached home safely. The British had achieved their objective of maintaining control of the central Mediterranean; the battle marked the effective end of the Italian surface fleet as a serious threat to the Royal Navy.

D. Macintyre, *The Battle for the Mediterranean*, London, 1962.

Cape Ortegal, Battle of
November 4, 1805

A sequel to the Battle of TRAFALGAR, October 21, 1805, during the Napoleonic Wars, 1803–15, involving four French ships that had managed to escape from the British. The DUGUAY-TROUIN, *Formidable*, *Mont Blanc* and *Scipion* were intercepted by a British squadron near Ortegal, in northwest Spain. Commanded by Captain Sir Richard

The British Mediterranean Fleet in action against the Italian navy at the Battle of Cape Matapan, off the southern coast of Greece
(Copyright © National Maritime Museum, Greenwich, London)

STRACHAN, the British squadron consisted of four ships of the line and four frigates. The French commander, Rear Admiral Dumanoir-Le-Pelley, tried to evade the superior enemy force, but after a protracted chase in poor conditions he was compelled to fight. It was a costly action for the French: Apart from sustaining some 750 casualties, their four ships were all badly damaged before their capture by the British. All four were salvaged and, following extensive repairs, were commissioned in the British service. This action underlined the strength of British naval power; Britain retained this dominant position for the rest of the war.

Cape Passaro, Battle of
August 11, 1718

The main naval engagement of the War of the Quadruple Alliance, 1718–20, was a direct result of Spain's reoccupation of Sicily in July 1718. A former Spanish colony lost in the War of the SPANISH SUCCESSION, 1701–14, Sicily had been ceded to Savoy by the Treaty of Utrecht, 1713. In response, England, France, Austria and Holland opposed the Spanish action, formed the Quadruple Alliance and demanded Spain's withdrawal from Sicily.

A large English fleet, which included 21 ships of the line, commanded by Sir George BYNG, was sent to the Mediterranean, arriving at Naples on August 1. Byng ap-

peared off Messina on August 9, disembarking a force of 3,000 Austrian troops that had been taken on board at Naples. They were landed in support of the Savoyards based in the fortress at Messina who retained a precarious hold on a small portion of Sicily.

The next day a Spanish fleet, under the command of Vice Admiral Don Antonio Castañeta, arrived in the area and sighted the British. His force was slightly smaller but much weaker than that of his opponent. It consisted of 11 ships of the line, 13 frigates and 21 other ships, including some galleys. The Spanish retreated rapidly in the face of a more powerful enemy without a shot being fired. Byng gave chase and, on August 11, the fleets came into contact off Cape Passaro on the southern tip of Sicily. A Spanish warship opened fire first and the action became general: The Spanish were heavily defeated in the unequal contest. By nightfall the surviving Spanish ships were in full retreat, with the British in close pursuit.

As many as 22 Spanish ships, including seven ships of the line, were captured or destroyed. Their commander, Castañeta, was taken prisoner and later died of his wounds. The victorious Admiral Byng was created Viscount Torrington for his services. With the seas under British control, Austrian troops were able to mount a land attack on Sicily, which fell in the autumn of 1719. The war did not finally end until the Treaty of The Hague was signed in 1720, but the Battle of Cape Passaro marked the effective end of hostilities at sea.

Cape St. George, Battle of

November 25, 1943

A battle fought in the South Pacific between American and Japanese naval forces southeast of New Ireland, an island in the Bismarck archipelago, on November 25, 1943, during WORLD WAR II, 1939–45. An American naval squadron commanded by Captain Arleigh BURKE, an able destroyer captain, intercepted a Japanese destroyer squadron of six ships in early morning darkness en route to Bougainville in the Solomon Islands. The Japanese squadron had been sent to resupply Japanese forces operating there, but Burke's six destroyers inflicted severe damage before they could do so. Three Japanese destroyers were sunk without a single American loss. Operations in the Solomons were completed shortly thereafter with the American capture of Bougainville on November 1, 1943.

Cape St. Vincent, Battle of

January 16, 1780

A naval engagement of the AMERICAN WAR OF INDEPENDENCE, 1775–83, known as the "Moonlight Battle," fought by British and Spanish forces south of Cape St. Vincent on January 16, 1780. Some two weeks earlier, on December 29, 1779, Admiral Sir George RODNEY (later First Baron Rodney) had left Plymouth, England, with 18 ships of the line and nine frigates. His mission had a dual purpose: to escort a convoy of reinforcements to Gibraltar, which was being besieged by the Spanish, and then to make for the West Indies, where Rodney was to take up his appointment as commander of the Leeward Islands station.

The British fleet first sighted the Spanish south of Cape Finisterre on January 8. A convoy of 16 merchantmen,

Nelson captures the Spanish warship *San Jozef* at the Battle of Cape St. Vincent, 1797   (*Copyright © National Maritime Museum, Greenwich, London*)

escorted by a ship of the line and six frigates under the command of Commodore Don Juan di Yardi, was headed for Cadiz. The British chased and captured the entire enemy force. Rodney then proceed toward Gibraltar according to plan, rounding Cape St. Vincent, a headland at the southwest extremity of Portugal, on January 16. Some 12 miles (19.3 km) south of the cape the British sighted another Spanish squadron—11 ships of the line and two frigates under the command of Admiral Don Juan de Langara—proceeding in a southeasterly direction.

The action began at about 4 P.M. as Rodney's ships engaged the enemy rear and continued in stormy weather during the night until about 2 A.M. One Spanish ship was destroyed almost immediately with the loss of almost all its crew of 600. As the battle progressed, the British captured six other Spanish ships, including the *Fénix*, Langara's flagship. Poor weather conditions the following morning forced the British to abandon two of the Spanish ships they had captured only hours before. However, even considering the numerical superiority of the British fleet, it was a notable victory against the Spanish—particularly as Admiral Rodney had been confined to bed with gout throughout the battle.

Cape St. Vincent, Battle of
February 14, 1797

Notable for the critical role played by Commodore Horatio NELSON, the Battle of Cape St. Vincent was a long-awaited British victory over a much larger Spanish force during the FRENCH REVOLUTIONARY AND NAPOLEONIC WARS, 1792–1815. The Spanish fleet, commanded by Admiral Don José de Cordova, consisted of 27 ships of the line and 12 frigates; it included the *SANTISSIMA TRINIDAD*, a 136-gun ship. Early in 1797 de Cordova's fleet had left Cartagena with orders to escort a convoy to Cadiz. He was then to proceed to BREST, where preparations were being made for a projected Franco-Spanish invasion of Ireland. The French naval component, under the command of Admiral the Comte de VILLANEUVE, had already left the Mediterranean in mid-December 1796 and reached Brest without incident.

The Spanish were not so fortunate. A British fleet commanded by Admiral John JERVIS was aware of the Spanish movement and had left its anchorage in the Tagus River, Portugal, on January 18 to intercept the enemy. Jervis's force, with 15 ships of the line and four frigates, was only about half the size of the Spanish. It was strengthened by the arrival of Nelson from Gibraltar with orders to take command of the *CAPTAIN*, a 74-gun ship of the line. On the same day, February 13, the British fleet received news of the approaching Spanish fleet. The next morning it was sighted near Cape St. Vincent, a headland at the southwest extremity of Portugal, moving toward

Cadiz in two divisions in heavy easterly winds. The unfavorable weather conditions saw the Spanish in some disarray and unprepared for combat.

The single column of British ships moved into the gap between the two enemy divisions. It first engaged the Spanish lee division but then turned to attack the larger weather division (those in the line of battle on the windward side). At about 1 P.M. the Spanish began to pass astern of the British column in order to escape to the north. At this point Nelson's decisive action saved the day. The *Captain*, which was the third ship from the rear, pulled out of line and moved across the path of the Spanish. Although there were risks—the *Santissima Trinidad*, the vast Spanish warship, was the leading ship—the *Captain* succeeded in forcing the enemy to change course. This enabled the other British ships to catch up. In the fight that followed, the British seized four enemy ships, including two—the *San Nicolas* and the *San Josef*—that Nelson had boarded.

Although the Spanish lee line remained intact, Admiral Jervis decided not to risk the gains that had already been achieved, and by the late afternoon the battle was over. The British did not pursue the defeated Spanish fleet, and Admiral de Cordova withdrew to Cadiz. The British victory was celebrated by Jervis' elevation to the peerage as Earl St. Vincent. The battle proved to be a great morale booster in Britain, where the population had become accustomed to a succession of defeats during the war with revolutionary France.

C. C. Lloyd, *St Vincent and Camperdown*, London, 1963.

Cape Spartivento, Battle of
November 27, 1940

WORLD WAR II, 1939–45, action in November 1940 that began as units of the Italian navy tried to intercept a British convoy south of Sardinia. Bound for Malta, the British convoy was escorted by FORCE H, which was commanded by Admiral Sir James SOMERVILLE. The British naval force included the AIRCRAFT CARRIER *ARK ROYAL*, the BATTLESHIP *RAMILLIES* and the BATTLE CRUISER *RENOWN*. They were accompanied by five cruisers and ten destroyers. The Italian units, commanded by Admiral Ingio Campioni, included the battleships *Vittorio Veneto* and *Giulio Cesare*, seven heavy cruisers and 14 destroyers. Warned of the Italian presence off Cape Spartivento by his carrier-based aircraft, Somerville sent the convoy away to the southeast and turned to meet the enemy.

During the action, which began at 12:20 P.M. with an exchange of gunfire between the two cruiser squadrons, the British cruiser *Berwick* and the Italian destroyer *Lanciere* were damaged. The action ended an hour later when Admiral Campioni ordered his fleet to turn and make for Naples. The Italian commander had become aware of the presence of the *Ark Royal* and wanted, following the TARANTO RAID, November 11, 1940, to preserve Italy's two remaining battleships from British air attack. As they retreated the Italians faced two air strikes from British torpedo-bombers, although neither was successful. The British convoy reached its destination safely, but the action off Cape Spartivento had been inconclusive.

Capelle, Eduard von
1855–1931

Appointed Germany's Secretary of State for the Ministry of Marine in March 1916, succeeding Grand-Admiral Alfred von TIRPITZ, Admiral Eduard von Capelle had worked in the German Navy Office for most of his career. He made his reputation as an expert on financial matters and played a leading role in facilitating the prewar expansion of the GERMAN NAVY. During WORLD WAR I, 1914–1918, he cooperated with the German chancellor, Theodore von Bethmann Hollweg, in opposing the reintroduction of unrestricted submarine warfare, but early in 1917 this policy was reversed in the face of strong pressure from naval and military leaders. Capelle's failure to respond adequately to the issues raised by the unrest among units of the HIGH SEAS FLEET in August 1917 significantly weakened his position, although he was retained in office for another year.

Capital Ship

The term "capital ship" refers to the most powerful unit to be found in the world's navies at any particular period in history. When it is equipped to fire nuclear missiles, the SUBMARINE must be regarded as the capital ship of contemporary navies. However, the period of dominance of the nuclear submarine has been relatively short compared with that of the SHIP OF THE LINE, which was the capital ship for nearly three centuries when the sailing ship was preeminent. As the rate of technological change accelerated, from the mid-19th century onward, there were much more rapid changes in capital ship types. The early IRONCLADS were quickly superseded by the iron BATTLESHIP, which itself did not survive for much more than a generation. It was replaced by the DREADNOUGHT and then the super-dreadnought battleship. The aircraft that were to bring the reign of the battleship to an end had already been invented by the time the first dreadnought was launched. Not until the 1940s did carrier-based aircraft develop sufficiently finally to sweep the battleship from the world's seas. The AIRCRAFT CARRIER was itself briefly a capital ship but was forced to share the title with the less vulnerable nuclear-powered and armed submarine, which

became the critical element in maintaining the nuclear balance of terror during the COLD WAR.

Captain, H.M.S.

The name of several notable British warships, including a strange mid-19th-century hybrid designed by Cowper Coles. Launched in 1870, this *Captain* was a steam-propelled IRONCLAD that had a full rig of sails. She was armed with four 12-inch (30-cm) and two 7-inch (18-cm) guns. One of her novel features was revolving gun turrets (located on the centerline) instead of the fixed batteries that were standard at the time. Another was twin screw propulsion, which reduced the risk of being stranded as a result of mechanical failure.

The *Captain* was designed with low freeboard to reduce the surface area presented to the enemy, but when fully loaded it was even lower in the water than had been intended. As a result, she was vulnerable to severe flooding in rough seas. Her instability was increased by the fact that she could carry very little coal and had to rely heavily on sails. These design weaknesses soon were graphically exposed: On September 6, 1870 she was caught in a squall and capsized while cruising in the Bay of Biscay. She went down very quickly, with her designer and most of the crew; only 18 men were saved.

An earlier and more effective *Captain* was the 74-gun ship commanded by Commodore Horatio Nelson at the Battle of CAPE ST. VINCENT, February 1797. She was one of five British ships at the heart of the battle. Nelson acted with great courage and initiative, boarding and capturing two large Spanish warships.

Caracciolo, Prince Francesco
1752–99

Neapolitan naval commander who first saw active service with the Royal Navy in the AMERICAN WAR OF INDEPENDENCE, 1775–83. Soon after Caracciolo returned to Naples, King Ferdinand appointed him supreme commander of the Neapolitan navy, with the rank of admiral. In December 1798, during the FRENCH REVOLUTIONARY AND NAPOLEONIC WARS, 1792–1815, Naples fell to the French and Caracciolo escorted the king and queen to safety in Palermo, Sicily. Shortly afterward, however, he returned to Naples and entered the service of the new republican administration, organizing operations against his former employer. In 1799, when Naples was recaptured from the French, Admiral Caracciolo was arrested quickly and tried on a charge of treason. A Neapolitan court-martial was held on board the *FOUDROYANT*, Lord Nelson's flagship. Caracciolo was found guilty and hanged on the ship on the following day.

Carcass

An iron shell containing inflammable materials. The carcass was used widely by the world's sailing navies from the late 17th century until the first part of the 19th century to set fire to the sails and rigging of an enemy ship. A notable example of the successful use of carcasses occurred in 1788 when the RUSSIAN NAVY, commanded by Sir Samuel BENTHAM, used them to destroy the Turkish fleet. The iron shell of the carcass was filled with a mixture of chemicals and had three vents to allow the chemicals to burn as the shell was being fired. Other incendiary devices, including heated cannonballs, were in use at the same time, but none could match the performance of the carcass.

Carden, Vice Admiral Sir Sackville
1857–1930

British vice admiral. Entering the navy in 1870, Carden saw service in Egypt, the Sudan and later in the Benin expedition of 1897. He was promoted to captain in 1899 and was advanced to the rank of rear admiral in 1908, serving for a year with the Atlantic Fleet before taking a desk job at the Admiralty. After more than 40 years' service in the ROYAL NAVY, Admiral Carden might have expected that his appointment to an administrative post in Malta in 1912 would be followed by retirement. However, WORLD WAR I, 1914–18, intervened, and he was recalled to active service. Carden replaced Sir Berkeley MILNE, commander of the British Battle Squadron in the Mediterranean, who had left his post following his failure to prevent the escape of the German warship GOEBEN to Turkey in August 1914.

Largely on Carden's advice, the British War Council decided to mount an operation to try to force the DARDANELLES in 1915 by naval power alone. The Anglo-French naval bombardment of the Turkish forts began on February 19, 1915, but it soon became clear that the Turkish defenses and minefields were much more formidable than had been envisaged and the disastrous Gallipoli landings were soon launched. The prospect of failure brought Carden, whose recent operational experience was extremely limited, to the verge of a nervous breakdown and, on March 16, 1915, he resigned. He was replaced by Admiral Sir John DE ROBECK, a much more able and effective officer.

The British armed merchant cruiser *Carmania*, formerly a Cunard transatlantic liner, was taken over by the Royal Navy at the start of World War I, 1914–18 *(Copyright © Imperial War Museum, London)*

Carmania

A British ARMED MERCHANT CRUISER OF WORLD WAR I, 1914–18, the *Carmania* was a former Cunard transatlantic liner of 19,600 tons and with a maximum speed of 21 knots. On the outbreak of war in 1914 she was taken over by the ROYAL NAVY and sent to the South Atlantic. During her patrols she soon came across the *Cap Trafalgar*, a German armed merchant cruiser of 18,700 tons coaling off an island near the Brazilian coast.

After an intensive engagement that lasted some 90 minutes, the *Cap Trafalgar* sank. The victorious British ship, which also sustained some damage, was the only armed merchant cruiser to sink a similar vessel during an engagement on the high seas during the war.

C. Simpson, *The Ship That Hunted Itself*, London, 1977.

Carnegie, William, Earl of Northesk
1758–1831

*T*hird in command of the British fleet at the Battle of TRAFALGAR, 1805, Admiral Lord Northesk had been appointed to the *BRITANNIA*, a three-decker, on the outbreak of the Napoleonic Wars in 1803. The *Britannia*, which was third in the weather line (those in the line of battle on the windward side), headed by Lord Nelson, was heavily involved in the battle and sustained substantial losses. Some six years earlier Lord Northesk had been caught up in the mutiny at the NORE, May 1797, as commander of the *Monmouth*, one of the ships directly involved. The mutineers imprisoned him for a while before commissioning him to go to London to present their demands to the king. The Admiralty rejected these demands out of hand and, unable to play any further role in the crisis, Northesk decided to relinquish the command of his ship.

Carrack

A type of sailing ship, in use from the late Middle Ages until the Elizabethan period. Originally a Mediterranean adaptation of the North European COG, the carrack was larger and had a fuller shape than its predecessor. First appearing early in the 14th century, it was carvel-built (i.e., had a flush hull) and had substantial outer wales (additional timbers) to strengthen the hull planking. The carrack was an example of a HIGH-CHARGED SHIP because its dominant feature was two massive deck castles located fore and aft high above the water line. Unlike the original cog design, the new vessel was three-masted. In addition to its center mast, it had a mizzen mast with a lateen sail and a short mast in the forecastle with a small square sail. Like its predecessor, it had a stern rudder on the centerline.

The "high-charged" carrack was the principal trading and naval vessel of the late Middle Ages and a forerunner of the galleon
(Copyright © National Maritime Museum, Greenwich, London)

Soon widely adopted in northern waters as well as in the Mediterranean, the design was used both as a merchantman and a warship. Small cannon were mounted on the castles and the upper decks, but the top-heavy vessel ran the risk of capsizing if it carried heavy artillery. With the introduction of the gunport, the center of gravity could be lowered by moving the larger guns from the castles into the hull, although the problem of instability was never completely resolved. As the carrack developed, larger versions of 1,000 tons or more eventually were built; these had a much greater gun-carrying capacity. For example, the HENRY GRACE À DIEU, Henry VIII's flagship, was a four-masted carrack of 1,000 tons that could carry 151 guns.

The weaknesses of the carrack led to the development of the GALLEON in the late 16th century. A LOW-CHARGED SHIP that was fast and maneuverable was more appropriate to a period when bombardment rather than boarding was the accepted naval tactic. Although the carrack was rendered obsolete in the age of the broadside, it was notable as the precursor of the three-masted ship that, in various forms, formed the heart of the sailing navy until the mid-19th century.

Robert Gardiner ed., *Cogs, Caravels and Galleons: The Sailing Ship 1000–1650*, London, 1994.

Carrier Air Group

Known to the UNITED STATES NAVY as the CAG, the carrier air group was the American designation for the aircraft—and their crews—that were assigned to a single AIRCRAFT CARRIER. These aircraft were grouped by type into squadrons or flights. During the early stages of WORLD WAR II, 1939–45, in the Pacific, the normal American CAG consisted of one fighter squadron, one reconnaissance squadron, one dive bomber squadron, one bombing squadron and one torpedo squadron. As the war continued, the mix of squadrons varied according to the tasks involved. For example, reconnaissance squadrons were dropped in favor of more fighters to protect the carriers from Japanese attacks. Other navies, including the British ROYAL NAVY, also employed the concept.

N. Friedman, *U.S. Aircraft Carriers*, Annapolis, 1983.

Carronade

An 18th-century Scottish naval gun developed by the Carron Iron Founding and Shipping Company, Falkirk, the carronade was a short-barreled light carriage gun that fired a heavy ball of 68 lbs. (30.6 kg) over a short distance. Known as the "smasher," it was first used in action by the ROYAL NAVY in 1779 and later was employed to great effect at the Battle of the SAINTS, 1782, during the AMERICAN WAR OF INDEPENDENCE, 1775–83. Ships with carronades could inflict severe damage on the enemy at short range but were at a serious disadvantage when opposed by standard guns with a conventional range. For this reason they were designed as an auxiliary weapon and were not intended as the main armament of a ship of the line. The carronade was widely used by the British and French navies during the FRENCH REVOLUTIONARY AND NAPOLEONIC WARS, 1793–1815, and was also used during the WAR OF 1812. Sometimes the carronade was used as the primary armament; in such cases, the ship could be outgunned by an opponent equipped with standard, longer-range weapons. The limited range of the carronade led to its eventual withdrawal from naval service.

Cartagena, Battle of
May 28, 1708

Battle fought between the English and Spanish in the West Indies during the War of the SPANISH SUCCESSION, 1701–14. On May 28, 1708 a British squadron consisting of three warships and a fireship under the command of Commodore Charles Wagner engaged the Spanish treasure fleet off the coast of Cartagena. The Spanish had 12 warships, including two ships of the line. During a short-lived action of about 90 minutes the Spanish ship *San Josef* blew up with the loss of her treasure and a crew of 600. Two other Spanish ships also were destroyed. Commodore Wagner achieved this outcome despite the withdrawal of the *Kingston* and the *Portland*, whose captains were later court-martialed for failing to support their commander and were removed from their commands.

Cartaret, Sir George
c. 1609–80

English naval commander and administrator who was an active supporter of the royalist cause during the English Civil War, 1642–51. Cartaret joined the navy early in the century and saw action against the Barbary pirates. He secured early promotion and soon received his first command. In 1639 he was appointed comptroller of the navy, but his career was interrupted by the Civil War. He turned down Parliament's offer of a command and retired to Jersey, which he held for the Royalists as governor, until 1651, when he was forced to surrender to Commonwealth forces. Nonetheless, he had provided valuable service to the Royalists by offering Jersey as a safe haven and by supplying arms. When the monarchy was restored in 1660, Cartaret returned to naval service and was rewarded with the office of treasurer of the navy. He continued in this post until the end of the Second ANGLO-DUTCH WAR, 1665–

67, when he was appointed deputy treasurer of Ireland. In 1673 he became a Lord Commissioner of the Admiralty and finally reached the summit of English naval administration.

Cartaret, Philip
c. 1738–96

*E*nglish naval commander and notable explorer who made two complete circumnavigations of the globe in expeditions sponsored by the ROYAL NAVY. Cartaret participated in Captain John BYRON's voyage round the world in 1764–66 as a lieutenant on the *DOLPHIN*. Almost as soon as he returned he was dispatched again on a second circumnavigation, commanded by Captain Samuel Wallis, but on this voyage he was given the command of the *Swallow*. As the ships passed through the Straits of Magellan, Cartaret lost contact with the *Dolphin*, which was also making the voyage for a second time. Cartaret pressed on alone and discovered a number of important Pacific Islands in the Polynesian and Melanesian groups. He returned via the Philippines, where he made some surveys, and reached England in 1769. During the AMERICAN WAR OF INDEPENDENCE, 1775–83, Cartaret, now a rear admiral, fought in the West Indies under Admiral Lord RODNEY. He retired in 1794.

Casabianca, Louis de
1752–98

*F*rench naval officer descended from a noble Corsican family who entered the navy as the AMERICAN WAR OF INDEPENDENCE, 1775–83, was beginning. Casabianca was involved in escorting a convoy of French troops across the Atlantic and participated in several naval actions against the British off the North American coast. Promoted to the rank of captain in 1790, he was appointed to the command of *L'ORIENT*, a SHIP OF THE LINE, during the French Revolutionary Wars, 1792–1802. At the Battle of the Nile, August 1, 1798, *L'Orient* served as the flagship of Vice Admiral François Paul BRUEYS D'AIGAILLIERS. When the French commander was killed, Casabianca assumed overall command—but this opportunity was short-lived. British guns had started a fire on deck that quickly caused the magazine to explode, killing both Casabianca and his ten-year-old son, who had refused to leave the ship, as well as many of the crew.

Catamaran

A type of sailing vessel. The term "catamaran" may be applied to any vessel that has two hulls and can be powered by steam or sails. Although the catamaran, which is notably difficult to capsize, often is associated with stability, speed and smoothness, its naval applications have been periodic and limited. The design was used by the ROYAL NAVY to produce several experimental gunboats during the late 18th century. It was also the basis of the *DEMOLOGUS*, the UNITED STATES NAVY's first steam-powered warship. The catamaran's more limited maneuverability and the real possibility of structural weakness may have been what curbed naval enthusiasm for this type. A special kind of catamaran—essentially a large chest packed with explosives—was developed by the British in 1804 during the Napoleonic War, 1803–15. Fitted with a delayed action bomb, the catamaran was towed to the enemy's position and was, therefore, particularly vulnerable to countermeasures. Today the catamaran design is used almost exclusively for racing yachts and, in a larger motor-powered version, for some passenger ferries.

Centurion

*F*amous as Commodore George ANSON's flagship during his circumnavigation of the globe, 1740–44, the *Centurion* was a fourth-rate ship (see RATING OF SHIPS) that was launched at Portsmouth, England, in 1732.

During a remarkable voyage, this 56-gun English vessel captured considerable quantities of booty; in fact, it was the most profitable operation of its kind ever undertaken. Her greatest moment came when she captured the Spanish treasure galleon *Nuestra Señora de Covadonga* as the latter sailed from Acapulco, Mexico to Manila with a cargo of silver. In a notable engagement the two ships struggled for two hours until the *Centurion*, the larger vessel, prevailed with very few casualties among her crew.

Eventually returning home against all odds—Anson barely evaded a hostile French fleet in the English Channel—the *Centurion* saw active again during the SEVEN YEARS' WAR, 1756–63. She was present at the capture of QUEBEC, 1759, and the taking of Havana, 1762. Her career finally came to an end in 1769 when she was broken up.

Cervera y Topete, Pascual
1839–1909

*S*panish admiral and chief of staff who commanded a squadron during the SPANISH-AMERICAN WAR of 1898. Following the American declaration of war in April 1898, Cervera was appointed to command a squadron that had been ordered to Cuba to strengthen Spain's presence there. The squadron consisted of four outdated and poorly equipped cruisers and two destroyers. Cervera reached Santiago de Cuba on May 19 and was immediately blockaded by a more powerful American force commanded by Admiral William SAMPSON.

Cervera remained in harbor and did not leave until forced to do so by the pressure of events on land, following the American invasion on June 22. On July 3 he departed from Santiago but almost immediately ran into the American fleet. The Battle of SANTIAGO resulted in the almost complete destruction of the Spanish force; some 1,800 survivors, including Cervera himself, were taken prisoner. The Spanish had been overwhelmed by a more powerful enemy, and no blame could be attached to their unlucky commander.

David F. Trask, *The War with Spain in 1898*, 1981.

Ceylon, Battle of
April 5–9, 1942

As the Japanese advanced through southeast Asia in the opening phase of WORLD WAR II (1939–45) in the Pacific, the British became increasingly concerned about the threat to the security of Ceylon. The British believed that the Japanese might want to use their island colony off the southeast coast of India, now known as Sri Lanka, as a key naval base and a source of rubber. A Japanese attack was expected on April 1, 1942, and the British Eastern Fleet, commanded by Admiral Sir James SOMERVILLE, was ordered to intercept the enemy fleet. Somerville's fleet consisted of five battleships (four of which were obsolete), three carriers, eight cruisers and 15 destroyers.

On April 1 Somerville was notified that an enemy carrier force, commanded by Admiral Chuichi NAGUMO, had been sighted 350 miles (563 km) south of Ceylon. The Japanese First Air Fleet consisted of five carriers and some 360 aircraft, four battleships, three cruisers and nine destroyers. The British commander responded by sending a fast squadron—consisting of three battleships, four cruisers and six destroyers—in search of the enemy. On April 5, when the Japanese attacked Colombo, the capital of Ceylon, the British were still some 500 miles (805 km) away. The Japanese inflicted heavy damage on the port and its facilities but were able to destroy only an auxiliary cruiser and a destroyer. Other British warships escaped before the Japanese arrived, although two heavy cruisers were attacked and sunk at sea later the same day.

From April 5 to 8, Somerville searched for Nagumo while three Japanese raiding squadrons sank 19 merchant ships in quick succession. Before finally withdrawing Nagumo attacked the British naval base at Trincomalee, on the northeast coast of Ceylon, and sank the aircraft carrier *HERMES*, a destroyer and a corvette as they fled. Somerville did not succeed in bringing the enemy to battle, and the heavy losses sustained by the Royal Navy at Colombo and Trincomalee went unpunished for a time.

Chain-Shot

During the age of the European sailing navies, the impact of a cannon ball or shot (a solid round ball) on an enemy target often was increased by using two balls or shots in combination, joined together by a substantial iron chain. When fired from a naval gun, the chain-shot revolved at high speed as it traveled toward its target. This weapon was used mainly against an enemy ship's masts and rigging, but it also had an antipersonnel capability. Another projectile with a similar purpose was know as a bar-shot. This consisted of two half cannonballs joined by a bar and operated on the same basis as chain-shot. Opposing ships also used canisters containing pieces of iron that scattered when fired. Another weapon was case-shot, which consisted of a container that fired small iron bullets at the enemy. Grape-shot was a cluster of iron balls clamped together in a frame. Like case-shot, all these weapons were intended for use against a ship's rigging or her crew.

Channel Dash
1942

A carefully planned German operation (officially designated Operation Cerebus) during WORLD WAR II, 1939–45, in which the German BATTLE CRUISERS *SCHARNHORST* and *GNEISENAU* and the heavy cruiser *PRINZ EUGEN* broke out from BREST on February 11, 1942. The two battle cruisers had taken refuge there following a successful campaign against Allied shipping in the Atlantic, while the *Prinz Eugen* had run short of fuel while accompanying the ill-fated *BISMARCK*. Heavy Royal Air Force bombing quickly made their position at Brest untenable and they planned to return to the Baltic. With full support from the Luftwaffe, the three ships left Brest in daylight. They were not spotted by the British for some hours, but eventually a lone Spitfire found them as they sailed through the English Channel at an average speed of 27 knots.

Heavy German naval protection and air cover made an effective British response difficult. The Germans easily repelled action by the Royal Navy, and fire from British coast defense guns proved ineffectual. The battle cruisers sustained some damage from mines but made good their escape, arriving back in Germany on February 13. The success of Operation Cerebus was a short-term humiliation for the British and revealed weaknesses in their naval planning and coordination. At the same time, however, the two battle cruisers were no longer an immediate threat to Allied convoys crossing the Atlantic.

Chariot

Widely described as a human torpedo, the chariot was in fact a small British submersible craft of WORLD WAR

II (1939–45) operated by two men, equipped with oxygen, who rode astride the craft on saddles. Its main purpose was to penetrate harbor defenses and attack enemy warships. Developed from an earlier Italian design, which had been found after the Italian attack on Alexandria, Egypt in 1941, these British-made vessels had a length of 25 feet (7.65 m) and a displacement of 1.5 tons (1,524 kg). The body housed a battery-powered motor and a 700-pound (317-kg) detachable warhead in the nose-cone. The front operator drove the chariot, which a conventional submarine always brought to the scene of operations in a special watertight container. The rear operator released the warhead underneath the target or attached it directly to the hull. They would then return to the mother submarine.

The first chariots were intended for use against the German battleship *TIRPITZ*, which was operating from Norwegian fjords, but the water proved to be far too cold for their crews to survive in. The chariots operated more effectively in Mediterranean waters and achieved a number of spectacular successes against the Italian navy, including the destruction of three cruisers.

Charles XIII
1748–1818

*T*he son of King Adolph Frederick of Sweden and younger brother of King Gustav III, Charles was King of Sweden, 1809–18, and of Norway, 1814–18, as well as a distinguished naval commander. As high admiral of the Swedish fleet he made an important contribution to the RUSSO-SWEDISH WAR, 1788–90. Using the title "Duke of Södermanland" (or Duke Carl), Charles fought with great bravery in a series of naval engagements in 1788–89, but he was badly served by some of his subordinates and the initial outcome was not as favorable as it might have been. Despite these difficulties the Swedish fleet defeated the Russians at the concluding Battle of SVENSKUND, July 1790. Charles was regent from 1792 to 1796 during the minority of his nephew Gustav. When Gustav was deposed in 1809, Charles succeeded him.

Charts and Maps

*B*y the time national navies emerged in Europe in the 16th and 17th centuries, the preparation of maps and charts had reached standards of accuracy unknown in the Middle Ages. The publication of Mercator's map of the world in 1569 represented a considerable step forward, particularly for the navigation of the seas. Henry the Navigator, 1394–1460, the Portuguese prince who organized charts of the seas around Europe and beyond, was an important early influence on the charting of the oceans. In the late 16th century Dutch mapmakers led in this field;

their collection of sea charts was published in England as the *Mariner's Mirrour*, 1588. A chart is a map of an area of sea that includes details of coastlines, rocks, buoys and other landmarks, together with information about water depths.

In time the requirements of organized naval warfare provided a considerable boost to the preparation of more accurate charts, which were facilitated by the invention of new navigational aids. Beginning in the late 17th century substantial naval resources were devoted to HYDROGRAPHY, and most navies established their own departments during the 18th century. In Britain the Admiralty began survey work only during the FRENCH REVOLUTIONARY AND NAPOLEONIC WARS, 1792–1815, and the first British chart was not issued until 1801. Since then a large number of Admiralty surveys have been completed and several thousand charts issued, but even today nautical charts do not provide comprehensive coverage of the world's oceans, particularly of the areas distant from a substantial landmass. Maps and charts are still a vital part of a warship's navigational tools, even though RADAR and the satellite are widely used to establish a vessel's position.

Chasse-Marée

A French two- or three-masted flush-deck sailing ship of the 18th and 19th centuries that was used for a variety of purposes. Particularly associated with the Brittany region of France, it was a coaster and a fishing vessel as well as a privateer and a small warship. The term "chasse-marée" means "tide chaser." The vessel's lug rig provided it with the ability to travel at high speed in the right conditions; however, when running before the wind, the chasse-marée was likely to be slower than its square-rigged equivalent. On the three-masted version, the center mast was raked aft and carried a very large lugsail with a topsail above. The other masts carried the same type of rig, although their sail area was much reduced. These large sails required additional crew members to lower and maneuver them in bad weather. Armed and carrying a gun crew, the chasse-marée often was used for privateering and smuggling. Chasse-marées saw regular naval duty as well, and were employed extensively by the French Navy during the FRENCH REVOLUTIONARY AND NAPOLEONIC WARS, 1792–1815.

Château-Renault, François Louis de Rousselet, Marquis de
1637–1716

*F*rench admiral who was created a marshal of France in 1703 in recognition of his services in the wars of Louis XIV against Britain and the Netherlands. Château-

Renault joined the French Navy in 1661 after a brief period in the army and was promoted quickly to the rank of captain. In 1689, during the War of the GRAND ALLIANCE, 1688–97, he was responsible for transferring French troops to Ireland in support of James II's attempt to regain the English throne. Following his arrival in BANTRY BAY on May 1, he engaged a smaller English force under Admiral Arthur HERBERT, Earl of Torrington. Château-Renault was unable to inflict a decisive defeat on the enemy partly because some of his FIRESHIPS were still unloading and therefore unavailable for battle. Disagreements with his subordinate commanders also weakened his position. In June 1690 he led the van of the fleet under the Comte de TOURVILLE that defeated an Anglo-Dutch force under Torrington at the Battle of BEACHY HEAD. Château-Renault became vice admiral of France on Tourville's death in 1701.

In 1702, during the War of the SPANISH SUCCESSION, 1701–14, he commanded a French squadron that escorted the Spanish treasure fleet from the West Indies. On his arrival at VIGO he fortified the harbor in anticipation of an enemy assault. It was soon forthcoming. An Anglo-Dutch fleet under Sir George ROOKE attacked on October 22, 1702, inflicting a serious defeat on the outnumbered French and seizing a large quantity of treasure. As a result of severe losses, Château-Renault's squadron effectively ceased to exist. He was absolved of blame for the disaster but never again commanded a fleet at sea.

J. J. R. Calman-Maison, *La maréchal de Château-Renault*, Paris, 1903.

Chatfield, Alfred Ernle Montacute, First Baron
1873–1967

British naval commander who headed British naval administration for much of the interwar period. Chatfield first made his mark during WORLD WAR I, 1914–18, serving as flag captain to Admiral Sir David BEATTY in the British battle cruiser *Lion*. He was present at the battles of HELIGOLAND BIGHT, 1914, DOGGER BANK, 1915, and JUTLAND, 1916. In 1916, when Beatty was promoted to commander in chief of the GRAND FLEET, Chatfield continued to serve him as flag officer. Their association was maintained in peacetime when Beatty was appointed First Lord of the Admiralty and Chatfield joined him on the naval staff.

Following two periods in command of the Home and Mediterranean fleets, Chatfield was appointed First Lord of the Admiralty in 1933. During a five-year term he oversaw the development of the British fleet in response to the growing naval threat from Germany. However, he misunderstood the nature of that threat and the future shape of naval warfare, which was to be dominated by the submarine and the aircraft. His preoccupation with the construction of large gun battleships, which were becoming obsolete, won him few allies. On leaving the Admiralty he was appointed Minister for the Coordination of Defence; when WORLD WAR II, 1939–45, was declared he was appointed to the War Cabinet. Chatfield proved to be ill-equipped to operate in a purely political environment and retired when his post was abolished in 1940.

Chatham, Dutch Attack on
June 17–24, 1667

A surprise attack against the British at the end of the Second ANGLO-DUTCH WAR, 1665–67, which directly influenced the outcome of the long-drawn-out peace negotiations that were then in progress. In mid-June 1667 the Dutch fleet, commanded by Admiral Michiel de RUYTER and Corneliszoon de WITT, crossed the North Sea, entered the Thames River and seized the fort at Sheerness, Kent, at the mouth of the Medway River. It then sailed up the Medway to Chatham, where the English fleet already had been laid up and its crews disbanded.

The Dutch attacked the English warships as they lay at anchor in the royal docks. The *Royal Charles*, the English fleet flagship, and four others were burned and two more were captured and towed back to Holland. The Dutch withdrew after laying siege to Chatham for a month. Their expedition, which had advanced to within 20 miles (32 km) of London, caused considerable concern in the capital; Samuel PEPYS was not alone in sending his family out of the city and placing his money in safekeeping. The action put direct pressure on the English negotiators to reach an agreement with the Dutch. Terms were finally reached and embodied in the Treaty of Breda, July 21, 1667.

Chauncey, Isaac
1772–1840

American naval officer, born in Black Rock, Connecticut in 1772. Chauncey entered the merchant service in 1791 before being commissioned as a lieutenant in the young UNITED STATES NAVY in 1798. He served as a first lieutenant on the *President* in the West Indies during the QUASI-WAR, 1798–1800, with France. Between 1802 and 1805 he sailed with the squadron that operated in the Mediterranean against the Barbary states. In September 1812, with the United States at war with Britain, he was given command of the American forces on the Great Lakes (see WAR OF 1812.) Giving particular priority to defensive activities on Lake Ontario, he built up naval forces to oppose British attempts at gaining control of the lake. However, although both he and his British counterpart engaged in much naval construction, there was relatively little real action, except for an American attack on York (now Toronto) in April 1813 and an engagement on the Niagara River in May. Nothing decisive occurred to break the stalemate on Lake Ontario, which lasted until the end of the war. After the war, Chauncey again served in the Mediterranean, commanding the squadron that concluded a treaty with Algiers. He held important positions in the navy's administration until his death in 1840.

Edward K. Eckert, "Isaac Chauncey," in *Dictionary of American Military Biography, Vol. 1*, ed. Roger J. Spiller et al., Westport, Conn., 1984, pp. 167–170.

Chemulpo, Battle of
February 9, 1904

*A*ction between elements of the Russian and Japanese navies during the RUSSO-JAPANESE WAR, 1904–5. As the main Japanese battle fleet appeared off Port Arthur, China, at the beginning of the war, a naval engagement was in progress in the Korean port of Chemulpo (Inchon), on the western coast. The port was the destination, on February 8, of a convoy of Japanese troopships escorted by a Japanese armored cruiser squadron under the command of Vice Admiral Hikonojo Kamimura. The transports left after the Japanese ground troops were landed. Kamimura then turned his attention to the two Russian warships anchored in the harbor, informing their commanders that war had just been declared and that they would be attacked if they did not leave their anchorage by noon. However, as the Russian vessels tried to break out before the deadline, they came under fire from the Japanese cruisers. The Russian cruiser *Varyag* sustained heavy damage, and both she and the sloop *Korietz* were forced back into Chemulpo harbor. The two ships were scuttled in the harbor to prevent them from falling into Japanese hands.

Cherbourg

A major French seaport and naval base on the Normandy coast, over the centuries Cherbourg often was the scene of Anglo-French engagements. It was not until 1450, when King Charles VII of France secured Cherbourg, that the question of its disputed ownership was finally settled. However, that did not prevent the English from occupying it temporarily in 1758 during the SEVEN YEARS' WAR, 1756–63. Its key position on the English Channel had long made Cherbourg an obvious site for a naval base and shipbuilding capability. It had the added advantage of being in a sheltered position on a bay, with natural protection on three sides. During the 17th century, separate naval dockyards were developed and naval education facilities were provided. In 1686 Sébastien de Vauban prepared plans for fortifications to protect these valuable facilities, but they were not completed until the mid-19th century.

Cherbourg suffered heavy damage during WORLD WAR II, 1939–45, and was under German occupation for much of the war, but in the postwar period it reestablished itself as a major naval facility where nuclear-powered submarines are built.

Chesapeake, U.S.S.

*A*n American frigate that fought in the most celebrated engagement of the WAR OF 1812, the *Chesapeake's* construction as one of the first six frigates in the UNITED STATES NAVY had been authorized in 1794. She was armed with 36 guns. During her engagement with a British frigate in 1813 she was captured and spent the rest of her days in the service of the Royal Navy.

The *Chesapeake* first met the British in 1807, when she was stopped in the Atlantic east of Cape Henry, at the entrance to Chesapeake Bay, by H.M.S. *Leopard*, which was searching for British deserters. At first the *Chesapeake's* captain, James BARRON, refused to give way, but he capitulated as soon as the British opened fire and handed over the alleged deserters. On his return to the United States, Barron faced a court-martial for cowardice.

The "Chesapeake incident," as it came to be known, was a contributory cause of the War of 1812, which led to the *Chesapeake's* second and even more damaging encounter with the British. On June 1, 1813 she was in Boston harbor when the *Shannon*, a British frigate lying offshore, challenged her to battle. James LAWRENCE, who was then captain of the *Chesapeake*, unwisely decide to fight. Within 15 minutes of leaving the safety of his harbor moorings, the British ship, which was better armed and had a more experienced crew, had secured the surrender of her opponent. There were 146 American casualties, including Lawrence, who was mortally wounded. Eventually the *Chesapeake* was taken to Britain and remained in the Royal Navy until 1819, when she was decommissioned.

Chesapeake, First Battle of
March 16, 1781

*O*n March 8, 1781, as the AMERICAN WAR OF INDEPENDENCE, 1775–83, entered its final phase, a French naval squadron based at Newport, Rhode Island, responded to an appeal for assistance from General George Washington, who was fighting the British in Virginia. Commanded by Admiral Sochet Destouches, the squadron—consisting of eight ships of the line and two frigates—sailed for Chesapeake Bay, where it was to operate in support of hard-pressed American land forces. The Royal Navy was aware of the French movements and a British squadron, commanded by Vice Admiral Marriot ARBUTHNOT, left Gardiner's Bay, Long Island, on March 10.

Six days later the two squadrons met some 40 miles (64 km) northeast of Cape Henry, at the mouth of Chesapeake Bay, in poor conditions. The French commander proved to be more able than his adversary, who followed the official guidelines on tactics far too closely to be an effective commander. Vice Admiral Arbuthnot failed to give the signal for close action, forcing his subordinates to maintain their position in the line of battle and preventing them from attacking the French ships individually. Three British van ships were badly damaged by the French. However, by the late afternoon the French were lost in foggy conditions and Admiral Destouches was forced to return to Newport, leaving the British in command of the sea. Arbuthnot, who was unable to pursue them, entered Chesapeake Bay. Despite its failure, the Royal Navy nonetheless had denied the French access to the bay, which had been their main objective.

Chesapeake, Second Battle of
September 5, 1781

*T*he outcome of this naval battle, the second to be fought in the area within a few months, proved to be a turning point in the AMERICAN WAR OF INDEPENDENCE, 1775–83. It led directly to the final surrender of the British army at Yorktown (on the York River, near Chesapeake Bay), where some 7,000 troops under the command of General Earl Cornwallis were besieged by American and French forces. Without fresh supplies, which would have to be brought by sea, they would starve. Consequently, a British fleet consisting of 19 ships of the line was loaded with supplies at New York and, on August 31, sailed for Chesapeake Bay. The relief fleet was commanded by Admiral Thomas GRAVES who raised his flag in the 98-gun ship *London*. Graves's immediate subordinates were Rear Admiral Drake, who headed the van, and Rear Admiral Samuel HOOD, who led the rear division.

On September 5 they arrived off Chesapeake Bay, some 12 miles (19 km) east of Cape Henry, only to find that a French fleet, under the command of Vice Admiral the Comte de GRASSE, was at anchor just inside the bay. Consisting of 24 ships of the line, its task was to reinforce the besieging armies. Alerted to the British threat, the French ships left their anchorage as soon as possible. Although the weather favored the British, their naval commanders were slow to respond and used traditional textbook tactics that allowed the French to seize the initiative. It was not until 4 P.M., nearly four hours after the French weighed anchor, that the opposing fleets opened fire. The battle, which lasted two and one-half hours, ended inconclusively, although the British lost one ship of the line and several others were damaged.

The two fleets remained in contact for the next four days, but Admiral Graves did not engage the enemy again.

On September 10 the British fleet, itself running low of essential supplies, returned to New York. De Grasse reentered Chesapeake Bay the following day and blockaded it. The outcome was a disaster for the British. Cornwallis knew that he could not survive without being resupplied, and on October 19 he was forced to surrender. This decisive event marked the end of the struggle for American independence.

Harold A. Larrabee, *Decision at Chesapeake*, New York, 1964.

Choiseul, Étienne François, Duc de
1719–85

*F*rench politician and minister of King Louis XV who spent his early career as a soldier during the War of the AUSTRIAN SUCCESSION, 1740–48, rising to the rank of lieutenant general through the influence of Madame de Pompadour, the king's mistress. The Duc de Choiseul became a diplomat and, in 1756, was responsible for arranging an alliance between France and Austria against Frederick the Great. In 1758 he received the wartime appointment of Minister of Foreign Affairs, including control of the naval and war ministries. There was, however, a limit to what he could do to reform the French navy while the SEVEN YEARS' WAR, 1756–63, was still in progress. Responsible for negotiating peace terms at the end of the war, Choiseul resolved to secure the return of the French territory—particularly in Canada and India—that had been lost to Britain. To this end he oversaw the reconstruction of the French navy after the war and the adoption of new tactical doctrines. However, as a result of a court intrigue, he was ousted from his post before these changes could be tested operationally, although they restored the French navy as an effective fighting force.

Churchill, Sir Winston Leonard Spencer
1874–1965

*B*ritish statesman and war leader who served not only as prime minister during WORLD WAR II, 1939–45, but was also political head of the navy on two separate occasions. Churchill, who had first displayed an interest in naval affairs before WORLD WAR I, 1914–18, was initially offered the post of First Lord of the ADMIRALTY in 1908 but turned it down then in favor of another ministerial post. In 1911, when the office was again offered to him, Churchill accepted it, and a period of naval reform and modernization followed. He was instrumental in improving the pay and conditions of the lower ranks, in creating a naval staff to oversee operations at the Admiralty and in supporting the development of naval aviation.

Believing that armed conflict in Europe was imminent, Churchill also increased the size of the navy and ensured that it was ready at its war stations when World War I broke out in 1914. However, his success in laying the wartime foundations of the ROYAL NAVY was not matched by his role in the war itself. His support for the disastrous Gallipoli operation, 1915, led to his dismissal from the Admiralty in May 1915 (See DARDANELLES.) His link with the navy severed, he joined the army on active service in France. In the interwar period Churchill's direct connections with the navy were tenuous, and as Chancellor of the Exchequer, 1924–29, he inevitably sought to reduce military budgets rather than increase them in a period of financial crisis. His main objective during this period was to protect the funding of the Royal Air Force.

When World War II began, Prime Minister Neville Chamberlain appointed Churchill First Lord of the Admiralty with the task of preparing the Royal Navy for combat. Despite his relative lack of support for the navy between the wars, his appointment was welcomed by the service and his role in raising morale turned out to be highly significant. He continued to support the cause of naval reform and the need for further technological development. He left the Admiralty in May 1940 when he became prime minister but retained a direct interest in naval strategy and the outcome of major naval issues until the end of the war and his departure from office. He gave particular priority

Sir Winston Churchill, British statesman, in naval uniform; he served twice as First Lord of the Admiralty *(Copyright © National Maritime Museum Greenwich, London)*

to the crucial struggle against the U-BOAT and to British participation in the Pacific War. As prime minister in the first postwar Conservative administration, 1951–55, he supported the case for a strong conventional navy.

Peter Gretton, *Former Navy Person: Winston Churchill and the Royal Navy,* London, 1968; Stephen Roskill, *Churchill and the Admirals,* London, 1977.

Clue Sabran, M. de la

c. 1703–59

French naval commander whose recorded service focused on operations against the British during the SEVEN YEARS' WAR, 1756–63. At the Battle of MINORCA, 1756, he was a commodore serving with the squadron that prevented an English naval force commanded by Admiral John BYNG from reaching the besieged British garrison on the island. The island soon fell to the French, and De La Clue was one of the officers rewarded with promotion. In 1759, as a vice admiral, he was appointed to the command of a squadron based at Toulon. Consisting of ten ships of the line and five other warships, it soon left for BREST, where it was to join the main French fleet to mount an invasion of England. Pursued by a Gibraltar-based British squadron under Admiral Edward BOSCAWEN, De La Clue was next sighted off the Portuguese coast on August 18. After a five-hour battle, the six surviving French ships (seven had fled to Cadiz) were driven into LAGOS Bay, Portugal. Fighting continued the following day when two more of De La Clue's ships were captured and two others, including his flagship, the *Océan,* were wrecked. De La Clue himself was severely wounded and later died of his injuries at Lagos.

Coastal Motor Boat

A small, fast surface warship used by the ROYAL NAVY during WORLD WAR I, 1914–18, the coastal motor boat (CMB) was designed and mainly produced by the British manufacturer Thornycroft. Coastal motor boats were first introduced in the summer of 1916 and were made in three sizes: 40 feet (12 m), 55 feet (16.8 m) and 70 feet (21 m). All three designs had hydroplane hulls, were constructed of wood and were powered by gasoline engines of varying types. The 55-foot version, for example, had twin power plants and a maximum speed of 42 knots. Normally they were armed with torpedoes, which were launched tail-first over the stern. The 40-foot version held one, the 55-foot two, and the 70-foot boats as many as six 18-inch (46-cm) torpedoes. Some models carried mines instead: Several 70-foot boats were built exclusively as minelayers. When employed in an antisubmarine role, the

CMBs also carried depth charges. Cruisers often carried the smaller boats, but the larger versions were operated independently and made a real contribution to the British naval war effort. During the interwar period the CMB was succeeded by the motor TORPEDO BOAT (MTB), produced by Britain, Germany, Italy and other nations.

Cochrane, Thomas, Tenth Earl of Dundonald
1775–1860

British naval commander, notable both for his eccentricity and creativity, whose eventful career included service as an admiral in the navies of Chile, Brazil and Greece. Cochrane entered the Royal Navy in 1793 and soon established his reputation as the commander of a brig sloop, capturing a Spanish frigate and a number of other prizes in 1800–1. Another major triumph was the Battle of BASQUE ROADS, 1809, during the Napoleonic Wars, 1803–15, when he led the FIRESHIP attack. Cochrane might have enjoyed even more success in this battle if Lord GAMBIER, who was in command, had not failed to provide support. On his return home Cochrane, a member of Parliament since 1807, did not hesitate to publicize his superior's weaknesses. His relations with the ADMIRALTY were already strained because of his earlier campaigns against abuses in the navy, and as a result of these new attacks he was deprived of any further employment at sea. Silencing him completely proved to be more difficult, but in 1814 he was imprisoned after being falsely accused of fraud; he also was dismissed from the navy and expelled from Parliament.

Cochrane eventually decided to escape this hostile environment, accepting, in 1817, an offer from the Chilean government to command its new navy in the war of independence against Spain. A brilliant tactician, he secured a series of victories that led to the liberation of Chile (and Peru) from Spanish control. In 1823, having quarreled with his Chilean paymasters, he was offered the supreme naval command by Brazil, which was fighting a war of independence against Portugal. Upon his arrival in Europe in 1825 he took command of the fledgling Greek navy in the Greek struggle for independence against Turkey, but with few ships at his disposal he was able to do little.

Finally returning to Britain, he eventually secured his reinstatement in the Royal Navy in 1832. During this last phase of his career he made important contributions to the technology of naval warfare. He pioneered the use of steam power in warships, introduced smokescreens and was an advocate of screw propulsion. Because of his advanced age he was deprived of a last opportunity of command in the CRIMEAN WAR, 1853–56, but his secret plan for a sulfur attack on Sebastopol was seriously considered before being rejected on ethical grounds. This intervention marked the end of Cochrane's unconventional career, during which he had distinguished himself as a brilliant tactician, innovator and naval reformer.

C. C. Lloyd, *Lord Cochrane: Seaman-Radical-Liberator*, London, 1947.

Cockburn, Sir George
1772–1853

British admiral responsible for the attack on Washington, D.C., during the WAR OF 1812. After many successful operations against the French, Cockburn was appointed in late 1812 to the command of the British squadron operating on Chesapeake Bay. He planned and participated in the joint naval and military expedition that led to the capture of Washington in 1814. The combined force set fire to the White House and other public buildings before moving north to Baltimore. On his return home at the end of the war Cockburn was given the command of the squadron that took Napoleon into exile on the island of St. Helena following the latter's final defeat at Waterloo, 1815.

Codrington, Sir Edward
1770–1851

British naval commander who won the Battle of NAVARINO, 1827, against the Turks—the last fleet engagement under sail and a turning point in the Greek War of Independence, 1821–32. During his early career Codrington had served with Admiral Earl HOWE and Admiral Lord NELSON, rising steadily during the war with France. He commanded a SHIP OF THE LINE at the Battle of TRAFALGAR, 1805, and was a rear admiral by the end of the FRENCH REVOLUTIONARY AND NAPOLEONIC WARS, 1792–1815.

Shortly after his appointment in 1827 as commander in chief of the Mediterranean fleet, the opportunity for active service offered itself when, in July, Britain and its allies (France and Russia) agreed to bring the Greek War of Independence to an end. Codrington was sent to Navarino, the port that supplied Turkish forces in the Peloponnese, with the main objective of preventing reinforcements arriving there. At the same time, however, he was ordered not to attack the enemy fleet.

With the Allied blockading force in place, the situation on land deteriorated. Local negotiations to arrange a ceasefire between the two armies broke down and, Codrington decided to increase pressure on the Turks. He moved his joint force of British, French and Russian ships into Navarino Bay, where the enemy fleet was anchored in an extended horseshoe formation. Events then moved forward more rapidly than the British commander had expected. As they anchored, a dispatch boat from a British frigate was attacked at close range and the allies returned fire. The action soon became general with a heavy bombardment that lasted for three hours, and ended with the decisive defeat of the Turks. Codrington himself was unable to celebrate his victory because he was ordered to return to London, where he was charged with disobeying his orders not to engage the enemy. An inquiry cleared him of blame. He spent the rest of his career uneventfully in home waters.

Cod War
1972–73

*I*celand's unilateral action in extending its fishing limits from 12 to 50 (19 to 60 km) miles early in 1973 led to a 14-month period of tension with Britain and West Germany. British and German trawlermen, whose livelihood was at stake, soon tested Iceland's resolve by continuing to fish within the new limits. They quickly provoked a reaction from the Icelandic navy, whose gunboats intervened in an effort to prevent these infringements; several incidents resulted. At first the Icelandic action was confined to trying to cut the trawlers' fishing nets, but in March 1973 the first warning shots were fired. The British government was forced to take more assertive action, deploying several Royal Navy frigates in the disputed area to protect British trawlers while they fished. This did not prevent an Icelandic warship from opening fire and slightly damaging a British gunboat on May 26. A few days later a British frigate collided with the same Icelandic gunboat. The damage was once more slight, but the prospect of further escalation in the conflict forced the two governments to reach a compromise agreement later in the year.

Cog

*T*he principal North European sailing vessel of the 13th to 15th centuries, the cog was used for trade, transport and military purposes. It is particularly associated with the development of the Hanseatic League, which employed the ship intensively, usually operating it in an armed convoy. The cog was keeled, and clinker-built (the outer boards of the hull overlapped one another) with a rounded bow and stern; the rudder was attached at the center of the stern. A typical medieval round ship, it was very broad in the beam and had a square sail mounted on a high mast amidships. In later examples, which had a displacement of up to 600 tons and an average length of some 100 feet (30.48 m), two smaller masts were added fore and aft. Other new features, including carvel construction (a flush hull), were introduced during the ship's long life. A French development of the cog, with full rigging, was known as the NEF.

A distinctive feature of the cog and of the HIGH-CHARGED SHIPS that followed it were the large castles (superstructures) mounted fore and aft, with a third at the masthead used as an observation platform. Not only did these provide accommodation for the ship's crew, but they also had a major military purpose when the ship functioned as a floating fort. Archers and musketeers operated their weapons from these protected positions when battles at sea were fought at close quarters, the objective being not to sink an enemy vessel by gunfire but to board it and set it on fire. During the 15th century the CARRACK, a development of the cog, gradually replaced the cog as the main dual purpose merchantman and warship operating in European waters.

Robert Gardiner, ed., *Cogs, Caravels and Galleons: The Sailing Ship 1000–1650*, London, 1994.

Colbert, Jean Baptiste
1619–83

*F*rench statesman, born at Reims, who served during the reign of King Louis XIV. Colbert was responsible

Jean Baptiste Colbert, French statesman and naval reformer, revived the French navy during the 17th century
(Copyright © National Maritime Museum Greenwich, London)

for reorganizing state finances and increasing state revenues. He restructured trade and industry according to the economic principles of mercantilism. In 1669 Colbert was appointed minister of marine. Under his direction, networks of canals were built and the naval base at Toulon was reconstructed. A new naval port was built at Rochefort, which was also one of the sites of three new naval schools opened during this period. Colbert greatly increased the strength of the FRENCH NAVY, overseeing the construction of several new warships during his tenure of office. He reformed the manning of the navy; improved terms of service encouraged recruitment. Much of the benefit of his financial reforms was to be lost, however, because of the king's general extravagance and the cost of his various foreign wars, which damaged the economy and undermined Colbert's reputation. Nonetheless, there is little doubt that the changes Colbert introduced as a naval reformer had a long-term benefit even though, in the latter part of his reign, Louis XIV tended to give more priority to army expenditure.

Ines Murat, *Colbert,* translated by Robert Cook and Jeannie Van Asselt, London, 1984.

Cold War, Naval Aspects

*F*or some 45 years following WORLD WAR II, 1939–45, international relations were dominated by the state of Cold War that existed between the former Soviet Union and the Western powers. Although the term was first used in 1947, the sources of friction between the two camps go back to World War II or even earlier. Indeed, an underlying cause of the Cold War was the competition between two rival socioeconomic systems, each of which sought to undermine the other.

The conflict was fueled by America's sole possession of the atomic bomb in the immediate postwar period and by the massive Soviet presence in Eastern Europe. It took the form of aggressive political and diplomatic maneuvering, economic warfare, propaganda and subversion, and indirect and limited war of various kinds. Periods of high tension (of which the CUBAN MISSILE CRISIS, 1962, and the U.S. naval BLOCKADE of Cuba are key examples) were interspersed with periods of détente. Certain tensions between Russia and the West, which are now fueled by conflicting national aspirations, remain clearly evident, but the ideologically driven Cold War conflict of the postwar period is now over.

A central feature of the Cold War was the absence of direct warfare between the major powers themselves. This is largely explained by the fact that, by the mid-1950s, both sides possessed the hydrogen bomb. Acquisition of the hydrogen bomb by both nations marked the beginning of a massive arms race that led to a significant overproduction of nuclear weapons, ballistic missiles, bombers, subma-

rines and other military hardware but did not ever seriously undermine the basic principle of deterrence—that no nuclear power could destroy another without itself suffering unacceptable damage. The world's major navies played a critical role in ensuring that this "balance of terror" was preserved. The introduction of intercontinental ballistic missiles such as POLARIS, which can be launched from a submerged submarine, strengthened significantly the deterrent effect of nuclear weapons. A potential aggressor would be unable to destroy every enemy submarine in a first strike and would, therefore, have to face the prospect of unacceptable damage from a retaliatory strike.

Naval forces also have been ascribed a key role by both Russia and the Western powers in the event of a conventional war occurring between the superpowers. During the postwar arms race, the former Soviet Union developed the world's second-largest navy. The UNITED STATES NAVY, together with its naval allies in the North Atlantic Treaty Organization (NATO), produced the fleets to defeat it. The opposing fleets closely monitored each other's actions using submarines or electronic surveillance ships. The Western navies also were intended to operate against Warsaw Pact troops invading Western Europe by attacking them from the Arctic Sea to their rear.

A major feature of the Cold War was the occurrence of limited war—from the KOREAN WAR, 1950–53, to the VIETNAM WAR, 1964–75, where the use of nuclear weapons was tacitly excluded. Some local wars were a direct product of the Cold War, while others have provided an opportunity for superpower rivalry. These included "proxy wars"—conflicts between (or within) Third World countries, with local Communist and anti-Communist forces supported by the respective superpowers. In some cases, however, the superpowers sought jointly to stop these wars or prevent them from spreading. The naval role in these operations has varied in importance, but the increasing ability of navies to affect the course of events on land will ensure that they continue to play a significant role.

Geoffrey Till et al., *Maritime Strategy in the Nuclear Age,* London, 1984.

Collingwood, Cuthbert, First Baron
1750–1819

*E*nglish naval commander, born in Newcastle-upon-Tyne. Collingwood entered the Royal Navy at the age of 11, but without influential patrons, he did not obtain his commission until he won it for gallantry at the Battle of Bunker Hill, 1775, during the AMERICAN WAR OF INDEPENDENCE, 1775–83. From this period his career was closely associated with that of Admiral Lord NELSON, who became his closest friend. They served together in the West Indies for a time and their careers progressed in parallel. Nelson, who was ten years older, always remained one step ahead and often overshadowed Collingwood's achievements.

During the first phase of the FRENCH REVOLUTIONARY AND NAPOLEONIC WARS, 1792–1815, Collingwood served with distinction at the Battle of the GLORIOUS FIRST OF JUNE, 1794, and at the Battle of CAPE ST. VINCENT, 1797. His ships were always noted for their good discipline (although Collingwood avoided using excessive flogging) and their effective gunnery. Collingwood's active service resumed during the Napoleonic Wars, 1803–15, and continued until his death in 1810. As a vice admiral, Collingwood was second in command to Lord Nelson at the Battle of TRAFALGAR, 1805. Flying his flag in the Royal Sovereign, he led the lee column, which first broke the enemy line. On Lord Nelson's death, Collingwood assumed command of the English fleet. For his service at Trafalgar, he was rewarded with a peerage.

Collingwood remained in command of the British Mediterranean fleet for the rest of his life. In difficult circumstances he was successful in maintaining the fleet's dominant position without facing a full-scale engagement with the enemy. He died at sea on his way home to retirement and was buried beside his friend Lord Nelson in St. Paul's Cathedral, London.

E. Hughes, *The Private Correspondence of Admiral Collingwood*, London, 1957; O. Warner, *Life and Letters of Vice-Admiral Lord Collingwood*, London, 1968.

Colomb, Philip Howard

1831–99

*B*ritish admiral and author who made important contributions to the development of naval warfare. Entering the ROYAL NAVY in 1846, he served in the Second Burmese War, 1852–53, and later in China, 1874–77. Early in his career he developed an interest in naval SIGNALING and developed a system for use at night. This system, which was published in 1858 as Colomb's Flashing Signals, used short and long flashes from a lantern to convey the dots and dashes of the Morse code. Colomb carried out research on the causes of collisions at sea, and his conclusions led to changes in international regulations. Colomb also was deeply interested in the development of naval tactics as well as the more practical aspects of war. In 1891 he published the influential book *Naval Warfare*, which analyzed the impact of steam power and other revolutionary changes of the Victorian period on the conduct of war at sea. His achievements were rewarded with his promotion to vice admiral in 1892.

Colossus, H.M.S.

*T*he only battleship of the British GRAND FLEET to be hit at the Battle of JUTLAND, 1916, during WORLD WAR I, 1914–18, the *Colossus* was one of eight capital ships constructed as part of the Admiralty's 1909 building program. Originally only four new ships were planned, but the number was doubled in response to fears that Germany was secretly building DREADNOUGHTS. The *Colossus* and her sister ship *Hercules* were generally similar to their half-sister *Neptune*, with a number of minor differences, including improvements to the arrangement of the secondary armament, an increase in side armor and 21-inch (53 cm) torpedo tubes rather than 18-inch (46-cm) ones.

The *Colossus* served with the Grand Fleet throughout World War I and became the flagship of the First Battle Squadron in August 1914. After the damage sustained at Jutland had been repaired, she served the remainder of the war with the Fourth Battle Squadron. The *Hercules* was also part of the Grand Fleet during World War I. After the Armistice in November 1918 the *Hercules* transported the Allied Naval Commission to Kiel, Germany.

Commerce Raiding

*A*ttacks on an enemy's seaborne trade have been an important feature of naval warfare since the Middle Ages. The early history of commerce raiding was dominated by PRIVATEERS who were given official endorsement by a LETTER OF MARQUE. However, with the growth of national navies in the 17th century, commerce raiding became an increasingly important official naval function. At the same time, commerce raiding by private individuals continued and was not finally banned by international agreement until 1856. The United States refused to ratify the agreement, and private commerce raiding, authorized by the Confederacy, was an important feature of the AMERICAN CIVIL WAR, 1861–65.

Commerce raiding by a major naval power first occurred on a significant scale during the three ANGLO-DUTCH WARS of the 17th century, when the English destroyed large numbers of Dutch merchant ships. It was an important feature of the European wars of the 18th century and often was used as a substitute for full-scale naval operations. This option might be adopted if the main fleet was in poor condition or if a government was unwilling to expose it to unnecessary risks. During the first phase of the FRENCH REVOLUTIONARY AND NAPOLEONIC WARS 1792–1815, the disorganized state of the FRENCH NAVY forced it to concentrate on commerce-raiding operations rather than fleet actions. Supplemented by the efforts of French privateers, attacks were made across the globe; between 1793 and 1801, 5,537 British merchant ships were captured. The British were forced to take a variety of countermeasures, including the introduction of CONVOYS and the more extensive use of naval patrols. As a result, British maritime trade continued to grow and the French suffered mounting losses.

When the war resumed in 1803, the French Navy's ability to operate globally as a commerce raider was quickly eroded, and the number of British merchant ships captured fell rapidly. Despite its promising start, commerce raiding had no real impact on the final outcome of the war.

It was not until WORLD WAR I, 1914–18, that naval commerce raiding played a critical role in the outcome of a war. During the first few months of the war, German cruisers operated against Allied merchant shipping in the Atlantic and Indian oceans with mixed results. (See the EMDEN.) By the beginning of 1915, the Royal Navy cleared them from the seas; the only German surface raiders still operating were a small number of disguised merchantmen. The Germans were forced to turn to the SUBMARINE in their efforts to disrupt British trade. (See Battle of the ATLANTIC, 1914–18.) By 1917, unrestricted submarine warfare in the Atlantic was producing unsustainable losses to Allied merchant shipping and only the belated introduction of a range of counter-measures, including the convoy, in 1917, turned the tide in Britain's favour.

History repeated itself during WORLD WAR II, 1939–45, when the German U-BOAT war was the principal weapon against Allied merchant shipping. Once again German surface ships made relatively little impact. (See Battle of the ATLANTIC, 1939–45). Both sides made tactical innovations during the extended battle in the North Atlantic, but the Allies' introduction of full air cover as well as SONAR and RADAR detection helped to neutralize the U-boat threat by 1943. The UNITED STATES NAVY also used the submarine with considerable success against Japanese merchant shipping in the Pacific, and the British operated effectively against enemy merchant ships in the Mediterranean. (See also ARMED MERCHANT CRUISER.)

J. S. Bromley, *Corsairs and Navies, 1660–1760*, London, 1987.

Confederate Navy

The naval force created by the Confederate States when they seceded from the Union and set in train the AMERICAN CIVIL WAR, 1861–65. Because the South lacked a maritime tradition and had a limited capacity to build ships, the odds were stacked heavily against it. At the same time, by contrast, the small Union navy was fully operational and was supported by the industrial power of the North. Despite these unpromising circumstances, the Confederate Navy was associated with the production and use of the latest weapons technology, including water mines, submarines and armored ships. One of these latter vessels, the *Virginia*, was used, on March 8, 1862, to break through the Union blockade at Newport News and sink two enemy warships. The next day she fought the Union

IRONCLAD *MONITOR* to a draw at the Battle of HAMPTON ROADS; it was the first occasion on which two ironclads had fought.

The Confederates also destroyed 37 Union ships with various types of water mine, which they deployed extensively. Their fleet of cruisers made an impact as well; for example, the *ALABAMA,* which sought out enemy merchant ships around the globe. However, the Confederate Navy enjoyed few other successes as it faced an increasingly effective BLOCKADE and a series of combined operations in which the Union navy worked in close cooperation with the army. Naval support was critical in securing Union control of the Mississippi and Tennessee rivers. The Confederate failure at the Battle of MOBILE BAY, August 1864, deprived blockade runners of one of their few remaining safe harbors. At the end of the war the Confederate Navy ceased to exist and its assets were transferred to the Union navy.

Tony Gibbons, *Warships and Naval Battles of the U.S. Civil War*, London, 1989.

Conflans, Hubert de Brienne, Comte de
1690–1777

French naval commander whose long and meritorious career ended in defeat at the Battle of QUIBERON BAY, November 20, 1759, during the SEVEN YEARS' WAR, 1756–63. Conflans joined the navy at the turn of the century and had a particularly distinguished record during the War of the AUSTRIAN SUCCESSION, 1740–48. By the time of the Seven Years' War, he was a marshal of France with over 50 years of naval service behind him. At this point he became vice admiral in command of the BREST fleet, which, in 1759, was earmarked to escort an invasion force across the English Channel. However, the fear of a French invasion of England led the English to maintain a close BLOCK-ADE against the French fleet at Brest.

The Royal Navy's Western Squadron, commanded by Admiral Sir Edward HAWKE, had remained on station during the summer and autumn but, on November 9, poor weather had forced him to shelter in Torbay. By the time Hawke returned to Brest some five days later, he found that Conflans's frigates had already escaped. Hawke pursued Conflans toward Vannes and attacked him in the confined conditions of Quiberon Bay, which the French had wrongly believed offered them some protection. During a long and muddled fight, the French lost seven ships of the line and sustained some 2,500 casualties. English losses were light. This major English victory ended French invasion plans and significantly weakened their naval power during the remainder of the Seven Years' War; it also marked the end of Conflans's long naval career.

Congress, U.S.S.

One of the victims of the Confederate IRONCLAD *Merrimack* during the AMERICAN CIVIL WAR, 1861–65, the *Congress* was a sailing frigate that had been launched in 1841. This Union warship was no match for her heavily armed and well-protected opponent. On March 8, 1862, the *Congress* and the *Cumberland* were blockading the estuaries of the York and James rivers in Virginia when they were attacked. The *Merrimack* first rammed the *Cumberland* and sank her. The *Merrimack* then attacked the *Congress*, firing cannonballs into her at a range of 200 yards (183 m) until the Union frigate caught fire and sank. Only hours later, on March 9, the *Merrimack*'s famous encounter with the *MONITOR* began in Hampton Roads.

An earlier *Congress*, authorized in 1794, was one of the original six frigates that formed the new UNITED STATES NAVY.

Conqueror, H.M.S.

A British hunter-killer nuclear submarine of 4,900 tons. During the FALKLANDS WAR, April–May 1982, H.M.S. *Conqueror* served with other British nuclear submarines in the South Atlantic—but none could match the high public profile she achieved as a result of a highly controversial action against the Argentine navy. On May 2, acting on specific instructions from the Ministry of Defence, the *Conqueror* fired two of her wire-guided Tigerfish torpedoes at the Argentine cruiser *GENERAL BELGRANO*, even though the *Belgrano* was some 36 (58 km) miles outside the 200-mile (322-km) exclusion zone imposed by the British. The Argentine vessel, which had a displacement of 13,645 tons—the largest warship lost in action since WORLD WAR II—sank with the loss of 368 lives.

Constellation, U.S.S.

The UNITED STATES NAVY's longest-serving ship, the *Constellation* was commissioned in 1798. She was one of the six frigates that formed the original nucleus of the new naval service. Her name was derived from the "new constellation of stars" that appeared on the stars and stripes, the national flag of the United States of America. Commanded by Thomas TRUXTON, the new frigate was soon in action during the QUASI-WAR, 1798–1800, with France, capturing an enemy ship in February 1799 and defeating another a year later.

The *Constellation* was rebuilt several times during her long career, which encompassed the AMERICAN CIVIL WAR, 1861–65, when she operated against Confederate commerce raiders in the Mediterranean, and a period as a training ship. During WORLD WAR II, 1939–45, she was recommissioned and served as a flagship of the U.S. Atlantic Fleet. Eventually the *Constellation* was returned to Baltimore, where she was originally built, for permanent preservation as a National Historic Landmark.

Constitution, U.S.S.

One of the original six frigates of the UNITED STATES NAVY, the *Constitution* was launched in 1797. During the WAR OF 1812 she was nicknamed "Old Ironsides" because of her apparent indestructibility in the face of enemy fire. The *Constitution* had a displacement of 2,200 tons and was armed with up to 55 guns. During her long career she also fought against France in 1798 and against the Barbary pirates of Tripoli between 1801 and 1805.

It was, however, during the War of 1812, when the Americans were heavily outnumbered by the ROYAL NAVY, that the *Constitution* established her fame, defeating the British on three separate occasions. In the first major engagement of the war, the *Constitution*, under the command of Isaac HULL, forced the surrender of the British frigate *Guerriere* on August 19, 1812, after a half-hour action off Nova Scotia. Under William BAINBRIDGE's command she defeated the British frigate *Java* off the coast of Brazil in December 1812. Finally, on February 20, 1815, she captured the British frigate *Cyane* and the sloop *Levant* in a four-hour battle.

After the war she was retained as a naval training ship for many years. Eventually she returned to Boston, where she had been built. Generally accepted as the most famous ship in American naval history, the *Constitution* has been on permanent exhibition there since 1934.

Convoy

A group of ships traveling together in order to provide mutual protection and ensure that the greatest number possible reach their destination safely. The extreme vulnerability of merchant ships to attack in time of war meant that they often traveled in convoy under the protection of one or more naval vessels. An established practice since ancient times, the convoy has been an important feature of naval warfare in the age of the sailing navies and beyond. A notable early example of a convoy was the SPANISH ARMADA, 1588, when 37 warships escorted 93 transports through the English Channel.

During the AMERICAN WAR OF INDEPENDENCE, 1775–83, and FRENCH REVOLUTIONARY AND NAPOLEONIC WARS, 1792–1815, the principal combatants were forced to introduce well-organized convoy systems to protect their merchant fleets from ever-rising losses. Together with the ARMED MERCHANT CRUISER, the unrestricted SUBMARINE warfare of the two world wars presented major new dangers to merchant shipping. Initially, the combatants were ill-

The U.S.S. *Constitution*, preserved at Boston, is a famous American warship that fought the British in the War of 1812 *(Copyright © National Maritime Museum, Greenwich, London)*

prepared for this challenge. When the steam IRONCLAD replaced the sailing warship, the lessons of naval history were cast aside and the convoy concept was neglected. Therefore, during WORLD WAR I, 1914–18, it was not surprising that the British were slow to react even though, by the beginning of 1917, shipping losses were reaching unsustainable levels. When the Admiralty's opposition to the convoy system was eventually overcome, its introduction in June 1917 had an immediate benefit in cutting shipping losses. When many merchantmen traveled in a few large groups rather than individually, they were much more difficult to detect. Surface attacks became much more problematic because of the presence of naval escorts, and enemy submarines were forced to strike with torpedoes when submerged.

In WORLD WAR II, 1939–45, the balance of advantage between the convoy system and its attackers oscillated. Learning from the errors of World War I, the Allies introduced the convoy system without delay at the beginning of the war. Notable examples include the Atlantic, MALTA and ARCTIC CONVOYS. At first, convoys suffered from a lack of prewar preparation and a shortage of escort vessels. At the same time, however, the enemy's offensive techniques were relatively undeveloped and, initially, its submarine force was small. This changed rapidly as the German fleet grew in size and U-BOATS were increasingly deployed in groups—known as WOLF PACKS—working in cooperation with long-range aircraft. These tactics resulted in mounting losses for Allied merchant ships, and it was not until 1943 that effective countermeasures—including RADAR, improved air support and faster escorts—began to be introduced. Meanwhile, in the Pacific, the Japanese failure to invest in such techniques resulted in heavy Japanese merchant shipping losses.

Since World War II, the balance of advantage seems to have moved against the convoy, which is now vulnerable to satellite detection as well as to high-performance nuclear submarines and torpedo systems. See also Battle of the ATLANTIC, 1914–18, 1939–45.

J. Winton, *Convoy: Defence of Sea Trade, 1890–1990*, London, 1983.

Convoy PQ-17

One of the Allied Arctic convoys that transported supplies to the Soviet Union during WORLD WAR II, 1939–

45, PQ-17 left Iceland on June 27, 1942, bound for Archangel. It consisted of 34 Allied merchantmen accompanied by Royal Navy vessels that provided a close escort and a covering force. The close escort, headed by Commander J. E. Broome, consisted of six destroyers, four corvettes and two antiaircraft ships. The covering force consisted of four cruisers and three destroyers. Additional support was provided by the British Home Fleet under the command of Admiral Sir John TOVEY.

The convoy was first detected by German reconnaissance aircraft on July 1 as it passed Jan Mayen Island, to the north-east of Iceland. Within 24 hours a German force had left the Norwegian coast to intercept the convoy. It initially consisted of the battleship TIRPITZ, two pocket-battleships—the ADMIRAL SCHEER and the Lützow—a cruiser, the Admiral Hipper, and accompanying destroyers. However, the Lüzow and three destroyers ran aground as they were leaving their base and were unable to participate in the operation. The German force moved cautiously in view of Hitler's instruction that it should not proceed if any British aircraft carriers were within range. On July 4 the German ships dropped anchor at Alten Fjord.

The British were aware of the German movement. In London, Sir Dudley POUND, the First Sea Lord, decided to withdraw the cruisers protecting the convoy, and he ordered the merchantmen to disperse. They were to proceed independently to the Soviet Union. The reason for this controversial decision was the fact that the close escort and covering force would have been no match for the powerful enemy naval units; moreover, the Home Fleet was too far away to intervene in time. Whatever the reasons, the merchantmen suffered severely. The Germans in Alten Fjord weighted anchor on July 5, but their role was already redundant: 23 merchant ships were to be sunk by German U-boats or aircraft; only 11 survived to reach the ports of the northern Soviet Union.

David Irving, *The Destruction of Convoy PQ17*, London, 1980.

Conyngham, Gustavus
c. 1744–1819

*A*merican naval officer, born in County Donegal, Ireland, whose early career at sea was spent in the merchant service. When his civilian sea career was disrupted by British action during the AMERICAN WAR OF INDEPENDENCE, 1775–83, Conyngham decided to volunteer for active naval service. In 1777 he was appointed to the command of the American lugger *Surprise* and quickly seized two British merchant ships. As commander of the *Revenge* he secured a great many more successes often in waters close to the English mainland and, as a result, became known as "*la terreur des anglais*"—the terror of the English.

Conyngham later transferred his activities to the West Indies, taking as many as 60 prizes during an 18-month cruise before returning to Philadelphia in February 1779. During a second voyage, however, the *Revenge* was captured and its crew imprisoned in England. Conyngham was subject to harsh treatment during his captivity but managed to escape on his third attempt. On the homeward journey his ship was captured by the British and he was returned to the same prison from which he had escaped. He was released too late for him to play any further part in the war.

Cook, James
1728–79

*E*nglish naval officer and explorer, born in Marton, Cleveland, Yorkshire, the son of a farm laborer, who made three voyages of exploration in the South Pacific and the coastal waters of North America. In 1755, following a three-year period in the merchant service, Cook enlisted in the Royal Navy and advanced rapidly, being appointed master in 1759. From 1756 to 1767 he was involved in charting the coastal waters off Newfoundland, Nova

James Cook, British explorer of the Pacific, made the first circumnavigation of the globe in an easterly direction
(Copyright © National Maritime Museum, Greenwich, London)

Scotia, and the St. Lawrence River, establishing his reputation as a navigator and surveyor.

In 1768 Cook was appointed to the command of the ENDEAVOUR and left on his first major voyage of exploration. Traveling across the Pacific, he stopped at the newly discovered island of Tahiti, where an expedition to observe the transit of Venus was to be based. He then continued to New Zealand in search of the southern continent of Terra Australis Incognita, centered on the South Pole, which was then generally believed to exist. He established that New Zealand was not linked to a southern continent and also accurately charted some 2,400 miles (3,860 km) of coastline for the first time. In 1770 he discovered the eastern coast of Australia and claimed it for England; he also established that it was an island continent. In 1771 Cook returned home and was promoted to the rank of commander.

A year later he set out in command of a second great expedition in the RESOLUTION and the ADVENTURE with the aim of continuing the search for Terra Australis Incognita. Cook reached the edge of the Antarctic ice block and, in January 1773, he made the first recorded crossing of the Antarctic Circle. In 1773–74, during extensive travels in the Pacific, he discovered many new islands, including the group that was subsequently named after him. He also discovered that there was no missing continent to be found there. Remarkably, there was only one death during the expedition. This was attributable to Cook's concern for a balanced diet, which reduced the incidence of scurvy. Cook returned to England in July 1775 and was promoted to the rank of post captain.

A year later he left on a new expedition. His aim was to determine whether the Atlantic and Pacific oceans were linked by a Northwest passage. The expedition included a visit to the mid-Pacific, where he discovered a group of islands—then called the Sandwich Islands, later to be named the Hawaiian Islands. Forced by ice to abandon his search for the Northwest Passage, he returned to the Sandwich Islands, where he was killed by natives in a dispute over a stolen boat. Cook was one of England's greatest seamen and navigators. His circumnavigations of the globe added substantially to knowledge about the southern hemisphere.

Richard Hough, *Captain James Cook*, London, 1994.

Coontz, Robert Edward
1864–1935

American naval officer, born in Hannibal, Missouri on June 11, 1864. Coontz was trained at the United States Naval Academy. During the SPANISH-AMERICAN WAR of 1898 he was on board the *Charleston* when it captured the small but strategically located Spanish-held Pacific island of Guam. He served as the executive officer on the

Nebraska with the GREAT WHITE FLEET during its circumnavigation of the globe to demonstrate American power. During the 1914 hostilities between the United States and Mexico, he commanded the *Georgia* off Vera Cruz, and in WORLD WAR I, 1914–18, he served as acting chief of naval operations while Admiral William S. BENSON was absent in Europe. Following a period in command of a division of the Atlantic Fleet, Coontz held the navy's top professional post as chief of naval operations from 1919 to 1921, playing a key role in the naval disarmament talks and negotiations that followed World War I. Returning to sea as commander in chief of the newly created U.S. Fleet, he retired in 1928 and died in Bremerton, Washington in 1935, with a reputation as a sound if not inspiring naval leader and an effective naval administrator.

Lawrence H. Douglas, "Robert Edward Coontz," in *The Chiefs of Naval Operations*, ed. Robert W. Love, Jr., Annapolis, 1980.

Copenhagen, First Battle of
April 2, 1801

In December 1800 Russia, Sweden, Denmark and Prussia created the alliance of the Armed Neutrality of the North in response to Britain's insistence on the right to search neutral shipping during the FRENCH REVOLUTIONARY AND NAPOLEONIC WARS, 1792–1815. The agreement led to a Danish embargo on British vessels, the closure of the Elbe River and the disruption of trade between England and northern Germany. The British dispatched a powerful naval force to Copenhagen in support of its diplomatic efforts to dissolve the Armed Neutrality of the North. Commanded by Admiral Sir Hyde PARKER, it consisted of 18 ships of the line and 35 other warships. With Admiral Lord NELSON as second in command, the fleet left Yarmouth Roads on March 12 and reached Copenhagen 18 days later.

The city was well protected, with a fortress and four ships of the line guarding the entrance to the harbor. Floating batteries and 18 warships plus other supporting vessels protected the city's eastern shore. Lord Nelson launched an attack on these defenses on April 2 after securing Parker's agreement to early action. He deployed 12 ships of the line and seven lesser warships as well as five bomb-vessels and two fireships. Leaving his anchorage in the outer channel, some two miles from the Danish fleet, Nelson planned to strike at the heart of the enemy defenses. He would move around Middle Ground Shoal and pass into King's Deep Channel, where a Danish flotilla, including warships, floating batteries and armed hulks, was anchored. Nelson's ships would take up position opposite them.

The operation did not go entirely according to plan. Shortly after it began, at 10:00 A.M., Nelson lost three ships of the line: Two were stranded in the Middle Ground

Shoal and the third was unable to make progress because of strong currents. The rest of Nelson's force moved into position, and there was an intense exchange of fire. The Danish flagship *Dannebrog* was an early victim, but otherwise the British made little headway at first. As the battle continued, Parker, alarmed by the strength of the Danish resistance, signaled Nelson to discontinue the engagement. In a notable response, Nelson disregarded the order: He put a spyglass to his blind eye and said he could not see his commander in chief's signal. Nelson's judgment proved correct. Danish resistance slowly eased and by 2:30 P.M. it was nonexistent.

Nelson, who soon replaced Parker as commander in chief, hoped to proceed east to Reval (Tallinn) to destroy the Russian fleet, but an armistice interrupted plans for further operations. On June 17 a convention was signed that brought hostilities to a close.

D. Pope, *The Great Gamble: Nelson at Copenhagen,* London, 1972.

Copenhagen, Second Battle of

September 2–5, 1807

*I*n 1807, during the Napoleonic Wars, 1803–15, Britain became increasingly concerned that Denmark was about to join the Franco-Russian alliance and would, as a result, pose a serious threat to its trading interests in the Baltic. Although not officially at war with Denmark at this time, in August 1807 Britain sent a combined naval and military expedition under Admiral James GAMBIER and General Lord Cathcart, bound for Copenhagen. When they arrived, a landing force under the command of Arthur Wellesley, Duke of Wellington, was disembarked and Copenhagen was besieged. A Danish counterattack was beaten back. When the Danish authorities refused to negotiate, the city was heavily bombarded from the land and sea for four days (September 2–5). The city suffered severe fire damage, and the Danes were forced to agree to an armistice. The major units of the Danish navy were surrendered to the British, and the Danish ships were taken to Britain with the expeditionary force. British ground troops were withdrawn from Denmark a month later, and the successful British operation was concluded.

Coral Sea, Battle of the

May 7–8, 1942

A key battle between Japanese and American naval forces in the Pacific during WORLD WAR II, 1939–45, in which Japan's drive south was halted; never again would Japan progress as far as the Coral Sea. The battle was occasioned by a Japanese offensive, code-named Mo, that was designed to capture three targets in the Coral Sea: the Australian base at Port Moresby, New Guinea; the Louisiade Islands; and the port of Tulagi, Solomon Islands. A successful operation would allow the Japanese to launch air attacks on Australia and isolate it from the United States. The Japanese fleet, commanded by Vice Admiral Shigeyoshi Inouye, included heavy cruisers, destroyers and an invasion flotilla. Rear Admiral Takeo Takagi's carrier strike group, which consisted of three AIRCRAFT CARRIERS and 125 aircraft, was to cover the entire operation.

American intelligence soon learned of the Japanese plans, and an Allied task force under Admiral Frank FLETCHER was quickly assembled. It consisted of Task Force 11, Task Force 17 and Task Force 44 (which was under British command) and included the carriers *YORKTOWN* and *LEXINGTON.* A group of Australian and American cruisers under Rear Admiral Sir John Crace also took part. On May 2 the Japanese landed on Tulagi; when Fletcher learned of this the next day, he went to intercept, causing some damage to the Japanese before rejoining the Allied fleet to the south. This fleet was to oppose the second Japanese invasion force, which was heading for the Louisiades en route to Port Moresby. On May 7 American carrier planes located this force and sank the Japanese light carrier *Shoho.* Without full air cover, Admiral Inouye was unwilling to risk his invasion fleet and ordered it to return to Rabaul.

It was not until May 8, after a two-day search, that the opposing carrier forces established their respective positions. The battle that followed—the first naval engagement in which the opposing warships remained out of sight—was conducted exclusively by carrier aircraft. In two attacks the Americans lost 33 aircraft but seriously damaged the Japanese carrier *Shokaku.* The Americans suffered heavier losses during a counterattack by 70 Japanese planes in which the carrier *Lexington* was lost and the *Yorktown* was damaged. Although the Americans suffered the major loss of a fleet carrier, the Battle of the Coral Sea represented a strategic victory for the U.S. Navy. The Port Moresby invasion force had to withdraw and Australia remained beyond the reach of Japanese bombers. The Japanese navy would never enter the Coral Sea again. The damage to Japanese ships and the heavy loss of naval aircraft weakened their position at the decisive Battle of MIDWAY, which occurred a month later.

Edwin P. Hoyt, *Blue Skies and Blood: The Battle of the Coral Sea,* New York, 1976.

Cornwallis, Sir William

1744–1819

*B*ritish admiral (brother of Charles, Earl Cornwallis, 1738–1805, commander of British land forces in the American War of Independence and later Governor General of India) who played a major role in frustrating French plans for the invasion of England during the Napoleonic Wars, 1803–15. Following his appointment to the command of the Channel Fleet in 1801, he imposed a long and successful BLOCKADE of BREST, which trapped a large and powerful French squadron.

A close friend of Lord NELSON, Cornwallis also had served in the AMERICAN WAR OF INDEPENDENCE, 1775–83, and as naval commander in chief in the East Indies. He was known as "Billy Blue" because of his habit of flying the Blue Peter flag (a blue flag with a white square in the center, normally hoisted as a signal that a ship was ready to sail). Cornwallis retired from the Royal Navy in 1806 after a career of solid achievement rather than spectacular success.

G. Cornwallis-West, *The Life and Letters of Admiral Cornwallis*, London, 1927.

Coronel, Battle of
November 1, 1914

When Japan entered WORLD WAR I, 1914–18, on the Allied side in August 1914, the East Asiatic Squadron of the GERMAN NAVY moved away from Far Eastern waters. Under the command of Vice Admiral Maximilian von SPEE, the squadron crossed the Pacific to the west coast of South America, where its two armored cruisers (the *SCHARNHORST* and the *GNEISENAU*) and three light cruisers (the *DRESDEN, Leipzig* and the *Nürnberg*) could operate against British shipping. Von Spee was at Valparaiso, Chile when, on October 31, he heard that the *Glasgow*, a British warship, was at Coronel, a port some 200 miles (322 km) to the south.

The Royal Navy had in fact already been alerted to Spee's journey across the Pacific, and Rear Admiral Sir Christopher CRADOCK, in command of the South American station, was ordered to respond. Based in the Falkland Islands, his squadron consisted of the *Good Hope*, an armored cruiser that served as flagship, the cruiser *Monmouth*, the light cruiser *Glasgow*, and the *Otranto*, an ARMED MERCHANT CRUISER. Because the British force was greatly inferior to von Spee's, a pre-dreadnought battleship, the *CANOPUS,* had been dispatched from England to strengthen it. Unfortunately, the *Canopus* had not arrived by the time Cradock left the Falklands on October 23.

The Germans moved south from Valparaiso to attack the *Glasgow* as the British squadron moved north. On November 1, at about 5 P.M., the two forces met some 50 miles (80 km) off Coronel. Cradock was outnumbered and outgunned, but with the memory of the escape of the *GOEBEN* to neutral Turkey and of Rear Admiral Sir Ernest TROUBRIDGE's failure to engage the enemy fresh in his mind, he decided to fight even though he had the opportunity to escape south. Spee's ships used their superior speed

to their own advantage. With the British ships silhouetted against the setting sun, von Spee attacked them at long range with superior guns. Rough seas prevented the British ships from using their secondary guns. The *Good Hope*, which was hit many times, blew up and sank at about 8 P.M. Soon after the *Monmouth* went down, but the *Glasgow* and the *Otranto* managed to escape. There were no survivors from either of the lost British ships, and some 1,600 British seamen, including Cradock, were killed. The German squadron escaped with virtually no damage and only two casualties.

This major British defeat must be attributed largely to Cradock's failure to act in concert with the *Canopus*, in disregard of specific orders to the contrary issued by the ADMIRALTY. However, the failure at Coronel was redeemed only five weeks later at the Battle of the FALKLAND ISLANDS, when von Spee's force was destroyed.

G. Bennett, *Coronel and the Falklands*, London, 1962.

Corsair

Term used to refer to the privateers who operated from the Barbary coast of North Africa from the early 16th century until the year 1830. The rulers of these North Africa satellites—Algiers, Morocco, Tripoli and Tunis—which formed part of the Ottoman empire, depended for their existence on the prizes captured by the corsairs, who preyed on merchant shipping in the Mediterranean and sometimes farther afield. Like those of the PRIVATEER, the corsair's activities were normally licensed by the government—in this case, the Turkish administration at Constantinople. The word "corsair" also was used to describe the ships in which these men operated.

The navies of countries affected by corsairs tried to bring their activities to a halt, but efforts proved largely ineffectual until an Anglo-Dutch force intervened decisively in 1816. Operations had intensified in the early years of the 19th century. An American war against Tripoli, 1801–5, included an ineffective two-year BLOCKADE of Tripoli in which the frigate U.S.S. *Philadelphia* was lost. It was followed by another, more significant American operation against Algiers in 1815. Commanded by Stephen DECATUR, the expedition was successful in securing guarantees on the cessation of corsair activity. Following corsair attacks on British shipping, a squadron of the Royal Navy, commanded by Admiral Edward PELLEW, First Viscount Exmouth, successfully bombarded Algiers in 1816. Assisted by a Dutch squadron, he succeeded in destroying the Algerian fleet. This largely ended corsair raids, although some residual activity continued until the French blockaded and then finally occupied Algiers in 1830.

Geoffrey Fisher, *Barbary Legend: War, Trade and Piracy in North Africa, 1415–1830*, Oxford, 1957.

Corvette

A three-masted full-rigged warship of up to 600 tons that was smaller than a frigate. Fast and maneuverable, the corvette first appeared during the 17th century. Typically less than 150 feet (45.72 m) in length, it was operated by up to 130 men and normally was armed with 18 to 24 cannon mounted on the upper flush deck that was a standard feature of this design. When more guns were carried, additional short upper decks were fitted. Like frigates, corvettes were used to perform miscellaneous tasks: scouting for the fleet, carrying dispatches and operating as "repeating" ships (to relay a commander's signal).

Corvette is a French word, and the ship was used extensively by the FRENCH NAVY between the 17th and 19th centuries. In the UNITED STATES NAVY this design was known as the sloop of war. Equivalent English ships were the sloop and the sixth-rate post ship (see RATING OF SHIPS), although the Royal Navy eventually adopted the term "corvette." The name also was used briefly in England in the 1870s in reference to the steam warship that was to become known as the cruiser. Generally, however, the name "corvette" disappeared as the age of the sailing navy came to an end.

The term was revived during WORLD WAR II (1939–45) in 1940, to describe a series of small antisubmarine escort vessels, armed with DEPTH CHARGES and one or more 4-inch (10-cm) guns in service with the Royal Navy. Based on the design of a whaling ship, more than 150 were built during the war. They played a key role in the fight against the Germans during the Battle of the ATLANTIC, 1939–45. The name "corvette" is still in use today in some navies to describe small surface warships next in size after the frigate. They are used for antisubmarine warfare and are often equipped with guided missiles.

Cossack, H.M.S.

A British DESTROYER of WORLD WAR II, 1939–45, that intercepted the German tanker ALTMARK in Norwegian territorial waters and secured the release of the 299 British prisoners on board. She was a Tribal-class destroyer of 1,870 tons, launched in 1938; she was armed with eight 4.7-inch (12-cm) guns and four torpedo tubes. Operated by a crew of 186, she was 362 feet 9 inches (110.57 m) in length and had a beam of 35 feet 9 inches (10.9 m). In February 1940, under the command of Captain (later Admiral Sir) Philip VIAN, she entered a remote Norwegian fjord in pursuit of the ship that had supplied the ill-fated German pocket-battleship ADMIRAL GRAF SPEE, which had been scuttled after the Battle of the RIVER PLATE, December 13, 1914. The *Altmark* was returning to Germany with the British prisoners seized during the *Graf Spee*'s brief cruise. In the fjord where the German tanker was shelter-

ing, the *Cossack*'s crew boarded her and, after fierce hand-to-hand fighting, seized the ship. The British captives were freed and the *Cossack* quickly left Norway's neutral waters. She was to return to Norway in April in support of the Allied landings and was damaged during the second Battle of NARVIK. The *Cossack*'s end came in October 1943 when she was sunk by a U-BOAT off Gibraltar.

Courageous, H.M.S.

L aunched in 1916, the *Courageous* and her sister ship, the *Glorious*, were British light BATTLE CRUISERS of WORLD WAR I, 1914–18, that were deemed "surplus to requirements" in the postwar period. To use its allocations under the terms of the Washington Naval Treaty, 1922 (see WASHINGTON NAVAL CONFERENCE, 1921–22), the Royal Navy decided to convert them for use as AIRCRAFT CARRIERS; conversion work began in 1924. The *Courageous* was completed in 1928 and her sister ship followed two years later. Equipped with an island superstructure, the *Courageous* had a displacement of 22,500 tons, an overall length of 786 feet 3 inches (240 m) and a beam of 90 feet 6 inches (28 m). She was capable of a maximum speed of 30.5 knots. Armament included 16 4.7-inch (12-cm) antiaircraft guns, and each vessel could carry 48 aircraft. The *Courageous*'s main weakness was her lack of armor protection. She was notable as the first major British naval loss of WORLD WAR II, 1939–45, when she was sunk by *U-29* west of Ireland on September 17, 1939. The *Glorious* also met disaster at the hands of the Germans. Returning from Norway with Royal Air Force aircraft and pilots, she was intercepted by the battle cruisers SCHARNHORST and GNEISENAU on June 8, 1940. Together with two accompanying destroyers (the *Ardent* and the *Acasta*), she was sunk by heavy German gunfire.

Courbet

T he French navy's first dreadnought-type BATTLESHIPS, the Courbet class was not completed until 1913–14, by which time it already had been superseded by more advanced British and American designs. The main armament consisted of 12 12-inch (30-cm) guns rather than the larger-caliber weapons common elsewhere. Powerful secondary weapons were mounted in wing turrets that were not well positioned. Although armor protection was improved in comparison with previous French battleships, it was thinner than that provided in contemporary Allied warships. The *Courbet* and her three sister ships—*France*, *Jean Bart* and *Paris*—served in the Mediterranean throughout the war. The *Courbet* was the flagship of the French Mediterranean fleet in 1914–15, as was the *France* in 1916.

Court-martial

Naval personnel accused of a wide range of offenses, from relatively trivial cases of petty theft to misconduct and cowardice in action, are subject to trial by court-martial. In England the right to constitute a court-martial, as well as its powers and composition, was first laid down by Act of Parliament in 1661. The legislature also determined the punishments that a court-martial was empowered to use and specified whether they should be varied in wartime. During the age of sail, the range of punishments available in the Royal Navy included death, imprisonment, a specified number of lashes, dismissal from the service or a reprimand. The wide range of offenses tried included theft, neglect of duty, misconduct, mutiny and desertion. A court-martial consisted of up to five officers who sat without a jury.

A court-martial always was held when an English warship was lost even if there was no suggestion that the commanding officer was blameworthy; in this context, it was acting as a court of inquiry rather than trying a specific offense. Among the most serious of wartime offenses was a failure to engage the enemy to the fullest extent. In a notable English court-martial Admiral John BYNG was found guilty of failing to save Minorca from the French in 1756 and was sentenced to death. The government could have changed the sentence passed in this case (or in any other), but, for political reasons, it decided not to do so.

Coventry, H.M.S.

A British Type-42 guided missile destroyer of 4,250 tons, completed in 1972. She was 136 feet 8 inches (125 m) in length and was powered by gas turbines. Her armament consisted of one 115-mm gun (4.5-inch), a twin Sea Dart surface-to-air missile launcher, two 20-mm (10.79-inch) antiaircraft guns and antisubmarine torpedoes launched by helicopter. The *Coventry* served in the FALKLANDS WAR, April–June 1982. On May 25, 1982 she was sunk off West Falkland by four 1,000-pound (454-kg) bombs from an Argentine air force McDonnell-Douglas A-4 Skyhawk attack bomber, with the loss of 19 lives. Three weeks earlier another Type-42 destroyer, the *SHEFFIELD*, had been severely damaged by an EXOCET MISSILE and was later sunk with explosives.

Cowan, Sir Walter
1871–1956

British naval commander whose long service at sea and on land began in the closing years of Queen Victoria's reign. He served in various capacities in the GRAND FLEET during WORLD WAR I, 1914–18, and was promoted to the rank of rear admiral in 1918. Cowan continued on active service after the Armistice, November 1918, because he was appointed to the command of the British naval forces sent to the Baltic to operate against the Bolsheviks during the Russian Civil War, 1918–22. Cowan's specific task was to act in support of the Baltic states of Estonia, Latvia and Lithuania. In this he achieved a large measure of success. In August 1919 his surprise attack on the Russian fleet at KRONSTADT using COASTAL MOTOR BOATS caused significant damage. Cowan retired from the Royal Navy in 1929 but sought to return to the sea on the outbreak of WORLD WAR II, 1939–45. Refused on the grounds of age, he was permitted to serve on land until the end of the war.

Crace, Rear Admiral Sir John
1887–1968

British naval commander who served with Australian naval forces for part of WORLD WAR II, 1939–45. He was appointed to command a squadron of cruisers that operated in support of the United States Navy in the Pacific. As commander of Task Force 44, which consisted of three cruisers and one destroyer, he served in the Battle of the CORAL SEA, May 1942, operating off the southeastern corner of New Guinea. He had a narrow escape when he came under heavy attack by Japanese aircraft. Crace returned to England shortly after this battle, retiring from active service to become superintendent of the naval dockyard at Chatham.

Cradock, Sir Christopher
1862–1914

An early British casualty of WORLD WAR I, 1914–18, Sir Christopher Cradock joined the ROYAL NAVY in 1875 and gained much of his early experience in a succession of colonial operations. He rose steadily and in 1910 was appointed to flag rank after 35 years in the service. Just before World War I he was appointed commander of the North America and West Indies station. His principal wartime responsibility in this command was the protection of the main British trade routes in the region. In August 1914 he forced the German cruisers DRESDEN and *Karlsruhe* away from his area and into the South Atlantic, having only just failed to destroy the latter.

Cradock himself was then ordered south, with instructions to search for Vice Admiral Maximilian von SPEE's East Asiatic Squadron, which was expected to appear soon off the west coast of South America. Although promised reinforcements in the shape of the battleship *CANOPUS* had not yet arrived, Cradock decided to engage Spee's vastly superior forces. Impetuous by nature, Cradock was determined to avoid Rear Admiral Sir Ernest TROUBRIDGE's mistakes in the Mediterranean when two German cruisers had escaped to Turkey because of the Royal Navy's inaction. His ships uncountered the German force off CORONEL, some 200 miles (322 km) south of Valparaiso.

The battle began in the afternoon of November 1. Within an hour, two British cruisers, including the *Good Hope*, Cradock's flagship, had been sunk. Cradock, who went down with his ship, received the public blame for the disaster, which was attributed to his recklessness in engaging a much stronger opponent.

G. Bennett, *Coronel and the Falklands*, London, 1962.

Crimean War
1853–56

A costly war on land and at sea, 1853–56, with British, French and Turkish forces opposing the Russians. The main cause of the Crimean War was the growth of Russian influence in the Balkans and its wish to control access to the Black Sea by occupying Constantinople. The failure of negotiations with the Ottoman empire led to the Russian occupation of two Ottoman provinces. The Ottoman sultan, who was expecting English and French support, responded by declaring war on Russia on October 4, 1853. On November 30 the Russian fleet attacked and destroyed the Turkish fleet at the Battle of SINOPE in the Black Sea.

In response, a combined Anglo-French fleet arrived in the area in January 1854, but it was not until March that England and France formally declared war on Russia. Besides refusing to withdraw from occupied Ottoman territory, Russia had invaded Bulgaria with the aim of attacking the Turks. The Allied naval forces were sent into action. Odessa was bombarded and Varna, another Black Sea port, was occupied. Under pressure from Austria, Russia soon decided to withdraw from Bulgaria and sue for peace. By this time, however, it was too late: The allies had decided to punish Russia and destroy its naval power in the area. Their target was the port of Sebastopol in the Crimea, which was the headquarters of the Black Sea Fleet.

An allied expeditionary force, consisting of British, French, Turkish and Sardinian troops, was landed in September and began a year-long campaign to capture Sebastopol. The warfare was marked by general incompetence on both sides. Sebastopol eventually fell on September 9, 1855 following a siege in which naval bombardments had played a significant part. When the Austrians threatened to intervene on the allied side, the Russians were forced to agree to peace negotiations. The result was the Peace of Paris, March 1856, in which Russia was forced to make major territorial and other concessions, including a commitment not to maintain a naval force in the Black Sea.

Chronological List of Naval Events

1853

October 4	Turkey declares war on Russia
November 30	Action at Sinope: Russians defeat Turkish squadron

1854

January 3	Anglo-French fleet arrives in the Black Sea
March 28	British and French declare war on Russia
August 16	French capture Bomarsund, a Russian fortress on the Aland Islands in the Baltic
September 13	Allied armies start landing in the Crimea, a fleet of 150 warships having conveyed them from Varna
October 17	Naval bombardment of Sebastopol begins

1855

August 9–11	Anglo-French fleet bombards the Baltic fortress of Sveaborg
September 9	Sebastopol falls to the allies: Russians scuttle their Black Sea Fleet prior to evacuation
October 16	Allied bombardment of Kinburn; ironclad warships are used in a fleet action for the first time

1856

March	Peace of Paris

Philip Warner, *The Crimean War: A Reappraisal*, London, 1972

Crossing the *T*

A naval warfare tactic that came into its own during the age of the sailing navies and was widely used during the FRENCH REVOLUTIONARY AND NAPOLEONIC WARS, 1792–1815, and the WAR OF 1812, 1812–15. It involved moving across a line of enemy ships at right angles to their line of advance, and normally conferred a clear advantage on the attacking fleet. (In contrast, earlier, when the GALLEY was the main naval unit, this tactic had favored the defense because the attacking ships exposed their most vulnerable point—their oars—when they crossed the *T*.) The sailing ships crossing the *T* were able to train their port or starboard guns on the enemy and fire a full BROADSIDE against it. The enemy's firepower was much more limited—only its bow guns could be used. The number of bow guns it could deploy depended on whether it was sailing in line-ahead or line-abreast formation, but its main preoccupation was to turn away from its opponent. This tactic did not disappear with the end of the sailing navies, although it became more difficult to employ when the enemy had the power to turn away quickly. This was the reaction of the German navy at the Battle of JUTLAND, 1916, but at the Battle of TSUSHIMA, 1905, the Japanese fleet had sufficient power to cross the Russian *T* before the Russians could respond.

Cruise Missile

A low-altitude guided "flying bomb" that is designed to escape detection by an enemy's air defence radar system. Ballistic missiles are also guided but have a high flight trajectory. Originating with the German V-I of WORLD WAR II, 1939–45, the cruise missile (or pilotless aircraft) was first developed for naval use by the postwar UNITED STATES NAVY. (See also GUIDED MISSILE). The performance of its Chance Vought Regulus missiles, 1953–58, which were designed to be fired from submarines and warships, was disappointing. Their guidance systems were inaccurate, while their size—57 feet 6 inches (18 m) in length—and flying altitude—60,000 feet (18,300 m)—made them vulnerable to attack. Attention turned to ballistic designs until technological changes improved the prospects of the cruise missile.

More recently developed terrain contour inertial guidance systems (TERCOMs) use a radar map stored in the missile's computer to compare it with the ground over which the weapon is passing. Any adjustments to the direction of travel can then be made. This system allows cruise missiles to fly at low altitudes and hit targets with great accuracy. The accurate use of this weapon from a moving ship at sea is more problematic, partly because its successful use depends on a precise starting point being set. Despite these constraints, the performance of the naval version of the United States Tomahawk cruise missile has been impressive.

During the GULF WAR, 1991, sea-launched Tomahawks achieved some significant successes against land targets in Iraq, including command centers and radar stations. Known as the BGM-109 Tomahawk Land Attack Missile, it can be used by both surface ships and submarines. It carries a 264-pound (119.7-kg) high-explosive warhead for 552 miles (888 km) at a speed of 548 mph (881 kph). Later versions can carry a 700-pound (318-kg) warhead for 1,000 miles (1,609 km). A second naval variant is the Tomahawk antiship missile, which is for use against surface ships. It has a range of 285 miles (459 km) and carries a 1,000-pound (454-kg) warhead. This variant does not require a ground-matching system because it operates only over the sea.

Cruiser

Originally defined as a general-purpose warship whose task was to cruise independent of the main fleet on patrol and scouting duties. Fast and maneuverable, cruisers were to report back to the fleet when the enemy had been sighted. In the days of sail they were large frigates whose primary role was to identify and report on the enemy. Following the introduction of the steam-powered, armor-protected warship in the mid-19th century, two principal types of cruiser were developed. The big armored cruiser, which was designed to form part of the battle fleet, had a displacement of up to 15,000 tons. Rendered obsolete by the development of the BATTLE CRUISER (itself originally described as a fast armored cruiser) in 1907, some were still in service during WORLD WAR I, 1914–18. Their ability to escort and assist battleships was limited by their relatively low speed, small guns and inadequate armor protection. Three British cruisers of this type were lost at the Battle of JUTLAND, 1916.

The second type—protected cruisers—had improved performance as a result of their reduced armor, which was confined to the steel decks covering the vital lower levels. At the beginning of the World War I these elderly ships were used to escort TROOPSHIPS and guard the world's trade routes. Supported by ARMED MERCHANT CRUISERS, their role declined as the activities of the German raiders lessened. The appearance of the battle cruiser did not, however, mean that there was no place for a standard cruiser. The new ships were far too costly to be produced in sufficient numbers to protect merchant shipping, while destroyers did not have adequate defensive firepower for scouting duties. New classes of light cruisers, which could attack enemy destroyers and operate for long distances, were already under construction by the principal naval powers at the beginning of World War I.

In the war's opening stages, the German navy used the detached light cruiser as a commerce raider; the well-publicized exploits of the EMDEN in the Indian Ocean were the most notable. However, their primary employment was in the war of attrition in the North Sea: at the Battle of HELIGOLAND, 1914, they played a critical role, while at Jutland and the DOGGER BANK, 1915, light cruisers made the initial contact between the opposing forces. Cruisers were also an important factor in two other major naval engagements of the war, CORONEL and the FALKLANDS. During the interwar period aircraft assumed some of the antireconnaissance duties of the cruiser which was now classified in two main types according to the size of the guns: The heavy cruiser was armed with eight-inch (20-cm) guns, while those of the light cruiser were no larger than six inches (15 cm). The British and American navies both produced an antiaircraft variant of the light cruiser. All types could normally carry seaplanes. During WORLD WAR II, 1939–45, the cruiser performed a variety of roles,

The 6-inch guns of a British World War II cruiser   *(Copyright © National Maritime Museum, Greenwich, London)*

including convoy support, the pursuit of commerce raiders and the provision of a defensive screen for larger warships.

The postwar role of the cruiser is less clear. In some respects, the cruiser has been displaced by the destroyer, which is far less costly to produce. However, armed with guided missiles and helicopters, cruisers have played a valuable role in supporting amphibious operations and in trade protection activity. The modern cruiser can attack aircraft, submarines and missiles as well as surface ships.

Peter C. Smith and John R. Dominy, *Cruisers in Action, 1939–45*, London, 1981; Gregory Haines, *Cruisers at War*, London, 1978.

Crutchley, Sir Victor
1893–1986

*B*ritish rear admiral who first gained distinction in WORLD WAR I, 1914–18, when he won the Victoria Cross for his part in the operation to obstruct Ostend with BLOCKSHIPS in 1918. At the beginning of WORLD WAR II, 1939–45, he served as captain of the battleship *WARSPITE* before moving to a shore command at Devonport barracks. In 1942 he was appointed to command the Australian naval squadron serving with the U.S. Pacific Fleet against the Japanese. In August, while stationed off Savo Island,

where he was responsible for the protection of Allied transports, Crutchley's force suffered a surprise Japanese attack. Later known as the Battle of the Five Sitting Ducks, the unequal battle resulted in the loss of five Allied warships. After he left the command of the Australian squadron in 1944, Crutchley served as flag officer at GIBRALTAR, 1945–47.

Cuban Missile Crisis
1962

*T*he prospect of nuclear war had never seemed closer than in the autumn of 1962 when the United States opposed the Soviet Union's plans to construct several missile sites on Cuba, bringing ballistic missiles with atomic warheads within easy range of virtually every American city. As a visible expression of American power in the region at the height of the COLD WAR, the United States Navy was to play an important role in deterring the Soviets from any precipitate action during the crisis. During the summer of 1962, Soviet technicians had arrived in Cuba to work on the missile project and, by mid-October, American U-2 spy planes had uncovered evidence of construction work. Within a few days the U.S. government announced publicly that the installation on Cuba of medium-range rockets, which had the capability to carry atomic warheads, posed a direct threat to America's security. President John F. Kennedy demanded the withdrawal of the missiles.

U.S. troops massed at various locations and statements were made that any rocket attack from Cuba would result in massive nuclear retaliation on the Soviet Union itself. On October 22 the U.S. Navy was ordered to impose a BLOCKADE of Cuba to prevent the arrival of further rocket equipment, as a convoy of 25 cargo ships was already on its way from the Soviet Union. The navy moved 183 warships (including eight aircraft carriers) into position as the first eight Soviet freighters (with accompanying submarines) approached the blockade line on October 24. The Soviet ships turned away when challenged, marking a turning point in the crisis. There had been a real possibility that these events would lead to a nuclear war, but the firm American response had persuaded Nikita Khrushchev, the Soviet leader, to give way and order the convoy to turn back. Further, in return for an American assurance that it would not invade Cuba, the Soviets agreed to dismantle the missile bases there under United Nations supervision and to ship them back to the Soviet Union. By November 20 this work had been completed and the U.S. naval blockade of Cuba was lifted, even though Fidel Castro, the Cuban leader, had refused the United Nations access to the missile sites.

Herbert S. Dinerstein, *The Making of a Missile Crisis: October 1962*, Baltimore, 1978.

Cuddalore, Battle of
April 29, 1758

An engagement between French and English forces in the Indian Ocean during the SEVEN YEARS' WAR, 1756–63. A French squadron, consisting of eight EAST INDIAMEN and a SHIP OF THE LINE, commanded by Admiral the Comte d'Aché, appeared on the Coromandel coast early in 1758. It operated from the French naval base at Pondicherry and posed a threat to Cuddalore, where the British East India Company operated a factory. In response, on April 17 a British squadron of seven ships of the line, commanded by Vice Admiral Sir George Pocock, left Madras for its home base of Cuddalore. At first, the squadron was unsuccessful in locating the French fleet, and the French ships were not sighted until the squadron reached Cuddalore on April 29.

The French had arrived off Cuddalore on April 27 and had forced two patrolling British frigates to withdraw to port. Two days later d'Aché dispatched two ships northward in search of Pocock's squadron, but soon after he gave the order the squadron appeared in the distance. The French had time to weigh anchor before the British

attacked, and were chased out to sea, where both sides formed into a line of battle. Both the British and French squadrons sustained damage during a fierce but inconclusive battle, which ended when the French withdrew north toward Pondicherry; the British squadron was unable to follow, and the battle came to an end.

Cuddalore, Battle of
June 20, 1783

The last in the series of five battles fought between English and French naval forces in the Indian Ocean during the AMERICAN WAR OF INDEPENDENCE, 1775–83. In 1783 the British launched a new counteroffensive against the French forces that had been in possession of Cuddalore on the Coromandel coast since early in the previous year. By June 1783 Admiral Edward HUGHES had deployed 16 ships of the line in support of the operation. As soon as Admiral Pierre de SUFFREN, who was based at Trincomalee, on the island of Ceylon, learned of the British operation, he sailed north with 15 ships of the line under his command.

As the French approached, Hughes weighed anchor and sought an opportunity to attack. At first Admiral Suffren eluded the British and anchored off Cuddalore. He managed to take on board some 1,200 men from the Cuddalore garrison to help his crews operate their guns. The two squadrons eventually came to battle in a three-hour engagement on June 20. Although neither side lost any ships, both sides suffered significant casualties. The British abandoned their BLOCKADE and withdrew to Madras the following day. Shortly afterward the opposing navies learned that the war had recently ended with the signing of the Treaty of Versailles, 1783.

Culverin

A long-barreled naval CANNON widely used in the 15th and 16th centuries. It had a small 5-inch (13-cm) caliber and a relatively long range of 1.25 miles (2 km), although its effective operating distance was probably no more than 350 yards (320 m). The culverin fired a 17-pound (7.7-kg) or 18-pound (8.1-kg) shot (compared with the 50-pound (23-kg) shot fired by a full-size cannon) and its barrel varied in length from 8 feet (2.4 m) to 13 feet (3.96 m). The weapon was favored by the main navies of the period because it was relatively light and maneuverable compared with a full-size cannon. Probably it was the main armament of the English fleet at the time of the SPANISH ARMADA, 1588. There were a number of smaller variants including the demi-culverin, the saker, the minion, and the falcon and falconet.

Cunningham, Andrew Browne, First Viscount Cunningham of Hyndhope

1883–1963

Distinguished British naval commander who entered the Royal Navy in 1898 and soon saw action in the Naval Brigade during the South African War, 1899–1902. He served as a destroyer commander during WORLD WAR I, 1914–18, and for much of the interwar period. Cunningham then commanded the battleship RODNEY before moving to the ADMIRALTY as a vice admiral. On June 1, 1939, shortly before the outbreak of WORLD WAR II, 1939–45, he was appointed commander in chief of the British Mediterranean fleet. When Italy entered the war, his main strategic objectives were to defeat the Italian navy and keep open the lines of supply to Egypt and Malta. Cunningham's preemptive strike against the Italian fleet at TARANTO, November 1940, resulted in severe damage to three enemy battleships and a permanent shift in the naval balance of power in the Mediterranean.

At the Battle of CAPE MATAPAN, 1941, Cunningham finally destroyed the Italian navy's hopes of dominating the Mediterranean. More difficult circumstances faced him in subsequent operations off Crete in which the British lost nine warships. In May 1942 he went to Washington as a British representative on the Joint Chiefs of Staff. He was back in the Mediterranean in November 1942 as chief of Allied naval operations, under the supreme command of General Dwight D. Eisenhower, for the Torch landings in French North Africa and the SICILY LANDINGS. In September 1943, shortly before his return to London, he received the formal surrender of the Italian navy on board the WARSPITE. In October he succeeded Sir Dudley POUND as First Sea Lord and Chief of the Naval Staff and was promoted to the rank of admiral of the fleet, a post he held for the remainder of the war. Cunningham retired in 1946 when he was made a viscount.

Andrew Browne, First Viscount Cunningham, *A Sailor's Odyssey*, London, 1951; S. W. C. Pack, *Cunningham the Commander*, London, 1974.

Admiral Andrew Cunningham, British naval commander, won several great victories in the struggle for the control of the Mediterranean in World War II   *(Copyright © National Maritime Museum, Greenwich, London)*

Cunningham, Sir John

1885–1962

British admiral of the fleet whose first major action during WORLD WAR II, 1939–45, was the support of a Free French action in West Africa. Cunningham was asked to cover the landing of French troops at Dakar in an attempt to overthrow the local Vichy authorities in September 1940. The initial landings were repulsed and the operation was quickly abandoned. He then returned to the ADMIRALTY as Fourth Sea Lord. In late 1942 he became commander in chief of the Levant, and was appointed to the head of the Mediterranean fleet when the two commands were merged in October 1943. He succeeded Admiral Andrew CUNNINGHAM, to whom he was not related. After the end of the war he was appointed First Sea Lord, 1946–48, and was responsible for managing the postwar naval retrenchment.

Cushing, William Barker

1842–74

American naval officer, born in Delafield, Wisconsin, who served with distinction on the Union side in the AMERICAN CIVIL WAR, 1861–65. Cushing had entered the United States Naval Academy in 1857 but failed to graduate. The Civil War gave him a second chance at a naval career: He entered the navy as an acting master's mate. He was soon involved in the capture of a Confederate BLOCKADE runner, and his efforts were rewarded by his promotion to acting midshipman. Cushing became a member of the North Atlantic Blockading Squadron and conducted many successful raids on the enemy, earning the praise of U.S. Secretary of the Navy Gideon WELLES for his courage and enterprise. Cushing's most notable and dangerous operation involved the destruction of the *Albemarle,* a Confederate IRONCLAD ram, which had just been built on the Roanoke River in North Carolina. On October 28, 1864, using an improvised TORPEDO BOAT, Cushing and 15 volunteers approached their target under heavy small arms fire. They successfully drove the torpedo under the *Albemarle,* and the resulting explosion sank the Confederate vessel quickly. Cushing and one other crew member were the only survivors. Cushing continued in the U.S. Navy after the war and reached the rank of commander.

Cutlass

A broad, curved naval sword carried on board ship during the age of the sailing navies. It was used by ship's company rather than by the officers when attacking or boarding an enemy ship or fighting on land. A typical cutlass of the 18th century might have been a saber that was some 30 inches (76 cm) long and 1.5 inches (38 mm) wide with an ivory grip. Later 19th-century designs had a short, straight blade with an iron grip and guard. These weapons, which were by then little different from sword designs in army use, continued in service into the 20th century in the ROYAL NAVY, long after any combat need for them had disappeared.

Cutter

A small sailing ship developed in England during the first half of the 18th century. Single-masted, it had a large mainsail and several smaller sails. In comparison with other sailing ships, it had a relatively deep draft and low tonnage. The cutter, which had excellent sailing and seagoing qualities and was noted for its speed, was soon adopted by the ROYAL NAVY. Equipped with up to 12 4-pounder (1.8 kg) guns and supporting weapons, it was employed as an auxiliary to the fleet during the 18th and 19th centuries. The cutter was used to carry dispatches as well as for patrol duties, particularly close inshore where it could operate with ease. A clinker-built ship's boat, equipped for rowing and sailing that was carried on a warship in the age of sail, was also referred to as a cutter. (In a clinker-built boat the outer boards of the hull overlap one another.) The cutter was the precursor of the modern racing yacht. Modern-day cutters—fast motor patrol boats—are a mainstay of the U.S. Coast Guard and are used for ocean rescue and to intercept suspected smuggling craft.

Dahlgren Gun

One of the most notable naval guns of the AMERICAN CIVIL WAR, 1861–65, the 11-inch (28-cm) Dahlgren smoothbore shell gun was used extensively by the UNITED STATES NAVY during this period. The creation of Admiral John DAHLGREN, 1809–70, it first appeared in 1850 in a 9-inch (23-cm) version. Cast in iron, it was originally designed to operate against the wooden warship but was sufficiently robust to be used effectively in the age of the IRONCLAD. Larger 15-inch (38-cm) models were produced, but the 11-inch (28-cm) version was the only one to be made in quantity. Dahlgren also created 12- (5.4-kg) and 24-pounder (10.9-kg) bronze boat howitzers. Designed primarily for use against land targets, they were produced in quantity during the Civil War. Dahlgren's final contribution to naval ordnance was the iron rifle. These were produced in three main sizes—50- (22.7-kg), 80- (36.3-kg) and 150- (68-kg) pounders—although the 50-pounder (22.7 kg) was the only widely used model. Like other Dahlgren designs, the iron rifle had a tapered barrel, the result of research on variations in pressure at various points.

Dahlgren, John Adolphus Bernard
1809–70

The man most closely connected with 19th-century American naval ordnance, Dahlgren was born in Philadelphia, Pennsylvania, on November 13, 1809. Entering the navy in 1826, his career showed no particular promise until 1847, when as a lieutenant he saw special ordnance duty at the Washington Navy Yard. It was then that his naval career became synonymous with gunnery. Within a year of reporting to the Washington Navy Yard to work on rockets, he had assumed control and command of all work there on ordnance. He conducted many experiments that resulted in the improvement of naval ordnance and

the invention of new ordnance, including the famous 11-inch (28-cm) cast-iron smoothbore gun named after him and used extensively during the AMERICAN CIVIL WAR, 1861–65. (See DAHLGREN GUN.)

With the numerous resignations and subsequent dismissals of all superior ranking officers at the Washington Gun Factory and Navy Yard at the outbreak of war in 1861, Dahlgren found himself in command of the Washington Yard along with additional duties as chief of the Bureau of Ordnance. Rewarded by Congress with an additional ten years of active duty and the rank of rear admiral for his developments of naval ordnance, he left the Navy Yard in July 1863 to assume command of the South Atlantic Blockading Squadron, which helped to close the port of Charleston, South Carolina. He remained in that billet until the close of the war. Dahlgren died at the Washington Navy Yard on July 12, 1870.

Clarence S. Peterson, *Admiral John A. Dahlgren, Father of U.S. Naval Ordnance*, 1945.

Dale, Richard
1756–1826

American naval officer, born in Norfolk County, Virginia, who served with John Paul JONES during the AMERICAN WAR OF INDEPENDENCE, 1775–83. Dale began his long career at sea at the age of 12 and in 1776 joined the Continental navy. He was soon captured by the British and taken to England, where he was held prisoner near Plymouth. Escaping to France, he joined the BONHOMME RICHARD as first lieutenant under John Paul Jones. On September 23, 1779 Jones intercepted a CONVOY escorted by the British warship *Serapis* off Flamborough Head on the east coast of England. Dale fought effectively during the battle and was the first American to board the *Serapis* when she surrendered. Although the *Bonhomme Richard* was sunk during the action, Dale continued his association with Jones in other ships. At the end of the war he transferred to the merchant service and later operated in the East Indies, 1783–94. In 1794 he was appointed as a captain in the first American Navy and, in 1801–2, served as a squadron commander in the Mediterranean, protecting American shipping against the Barbary corsairs. He flew his commodore's pennant in the frigate PRESIDENT. Following a dispute with its Navy Department, he retired from the navy in 1802, the third most senior officer in the service.

Dampier, William
1652–1715

*B*ritish naval captain, hydrographer and explorer, born at East Coker, Somerset. He went to sea at an early age as a merchant seaman and later saw action as a volunteer in the ROYAL NAVY during the Third ANGLO-DUTCH WAR, 1672–74. Dampier then worked on a Jamaica plantation before joining a group of BUCCANEERS operating in the Caribbean and along the Pacific coast of South and Central America, 1679–81. By now an experienced pirate, Dampier formed more ambitious plans; over the next eight years he sailed around the world, exploring places as far apart as Virginia, Australia, China and Cape Horn. He kept a detailed account of his travels, which he concealed in hollow bamboos, and established his reputation as an explorer and hydrographer as well as a pirate.

Returning to England in 1691, he published *A New Voyage Round the World* (1697) and *A Discourse of Winds* (1699). In 1699, as a captain in the Royal Navy, he was given command of the *Roebuck* and dispatched on a voyage of exploration to the South Seas. Exploring Australia and New Guinea, his discoveries included New Britain and the Dampier Archipelago, a group of islands off northwest Australia. During this dangerous voyage the crew mutinied; on his return to London in 1702, Dampier was court-martialed and found guilty of cruelty to his subordinates. Although his leadership qualities had been found wanting, Dampier still enjoyed a high reputation as a navigator.

In 1703 he commanded a privateering expedition to the South Seas that ended in failure and dissension. Among the many incidents that followed, the most notable was the occasion when a crew member, Alexander Selkirk, asked to be marooned in the Juan Fernandez Islands. His adventures were to inspire the English novelist Daniel Defoe to write the novel *Robinson Crusoe* (1719). Dampier returned home in 1707, having completed his second circumnavigation of the world. He made only one more privateering expedition (1708–11), serving as a pilot. His third and final voyage round the world was a great financial success, and it also achieved Selkirk's rescue from the Juan Fernandez Islands. In March 1715 Dampier died in poverty in London. (See also PIRACY.)

C. C. Lloyd, *William Dampier*, London, 1966.

Dance, Sir Nathaniel
1748–1827

*E*nglish seaman who began employment in the naval service of the East India Company in 1759 and was first appointed to the command of a ship in 1787. In January 1804 he left Canton, China, in the *Earl Camden* with 15 EAST INDIAMEN and 12 other ships. Although these ships had some arms, they had no escort and were vulnerable to French attack at a time when the Napoleonic Wars, 1803–15, were in progress. Dance's convoy was intercepted off the southern entrance of the Malacca Straits by a French squadron commanded by Rear Admiral Durand Linois. The French force, which consisted of a SHIP OF THE LINE, three heavy FRIGATES and an armed BRIG, was much more powerful in terms of firepower. However, Dance proved to be more than a match for his opponents. A display of expert maneuvering convinced the French that there were British warships protecting the convoy and after a brief action they fled. They were pursued briefly by Dance's convoy, which soon resumed its homeward journey. On his return to London, Dance was knighted for his action.

Daniels, Josephus
1862–1948

*A*merican politician who was a controversial Secretary of the Navy in the Woodrow Wilson administration. Born in rural North Carolina in 1862, Daniels became a journalist and newspaper editor, rising in the local Democratic party before becoming involved in national politics. A leading advocate for reform, including prohibition, he became a chief spokesman for the Democratic party's progressive wing. An early supporter of Woodrow Wilson, he was appointed Secretary of the Navy after Wilson took office in 1913, remaining as such throughout Wilson's two terms and thus during WORLD WAR I, 1914–18. As Secretary of the Navy he instituted considerable reforms, many of which proved very unpopular with the naval establishment but were supported by the enlisted ranks. As Secretary he oversaw both the navy's expansion as part of the 1915 and 1916 Navy Acts and America's naval involvement in World War I. After the war, in his native North Carolina, he remained an advocate for progressive reforms. Appointed by his former Assistant Secretary of the Navy, Franklin D. ROOSEVELT, Daniels served as Ambassador to

Mexico during the years leading up to America's entry into World War II. He died in 1948.

Joseph L. Morrison, *Josephus Daniels: The Small-d Democrat*, Chapel Hill, N.C., 1966.

Dante Alighieri

Completed in 1913, Italy's first dreadnought was claimed to be the world's fastest BATTLESHIP, with a maximum speed of 22–23 knots. However, there are doubts about this claim—there is no firm evidence that the ship ever reached this speed. One fact about which there is no doubt is that the *Dante Alighieri* was also the world's first warship to carry its heavy armament in triple turrets. She had 12 12-inch (30-cm) guns, mounted in four turrets on the centerline. Also novel was the positioning of some of her 4.7-inch (11.9-cm) medium-caliber guns in turrets rather than in side batteries. With a displacement of 19,500 tons, she was 471 feet (144 m) in length and was operated by a crew of 410. The *Dante Alighieri*'s WORLD WAR I, 1914–18, service in the Mediterranean proved to be uneventful, her only action being the bombardment of Durazzo shortly before the Armistice in November 1918. She was scrapped between the world wars.

Dardanelles, Operations in

February 19–March 18, 1915

During WORLD WAR I, 1914–18, the ill-fated Gallipoli expedition was preceded by an Allied naval operation that attempted to force a passage through the Dardanelles by sea power alone. According to the Allied plan, Constantinople could then be attacked and seized, forcing Turkey out of the war and allowing a secure supply route to be established. An Anglo-French fleet, under the command of British Vice Admiral Sir Sackville CARDEN, was made ready at Mudros Bay on Lemnos, 50 (80 km) miles west of the Dardanelles. It consisted of 14 pre-dreadnoughts, four old French battleships, a battle cruiser and a super-dreadnought.

The attack began on February 19, 1915, initially with a long-range bombardment of the outer forts at Cape Helles and Kum Kale, which eventually were put out of action on February 25. Marines landed almost immediately to destroy whatever Turkish fortifications remained intact. Five battleships and a battle cruiser had taken part in the operation, but the 15-inch (38-cm) guns of the British super-dreadnought *Queen Elizabeth* had made the decisive impact.

The next stage, which was much more difficult, involved silencing the intermediate Turkish defenses, which could

The British battleship *Queen Elizabeth* at Gallipoli as Allied troops are finally withdrawn in December 1915   *(Copyright © National Maritime Museum, Greenwich, London)*

be attacked only from inside the Narrows, where the danger from mines was ever present. Continuous heavy fire from Turkish shore positions severely restricted the effectiveness of the preliminary shelling and minesweeping activities, which extended over a period of days. At this point the ineffectual Carden, whose health had broken under the strain of command in the Dardanelles, was replaced by British Vice Admiral Sir John DE ROBECK, a much more able commander. This leadership change was rapidly followed by an all-out attack on the enemy's positions on October 18. Sixteen battleships and many other smaller ships were involved in the massive bombardment that extended to six miles up the straits. Even so, the Turkish batteries could not be silenced, and disaster soon occurred when the French battleship *BOUVET* hit a Turkish mine and sank. She was soon followed by the *Irresistible* and the *Ocean,* which were also lost. Three other British and French capital ships were seriously damaged by mines or gunfire.

At this point De Robeck canceled the operation. Although some British officers believed that the enemy was close to collapse after their attack, the British commander was unwilling to take any further risks. Winston CHURCHILL, First Lord of the Admiralty, who had sent replacement ships to the Dardanelles, also wanted the naval attack renewed but found no support within the Admiralty. The Turkish guns and minefields were, in fact, still largely intact and, as a result, the purely naval phase of the operation was ended. An amphibious landing would be needed; a combined assault on Gallipoli began a month later, with disastrous results.

R. Rhodes James, *Gallipoli,* London, 1965.

Darlan, Jean François
1881–1942

French naval commander and gunnery specialist who entered the navy in 1899, establishing his reputation during WORLD WAR I, 1914–18. He was promoted to the rank of rear admiral in 1929 and held a number of important commands during the interwar period, including that of the Atlantic Squadron. In 1936 he was appointed chief of the naval staff. Promotion to full admiral and appointment as commander in chief of the French navy came in 1939 as WORLD WAR II, 1939–45, began.

On the fall of France in June 1940 Darlan was appointed Minister of Marine Affairs in Marshal Philippe Pétain's government at Vichy. This called into question the commitment he had given Winston CHURCHILL that the French navy would not fall into German hands. At one time there had been a possibility that the French fleet might have sailed for England, but it was now moved to Mers-el-Kebir in North Africa. In July 1940 the British successfully attacked the fleet to ensure that it could not be used by the enemy.

Darlan was appointed deputy premier of France in the Vichy government in February 1941. He was subsequently commander in chief of the French armed forces and, in 1942, was sent to Algiers as High Commissioner for France in North Africa. Darlan was recognized by the United States as French head of state when Algeria was invaded by Anglo-American forces on November 8, 1942. By this time his reputation had been irretrievably damaged by his willingness to collaborate with the Germans. He was assassinated by a French monarchist on Christmas Eve, 1942.

David-Class Submarine

The American Confederate David-class submarines, which appeared during the AMERICAN CIVIL WAR, 1861–65, were among the first to be used during wartime. Constructed from steel cylinders with tapered ends, most were powered by steam engines, although some, including the *H. L. HUNLEY,* were equipped with a crankshaft driven by hand. They were armed with SPAR TORPEDOES—explosive charges fixed to long poles—that were mounted on their bows. Ballast tanks enabled the David-class boats to move with only the engine funnel and hatchway above the waterline. Strictly speaking, they were submersibles or semisubmersibles rather than true submarines because they could not dive. The name "David" refers to the story of David and Goliath, with the latter representing the Union giant.

During the Civil War, the David class, which was commissioned by the CONFEDERATE NAVY, provided an early indication of the future potential of the submarine as well as of some of the problems associated with it. On October 5, 1853 the Northern warship *New Ironsides* became the first vessel to be damaged in a submarine attack. However, the shock waves caused by the explosion sank the attacking Confederate submarine. The hand-powered *H. L. Hunley* fared no better when, in February 1864, she attacked the Federal frigate *Housatonic,* which became the first ship to be sunk by a submarine: The *H. L. Hunley* was taken down with her.

Davis, Charles Henry, Sr.
1807–77

American naval officer who enjoyed a reputation as a scientist as well as a wartime commander. Born in Boston, Massachusetts on January 16, 1807, Davis attended Harvard University for two years before entering the navy in 1823. (He eventually completed his degree from Harvard in mathematics in 1842.) One of the brightest naval officers of the mid-19th century, he specialized in hydrography, publishing numerous works on tides and other related subjects. He became the first superintendent of the Nautical Almanac Office at Harvard University, contributing to its development as a center of American scientific activity. In the same vein, he helped found in 1863 the National Academy of Sciences.

A commander at the outset of the AMERICAN CIVIL WAR in 1861, he was influential in developing war plans, especially those regarding the U.S. Navy's efforts to BLOCKADE the Confederate coastline. In 1862 he assumed command of the Upper Mississippi Squadron, seeing the surrender of Memphis, Tennessee. Returning to Washington later that year as Chief of the Bureau of Navigation, he remained in that important policy and administrative position until the end of the war. Pursuing his love of science, he then twice served as superintendent of the Naval Observatory in Washington, D.C., dying there while on duty on February 18, 1877. His son, Charles Henry DAVIS, Jr., similarly followed a distinguished naval and scientific career.

Charles Henry Davis, *Life of Charles Henry Davis, Rear-Admiral, 1807–1877*, 1899.

Davis, Charles Henry, Jr.
1845–1921

*A*merican rear admiral who was born in Cambridge, Massachusetts on August 28, 1845, the son of famed hydrographer and scientist, Rear Admiral Charles Henry DAVIS, USN (1807–77). Entering the navy in 1861, he became, like his father, a notable scientist, working principally on astronomical and geodetic activities while connected with the Naval Observatory and the Hydrographic Office in Washington, D.C. He was involved with several expeditions to determine differences of longitude by laying submarine telegraph cables. He also served as chief of naval intelligence and, for lengthy periods, as superintendent of the Naval Observatory.

During the SPANISH-AMERICAN WAR of 1898, he commanded the converted cruiser *Dixie*, which received the surrender of Ponce, Puerto Rico, from the Spanish in July 1898. He was promoted to rear admiral in 1904. While commanding the BATTLESHIP squadron of the North Atlantic Fleet on board the *ALABAMA*, he served as the American representative on the international commission at Paris that investigated the DOGGER BANK INCIDENT, 1904. He assisted in the relief of earthquake victims in Jamaica in January 1907, while commanding the Second Squadron of the North Atlantic Fleet. After his retirement that year, he produced several biographical and scientific works. He died on December 27, 1921 in Washington, D.C.

William B. Cogar, *Dictionary of Admirals of the U.S. Navy, Vol. 2, 1901–1918*, Annapolis, 1991.

Davis, John
c. 1550–1605

*E*nglish navigator and naval commander, born near Dartmouth, Devon. Davis went to sea at an early age and soon acquired a strong interest in exploration. In 1585 he headed an expedition to discover the Northwest Passage, the route from the Atlantic to the Pacific Oceans that was presumed to exist through North America. Two further voyages followed in 1586 and 1587. Although he did not achieve his main objective during these explorations, he discovered the Davis Strait, which separates Greenland from North America. On his return he served with the English navy as it fought the SPANISH ARMADA, 1588, commanding the warship *Black Dog*. Davis later served at the Battle of the AZORES, August 1591, and in Sir Walter RALEIGH's successful expedition against Cadiz in 1596.

Davis's first priority remained exploration, and, in 1591, he joined a privateering expedition around the world under Thomas Cavendish. Although the expedition was soon abandoned in the Strait of Magellan, Davis discovered the Falkland Islands as he returned home. In his final few years Davis spent much time exploring the Far East. He was killed by Japanese pirates in 1605. His legacy included books on navigation and the invention of the back-staff or Davis's quadrant, which remained a key navigational instrument for some 150 years.

D-Day   *See* NORMANDY LANDINGS.

Deane, Richard
1610–53

*B*ritish naval commander who served in Oliver Cromwell's army for much of the English Civil War, 1642–49, before turning to the sea. He was one of the commissioners for the trial of King Charles I and in that capacity signed the warrant for the king's execution in 1649. Shortly afterward he became one of three generals-at-sea, all trusted officers who were politically reliable. Deane's patrols around the British coast were interrupted by the uprising against Oliver Cromwell in Scotland, 1650–51, and in the autumn of 1651 he became commander in chief of the army there.

He was recalled to the navy toward the end of 1652 as the First ANGLO-DUTCH WAR, 1652–54, began and was present at the Battle of PORTLAND, 28 February–2 March 1653, when he commanded the fleet jointly with Admiral Robert BLAKE. During the months that followed the battle Deane prepared for further combat with the Dutch and gave priority to improving the working conditions of those under his command. He was in action again in the autumn of 1653 at the Battle of the GABBARD (or North Foreland), where he was killed. At the beginning of the engagement, according to an eyewitness account, a Dutch shot "struck him full in the body, cutting it nearly in two," and bringing the naval career of Cromwell's loyal servant to an abrupt end.

Decatur, Stephen
1779–1820

American naval officer, born near Berlin, Maryland on January 5, 1779. The son of a naval officer, Decatur was commissioned as a midshipman in the young United States Navy in 1798, advancing quickly to assume command in 1803. In the same year he was attached to the squadron under Edward PREBLE sent to suppress the Barbary CORSAIRS, restore American honor and offer protection to commerce in the Mediterranean area. Decatur gained international notoriety when he led a cutting-out party that retook the *Philadelphia* (which had been captured in Tripoli harbor when it was run aground by William BAINBRIDGE) and burned the vessel to prevent her from

Stephen Decatur, early 19-century American naval commander, fought the Barbary pirates and later the Royal Navy
(Copyright © National Maritime Museum, Greenwich, London)

being used by the Tripolitans. His act inspired Lord NELSON to declare it "the most bold and daring act of the age."

A hero in the eyes of America, he sat on a court-martial board that suspended Commodore James BARRON after the 1807 *CHESAPEAKE-Leopard* Affair. In the WAR OF 1812, he commanded the frigate *UNITED STATES,* which defeated the frigate H.M.S. *Macedonian* off Madeira in October 1812. Blockaded in New London by the British, he tried to run the BLOCKADE but was forced to surrender in early 1815, just as the war was ending. Later that year he was given command of a squadron that dictated terms to Algiers, Tunis and Tripoli, thereby ending the annual tribute paid by the United States to the Barbary States, as well as forcing a restitution for injuries they had inflicted on Americans. Known for his fervent patriotism, reckless bravery and exaggerated pride, Decatur was mortally wounded in a duel with the aforementioned James Barron in 1820.

John H. Schroeder, "Stephen Decatur: heroic ideal of the young navy," in *Command Under Sail. Makers of the American Naval Tradition, 1775–1850,* ed. James C. Bradford, Annapolis, 1985.

Defence, H.M.S.

The most famous of the six British warships named *Defence* was a third rate (see RATING OF SHIPS) of 74 guns that was launched at Plymouth in 1763. During nearly 50 years of service with the Royal Navy, she fought under a succession of leading commanders, including George RODNEY, Richard HOWE and Horatio NELSON, playing a key role in several major engagements. Among these were the Battle of the GLORIOUS FIRST OF JUNE, 1795 (where she was the first to break the enemy line), the NILE, 1798, and COPENHAGEN, 1801. At the Battle of TRAFALGAR, 1805, she captured the Spanish warship *Ildefonso*. The *Defence*'s long career ended in December 1811 when she was lost off the coast of Jutland while returning from the Baltic. Most of her crew of 550 went down with her.

Defensively Equipped Merchant Ships (DEMS)

During both world wars the Royal Navy armed British merchant ships to protect them against enemy attack. The United States Navy made similar arrangements for U.S. Merchant Ships. At the beginning of WORLD WAR II, 1939–45, most such ships were equipped with obsolete weapons, but in time many merchant ships were armed with current equipment, typically a single medium-size antisubmarine gun on the stern plus several antiaircraft guns elsewhere. DEMS was the name for the British organization responsible for this program—its American equivalent was the U.S. Navy Armed Guard—and its functions included the provision of gun crews for merchant ships. These crews could be service personnel or merchant seamen. Within 18 months nearly 4,500 merchant ships had been armed, with others receiving temporary protection on particularly dangerous routes. Although it is difficult to assess the effectiveness of DEMS, undoubtedly it reduced the number of surface attacks by German submarines.

Delavall, Sir Ralph
c. 1642–1707

British naval commander who was held primarily responsible for the loss of the Smyrna convoy in 1693. Delavall (or Delaval) served in the ANGLO-DUTCH WARS of 1665–67 and 1672–74 but first came to prominence after the Glorious Revolution of 1688. On the accession of William and Mary to the English throne, he was selected to affirm in person the fleet's loyalty to the new monarchs.

Delavall was promoted to the rank of vice admiral and played a leading role in the Battles of BEACHY HEAD, 1690, BARFLEUR and LA HOGUE, 1692, during the War of the GRAND ALLIANCE, 1688–97. As commander of the Channel Fleet, Delavall was ordered to protect a large convoy of some 400 ships that left England for Smyrna in 1693. Unfortunately, he had failed to establish whether the French fleet based at BREST had already left port, and when it attacked the convoy over 100 ships were lost. Delavall was accused of acting in the interest of King James II (who had been deposed by the Glorious Revolution and who was plotting with the French to resume the throne) and was removed from his command. He never went to sea again.

Delaware, U.S.S.

The Delaware and her sister ship, the North Dakota, which were completed in 1910, were the much larger successors of the South Carolina class. In fact, they were the first American BATTLESHIPS with a displacement that exceeded 20,000 tons. Each had a length of 518 feet 9 inches (158.1 m), a beam of 85 feet 3 inches (26 m) and carried a crew of 946. Major changes from their predecessors included an additional twin 12-inch (30-cm) turret on the centerline and an improved speed of 21 knots. For the first time, therefore, the United States Navy possessed ships that were comparable in standard to the British dreadnoughts. However, unlike their counterparts in the Royal Navy, the Delaware and North Dakota had a heavy secondary battery of 14 5-inch (13-cm) guns, giving them a relative advantage. Along with the New York, Wyoming and Florida, the Delaware served with the Sixth Battle Squadron of the British GRAND FLEET following American intervention in WORLD WAR I, 1914–1918, in April 1917 and was employed on convoy and escort duties until July 1918. The Delaware and the North Dakota were declared surplus to fleet requirements under the Washington Treaty, 1923 (see WASHINGTON CONFERENCE) and subsequently were scrapped.

Demologus

The world's first steam-powered and armored warship, the Demologus, which had a double hull, was designed by Robert FULTON and launched at New York in 1814. This experimental vessel was not intended to be seagoing and had a maximum speed of only 7 knots. Power was provided by a single-cylinder 120-horsepower steam engine that drove a paddle wheel mounted in a well in the middle of the ship. With a displacement of 38 tons, the Demologus was armed with 30 guns (32-pounders [14.5 kg]) that could fire shot heated in the ship's boiler. She also was equipped with guns that could fire 100-pound (45.36-kg) projectiles below the waterline. The warship was claimed to be invulnerable to enemy attack because her wooden sides, which were 5 feet (1.52 m) thick, were protected by iron plates. The Demologus was not completed until after the WAR OF 1812 had ended, and her novel features were never tested in action. Later renamed the Fulton after her architect, she survived until her destruction in an accidental explosion, in 1829, in the Brooklyn Navy Yard.

Deptford

Situated on the south bank of the Thames River in southeast London, Deptford was a naval dockyard for nearly 400 years until its final closure in 1869. Dating back to the late 15th century, when Henry VII was on the throne, it was almost certainly the first English naval dockyard. It played a key role in the development of a permanent English navy and had a preeminent position during the 17th century. During this period many of the largest SHIPS OF THE LINE were built at Deptford, under the direction of members of the PETT family, who were master shipwrights. Deptford also was associated with the manufacture and storage of naval supplies, including food and clothing—a function that continued until 1965. In addition, Deptford was the headquarters of the Victualling Board, the body responsible for purchasing food, clothing and other supplies for the Royal Navy until its closure in 1832.

Depth Charge

A British creation of WORLD WAR I, 1914–18—it first appeared in 1916—the depth charge is an explosive weapon used to attack submerged submarines. Its first major victim was the German submarine UC-19, which was sunk in the Dover Straits by a British destroyer in December 1916. The depth charge consisted of a hollow cylindrical canister containing explosive that was detonated at a preselected depth by means of a hydrostatic valve operated by water pressure. It could be dropped or launched (using a thrower) from the stern of a ship as it passed over the target.

The invention of the depth charge thrower enabled ships to fire the weapon according to a preset pattern, maximizing the charge's destructive effect. A direct hit was not necessary: An enemy submarine would be damaged by the concussion waves produced by several explosions if the depth charges were detonated close enough to the target. During World War I, the depth charge was widely employed by the Royal Navy as its struggle with the U-BOAT during the Battle of the ATLANTIC, 1915–17, reached a climax in 1917. It was also quickly adopted by the United States Navy, which nicknamed it the "ashcan," and by other navies.

In the interwar period much heavier depth charges capable of reaching targets up to 900 feet (274 m) under the sea were developed. This was later extended to 1,500 feet (457 m). Depth charges of this size had to be fired like torpedoes from deck-mounted tubes. Aerial depth charges also were developed and used during WORLD WAR II, 1939–45. These were dropped from aircraft like bombs and were set to explode within 25 feet (7.62 m) of the surface. Another wartime development was the gradual replacement of stern-fired depth charges by forward-firing versions. Known as the HEDGEHOG and Mousetrap, these mortar-based systems were developed because stern firing interrupted sonar detection systems. They were followed by the SQUID and the Limbo. These developments marked the end of the original depth charge design.

The depth charge remained in use in this new form in postwar navies, although it has been subject to continuous improvement, such as the introduction of automatic depth setting. The Soviet Navy supplemented the depth charge with rocket-propelled bombs; both superpowers developed the nuclear depth charge, which, like the early versions, involves heavy detonation at a considerable depth. It has never been used in action.

N. Friedman, *U.S. Naval Weapons. Every Gun, Missile, Mine and Torpedo Used by the U.S. Navy from 1883 to the Present Day*, Annapolis, 1982.

Derfflinger

The last German BATTLE CRUISERS to be produced before WORLD WAR I, 1914–18, the *Derfflinger* and her sister ships were highly successful CAPITAL SHIPS that were superior to contemporary British designs. The ships of the Derfflinger class differed considerably from the *SEYDLITZ*, their immediate predecessor. Their decks were flush, and their twin 12-inch (30-cm) turrets were arranged in superfiring pairs fore and aft. Heavy secondary armament,

British destroyers dropping depth charges during World War II *(Copyright © National Maritime Museum, Greenwich, London)*

consisting of 12 5.9-inch (15-cm) guns, was located in an upper deck battery. With a displacement of 26,181 tons, the Derfflinger-class ships were 689 feet (210 m) in length, had a beam of 95 feet (29 m) and were operated by a crew of 1,112. They had a maximum speed of 28 knots. These ships had excellent firepower; at the Battle of JUTLAND, 1916, the Derfflinger claimed the battleship H.M.S. Queen Mary while the Lützow claimed at least one other British capital ship. Moreover, not only were they powerful offensive weapons, but they also had an invaluable ability to absorb considerable damage because of the quality of their armor protection. The Derfflinger sustained light damage at the Battle of DOGGER BANK, 1915, but suffered much more severely at the Battle of Jutland, during which she was hit by 21 shells. She survived the resulting fires and 3,350 tons of flood water; subsequently she was repaired and resumed operational service. However, the Lützow, the Derfflinger's sister ship, was even more badly affected by enemy action at Jutland and was sunk on the orders of Admiral Franz von HIPPER. She was the only German battle cruiser lost during World War I. The Hindenburg—the third member of the Derfflinger class—was not completed until late in 1917 and had a less eventful war than her sister ships. However, like the Derfflinger, the Hindenburg was interned at SCAPA FLOW by the British at the end of the war and scuttled there on June 21, 1919.

De Robeck, Sir John
1862–1928

British naval officer. Having joined the Royal Navy in 1877, Sir John De Robeck was already an experienced officer when he was given his great opportunity a few months after WORLD WAR I, 1914–18, was declared. In January 1915 he was appointed second in command of the naval forces at the DARDANELLES headed by Vice Admiral Sir Sackville CARDEN. He participated in the successful bombardment of the outer forts at the end of February and in the failure to negotiate the minefields across the Narrows in early March. The strain of these difficult operations damaged Carden's health, and he was succeeded by De Robeck on March 17, 1915. On the very next day the new commander led the disastrous Anglo-French assault that resulted in the destruction of three Allied battleships and other serious losses.

Now convinced that the Dardanelles could not be taken by naval force alone, De Robeck suspended all offensive action while the combined assault on Gallipoli was being prepared. De Robeck was in command of the naval side of the Gallipoli operations, and both his handling of the initial landings on April 25 and the eventual withdrawal of Allied troops early in 1916 won him high praise. He spent the remainder of the war in home waters in command

of a battle squadron of the Grand Fleet. In the postwar British navy he was appointed commander in chief in the Mediterranean and subsequently in the Atlantic; he was promoted to the rank of admiral of the fleet in 1925.

Destroyer

First developed in Britain in the last decade of the 19th century, the destroyer was originally produced as a "TORPEDO BOAT catcher." Speed was the key to the success of this light, fast warship, and the introduction of the turbine engine helped to produce the required margin over the torpedo boat. Armed with guns and torpedo tubes, the typical British destroyer of WORLD WAR I, 1914–18, had a displacement of more than 1,000 tons, a crew in excess of 70 and a maximum speed of around 30 knots. The destroyer's main defensive function during the war was to protect the fleet against the SUBMARINE and increasingly the aircraft, which by this time had superseded the torpedo boat as the main threat. Standard equipment for ANTISUBMARINE WARFARE included hydrophones and DEPTH CHARGES.

As the destroyer's size and performance increased, it was used offensively against the main battle fleet. At the Battle of JUTLAND, 1916, for example, some 60 British destroyers were ranged against the BATTLESHIPS and BATTLE CRUISERS of the HIGH SEAS FLEET. Although they repelled several attacks successfully, the price was high, with eight British destroyers sunk and almost all the rest damaged to some degree. The Jutland experience demonstrated the need to reduce destroyer vulnerability and proved to be an important influence on their future design. The growing antiaircraft role of the destroyer in the interwar period was another major influence on its development. Size increased so that destroyers could accommodate the necessary cannon and machine guns. Some also were used as air-direction ships that controlled the operation of aircraft on carriers or on shore. These changes meant that average displacements had risen to more than 2,000 tons by the late 1930s. Some countries, notably Germany and Japan, built "super-destroyers," which were specifically designed to operate against cruisers and capital ships.

During WORLD WAR II, 1939–45, the destroyer continued to perform various functions, including convoy escort, but fleet defense, using its antiaircraft and antisubmarine capabilities, remained one of the most important duties. In the postwar period, the destroyer—now designated the guided missile destroyer—has continued to grow in size; and typically displacement now is between 5,000 and 8,500 tons. It is smaller and faster than a cruiser but larger than a frigate. Although the term "destroyer" now has no precise meaning, the ship retains its multipurpose role, with antiaircraft, antisurface and antisubmarine capabilities. Typically it is equipped with guns, guided missiles, torpedoes and antisubmarine helicopters, and is operated by a crew of some 400.

Peter Hodges and Norman Friedman, *Destroyer Weapons of World War II*, London, 1981; P. C. Smith, *Hard Lying. The Birth of the Destroyer, 1893–1913*, Annapolis, 1971.

Deutschland

The name of two German battleships that served in WORLD WAR I (1914–18) and WORLD WAR II (1939–45) respectively. The first *Deutschland* was one of Germany's last five pre-DREADNOUGHTS that were launched in 1904–5. Although these Deutschland class ships were rendered obsolete with the appearance of the "all-big-gun" dreadnought BATTLESHIP, they served with the HIGH SEAS FLEET during the first phase of World War I. They were present at the Battle of JUTLAND, 1916, but by this time it was evident that they contributed little to the strength of the German fleet. As a result the *Deutschland* and her surviving sister ships were withdrawn before the end of 1916.

A more famous *Deutschland* was the POCKET-BATTLESHIP built by the GERMAN NAVY between the wars. One of three such ships, she was a commerce raider with a nominal displacement of 11,000 tons. She was armed with two triple 11-inch (28-cm) turrets and eight 5.9-inch (15-cm) guns and had some armor protection. Her diesel engines gave a maximum speed of 28 knots. Shortly after the beginning of World War II, she was renamed the *Lützow*, a change prompted by the sinking of her sister ship, the *ADMIRAL GRAF SPEE*, in December 1939. In the event of her sinking, Hitler wanted to avoid the damage to civilian morale that would inevitably result from the loss of a ship named "Germany."

As the *Lützow* she was involved in the Norwegian campaign, 1940, and later operated, in company with the *TIRPITZ* and the *SCHARNHORST*, against the Allied convoys to the Soviet Union. In December 1942, together with the *Admiral Hipper*, she attacked a convoy defended by eight Allied destroyers; the German vessels' poor performance led Hitler to threaten to disband the entire German surface fleet. The action provided further evidence of the limitations of the pocket battleship design. The *Lützow* later served in the eastern Baltic. She was scuttled in May 1945 after being damaged by Royal Air Force bombs.

Devastation, H.M.S.

Launched in 1871, this British seagoing IRONCLAD was the first operational warship to be powered by steam alone. Although she was quickly followed by another British steam-powered ship and a similar Russian design, it was the *Devastation* that finally brought the age of the sailing warship to an end. This revolutionary ship avoided the design errors—low freeboard and heavy tripod masts—that had caused the CAPTAIN, her unfortunate predecessor, to capsize in 1870.

The *Devastation* had a displacement of 9,330 tons and was 285 feet (86.87 m) in length; her twin screw engine gave a maximum speed of about 13 knots. Main armament consisted of four 12-inch (30-cm) guns housed in two twin turrets, one forward and one aft. (These were replaced with more powerful 10-inch [25-cm] weapons in 1891.) The *Devastation*'s turrets and hull were protected by armor plate that was 10 to 14 inches (25 to 36 cm) thick. Operated

A British destroyer sinking a submarine in 1943   (Copyright © National Maritime Museum, Greenwich, London)

by a crew of 358, the service career of the first "mastless warship" passed without incident in the Mediterranean and in home waters; she was eventually decommissioned in 1908.

Devereux, Robert, Second Earl of Essex
1567–1601

English soldier and naval commander, a favorite of Queen Elizabeth I, who first sought action at sea when he joined Sir Francis DRAKE's unsuccessful expedition to Portugal in 1589. He already had fought overseas in the Earl of Leicester's expedition to Holland in 1585. Essex later was heavily involved in the preparations for the naval attack on Cadiz in 1596. Led by Lord HOWARD of Effingham, the Earl of Essex commanded the English ground forces that captured Cadiz, and on his return home his reputation was high.

The following year he was appointed to the command of a force of 27 ships sent to the Azores to capture the Spanish treasure fleet. The expedition, which failed to produce the promised booty, was not a success and revealed serious weaknesses in Essex as a naval leader. As he was regarded as little more than an adventurer, his reputation began to decline and was further damaged by his subsequent failure as Governor General of Ireland. Unable to restore close relations with the queen, Essex led a rebellion in the City of London that resulted in his arrest and execution for treason early in 1601.

Devonport

Dating back to the end of the 17th century, Devonport, in the west of England, lies on the Devon side of the estuary of the Tamar River and began life as an extension to Plymouth. Devonport naval dockyard, which originated in 1689 as Plymouth Dockyard, was renamed in 1824. Since then it has been a major naval facility, particularly from the mid-19th century, when it was adapted to take steam-powered warships. In the early years of the 20th century it was equipped to maintain the new dreadnoughts and super-dreadnoughts. In the postwar period it developed a facility for refitting nuclear submarines, and it recently won the contract to maintain the TRIDENT submarine. Devonport, which is the largest naval base in Western Europe, also has served as a sheltered anchorage for the fleet, an expanse of water which is known as the Hamoaze; while onshore it has accommodated several naval educational establishments, including the Royal Naval Engineering College.

Dewey, George
1837–1917

American naval officer, celebrated for his victory over the Spanish during the SPANISH-AMERICAN WAR, 1898. Born on December 26, 1837 in Montpelier, Vermont, Dewey entered the service in 1854. First seeing action in the AMERICAN CIVIL WAR, 1861–65, he was executive officer of the *Mississippi* in April 1862, navigating that vessel past Confederate-held Fort Jackson and Fort St. Philip as part of the fleet that took New Orleans and closed the bottom portion of the Mississippi River. During the run past Confederate Port Hudson, the *Mississippi* ran aground and had to be burned to avoid capture. Dewey received praise for his efforts evacuating the crew while under enemy fire.

Various shore and sea duties followed, including the post of chief of the Bureau of Equipment and Recruiting from 1889 to 1893, but it was the overwhelming victory at MANILA Bay, May 1, 1898, during the Spanish-American War of 1898, that assured Dewey's place as an American naval hero. With the rank of commodore he commanded the Asiatic Squadron, which consisted of five cruisers and two gunboats, taking it to Manila when war broke out between America and Spain. Without the loss of a single man Dewey attacked and destroyed the entire Spanish squadron of eight ships, which had inferior guns. In March 1899 he was promoted to the rank of rear admiral; in the following year he became the first and only president of the navy's General Board, which was established to advise the Secretary of the Navy on matters such as war strategies, construction programs, the acquisition of overseas naval bases and the construction of a canal across the Isthmus of Panama. In 1903 Congress commissioned him admiral of the navy, a rank created especially for him and unprecedented in American naval history. Dewey remained on active duty—and tremendously influential—until his death on January 16, 1917.

Ronald Spector, *Admiral of the New Empire: The Life and Career of George Dewey*, Baton Rouge, 1974.

Dieppe Raid
1942

A notably unsuccessful AMPHIBIOUS operation by Allied forces against the German-occupied French seaport of Dieppe during WORLD WAR II, 1939–45. This raid across the English Channel, known as Operation Jubilee, was planned by the British Combined Operations Headquarters. It was launched on the night of August 18–19, 1942. Partly designed to allay American concerns about British willingness to open a second front in Europe, it also was intended to give the Allied troops involved vital battle experience and to test amphibious landing techniques.

The landing force consisted of 5,000 men of the Second Canadian Division accompanied by 1,000 men of No. 3 and No. 4 Commando of the British army, supported by several tanks. The invasion fleet included 179 landing craft and 73 naval ships.

Eight separate landings were planned with the aim of destroying German coastal batteries in the Dieppe area. Only one landing, on the western flank, which took place shortly before dawn, succeeded. Elsewhere, the Germans were well prepared and the landing craft came under heavy fire, with most troops pinned down on the beaches. Fighting continued for some hours after a decision to withdraw was made at 9:00 A.M. Allied losses were heavy with some 4,000 men being killed, wounded or captured. The Royal Navy lost 34 ships, including a destroyer, the *Berkeley*, which had to be torpedoed to prevent it from falling into German hands. Although the Allies fared very badly at Dieppe, the raid provided lessons on the future conduct of amphibious operations that were to prove invaluable in planning the NORMANDY landings, 1944. The experience at Dieppe proved that the premature launch of a major invasion of Western Europe would end in disaster.

Ronald Aitkin, *Dieppe 1942: The Jubilee Disaster*, London, 1980.

Digby, Sir Kenelm
1603–65

*B*ritish author and diplomat whose reputation as a naval commander is based on a sole privateering expedition to the Levant in 1627–29 during the time of the Anglo-French War, 1626–30. Digby's plan was to attack French shipping in the Venetian harbor of Scanderoon, in the eastern Mediterranean, and he proposed to lead the expedition himself. Opposition from the Duke of Buckingham, who was the Lord High Admiral and an enemy of Digby's at court, meant that he went as a private adventurer under a LETTER OF MARQUE rather than as head of an official naval expedition.

Digby's two ships left Deal late in 1627 and attacked some Spanish vessels off Gibraltar on their way east. It was nearly six months before he arrived at Scanderoon. On June 11, 1628, after three hours' hard fighting, Digby captured several French and Venetian ships and obtained much prize money. He arrived back in England early in 1629 to a warm reception from Charles I, although some of the king's advisers were concerned about the possible effects of the raid on the position of English merchants in the Middle East. Following complaints from the Venetian ambassador about Digby's conduct, the British government disavowed the raid. Digby did not return to sea again and spent much of his time writing and conducting scientific experiments.

Dilke, Sir Thomas
1667–1707

*E*nglish rear admiral who succeeded Sir Clowdisley SHOVELL as commander in chief of the British Mediterranean fleet in 1707 during the War of the SPANISH SUCCESSION, 1701–14. Dilke established his reputation during the War of the Grand Alliance, 1688–97, when he had commanded the *Adventure*, a 50-gun ship, at the Battles of BARFLEUR and LA HOGUE, 1692. As the war drew to a close he was dispatched to the West Indies in command of the 60-gun ship *Rupert*.

During the War of the Spanish Succession he was soon promoted to the rank of rear admiral in command of a squadron operating in the English Channel, where he achieved a notable success against a large French convoy. He commanded the White Squadron at the Battle of MALAGA, 1704, and was rewarded with a knighthood. Following service with Sir John LEAKE in defense of the newly acquired British possession of GIBRALTAR, he was appointed second in command of the British Mediterranean fleet under Clowdisley Shovell. He acceded to the command when Shovell left for England on a journey that was to end in disaster. Dilke himself was little more fortunate: He was taken ill and also died later the same year.

Director Fire Control System

*R*apid changes in naval gun design in the second half of the 19th century were not matched by improvements in the range at which these guns had any real chance of scoring hits. Guns continued to be operated individually, with little guarantee that they would be fired accurately or even aimed at the correct target. With the development of the all-big-gun dreadnought BATTLESHIP, a solution to these problems became even more urgent. British Admiral Sir Percy SCOTT, who had been working on gun control for some time, produced an answer in 1910.

Scott's director firing system was based on a single telescopic sight mounted on a masthead where it would be unaffected by smoke from the funnels or guns. This central sight was connected electrically to the sights of each gun. All the ship's guns could be fired simultaneously in exactly the same direction from the masthead observation position. Tests conducted by the ROYAL NAVY quickly established the superiority of this method, and it was soon installed on many of the world's battleships. The system remained in use until it was replaced by RADAR in the 1940s.

In the period immediately before 1914, the introduction of plotting machines further enhanced the accuracy of naval gunnery. Designed to plot the course of a target in relation to the course of the ship in pursuit, these fire control systems were based on a rangefinder mounted on a table that was stabilized by a gyroscope. The results of the machine's calculations were passed continuously to the director sight, which was adjusted accordingly. These devices were introduced widely during WORLD WAR I, 1914–18.

Discovery, H.M.S.

The name of several British naval ships that, appropriately, contributed to the exploration of the globe at different periods. The first *Discovery*, which was operated by the British East India Company, was used to explore the Hudson Strait in 1602 and to search for a northwest passage in 1610. Another famous *Discovery* was the converted Yorkshire collier that served with the *Resolution* on Captain James COOK's third voyage around the world in 1776–79. *Discovery* was also the name of the specially constructed wooden ship of 485 tons that conveyed Captain Robert Falcon Scott on his first Antarctic expedition, 1901–4. Based on an earlier H.M.S. *Discovery*, a strengthened whaler used in an expedition to the North Pole in 1875–76, Scott's ship was used in other expeditions to the South Pole and survives today as an Antarctic Museum and training facility on the Thames River in London.

Diu, Battle of
February 21, 1509

The arrival of a small Portuguese squadron headed by Vasco de Gama on the Malabar coast (the west coast of southern India) in 1498 marked the beginning of a new trading relationship between India and Europe. Trade links that were developing between western India and Portugal at the time were facilitated by the establishment of Portuguese trading posts along the coast. These posts often had to be established by force, and two rival adventurers—Francisco de Almeida and Alfonso d'ALBUQUERQUE—were jointly responsible for achieving Portuguese naval and military dominance over a large area of India. In 1508 Muslim naval forces, in alliance with Egypt, assembled a fleet to prevent continuing Portuguese interference with their own trading routes between India and the Red Sea. In an inconclusive engagement at Dabul, 1508, the commander of the Portuguese squadron, Lorenzo Almeida, the son of Francisco de Almeida, was killed. Francisco made plans to avenge his son's death and sailed north from Cochin, in southwest India, in search of the Muslim fleet. On February 2, 1509 he found it anchored at Diu, an island off the northwest coast of India. He launched a strong attack and, after heavy fighting, completely destroyed the Muslim fleet. This victory marked the firm establishment of Portugal's

territorial presence in India, which was to last for some 450 years.

Dogger Bank, Battle of the
August 5, 1781

An engagement between English and Dutch naval forces that took place some nine months after Holland entered the AMERICAN WAR OF INDEPENDENCE, 1775–83, on the American and French side. Two opposing British and Dutch squadrons, both escorting merchantmen, met in the North Sea off the Dogger Bank, a shoal in the North Sea 60 miles (96 km) off Britain's northeast coast, during the early hours of August 1, 1781. Vice Admiral Sir Hyde PARKER, with seven ships of the line under his command, was returning from the Baltic when he met a Dutch force of similar size commanded by Rear Admiral Johann Zoutmann. The engagement began at 8:00 A.M. and lasted for over three hours. As the British and Dutch convoys dispersed in opposite directions, the two squadrons struggled for supremacy but neither side could gain the advantage, and both sides eventually abandoned the battle. Casualties on both sides were heavy, but the only ship lost was a Dutch vessel, the *Hollandia*, which sank the day after the battle.

Dogger Bank, Battle of the
January 24, 1915

This WORLD WAR I, 1914–18, engagement began with the departure of the German First Scouting Group, under the command of Rear Admiral Franz von HIPPER, from Wilhelmshaven, Germany during the night of January 23, 1915. His destination was the Dogger Bank, a shoal in the North Sea about 60 miles (96 km) off Britain's northeast coast. The German force consisted of four battle cruisers—SEYDLITZ (the flagship), *MOLTKE*, *DERFFLINGER* and *BLÜCHER*—and accompanying light cruisers and torpedo boats.

The Germans planned to attack British patrols and fishing boats near the bank on the following day. However, the element of surprise had disappeared because the German plan was already known to British naval intelligence and the ROYAL NAVY's Battlecruiser Force, commanded by Admiral David BEATTY, had left its base at Rosyth, in Scotland, to intercept the enemy. Beatty's squadron, which consisted of the *LION* (the flagship), *TIGER*, *Princess Royal*, *New Zealand* and *INDOMITABLE*, was to rendezvous with the Harwich Force, under the command of Commodore Reginald TYRWHITT, northeast of the Dogger Bank, at dawn on January 24.

Shortly after the two British units rendezvoused, the Germans were sighted heading west; but as soon as von Hipper saw the larger enemy force, he changed course and headed for home. As the faster British ships closed the distance between them, the *Lion*, at the head of the British line, opened fire at extreme range (20,000 yards; 18,288 m). In a running battle the *Lion* hit the slow-moving *Blücher* at a range of about 10 miles (16 km). The *Tiger* attacked the *Seydlitz*, and the *Princess Royal* hit the *Derfflinger*. The *Seydlitz* and the *Derfflinger* were both badly damaged, while the *Blücher* was crippled. The *Tiger* was then hit by a shell and Beatty's flagship was forced to retire. Rear Admiral Arthur Moore on the *New Zealand* temporarily took command, but he misinterpreted Beatty's instructions: Instead of pursuing the enemy fleet, he abandoned the chase to concentrate on the *Blücher*, a task that previously had been allocated to the *Indomitable*.

By the time an angry Admiral Beatty was able to resume the pursuit, it was too late—all the surviving German ships had escaped. The loss of the *Blücher* accounted for most of the 954 fatalities; British casualties amounted to no more than 15 killed and 80 wounded. Although the battle was technically a British victory, the opportunity to destroy four German warships had been missed. Admiral Moore was quickly removed from command. One of the most important outcomes of the battle was the German discovery of the vulnerability of ships' ammunition chambers to the flash of bursting shells. They lost no time in fitting antiflash devices to their own vessels, while the British were to lose five ships during the Battle of JUTLAND, 1916, through unprotected magazines.

Geoffrey Bennett, *Naval Battles of the First World War*, London, 1968.

Dogger Bank Incident
1904

An incident during the RUSSO-JAPANESE WAR, 1904–5, that occurred as the Russian Baltic Fleet passed through the North Sea on its way to the Far East. Under the command of Admiral Zinovi ROZHESTVENSKY, the fleet received intelligence reports about Japanese TORPEDO BOATS operating in the area. These unlikely reports turned out to be faulty, but before their accuracy could be checked the Russians opened fire on a group of British fishing trawlers operating from Hull, believing them to be enemy ships. One trawler sank and two crew members were killed. The incident, which occurred because of faulty Russian intelligence and badly trained crews, caused a diplomatic crisis and nearly led to war between Britain and Russia, although the crisis soon subsided. The Russians accepted responsibility for the error and agreed to pay compensation. The officers directly involved in this incident were put ashore at Vigo pending a settlement of the incident, and

the Russian fleet continued on its journey to the Far East, where it was destroyed by the Japanese at the Battle of TSUSHIMA, May 27–28, 1905.

Richard Hough, *The Fleet That Had to Die*, London, 1958.

Dolphin, H.M.S.

The British warship that participated in the circumnavigations of the globe led by John BYRON in 1764 and by Samuel Wallis in 1766–68. Launched at Woolwich in 1761, the *Dolphin* had a displacement of 511 tons and was armed with 24 guns. She had previously served during the SEVEN YEARS' WAR, 1756–63, and was finally scrapped in 1777.

Dolphin is also the name of the ROYAL NAVY's land-based submarine headquarters at Fort Blockhouse, Gosport, Hampshire. It is derived from another *Dolphin*, the first submarine depot ship to be based there just before WORLD WAR I, 1914–18.

Dominica, Battle of
April 17, 1780

A naval engagement between the British and French squadrons in the Caribbean during the AMERICAN WAR OF INDEPENDENCE, 1775–83. The French commander Admiral Luc-Urbain de GUICHEN had arrived at Martinique early in March 1780 with a convoy and naval reinforcements. On April 13 he left Fort Royal with the aim of capturing Barbados. His force consisted of 23 ships of the line and five frigates that protected a convoy carrying 3,000 ground troops. As the French passed through the channel between Martinique and Dominica, they were sighted by a British squadron under the command of Admiral George RODNEY, who had just taken up the command of the Leeward Islands station.

By April 17 the opposing fleets were moving north on a parallel course. Rodney planned to attack when a suitable opportunity arose, but before he could do so Admiral de Guichen, who was aware of the danger he was in, quickly changed direction and headed south. Rodney followed suit and issued an order that every British ship should "bear down and steer for her opposite in the enemy's line." This apparently clear order led to a misunderstanding among Rodney's captains, who interpreted it as an instruction to seek out their equivalent in terms of the number of guns carried. Not surprisingly, the impact of the action was lost and an indecisive battle followed. The French eventually dispersed, and Admiral Rodney, whose flagship the *Sandwich* was badly damaged, strongly criticized the actions of his subordinates. However, despite their shortcomings, Rodney had saved Barbados from the French.

Dominica, Battle of
April 9, 1782

Following Admiral Samuel HOOD's brilliant defense at ST. KITTS, January 25–26, 1782, during the AMERICAN WAR OF INDEPENDENCE, 1775–83, the English did not next engage the French in the Caribbean until well over two months later. During this period the French were preparing for an attack on Jamaica in collaboration with the Spanish. They were reinforced from Europe. By the end of March, Admiral the Comte de GRASSE, who was based at Fort Royal, Martinique, had a squadron of 35 ships of the line available. The British, aware of the enemy's plans, were waiting at Castries, St. Lucia, some 36 (58 km) miles away. Commanded by Admiral George RODNEY, the squadron consisted of 36 ships of the line.

The British pursued de Grasse as he left Fort Royal harbor with several troop transports on April 8. The next day the French commander was becalmed under the lee of Dominica; Rodney soon suffered the same fate. The Comte de Grasse's van, commanded by Rear Admiral the Marquis de Vaudreuil, had managed to press on to the north of Dominica, aided by the trade wind in the channel. The British van, commanded by Rear Admiral Sir Samuel Hood, edged forward toward Vaudreuil, but the entire rear division and some ships in the center were unable to participate in the battle. Hood, who was isolated from the rest of the British squadron, opened fire at 9:30 A.M. The French van returned fire for four hours, but the rest of the French fleet took no action until it was too late. By 1:15 P.M. Rodney was able to move as the wind picked up and reinforced his van division. At this point the evenly balanced forces suspended action because there was no prospect of a decisive outcome, and the French withdrew to the north. The opposing fleets met again three days later at the decisive Battle of the SAINTS.

Donegal, Battle of
October 12, 1798

An Anglo-French engagement off the northwest coast of Ireland during the first phase of the French Revolutionary and Napoleonic Wars, 1792–1815, occasioned by an abortive French attempt to land troops at Lough Swilly in support of Irish revolutionaries. It followed an earlier French expedition to Bantry Bay in December 1796, which also was unsuccessful in landing troops. The second expedition left BREST in September 1798 under the command of Commodore Jean Bompard. Consisting of the *Hoche*, a 74-gun ship, and 9 frigates, it carried 3,000 French troops and the Irish revolutionary leader Wolfe Tone. The British soon became aware of French intentions, and a British squadron commanded by Rear Admiral Sir John WARREN made plans to intercept the enemy.

Warren's squadron, consisting of three ships of the line and five frigates, first sighted the enemy off Tory Island, Donegal, at about noon on October 11. The chase that followed extended into the following morning, with the British bringing the French to action at 7:00 A.M. After a brief but intense fight the French flagship surrendered and Wolfe Tone fell into English hands; over the next three days most of the French frigates were captured, with only two managing to escape back to France. This successful British operation, also known as "Warren's action," severely damaged the prospects of the Irish nationalist movement and led to the loss of its leader, Tone, who died in jail.

Dönitz, Karl
1891–1980

German naval commander and Nazi politician, born in Grunau, near Berlin, who briefly succeeded Adolf Hitler as Führer at the end of WORLD WAR II, 1939–45. Dönitz entered the Imperial German navy as a cadet in 1910, and

Karl Dönitz: commander in chief of the German navy and Führer during the final days of the Third Reich *(Copyright © Imperial War Museum, London)*

when WORLD WAR I, 1914–18, began he was serving on the light cruiser *Breslau*. This ship, together with the *GOEBEN*, escaped through the Mediterranean to the Dardanelles. In 1916 Dönitz transferred to the submarine service; in October he commanded a submarine, *U-68*, that was sunk by the British in the Mediterranean. He was held as a prisoner of war in Britain until 1919.

Dönitz was a leading advocate of the U-BOAT during the interwar years and played a key role in developing a new German submarine service, which officially came into existence in 1935. He was appointed to command it in 1936 and remained in post until early in 1943. The first half of World War II was the period in which the U-boat fleet enjoyed its greatest success. Dönitz oversaw the massive wartime expansion of the submarine fleet and played a critical role in the development of U-boat tactics. This included the concept of the WOLF PACK, with U-boats cooperating to locate and attack the enemy. He favored surface attacks at night when the U-boat could operate at higher speeds and could not be detected by SONAR.

Early in 1943 Dönitz was appointed commander in chief of the navy, succeeding Admiral Erich RAEDER, who had resigned after disagreeing with Hitler's order to withdraw from operational use the remaining German heavy surface ships. Soon after Dönitz's appointment the tide turned against Germany in the U-boat war: Allied airpower and other countermeasures were soon to reverse the German navy's fortunes. Although Dönitz presided over the navy's decline in the latter stages of the war, he never lost Hitler's confidence in the way that the German army and Luftwaffe did. The Führer remained loyal to his naval chief, and in his political testament he appointed Dönitz as his successor as chancellor. When Hitler committed suicide on April 30, 1945, Dönitz succeeded him and was responsible for the final surrender to the Allies a week later. On May 23 he was arrested by the British in the town of Flensberg, which had been the final seat of government of the Third Reich. At Nuremburg he was convicted of war crimes and sentenced to ten years' imprisonment.

K. Dönitz, *Memoirs: Ten Years and Twenty Days*, London, 1958.

Doria, Andrea
c. 1466–1560

*G*enoese merchant, naval commander and political leader who was known as "father and liberator of his country." One of the leading GALLEY captains of his day, Doria saw varied service in different Italian navies before returning to his native Genoa in 1501. In 1513 he was appointed to the command of the Genoese fleet and, in 1519, gained a notable victory against Turkish corsairs off Pianosa. In 1522 he relinquished his command following the restoration of the imperialist faction in Genoa, to which he was opposed.

Seeking refuge with the French, Doria entered the service of King François I and eventually became high admiral of the Levant. In this capacity he defeated Charles V, the Holy Roman Emperor, in Provence and then blockaded Genoa, where he established a nominally independent republic. In 1528, fearing French domination of the republic, he ejected his former allies from Genoa and transferred his loyalty to the emperor. Doria continued to command the Genoese fleet in several successful operations against the Turks and the Barbary pirates. (See PIRACY.) In 1535, for example, he escorted Charles V's amphibious expedition to Tunisia and defeated his great adversary, BARBAROSSA, admiral of the Turkish fleet, in a battle off the coast. He did not give up command until extreme old age, his last sea service being operations against the French in 1555.

John F. Guilmartin, *Gunpowder and Galleys*, New York, 1975.

Douglas, Sir Charles
1725–89

*B*ritish rear admiral who served in the SEVEN YEARS' WAR, 1756–63, and the AMERICAN WAR OF INDEPENDENCE, 1775–83. Douglas had a number of operational successes to his credit, including the relief of QUEBEC, 1776, but his reputation was largely based on his innovations in naval gunnery. Among the changes he introduced, largely at his own expense, were improvements to check recoil, the use of flintlocks rather than the "slow match," which involved lighting a fuse; and modified cartridges that did not deposit debris in the bore.

Douglas also gave priority to increasing the rate of fire of naval guns, and his methods were widely applied throughout the fleet. His work had a direct impact at the Battle of the SAINTS, 1782, where the superiority of British gunnery was clearly evident. Douglas was present at the battle as Admiral George RODNEY's flag captain. He is said to have advised his commander to break the enemy line of battle—the first time that this tactic, which proved to be effective in disrupting the French, had been employed. This tactic represented a welcome revision of the rigid line-ahead formation and soon was adopted officially by the ROYAL NAVY.

Dover

*E*nglish Channel seaport in Kent in southeast England that has featured periodically in English naval history. Following the Norman conquest, Dover became one of the "Cinque ports"—that is, one of the five ports that had an obligation to supply men and ships to the crown in time of war. In return they received certain guaranteed trading privileges. In 1652 the opening battle of the First ANGLO-DUTCH WAR, 1652–54, was fought off Dover and resulted in an English victory. Dover had been long established as a major gateway between Britain and the European continent by time the Royal Navy decided, in the late 19th century, to establish a naval base there. This growing naval presence led to the construction of a mole (a long breakwater) that has formed Dover harbor ever since. During WORLD WAR I, 1914–18, Dover harbor served as the base for the Dover Patrol, a flotilla that was responsible for keeping the Straits of Dover free of German submarines and gunboats. In WORLD WAR II, 1939–45, Dover played a key part in the evacuation of DUNKIRK, 1940, and other operations despite the fact that it was within range of German land-based guns at Cape Gris-Nez on the French coast.

Dover, Battle of
May 19, 1652

The First ANGLO-DUTCH WAR, 1652–54, was the product of bitter maritime competition between England and Holland. It began as the rival fleets clashed off DOVER in May 1652. War had not yet been formally declared, but both sides were eager to fight. On May 18 a Dutch fleet of 42 ships under Admiral Marten TROMP had been forced to shelter under the South Foreland near Dover because of bad weather. A smaller English squadron, under the command of Admiral Robert BLAKE, was anchored down the coast at Rye but was soon warned of the Dutch presence. During the following day, as Blake approached, Tromp left for the open sea because he did not wish to comply with the requirement that all foreign ships should salute the English flag when it was encountered in English waters.

As he sailed in the direction of Calais, Tromp met a small Dutch warship that informed him of a recent incident between the ROYAL NAVY and a Dutch convoy that had occurred off the English coast. The Dutch commander reversed direction at once. In the late afternoon he ran into Blake's squadron but deliberately did not lower his flag immediately, as convention dictated. The English, who were expecting an attack after Tromp's sudden reversal of course, fired three warning shots. In reply they received a broadside from Tromp's flagship, the *Brederode*, and a fierce fight, lasting five hours, ensued. It ended when the Dutch, who lost two ships, withdrew. War was formally declared between the two countries in July 1652 after a retaliatory British attack on the Dutch herring fleet. The two fleets met again in August in an indecisive engagement off PLYMOUTH, but the first major action after Dover was the Battle of KENTISH KNOCK in September 1652.

Downs, Battle of the
October 11, 1639

A decisive Dutch naval victory during the long war of independence against Spain (the Eighty Years' War, 1567–1648). On September 16, 1639 Dutch Admiral Marten TROMP, commanding a squadron of 20 ships in the Straits of Dover, intercepted a much larger fleet of 70 Spanish and Portuguese ships that were taking reinforcements and supplies to Spanish forces fighting in the Netherlands. The Spanish-Portuguese flotilla was under the command of Admiral Antonio de Oquendo.

During a short initial artillery duel Oquendo's flagship, the *Santiago*, was damaged and, despite their numerical superiority, the Spanish were forced to retreat toward the English coast. They anchored off Dover, where they were monitored by an English squadron under the command of Sir John Pennington who was under orders to protect English neutrality. There they carried out repairs and replenished their supplies. Meanwhile Tromp, who now blockaded the enemy, delayed a further attack until reinforcements had arrived from Holland. Within a month his fleet had expanded to 100 ships.

Tromp now outnumbered the Spanish, and, on October 21, with a favorable wind, he decided to attack. His fleet was divided into six squadrons, one of which was used to keep the English squadron under observation. The Spanish fleet, still anchored in the Downs, was taken by surprise: It had not expected the Dutch to attack with the English in such close proximity, and was unable to respond effectively in time. Eleven Dutch FIRESHIPS found a number of victims while others were captured or run aground. However, 13 enemy vessels, including the *Santiago* (and Oquendo himself) managed to escape. Over 7,000 Spaniards were killed or wounded and nearly 2,000 captured. In contrast, the Dutch lost some 500 men and just a single ship. The Battle of the Downs marked the end of Spanish supremacy in northern Europe.

Drake, Sir Francis
c. 1540–1596

English navigator, pirate and naval commander, born near Tavistock, Devon. Drake, who first went to sea at the age of 13, soon graduated from the English coastal trade to the SPANISH MAIN, where he first arrived in 1565. He returned there two years later as a member of the slave-trading expedition commanded by his cousin Sir John HAWKINS. Although Drake and his ship the *Judith* survived, the voyage ended in disaster at the hands of the Spanish. In 1570 and again in 1571 he returned to the area with his mind set on revenge, and he was able to recover some of his losses. He added to his successes in 1573 when he captured a Spanish treasure train as it crossed the isthmus

Sir Francis Drake: English privateer and admiral *(Copyright ©*
National Maritime Museum, Greenwich, London)

of Panama. During this raid he became the first Englishman
to see the Pacific Ocean.

In 1577 he was given the opportunity to explore the
Magellan Straits and the Pacific Ocean beyond when a
syndicate headed by Queen Elizabeth commissioned him
to circumnavigate the globe. He left in the *Pelican*, a 100-
ton ship that Drake renamed the *Golden Hind*, accompanied by four other vessels. Having dealt with a potential
munity as they reached the Magellan Straits, Drake encountered severe weather on entering the Pacific and was
forced to press on north without his accompanying ships.
Unable to find the Northwest Passage, the presumed route
back to the Atlantic, Drake turned west across the Pacific
and eventually returned to England via the Cape of Good
Hope, thus becoming the first Englishman to circumnavigate the world. Arriving home in 1580 with treasure valued
at £500,000, he was knighted by Queen Elizabeth. In
1585 he returned to the West Indies and operated against
Spanish interests there and on the coast of North America.
Two years later he continued hostilities against the Spanish, leading a naval operation against Cadiz. The sack of
the port put back Spain's Armada preparations for a year.

At the time of the SPANISH ARMADA, 1588, Drake was
appointed vice admiral under Lord HOWARD of Effingham.

Drake played a leading part in the actions against the
Spanish fleet as it passed through the English Channel. He
was said to have been playing a game of bowls on Plymouth
Hoe when news of the Armada's arrival reached him on
July 19. Whether he completed the game, as legend suggests, or left for sea immediately remains unclear. Among
his achievements was the capture of a Spanish galleon,
the *Rosario*, near Portland and his role in the battle off
Gravelines, France on July 29. Drake's involvement in a
raid against Lisbon and Corunna in 1589 with the aim of
destroying the remains of the Armada was a failure, and
he was not employed again by the crown for five years. He
later returned to privateering as joint commander with Sir
John HAWKINS of an expedition to the West Indies, but
his life of adventure came to an end when he died of
yellow fever at Porto Bello in 1596. The greatest seaman
of his age, Drake was notable for his opposition to the
Spanish monopoly in the New World and for his zealous
defense of Protestantism. He was a fine leader and tactician
who achieved great fame in his lifetime.

J. Cummins, *Francis Drake*, London, 1995.

Dreadnought, H.M.S.

*L*aunched at Portsmouth, England, in 1906, the *Dreadnought* was the world's first all-big-gun battleship and
marked a major turning point in the design of CAPITAL
SHIPS.

Based on revolutionary ideas developed by Admiral
Jackie FISHER, her powerful primary armament consisted of
ten 12-inch (30-cm) guns that were intended to be fired in
salvoes against targets at long distances. The *Dreadnought*'s
secondary armament was confined to antitorpedo guns
only. She was the first capital ship to have an all-turbine
power plant, and her maximum speed of 21 knots was
unmatched by any of her contemporaries. However, it was
necessary to reduce armor protection significantly in order
to achieve the required performance figures, and thus she
had a displacement of only just over 18,000 tons. She had
a length of 527 feet (161 m), a beam of 82 feet (25 m)
and was operated by a crew of 770. The *Dreadnought* also
was notable for the fact that she had been built in only
366 days, a record that has never been beaten for a ship
of this size.

The appearance of the *Dreadnought* rendered all existing
battleships obsolete, and she gave her name to a type of
capital ship (the dreadnought battleship) that followed
her. Despite her powerful armaments, the *Dreadnought* had
a relatively uneventful career in the Royal Navy. During
much of WORLD WAR I, 1914–18, she served with the Third
Battle Squadron, Home Fleet. She rammed and sank the
German submarine *U-29* in the North Sea on March 18,
1915 but otherwise saw no action.

John Wingate, *HMS Dreadnought*, Windsor, 1971.

H.M.S. *Dreadnought*, the first all-big-gun battleship, revolutionized warship design   *(Copyright © National Maritime, Museum Greenwich, London)*

Dresden

German light cruiser, completed in 1908. She and her more famous sister ship, the EMDEN, constituted the two ships of the Dresden class. The *Dresden* had a displacement of 3,650 tons, a maximum speed of 25 knots and ten 4.1-inch (10-cm) guns. She had three equally spaced funnels. Operated by a crew of 361, she was 389 feet (119-m) in length and had a beam of 44 feet (13.4 m).

After completion both ships went to the Far East and on the outbreak of WORLD WAR I, 1914–18, formed part of Admiral Maximilian von SPEE's East Asiatic Squadron. Soon thereafter the whole squadron, except for the *Emden*, left its base at Tsingtao, China, for a journey across the Pacific and ultimately back to Germany. A victory against the British off CORONEL in November was followed by disaster for the Germans five weeks later at the Battle of the FALKLAND ISLANDS, when most of von Spee's squadron was sunk. Although the *Dresden* was damaged, she was the only German ship to escape from the battle.

Reentering the Pacific, she eluded capture for three months. On March 14, 1915 she was trapped in the Juan Fernandez Islands by the British cruisers *Kent* and *Glasgow* and by the ARMED MERCHANT CRUISER *Orama*. The *Dresden* was scuttled to prevent her capture.

Duckworth, Sir John Thomas

1748–1817

British naval commander who joined the Royal Navy in 1759 at the age of 11. At the beginning of more than 50 years' active service, Duckworth saw action under Admiral Edward HAWKE during the SEVEN YEARS' WAR, 1756–63, and was present at the battles of Lagos Bay and QUIBERON BAY in 1759. He served actively during the *American War of Independence*, 1775–83, but it was not until the FRENCH REVOLUTIONARY AND NAPOLEONIC WARS, 1792–1815, that he achieved wider recognition. He received the thanks of Parliament and a gold medal for his contribution to the British victory at the Battle of the GLORIOUS FIRST OF JUNE, 1794, when he flew his flag in the *Orion*. Further recognition was given, in the form of the Order of the Bath and a pension, for the capture of Danish and Swedish possessions in the West Indies in 1801. With his long period of active service concluded, Admiral Duckworth was appointed governor and commander in chief of Newfoundland.

Duff, Robert

1720–87

British vice admiral who played a key role in the events leading to the Battle of QUIBERON BAY, 1759, although neither he nor his squadron took any part in the actual fighting. Duff, who had established his reputation during earlier operations of the SEVEN YEARS' WAR, 1756–63, was involved in Admiral Edward HAWKE's blockade of the west coast of France in 1759. Duff's task was to watch the port of Morbihan, which was the base for the French troop transports that were to be used in a planned invasion of Ireland.

In November 1759 storms forced Hawke to withdraw across the English Channel. The French fleet, under the command of Admiral the Comte de CONFLANS, took this opportunity to escape from BREST, which previously had been blockaded. Duff, who had remained at his station, was pursued by the French as they arrived off Morbihan to escort the transports to Ireland. Hawke was intercepted by Duff as he returned from England, but the English commander had already sighted the French in pursuit. The English fleet defeated Conflans almost immediately in Quiberon Bay. In his later career Duff was rewarded with several important commands and was appointed vice admiral in 1778.

Duguay-Trouin

A 74-gun French warship, named after René DUGAY-TROUIN, one of the great admirals of France, the *Duguay-Trouin* was launched in 1801 and served during the Napoleonic Wars, 1803–15. During an engagement with the British off Ferrol, November 1805, she was captured along with several other French ships that had escaped from the Battle of TRAFALGAR and taken to England. On joining the ROYAL NAVY, where she served until 1855, she was renamed the *Implacable*.

Her subsequent role as a British training ship lasted until well into the 20th century, and, apart from the VICTORY, she was notable as the last wooden SHIP OF THE LINE to survive. The *Implacable* was used as a depot ship during WORLD WAR II, 1939–45, but by then her timbers were in such poor condition that she was beyond permanent preservation. As a result, in 1949 naval authorities decided to sink her in the English Channel.

Duguay-Trouin, René
1673–1736

Notable French corsair and naval commander, born at St. Malo. Duguay-Trouin, who first went to sea at an early age in the privateer *La Trinité*, demonstrated sufficient skill and courage to be entrusted with the command of his own ship at the early age of 18. During the War of the GRAND ALLIANCE, 1688–97, Duguay-Trouin first saw service as a PRIVATEER, but he later fought the English as a member of the French navy. In 1694, while in command of the *Diligente*, a 40-gun FRIGATE, an English squadron forced him to surrender. He was imprisoned at Plymouth Castle but soon escaped back to France.

Appointed to the command of a 48-gun ship, he took his revenge by capturing two English warships. His success was rewarded by his promotion to the rank of *captaine de frégate* (commander) and, in 1705, to *captaine de vaisseau* (captain). In 1711, during the War of the SPANISH SUCCES-SION, 1701–13, he commanded a squadron of seven SHIPS OF THE LINE in a successful expedition to Rio de Janeiro, which he seized, sacked and held to ransom. His efforts during the war were rewarded by his promotion to rear admiral in 1715. In a final operation, in 1731, Duguay-Trouin, now a vice admiral, commanded a squadron that successfully moved against the Barbary CORSAIRS in the Mediterranean.

Yves Marie Rudel, *Duguay-Trouin: corsaire et chef d'escadre, 1673–1736*, Paris, 1973.

Duilio

Launched in 1876, the 10,962-ton battleship *Duilio* was the first warship to be built in Italy without sails, but her most important feature was her four large Armstrong guns. These 17.7-inch (45-cm) weapons were the largest guns then mounted in a ship; it was not until the Japanese battleships YAMATO and *Musashi* appeared during the WORLD WAR II, 1939–45, that they were exceeded in size.

Armstrong, the British gun manufacturer, had offered larger guns to the ROYAL NAVY in 1871 but had been rejected. The company had more success with the Italians. Benedetto BRIN, Minister of Marine, who was developing the navy of the newly created state of Italy, adopted the new guns in a design for a heavily armored warship capable of up to 15 knots. The *Duilio*'s four guns were mounted in two diagonal turrets, giving an almost free field of fire in all directions. She was 358 feet (109 m) in length, had a beam of 64 feet 9 inches (19.7 m) and was operated by a crew of up to 515.

The *Duilio* and her sister ship the *Dandolo* were regarded at the time as outstanding achievements in marine engineering. In a rapid response, Britain built the INFLEXIBLE, launched in 1881, which drew heavily on the design of the two Italian ships and included four 16-inch guns. The *Duilio* served with the Italian navy until she was decommissioned in 1909.

Duisburg Convoy
November 9, 1941

An Italian naval convoy that left Messina, in Sicily, for Tripoli on November 9, 1941 to resupply German and Italian ground forces in North Africa. It consisted of seven merchantmen, including the German ship *Duisburg*, and was accompanied by a close escort of seven Italian destroyers. Further protection was provided by a covering force of two cruisers and four destroyers. British reconnaissance aircraft soon detected this large convoy, commanded by Vice Admiral Bruno Brivonesi. In response, the Royal Navy's Force K, which consisted of two cruisers and two destroyers, was dispatched from Malta to intercept the Italian convoy. Contact was made shortly after midnight on November 9.

In a successful British operation lasting just over an hour, the Italians suffered heavy losses. The covering force was, at this point, some distance from the convoy, and the action largely fell on the close escort. An Italian destroyer was lost and two damaged before Force K sank every merchant ship in the Duisburg convoy. Another Italian destroyer was sunk later the same day by a British submarine. As a result of this action German and Italian forces in North Africa were deprived of much-needed fuel supplies and their offensive plans had to be modified.

Duke of York, H.M.S.

A British BATTLESHIP of 35,000 tons that was completed in 1941. One of five King George V–class battleships, she was armed with ten 14-inch (36-cm) and 16 5.25-inch (13-cm) guns as well as antiaircraft guns and DEPTH CHARGE throwers. The *Duke of York* had a maximum speed of 29 knots, carried four aircraft and had a crew of 1,558 men. She was 745 feet (227 m) in length and had a beam of 34 feet 6 inches (10.5 m)

The *Duke of York* was part of the British Home Fleet for much of WORLD WAR II, 1939–45, and her duties included providing cover for convoys to the Soviet Union. It was as flagship of Admiral Sir Bruce FRASER, commander in chief, Home Fleet, that she sank the German battle cruiser *SCHARNHORST* on December 26, 1943. The *Scharnhorst* had been planning to attack a Soviet convoy but British cruisers had prevented her from doing so. As she returned to her Norwegian base, she was intercepted by the *Duke of York*, which had been covering the convoy to the south.

During a three-hour night battle, known as the Battle of NORTH CAPE, December 26, 1943, the *Duke of York* and other ships from the covering force attacked the *Scharnhorst*. The *Duke of York*'s radar-controlled gunnery proved to be accurate, and the German battle cruiser suffered heavy damage. Successive torpedo hits eventually caused the *Scharnhorst*'s magazines to explode and she sank very rapidly. Toward the end of the war the *Duke of York* was sent to the Pacific, where she was briefly flagship of the British Pacific Fleet. She was scrapped in 1957.

Duncan, Adam, First Viscount
1731–1804

B ritish admiral who defeated the DUTCH NAVY at the Battle of CAMPERDOWN, 1797, during the French Revolutionary and Napoleonic Wars, 1792–1815. Duncan gained his early operational experience during the AMERI-CAN WAR OF INDEPENDENCE, 1775–83. He was present at the Battle of CAPE ST. VINCENT, 1780, and at the relief of GIBRALTAR, 1782. Duncan did not see service again until he was appointed commander in chief in the North Sea in 1795. His main assignment was to blockade the Dutch fleet at Texel, as the Netherlands had been compelled by force of arms to align itself with France.

Duncan's task was complicated by the outbreak of MUTINY in the ROYAL NAVY in 1797. Trouble had spread from Spithead and the Nore (see NORE MUTINY) to his own base in Yarmouth Roads. As a result, his fleet was depleted for a time, but his astute handling of his disaffected crews minimized the effects of the action. The need to resupply the British fleet, in October 1797, after five months at sea, gave the Dutch their chance to break out from the Texel. On learning of their escape, Duncan returned without delay to the Dutch coast where, on October 11, he engaged the Dutch under Admiral Jan de WINTER. After more than three hours' heavy fighting, Duncan and his more powerful fleet emerged victorious from the Battle of CAMPERDOWN. It was a triumphant conclusion to a distinguished career, and he was immediately raised to the peerage as Viscount Duncan.

Dungeness, Battle of
November 30, 1652

F ollowing Admiral Witte de WITT's defeat by the British at the Battle of KENTISH KNOCK, September 28, 1652, the second major encounter of the First ANGLO-DUTCH WAR, 1652–54, Admiral Marten TROMP was recalled to command the Dutch fleet. With a reinforced squadron of 78 ships, Tromp appeared off the Goodwin Sands, at the entrance to the straits of Dover, on November 29 in search of the British fleet. British commander Admiral Robert BLAKE, who was anchored in the Downs, a roadstead in the Straits of Doves, had only 42 ships available but did not avoid an engagement. Poor weather prevented any immediate action, and both fleets were compelled to find shelter: Tromp moved under the cliffs of South Foreland and Blake anchored in Dover Roads.

On November 30 conditions improved, and both fleets moved in parallel west along the Kent coast. As they approached Dungeness, the changing direction of the coastline forced the English van to close on the Dutch. Blake soon came under heavy attack, with three British ships being sunk and two captured. Blake's flagship, the *Triumph*, was damaged, but several English ships to the rear failed to join the fighting. This decisive Dutch victory allowed their convoys to pass freely through the English Channel. It was not until the Battle of PORTLAND, February 1653, that the Dutch faced a serious British challenge.

Dunkerque

A French BATTLE CRUISER of 30,750 tons, launched in 1932. Together with her sister ship the *Strasbourg*, the two ships of the Dunkerque class were designed as the first replacements for France's aging dreadnought battleships. The *Dunkerque* was an elegant, powerful warship armed with eight 13-inch (33-cm) guns in two quadruple turrets forward. She had a maximum speed of 30 knots, but her armor protection was much less impressive. Her equipment included four Louis Nieuport 130 seaplanes.

The *Dunkerque*'s operational career during WORLD WAR II, 1939–45, was short-lived. On July 3, 1940 the *Dunkerque* and her sister ship, together with other French warships, were lying at MERS-EL-KEBIR, near Oran. Concern that the French fleet was about to fall into German hands led to an attack by the British FORCE H, under the command of Admiral Sir James SOMERVILLE. The *Dunkerque* was badly damaged by British shellfire but managed to slip away. Some two days later she was intercepted by Swordfish bombers from the British aircraft carrier ARK ROYAL. Hit

by a torpedo, she sustained nearly 1,000 casualties. The *Dunkerque* eventually joined the *Strasbourg*, which had escaped undamaged to Toulon, but she was scuttled there in November 1942.

Dunkirk Evacuation

May–June 1940

The evacuation from continental Europe to Britain of a large number of British and other Allied soldiers in the face of a German onslaught. Dunkirk was the seaport in northern France from which the remnants of the British Expeditionary Force, commanded by Lord Gort, escaped to England as the first phase of WORLD WAR II, 1939–45, came to an end in May 1940. As the Allied land forces collapsed under the weight of the rapid German advance through Belgium and France, Gort decided to withdraw to Dunkirk. There he would seek to hold a defensive position while some 400,000 troops were evacuated. The escape from

Some of the many small ships involved in the British evacuation of Dunkirk, 1940   *(Copyright © National Maritime Museum, Greenwich, London)*

Dunkirk, which was code-named Operation Dynamo, was planned by Vice Admiral Bertram RAMSAY, who was flag officer, Dover. Within a few days he had assembled over 1,000 British, Dutch, Belgian and French vessels of all types, including destroyers and minesweepers as well as civilian ferries, trawlers and various small private craft.

The operation began on May 26 and lasted until June 4. During that period over 338,000 troops were ferried across the English Channel from Dunkirk and the surrounding area. This was a larger number than had been expected, particularly as the whole evacuation was carried under the threat of constant Luftwaffe attack. The British naval and merchant ships involved in the operation sustained heavy losses, including the sinking of nine destroyers and over 200 other ships. Despite this heavy toll, the overall success of the operation was important in maintaining British morale during a very difficult period of the war and also in denying Adolf Hitler complete victory in his blitzkrieg across Western Europe. The Dunkirk evacuation remains a symbol of bravery and perseverance in the face of overwhelming adversity.

Robert Jackson, *Dunkirk: The British Evacuation, 1940*, London, 1976.

Du Pont, Samuel Francis
1803–65

*A*merican naval officer, born on September 27, 1803 at Bergen Point, New Jersey. Entering the navy at age 12 in 1815, Samuel Du Pont saw varied service at sea and on shore. In 1845 he sat on the board that supported Navy Secretary George BANCROFT's idea of establishing a single naval school—the future United States Naval Academy—in ANNAPOLIS, Maryland.

In the Mexican War, 1846–48, Du Pont commanded the sloop *Cyane*, clearing the Gulf of California of Mexican naval forces and landing American troops that captured San Diego, La Paz and Mazatlán, among other places. For these efforts Du Pont received an official commendation. Following the war, he worked for improvement of the Naval Academy and for development of steam power in the navy. In 1855 he headed the Naval Efficiency Board, a controversial attempt at reform by recommending the retirement of many naval officers deemed unfit to continue service. As such, his efforts assisted in developing a retirement policy for the navy where none had existed before.

As one of the highest-ranking naval officers at the outset of the AMERICAN CIVIL WAR, 1861–65, Du Pont was very influential in planning the navy's strategy and operations. As commander of the South Atlantic Blockading Squadron, he successfully directed the capture of Port Royal, South Carolina, in late 1861, converting it into the Union's future base for blockading operations on the Atlantic. This made the BLOCKADE tighter and more effi-

cient. Under tremendous government and public pressure to take Charleston, South Carolina, the cradle of secession, he led an unsuccessful IRONCLAD attack against the city in April 1863. Embittered by his failure, he requested inactive duty through most of the war, dying in Philadelphia, Pennsylvania on June 23, 1865, little more than two months after the war's end.

James M. Merrill, *Du Pont, The Making of An Admiral: A Biography of Samuel Francis Du Pont*, Northbrook, Ill., 1987.

Duquesne, Abraham, Marquis
1610–88

*F*rench naval commander who served with distinction in the operations against Spain, 1637–43, during the Thirty Years' War, 1618–48. Born in Dieppe, Duquesne spent his early career in the French merchant fleet but joined the navy in 1637 to avenge the death of his father at the hands of the Spanish. He saw much action in a series of battles beginning with Guetaria, 1638, and ending with Cabo de Gata, 1643. Shortly afterward employment needs forced him to transfer his loyalties to the Swedish navy, where he was appointed a vice admiral. He was victorious in two major battles against the naval forces of Holland and Denmark, which had formed an alliance against Sweden.

In 1647 Duquesne returned to France where, in 1650, Bordeaux had declared for the Fronde (a series of civil revolts against the authority of the French crown, 1648–53) and was supported by arms supplied by Spain. He assembled a squadron of ships that blockaded the mouth of the Gironde River and eventually forced Bordeaux to surrender. Years of routine operations against the corsairs in the Mediterranean followed, and it was not until the third ANGLO-DUTCH WAR of 1672–78 that Duquesne was to distinguish himself again. He was victorious in an important action—the naval Battle of Messina—on April 22, 1676 against a Spanish-Dutch fleet commanded by Admiral Michiel DE RUYTER, Holland's greatest admiral, off the east coast of Sicily. His reputation secured, Duquesne was appointed a marquis by King Louis XIV in recognition of his achievement. He continued to serve in the navy until his death.

Dutch East Indies Campaign
January–March 1942

*T*he Dutch East Indies—now Indonesia—was a primary target for the Japanese as they advanced westward during WORLD WAR II, 1939–1945. The Dutch colony was oil-rich and could provide the fuel to sustain the Japanese war effort. While their conquest of Malaya and the Philippines was still in progress, the Japanese mounted a three-pronged seaborne invasion of the Dutch East Indies that would be over within two months. Three invasion fleets were formed: The western force would invade southern Sumatra, western Java and north Borneo, the central force would attack eastern Borneo, and the eastern force would take Celebes and then eastern Java.

The joint Allied command, headed by British General Sir Archibald Wavell, had more ground troops (98,000) than the Japanese, but the latter had superiority at sea and in the air. The Allies had no more than three cruisers and 12 destroyers and submarines for use against their opponents. The Japanese first landed in eastern Borneo on January 13 and made steady progress south. By February 9 they had arrived in the south of Celebes, despite the orders given to Dutch Rear Admiral Karel Doorman to intercept the invasion fleet. At the same time the western force, commanded by Admiral Jisaburo Ozawa, was in sight of Sumatra, and again Rear Admiral Doorman was unable to prevent a Japanese landing. On February 19–20 the Japanese invaded Bali and Timor despite Doorman's efforts at the Battle of Lombok Strait.

As Allied opposition collapsed under the weight of the Japanese advance, Wavell's command disappeared and all ground and naval forces were placed in Dutch hands, with Vice Admiral Helfrich becoming overall commander of the naval forces present there. As the Japanese moved a large invasion force toward Java, the allies made a final attempt to stall it at the Battle of the JAVA SEA on February 27. A disastrous Allied defeat simply confirmed that the Japanese were in the ascendant, and by March 8 Dutch resistance on Java (and the rest of the Dutch East Indies) had ended.

Dutch Navy

The Dutch navy traces its origins to the start of the Eighty Years' War, 1567–1648, when the SEA BEGGARS attacked the Spanish at Brill in 1572. This group of PRIVATEERS operated against Spanish shipping and mounted AMPHIBIOUS operations with considerable success. During the course of the war other local fleets were created, and it was not until 1597, following the formation of the Dutch republic, that a national navy was created. Headed by an admiral in chief, it drew heavily on the experience and personnel of the irregular forces that preceded it. It was organized in five regional headquarters, of which Amsterdam came to be the most important.

The Dutch navy continued the record of success against the Spanish that the Sea Beggars had enjoyed. In 1628 the Dutch under Piet HEIJN had a notable success in capturing the Spanish treasure fleet off Havana. At the Battle of the DOWNS, 1639, Admiral Maarten TROMP ended Spanish dominance of north European waters. During the war with Spain the Dutch navy played a critical role in protecting Holland's rapidly expanding trade routes to the East Indies, routes on which the Netherlands' 17th-century prosperity was based. Commercial and colonial rivalry between Britain and the Netherlands beginning in the mid-17th century led to three naval wars. Although these wars failed to produce a decisive outcome, the Dutch were successful in protecting their vital interests and gained some concessions from the English. The critical leadership role was played by Admiral Michiel de RUYTER, the greatest figure in Dutch naval history. De Ruyter also played a leading part in the First Northern War, 1657–60, successfully blocking a Swedish plan to control access to the Baltic. Dutch naval successes reflected the quality of their warships as well as of their admirals. Dutch ships were typically faster and more maneuverable than other comparable vessels. Despite the fact that they were lighter than their English equivalents and more likely to sustain damage in an attack, they were used as a model by several other European naval powers.

During the 18th century the Netherlands entered a long period of economic decline; this was reflected in a gradual contraction in naval activity. Despite these less favorable circumstances, the Dutch participated in some of the major wars of the century, including the War of the SPANISH SUCCESSION, 1701–14, when their navy fought with the English against the French. Dutch naval forces were to engage the British on two more occasions. At the Battle of the DOGGER BANK, August 5, 1781, during the American War of Independence, 1775–83, Admiral Johann Zoutmann fought Admiral Sir Hyde PARKER to a draw. During the French Revolutionary Wars, 1792–1802, when Holland was occupied by the French, the Dutch and English fleets fought at the Battle of CAMPERDOWN, 1797. This was the last occasion on which the two countries fought against each other at sea. The Dutch navy fought alongside the British and Americans in the Pacific during WORLD WAR II, 1939–45. Since then, Dutch naval activities have been coordinated with their allies through the North Atlantic Treaty Organization (NATO).

Jaap R. Bruijn, *The Dutch Navy of the Seventeenth and Eighteenth Centuries*, Columbia, S.C., 1993.

Eagle

$\mathcal{A}$ name given to two British aircraft carriers. The first of these was a converted battleship that was under construction in Britain for the Chilean navy when it was taken over by the British Admiralty during WORLD WAR I, 1914–18. She was launched as an AIRCRAFT CARRIER in June 1918. The *Eagle* was fitted with a flight deck that was 654 feet (199.3 m) in length and enclosed a large hangar. A single starboard-side island superstructure was employed for the first time and was a feature to be adopted in almost all the carrier designs that have followed. She had a displacement of 21,850 tons, a maximum speed of 24 knots, a crew of 744 and could accommodate 21 aircraft. Completely refitted in 1921, she spent much of her 18-year career in the Mediterranean. During WORLD WAR II, 1939–45, in February 1942, she joined FORCE H at Gibraltar and was used to transport aircraft to Malta. On August 11, 1942 she was hit by four torpedoes from a German U-BOAT some 580 miles (933 km) from Malta while escorting the Pedestal convoy. She sank within four minutes with the loss of 160 crew.

The second British *Eagle*, together with her sister ship, the ARK ROYAL, formed the nucleus of the ROYAL NAVY's carrier fleet in the postwar period. With a displacement of 43,060 tons, a crew of 2,637 and 34 aircraft, she was much larger than her predecessor. This later *Eagle* was notable because she embarked the Royal Navy's first operational squadron of jet fighters and was the first carrier to be fitted with a mirror landing sight. The *Eagle* entered service in 1952 and was fully employed during a 20-year career in the Royal Navy, which included the SUEZ landings, 1956, and the confrontation with Indonesia in 1964.

Another famous *Eagle* is the three-masted training ship used by cadets attending the United States Coast Guard Academy. With the full name of *Bark Eagle*, this ship was built in Germany as the *Horst Wessel* in 1935. She was transferred to the United States at the end of World War II and was allocated to the academy as a training ship in 1947.

East Indiaman

$\mathcal{B}$uilt and operated by the English, Dutch and French East India Companies, East Indiamen were the ships used on the trade routes from Europe to the east from the early years of the 17th century. Developed from the GALLEON and the Dutch FLUYT, they were large three-masted, square-rigged sailing ships constructed to a high standard.

East Indiamen were in fact the finest ships of their time and were symbols of commercial success and national prestige. They had luxurious accommodation for officers and passengers and elaborate carvings and gilding. During the 17th century these two-decker ships had a displacement of about 700 tons, but by the 1800s this had increased to some 1,200 tons. The hull was always designed to carry as much cargo as possible; a large crew also had to be accommodated to operate and maintain the ship during extended journeys. Long distances were covered at very low speeds, as East Indiamen were capable of little more than eight knots an hour.

The real risk of attack from pirates or from the ships of rival companies or foreign navies meant that East Indiamen always carried guns. These were located on their flush upper deck, but a row of dummy gunports often was painted on the lower deck to give them the appearance of two-decker warships. In wartime East Indiamen were employed as fighting craft, and some were built and armed as full men-of-war. The large ships of the Dutch East India Company, for example, certainly fell into this category. A typical example was the *Den Ary*, a 54-gun East Indiaman built in 1725. The abolition of the British East India Company's monopoly of trade with India and China in 1833 and the need for faster ships marked the end of the

An East Indiaman, an armed ship in the service of the British East India Company, off the Cape of Good Hope in 1790 *(Copyright ©
National Maritime Museum, Greenwich, London)*

East Indiaman and its replacement first by the Blackwall frigate and later by the clipper.

Eastern Solomons, Battle of the

August 24–25, 1942

After the Battle of SAVO ISLAND, August 9, 1942, the American and Japanese fleets continued their fight during WORLD WAR II, 1939–45, for control of the SOLOMON ISLANDS at the Battle of the Eastern Solomons, August 24–25. The battle was occasioned by the Japanese plan to land troop reinforcements on GUADALCANAL in order to strengthen their resistance to American landings on the island. Some 1,500 troops were dispatched in old destroyers escorted by the *Jintsu* (Admiral Raizo TANAKA's flagship) and four cruisers commanded by Vice Admiral Gunichi Mikawa. They were accompanied by two carriers, commanded by Admiral Chuichi NAGUMO and an advance force of six cruisers, headed by Vice Admiral Nobutake KONDO, the tactical commander. A small carrier, the *RYUJO*, with a cruiser and two destroyers, was sent ahead of the main convoy to act as bait to induce the U.S. fleet into the area.

The *Ryujo* was spotted by American reconnaissance, and Rear Admiral Frank FLETCHER's Task Force 61—consisting of the carriers *SARATOGA, ENTERPRISE* and *WASP*, the battleship *NORTH CAROLINA*, nine cruisers and 17 destroyers—was ordered into the Eastern Solomons. On August 23 American reconnaissance aircraft spotted the convoy. Bombers took off from the *Saratoga*, but poor weather conditions obscured the enemy's position. At this point the *Wasp* was ordered south to refuel, reducing Fletcher's available strength considerably. Early the following day the *Ryujo* was discovered. A strike force left the *Enterprise* and succeeded in sinking her east of Malaita. At the same time the location of two other carriers—the *Shokaku* and *ZUIKAKU*—was determined, but the Americans were not able to mobilize sufficient aircraft to inflict more than minor damage. At the same time, Japanese aircraft were sent into action against Task Force 61 and several managed to penetrate its defenses. The *Enterprise* was damaged but soon was back in operation again.

This inconclusive battle came to an end at nightfall, by which time one Japanese troop transport and a destroyer had been sunk by American land-based planes. On the following day, August 25, the remaining Japanese ships were forced to withdraw after further heavy air attacks. The Americans had denied the Japanese the opportunity to reinforce their ground troops, and from then on they were forced to resupply Guadalcanal at night using the "Tokyo Express" (the nickname given to the Japanese convoys that made the dangerous journey through the Solomons to support the garrison at Guadalcanal). The Japanese also had suffered heavy losses of aircraft and crews that would prove to be difficult to replace.

Eilat

*T*he Israeli destroyer *Eilat* was unremarkable except for the fact that she was the first large warship to be sunk by a surface-to-surface guided missile. While cruising off the Egyptian coast, on October 21, 1967, during the Six Day War between Israel and several Arab states, she was hit by three Soviet-built SS.N.2 Styx missiles fired by a Komar-class missile craft of the Egyptian navy. At the time of the attack the Egyptian craft was positioned inside Port Said harbor some ten miles (16 km) from the *Eilat*. She sank rapidly; by the time a fourth Styx missile arrived in the target area, the *Eilat* had gone down.

This incident, which confirmed the value of fast patrol boats armed with antiship missiles, represented a turning point in modern naval warfare. The missile craft was the creation of the Soviet navy, which needed a fast and inexpensive alternative to the aircraft carrier and came up with the Komar. The Israeli navy also drew the appropriate conclusions from the loss of the *Eilat*. It developed its own fleet of fast missile boats armed with locally produced missiles. Their effectiveness was demonstrated during the Yom Kippur War, 1973, when the Israelis fought Egyptian and Syrian missile boats in the first direct engagement between missile-armed fleets. During the war the Israeli navy, which had developed effective missile-based counter-measures, destroyed 13 enemy boats without losing any of its own ships.

Elba, Battle of
August 28, 1652

A battle between Dutch and English forces in the Mediterranean in the opening stages of the First ANGLO-DUTCH WAR, 1652–54. At the time, the English Mediterranean fleet consisted of eight warships organized in two squadrons under the command of Commodore Henry Appleton and Admiral Richard Badiley. Appleton's squadron was anchored in Leghorn when a much larger Dutch fleet of 14 ships, commanded by Johan van Galen, arrived. The Dutch commander left four ships to blockade Leghorn, while the remainder departed to search for the English squadron commanded by Badiley. Opposing the ten Dutch ships were only four British ships that van Galen found off Elba escorting four Levant merchantmen.

Despite their relative weakness, the English fought gallantly and the battle extended throughout August 28. The Dutch captured the *Phoenix* and damaged the other British ships, which sought refuge on Elba when the battle ended. When van Galen tried to renew hostilities the following day, he was denied access by the governor and was unable to bring the engagement to a final conclusion. The opposing sides were to fight a second engagement (see Battle of LEGHORN) in March 1653.

Elizabeth Bonaventure

*T*he *Elizabeth Bonaventure*, a typical 600-ton GALLEON of the Tudor period, owned by the English crown, served as Sir Francis DRAKE's flagship during his successful raid on CADIZ in 1587. During the operation he destroyed 33 Spanish warships, "singeing the King of Spain's beard" and disrupting the preparations for the SPANISH ARMADA, 1588. The *Elizabeth Bonaventure*'s keel was just under 100 feet (30.48 m) in length, and the ship had a beam of some 30 feet (9.14 m). In Tudor times the word "bonaventure"— literally "good adventure"—was often used as a ship's name and normally was linked with the owner's Christian name. It was an appropriate designation for a warship of the period.

Elphinstone, George Keith, First Viscount Keith
1746–1823

*B*ritish admiral who succeeded Admiral John JERVIS, Earl St. Vincent, as commander of the Mediterranean fleet during the French Revolutionary Wars, 1792–1802. The most notable episode of his tenure in command was the successful British expedition to Egypt in 1801, which he led jointly with Sir Ralph Abercromby. During the Napoleonic Wars, 1803–15, his role in the defense of Britain as commander of the North Sea station and then of the Channel Fleet was important but unexciting. During his earlier career Elphinstone had served in the AMERICAN WAR OF INDEPENDENCE, 1775–83, and had played a major role in suppressing the naval mutinies at SPITHEAD and the NORE in 1797.

C. C. Lloyd, ed., *The Keith Papers*, 3 vols., 1927–55.

Emden

*T*he best-known and most successful of the German surface raiders of the WORLD WAR I, 1914–18, the *Emden* was a light cruiser of 3,544 tons. At the beginning of the war she left Admiral Maximilian von SPEE's East Asiatic Squadron and headed for the Indian Ocean. She bombarded Madras on September 22, 1914, but her main preoccupation was the destruction of enemy merchant shipping: She captured or sank 23 Allied victims with a combined displacement of 101,182 tons in the period up to November 9. She also sank a Soviet cruiser and a French destroyer as well as disrupting shipping movements across a wide area. Much of the success of the *Emden's* remarkable hit-and-run campaign can be attributed to the skill and courage of her captain, Karl von Miller.

The Allies had considerable difficulty in tracking the *Emden*. She eluded capture even when she was forced to undertake emergency repairs in the British Maldive Islands: The local population had no direct links with the rest of the world, and they had not yet heard that Britain and Germany were at war. Her final action was to sabotage the cable station on Cocos Island, but on November 9 her work was interrupted by the arrival of the *Sidney*, an Australian light cruiser. The *Emden* was an easy target and was quickly destroyed with the loss of 142 German lives.

Edwin P. Hoyt, *Last Cruise of the Emden*, London, 1967.

Empress Augusta Bay, Battle of
November 2, 1943

A night engagement between American and Japanese naval forces, part of the continuing struggle for the control of the Solomon Islands in the Pacific during WORLD WAR II, 1939–45. On November 1 the U.S. Third Marine Division landed on Bougainville Island, prompting an immediate Japanese response. A squadron commanded by Rear Admiral Sentaro Omori was sent from Rabaul to attack the American transports that were disembarking troops in Empress Augusta Bay, Bougainville. Consisting of two heavy cruisers, two light cruisers and six destroyers, the Japanese squadron was opposed by an American force that included four light cruisers and eight destroyers, commanded by Rear Admiral A. S. Merrill. Merrill positioned his forces across the mouth of the bay as the Japanese approached the area. American RADAR picked them up moving ahead in three columns, but shortly afterward Rear Admiral Omori was warned of the impending danger. He changed formation into line ahead as the Americans opened fire. The Japanese cruiser *Sendai* was sunk and three destroyers were damaged as they collided with one another—one fatally. Only one American destroyer was damaged. Rear Admiral Omori could not reach his target and was forced to withdraw before daybreak.

Endeavour, H.M.S.

*T*he famous British barque, acquired by the ROYAL NAVY in March 1768, in which Captain James COOK undertook his first great journey—a three-year voyage of exploration in the Pacific. The three masted *Endeavour* was originally a Whitby collier named the *Earl of Pembroke*,

built in 1764, that was used for carrying coal between England and Sweden. She was cat-built—the waterlines aft were very full—and was notable for the absence of a figurehead on her bows. The ship's keel was 81 feet (24.7 m) in length and she had a displacement of 366 tons. After the Admiralty acquired the *Endeavour*, some important modifications were made: She was armed with ten 4-pounder guns on carriages and 12 swivels, her quarter deck was extended and a square topsail was added to the mizzen mast.

The *Endeavour* left England on August 26, 1768 with a crew of 94. She returned in July 1771 after a highly productive voyage during which Cook discovered the Society Islands, mapped the entire New Zealand coast and explored the eastern coast of Australia. After Cook's return to England the *Endeavour* made three journeys to the Falkland Islands before she was sold by the Admiralty. She returned to work as a collier but later became a whaler. It was in this capacity that, in 1790, she ran aground off Rhode Island and was damaged beyond repair.

Endymion, H.M.S.

A British frigate, built in 1797, the *Endymion* was closely based on *La Pomone*, a captured French warship. She had a displacement of 1,277 tons, carried 46 guns (including 26 24-pounder [11-kg] guns) and was noted for her speed. The *Endymion* was a successful design and served in the Royal Navy for over 60 years. The most notable incident in her long career was the engagement during the WAR OF 1812 in which she fought the American frigate *President*. On January 15, 1815, in company with three other British ships, the *Endymion* attacked and captured her opponent after a long pursuit. The *President* was severely damaged as a result, and her commander (Stephen DECATUR) and crew were taken prisoner.

England, U.S.S.

*A*merican Buckley-class destroyer escort that served in the Pacific during WORLD WAR II, 1939–45, achieving a remarkable series of victories against the Japanese. Commissioned in 1943, the *England*, which was built to a British design, had a displacement of 1,400 tons and main armament of three 3-inch (8-cm) guns. She was also equipped with three 21-inch (53-cm) torpedo tubes and six 40-mm antiaircraft guns. Operated by a crew of 220, she had a length of 306 feet (93 m) and a beam of 37 feet (11 m). In May 1944 she was ordered to operate against the Japanese submarine line to Bougainville. Working with two other destroyer escorts, she destroyed her first enemy submarine with a HEDGEHOG mortar on May 19. During the next 12 days the *England* was responsible for the destruction of five more Japanese submarines. Although the *England*'s achievement was without precedent, it received little recognition at the time except for a signal from Admiral Ernest KING, the American commander in chief in the Pacific. The *England* was hit by a KAMIKAZE attack off Okinawa almost exactly a year later and forced to return to the United States, where she was written off as beyond repair.

Enterprise, U.S.S.

*S*everal ships in the United States Navy, including two notable AIRCRAFT CARRIERS, have gone by the name *Enterprise*. The first carrier, known as "Big E," was one of the YORKTOWN class, which also included the *Hornet* and the *Yorktown*. She had a displacement of 19,872 tons, a maximum speed of 15 knots and could carry 96 aircraft. Launched in 1938, she escaped destruction at PEARL HARBOR, 1941, and earned 20 battle stars during WORLD WAR II, 1939–45. The *Enterprise* was involved in virtually every major engagement of the Pacific war, including the Battles of MIDWAY, GUADALCANAL, the PHILIPPINE SEA and LEYTE GULF. She was badly damaged during the assault on OKINAWA in April 1945, being hit twice by KAMIKAZE aircraft, and saw no further service. Widely regarded as the most famous American warship of World War II, the *Enterprise* was decommissioned in 1947. Her sister ships were less fortunate: Both were lost in the Pacific in 1942.

The name *Enterprise* was revived by the U.S. Navy when the world's first nuclear-powered aircraft carrier was launched at Newport News, Virginia in September 1960. This *Enterprise*, which remains in service, has a displacement of 75,700 tons (89,600 tons when fully loaded), about equal in size to the later NIMITZ-class carriers. Her four steam turbines, which provide a cruising speed of 35 knots, are powered by eight water-cooled reactors. At 20 knots she can travel more than 400,000 miles (643,738 km) without refueling. The *Enterprise* has a crew of 3,100, with a futher 2,400 men to operate the 100 aircraft that can be carried. There are four steam catapults and four lifts give access to the hangars. She is equipped with short-range supersonic antiaircraft missiles for defensive purposes.

Ericsson, John
1803–89

*O*ne of the 19th century's most famous engineers and inventors, Ericsson played a significant role in the transformation of ships from wood to iron and from sail to steam. He developed the screw propeller and built the first armored turret warship. Born in Sweden in 1803, he trained as a cadet in the Swedish corps of mechanical engineers. Between 1826 and 1838 he worked in London, developing

mechanical inventions such as a steam locomotive, a steam fire-pumper and a screw propeller for steam vessels. He visited the United States in 1839 and eventually became a naturalized citizen. Energetic and prolific, Ericsson nevertheless had difficulty working with others, as evidenced in his stormy relations with Commodore Robert STOCKTON regarding the design and construction of the U.S.S. *PRINCETON,* America's first screw-propelled man-of-war.

Ericsson's greatest fame came in the AMERICAN CIVIL WAR, 1861–65, when he designed and built the famous IRONCLAD *MONITOR*, which fought the Confederate's *Virginia* (formerly the *MERRIMACK*) at HAMPTON ROADS in 1862; the action gave a foretaste of naval battles of the future. Ericsson received further orders for similar warships, and the Monitor type was to play a key role during the Civil War. Continuing his efforts after the war, he was instrumental in developing the modern TORPEDO BOAT or DESTROYER and also experimented with solar-powered engines.

William C. Church, *The Life of John Ericsson,* 2 vols., New York, 1890.

Essen, Nikolai von
1860–1915

*C*ommander of Russia's Baltic fleet from 1909 until his death in May 1915. Admiral Nikolai von Essen had established his reputation as one of the country's leading naval officers during the war against Japan, 1904–5. Briefly in command of a battleship, he then moved to shore duty, playing a key role in defending the entrance to Port Arthur in its capture by the Japanese in January 1905. During WORLD WAR I, 1914–18, he was constrained by the superiority of German naval forces and his main wartime task was to maintain Russia's Baltic defenses, giving first priority to the protection of St. Petersburg (Petrograd). A further bar to his ability to take offensive action—which was limited to the mining of German ports—was the fact that the Baltic fleet was subject to the overall control of the commander of the Russian Sixth Army. At the time of his death in May 1915 at a relatively early age, Essen was still seeking support for a more aggressive role for the Baltic Fleet. This situation was to last until 1917, when the Baltic Fleet became a focus of political unrest, fuelled in part by years of inaction by its crews.

Essex, U.S.S.

*A*n American frigate, launched in 1799, that operated in the Pacific Ocean during the WAR OF 1812. She previously had served in the Pacific in 1800, under the command of Edward PREBLE, protecting American merchantmen against French PRIVATEERS. Under the command of David PORTER during the War of 1812, the *Essex* was initially highly successful during her second period of service in the Pacific. In a 17-month cruise she captured a number of British merchantmen. In March 1814, however, the British took their revenge off the coast of Chile. A Royal Navy frigate and a sloop of war captured the *Essex*, now a "bloody, burning hulk," in a hard-fought action that lasted nearly three hours.

A second *Essex* was the name-ship of a class of American aircraft carriers of WORLD WAR II, 1939–45. More Essex-class carriers were built than any other carrier class. Improved versions of the Yorktown class, they had better protection and enhanced defensive armament. The *Essex* had a displacement of 27,100 tons, an overall length of 876 feet (267 m) and a beam of 93 feet (28.34 m). Capable of a maximum speed of 33 knots, she could accommodate 80 aircraft. Her armament included 12 5-inch (13-cm) and 68 40-mm (1.57-inch) antiaircraft guns. Fourteen Essex-class ships were eventually built, although not all of them were ready in time to see combat in World War II. The Essex-class carriers played a leading role in the Pacific War from November 1943 onward; remarkably, all survived the war.

Estaing, Charles Hector, Comte d'
1729–94

French admiral and politician who commanded the first French fleet sent in support of the American colonists during the AMERICAN WAR OF INDEPENDENCE, 1775–83. Estaing served as a soldier in his early career before joining the French navy in 1757 during the SEVEN YEARS' WAR, 1756–63. He was based in India at the time, but at the end of the war, as a lieutenant general, he became governor of the Antilles, 1763–66. Promoted to vice admiral in 1777, he was sent to America in July 1778 to support the fight against the British.

Estaing's caution and lack of experience limited the impact of his intervention. The British Admiralty ordered Admiral John BYRON to pursue Estaing, and there were inconclusive engagements in Boston Harbor and elsewhere before both fleets moved to the West Indies. Estaing captured the islands of GRENADA and St. Vincent from the British but failed to achieve a decisive victory over Byron's much smaller force. In 1779 the focus of Estaing's operations moved north once more as he supported the Americans' attempt to raise the siege of Savannah. He was unsuccessful and sustained serious wounds during the fighting. In 1783 he commanded the combined fleet of France and Spain but soon afterward turned his attention to politics. Elected to the Assembly of Notables in 1787, he was a moderate revolutionary who was guillotined in Paris during the Reign of Terror because he had intervened in favor of Marie Antoinette.

Euryalus, H.M.S.

A notable British 36-gun frigate, designed by Sir William Rule, surveyor of the navy, and completed in 1805. Built at Adam's Yard, Buckler's Hard, Hampshire, the *Euryalus* was to be known as "Nelson's Watch Dog." Joining the fleet during the Napoleonic Wars, 1803–15, she was commanded by Captain Henry BLACKWOOD. It was the *Euryalus*'s crew who first warned of approaching French and Spanish warships three days before the Battle of TRAFALGAR, October 21, 1805. She monitored enemy movements closely and relayed the information back to Admiral Lord NELSON, who personally acknowledged Blackwood's contribution to the preparations for battle. Admiral Lord COLLINGWOOD, who succeeded Lord Nelson as commander in chief, transferred his flag to the *Euryalus* at the end of the battle after his own ship, the *Royal Sovereign*, was badly damaged. It was here that Collingwood wrote his famous dispatch about the death of Lord Nelson and the valor of the British at Trafalgar. The later history of the *Euryalus* was much less glorious: She ended her days as a convict ship.

Evans, Edward, First Baron Mountevans
1880–1957

British naval officer. Evans entered the Royal Navy in 1895 and saw service in the Antarctic in 1902–4 and 1909–13. During his second Antarctic expedition, with the rank of lieutenant, he was second in command to Captain Robert Falcon SCOTT. Evans commanded the *Terra Nova*, which Scott later used on his final Antarctic expedition, 1910–12. During WORLD WAR I, 1914–18, he served as a destroyer commander; in the later stages of the war he operated in the *BROKE*, which formed part of the Dover Patrol. Accompanied by the *Swift*, he sank two German destroyers in a flotilla of six in a remarkable action in the Straits of Dover during the night of April 20–21, 1917. His victory meant that there would be no more German raids into the Straits of Dover until 1918. Now known as "Evans of the *Broke*," he was promoted to captain and was soon appointed to the command of the cruiser *Active*. Despite his wartime achievements he was not promoted to rear admiral until 1928. At this point he was given the command of the Australian squadron, where he remained for two years before holding various appointments as local commander in chief.

Evans, Robley Dunglison
1846–1912

American naval officer, born in Floyd County, Virginia, on August 18, 1846. In order to receive an appointment to the U.S. Naval Academy, he moved west and established residency in Utah. (Each state had a limited allotment of places to the Academy, and there would be less competition for a place in Utah.) Nicknamed "Fighting Bob" Evans, he epitomized the changing nature of the U.S. Navy from the period of the AMERICAN CIVIL WAR 1861–65, to the years preceding WORLD WAR I, 1914–18. He was severely wounded while commanding a company of marines during an assault on Fort Fisher, North Carolina on January 15, 1865. Forcibly retired by a navy medical board, he eventually recovered, successfully appealed the board's decision and returned to active duty. As the navy's chief inspector of steel in 1885, he assisted in building the new steel ships, marking America's entry into the ranks of a naval power.

In August 1891 he captained the gunboat *Yorktown*, sent to Valparaiso, Chile, where he skillfully handled a diplomatic crisis over the killing of two American sailors from the U.S.S. *Baltimore* and the use of the American legation as an asylum for political refugees. During the SPANISH-AMERICAN WAR of 1898, he commanded the *Iowa* at Puerto Rico and at the decisive Battle of SANTIAGO, and was advanced in seniority for eminent conduct in battle. Promoted to rear admiral in 1901, he was given command of the GREAT WHITE FLEET during its voyage around the world, a command cut short by ill health. Retiring in 1908, he eventually wrote a two-volume autobiography before his death in Washington, D.C., on January 3, 1912.

Edwin A. Falk, *Fighting Bob Evans*, New York, 1931.

Evertsen, Cornelis
1642–1706

Dutch naval commander, born at Flushing, the Netherlands, into a notable Zeeland family that produced five admirals. He was the son of Cornelis Evertsen, 1610–66, who was killed during the FOUR DAYS' BATTLE, June 1–4, 1666; Admiral Jan EVERTSEN, 1600–66, who commanded the Dutch fleet at the Battle of SCHEVENINGEN, July 1653, after the death of Marten TROMP, was his uncle. Cornelis Evertsen also rose to high rank in the Dutch navy and was to command the fleet that escorted William of Orange to England in 1688. He first saw service in the Second ANGLO-DUTCH WAR, 1665–67, when he served during Admiral Michiel de RUYTER's raid on the Medway, 1667. He saw further action in the Third Dutch War, 1672–74, when, on July 30, 1673, he captured New York (and temporarily restored its original name, Nieuw Amsterdam), destroying a large number of British ships in the process. Cornelis Evertsen's career at sea concluded during the War of the GRAND ALLIANCE, 1688–97. Evertsen commanded 22 Dutch ships of the line at the Battle of BEACHY HEAD, July 10, 1690, under Admiral Arthur HERBERT, Earl of Torrington,

the British commander. However, the Anglo-Dutch fleet fared badly against the French, and the engagement did little for the reputations of either allied commander.

Evertsen, Jan
1600–66

Dutch naval commander, born at Flushing, the Netherlands. He was perhaps the most notable member of a family that produced five admirals. Progressing rapidly in his chosen profession, he was appointed to his first command at the age of 23. He first saw action at the Battle of the DOWNS, September 1639, when the Dutch fleet under Admiral Marten TROMP defeated the Spanish off the English coast at Dover. Evertsen was again in action during the First ANGLO-DUTCH WAR, 1652–54, serving at the battles of KENTISH KNOCK, 1652, DUNGENESS, 1652, and PORTLAND, 1653. His opportunity came at the Battle of SCHEVENINGEN, July 1653, when he flew his admiral's flag in the *Brederode*. The Dutch commander, Marten Tromp, was killed during the battle, and Evertsen succeeded him immediately. After a fierce fight the Dutch were forced to give way. Evertsen himself was killed at the Battle of ORFORDNESS, July 1666, during the Second Anglo-Dutch War, 1665–67. His son Cornelis EVERTSEN, 1628–79, who also became an admiral in the DUTCH NAVY, served in all three Anglo-Dutch wars and commanded his father's flagship, the *Brederode*, at the Battle of Scheveningen.

Excellent, H.M.S.

The first British warship to be named *Excellent* was a third rate (see RATING OF SHIPS) of 75 guns, launched in 1787. After a long period of active service in the ROYAL NAVY during the FRENCH REVOLUTIONARY AND NAPOLEONIC WARS, 1792–1815, she became the base for the naval gunnery training establishment when it was formed at Portsmouth in 1830. Several generations of young British officers and seamen learned the theory and practice of gunnery on board the *Excellent*. Although the *Excellent* has long since been broken up, in keeping with the British tradition of naming naval bases after ships, she gave her name to the Royal Navy's land-based school of gunnery, which has been based on Whale Island in Portsmouth harbor since it moved ashore in 1891.

Exeter, H.M.S.

British heavy cruiser of WORLD WAR II, 1939–45, completed in 1931, the *Exeter* had a displacement of 8,390 tons and six 8-inch (20-cm) guns. She was 575 feet

(175.26 m) in length and had a beam of 58 feet (17.6 m). Operated by a crew of 600, she had a maximum speed of 32 knots and was equipped with six 21-inch (53-cm) torpedo tubes. The Exeter was badly damaged by the POCKET BATTLESHIP ADMIRAL GRAF SPEE during the Battle of the RIVER PLATE, December 1939, in which she played a major role. She fought in company with the AJAX and ACHILLES, but enemy fire was concentrated on her because she was the most powerful British unit. Only the fact that many of the German 11-inch (28-om) shells were faulty saved her. After undergoing extensive repairs, the *Exeter* served briefly in the Home Fleet, 1940–41, before participating in Allied operations in the Dutch East Indies. On March 1, 1942, following the Battle of the JAVA SEA, she was hit by gunfire from Japanese warships in the South Java Sea and sank. Her sister ship, the *York,* also met a premature end. Serving with the Mediterranean fleet, she was severely damaged by the Italians while anchored in Suda Bay, Crete in March 1941. When the British withdrew from Crete two months later, they were forced to blow her up to prevent her from falling into enemy hands.

Exocet Missile

*F*rench-built antiship missile with radar homing, first used in the IRAN-IRAQ WAR, 1980–88. Manufactured by France's SNI Aerospatiale, it carries a 364-pound (165-kg) warhead at a speed of almost Mach 1 (the speed of sound). The Exocet can be launched from surface ships, submarines, aircraft or the ground and has a range of 25 to 42 miles (40–67 km) depending on type. As a result of its established record, this missile has been widely adopted by the world's naval forces. It was used with notable effect by Argentina in the FALKLANDS WAR, 1982, although a number failed because of poor maintenance. Air-launched versions claimed the British destroyer *SHEFFIELD* and the aviation auxiliary *ATLANTIC CONVEYER,* a 15,000-ton container ship. The destroyer *GLAMORGAN* was damaged by a land-based Exocet. In 1987, during the Gulf of Hormuz crisis, an Iraqi Exocet caused serious damage to the American Warship *Strand*.

Exploration and Discovery

*T*he exploration of the earth's surface by sea was an extended process dating back to the earliest periods of recorded history. Naval forces have played a key part in this exploration. The critical phase of exploration was the period of European discovery by sea in the 15th and 16th centuries. During the age of discovery, as it became known, individual pioneers made rapid progress in completing the map of the world, even though often they were motivated more by the desire for wealth than by the quest for knowledge.

The age of discovery began in 1415 with the Portuguese explorations of the west coast of Africa organized by Prince Henry the Navigator. These early voyages were followed by the discovery of the southern tip of Africa by Bartolomeu Diaz in 1487. Another Portuguese explorer, Vasco de Gama, opened a sea route to India in 1497. Several distinguished explorers also ventured westward from Europe. The Italian navigator Christopher Colombus, in the service of Spain, explored the Americas (1482–1504), as did Amerigo Vespucci (1499–1502), Giovanni Caboto (John Cabot; 1497–98) and the Frenchman Jacques Cartier (1524–42). Ferdinand Magellan also sailed west in 1519 and reached the Philippines, where he was killed. One of his captains continued the expedition and returned to Spain in 1522, completing the first circumnavigation of the globe. The English seaman Sir Francis DRAKE successfully completed a similar voyage around the globe in 1577–80.

During the 17th century, explorers focused their efforts on finding a route from the Atlantic to the Pacific using either a Northwest or Northeast Passage. The Dutch explorer Abel Tasman discovered Tasmania and New Zealand in 1642 and proved that Australia was an island. By the eighteenth century, national navies had become heavily involved in voyages of exploration, providing ships, personnel and other resources. In some cases they more were concerned with engaging enemy ships in remote locations than with exploration and scientific investigation. When British Admiral Lord ANSON circumnavigated the globe in 1744, he devoted as much attention to attacking the Spanish as he did to exploration. The ROYAL NAVY also supported the scientific voyages of Captain James COOK, 1768–79, in which the coasts of Australia and New Zealand were surveyed and mapped. Charles Darwin's later voyage in H.M.S. *BEAGLE* also benefited from the support of the Royal Navy. In 1768–69 Antoine de BOUGAINVILLE, a French naval officer, completed the first French circumnavigation of the globe.

During the 19th and early 20th centuries explorers switched their attention to the Arctic and Antarctica. The efforts of British, Russian and American explorers all contributed to an understanding of the vast polar regions, and naval officers played an important role. In 1909 Robert PEARY, a U.S. naval officer, led the first expedition to reach the North Pole. A fellow American officer, Admiral Richard BYRD, was the first person to fly over the North Pole in 1926. In 1958–59 an American nuclear-powered submarine made two journeys under the polar ice of the Arctic Ocean. There was also a tradition of British naval involvement in expeditions to Antarctica, although Captain Robert SCOTT, a serving officer in the Royal Navy, failed in his attempt to reach the South Pole before Norwegian Ronald Amundsen in December 1911. In 1929, Admiral Byrd claimed to be the first to reach the South Pole by plane, although doubts about this record continue to be expressed. The exploration of Antartica closed the last significant gap in the exploration of the earth.

In the postwar period, the traditional naval role in exploration has been continued by individual American naval officers (such as Alan Shepard) who have trained as astronauts and participated in the U.S. space program.

Samuel E. Morison, *The European Discovery of America,* 2 vols., London, 1971–74; John H. Parry, *The Age of Reconnaissance,* London, 1963.

Falkland Islands, Battle of the

December 8, 1914

A WORLD WAR I, 1914–18, engagement that restored British prestige after their disastrous defeat, on November 1, 1914, at the Battle of CORONEL, off the coast of Chile. The victorious German commander, Admiral Maximilian von SPEE, had returned briefly to Valparaiso before proceeding south to Cape Horn en route for Germany. Because of poor weather and a shortage of coal his progress was slow, but early in December he decided to attack Port Stanley in the Falkland Islands. This British communications center and coaling station was, von Spee thought, undefended, and he planned to destroy the wireless station there.

Admiral von Spee soon found that his information was hopelessly inaccurate. After the Coronel disaster, the Royal Navy reinforced the available British warships in the South Atlantic with two battle cruisers (the INVINCIBLE and the INFLEXIBLE) from the GRAND FLEET. They had left England on November 11 in readiness for a further engagement with von Spee. The whole force was placed under the command of Admiral Sir Doveton STURDEE and concentrated in the Falklands, where it arrived on December 7.

Von Spee reached his target during the early hours of the following day, December 8. The GNEISENAU and the Nürnberg—the advance guard of the squadron—were sent to reconnoiter and discovered the much more powerful British force at anchor. Von Spee was compelled to head southeast at full speed. The British fleet pursued as soon as its coaling operations were completed. The long chase began at 11:00 A.M. on December 8 in excellent weather conditions. As the British came in range of the Leipzig, the slowest German ship, at about 1:00 P.M., von Spee ordered his light cruisers to break away and a number of separate actions developed.

The British battle cruisers soon dealt with the enemy's principal ships, sinking the SCHARNHORST at 4:15 and the Gneisenau almost two hours later. The Leipzig was pursued and sunk by the Glasgow and the Cornwall, while the Nürnberg was destroyed by the Kent. The Dresden, the only German warship to escape, was scuttled three months later after a brief engagement with the Kent and the Glasgow in the South Pacific. The Germans, who fought with great bravery and determination, lost almost 2,000 men, including their commander, while the British suffered virtually no casualties. As a result of this battle, which was won by a much superior naval force, Britain's surface fleet controlled the seas.

G. Bennett, *Coronel and the Falklands*, London, 1962.

Falklands War

1982

This brief war between the United Kingdom and Argentina was precipitated by the Argentinian occupation of the Falkland Islands, a British colony in the South Atlantic. The Argentines, who had long claimed sovereignty over the islands, began an invasion on April 2, 1982, believing that Britain would not take any effective counteraction. It soon became evident that General Leopoldo Galtieri, head of the military junta that ruled Argentina, had seriously miscalculated. The British government, headed by Prime Minister Margaret Thatcher, decided to reoccupy the Falklands, and a ten-week military campaign followed. The severe difficulties in conducting an operation some 8,000 nautical miles from Britain were eased to some extent by British access to an American base on Ascension Island, and by the end of April an AMPHIBIOUS task force was in place off the Falklands.

Commanded by Rear Admiral John Woodward, the British force consisted of two aircraft carriers—the Hermes and the Invincible—and some 50 other warships as well as requisitioned merchant ships. The latter category included the passenger liners QE2 and CANBERRA, which served as troopships during the campaign. The arrival of the main force had been preceded by an advance guard of ships and submarines that imposed a BLOCKADE of the Falklands, enforcing a 200-mile exclusion zone around the islands. The arrival of the *CONQUEROR,* a nuclear submarine, quickly neutralized the Argentine fleet. On May 2 it sank the Argentinian cruiser *GENERAL BELGRANO* and forced the rest of the enemy fleet, which had no effective ANTISUBMARINE WARFARE capability, to remain in port for the duration of the war. Following the arrival of the task force, a series of initial air and commando attacks were made against enemy forces on the islands. The main operation began on May 21 when 10,000 ground troops were landed at San Carlos Water. During this landing British naval forces came under sustained attack from Argentinian aircraft armed with EXOCET missiles. However, the Argentinians were unable to prevent the successful completion of the landing. After the landings, ground troops advanced toward Port Stanley, the capital, which fell on June 14, bringing the war to an end.

Argentinian losses were heavy, including 109 aircraft, although the Royal Navy also suffered badly. Its losses included the destroyer *SHEFFIELD,* two frigates, a transport ship and two landing ships, demonstrating that modern warships were vulnerable to attack by advanced missiles. Total British and Argentinian casualties amounted to 1,000 men.

D. Brown, *The Royal Navy and the Falklands War,* London, 1987; M. Middlebrook, *The Fight for the Malvinas: The Argentinian Forces in the Falklands War,* London, 1989.

David Farragut: America's first rear admiral and Civil War hero   *(Copyright © National Maritime Museum, Greenwich, London)*

Farragut, David Glasgow
1801–70

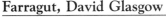

*T*he first American naval officer to reach the rank of rear admiral, Farragut was born near Knoxville, Tennessee, on July 5, 1801. Adopted by Commodore David PORTER in 1808, and thus the adopted brother of future Admiral David Dixon PORTER, he entered the navy at age nine. Serving under his famous new father on board the *Essex* during the WAR OF 1812, he was subsequently made—at the age of 12—prize captain of the British warship *Alexander Barclay.* When the *Essex* was captured at Valparaiso in March 1814, the young Farragut remained a prisoner-of-war until the following November. He subsequently saw service in the West Indies, attacking nests of pirates in and around Cuba during the 1820s.

A wide variety of shore and sea duties followed until the outbreak of the AMERICAN CIVIL WAR, 1861–65. Although a Southerner by birth and residence, Farragut resisted family and peer pressure to side with the Confederacy: He remained loyal to the Union, assuming command early in 1862 of the important West Gulf Blockading Squadron.

With orders to attack the southern Mississippi River and cut the Confederacy in half, Farragut succeeded in running past the defending Fort Jackson and Fort St. Philip, taking New Orleans and securing the Mississippi Delta area. For this action, Congress created the new rank of rear admiral and promoted Captain Farragut to become America's first flag officer. He remained in command on the Gulf, eventually taking Vicksburg, Mississippi and thus controlling the entire Mississippi River by late summer 1863. In August 1864 he and his forces proceeded, amid mine-infested waters, past the two defending fortresses at Mobile Bay, Alabama, and after a sharp contest with a Confederate IRONCLAD force, won the Battle of MOBILE BAY and thus closed the last significant Confederate port on the Gulf of Mexico. (During the battle, Farragut is reputed to have declared, "Damn the torpedoes [mines]! Full speed ahead!" The expression soon entered American naval lore.) He subsequently was promoted to vice admiral and in 1866 to full admiral. Farragut remained on active duty until his death in Portsmouth, New Hampshire on August 14, 1870.

Edwin P. Hoyt, *Damn the Torpedoes! The Story of America's First Admiral: David Glasgow Farragut,* 1970.

Fatshan Creek, Battle of

June 1, 1857

British attack on enemy ships during the Second China War, 1856–60, that resulted in heavy Chinese losses. The British target was a fleet of 70 armed junks at Fatshan Creek, an anchorage south of Canton. The action was launched on June 1 by a British squadron consisting of two paddle-tenders, seven gunboats and lesser craft, under the command of Rear Admiral Sir Michael Seymour. The squadron's passage into the creek was barred by a fort commanding the entrance, but this was quickly captured. As the squadron entered the creek a further barrier—submerged junks filled with rocks—appeared and proved to be more formidable. The smaller British boats continued into the creek under a heavy exchange of fire. Superior British gunnery quickly took its toll, and most of the junks soon surrendered. Some 20 junks escaped upstream but were soon seized by the British. (See also OPIUM WARS.)

Fegen, Edward

1895–1940

British naval officer who commanded the JERVIS BAY, an ARMED MERCHANT CRUISER, at the beginning of WORLD WAR II, 1939–45. On September 5, 1940, while escorting a 37-ship convoy across the North Atlantic, he was intercepted by the German POCKET-BATTLESHIP ADMIRAL SCHEER. Fegen ordered his convoy to scatter. Without fear for his own position, he engaged the battleship in an unequal duel in which he was completely outgunned. The fight could have only one outcome: The Jervis Bay was soon destroyed and Fegen went down with his ship. However, as a result of his brave action, most of the convoy escaped and only five ships were lost. Fegen was awarded a posthumous Victoria Cross.

Fighting Instructions

Official tactical rules that largely determined how the British navy fought at sea during the 17th and 18th centuries. First introduced in 1653, the earliest edition of the Fighting Instructions sought to impose a consistency of approach in the tactics employed by British officers at sea and, in particular, in the use of the line-ahead formation. Successive editions amplified and modified the instructions in the light of the experience gained fighting the Dutch and other naval powers in the second half of the 17th century. Shortly before the 1691 edition appeared, a similar guide was issued by the French navy.

The initial advantages of improving tactical discipline were gradually outweighed by the disadvantages of rigid adherence to a code that might not be appropriate in every circumstance. Indeed there were several notable examples, including the Battle of MINORCA, 1756, where following the fighting instructions led to an avoidable defeat. Some admirals were more willing than others to modify the rules. If an admiral wished to deploy his ships more flexibly than the instructions allowed, he was able to issue fresh orders using the new systems of signaling that were developed during the second half of the 18th century. As a result, the Fighting Instructions gradually fell into disuse and were replaced by more flexible tactical guidance that was developed during the late 18th century.

J. S. Corbett, ed., Fighting Instructions, 1530–1816, London, 1905.

Fireship

A small ship, packed with combustible material, that was set on fire after she had been attached to an enemy ship with the aim of destroying her. An important and often effective weapon in the age of the wooden warship, the fireship scored some notable successes. The attack on the SPANISH ARMADA, 1588, by British fireships is one major example of their effective use. As it was anchored off Calais during the night of July 28–29, the Spanish fleet was attacked by eight British fireships. The Spanish were compelled to abandon their anchorage in great haste and confusion. The following day they were brought to battle at Gravelines—a battle that produced a decisive British victory. The Royal Navy continued to use fireships over the next 200 years; they were last employed by the British during the Napoleonic Wars, 1803–15. Fireships gradually disappeared from the naval scene elsewhere as iron replaced wood in the construction of ships, but they were still in use during the AMERICAN CIVIL WAR, 1861–65.

Fireships had been used in naval warfare since ancient times but their basic components remained unchanged. A redundant vessel would be filled with flammable materials, which might include oil, pitch, tallow or even gunpowder. The DUTCH NAVY used these "explosion" or BOMB VESSELS during the 17th century and in one instance packed a ship with 18,000 pounds (8,165 kg) of explosive in a successful action against a Spanish BLOCKSHIP off Antwerp. A prepared fireship would be moved near to the enemy fleet, which might be engaged in battle or anchored in harbor. The correct positioning of the fireship was critical. Propelled by favorable winds or currents, it would drift into the enemy fleet. However, if the wind changed direction unexpectedly, there was a risk that the fireship could drift backward and endanger its own fleet. The fireship crew would seek to attach the fireship to its intended victim with grappling irons. They would then set light to the ship before abandoning it, returning to their own ships in small boats. The aim was first to destroy the rigging of the enemy ship and then the ship itself, although a bomb vessel might accomplish the whole task more directly.

Fisher, John, First Baron
1841–1920

Outstanding British naval administrator whose major reforms and improvements in efficiency gave the Royal Navy supremacy at sea at the beginning of WORLD WAR I, 1914–18. Entering the navy in 1854, at age 13, Fisher established a reputation as a gunnery and torpedo expert. He received regular promotion and by 1901 was an admiral in command of the Mediterranean Fleet, where he revolutionized training and tactics. His appointment, later in the same year, as Second Sea Lord in charge of personnel produced a new program of training for the service and the establishment of two new naval colleges.

As First Sea Lord, 1904–10, Jackie Fisher (as he was always known) introduced the world's first all-big-gun BATTLESHIP, the DREADNOUGHT, as well as the new BATTLE CRUISER. Ships with limited fighting power were scrapped as the new dreadnoughts appeared in the competition with Germany for naval supremacy. Fisher concentrated the fleet in home waters, where the main threat was likely to materialize, rather than in the Mediterranean. Entry to the officer corps was widened and its training improved to reflect fundamental changes in warfare and technology. At the same time, Fisher's aggressive personality made him many enemies, and he was involved in a damaging dispute with Lord Charles BERESFORD, commander in chief of the Channel Fleet. In 1909 he was raised to the peerage, and he retired from the navy early in the following year.

Fisher returned to the Admiralty as First Sea Lord on October 29, 1914, at the request of Winston CHURCHILL, then First Lord of the ADMIRALTY. Fisher soon had evidence that his own earlier work to improve the war readiness of the British fleet had been successful. Following the Battle of CORONEL, November 1, 1914, he detached two battle cruisers from the Grand Fleet and sent them to the South Atlantic to engage Admiral Maximilian von SPEE's squadron, which was destroyed at the Battle of the FALKLAND ISLANDS on December 8, 1914. He also was responsible for the introduction of a vast naval construction program that paid substantial returns later in the war. Fisher also promoted the development of semirigid airships ("blimps") that were used effectively against German U-BOATS.

Fisher's relations with Winston Churchill were good at first but soon deteriorated: Churchill's intervention in purely professional matters was an irritant, as were both men's volatile temperaments, but the DARDANELLES operation, 1915, was the major cause of conflict between them. Fisher's original lukewarm support for the plan turned to

Architect of the Royal Navy in World War I, Admiral John (Jackie) Fisher clashed with Winston Churchill, First Lord of the Admiralty, about strategy   *(Copyright © National Maritime Museum, Greenwich, London)*

opposition when it proved to be a significant drain on resources in the North Sea, and he resigned on May 15, 1915 in response to Churchill's demand for substantial new reinforcements for the Mediterranean. He never held high office again. Churchill himself later acknowledged the value of Fisher's work in sustaining the "power of the Royal Navy at the most critical period in its history."

A. J. Marder, ed., *Fear God and Dread Nought: The Correspondence of Lord Fisher*, 3 vols., London, 1952–59; *From the Dreadnought to Scapa Flow*, 3 vols., London, 1961–69.

Fiske, Bradley Allen
1854–1942

Born in Lyons, New York on June 13, 1854, Allen Fiske was probably America's greatest naval inventor as well as one of the most progressive and reform-minded officers in the military. He was instrumental in bringing the U.S. Navy into the modern period. Fiske entered the navy in 1870, reaching the rank of rear admiral in 1911, when he became the first admiral to leave and return to a ship by an aircraft. His many inventions included an electrical ammunition hoist, a system for detaching and lowering boats from larger vessels, an electrical mechanism for turning gun turrets, an electric range-finder and telescopic sights for naval guns, a speed and direction finder, a shipboard electric communications system, a submarine detection device, torpedo design improvements and, in 1912, the means for creating torpedo-launching airplanes. In the course of his career he registered more than 60 patents.

Opposition to his reforms by the naval establishment led Fiske to advocate changes in naval education and officer training. He urged the creation of a naval general staff and a national security council that would encompass all national policies in one centralized body. Partly as a result of Fiske's recommendations, the office of chief of naval operations was created in 1915. He campaigned vigorously for the administrative departments of the U.S. Navy to be consistently ready for war with specific plans. A prolific writer, he used his position as president of the U.S. Naval Institute, 1911–23, as a means to publish many works. Besides scores of articles, he wrote five books, including *Electricity in Theory and Practice* (1883, with at least 21 subsequent editions), *The Navy as a Fighting Machine* (1916, 1918), and *The Art of Fighting: Its Evolution and Progress* (1920). He retired in 1916 and died in New York City on April 6, 1942.

Paolo E. Coletta, *Admiral Bradley A. Fiske and the American Navy*, Lawrence, Kans., 1979.

Fitch, Aubrey Wray
1883–1948

*A*merican naval officer, born on June 11, 1883 in St. Ignace, Michigan, who has been described as among the least well known of the major commanders of WORLD WAR II, 1939–45. Most of Fitch's naval career was spent in surface and torpedo warfare until he switched to naval aviation in 1930. He participated in the aborted Wake Island Relief Expedition in December 1941. Commanding his carrier force on board the *Lexington*, he participated in the Battle of the CORAL SEA on May 7–8, 1942 that stopped the Japanese advance in the southeastern Pacific, although he lost his ship in the action. The Coral Sea was the first sea battle in which opposing ships never saw each other or exchanged a shot, signaling the role that air power subsequently would play in the Pacific Theater of World War II.

Beginning in September 1942, Fitch was placed in command of all aircraft in the South Pacific Area. Forces under his command began the advance against Japanese-held islands and against Japanese naval forces, destroying

in the air and on the ground over 3,000 Japanese aircraft by the time he left that post in August 1944. He served as deputy chief of naval operations until the end of the war. He then became superintendent of the U.S. Naval Academy, the first qualified naval aviator to hold that position and the first with the rank of vice admiral. He completed his career as a special assistant to the secretary of the navy. Fitch died on May 22, 1948 in Newcastle, Maine.

Clark G. Reynolds, *Famous American Admirals*, New York, 1978.

Flagship

*T*erm used for the vessel carrying the highest-ranking officer in command of a fleet, squadron or other naval formation and flying his flag of command. From this ship the flag officer exercises his command at sea and confers with his immediate staff, who also are accommodated on board. Notable flagships of the age of sail include the British warships *Royal Sovereign*, originally named the *Sovereign of the Seas* (Prince Rupert's flagship) and VICTORY (Lord NELSON's flagship). Equally important in Dutch naval history was the ZEVEN PROVINCIEN, the flagship of Admiral Michiel de RUYTER during the wars against the English in the 17th century. In the UNITED STATES NAVY, the sloop *Hartford* served as Admiral FARRAGUT's flagship during the AMERICAN CIVIL WAR, 1861–65, while the BATTLESHIP *New York* was Admiral SAMPSON's flagship during the SPANISH-AMERICAN WAR of 1898.

Fleet Air Arm

*T*he aviation branch of the British navy. During WORLD WAR I, 1914–18, it was called the Royal Naval Air Service (RNAS), but with the creation of the Royal Air Force (RAF) in 1918, it ceased to be a separate arm. As the importance of AIRCRAFT CARRIERS became apparent, the Royal Navy insisted that it should once again have its own air service and, in 1924, the Fleet Air Arm (FAA) was created. This was a compromise arrangement, in which the FAA came under operational control of the navy while its shore bases remained in RAF hands. Consequently, the FAA had no repair and maintenance facilities of its own. A further problem was that, during the interwar years, financial restrictions and interservice jealousies prevented any new aircraft from being designed specifically for FAA use. Instead, the FAA was obliged to accept hybrid designs. As a result, all FAA aircraft were unsuitable or obsolete at the start of WORLD WAR II, 1939–45. The FAA overcame the problem by buying UNITED STATES NAVY aircraft such as the Wildcat, Hellcat, Corsair and Avenger. Many of these designs remained in service long after the war had ended.

In the postwar period there were ambitious plans to expand the FAA's carrier force, but only two 42,000 ton carriers—the EAGLE and ARK ROYAL—appeared. Three Gibraltar-class carriers, equivalent in size to the American Midway-class carriers, were canceled. However, the FAA was in the forefront of carrier development and, in 1945, the Vampire jet fighter made the first takeoff from a carrier by a jet aircraft. This led to the FAA's inventions of the angled deck (which allowed aircraft to overshoot the carrier's runway in safety), the steam catapult and the automatic landing system (Mirror Landing Sight), all of which were quickly adopted by the U.S. Navy.

As the cost of aircraft carriers increased, successive British governments examined the FAA's future role in the context of diminishing defense budgets and political commitments outside the North Atlantic Treaty Organization (NATO). In the 1970s the government decided to phase out the carrier and fixed-wing aircraft; as a result, the last British conventional carrier, the Ark Royal, was scrapped in 1978. However, a political compromise followed, and a new type of cruiser, equipped with an extended flying deck, was developed. Initially this was designed to carry helicopters only, thus preserving some role for the FAA. In 1975 the development of the Sea Harrier vertical takeoff and landing (VTOL) aircraft was authorized; it went into FAA service in September 1979 on board the INVINCIBLE and later on a second carrier, the Illustrious.

By 1981 the United States was deeply concerned at the continued rundown of British naval forces outside the North Atlantic area. It offered the British two 45,000-ton U.S. Navy carriers, the Oriskany and the Hancock. The offer was rejected because of the cost of reestablishing a new fixed-wing FAA. Indeed, by 1982, plans were well advanced to sell the Invincible to the Australians and to scrap the HERMES, an old carrier. At this point, however, Argentina invaded the FALKLAND Islands and Britain was obliged to send a large task force to the South Atlantic. The operation to recapture the islands was achieved with the help of all the FAA's Sea Harriers, which performed brilliantly, achieving 95% availability throughout the war. They shot down 24 Argentine aircraft with their Sidewinder missiles. At the end of the war the FAA's future was secured, and a third carrier—the new ARK ROYAL—was built. Today the FAA has three squadrons of Sea Harriers and 160 helicopters of various kinds.

Geoffrey Till, Air Power and the Royal Navy, 1914–45, London, 1979.

Fletcher, Frank Friday
1855–1928

*A*merican naval officer. Born in Oskaloosa, Iowa, on November 23, 1855, Fletcher entered the navy in 1870. He served aboard the *Ticonderoga* from 1878 to 1881 on special service circumnavigating the world as part of U.S. efforts to open new commercial ties and to expand existing ones. A scientist and advocate of reforms at the time that the U.S. Navy began to build its steel fleet, he saw special service on the expedition (September 1883– June 1884) to determine longitudes. While attached to the Bureau of Ordnance from 1887 to 1892, he contributed to the design and manufacturing of gun mechanisms, which increased the speed of rapid-fire guns. He also campaigned for the implementation of range lights for all naval vessels, which the navy finally adopted in 1890. Three years later he developed the first American doctrine on the use of TORPEDO warfare.

Commanding the *Vermont* as part of the GREAT WHITE FLEET from November 1908 to February 1910, he was promoted to rear admiral the following year, and captained some of the navy's newest ships between 1912 and 1914, including the *Ohio, Minnesota, Louisiana, Rhode Island* and *Florida*. As commander of American forces off the west coast of Mexico in April 1914 during the crisis between the United States and Mexico, he was ordered by President Woodrow Wilson to seize the customs house at Vera Cruz. For this action he was subsequently awarded the Congressional Medal of Honor. Promoted to admiral in 1915, he served a valuable role as a member of both the Army-Navy Joint Board and the War Industries Board during WORLD WAR I. Retiring in November 1919, he died in New York City on November 28, 1928.

William B. Cogar, *Dictionary of Admirals of the U.S. Navy, Vol. 2, 1901– 1918*, Annapolis, 1991.

Fletcher, Frank Jack
1885–1973

*A*merican naval officer, born on April 29, 1885 in Marshalltown, Iowa, the nephew of Admiral Frank Friday FLETCHER. Like his uncle, he participated in the Vera Cruz affair, 1914, overseeing the evacuation of refugees from a passenger vessel, for which he was awarded the Congressional Medal of Honor. His major fame came some 28 years later as the commander of the carrier task forces during the pivotal battles of the Pacific War in 1942. Commanding Task Force 17 and flying his flag in the *YORKTOWN,* he launched air attacks against Japanese forces in the Gilbert and Marshall Island groups in February 1942, followed by raids on Japanese vessels at Lae and Salamaua in New Guinea. With Rear Admiral Aubrey W. FITCH's Task Force 11, Fletcher's carrier force stopped the Japanese thrust at the Battle of the CORAL SEA on May 4–8, 1942.

He was then given tactical command (thus becoming senior task force commander) of the three carriers sent to repel the Japanese attack on MIDWAY ISLAND in June. Securing a decisive victory, Fletcher's flagship, the *Yorktown*, was severely crippled and later sank, forcing him to yield his command to Rear Admiral Raymond A. SPRUANCE. As commander of Task Force 6, he sailed in the *SARATOGA* and directed the GUADALCANAL landings in August 1942. Soon afterward his carriers fought the Japanese at the Battle of the EASTERN SOLOMONS and denied them the opportunity to retake Guadalcanal. However, he was severely criticized for abandoning the *Yorktown* at Midway and for tactical decisions off Guadalcanal that resulted in heavy losses. Although he tried to secure another active sea command, he was given instead, in late 1943, the relatively inactive command of the North Pacific area, overseeing combat operations in Alaskan and Aleutian waters. In the last month of the war, Fletcher's forces occupied the northern Japanese islands of Honshu and Hokkaido. He died in Bethesda, Maryland on April 25, 1973.

Stephen B. Regan, *In Bitter Tempest: The Biography of Admiral Frank Jack Fletcher*, Ames, IO, 1994.

Floating Battery

*I*n use during the 18th and 19th centuries, a floating battery typically consisted of the modified hull of an old sailing ship or, in a later form, a specially designed structure that was used as a mobile gun platform. Floating batteries were used for attacking enemy positions on shore and were subject to heavy retaliatory fire. Following the strong Russian response when the British and French used floating batteries in the CRIMEAN WAR, 1853–56, the batteries were fitted with protective armored plating. Small steam engines also were added to enable them to be transported to and from the battle zone more easily. Floating batteries were superseded by the MONITOR, a ship specifically designed for bombardment purposes, which first appeared during the AMERICAN CIVIL WAR, 1861–65.

Flotilla

A group of small warships typically under the overall command of a captain. The term has Spanish origins and means "little fleet." The word often refers to a group of ships of the same kind—destroyers, submarines or torpedo boats, for example. The ship carrying the officer in command of a destroyer flotilla was known as the flotilla leader. This command ship normally was larger than the rest of the flotilla and better armed. In the late 20th century the word "squadron" is normally used to describe a group of small warships, and the term "flotilla" is no longer widely used.

Fluyt

A Dutch three-masted sailing ship that was in use from the late 16th century until well into the 18th century. It proved to be a highly successful design and became one of the principal merchant ships of northern Europe. The fluyt had a larger-than-average tonnage and was longer than most of its contemporaries, with the typical length-to-beam beam ratio being increased from 3 to 1 to 6 to 1 to enlarge its carrying capacity. It had a shallow draft and a distinctive rounded stern with a large opening for the tiller. The main mast and foremast were square-rigged with a mainsail and a topmast. A lateen sail was fitted to the mizzen mast.

Although the fluyt was employed primarily as a merchant ship, inevitably such a successful design was soon adapted for a variety of other uses by the navies of northern Europe. A typical naval fluyt of the 17th or 18th century would carry fewer than 20 guns, with most positioned on the main deck and a smaller number at the stern and forecastle. Otherwise it was much the same as its commercial counterpart. It was operated by a small crew of up to 20 men and could carry a considerable volume of naval supplies.

Foote, Andrew Hull
1806–63

*A*merican admiral, born in New Haven, Connecticut, who served with distinction during the AMERICAN CIVIL WAR, 1861–65. A brief period at West Point in 1822 ended when Foote decided to join the navy as a midshipman. He saw action on land against Chinese nationalist forces during his command of the *Portsmouth*, 1856–58, at Canton. As the Civil War began he was appointed to the command of a naval FLOTILLA on the upper Mississippi, where he was to act in concert with the Union army units under General Ulysses S. Grant. Foote succeeded in advancing southward and was able to split the Confederacy in two, interrupting its supply routes from the west.

Early in 1862 combined operations continued with the capture of Fort Henry and then of Fort Donelson, forcing the Confederates to abandon large areas of Kentucky and Tennessee. Foote's naval forces were solely responsible for the victory at Fort Henry, although the army must receive the credit for the conquest of Fort Donelson, where the navy was forced to withdraw with heavy damage and Foote himself was badly injured. Eventually he was forced to give up his command and transferred to a naval office in Washington, D.C. In 1863 he was appointed head of the South Atlantic Blockading Force but died before he could take up the post.

Forbes, Sir Charles Morton
1881–1960

British naval commander and gunnery expert who enjoyed short-lived prominence as the head of the British Home Fleet at the beginning of WORLD WAR II, 1939–45. Earlier in his career Forbes had served on the staff of Sir John JELLICOE when he was commander in chief of the GRAND FLEET during WORLD WAR I, 1914–18. During the interwar period he was a battleship commander, held various staff commands and served in the Mediterranean as second in command of the British fleet. He reached the rank of admiral in 1936 and in 1938 was appointed to the command of the Home Fleet.

Following the outbreak of World War II, Forbes was fully involved in the Norwegian campaign of April 1940. He was held partly responsible for the Home Fleet's slow response to German action against Norway because of doubts about the accuracy of its intelligence about the enemy's intentions. Nevertheless, this did not prevent his promotion to admiral of the fleet in May 1940. However, within six months he had been replaced as commander of the Home Fleet by Admiral Sir John TOVEY. Forbes's final three months in command were overshadowed by a dispute with the ADMIRALTY over the removal of some of his cruisers and destroyers to protect the coast of southern England against a possible German invasion attempt. He spent the last two years of his naval career in command at Plymouth and was involved in planning the ST. NAZAIRE RAID, March 1942.

Forbin, Claude de
1656–1733

French naval officer who distinguished himself during Louis XIV's wars and who recorded his exploits in his *Mémoires*, published in 1730. Once Forbin gained basic experience at sea, his promotion was rapid and, in 1686, he was sent on a French mission to the King of Siam. He held office as grand admiral of the King of Siam's fleet for two years, 1685–87, before returning home to serve in a privateer with Jean BART. They were captured by the English and imprisoned at Plymouth but later managed to escape back to France.

During the War of the SPANISH SUCCESSION, 1701–14, Forbin commanded a squadron in the Adriatic and cut the supply lines of imperial forces operating in Italy. He later served in the French northern squadron and operated successfully against Dutch and English ships in the North Sea. In 1708, following the failure of an expedition under his command to land James, the Old Pretender (the son of the deposed King James II and claimant to the English throne) in Scotland, Forbin resigned from the navy.

Force H

A British naval force of WORLD WAR II, 1939–45, formed in June 1940, that was based at Gibraltar. By establishing a powerful naval presence in this area, Force H was intended to compensate for the collapse of France and to take account of Italy's entry into the war. Commanded by Admiral Sir James SOMERVILLE, the composition of the force varied, but at its formation it included the aircraft carrier ARK ROYAL, the battleships *Valiant* and *RESOLUTION* and the battle cruiser *HOOD*. For the next three years it was the main British naval force in the western Mediterranean and Atlantic.

One of its first duties was to neutralize the French fleet based at MERS-EL-KEBIR, 1940, which was achieved without any loss. When the BISMARCK sank the *Hood* in May 1941, the *Ark Royal*, RENOWN and SHEFFIELD went in search of her. Swordfish aircraft from the *Ark Royal* attacked and hit the *Bismarck*, damaging her steering gear beyond repair; this decisive action slowed the enemy battleship down before her final destruction. Force H played a key role in escorting the MALTA CONVOYS and took part in the landings in North Africa, 1942, and in SICILY and SALERNO, 1943. With its work in the Mediterranean completed, Force H was disbanded in October 1943 and its ships were allocated to other British naval units.

D. Macintyre, *The Battle for the Mediterranean*, London, 1962.

Force Z

A British squadron sent to the Far East in December 1941 following Japan's entry into WORLD WAR II, 1939–45, in order to provide Malaya and Singapore with a defense against enemy attack. Commanded by Admiral Tom PHILLIPS, Force Z consisted of the battleship *PRINCE OF WALES*, the battle cruiser *Repulse* and several destroyers. Admiral Phillips arrived in Singapore on December 2 with orders to prevent enemy landings on the coast of Malaya. Although he had no air cover, he put to sea without delay on December 8 in order to intercept enemy convoys that were supporting Japanese landings at Kota Bharu, near the northeast tip of Malaya. Force Z was spotted by a Japanese submarine during the following afternoon, but Phillips' staff were not aware of the enemy's presence until they saw a reconnaissance aircraft just before sunset. Unwilling to take any further risks with his unprotected ships, Phillips returned south along the Malayan coast.

On December 10 Japanese bombers from the Twenty-second Air Flotilla were sent to bomb Force Z as it returned to Singapore. Both capital ships were sunk, although more than 2,000 survivors were picked up by the escorting destroyers. The loss of Force Z represented a major blow to British prestige and confirmed the obvious rule that naval units should not be sent into battle unless they have the necessary air protection. Except for three American aircraft carriers, there were now no Allied capital ships in service in the Pacific.

Richard Hough, *The Hunting of Force Z*, London, 1963; D. Macintyre, *The Rise and Fall of the Singapore Naval Base, 1919–1942*, London, 1979.

Formidable, H.M.S.

*B*ritish aircraft carrier, the second ship of the Illustrious class, launched in 1939. With a displacement of 23,000 tons, she had greater protection and better armament than previous British carriers. Some 1,400 men were needed to operate her, and she could accommodate 36 aircraft. She was 673 feet (205 m) in length and had a beam of 95 feet 9 inches (29 m). The *Formidable*'s WORLD WAR II, 1939–45, service was divided between the Mediterranean and the Pacific; she saw much action in both theaters. Present at the Battle of CAPE MATAPAN, 1941, she assisted in the evacuation of mainland Greece and Crete soon afterward. The *Formidable* sustained major damage during a German air attack off Crete on May 26, 1941 and went to the United States for repairs.

Later service in the Mediterranean included support for the Allied invasions of North Africa, October 1942, and Italy, 1943. In 1945 the *Formidable* was sent to the Pacific, where she was damaged in a KAMIKAZE attack. An accident later destroyed many of her aircraft, but she was still able to participate in some of the final attacks on the Japanese. She finally was scrapped in 1953.

The name "Formidable" originally had been adopted by the ROYAL NAVY when the French warship *Formidable* was captured at the Battle of QUIBERON BAY, 1759, during the SEVEN YEARS' WAR, 1775–63. She was added to the British fleet. A later British *Formidable*, a second rate (see RATING OF SHIPS) of 90 guns, was launched in 1777. She served as Admiral Sir George RODNEY's flagship at the Battle of the SAINTS, 1787.

Forrestal, James Vincent
1892–1949

*A*merican businessman and public official who served as U.S. Under Secretary of the Navy during WORLD WAR II, 1939–45, then Secretary of the Navy and finally as first Secretary of Defense. Born on February 15, 1892 in Matteawan, New York, Forrestal was educated at Dartmouth College and Princeton University. He entered business as an investment banker, rising in stature as a man of high abilities and talents. Asked in 1940 by President Franklin D. Roosevelt to be a special administrative aide, he became Under Secretary of the Navy, overseeing the procurement program for the war and, despite considerable

opposition from within the navy, asserting civilian authority over the Navy Department. In 1944 he was appointed Secretary of the Navy following the death of the then-secretary Frank Knox.

An initial opponent of the proposed unification of the armed services following World War II, Forrestal recognized the inevitable and supported the National Security Act of 1947 but campaigned hard and successfully to ensure that the individual services, and especially the navy, each retained a large degree of autonomy. In July of that year he became the first Secretary of Defense, but after nearly two years of interservice squabbling and differences with President Harry Truman, he resigned in March 1949. Suffering from severe depression, he committed suicide later that year.

Townsend Hoopes and Douglas Brinkley, *Driven Patriot: The Life and Times of James Forrestal*, New York, 1992.

Forrestal, U.S.S.

*L*aunched at Newport News, Virginia in 1954, the *Forrestal* was the first American AIRCRAFT CARRIER built after WORLD WAR II, 1939–45. At the time of her completion, she was the biggest warship in the world and the largest ship ever to have been built in the United States. Named after James FORRESTAL, Secretary of Defense, 1947–49, she had a displacement of 59,650 tons (75,900 tons when fully loaded) and carried a crew of 2,790. Another 2,150 men were needed to operate and maintain her 70 aircraft. The *Forrestal* was 1,086 feet (331 m) in length and had a beam of 129 feet (39.3 m); her flight deck was 252 feet (76.8 m) wide. She had a maximum speed of 33 knots.

The *Forrestal*'s structure incorporated two recent British innovations in carrier design. The first was the angled flight deck, which enabled an aircraft to go around again if it missed the arrester wire during a landing attempt. She also had a steam catapult to help launch her aircraft; the catapult compensated for the jet engine's relatively slow acceleration and gave it a safe takeoff speed. These improvements, new at the time she was built, have been a feature of all later carriers, including three other ships of the Forrestal class—the *Saratoga*, *Ranger* and *Independence*. During her service in the VIETNAM WAR, 1965–73, the *Forrestal* was damaged and 60 of her aircraft destroyed when an explosion on the flight deck caused a serious fire. Following repair and modernization, she continued in service with the UNITED STATES NAVY but was stricken in 1993.

Foudroyant, H.M.S.

A British second-rate (see RATING OF SHIPS) warship, launched in 1798, the *Foudroyant* became Admiral

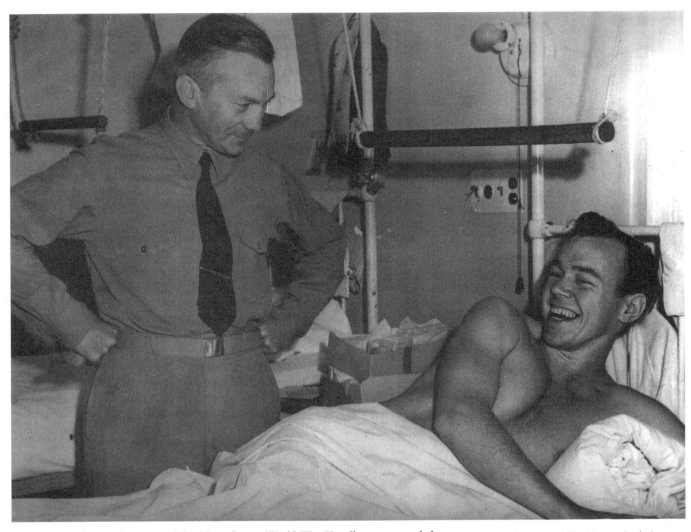

James Forrestal, U.S. Secretary of the Navy during World War II, talks to a wounded marine   *(Copyright © Imperial War Museum, London)*

Horatio NELSON's flagship at Palermo in 1799, during the FRENCH REVOLUTIONARY AND NAPOLEONIC WARS, 1792–1815. She served in this capacity until her return to London during the following year. She later acted as the FLAGSHIP of Lord Keith (see ELPHINSTONE) and was present at the surrender of the French at Alexandria in 1801. A later *Foudroyant* (originally named the *Trincomalee*) was a fifth rate, launched at Bombay in 1819, that eventually became a famous training ship.

The name *Foudroyant* derived from a famous French warship of 80 guns that was captured by the British in a notable single-ship action during the SEVEN YEARS' WAR, 1756–63. Early in 1758 the *Monmouth*, a much smaller vessel, gave chase and fought the *Foudroyant* in the western Mediterranean. After an intense engagement, the French surrendered and the *Foudroyant*, which was Admiral the Marquis DUQUESNE's flagship, was seized. The ROYAL NAVY retained her name and employed her for the rest of the war, returning her to active service during the AMERICAN WAR OF INDEPENDENCE, 1775–83. After a notable second career she was finally broken up in 1787.

Four Days' Battle

June 1–4, 1666

The second major battle of the Second ANGLO-DUTCH WAR, 1665–67, the Four Days' Battle was one of the longest in naval history. It took place almost exactly a year after the war's opening battle off LOWESTOFT. In January 1666 the French had entered the war on the Dutch side; in response, the English fleet was divided. Prince RUPERT's White Squadron of 24 ships was sent down the English Channel to intercept a French naval force that was expected to be dispatched to help the Dutch. As a result the main fleet under George MONCK, Duke of Albemarle, was under strength, having only 56 ships remaining, compared with the 85 warships available to the Dutch.

Commanded by Admiral Michiel de RUYTER, the Dutch fleet was sighted off North Foreland on June 1, in poor weather conditions. Albemarle attacked just after noon; the battle continued that day until 10 P.M. As the two sides moved toward Dunkirk during a running fight, both suffered heavy damage, and each lost two or three ships. Monck renewed the fight on June 2, but his damaged and outnumbered fleet was forced to retreat west after hours of hard combat. Losses were similar to those on the first day.

On the third day the English retreat continued, their fleet now reduced to fewer than 30 operational ships. Monck was forced to destroy three of his own badly damaged vessels, while the *Royal Prince*, a fine 90-gun ship, ran aground and was captured. The Dutch continued their pursuit but did not renew the fight. Fortunately for Monck, Prince Rupert's White Squadron rejoined the English fleet at this point, ending his abortive search for the French and increasing the number of English ships available to 60—only 18 fewer than the Dutch. This number, however, was not enough to reverse English fortunes. Fighting was renewed on the fourth day, and in a melée lasting some two hours losses mounted rapidly on both sides. The Dutch finally withdrew in a state of exhaustion and the battle came to an end. The Four Days' Battle was a major defeat for the English, whose losses were heavy—17 ships and 8,000 casualties. The Dutch lost seven ships and 2,000 officers and men killed or wounded. However, despite their setback, the English were to recover quickly, winning the Battle of ORFORDNESS only seven weeks later.

Fox, Gustavus Vasa
1821–83

*A*merican naval administrator, born at Saugus, Massachussetts in June 1821. Fox trained at the United States Naval Academy, ANNAPOLIS, and served in the navy from 1838 to 1856, leaving with the rank of lieutenant. Through influential family connections he was involved in the attempt to resolve the crisis at Fort Sumter, South Carolina in the opening stages of the AMERICAN CIVIL WAR, 1861–65. As a result of his contribution, he was invited to rejoin the navy and became chief clerk in the Navy Department. Within a few weeks he had become assistant navy secretary, working in partnership with Secretary of the Navy Gideon WELLES, with the aim of creating an effective naval force in the North. Fox served in this capacity throughout the war and established an effective naval administration. He was also active in improving procurement methods, modernizing the curriculum at Annapolis and supporting the use of IRONCLADS in battle. Fox

resigned from his post in May 1866 and died in New York City on October 29, 1883.

Fraser, Bruce Austin, First Baron Fraser of North Cape
1888–1981

*B*ritish naval commander whose name is associated with the destruction of the German battle cruiser *SCHARNHORST* during WORLD WAR II, 1939–45. Fraser entered the Royal Navy in 1902 and specialized in gunnery at an early stage in his career. Periods at sea were punctuated by service in the ordnance arm of the ADMIRALTY. He was appointed to flag rank in 1938 and became chief of staff to Admiral Sir Dudley POUND, commander in chief of the Mediterranean fleet. At the beginning of the war Fraser was Third Sea Lord and Controller with the rank of vice admiral. In 1943 he returned to sea as commander in chief of the Home Fleet. His victory at the Battle of NORTH CAPE, December 26, 1943, resulted in the loss of the German battle cruiser *Scharnhorst*.

Promoted to the rank of admiral in August 1944, Fraser exchanged the Home Fleet for the Eastern Fleet, replacing Admiral Sir James SOMERVILLE as commander in chief. Only three months later he was appointed to the command of the British Pacific Fleet, which joined with the Americans in the final actions against the Japanese in 1944–45. He was a British signatory at the Tokyo Bay Peace Ceremony on board the American battleship *Missouri*. In the immediate postwar period he received a succession of honors, being raised to the peerage and promoted to admiral of the fleet. Fraser served as First Sea Lord, 1948–51, before his final retirement from the navy.

Richard Humble, *Fraser of North Cape: The Life of Admiral of the Fleet Lord Fraser (1888–1981)*, London, 1983.

Fremantle, Sir Thomas
1765–1819

*B*ritish vice admiral who served with Admiral Lord NELSON during the wars against France, 1792–1815. Fremantle joined him in Corsica in 1794 and, as commander of the *Seahorse*, took part in the attack on Santa Cruz in 1797. He was involved in the Battle of COPENHAGEN, 1801, and was present at the Battle of TRAFALGAR, 1805, in command of the *Neptune*, a first rate (see RATING OF SHIPS) SHIP OF THE LINE and the third vessel in the weather line (those ships in the line of battle on the windward side). He spent much of the remaining years of his career in the Mediterranean where, shortly after the war, he was briefly commander in chief. His wife, Betsy Wynne, whom he married in 1797, was a notable diarist

British and Dutch fleets clash at the Four Days' Battle, 1666, during the Second Anglo-Dutch War, 1665–67   *(Copyright © National Maritime Museum, Greenwich, London)*

French Navy

Although it was always primarily a Continental land power, France has maintained a powerful navy since the first part of the 17th century. The French navy has had a checkered history, although it was to intervene decisively in the AMERICAN WAR OF INDEPENDENCE, 1775–83, produce major contributions to naval science and, during the age of sail, construct warships of high quality.

France first emerged as a major naval power under Cardinal Richelieu, 1585–1642, who assembled a Dutch-built fleet that could match the performance of the English GALLEONS of the day. France soon developed a shipbuilding capacity of her own. When Jean Baptiste COLBERT revived the fortunes of the fleet later in the 17th century, he could turn to local shipwrights to produce new designs. The main purposes of the French fleet included home defense and the protection of trade as well as support for the acquisition of a colonial empire in the West Indies and elsewhere. In the Mediterranean, the French navy also was charged with the defense of French trading links and, until the early 18th century, used GALLEYS for this purpose.

An early test of its performance came during the Third DUTCH WAR, 1672–78, when, unusually, it worked in alliance with the English fleet. At the Battle of Augusta, April 22, 1676, Admiral Abraham Marquis DUQUESNE defeated the Dutch fleet, whose commander, Admiral Michiel de RUYTER, was mortally wounded. During the War of the GRAND ALLIANCE, 1688–97, France and England were on opposite sides. The French navy's success at the Battle of BEACHY HEAD, 1690, was overshadowed by Admiral de TOURVILLE's defeat at LA HOGUE two years later. In the series of major European land wars that followed, the English and French fleets fought several major engagements in which the Royal Navy's dominant position remained secure. The SEVEN YEARS' WAR, 1756–63, was notable for several French naval defeats at the hands of the British, leading to a significant reduction in the size of her colonial empire.

However, restored by the Comte de Sartine, the navy had the opportunity to avenge itself during the American War of Independence, although by the end of conflict the English fleet had reestablished its dominant position, defeating the enemy at the Battle of the SAINTS, 1782. The French navy also let the opportunity of invading England pass during a brief period when it dominated the English Channel. The French navy's principal ally, Spain, was heavily defeated at the Battle of CAPE ST. VINCENT, 1781. Against this must be set the outcome of the second Battle of CHESAPEAKE, September 5, 1781, when Admiral the Comte de GRASSE defeated an English fleet under Admiral Thomas GRAVES. As a result, Graves was unable to resupply the English land forces under General Cornwallis who were besieged and in a desperate position at Yorktown. Cornwallis was forced to surrender within a few weeks and American independence was secured. De Grasse's victory marked the greatest moment in the history of the French navy. Britain and France were to be at war again less than ten years later, but this time the outcome would be much less favorable to the French.

Although the FRENCH REVOLUTIONARY AND NAPOLEONIC WARS, 1792–1815, were primarily land-based, considerable resources were tied up in naval operations. As in the past, the French navy was responsible for maintaining essential supplies by sea in the face of a British blockade. The Royal Navy sought to engage the enemy whenever it could and in one notable example defeated the French fleet under Admiral Louis VILLARET-JOYEUSE at the Battle of the GLORIOUS FIRST OF JUNE, 1794, although most of the grain ships he was protecting escaped to complete their journey. It was also involved in a major AMBHIBIOUS operation—landing 40,000 men in Egypt—although it suffered a major defeat shortly afterward at the Battle of the NILE, 1798. The French navy also took part in preparations for more than one planned invasion of England. Although these plans came to nothing, the British army devoted considerable effort to making the necessary defensive arrangements. Working in alliance with the Spanish fleet, the French navy remained a potential threat to England until Admiral Lord NELSON's decisive victory at the Battle of TRAFALGAR, October 1805. From that point the French navy continued to represent a danger to enemy merchant shipping but was unable to challenge British dominance of the seas. A variety of reasons—ranging from poor morale and internal conflict to inferior guns—explain the French navy's failures in these wars.

France quickly rebuilt its navy after 1815 and, like Britain, intervened against Turkey in the Greek War of Independence, 1821–32, with both navies fighting side by side at the decisive Battle of NAVARINO, 1827. They were to do so again during the CRIMEAN WAR, 1853–56 although the French navy's main role in the 19th century was maintaining France's colonial empire. With one or two notable exceptions—for example, the DARDANELLES operation, 1915—France, in contrast to Britain, played a relatively minor role in the war at sea in WORLD WAR I, 1914–18. The German invasion of France and the subsequent attack on its fleet at Oran meant that its naval contribution to WORLD WAR II, 1939–45, was even more restricted, although some units did serve with Allied naval forces.

The French navy always has been closely associated with technological innovation, especially from the time it produced LA GLOIRE, the world's first IRONCLAD ship, in 1859. Other examples included a high-speed destroyer of the 1920s and the advanced submarine SURCOUF, which was lost in 1942. In the postwar period, France has remained at the forefront of submarine design. It has developed and maintained an independent nuclear deterrent, using submarine-launched ballistic missiles, which forms the basis of its defense policy outside the North Atlantic Treaty Organization (NATO). In other respects the capability of the present-day French navy reflects France's position as a medium-size European power with continuing global interests.

Ernest H. Jenkins, *A History of the French Navy, from the Beginnings to the Present Day*, London, 1979.

French Revolutionary and Napoleonic Wars
1792–1815

*I*n 1792 France was proclaimed a republic and embarked on a war that was to engulf most of Europe for over 20 years. Britain entered the war early in 1793, and its naval forces soon were deployed on active service against the French. In August French royalists surrendered the port of Toulon to the British Mediterranean Fleet, which was to hold it for some four months before it was evacuated. With France in the hands of the Convention, Britain imposed a close BLOCKADE of its ports to ensure that essential supplies were disrupted. The first major naval battle of the war—the GLORIOUS FIRST OF JUNE, May 29–June 1—was fought as the Royal Navy sought to intercept an Atlantic convoy on its way to Brest with essential grain supplies. Although the French navy suffered a tactical defeat, the grain convoy managed to reach its destination.

As the war progressed, the blockade was extended to cover Dutch and Spanish ports, with each location being allocated to a separate British squadron, which would abandon its position only in a severe storm. The Royal Navy stopped and searched neutral merchant ships, severely disrupting normal trade for much of the war. It sought to maintain its dominant position in the English Channel and thus protect its coast from threatened invasion. A major French landing in Ireland was thwarted when the accompanying Dutch fleet was defeated at the Battle of CAMPERDOWN, October 1797. The British fleet also was involved in several amphibious operations; these met with varying degrees of success, although only the WALCHEREN expedition, 1809, was a complete disaster.

In the Mediterranean the opposing fleets fought on several occasions, and the British achieved a notable early success when they captured Corsica in 1795. However, this was to be a short-lived victory because of Spain's entry into the war on the French side in 1796. This posed a potentially serious threat to the British Mediterranean fleet, which was forced to abandon Corsica and Elba. However, within a few months Admiral Sir John JERVIS had defeated the Spanish fleet at the Battle of CAPE ST. VINCENT, 1797, and blockaded the surviving enemy units in Cadiz. In 1798 the Mediterranean continued as a focus of naval activity when the French Mediterranean Fleet, commanded by Admiral François de BRUEYS, escorted Napoleon and his army to Egypt. Admiral Horatio NELSON was dispatched to search for the French and eventually fought them at the Battle of the NILE, August 1798. The French were heavily defeated and their army was cut off in Egypt. Nelson again displayed his brilliance at the Battle of COPENHAGEN, November 1801, the last significant engagement of the French Revolutionary Wars, which were concluded by the Peace of Amiens, 1802.

When war resumed in 1803, the British quickly reimposed their blockade of French ports and took early action to thwart Napoleon's plans to invade England. In October a French invasion force that had been assembled at the mouth of the Rhine was badly damaged by British naval forces, but the threat remained. In 1805 Nelson was ordered to locate and destroy the French fleet, commanded by Admiral Pierre VILLENEUVE, that would be needed to support an invasion. Following an extended pursuit across the Atlantic, this Franco-Spanish fleet was defeated at the Battle of TRAFALGAR, October 1805, when Nelson used his preferred tactic of concentrating his force to break the enemy line.

The French navy failed during the war for a whole variety of reasons, ranging from internal divisions to inferior gunnery. This decisive victory meant that from this point the British had effective control of the seas, which they were to maintain unchallenged until the end of the war in 1815. The British mounted a number of smaller operations, including a second attack on COPENHAGEN in 1807, but there were no further naval battles on the scale of those fought by Nelson and his captains.

Chronological List of Naval Events

1793

August 27–December 19	British naval siege of Toulon; continuing blockade of Toulon, Brest and other French ports during the war
1794	
April	British admiral Sir John Jervis occupies the French islands of Martinique, St. Lucia and Guadeloupe
May 29–June 1	Battle of the Glorious First of June between Britain and France

1795	British and French campaigns against merchant shipping in the Atlantic and elsewhere begin
1796	
August 19	Spain joins France in the war against Britain, threatening the position of the British Mediterranean Fleet
December 5	French invasion fleet leaves Brest for Ireland but abandons plan because of bad weather
1797	
February 14	Battle of Cape St. Vincent ends the Spanish naval threat to Britain
April 16	British naval mutiny at SPITHEAD which later (May 12) spreads to the NORE
October 11	Battle of Camperdown
1798	
August 1	Battle of the Nile: Nelson defeats the French fleet that brought Napoleon to Egypt
August 22	French invasion of Ireland (defeated by October 12)
1799	
August	British forces landed in Holland; the Dutch fleet at the Texel surrenders to the Royal Navy
1801	
March 8	Amphibious British landing at Aboukir, Egypt
April 2	Battle of Copenhagen
August 6 & 12	Battles of Algeciras
1802	
March 27	Peace of Amiens
1803	
May 16	Hostilities resume. British reimpose a blockade of Europe
October 2	French invasion fleet badly damaged by the British at the mouth of the Rhine
1805	
April–July	Nelson pursues the French fleet commanded by Admiral Pierre Villeneuve
July 22	Action off Cape Finisterre

October 21	Battle of Trafalgar
1806	
January 8	British capture Cape Town
February 6	Battle of Santo Domingo
June 17	British Admiral Sir Home Riggs POPHAM occupies Buenos Aires
June–July	British amphibious operation against Calabria
1807	
February–March	British action against Constantinople repelled
July	British occupy Montevideo
September 2–7	Second Battle of Copenhagen
1809	
July–October	Walcheren expedition
1815	
June 21	Napoleon abdicates; the war ends

Brian Lavery, *Nelson's Navy: The Ships, Men and Organisation, 1793–1815*, London, 1989; Piers Mackesy, *The War in the Mediterranean, 1803–10*, London, 1957; C. Northcote Parkinson, *Britannia Rules. The Classic Age of Naval History, 1793–1815*, London, 1977.

Frigate

*O*riginally used to describe a fast, open-decked sailing vessel operating in the Mediterranean, the term came into general naval use in the 18th century. At that time a frigate was defined as a fourth- or fifth-rate (see RATING OF SHIPS) ship that was too small to serve in the line of battle. A fast warship that could operate with the fleet or independently, it was used on reconnaissance, commerce protection and raiding duties. The frigate was a three-masted, square-rigged vessel with one deck and from 24 to 38 guns, although Britain was to develop a 44-gun frigate during the FRENCH REVOLUTIONARY AND NAPOLEONIC WARS, 1792–1815. The frigate provided the mainstay of the early UNITED STATES NAVY, with individual frigate actions dominating the naval side of the WAR OF 1812. When the steam engine replaced the sail, the frigate passed into history and its functions were taken over by the CRUISER and the DESTROYER.

During WORLD WAR II, 1939–45, in 1942, the term was revived by Britain to describe a warship of about 1,000 tons that was smaller and lighter than a DESTROYER but larger than a CORVETTE. Such frigates were used extensively on escort duties and in antisubmarine roles. They contin-

ued to perform these roles (and others) in the postwar period, although their specification and size has varied considerably in different navies. Reflecting their general-purpose role, they have a mixed armament of missiles, torpedoes and guns as well as antisubmarine helicopters and rockets. Some American variants are driven by nuclear power; U.S.S. *Bainbridge*, which was commissioned in 1962, was the first nuclear-powered frigate.

James Henderson, *The Frigates: An Account of the Lesser Warships of the Wars from 1793–1815*, London, 1970.

Frobisher, Sir Martin
c. 1534–94

*E*nglish explorer and naval commander who came to public notice as the leader of three expeditions (1576–78) in search of the Northwest Passage to China, from the Atlantic to the Pacific via the north of Canada. He discovered the strait that was to be named after him and also returned with some stones that appeared to contain gold. The possibility of finding gold in the area led to two more expeditions under Frobisher's command, but the evidence finally proved to be false and no more attempts were made. As a result of this failure, Frobisher's career was eclipsed for a period; eventually he was restored to official favor with his appointment as vice admiral in Sir Francis DRAKE's expedition to the West Indies, 1585–86. The strong-willed Frobisher later threatened his commander's life in a bitter argument over the distribution of prize money during the SPANISH ARMADA, 1588.

Frobisher played a leading role in the fight against Spain, commanding the *TRIUMPH*, the largest ship in the English fleet, in 1588. In recognition of his major contribution during the battles in the English Channel, Frobisher was knighted by Lord HOWARD of Effingham on board the *ARK ROYAL*. He renewed operations against the Spanish in European waters in 1590 and 1592 but failed to intercept any enemy treasure ships on their way home. In 1594 he went to sea for the last time, commanding a squadron that was to assist the French in expelling Spanish forces from the Brest area. Mortally wounded during the successful landing, Frobisher died a few weeks after his return to England.

William McFee, *Sir Martin Frobisher*, London, 1928.

Fuchida, Mitsuo
1902–76

*E*xperienced Japanese naval pilot, with the rank of commander, who coordinated the various waves of aircraft from the First Carrier Division involved in the attack on PEARL HARBOR, December 7, 1941, during WORLD WAR II, 1939–45. As Air Group Commander, Mitsuo Fuchida led the first wave of bombers in person, flying a Nakajima B5N2 "Kate." He directed the attack on the enemy warships before returning to the aircraft carrier AKAGI. He was unsuccessful in his attempts to persuade Vice Admiral Chuichi NAGUMO to mount a further attack on the surviving American ships. Fuchida served in the Imperial JAPANESE NAVY throughout the war, although he was taken ill during the critical Battle of MIDWAY, June 1942. He was later appointed to a staff post as air operations officer of the combined fleet.

Mitsuo Fuchida, *Midway: The Battle That Doomed Japan*, New York, 1955.

Fulton, Robert
1765–1815

Generally considered the inventor of the steamboat, Robert Fulton was a mechanical genius with numerous other talents. Among other things, he was an expert gunsmith, a landscape and portrait painter, and a maker of torpedoes and submarines. Born in Lancaster County, Pennsylvania on November 14, 1765, he went to London in 1786, following a period of ill health. He lived with Benjamin West, the painter, an old family friend. Fulton devoted his time to engineering projects with the aim of developing new mechanical devices. Some of his patented machines included a device to raise and lower canal boats, and a dredge to cut channels and various inexpensive aqueducts and canals. Fulton did not return to the United States until 1806.

Between 1798 and 1806, he was involved in the development of submarine MINES and the TORPEDO, doing much of his experimentation in BREST, France. He also invented a submarine, the *NAUTILUS*, that could submerge to 25 feet (7.62 m), steer under water and remain submerged for over four hours. He offered the submarine to the French, who lost interest in his project after his invention failed to capture any enemy prizes. Returning to the United States, he built the *Clermont*, the first commercially successful steamboat in America. It was launched and operated on the Hudson River. During the WAR OF 1812, he designed a steam vessel for defense of New York Harbor. The *Fulton the First* was 156 feet (47.54 m) long and carried 30 32-pound guns. Fulton died in New York in 1815.

Wallace S. Hutcheon, Jr., *Robert Fulton: Pioneer of Undersea Warfare*, Annapolis, 1981.

Furious, H.M.S.

A British warship that was a notable development in modern naval history. Launched in 1916 as a light

BATTLE CRUISER of the Courageous class, she was converted for service as a fleet seaplane carrier. A flying-off deck and hangar were constructed on her forecastle, and her main armament consisted of a single 18-inch (46-cm) gun, the largest ever mounted in a British ship.

In July 1917 the *Furious* joined the GRAND FLEET, but she also was used for experimental purposes. She was designed to launch aircraft, although they could not land on her. Seaplanes would be recovered from the sea, while conventional wheeled aircraft had to return to land. Trials therefore focused on the potential of the *Furious* for landing aircraft. On August 2, 1917 Commander E. H. Dunning made the first landing by an aircraft on a moving ship in a Sopwith Pup. However, when Dunning repeated the experiment a few days later, high winds blew his aircraft over the side and he was killed. Nonetheless, the ship's potential had been demonstrated and a second flight deck was built over the aft section of the *Furious* so that aircraft could land there. After conversion she rejoined the Grand Fleet as the world's first operational AIRCRAFT CARRIER. Several successful operations were launched from her decks before the end of WORLD WAR I, 1914–18, and experiments in landing techniques continued.

In the 1920s the *Furious* was reconstructed to provide a full-length flight deck; in the process, her original superstructure was removed. Command positions were provided under the forward end of the flight deck; no island superstructure was thought necessary, although a small structure was added in a later refit. The refurbished *Furious* had a flight deck of 700 feet (213 m), a displacement of 22,450 tons and could carry 33 aircraft.

During WORLD WAR II, 1939–45, the *Furious* served with the Home Fleet and was to be the only first-generation British aircraft carrier to survive until the end of the war. Her wartime service included convoy escort duties in the Mediterranean and the Atlantic as well as action against the battleship *TIRPITZ* in 1944. The *Furious* was not finally scrapped until 1949.

C. A. Jenkins, *HMS Furious, 1917–25*, Windsor, 1973.

Fuso

Japanese dreadnought BATTLESHIP. The *Fuso* and her sister ship *Yamashiro* were built under Japan's 1911–12 naval expansion program. Completed in 1915, the *Fuso* had a displacement of 29,330 tons and main armament of 12 14-inch (36-cm) guns in six twin turrets on the centerline. Operated by a crew of 1,193, she was 673 feet (205 m) in length and had a beam of 94 feet (28.65 m). Her 39,452-horsepower engines produced a maximum speed of almost 25 knots. She was modernized during the 1930s with updated engines, improved armament and the addition of aircraft-handling facilities. These changes increased her displacement to 34,700 tons but caused problems of stability that were solved only by widening her bulges.

The *Fuso*'s WORLD WAR II, 1939–45, career was largely uneventful. For much of the time she was confined to second-line duties. As Japanese AIRCRAFT CARRIER losses mounted, there were plans to turn the *Fuso* into a carrier, but these plans foundered because of a growing shortage of pilots. Both the *Fuso* and her sister ship were lost at the Battle of LEYTE GULF, October 25, 1944. The *Fuso* was sunk by American destroyer torpedoes during the prelude to the battle; she blew up and broke in two.

Gabbard, Battle of the

June 2–3, 1653

A major engagement of the First ANGLO-DUTCH WAR, 1652–54; also known as the First Battle of North Foreland after the area where much of the fighting actually took place. After its defeat at the Battle of PORTLAND, February 19–20, 1653, the Dutch fleet under Admiral Marten TROMP had to wait until the beginning of June before it could strike again at the English.

The opposing sides first sighted each other at the Gabbard, a sandbank off Orfordness on the Suffolk coast, at daybreak on June 2. The Dutch fleet consisted of 98 ships and six FIRESHIPS, with Michiel de RUYTER and Witte de WITT as vice admirals. The English had 100 ships and five fireships under the command of Generals-at-Sea George MONCK and Richard DEANE. (The rank of general-at-sea, which was equivalent to that of admiral, was used during the time of the Protectorate, 1653–59.) Action did not begin until 11 A.M. because of light wind; then it lasted until about 6 P.M., when the Dutch withdrew with the loss of three ships. At noon on the following day, the battle was renewed, with the English reinforced by a squadron of 18 ships commanded by Admiral Robert BLAKE. After four hours the Dutch fleet retreated in disarray. They were pursued by the British until dark.

Tromp lost about 20 ships in total, with nine captured and the rest destroyed. Some 1,360 prisoners were taken by the English, who lost none of their ships and had few casualties, except for General Deane, who was killed by the first BROADSIDE. Superior English gunpowder, which kept the Dutch at a safe distance, was one explanation for their success. Another was the impact of the new *FIGHTING INSTRUCTIONS*, issued in March 1653 by the ADMIRALTY in London, which provided for line-ahead formations. Following Monk's victory Holland was blockaded and the Dutch were forced to discuss peace terms, although they made a final effort to turn the war in their favor at the Battle of SCHEVENINGEN, July 31, 1653.

Galeasse

A Mediterranean warship type, developed in Venice at the beginning of the 16th century, that combined the oars of the GALLEY with the sails of the large sailing vessel of the day.

The galeasse was developed in response to the need for a fast and maneuverable warship that could carry a large number of heavy guns. Enlarged galleys, which appeared first, were too heavy to be rowed over long distances. The supplementary sail power of the galeasse overcame this problem, and the galeasse eventually became the dominant ship type in southern waters. It had a deeper draft and a broader beam than its predecessor in order to accommodate two or three lateen-rigged masts. A typical galeasse had a displacement of at least 600 tons and was armed with over 40 guns, the heaviest of them being mounted forward. It required a crew of up to 300 as well as extra men to operate the oars, which made their greatest impact once a battle had begun. There were up to 30 oars on each side, with each oar requiring the effort of at least five men.

In terms of its seagoing qualities, firepower and range, the galeasse represented a considerable improvement over the galley. A notable example of its significant impact on the naval warfare of the period was its critical contribution to the Venetian victory over the Turks at the Battle of LEPANTO in 1571, when 26 galeasses were used. In 1588, four powerful Neapolitan galeasses joined the SPANISH ARMADA against England, although they performed less well in the stormier conditions of northern waters. The galeasse remained the leading Mediterranean warship until well into the 17th century, when it was finally superseded by the advanced sailing man-of-war, whose guns and speed it could not match.

Galeote

A reduced version of the medieval GALLEY, the galeote (or galliot) remained in naval use in Europe until well into the 18th century. It had up to 20 oars on each side; each oar was normally operated by one man, although sometimes two or three might be used. The galeote also was usually fitted with a single mast and sail. It was equipped with several bow guns and the crew, which might include soldiers, normally were armed with muskets. Faster and more maneuverable than the galley, the galeote's main wartime function was to pursue and capture enemy ships, with its armed crew forming the boarding party. Its excellent performance meant that the galeote also was widely used by Mediterranean pirates and traders.

Galiot

A small one- or two-masted sailing vessel originally developed in the Netherlands during the 17th century. It had a steeply rising stern and a rounded bow; there was a large gaff sail on the mainmast and sometimes another on a smaller mizzen mast. Its length was between 59 feet (18 m) and 98 feet (30 m) and its beam 13 feet (4 m) to 36 feet (7.5 m). Although the galiot was primarily a trading vessel, it also was used by several European navies. In France, for example, galiots were equipped with mortars and were used as BOMB VESSELS. In the navies of the Baltic states, where galiots were used on patrol duties, they were often schooner-rigged. The galiot hull-form survived in various guises well into the 19th century.

Galleon

A large sailing ship of the late Middle Ages and early Renaissance. Although "galleon" is a Spanish term, the galleon was in fact developed in England, in the late 16th century, as a direct response to the limitations of the CARRACK. As a warship, the carrack—a HIGH-CHARGED ship with castles at bow and stern—had become obsolete when bombardment rather than boarding had become the dominant naval tactic. The carrack's high forecastle also made it difficult to maneuver: It had a tendency to push the bows to leeward, making steering a straight course difficult.

Sir John HAWKINS, the English naval commander, sought to correct these problems by creating, in 1570, a

An Elizabethan galleon   (*Copyright © National Maritime Museum, Greenwich, London*)

new design in which the high, overhanging castles of the carrack disappeared and were replaced by a reshaped hull that was long and slender, and could travel at higher speeds. His design was not dissimilar to the lines of a galley, although it stood higher out of the water. The stern was squared and its forecastle was set well back from the stem of the ship. It was fitted with a low, projecting beakhead (the space in front of the forecastle). The new design was also equipped with rows of gunports through which BROADSIDE guns were fired. A typical galleon of the Elizabethan period had a keel of some 100 feet (30.48 m), and its length from stem to stern was about 135 feet (42 m). With a beam of some 38 feet (11.58 m), it had a crew of about 250 and carried some 50 guns.

The new design reached Spain some 17 years later, and 20 of these vessels were made in time for the SPANISH ARMADA of 1588. It became known in Spain as the galleon although this term was never used at the time in England or in the neighboring countries of Western Europe. The galleon established the essential features of the sailing SHIP OF THE LINE and was the CAPITAL SHIP of the world's navies until it was displaced by the steam-powered IRONCLAD in the mid-19th century. See also ARK ROYAL, ELIZABETH BONAVENTURE, GOLDEN HIND, GOUDEN LEEUW, VANGUARD and ZEVEN PROVINCIEN.

Robert Gardiner, ed., *Cogs, Caravels and Galleons: The Sailing Ship 1000–1650*, London, 1994; F. Howard, *Sailing Ships of War, 1400–1860*, London, 1979.

Galley

*A*n oared fighting ship of the Mediterranean that dates back to at least 3,000 B.C., the galley was still employed during the age of the sailing navies and survived until the early years of the 19th century. Equipped with supplementary sails, it was a long, narrow ship with a shallow beam and low freeboard. There were no standard specifications; galleys varied, for example, according to the number of oar banks and the number of oarsmen per oar. A galley with two banks of oars was known as a bireme; one with three banks was called a trireme. Operated by up to 500 crew, with as many as eight men to a single oar, a galley could achieve a maximum speed of about nine knots, although the top speed could be attained only in short bursts; typically the cruising speed would be no more than half that figure. Additional power was provided by the lateen sails with which the two- or three-masted galleys were rigged.

First developed by the Phoenicians from earlier Egyptian designs, the galley was the principal warship of the Greeks and Romans. It outlived the collapse of these empires and during the Middle Ages, Venice became the main center of galley design and construction. By the 1570s some 16,000 men were employed in this work. A typical 17th-century galley might have a displacement of 200 tons, a length of 54.6 yards (50 m) and a beam of 6.6 yards (6 m). It was armed with a bow ram that served several purposes: It could be used to destroy the oars of an opponent, to RAM an enemy ship or as a bridge for boarding. From the 16th century onward, the galley was equipped with guns on a platform above the oar banks, but their position was fixed and their aim could not be adjusted.

A major disadvantage of the galley was its instability and vulnerability in heavy seas. It could stay at sea only for a short time because there was very little space to store supplies. By contrast, the sailing ship offered greater range, increased armaments and a smaller crew. On the other hand, the galley was maneuverable and could operate in

A 14th-century Venetian galley with a single bank of oars   *(Copyright © National Maritime Museum, Greenwich, London)*

calm conditions or when the wind was against it. Despite the sailing ship's advantages, it did not entirely supersede the galley, which remained in limited use in the Mediterranean and the Baltic during the 17th and 18th centuries. The last major engagement between galley fleets in the Mediterranean occurred at the Battle of LEPANTO, October 7, 1571.

Beeching, Jack, *The Galleys at Lepanto*, London, 1982.

Gambier, James, Lord
1756–1833

*B*ritish admiral and naval administrator who commanded the fleet during the bombardment of COPEN-HAGEN, 1807, which resulted in the surrender of the Danish navy. Gambier's active service dated back to the AMERICAN WAR OF INDEPENDENCE, 1775–83, but he had first distinguished himself in the Battle of the GLORIOUS FIRST OF JUNE, 1794, when his ship, the *Defiance,* was the first to break the French line. His record as a naval leader was, however, mixed. In 1809, while in command of the Channel Fleet, his unsuccessful attempt to destroy the French fleet in the Basque Roads revealed his limitations at sea. He ended the operation prematurely because of his moral objections to the use of FIRESHIPS and his personal antipathy to Thomas COCHRANE, one of his subordinate commanders. After a court-martial that found in his favor, Gambier's wartime naval service continued until 1811.

Ganges, H.M.S.

*T*he *Ganges* was the last sailing SHIP OF THE LINE to remain in British service. Armed with 84 guns, she was launched at Bombay in 1821—one of the many warships built of teak in India or Burma for the Royal Navy during the 18th and 19th centuries. She finally was taken out of naval service in 1861. By that time there were no other sailing ships of this type still operating in the ROYAL NAVY, and thus her retirement marked the end of an era. After being decommissioned the *Ganges* was used, from 1866, as a training ship and was moored in Falmouth Bay for many years.

Gangut

*C*ompleted in 1914, the *Gangut,* which had a displacement of 23,000 tons, gave her name to the Gangut class, the first Russian-produced dreadnoughts. With a maximum speed of 23 knots, she was relatively powerful, but this advantage was achieved at the price of thinner

than normal armor protection. Armament consisted of 12-inch (30-cm) Obukhov guns, mounted in four triple turrets on the centerline. These weapons were highly accurate and gave a significantly greater weight of broadside than the best contemporary battleships. Operated by a crew of 1,125, the *Gangut* was 600 feet (183 m) in length and had a beam of 88 feet 3 inches (26.9 m). The *Gangut* and her sister ships—the *Poltava, Sevastopol* and *Petropavlovsk*—formed the First Battleship Brigade of the Baltic Fleet and were based at Helsinki during WORLD WAR I, 1914–18. However, the Russian High Command was unwilling to risk the dreadnoughts unnecessarily and confined them to uneventful patrols in the Gulf of Finland. The *Petropavlovsk* was active during the Russian Civil War, 1917–22, and was torpedoed by the British at Kronstadt in August 1919. Salvaged and restored, she rejoined other members of the Gangut class in the SOVIET NAVY. With the exception of the *Poltava,* which was severely damaged by fire in 1922, the Gangut-class ships survived service in WORLD WAR II, 1939–45, and were not scrapped until the 1950s.

Ganteaume, Comte Honoré
1755–1818

*F*rench vice admiral who entered the navy in 1778 following a period at sea in the merchant fleet. He served in the West Indies during the closing stages of the AMERICAN WAR OF INDEPENDENCE, 1775–83. Ganteaume later commanded a French East Indiaman but resumed his naval service as the French Revolutionary Wars, 1792–1802, began. He was wounded three times at the Battle of the GLORIOUS FIRST OF JUNE, 1794. In 1798, at the Battle of the NILE, 1798, where he served as Admiral François BRUEYS D'AIGAILLIERS' chief of staff, he was much more fortunate. Ganteaume managed to reach shore when *L'O-RIENT,* the fleet FLAGSHIP, blew up. Napoleon promoted Ganteaume to rear admiral and attached him to his staff during the campaign in Syria. In 1799 he accompanied Napoleon back to France in *La Muiron.* He was in command of the Brest fleet in 1800–2 and made two unsuccessful attempts to evacuate the French army from Egypt.

In 1802 Ganteaume led a successful expedition to the West Indies with the object of resupplying Haiti and Santo Domingo. Promoted to vice admiral in 1804, he returned to Brest in 1804–5, where he was blockaded by the British and prevented from joining the TRAFALGAR campaign. He later moved to the Mediterranean command, 1808–10, where he kept the French garrison on Corfu supplied. Ganteaume left his final sea command to become Minister of Marine, 1810–14, and subsequently supported the restored monarchy during Napoleon's final campaign. Ganteaume was an able commander who supported Napoleon effectively in Egypt, but he never had the opportunity to demonstrate that he was a naval leader of real distinction.

General Belgrano

*T*he *General Belgrano* began life as the American light cruiser *Phoenix*, which was launched in 1935 and completed three years later. This Brooklyn-class ship had a displacement of 13,645 tons, was 608 feet 3 inches (185.4 m) in length and had a beam of 61 feet 9 inches (19.75 m). Capable of over 32 knots, her main armament consisted of 15 6-inch (15-cm) guns in five triple turrets; she could accommodate a wartime crew of 1,200 men. She served in the Pacific during WORLD WAR II, 1939–45.

In 1951, following modernization, the *Phoenix* was purchased by Argentina and renamed the *Diecisiete de Octubre*. At the time of the FALKLANDS WAR, 1982, she was still in service but had been earmarked for scrapping. On May 2, 1982 the *General Belgrano* (as she had been named since 1956) was torpedoed by the British nuclear submarine HMS CONQUERER in the South Atlantic some 36 miles outside the 200-mile maritime "exclusion zone" around the Falkland Islands that had been imposed by the British government on April 7. She was thought to be a threat to the British carrier group positioned to the east of the Falklands, and the ADMIRALTY in London approved her sinking. Hit by two wire-guided Tigerfish torpedoes fired by the *Conqueror*, she was the largest ship to be destroyed in action since World War II; 368 lives were lost. The decision to attack the *General Belgrano* well outside the exclusion zone will always be controversial.

Arthur L. Gorshov, *The Sinking of the Belgrano*, London, 1984.

George Washington, U.S.S.

*T*he world's first nuclear-powered ballistic-MISSILE submarine. Launched at Groton, Connecticut in 1959, the U.S.S. *George Washington* had a displacement of 5,400 tons, a length of 380 feet (115.8 m) and was operated by a crew of 112. She had a distinctive whale-shape hull and was powered by a single pressurized, water-cooled nuclear reactor that could drive her at a maximum speed of over 30 knots submerged. The submarine also had a conventional power plant for use in an emergency.

The *George Washington* was armed with 16 POLARIS missiles fired from vertical launching tubes arranged in parallel rows behind the conning tower. All 16 missiles, which had a range of 1,500 miles (2,413 km), could be fired within a period of 15 minutes. She was also equipped with six 21-inch (53-cm) torpedo tubes. The success of the design was confirmed, in 1960, when the *George Washington* became the first submarine to launch a ballistic missile while submerged. She set another standard when she remained submerged on patrol for a period of 66 days and 10 hours. The *George Washington* and her four sister ships were refitted during the 1960s. She was decommissioned in 1985.

German Navy

*A*t the outbreak of WORLD WAR I, the German navy was the world's second largest, with 17 capital ships to Britain's 27. During the previous 20 years Germany's industrial power had transformed its maritime capability from a minor coastal defense force to an oceangoing navy under the direction of Grand Admiral Alfred von TIRPITZ, the "father of the German navy." Its aim of becoming a powerful opponent of the Royal Navy became more realistic with the appearance in 1906 of H.M.S. DREADNOUGHT, which rendered all existing battleships obsolete and reduced Britain's relative advantage as a great naval power. The new design forced all naval powers, including Britain, to start from scratch and marked the beginning of a costly arms race. German battleship design in the prewar period proved to be superior to the British in many respects, particularly in terms of protection, gunnery and machinery.

Despite these advantages, sheer weight of numbers meant that the Royal Navy quickly brought the German navy's surface operations outside northern Europe to an end soon after the start of World War I. British wartime policy throughout the war was to confine the German navy's principal fleet—the HIGH SEAS FLEET—to the North Sea by means of a distant BLOCKADE. This fleet, which included 15 dreadnoughts and four battle cruisers, was used with extreme caution: The kaiser had decided that it should not be risked unnecessarily. He expected the land war in Europe to end quickly, and he wanted to use the intact fleet as a lever in peace negotiations. Although this expectation soon proved to be unrealistic, restrictions on the use of the fleet continued. Limited operations were, however, authorized in an attempt to reduce the British GRAND FLEET's superiority, although all such operations were suspended after the narrow German escape at the Battle of the DOGGER BANK, January 24, 1915. With Admiral Rheinhard SCHEER's appointment as commander of the High Seas Fleet in January 1916, a more aggressive policy was pursued, leading to the Battle of JUTLAND, May 1916, when the main fleets of Britain and Germany clashed. Although inconclusive, this battle confirmed British dominance of the North Sea. Consequently, the High Seas Fleet ventured there only three other occasions before the end of the war. The transfer of personnel to the expanding U-BOAT fleet and MUTINY progressively reduced the efficiency of the High Seas Fleet. Unrest in 1917 was followed by open mutiny in October 1918, marking the demise of the High Seas Fleet as a fighting force. After Jutland the German navy turned increasingly to the SUBMARINE as a means of defeating England, hoping to cut off the flow of supplies from North America and from the colonies. The U-boat war, which hit Allied shipping hard, might have succeeded had it not been for the Royal Navy's belated introduction of the CONVOY system, which reduced losses to manageable levels by the end of 1917. At the end of the war all 160 German submarines were surrendered and transferred to Britain. The Armistice also provided for the surrender of the High Seas Fleet to the Royal Navy on November 21, 1918 and its internment at SCAPA FLOW, where the fleet was scuttled by the Germans on June 21, 1919. It was the last act of the wartime German navy, and a final protest against the terms of the Treaty of Versailles, 1919.

The treaty reinforced the Allied victory by reducing the German navy to a coastal force once more and banning its use of submarines. Despite these constraints, secret German development work on submarines continued throughout the Weimar period. New warships were constructed that did not always meet the restrictions imposed by the treaty. The POCKET-BATTLESHIP is a key example of how the treaty's intentions were circumvented as the Germans sought to restore their naval power. These plans gained momentum after Adolf Hitler became chancellor in 1933. Plan Z, a ten-year construction program, was adopted in 1937 with the aim of constructing, between 1943 and 1948, a fleet that could match the Royal Navy. A fast surface fleet, including six battleships and eight heavy cruisers, would be complemented by an effective

submarine force of 233 boats that would dominate Britain's trade routes.

World War II came far too soon for these plans to be fully implemented, and the development of a surface fleet lagged far behind the construction of submarines. The navy had no air arm and made only limited use of RADAR. Moreover, its political influence under Grand Admiral Erich RAEDER, commander in chief, 1933–43, was limited, and it was never central to Hitler's war plans. The U-boat fleet was the most effective arm of the German navy during the war, sinking some 14 million tons of shipping. The Battle of the ATLANTIC, 1939–45, led to heavy Allied shipping losses, and the U-boats were not effectively defeated until mid-1943. Allied air attacks disrupted German plans to revive the submarine war with improved U-Boat designs. The German surface fleet had some initial successes against Allied merchantmen, but the early loss of the pocket-battleship *ADMIRAL GRAF SPEE* in December 1939 was a major blow to German prestige. Further losses were sustained during the invasion of Norway, 1940, although the navy did play a key part in this successful operation.

Following the German land invasion and occupation of France and the Low Countries, the navy could operate

The German High Seas Fleet on maneuver in 1906 *(Copyright © National Maritime Museum, Greenwich, London)*

from new bases with direct access to the Atlantic. It enjoyed a period of success in the Atlantic, although this came to an end with the sinking of the BISMARCK in May 1941. The increasing effectiveness of the Royal Air Force in the Atlantic made it difficult for the German surface fleet to operate there. The German navy had more impact in attacking the ARCTIC CONVOY route to the Soviet Union, but it was unable to satisfy Hitler's requirement for more spectacular successes. By the beginning of 1943 Hitler's decision to dismantle the surface fleet prompted Grand Admiral RAEDER's resignation. His successor, Admiral Karl DÖNITZ, U-Boat commander in chief, persuaded Hitler against this course of action, but the main surface fleet was effectively confined to Norwegian waters. The only exception were the achievements of the German motor TORPEDO BOATS—the E-boats—which secured numerous victories in British coastal waters until their activities were curtailed by Allied air superiority.

The remaining units of the Germany navy were deployed in the Baltic, where they transported large numbers of refugees and troops fleeing from the advancing Red Army. Very little of the navy's surface fleet survived the end of the war. Postwar Western Germany and, since 1990, the unified German State has maintained a more modest (though modern) fleet, which operates under the command of the North Atlantic Treaty Organization (NATO).

J. P. Mallmann Showell, *The German Navy in World War Two*, London, 1979.

Ghormley, Robert Lee
1883–1958

*A*merican naval officer, born on October 15, 1883, in Portland, Oregon. Ghormley enjoyed a noteworthy career, ultimately rising to the rank of vice admiral. Early on he developed a reputation throughout the U.S. Navy as an excellent staff officer. Rotating commands at sea with intervening staff positions, he became in 1938 director of the war plans division in the office of the Chief of Naval Operations. In 1939–40 he was Assistant Chief of Naval Operations to Admiral Harold R. STARK. This was followed by a tour as a special naval observer at the American embassy in London until April 1942, when he briefly assumed command of American naval forces in European waters. He went to the Pacific from June to October 1942 as commander of the South Pacific Force and area. In this capacity he was responsible for planning and executing the invasion of the SOLOMON ISLANDS and the assaults on GUADALCANAL, the first AMPHIBIOUS operation by American forces since the war against Spain in 1898. He then returned to Washington and duty with Admiral Ernest KING, Commander in Chief, U.S. Fleet. After a tour as commandant of the 14th Naval District and Commander, Hawaiian Sea Frontier, he was transferred, in November

Admiral R. L. Ghormley was a distinguished U.S. naval commander in the Pacific War, 1941–45   *(Copyright © Imperial War Museum, London)*

1944, to become Commander of U.S. naval forces, Germany, a duty that lasted until December 1945, during which he oversaw the demobilization of the German navy. He died on June 21, 1958, at Bethesda, Maryland.

Gibraltar

*T*he port of Gibraltar, located at a key point on the western edge of the Mediterranean, juts out into the sea from the south coast of Spain. Formerly part of Spain, it has been a British colony since July 24, 1704, when it was captured by English and Dutch naval forces, commanded by Admiral Sir George ROOKE, during the War of the SPANISH SUCCESSION, 1701–14; it has remained in British hands ever since. Its seizure from Spain was recognized in the Treaty of Utrecht, 1713, which brought the war to an end. Its great strategic value on the Straits of Gibraltar, where the Mediterranean Sea meets the Atlantic Ocean, has made it subject to periodic attack, and the British often have had to invest heavily in its defense. The most notable

British ships relieve Gibraltar in 1804 during the French Revolutionary War, 1792–1802 *(Copyright © National Maritime Museum, Greenwich, London)*

example occurred during the AMERICAN WAR OF INDEPENDENCE, 1775–83, when the Spanish and French besieged it for more than three years (1779–83). In September 1782 the British destroyed their opponents' floating batteries outside the harbor, but the siege did not end until the peace process was under way. During the 19th century Gibraltar developed as an important strategic naval base, repair facility and coaling station for the Royal Navy. Remaining a British colony, it played a critical role in the conflict at sea during two world wars. In WORLD WAR II, 1939–45, it was the starting point for many of the convoys that supplied Malta while it was under constant threat of Axis attack. Adolf Hitler made plans to capture Gibraltar with the aim of closing the Mediterranean to the Royal Navy, but he was never able to implement them. Gibraltar remains a British colony although Spain continues to assert its claim to the territory.

Dennis, Philip, *Gibraltar*, North Pomfret, Vt., 1977.

Gilbert Islands, Capture of
November 1943

The Gilbert Islands (now part of the small island nation of Kiribati) were occupied by the Japanese in 1941 as they advanced across the Pacific. The islands' recapture was a key American objective as they launched their central Pacific campaign in 1943. The campaign, which was code-named "Granite," was under the overall command of Admiral Chester NIMITZ. The naval forces assigned to this campaign were headed by Vice Admiral Raymond SPRUANCE and included the Fast Carrier Force commanded by Rear Admiral Charles Pownall. The latter included six fleet carriers, five light carriers and six battleships. On November 20, 1943 the two most westerly islands in the Gilbert group—Makin and Tarawa—were invaded from the sea. Makin was lightly defended and fell within four days, but Tarawa, a key island, was much better protected. The landing, which was preceded by a heavy bombardment from the sea and air, was complicated by the fact that Tarawa's coastal waters, which are enclosed by a coral reef, proved to be too shallow for landing craft. The U.S. Marine Corps had to wade ashore for several hundred yards under heavy fire. They faced determined Japanese resistance, which produced heavy losses on both sides but could not prevent the island from falling to the Americans on November 23. This victory allowed American naval forces to withdraw and to move on to the Marshall Islands, the next target in their "island-hopping" campaign against Japan.

Glamorgan, H.M.S.

British County-class guided-MISSILE destroyer with a displacement of 5,440 tons (6,200 tons full load). Launched in 1964, the Glamorgan was equipped with a combined steam and gas turbine propulsion system, operated by a crew of 471 and fitted with the Armstrong-

Whitworth Seaslug guided weapon system. The County-class ships were the first in British service to be equipped with guided missiles. The *Glamorgan* was later converted to carry four EXOCET surface-to-surface missiles. While serving in the FALKLANDS WAR, 1982, on June 11 she was operating in support of British ground troops fighting near Port Stanley when she was hit by a land-based Exocet. Fires broke out and nine crew members were killed. Although she suffered heavy damage, the quality of her construction enabled the *Glamorgan* to continue operations against the Argentinians.

La Gloire

Notable as the world's first seagoing IRONCLAD, the French frigate *La Gloire* was launched in 1859. Designed by Stanislas Dupuy de Lôme, she appeared in response to the growing vulnerability of wooden warships to improvements in gunnery. The limitations of wooden vessels had been increasingly evident during the CRIMEAN WAR, 1853–56, having been graphically demonstrated at the Battle of SINOPE, 1853, when Russian ships burned a squadron of Turkish ships.

La Gloire was constructed of oak in the traditional manner but had a belt of 4.7-inch (12-cm) armor along her sides. With a displacement of 5,600 tons, she was powered by steam but retained a full rig of sails. She was armed with 36 rifled guns. *La Gloire* was followed by other ironclads that formed the basis of an expansion of French naval power. France's progress in ship design compelled the ROYAL NAVY to develop an ironclad of its own—the *WARRIOR,* launched in 1860.

Glorious First of June

June 1, 1794

The first major naval engagement of the FRENCH REVO-LUTIONARY AND NAPOLEONIC WARS, 1792–1815, was occasioned by the appearance in the North Atlantic of a French convoy of 130 merchant ships that was bringing vital supplies of grain from the United States to France. A British squadron of 34 ships of the line, commanded by Admiral Richard, Earl HOWE, had been searching the western approaches to England in April and May 1794 with the aim of intercepting the convoy before it reached France. The convoy's safe passage was vital to France, whose population was facing starvation, and a French squadron left BREST on May 16 with the aim of preventing a British attack. Commanded by Rear Admiral Louis VIL-LARET-JOYEUSE, the French fleet consisted of 26 ships of the line. On May 28 it first sighted the British some 400 miles off Ushant in the North Atlantic. There was a brief engagement in rough seas the same day. Although the French had the wind advantage, one of their ships, the *Revolutionnaire,* was damaged by the British.

Fighting resumed the next day with the British still downwind, although they mounted a successful attack on the enemy's rear and cut off two ships of the line. Fighting was restricted during the next two days as fog closed in but resumed on June 1. Lord Howe planned a major attack designed to achieve a decisive result. Six British ships led the attack on the enemy from the windward position; but, in a series of misunderstandings, most of the others failed to respond to the order. In addition, a few British ships failed to break through the French line, which had been reinforced by a squadron of four ships of the line under Rear Admiral Neilly. In the general melée that followed, six French ships of the line were captured and one destroyed. Villaret-Joyeuse's FLAGSHIP, the *Montagne,* was severely damaged, with many casualties. Exhausted by the battle, the British were unable to renew hostilities against the French, who were in disarray. On June 9 Villaret-Joyeuse was able to repel a further attempt to intercept the convoy by a British squadron commanded by Rear Admiral Montagu. Although the French navy had suffered heavier losses than its opponent, both the convoy and its escort were to reach the safety of Brest without further incident.

Oliver Warner, *The Glorious First of June*, London, 1961.

Gneisenau

German Scharnhorst-class BATTLE CRUISER of WORLD WAR II, 1939–45, launched in 1936. With similar specifications and performance to her sister ship, the *SCHARN-HORST,* the *Gneisenau* first saw wartime service in the Atlantic. She worked with the *Scharnhorst* continously until February 1942, when the two vessels broke out from Brest in the CHANNEL DASH and returned to Germany. Shortly after her arrival at Kiel, the *Gneisenau* was damaged during a British bombing raid. Later she was moved to Gdynia (Gotenhafen), which was out of range of Allied bombers. Work to upgrade her main armament was begun but was later abandoned because of wartime supply difficulties. In March 1945 she was sunk as a BLOCKSHIP in Gdynia harbor with the aim of impeding the progress of Soviet forces.

Richard Garrett, *Scharnhorst and Gneisenau*, London, 1979.

Goeben

Few warships can have had as much impact on the course of modern history as the German BATTLE CRUISER *Goeben*, which was the instrument that brought Turkey into WORLD WAR I, 1914–18. An enlarged version

The Glorious First of June, 1794, was the first major naval engagement between British and French naval forces during the French Revolutionary War, 1792–1802 *(Copyright © National Maritime Museum, Greenwich, London)*

of the VON DER TANN, with a displacement of 23,000 tons, the *Goeben* had ten 11-inch (27.5 cm) guns, protection approaching battleship standards and a crew of just over 1,000. With a maximum speed of 25.5 knots, she was 612 feet (185 m) in length and had a beam of 96 feet 9 inches (29.3 m). The *Goeben* was completed in 1912 and at the outbreak of war was stationed in the Mediterranean under the command of Admiral Wilhelm SOUCHON. Her first wartime task, with the light cruiser *Breslau*, was to disrupt the flow of troops from Algeria to France by shelling the ports of Bone and Philippeville on August 4, 1914.

The *Goeben*'s reputation as the fastest warship in the Mediterranean was confirmed soon afterward when she eluded the British battlecruisers INDOMITABLE and INDEFAT-IGABLE, which had given chase. After coaling at Messina in then-neutral Italy, the *Goeben* headed for Constantinople, hoping that Turkey, which also was neutral, would cooperate and allow her to make good her escape from the powerful British naval presence. The ROYAL NAVY failed to intercept the ships as they sailed eastward. Rear Admiral

Sir Ernest TROUBRIDGE, commanding a squadron of four cruisers, was in a position to engage the *Goeben* and the *Breslau* off the western coast of Greece but did not do so. Unhelpful ADMIRALTY orders required him to avoid being drawn into battle with a force of superior strength, and subsequently he was forced to defend his rigid adherence to these orders at a famous court-martial.

On their arrival at Constantinople on August 11, the two German ships were nominally transferred to Turkey, although they retained their German crews and commander. Because Turkey was still neutral, the *Goeben*, renamed the *Yavuz Sultan Selim*, lay idle for some time, but, on October 29, Admiral Souchon carried out a surprise raid on the Russian fleet at Sebastopol. From the German point of view the action produced a handsome reward: Turkey had committed an act of aggression against Russia and was forced to declare war on Russia and the other Allied powers. The *Goeben* was based at Constantinople and was used from time to time against the Russian Black Sea Fleet and in the Mediterranean. In January 1918

British bombers put her out of action for the rest of the war.

Dan van der Vat, *The Ship That Changed the World: The Escape of the Goeben to the Dardanelles in 1914*, London, 1985.

Golden Hind

*D*uring the Elizabethan era, two English ships bore the name *Golden Hind*. The earlier, more famous *Golden Hind* was the ship in which Sir Francis DRAKE circumnavigated the globe. Originally known as the *Pelican*, this GALLEON had been renamed during Drake's epic voyage in 1577–80. She was about 75 feet (22.86 m) long, had a crew of over 100 men and was armed with about 30 artillery pieces. As she traveled across the globe, she was employed successfully in a number of highly profitable raids on Spanish ships and settlements on the coast of South America. Following her triumphant return, on September 26, 1580, she was placed on public display at Deptford dockyard, southeast London.

A second *Golden Hind,* a 50-ton English pinnace, was on scouting duty off The Lizard Peninsula, Cornwall in July 1588 when she sighted several Spanish warships. They were the first of 133 enemy ships that were to appear in English waters and meant that the long-expected SPANISH ARMADA finally had arrived. *The Golden Hind* returned quickly to Plymouth, arriving there on July 19. On hearing the news, the English fleet, under Lord HOWARD of Effingham and Sir Francis Drake, left almost immediately to intercept the Spanish.

Goodrich, Caspar Frederick
1847–1925

*B*orn in Philadelphia on January 7, 1847, Goodrich was one of the brightest American naval officers during the period of naval expansion, graduating first in his class from the U.S. Naval Academy at ANNAPOLIS in 1864. While an instructor of physics and chemistry at the academy from 1871 to 1874, he was instrumental in helping to found the Naval Institute, an independent forum that advocated reforms in the naval service. He served as that body's president, 1904–9. Goodrich also was instrumental in helping to establish the Naval War College in Newport,

Sir Francis Drake circumnavigated the globe in the *Golden Hind*   *(Copyright © National Maritime Museum, Greenwich, London)*

Rhode Island in 1884, serving twice as its president (1889–92; 1896–1898) as well as being a regular lecturer there. He served as naval attaché to British General Sir Garnet Wolsley during the bombardment of Alexandria, Egypt in 1882, participating also as an assault commander.

Advancing to the rank of captain in 1897, Goodrich took part in the decisive action at SANTIAGO BAY during the SPANISH-AMERICAN WAR in 1898, commanding the *St. Louis*. Promoted to rear admiral early in 1904, he last saw duty at sea as commander of the Pacific Fleet from 1904 to 1906 and retired in 1909. A prolific writer on various subjects from technical matters to naval history, contributing over 35 scholarly articles and several books, Goodrich died on December 26, 1925 in Princeton, New Jersey.

William B. Cogar, *Dictionary of Admirals of the U.S. Navy, Vol. 2, 1901–1918*, Annapolis, 1991.

Gorshkov, Sergei Georgievich
1910–88

*S*oviet admiral and commander in chief of the navy, 1956–88. In 1956 the SOVIET NAVY was little more than a coastal defense force. Under Gorshkov's leadership, the Soviet Union would become a world naval power following the rapid modernization and expansion of the fleet.

Born in Podolsk, Ukraine, Gorshkov entered the service in 1927. He graduated from the Frunze naval academy in 1931 and spent his early service with the Black Sea fleet. During WORLD WAR II, 1939–45, he commanded a destroyer squadron and was noted for his wartime exploits. Gorshkov was a beneficiary of Nikita Khrushchev's rise to power as First Secretary of the Communist Party and, in 1956, was appointed commander in chief of the Soviet navy. His initial task was to reduce naval expenditure in accordance with the new leader's general policies, but this period of retrenchment was short-lived.

As the COLD WAR intensified with the CUBAN MISSILE CRISIS, 1962, and the appointment of Leonid Brezhnev as Khrushchev's hard-line successor, military expenditure increased. The Soviet navy was to be increased significantly, giving it the ability to operate globally in support of Soviet foreign policy objectives. Gorshkov oversaw the development of Soviet aircraft carriers, nuclear submarines and battle cruisers that were capable of challenging equivalent Western designs. By the 1970s many of these plans had come to fruition and Gorshkov devoted more time to the changing tactics and strategy of modern naval warfare. The publication of his major study, *The Sea Power of the State*, 1976, confirmed his reputation as significant military thinker as well as the architect of modern Soviet naval power. He remained in command of the navy until his death in 1988.

Gouden Leeuw

*D*utch, "Golden Lion." The first *Golden Lion* was a British warship that served in Sir Francis DRAKE's attack on CADIZ, 1587, but there was also later, a famous Dutch man of war of the same name. Known in Dutch as the *Gouden Leeuw*, this three-masted GALLEON was commissioned by the Amsterdam admiralty during the Second DUTCH WAR, 1665–67. She was built at Amsterdam and was armed with 80 guns. The mainmast and foremast were square-rigged. The mainmast carried a mainsail, main topsail and main topgallant; the foremast carried a foresail, fore topsail and fore topgallant sail; and the mizzen mast carried a lateen sail and a square sail. The *Gouden Leeuw* served as the FLAGSHIP of the Dutch Admiral Cornelis TROMP, who fought under Admiral Michiel de RUYTER during the Third Dutch War, 1672–74. She was badly damaged in the struggle with Sir Edward SPRAGGE's division at the Battle of the TEXEL, 1673, but subsequently was repaired and returned to service. The *Gouden Leeuw* was finally decommissioned in 1686.

Graf Spee   See ADMIRAL GRAF SPEE.

Graf Zeppelin

*N*otable as the German navy's first AIRCRAFT CARRIER, the *Graf Zeppelin* was ordered in 1935 and launched in December 1938 but was never completed. By August 1940, when construction work was halted by wartime shortages, she was some 80 percent complete. Work was restarted in 1942 and again abandoned the following year. Her hull was scuttled at Stettin in 1945, but later she was refloated. In August 1947 she was lost at sea while being towed to Leningrad (St. Petersburg) under Soviet command. Planned as a 23,430-ton carrier, she would have had a maximum speed of 33.75 knots and the ability to carry 40 aircraft.

Intended to provide air cover for commerce raiders, the *Graf Zeppelin* was never completed because of severe design weaknesses and interservice rivalry. She would have had a limited range and her armor protection was poor because it had been sacrificed to provide heavy armament, including 16 5.9-inch (15-cm) guns. Her aircraft-carrying capacity was also low compared with other carriers of the time. Progress on her construction was constrained by the Luftwaffe's refusal to consider the formation of a separate naval air arm or to cooperate actively with the project by releasing the required aircraft. As a result of these problems, construction of the *Graf Zeppelin* was abandoned and a second carrier project also was scrapped.

Grand Alliance, War of the

1688–97

*A*lso known as the War of the League of Augsburg or the Nine Years' War, the War of the Grand Alliance was fought by the combined forces of England, the Netherlands and the Hapsburg empire against France. With strong leadership from King William III of England, the alliance opposed the territorial ambitions of Louis XIV, who sought to bring the whole continent under French control. France intended the Irish War, 1689–91, in which Louis XIV supported James II, the deposed Stuart king, to divert English military effort from the Continent.

The focus of the war was nine years' land combat in Europe, with operations being concentrated in the Netherlands, where a succession of sieges took place. With no breakthrough on land in sight, France intended to use its powerful naval forces to secure a decisive victory at sea. At the Battle of BEACHY HEAD, July 10, 1690, Admiral the Comte de TOURVILLE defeated an Anglo-Dutch fleet under Admiral Arthur HERBERT, Viscount Torrington. However, the French missed a real opportunity to build on this victory by failing to seize control of the English Channel, and the English and Dutch navies were able to build up their strength. At the Battle of LA HOGUE, May 29, 1692, the key naval battle of the war, the Anglo-Dutch fleet decisively defeated Admiral de Tourville. The French lost control of the English Channel and had to abandon their plans to invade England, although fears of an invasion were briefly revived in 1696. Although Admiral de Tourville inflicted heavy damage on an Anglo-Dutch convoy at the Battle of Lagos, June 27–28, 1693, the balance of naval power had shifted decisively in favor of the English and it was too late for the French to reverse it. Louis XIV's changing fortunes on land and his lack of success at sea persuaded him to enter secret peace negotiations with King William. This led to the Treaty of Ryswick, 1697, which concluded the war.

John P. W. Ehrman, *The Navy in the War of William III, 1689–97: Its State and Direction*, London, 1953; Edward B. Powley, *The Naval Side of King William's War*, London, 1972.

Grand Fleet

*T*he main fleet of the British navy during WORLD WAR I, 1914–18, the Grand Fleet consisted of four battle squadrons (21 dreadnoughts and eight pre-dreadnoughts), a battle cruiser squadron (four battle cruisers), two cruiser squadrons and a light cruiser squadron. From its bases at SCAPA FLOW and Rosyth in Scotland, the ROYAL NAVY's Grand Fleet, under the command of Admiral John JELLICOE, operated a policy of containing the less powerful German HIGH SEAS FLEET by means of a distant BLOCKADE. A close blockade of the German coast was ruled out because it would have resulted in unacceptable losses from German U-BOATS and MINES. Each navy wanted to bring the other to action, but the expected decisive fleet action in the North Sea did not materialize: Caution on both sides in the use of their forces led to long periods of inactivity.

The Battle of JUTLAND, May 1916, was the only occasion when the main British and German battle fleets fought each other. Although the Grand Fleet was unable to achieve anything more than a draw at Jutland, the Germans realized that their High Seas Fleet would never be able to defeat its stronger opponent. Now they were even more unwilling to risk their main battle fleet, which remained in port for much of the rest of the war. Under its new commander, Admiral David BEATTY, who was appointed in December 1916, the Grand Fleet was reorganized after Jutland: Improved protection to magazines, new shells and new methods of coordinated fire control were provided as the lessons of the battle were absorbed. Beatty maintained the distant blockade of Germany until the end of the war, but by 1917–18 the focus of British naval activity had shifted to neutralizing the U-boat threat and establishing an effective convoy system. The Grand Fleet did not long survive the war; the ROYAL Navy was reduced rapidly as economic pressures took their toll.

Grasse, François Joseph Paul, Marquis de Grasse-Tilly

1722–88

*F*rench naval commander who contributed to the fall of Yorktown to American forces in 1781 and thereby helped to determine the final outcome of the AMERICAN WAR OF INDEPENDENCE, 1775–83. Entering the French navy at the age of 11, the Comte de Grasse saw much action during the War of the AUSTRIAN SUCCESSION, 1740–48, and the SEVEN YEARS' WAR, 1756–63. Before the American War of Independence his career progressed relatively slowly, and he was not appointed captain until 1762. A commodore when France intervened in the war, he was present at the Battle of USHANT, July 1778. In 1781 he became commander in chief of the French Atlantic Fleet and was promoted to the rank of lieutenant general. In March he left for the West Indies with a large convoy of merchant ships, which he safely escorted to Port Royal, Jamaica.

Later he went north to the strategic waters of Chesapeake Bay, which he dominated before the British fleet under Admiral Thomas GRAVES was able to arrive from New York. During the Battle of CHESAPEAKE, September 5, 1781, the French maintained their position with great skill and the British were unable to relieve their main army under General Cornwallis at Yorktown, which fell to the

Americans. Sir George RODNEY took his revenge on behalf of the Royal Navy at the Battle of the SAINTS, April 12, 1782, but nothing could undermine the significance of the fall of Yorktown. The Comte de Grasse, whose flagship the *Ville de Paris* was captured, was taken prisoner by the British. On his return home he found that his reputation had not survived his defeat at the Battle of the Saints, and his naval career was over.

Charles Lee Lewis, *Admiral de Grasse and American Independence*, Annapolis, 1945.

Graves, Thomas, First Baron
1725–1802

*B*ritish naval commander, born in Cornwall, who progressed steadily through the naval hierarchy, reaching the rank of rear admiral in 1779, during the AMERICAN WAR OF INDEPENDENCE, 1775–83. Two years later he was appointed to the command of the British fleet blockading the eastern coast of North America. His responsibilities included providing support to the British army that was besieged by the Americans at Yorktown. With this objective in mind Graves, who had 19 ships, sailed from New York in August 1781 but arrived too late at the Chesapeake to prevent the French from securing their position.

Graves had expected to meet only a small enemy squadron, but instead Admiral Comte de GRASSE's entire French fleet of 24 ships came out to meet the British. During the extended but partial and inconclusive Battle of CHESAPEAKE, September 5, 1781, Graves failed to use the opportunities presented to him. The French, who outmaneuvered Graves, were able to reoccupy Chesapeake Bay; the British army at Yorktown was doomed and the war was lost. Graves had the opportunity to redeem his reputation during the FRENCH REVOLUTIONARY AND NAPOLEONIC WARS, 1792–1815, when he served with distinction at the Battle of the GLORIOUS FIRST OF JUNE, 1794, and was raised to the peerage as a result.

Great White Fleet

*T*he Great White Fleet consisted of 16 American battleships, painted brilliant white, that were sent on a 14-month cruise of the world, returning home on February 22, 1909. Planned by President Theodore ROOSEVELT as a major public relations exercise, it was intended to celebrate the United States' position as the world's third naval power, to deter potential aggressors and to boost the nation's prestige abroad. It also would be used in an attempt to silence the vocal domestic critics of Roosevelt's plans for the further expansion and modernization of the navy.

The 16 ships traveled together for a total of 46,000 nautical miles, visiting ports in South America and the Caribbean; in New Zealand, Australia and Japan; and then in China and the Mediterranean. The Great White Fleet was generally well received even in Japan, which was widely seen as a serious potential threat to American interests in the Far East. As he had intended, Roosevelt was able to use the positive impact of the fleet in different regions to underpin the case for greater investment in an American dreadnought program. Without such investment, the U.S. Navy would soon be overtaken by the navies of Germany and Japan. The Great White Fleet also succeeded in helping to boost American influence abroad; for the navy, it proved to be a valuable training exercise for the crews involved.

The fleet's return home in February 1909 coincided with Roosevelt's departure from the presidency. Its success was a fitting tribute to the politician who had turned the United States into a world naval power in less than a decade.

Greer, U.S.S.

A flush-decked DESTROYER of the Wickes class, built during WORLD WAR I, 1914–18. Used primarily for patrol duties in the period 1940–41 before the United States entered WORLD WAR II, 1939–45, the *Greer* was involved in an incident with the German navy on September 4, 1941 while transporting supplies to the U.S. garrison in Iceland. As she progressed toward Iceland she received a signal from a British Hudson bomber saying that the bomber was about to depth-charge a submerged U-BOAT (*U-652*) that was in the area. The U-boat assumed that the attack had been made by the *Greer* and responded by firing a torpedo at her. The torpedo missed; in retaliation the *Greer* dropped depth-charges. Described by President Franklin Roosevelt as an unprovoked German attack on a neutral vessel, the incident increased the likelihood of war between the United States and Germany. Although Adolf Hitler sought to avoid a direct confrontation with the U.S. Navy, incidents of this kind were almost inevitable in wartime. The possibility of confusion was even greater because Britain had taken a large number of former American destroyers into service with the ROYAL NAVY under the LEND-LEASE AGREEMENT.

Greif

*F*ormerly the German merchant vessel *Guben* of 4,963 tons, the *Greif* was an ARMED MERCHANT CRUISER employed by the German navy during WORLD WAR I, 1914–18. Operated by a crew of 306, she patrolled in disguise as a Norwegian merchantman and was, therefore, the equivalent of the British Q-SHIP. The *Greif*'s operational life was very limited. On February 29, 1916, less than a month after she had been commissioned, she was intercepted by the British armed merchant cruiser *Alcantara* while operating in the North Sea. The two ships exchanged fire at short range and both began to sink; the *Greif*'s fate was sealed by the *Andes*, another armed merchant cruiser and one of the three vessels that the *Alcantara* had summoned to help her. The *Andes* also rescued the *Greif*'s surviving crew of 220 men.

Greig, Sir Samuel
1735–88

Scottish naval commander, born in Inverkeithing. Greig served for much of his career in the RUSSIAN NAVY and played a key role in its development in the late 18th century. Spending his earliest seagoing service in the merchant fleet, he later transferred to the Royal Navy and saw action during the SEVEN YEARS' WAR, 1756–63. He was on board Admiral Edward HAWKE's flagship at the Battle of QUIBERON BAY, 1759. In 1763, shortly after Catherine the Great acceded to the throne, he transferred to the Russian navy where employment prospects were more favorable.

He was promoted to the rank of rear admiral during Russia's war with the Turks, 1768–72, and was present at the battle of Çeşme (Chesme) in July 1770. Not long afterward, in 1773, Greig was promoted to vice admiral, and in this capacity was involved in the modernization of the Russian fleet and dockyards over the next few years. He commanded the Russian fleet during the first stages of the Russo-Swedish War, 1788–90, in the Baltic, winning the key opening Battle of Hoglund, July 17, 1788, but died of natural causes before the end of the war. Greig's son, Alexis Samuelovich Greig, 1775–1845, also became an admiral in the Russian navy.

Grenada, Battle of
July 6, 1779

Following their failure to capture the island of St. Lucia, December 15, 1778, in an early naval engagement against the British during the AMERICAN WAR OF INDEPENDENCE, 1775–83, the French increased their naval activity against Britain in the Caribbean. Admiral the Compte d'ESTAING, the French commander, seized St. Vincent in June 1779; his next target was the island of Grenada. He assembled 25 ships of the line for the attack, which he carried out successfully. When Vice Admiral John BYRON, British commander of the Leeward Islands, learned of the French operation, he left his anchorage at St. Lucia with 21 ships of the line and other naval vessels.

As the British approached Grenada, on July 6, the stronger French force emerged from the harbor of George-town. Byron unwisely decided to engage the enemy, and the two forces met in St. George's Bay soon after dawn. Several British warships quickly sustained damage and four were disabled. By 11 A.M. the two fleets were in line-ahead formation, moving in a northerly direction. As Byron's van came under renewed pressure he was supported effectively by ships to the rear under the command of Admiral Sir Joshua Rowley. Fighting continued sporadically, but, fortunately for the British, the French never took full advantage of their stronger position. In the late afternoon the French broke off their action and withdrew to the south. Although the British had avoided a disastrous defeat, the battle marked a turning point in the Anglo-French naval struggle in the Caribbean, with the French securing a strategic advantage that they were to retain until their defeat at the Battle of the SAINTS, April 12, 1782.

Grenada Invasion
1983

A pro-Marxist military coup in the former British colony of Grenada in the Caribbean in October 1983 provided the immediate justification for U.S. intervention, although there had been considerable concern for some time about alleged evidence of growing Soviet and Cuban influence on the island. The course of political events on Grenada meant that it was perceived to be a threat to the security of the United States and required the installation of a more politically reliable regime.

On October 21 a U.S. naval task force, headed by the aircraft carrier *Independence*, was sent to the Caribbean on the orders of President Ronald Reagan with the stated purpose of evacuating American citizens from Grenada. At the same time U.S. Marines were landed on neighboring Caribbean islands. American intentions became clear four days later, on October 25, when operation "Urgent Fury" was launched, using the resources of the naval task force. Some 1,500 members of the 82nd Airborne Division and 400 marines, supported by helicopter gunships, landed on the island. Opposition by the Grenadian People's Revolutionary Army was fiercer than expected, although the worst of the fighting was over within four days and a new U.S.-backed administration was quickly established. Casualties were light but the political cost in terms of adverse international reaction was higher.

Grenville, Sir Richard
1542–91

English shipowner and naval commander whose most famous engagement is commemorated in Lord Tennyson's poem "The last fight of the *Revenge*." During his adventurous youth, Richard Grenville, who came from an old Cornish family (the Grenvilles of Mount Edgcumbe, Plymouth), killed a man in a duel and, in 1567, fought for Holy Roman Emperor Maximilian II against the Turks. In 1585 Grenville turned to the sea, making the first of two journeys to North America. There he established the ill-fated colony at Roanoke Island, Virginia—the inspiration of his cousin, Sir Walter RALEIGH. By the time of the SPANISH ARMADA, 1588, he was wealthy enough to contribute three ships to Lord HOWARD of Effingham's fleet at Plymouth. Grenville himself commanded a small naval force in the Irish Sea, hoping to intercept the enemy fleet on their way back home to Spain but failing to do so.

It was not until 1591 that a real opportunity for action arose. Grenville was appointed second in command of a squadron of seven ships, under Lord Thomas Howard, that was ordered to the Azores with the aim of intercepting the Spanish treasure fleet. Before they could act a superior enemy force, which had been sent out as an escort, arrived off the Azores. Howard was compelled to withdraw, and his entire fleet, except for Grenville's flagship, the *Revenge*, escaped successfully. Grenville had delayed his departure for too long in order to embark his many sick crew, and soon was surrounded by the enemy. In an epic 15-hour fight the *Revenge* held off 15 Spanish galleons, sinking one and badly damaging another. By the end of the battle the *Revenge* was severely damaged and Grenville was mortally wounded. He died on board the Spanish flagship *San Pablo* three days later. During the Battle of the AZORES, Grenville had demonstrated outstanding seamanship as well as an exaggerated sense of pride and honor in unnecessarily prolonging the action.

A. L. Rowse, *Sir Richard Grenville of the* Revenge: *An Elizabethan Hero*, London, 1937.

Guadalcanal, Battle of
November 12–15, 1942

*A*n extended and fiercely fought WORLD WAR II, 1939–45, engagement between American and Japanese naval forces that effectively settled the fate of the Pacific island of Guadalcanal. The island, a British protectorate, had been occupied by the Japanese early in the war. An American counterforce established a beachhead on the island in August 1942, and a battle for control had ensued. By October 1942 Admiral Isoroku YAMAMOTO had decided on a major naval assault that would end the American presence there. A bombardment force, which included the battleships *Hiei* and *Kirishima*, commanded by Vice Admiral Hiroaki ABE and escorted by the cruiser *Nagara* and fourteen destroyers, would destroy Henderson Field, the American-controlled airstrip. An amphibious force, commanded by Admiral Raizo TANAKA, would then land 13,500

reinforcements who would strike a decisive blow against the occupying American forces.

The Americans became aware of the Japanese plan, and Rear Admiral Daniel CALLAGHAN prepared to intercept Vice Admiral Abe's force as it passed between the northern coast of Guadalcanal and Savo Island during the night of November 12. Callaghan's force, which was moving on an opposite course, consisted of five cruisers and eight destroyers. Because of an American communications breakdown, Callaghan failed to open fire until the Japanese had done so. During a battle lasting 24 minutes, the *Atlanta*, an American light cruiser, and four destroyers were sunk and two admirals, including Callaghan, were killed. Three American cruisers were badly damaged, including the *Juneau*, which was torpedoed and sunk by an enemy submarine the next day. American fire was concentrated on the battleship *Hiei*, which withdrew only to suffer further air attacks; the *Hiei* was scuttled the following day. The Japanese also lost two destroyers.

Despite their heavy losses, the Americans had prevented Abe reaching Guadalcanal and had forced the Japanese to postpone the landing of reinforcements. Japan then sent a cruiser force commanded by Vice Admiral Gunichi Mikawa to carry out the bombardment mission that Abe had been unable to complete. Arriving off Savo Island during the night of November 13–14, Mikawa dispatched Rear Admiral S. Nishimura with three cruisers and six destroyers to attack Henderson Field. Mikawa provided a covering screen of three cruisers and two destroyers, although no American opposition was encountered during the attack. Nishimura fired 1,000 shells on the field but failed to put it out of action, The next morning the Japanese naval forces were pursued by American aircraft that sank the cruiser *Kinugasa* and damaged two other cruisers and a destroyer.

Meanwhile, Admiral Tanaka's reinforcement group, consisting of 11 transports and 11 destroyers, was progressing toward Guadalcanal under heavy air attack. With seven of his transports lost, Tanaka landed his remaining reinforcements during the night of November 14–15. At the same time another Japanese squadron was on its way to bombard Henderson Field. Under the command of Admiral Nobutake KONDO, it consisted of the battleship *Kirishima*, three cruisers and six destroyers, protected by an advance screen of a cruiser and three destroyers under the command of Rear Admiral Shintaro Hashimoto. The Japanese came into contact with an American task force, commanded by Rear Admiral Willis Lee, off Savo Island. Sent to replace Callaghan's cruiser squadron, it was comprised of the battleships *Washington* and *South Dakota* and four destroyers.

During the opening stages of the engagement, the Japanese hit and sank three American destroyers. The *South Dakota* also lost her electrical power. At the same time the *Washington* hit the *Kirishima* many times with her 5-inch

(13-cm) and 16-inch (40.64-cm) shells; the Japanese warship later was scuttled. Kondo soon withdrew from the area, ending the naval battle of Guadalcanal. The Japanese had sustained heavy losses and had failed in their objective of landing significant reinforcements on Guadalcanal. This marked a turning point in the struggle for control of Guadalcanal and the other SOLOMON ISLANDS.

S. B. Griffith, *The Battle for Guadalcanal*, New York, 1980.

Guardship

During the age of the sailing navies, a naval guardship was, as the name indicates, a vessel responsible for the protection of a port, naval dockyard or anchorage. In the British navy it was often the FLAGSHIP of the port admiral. Apart from generally monitoring activity within the installation, the guardship ensured that the guard boat carried out its nightly patrols of the fleet anchorage. It also was responsible for the security of warships that had been laid up and did not have a regular watch to protect them. In most European navies they also were the normal receiving point for press-ganged seamen before they were posted to a specific ship. A typical guardship might be a former man-of-war that was no longer seaworthy.

Guichen, Luc Urbain de Bouëxic, Comte de
1712–90

French fleet commander during the AMERICAN WAR OF INDEPENDENCE, 1775–83. Guichen entered the navy in 1730 as a garde de la Marine, the lowest commissioned rank. Progressing slowly through the hierarchy, he reached the rank of rear admiral in 1776. When France intervened in the American Revolution, Guichen raised his flag in the French Channel fleet. He was present at the Battle of USHANT, July 1778. Early in 1780 he was dispatched to the West Indies as an escort to 83 merchant ships. His 16 ships of the line, joined by Admiral the Comte de GRASSE's fleet, successfully defended French interests in the Caribbean against the British fleet commanded by Admiral Sir George RODNEY. Guichen met the enemy fleet on three occasions before returning to France but was unable secure a decisive outcome.

In December 1781 Guichen was ordered to return to the West Indies with supplies and reinforcements. As he passed through the Bay of Biscay, he was intercepted by a British squadron commanded by Admiral Richard KEMPENFELT. The British captured 20 French transport ships; the rest were dispersed. A second failure, in 1782, to prevent a British convoy from reaching GIBRALTAR proved to be Guichen's last opportunity to restore his reputation as a sound if uninspiring naval commander.

Guided Missile

Rockets that can be guided from launch until they reach their target. A wide range of different types has been used by naval forces since WORLD WAR II, 1939–45, including surface-to-surface missiles (SSMs), surface-to-air missiles (SAMs), air-to-air missiles (AAMs) and air-to-surface missiles (ASMs). SSMs vary from short-range tactical systems to the intercontinental ballistic missile systems of the POLARIS submarine that also can be fired from beneath the surface. The former have proved to be so effective in ship-to-ship engagements that they have largely replaced conventional naval guns and have led to the development of new classes of warship, such as the guided missile cruiser. They have been produced in a wide variety of forms, including the French-produced EXOCET and the American-made HARPOON, and typically have a range of up to 180 miles (290 km). A more recent SSM is the ship-launched CRUISE MISSILE, which has the capability to follow the ground over which it is traveling.

SAM systems also are widely used for defensive purposes against air attack, to destroy either the enemy aircraft or an incoming missile from whatever source. In the latter case a multiple-barrel quick-firing cannon also might be used. AAMs, which are standard equipment on naval aircraft, have replaced the machine gun as the principal weapon of aerial combat. The missile also has greatly increased the potential of the SUBMARINE, which continues to be the main threat to the surface ship. Apart from being a major weapon in the armory of deterrence, conventional underwater-launched missiles such as the Exocet (which is also produced in surface- and air-launched versions) have enlarged the antiship potential of the modern submarine. Capable of underwater launch, the missile can lock onto an enemy ship (or a land target) hundreds of miles away. The rapid evolution of the missile in the postwar period has underlined the cost and complexity of advanced naval forces and has meant that only the superpowers have the economic resources to exploit fully the real potential of this technology. See also SUBMARINE-LAUNCHED BALLISTIC MISSILE.

Gulf of Genoa, Battle of the
March 12–14, 1795

An engagement between British and French squadrons during the FRENCH REVOLUTIONARY AND NAPOLEONIC WARS, 1792–1815, that ended inconclusively. The events leading to the battle began with the departure of a French force of 15 ships of the line, commanded by Rear Admiral Pierre Martin, from Toulon. The squadron carried some 5,000 troops with the aim of recapturing the island of Corsica, which was then in British hands. On March 11 a British squadron of 14 ships of the line, commanded by

Rear Admiral William Hotham, sighted the enemy in the Gulf of Genoa. For two days the two opposing squadrons failed to make contact but, on March 13, the French 84-gun ship *Ça Ira* fouled the *Victoire*, the next ship ahead. The *Ça Ira* had lost her fore and main topmasts, and the British seized their opportunity, attacking her with two ships, including the AGAMMEMNON, which was commanded by Captain Horatio NELSON. Fighting continued the next day but it was inconclusive, and the French withdrew in a westerly direction. The British, who did not pursue the retreating French, had captured two enemy ships—the badly damaged *Ça Ira* and the *Censeur*, the ship that was towing her.

Gulf of Sirte Incident
August 1981

*F*ollowing a previous incident in 1979, a second unprovoked attack by Libyan air force planes against U.S. Navy aircraft occurred in August 1981. Two Libyan Sukhoi Su-22 fighters targeted two Grumman F-14 Tomcat aircraft that were engaged in exercises outside Libyan territorial waters in August 1991. The F-14s, which were multirole fighters, operated from the aircraft carrier U.S.S. NIMITZ. One of the Soviet-built Su-22s fired a missile, which its American target successfully evaded. In response, both American aircraft fired their AIM-9 Sidewinder missiles; the two Su-22s, which were outclassed by their opponents, were destroyed.

Gulf War
1990–1991

*O*n August 2, 1990, following a series of territorial disputes and disagreements over oil production, Iraq invaded the small oil-rich Persian Gulf emirate of Kuwait and rapidly gained control of the country. There was a swift military response from the United States, Britain and several other countries, which dispatched troops and naval units to the area in Operation Desert Shield, to prevent an Iraqi invasion of Saudi Arabia. The United Nations condemned the Iraqi action. It soon became evident that, despite intense diplomatic activity and the introduction of economic sanctions, the Iraqis would not withdraw fully from Kuwait unless military action were taken.

The remainder of the year was devoted to assembling the forces from 30 countries required to launch Operation Desert Storm on January 16, 1991 from land bases in Saudi Arabia and from ships in the Persian Gulf and other waters. The operation began with a massive air assault, which continued until February 24, on Iraqi positions in Kuwait and on the military and economic infrastructure of Iraq itself. The ground assault on Kuwait, which began on February 24, secured the country within a few days, with parts of the Iraqi army failing to put up any effective resistance.

Before Operation Desert Storm had begun, the coalition had assembled an impressive array of naval units, including six carrier battle groups, in the Persian Gulf. The U.S. Navy was the dominant naval power and had deployed ships in the Red Sea and the Mediterranean as well as the Gulf. The small Iraqi navy was no match for the allied naval forces, which took complete control of the sea on their arrival. A major naval contribution to the operation was the use of Tomahawk CRUISE MISSILES, fired from battleships, cruisers and frigates, against targets deep inside Iraq that were too dangerous for manned aircraft to reach. It was the first wartime use of the cruise missile. Carrier-based aircraft also made a major contribution to the fighting, supplementing the main allied air forces, which operated from bases in Saudi Arabia. Among the American ships involved in the war were the aircraft carriers *Midway* and *Theodore Roosevelt* and the Iowa-class battleships MISSOURI and WISCONSIN. The Gulf War is a clear example of the increasing influence of naval power on land operations in contemporary warfare.

L. Freedman and E. Karsh, *The Gulf War, 1990–91*, London, 1993.

Gunboat Diplomacy

*T*he overt display of naval force by a major power with the aim of influencing the course of political events in a lesser power or colony. The term "gunboat diplomacy" is particularly associated with the use of naval power by the major European imperial powers, especially Britain and France, and by the United States, in the latter part of the 19th century and the period before World War I. For example, during this period U.S. Navy vessels were frequently deployed in the Caribbean and off the coast of Latin America with the aim of dictating the outcome of internal events. A display of American naval force also was sometimes used to forestall intervention by a European power. The United States also practiced gunboat diplomacy in China and the Philippines, while the French used the technique in Indo-China and the British used it in Egypt. Gunboat diplomacy was a symbol of imperial strength, but it many cases it was not sufficient in itself to produce a satisfactory political outcome, and direct military intervention was often the result. (See also GREAT WHITE FLEET.)

Gundelow

A type of North American sailing river barge of the 18th century whose primary role was commercial transport, although it was adapted for naval use during the

AMERICAN WAR OF INDEPENDENCE, 1775–83. The gundelow had one tall mast that normally carried two square sails and a staysail, although some versions had a large lateen mainsail. Some gundelows were built with a high bow. A typical gundelow was about 19.68 yards (18 m) in length and over 5.47 yards (5 m) wide. It was lightly armed, with perhaps one gun on each side and a swivel gun. Both the British and Americans operated gundelows during the War of Independence. Together with frigates, schooners and galleys, they were used in battle on LAKE CHAMPLAIN and elsewhere.

Guns and Gunnery

The long reign of the muzzle-loading CANNON as the principal offensive weapon of the sailing warship came to an abrupt end in the mid-19th century. The use of a new explosive shell by the RUSSIAN NAVY at the Battle of SINOPE, November 30, 1853, demonstrated the vulnerability of wooden warships and stimulated the development of the IRONCLAD. France produced the first armored warship, the frigate LA GLOIRE, in 1859, and others quickly followed. This development forced the world's navies to abandon the muzzle-loading smooth-bore cannon that fired a shot with a charge of gunpowder. It was replaced with a more accurate, longer-range weapon that was more likely to pierce the protective armor with which warships were now fitted. This new weapon was a breech-loading rifled-bore gun that fired an explosive shell with a charge of cordite. It was constructed with reinforced wire-bound barrels enclosing the rifled tube to enable them to withstand higher firing pressures.

This change was accompanied by the abandonment of BROADSIDE firing through portholes. A smaller number of heavier breech-loaders were accommodated in rotating turrets fore and aft, which meant that guns could be fired simultaneously in several different directions. In the second half of the 19th century, naval gun design was constantly under review as improvements in armor were made with the aim of concentrating protection on the most vulnerable areas. For example, the adoption of new breech-loading mechanisms and changes in propellent helped to improve the performance of the naval gun. The introduction of DIRECTOR FIRE CONTROL marked the first major step in the efforts to produce more accurately targeted gunfire. The later Dreyer fire control table, which was used during WORLD WAR I, 1914–18, sought to bring together the different factors that affected the alignment of a gun sight on its target. Higher levels of accuracy were achieved only when RADAR and, later, the computer were used for naval gun control.

Despite these improvements, by the early years of the 20th century, it became evident that there were significant limitations to the large naval gun even though it formed the basis of the new all-big-gun dreadnought BATTLESHIP. Weaknesses in the design and production of ammunition as well as the problem of distorted barrels, which could have a caliber of up to 16 inches (40.64 cm), reduced their impact. The distance at which a big gun was effective was relatively short and fell well below the distance (12.4 miles; 20 km) at which warships typically fought during World War I. A battleship designed to an appropriate standard normally could withstand a direct hit unless its magazine was vulnerable to attack. Experience in World War I confirmed that the big gun was less effective than the torpedo and the mine in sinking enemy warships.

This lesson was not fully appreciated at the time but was reinforced in WORLD WAR II, 1939–45, when the aircraft became the effective adversary of the ship. Direct engagements between opposing ships were relatively uncommon, and large naval guns were more likely to be used against land-based targets during amphibious operations. In the postwar period, the big naval gun has become obsolete. It has been replaced by the GUIDED MISSILE, which provides—in its antiship and antiaircraft forms—the basis of modern naval armament.

Norman Friedman, *U.S. Naval Weapons: Every Gun, Missile and Torpedo Used by the U.S. Navy from 1883 to the Present Day*, Annapolis, 1982; Ian Hogg and John Batchelor, *Naval Gun*, Poole, 1978; Peter Padfield, *Guns at Sea*, London, 1973.

Hague Convention

1907

The second of two international conferences that aimed to reach an agreement that would limit the effects of war. The first conference, held in 1899, was called by Nicholas II, Tsar of Russia, and involved 26 countries. Although progress was more difficult to achieve than expected, several agreements were concluded, including one on the laws and customs of war, with references to sea warfare. There was an agreement to resolve disputes between states peacefully, and the first international legal machinery was created.

At the second conference at The Hague in 1907, organized on the initiative of American president Theodore ROOSEVELT, 44 participant countries met to renew most of the earlier agreements. Much effort was devoted to producing clear rules on the treatment of prisoners of war, and new agreements relevant to the conduct of naval warfare were made. Designed to mitigate the horrors of war, they included provisions about the declaration of war, the laying of naval mines, the position of neutrals at sea during wartime and naval bombardment. The convention had only limited success as the experience of naval warfare in WORLD WAR I, 1914–18, makes clear.

Halibut, U.S.S.

The U.S.S. *Halibut* was notable as the world's first SUBMARINE specifically designed and constructed to operate GUIDED MISSILES. Completed in late 1959 for the UNITED STATES NAVY, she was powered by a single pressurized water-cooled nuclear reactor that gave a maximum speed submerged of about 20 knots. The *Halibut* had a displacement of 3,800 tons and was operated by a crew of 98. She was equipped with five Regulus I subsonic weapons and six 21-inch (53-cm) torpedo tubes. Following the

end of the failed Regulus program, the *Halibut*'s missile equipment was removed. Reclassified as an attack submarine, she was equipped to operate deep submergence rescue vehicles (DSRVs) from her afterdeck while she was submerged. The *Halibut* was decommissioned in 1996.

Hall, Sir William

1870–1943

Director of British naval intelligence from November 1914 until the end of WORLD WAR I, 1918, Hall was an outstanding success who effectively employed every field of intelligence. A gunnery expert and former battle cruiser commander, he was generally known as "Blinker" Hall because of a pronounced facial twitch. At the center of his intelligence division was the group responsible for deciphering intercepted signals. This was the main source of information during the war about the German fleet, including the U-BOATS. Known as Room 40 OB, after the room in the War Office building in London where it operated, the deciphering group was brought within Hall's control early on in the war. He expanded it considerably, eventually employing more than 100 specialists.

Hall also gave priority to the interception of transatlantic diplomatic signals and had a number of notable successes, including the exposure of the famous Zimmerman telegram, which helped to bring the United States into the war, and information about the anti-British activities of the British nationalist Sir Roger Casement, who had sought German aid for an Irish uprising. Hall also established a network of agents and, in cooperation with the (London) Metropolitan Police, was involved in counterespionage activities in England. His development of naval intelligence made a significant contribution to the Allied naval victory, and he was knighted for his wartime services. Hall retired from the service at the end of the war and entered politics, serving as a Member of Parliament until 1929.

P. Beesly, *Room 40: British Naval Intelligence in World War I*, London, 1982.

Hallowell, Sir Benjamin
1760–1834

One of Admiral Lord NELSON's "band of brothers," Hallowell was a Canadian-born vice admiral of unusually heavy build and considerable personal strength. He entered the Royal Navy at an early age, and his connection with Nelson dated from 1794, when they were both in action on Corsica. At the Battle of the NILE, 1798, Hallowell commanded the *Swiftsure*, which, together with the *Alexander*, was responsible for the destruction of the French flagship *L'ORIENT*. After the battle Hallowell had a coffin made from the mainmast of this ship and presented it to Nelson in order that the great naval commander might be buried in "one of his own trophies."

Hallowell did not serve with Nelson again until he joined the fleet off Toulon some years later. In 1805 he took part in the chase of the French fleet to the West Indies and later kept watch on it at Cadiz before making for GIBRALTAR in October. Therefore, he was not present at the Battle of TRAFALGAR, October 1805. The remainder of his wartime career was occupied with routine operations in the Mediterranean.

Halsey, William Frederick, Jr.
1882–1959

American naval officer, one of the great wartime leaders of WORLD WAR II, 1939–45, and nicknamed "Bull" by the press for his pugnaciousness. Born on October 30, 1882, the son of a navy captain, Halsey entered the U.S. Naval Academy in 1900. He served on battleships as part of the GREAT WHITE FLEET's circumnavigation of the globe in 1907–9. Seeing service principally in torpedo boats, he commanded a destroyer during the 1914 Mexican intervention. During WORLD WAR I, he commanded destroyers operating from Queenstown (now Cobb, County Cork), Ireland, on antisubmarine patrol duty, receiving the Navy Cross for his service. After more commands of destroyers and destroyer squadrons, interrupted by tours as naval attaché in Europe, Halsey trained and earned his wings in 1935 at the advanced age of 52. He became a fervent advocate of naval air power and of fast carrier task forces, for which he would gain his greatest fame.

When the Japanese attacked PEARL HARBOR, December 7, 1941, Halsey, who commanded the aircraft carriers of the U.S. Pacific Fleet, was returning to base after having delivered planes to Wake Island. From his FLAGSHIP the

Admiral William Halsey (right), the victor of the Battle of Leyte Gulf, talks to Admiral Chester Nimitz   *(Copyright © Imperial War Museum, London)*

Enterprise, together with the YORKTOWN and supporting cruisers and destroyers, he conducted the first major offensive operation of the war by attacking the Japanese-held Marshall and Gilbert Island chains as well as Wake and Marcus Islands early in 1942. While inflicting minimum damage, his efforts provided his pilots with valuable experience in carrier tactics. He then led Task Force 16 on the famous air raid on TOKYO by army Lieutenant Colonel James Doolittle from the *Hornet* in April 1942. A forced hospital stay caused Halsey to relinquish his command, missing the Battle of MIDWAY in June 1942. He became commander of the South Pacific Force and Area, directing the victories in late 1942 and early 1943 off the SANTA CRUZ ISLANDS and GUADALCANAL. From 1943 and into much of 1944 he directed the Allied efforts in the SOLOMON ISLANDS. Appointed commander of the Third Fleet in June 1944, he helped formulate the plans for retaking the Philippine Islands. Controversy surrounds Halsey's role in the Battle of LEYTE GULF and specifically as commander of Task Force 38 at the Battle of Cape Engaño. While he succeeded in sinking all four Japanese carriers, his action nevertheless weakened American naval forces operating against the main Japanese force in the Leyte Gulf. Controversy also surrounded his action in leading his fleet into a typhoon in December 1944, in which three destroyers were lost.

Helping to plan the next operations in the Pacific, his command participated in the OKINAWA campaign and in the air attacks upon the Japanese home islands. The formal surrender took place on the deck of his flagship, the MISSOURI, in September 1945 in Tokyo Bay. The recipient of many medals and awards, foreign and domestic, Halsey was promoted to Fleet Admiral in December 1945, and retired on March 1, 1947. He died on August 16, 1959 in New York.

E. B. Potter, *Bull Halsey: A biography,* Annapolis, 1985.

Hamelin, François
1796–1864

*F*rench admiral who commanded France's fleet in the Black Sea during the CRIMEAN WAR, 1853–56. He worked closely with British naval forces and was involved in the bombardment of Sebastopol in 1854. Hamelin's long naval career, which began during the Napoleonic Wars, 1803–15, culminated in his term as a forward-looking minister of marine. He was a firm advocate of the IRONCLAD, and it was largely due to him that France produced the FRIGATE *LA GLOIRE,* the world's first seagoing ironclad warship.

Hampshire, H.M.S.

*O*n June 5, 1916, during WORLD WAR I, 1914–1918, the British armored cruiser *Hampshire* struck a mine and sank off the Orkney Islands. She was carrying Lord Kitchener, the Secretary of State for War, and his staff on a mission to Russia in an effort to encourage greater Russian resistance to the Germans. There were only 12 survivors, and Kitchener was not among them; his body was never recovered. The *Hampshire,* which had a displacement of 10,850 tons and a maximum speed of 22.5 knots, was completed in 1905. She had joined the Second Cruiser Squadron, GRAND FLEET, early in 1916 and had been present at the Battle of JUTLAND.

Hampton Roads, Battle of
March 8–9, 1862

*T*he outcome of the Battle of Hampton Roads, although notable as the first naval engagement between IRON-

CLADS, was in fact inconclusive and had little impact on the course of the AMERICAN CIVIL WAR, 1861–65. The engagement began as the ironclad *MERRIMACK* entered Hampton Roads on March 8, 1862. Originally a Union frigate, the *Merrimack* had been captured by Confederate forces at Norfolk, Virginia and converted into an ironclad named *Virginia* that was armed with ten heavy guns. She attacked a Union squadron in Hampton Roads and successfully destroyed two wooden warships.

The *Merrimack* planned to resume offensive operations the following day, March 9, but was surprised by the appearance of the Union ironclad *MONITOR,* which had just arrived from New York. Unlike the *Merrimack,* the *Monitor* had been specially built as an ironclad with heavy armor plating. Capable of a higher maximum speed than the *Merrimack,* she was equipped with a revolving turret and two 11-inch (28-cm) DAHLGREN guns. The two ships bombarded each other at close range for some four hours but neither sustained any serious damage. This first major naval battle of the American Civil War produced no clear advantage to either side but was a notable turning point in the history of naval warfare, proving the defensive value of iron construction. Both historic combatants were lost before the end of the year.

Hardy, Sir Thomas Masterman
1769–1839

*B*ritish admiral, one of Lord NELSON's "Band of Brothers." Born in Portisham, Dorset, Hardy first saw action in the Mediterranean during the French Revolutionary Wars, 1792–1802, serving under Nelson as a lieutenant. In 1796, shortly before the Battle of CAPE ST. VINCENT, he had a narrow escape when he lowered a boat in an attempt to rescue a seaman who had fallen overboard. With a Spanish squadron in pursuit of Hardy's boat, Nelson shouted: "I'll not lose Hardy!" Nelson gave orders for a maneuver that enabled Hardy to complete his rescue mission successfully. Hardy was appointed to the command of the *Mutine* in time for the Battle of the NILE, 1798, and shortly afterward he was transferred to the *Vanguard* as Nelson's flag captain.

At the Battle of COPENHAGEN, 1801, he served with Nelson on the *Elephant.* (The sea was too shallow for his own ship, the *St. George,* to participate.) In 1803 the battle with France—the Napoleonic Wars, 1803–15—resumed. On Nelson's appointment as commander in chief in the Mediterranean, once more Hardy accompanied him as flag officer. The two men served together until Nelson's death. Hardy was present with him on deck at the Battle of TRAFALGAR, 1805, when Nelson was mortally wounded. Hardy's services were rewarded with a baronetcy but he had to wait until the age of 56, in 1825, before he was promoted to rear admiral. This promotion had followed a five-year period as commander in chief of the South American station. Hardy concluded his career at the ADMIRALTY as First Sea Lord, 1830–34, reaching the rank of vice admiral in 1837. Universally regarded as a fine seaman and courageous officer, he had been an invaluable support to Lord Nelson in his great battles against the French.

John F. Gore, *Nelson's Hardy and His Wife,* London, 1935.

Hart, Thomas Charles
1877–1971

The commander of the doomed U.S. Asiatic Fleet when the United States entered WORLD WAR II, 1939–45. Born on June 12, 1877 in Genesee County, Michigan, Hart entered the U.S. Naval Academy in 1893; he would reach admiral rank in 1939. During the SPANISH-AMERICAN WAR of 1898, he saw service on board the converted yacht *Vixen* participating in the Battle of SANTIAGO on July 3, 1898. In WORLD WAR I, 1914–18, he commanded two U.S. SUBMARINE divisions, one based in the waters around the British Isles and the other in the Azores operating with British submarines against the German U-BOAT threat.

A submariner with great experience, in 1939 he became commander in chief of the Asiatic Fleet, headquartered at first at Shanghai and then at Manila as war with Japan became more likely. Working with British, Dutch and Australian forces, Hart was forced to move by submarine to the Dutch East Indies. With his pathetically small force he set about trying to stem the Japanese attack toward Southeast Asia and the Dutch East Indies. For political reasons as much as anything else, he was forced to relinquish command to the Dutch just before the disastrous Battle of the JAVA SEA in February 1942. After retiring from the service, he was appointed to complete a vacated Connecticut seat in the U.S. Senate, 1945–47. He died in Connecticut on July 4, 1971.

James R. Leutze, *A Different Kind of Victory,* Annapolis, 1981.

Hartford, U.S.S.

Notable as the FLAGSHIP of the Union naval commander Admiral David FARRAGUT, during the AMERICAN CIVIL WAR, 1861–65, the *Hartford* was a ship-rigged sloop that was launched in 1858. She had auxiliary steam power and was provided with armament, including 20 9-inch (22.8-cm) DAHLGREN guns, in 1862. The *Hartford's* finest hour came during the Battle of MOBILE BAY, August 5, 1864. Following the destruction of the *Tecumseh,* Farragut's leading MONITOR at the beginning of the battle, the *Hartford* led the fleet safely through a minefield that provided the only entrance into the bay. She tried to sink the Confederate IRONCLAD *Tennessee,* which soon surrendered, along with the defending forts. It was the *Hartford's* greatest victory.

Harwood, Sir Henry
1888–1959

British admiral who commanded the South American division of the Royal Navy on the outbreak of WORLD WAR II, 1939–45. Harwood's squadron included his FLAGSHIP, the cruiser *AJAX,* as well as the *ACHILLES,* and the *EXETER.* It soon became involved in the hunt for the German commerce-raider *ADMIRAL GRAF SPEE,* a POCKET-BATTLESHIP that had caused much disruption in the early weeks of the war. Harwood was to be proved correct in his expectation that the German ship would find the RIVER PLATE a fruitful hunting ground. It was there that the British ships lay in wait. Although Harwood was outgunned by his opponent, he saved the British position by dividing his ships and thereby dividing the fire against him.

Eventually the German ship was forced to withdraw to the neutral port of Montevideo, Uruguay, for essential repairs. While it was there British intelligence persuaded the Germans with false information that a large enemy force had assembled. To avoid capture, the *Admiral Graf Spee* was scuttled. In recognition of his achievement, Harwood was knighted and promoted to the rank of rear admiral. In 1942, after a period on the naval staff, Harwood was appointed commander in chief of the Mediterranean Fleet, succeeding Admiral Sir Andrew CUNNINGHAM, but he was compelled to leave his post within a year because of ill health.

Haus, Anton, Baron von
1851–1917

Austrian naval officer. Von Haus was commander in chief of the AUSTRO-HUNGARIAN NAVY from February 1913 until his death in February 1917. Stationed in the Adriatic Sea, he was involved in the BLOCKADE of the Montenegrin coast, and, in May 1915, he ordered the bombardment of the Italian coast. However, in operational terms his command during WORLD WAR I, 1914–18, was relatively uneventful and Austria's modern CAPITAL SHIPS were confined to Pola harbor for much of the war. His earlier naval service, which dated from 1869, included several years at the War Ministry, where he made a significant contribution in the prewar period to the creation of a modern battle fleet. In 1916 Haus's distinguished career was recognized when he became a grand admiral. The rank was never held by any other officer of the Austro-Hungarian navy.

Havana, Battle of
October 1, 1748

A battle between British and Spanish naval forces in the Caribbean during the War of the AUSTRIAN SUCCESSION, 1740–48. When he was informed that the Spanish treasure fleet was due at Havana, Rear Admiral Charles KNOWLES, commander in chief of the Jamaica station, left Port Royal. His squadron, consisting of six SHIPS OF THE LINE, had not located the treasure fleet when, on October 1, it met a small Spanish force of six warships under the command of Vice Admiral Reggio. The British delayed coming to battle partly because two of their ships had been too far astern and needed time to catch up to the rest of the squadron. Fighting eventually started at 2:30 P.M. and continued until 8:00 P.M. in the evening. By that time the Spanish, who had been under heavy pressure, were forced to withdraw with significant losses, including two ships. Despite the favorable outcome for the British, Admiral Knowles was court-martialed for not bringing his squadron to action earlier or in better order. He was found guilty and reprimanded.

Richard Pares, *War and Trade in the West Indies, 1739–63*, London, 1963.

Havock, H.M.S.

The high-speed TORPEDO BOAT, which first appeared in the 1870s, was a considerable success and represented a major potential threat to larger warships that needed to be countered as a matter of urgency. In response the British developed a "torpedo boat destroyer" that was better armed and even faster than its opponents.

The world's first real destroyers, the *Havock* and her sister ship *Hornet*, were built in Britain in 1892–93 and were quickly followed by two more—the *Daring* and the *Decoy*. The first example of this new type, the *Havock*, was 180 feet (54.9 m) long, had a displacement of 260 tons and a maximum speed of 27 knots. (The *Hornet*, with an improved boiler, was even faster with a top speed of 28 knots.) The *Havock* was armed with four guns and three torpedo tubes. The *Hornet*, the *Daring* and the *Decoy* were all similar in design and marked the beginning of a new class of warship that was to become the modern DESTROYER.

Hawke, Edward, First Baron Hawke
1705–81

English naval commander. Born in London, Hawke entered the Royal Navy in 1720. He rose rapidly through family influence and was a post-captain by the age of 29. He established his name during the War of the AUSTRIAN SUCCESSION, 1740–48, often disregarding the rigid official FIGHTING INSTRUCTIONS and developing his own more flexible general chase tactics. Hawke's most notable achievement was his defeat of a French squadron at the second Battle of CAPE FINISTERRE in October 1747. By this time he had been promoted to the rank of rear admiral, and it was evident that he enjoyed the patronage of King George II.

His service during the SEVEN YEARS' WAR, 1756–63, began with an unsuccessful period as commander in chief in the Mediterranean following Admiral John BYNG's failure to relieve MINORCA in 1756. This was followed by an expedition, of which he was joint commander, to capture Rochefort, which ended in failure. In 1759 Hawke redeemed himself when he was appointed to command the force blockading BREST, where the French fleet under Admiral the Comte de CONFLANS was anchored. Conflans was waiting to escort an invasion force across the English Channel. When Hawke had difficulty in maintaining the blockade in poor weather conditions, the French fleet escaped from Brest but was brought to battle off QUIBERON BAY, November 20, 1759. Hawke decisively defeated the French, confirming his reputation as one of England's great naval commanders. He was First Lord of the Admiralty, 1776–78, and was made a baron in 1776. Hawke was appointed admiral of the fleet as he left office.

R. F. Mackay, *Admiral Hawke*, Oxford, 1965.

Hawkins, Sir John
1532–95

English naval commander and navigator. Born in Plymouth, Hawkins became a wealthy man before the age of 30 as a result of his trading activities. In 1562 he became the first Englishman to traffic in slaves, transporting them from West Africa to the Spanish West Indies. He made two further journeys, in 1564–65 and 1567–68, in which he traded in slaves. Hawkins's final voyage, when he was accompanied by his cousin, Sir Francis DRAKE, ended in disaster when he was attacked by a Spanish fleet while anchored in a Mexican port. Only Hawkins's and Drake's ship survived. The incident marked a turning point in Anglo-Spanish relations.

On his return to England, Hawkins turned his attention to naval administration and, in 1577, was appointed Treasurer of the Navy. In this capacity he made a major contribution to the development of the Elizabethan navy and its preparation for war with the Spain. He introduced major improvements in warship design and armament and helped to establish better standards of food and hygiene on board ship. He was directly responsible for the creation of the GALLEON, which provided the basis for the sailing

Sir John Hawkins: English naval commander, reformer and creator of the galleon *(Copyright © National Maritime Museum, Greenwich, London)*

SHIP OF THE LINE over the next 300 years. Hawkins returned to sea during the SPANISH ARMADA, 1588, raising his flag in the *Victory*. He was knighted by Lord HOWARD of Effingham, the Lord High Admiral, during the battle. As comptroller of the navy from 1589, he strengthened his role in naval administration. In 1593, accompanied by Drake as joint commander, Hawkins returned to sea for the last time in an expedition to the West Indies. He fell ill and died at sea off Puerto Rico. Hawkins has a mixed reputation; his early slave-trading activities are offset by his contribution to the reform of the Royal Navy and his role in the victory against Spain. His son, Admiral Sir Richard Hawkins, 1562–1622, also served in the Royal Navy and, like his father, fought against the Spanish Armada, commanding the *Swallow*.

Hedgehog

*B*ritish antisubmarine weapon of WORLD WAR II, 1939–45, later adopted and developed by the UNITED STATES NAVY. Used operationally for the first time in January 1942, the Hedgehog was a multibarrel spigot mortar that fired a pattern of 24 DEPTH CHARGES ahead of the attacking ship. The bombs were armed with a charge of 35 pounds (15.9

kg) and were positioned in four rows of six each. The advantage of this system was that the attacking ship remained in SONAR contact with the target submarine as the charges were fired.

In a conventional depth-charge attack, contact with the target was lost prior to the attack: The sonar beam produced by the transducer could not scan directly below the ship to which it was attached as the depth charge was released over the stern. Rather, the depth charge had to be dropped by guesswork. Unlike conventional depth charges, the Hedgehog did not have a hydrostatic fuse that would enable it to explode at a preset depth; it only exploded on impact against a U-BOAT hull. This was its main weakness, because there could be no guarantee that the charge would hit the target. In practice, however, it increased the number of successful attacks on enemy submarines until it was replaced by the SQUID, which combined the advantages of the depth charge with the forward-throwing capability of the Hedgehog.

Heemskerk, Jacob Van
1567–1607

*D*utch naval commander and explorer, born in Amsterdam. He was notable as one of the SEA BEGGARS, who led the revolt against the Spanish occupation of Holland in the late 16th century. Early in his career he participated in two expeditions, in 1595 and 1596, in search of a passage through the Arctic to China. Although both expeditions ended in failure, they demonstrated his courage as a seaman and foreshadowed his role as one of Holland's first naval heroes. In 1607 he commanded a squadron of 26 ships in search of a stronger Spanish fleet, including ten GALLEONS. The enemy had set sail for the East Indies with orders to attack Dutch settlements. The two fleets met in Gibraltar Bay on April 25, 1607; the outcome was a decisive Dutch victory. Jacob van Heemskerk, who was one of the fatalities of the battle, achieved national prominence as a result.

Heijn, Piet
1578–1629

*D*utch naval commander, born in Delfshaven. His early maritime experiences were as a fisherman. When Heijn (or Heyn) was captured by the Spanish, he was employed as a galley slave for four years. On his release he became a merchant captain and created a profitable business. He also was associated with the Dutch East India company as a local director in Rotterdam and, in 1623, became vice admiral. In this capacity he led several operations against the Spanish; in 1624 he defeated the enemy near San Salvador. Heijn's most notable exploit was the capture, in 1626, of the Spanish treasure fleet off the Cuban coast. It was carrying silver valued at some 15 million florins and proved to be the largest haul of its kind ever.

Although the Dutch East India Company was the principal beneficiary of this operation, Heijn had established his reputation as one of Holland's great naval commanders. It therefore came as no surprise when, in 1629, he was appointed to command the DUTCH NAVY with the title of Admiral of Holland. At that time the navy's main task was to counter the activities of the PRIVATEERS of Dunkirk who operated on behalf of Spain in the English Channel and North Sea. In a sea fight in June 1629, the Dutch navy soundly defeated the privateers; but the victory cost the life of its famous commander, who was killed by a cannon ball.

Helicopter

Although the first practical helicopter design appeared in Germany in 1936, it was not until the 1940s that vertical landing and takeoff aircraft were first employed for naval and military purposes. At first their role was limited mainly to reconnaissance and light cargo duties because of their relatively poor performance; but with the adoption of lightweight gas turbine engines, larger and faster machines were introduced in the 1960s. Ship-based helicopters have become an important factor in war at sea. Less vulnerable to attack than their land-based counterparts, such helicopters have been deployed regularly against enemy mines and submarines.

When operating in an ANTISUBMARINE role, helicopters have the ability, when hovering, to lower sonar detectors into the sea to seek out their target. Once its location has been established, the helicopter can use its air-to-surface missiles or torpedoes against the enemy. Apart from general reconnaissance duties, providing logistic support and its search-and-rescue role, the naval helicopter also is used in amphibious operations. An early example is the British seizure of the Suez Canal during the SUEZ CRISIS in 1956. Naval helicopters were much in evidence in the FALKLANDS WAR, 1982, and during the GULF WAR, 1990–91. Improved navigational aids have given helicopters a much-enhanced capacity to operate at night or in poor weather conditions, and undoubtedly they will remain an important feature of modern naval warfare.

Heligoland Bight, Battle of
August 28, 1914

The first naval battle of the WORLD WAR I, 1914–18, originated in a British plan to attack German patrols in the Heligoland Bight, an area of the North Sea off the northwest coast of Germany. The raid was to be undertaken by the Royal Navy's Harwich Force, consisting of the light cruisers *Arethusa* and *Fearless* and two flotillas of destroyers, under the command of Commander Reginald TYRWHITT. They were to be covered by the First Battlecruiser Squadron under the command of Vice Admiral Sir David BEATTY, which had moved from SCAPA FLOW just before the operation began.

Tyrwhitt entered the Bight in the early hours of August 28, 1914. The action began at 7:00 A.M. when two German torpedo boats were sunk. The Germans, who had been aware of the possibility of a British attack, quickly moved in the *Frauenlob* and *Stettin* to support the stricken boats. They were later joined by four other light cruisers, including the *Köln*, the FLAGSHIP of Rear Admiral Maas.

During the morning's running battle, four of Tyrwhitt's ships were hit repeatedly, and with the arrival of the additional German ships, Tyrwhitt's whole force was outgunned. At 11:25 Tyrwhitt, who was forced to withdraw, called for urgent assistance from Beatty's battle cruisers, which were then some 40 miles (64 km) to the north. Traveling at top speed, they arrived in the Bight just in time, at 12:40 P.M. The *Mainz*, the *Köln* and the *Ariadne* were sunk and three other German cruisers were damaged. The remnants of the German force quickly withdrew under cover of mist, having lost 1,200 men. Their opponents, who had suffered only 35 fatalities as well as two damaged ships, then made for home.

Although the British had secured a success in their first battle with the Germans, the victory was overshadowed by the fact that the operation had revealed serious weaknesses in terms of planning, communications and coordination. These included several examples of confusion as to where— friend or enemy—the fire was coming from.

Henry Grâce à Dieu

An English-built CARRACK, launched in 1514, that was the largest warship then in existence and an important component of Henry VIII's expanding navy. She was in fact the first English vessel to be designed specifically as a warship, although she was to be used in action only once in 38 years. Early accounts do not provide a completely consistent specification of the "Great Harry," as she was popularly known, even though there is a contemporary illustration in the Anthony Roll (Magdalene College, Cambridge).

The *Henry Grâce à Dieu* had four masts, a "lofty spread of sail" and a displacement in the range of 1,000 to 1,500 tons. Her size meant that many harbors were inaccessible to her; this problem led to the construction of repair facilities at Deptford, southeast London, the first permanent dockyard in England. A HIGH-CHARGED SHIP, the *Great Harry* was built with four decks in the forecastle and three

Henry Grâce à Dieu: Henry VIII's greatest warship   (*Copyright © National Maritime Museum, Greenwich, London*)

in the poop. She was operated by a crew of about 650 (of whom 300 were mariners and the remainder soldiers). Well armed, the *Great Harry* carried 21 heavy brass cannon—a recent innovation in naval warfare—and more than 200 smaller weapons. Her armament was modified during rebuilding in 1540, but before it could be used in battle the entire ship was accidentally destroyed by fire at Woolwich in 1553.

Herbert, Arthur, First Earl of Torrington
1647–1716

*B*ritish admiral of the fleet whose reputation was undermined by failure during the War of the GRAND ALLIANCE, 1688–97. His active service began during the Second ANGLO-DUTCH WAR, 1665–67, and continued in operations against the Barbary CORSAIRS. Herbert returned home as the Third Dutch War, 1672–74, was beginning and he fought at the Battle of SOLEBAY, June 1672. During a further period of service in the Mediterranean, in 1680, he

reached flag rank, but in 1687 he was dismissed from the navy because of his failure to vote in Parliament for the repeal of the Test Act, which imposed religious tests on government officials. In consequence he joined Prince William of Orange and commanded his fleet during the Glorious Revolution of 1688. In recognition of his support he was appointed First Lord of the Admiralty and was soon to be created Earl of Torrington.

Herbert commanded the English fleet during the war that followed the Revolution. At the Battle of BANTRY BAY, May 1689, the English escaped destruction only because the French fleet, commanded by Admiral the Comte de CHÂTEAU-RENAULT, was understrength and its senior commanders were divided. Misfortune again struck at the Battle of BEACHY HEAD, June 1690, when Herbert's Anglo-Dutch fleet met a large French force under Admiral the Comte de TOURVILLE. Only the Dutch in the van and the English at the rear engaged the enemy. The center was kept out of the fighting. As a result it suffered heavy losses at the hands of the French, for which Herbert was blamed. Court-martialed for failing to engage the enemy, he defended himself successfully on the grounds of the weakness of the English fleet and the risk that even greater destruction might have occurred if all of his units had been committed. However, many still regarded him as a traitor and a coward, and he never again served at sea.

Hermes, H.M.S.

The name of two British AIRCRAFT CARRIERS, including the world's first aircraft carrier designed as such. Completed in 1923, this earlier *Hermes* had a displacement of 10,850 tons and a maximum speed of some 26 knots. Fitted with an island bridge and a single hangar, she could accommodate up to 15 aircraft. Beginning in 1936, she operated 12 Fairey Swordfish torpedo machines. By the late 1930s she had become a training ship, but on the outbreak of WORLD WAR II, 1939–45, she was recommissioned. In one notable incident her aircraft were responsible for inflicting serious damage on the new French battleship *RICHELIEU* at Dakar in 1940, in an effort to keep that ship from falling into German hands. She later served with the Eastern Fleet but was sunk by Japanese dive-bombers off Ceylon in 1942—the first British carrier to be sunk by an air attack.

The second British carrier named *Hermes* was completed in 1959 following a delayed construction period beginning in 1944. One of four Hermes-class ships, she was an unarmored medium-size carrier with a displacement of 18,400 tons. She could carry up to 45 aircraft and was operated by a crew of 1,380. Her flight deck included a port-side extension, and she was equipped with two steam catapults. During the first phase of her operational service with the Royal Navy, she operated Sea Vixen, Scimitar and Buccaneer aircraft. In 1973 she was reemployed as a commando carrier following the removal of her catapults and arrester gear. In the latter stages of her career she became an anti-submarine warfare carrier operating Sea King helicopters and then Sea Harrier jump-jets. Following service in the FALKLANDS WAR, 1982, she was sold to India in 1986.

Hermione, H.M.S.

A British frigate of 32 guns, launched at Bristol in 1782, that was the scene of a violent MUTINY off Santo Domingo in 1797. *Hermione*'s captain, Hugh Pigot, was a rigid disciplinarian whose brutal conduct had led to the deaths of two of his men. The crew responded by killing Pigot and most of his officers and taking control of his ship. To escape the attentions of the ROYAL NAVY, the mutineers sailed to La Guaira, on the northern coast of South America, where they handed the *Hermione* over to the Spaniards. She was refitted before being returned to operational use in the Spanish navy.

The British found her in the Caribbean harbor of Puerto Cabello some two years later, in October 1799. She was boarded by men from the frigate *Surprise*, commanded by Sir Edward Hamilton, who overpowered the *Hermione*'s larger Spanish crew and towed her away. When she rejoined the British fleet for service in the FRENCH REVOLUTIONARY AND NAPOLEONIC WARS, 1792–1815, the *Hermione* was appropriately renamed the *Retribution*. Her former British crew were pursued relentlessly for ten years, and more than 20 mutineers eventually were captured and hanged.

Hervey, Augustus John, Third Earl of Bristol
1724–79

British admiral. A hereditary peer who served in the Royal Navy during the SEVEN YEARS' WAR, 1756–63, he was later appointed a Lord of the Admiralty. He recorded his early experiences at sea in *Augustus Hervey's Journal* (published in 1953), but first came to notice because of his involvement in Admiral John BYNG's failed operation off MINORCA in 1756. Hervey was recalled home to give evidence in the trial that convicted Byng and sentenced him to death. He was later involved in a BLOCKADE of BREST in 1759, but it was in subsequent operations in the West Indies that he made a real impact. Serving under Admiral Sir George RODNEY, he was responsible for the capture of St. Lucia in 1761. A year later he was involved in the taking of Havana. Hervey concluded his wartime career with a period as commander in chief in the Mediterranean in 1763.

Hewitt, Henry Kent
1887–1972

American naval officer, born on February 11, 1887, in Hackensack, New Jersey. While serving on his first vessel, the *Missouri*, he sailed on a voyage around the world with the GREAT WHITE FLEET. While commanding the converted yacht *Eagle*, which was engaged on survey work, he protected American life and property during the 1917 Cuban revolution. In WORLD WAR I, 1914–18, he commanded two destroyers, engaging in convoy, escort and submarine patrol duty. Before the United States entered WORLD WAR II, 1939–45, he commanded the U.S. Atlantic Fleet's task groups that carried out neutrality patrols and later troop convoy escort work from mid-1941 into early 1942. He soon demonstrated his expertise in AMPHIBIOUS WARFARE.

Commanding the Atlantic Fleet's amphibious force, Hewitt was responsible for the amphibious landings in

1942 of General George S. Patton's I Armor Corps on the Moroccan coast beginning in November 1942 and for engaging French naval forces at Casablanca, including the JEAN BART. Subsequently commanding the 8th Fleet in northwest African waters, he planned and directed the Western Naval Task Force in America's part of landings in SICILY, in July 1943, and at the assault at SALERNO, Italy, in September. He then commanded the Allied naval forces that landed the U.S. 7th Army in southern France in August 1944. A year later he became commander of U.S. Naval Forces, Europe, with the rank of admiral. Retiring in 1949, he died on September 15, 1972.

John Clagett, "Admiral H. Kent Hewitt, U.S. Navy: High Command," *Naval War College Review* 28 (Fall 1975), 60–86.

High-Charged Ship

A distinctive feature of the large sailing warships of northern Europe that preceded the introduction the GALLEON in the 1570s were the large "castles" mounted fore and aft, with a third at the masthead used as an observation platform. These high superstructures not only provided accommodation for the ship's crew, they also had a major military purpose as the ship functioned as a floating fort. Archers and musketeers operated their weapons from these protected positions during a period when battles at sea were fought at close quarters, the objective being to board an enemy ship and set it on fire. Major examples of the high-charged ship, which took its name from its tall superstructure, include the COG and the CARRACK. During the late 16th century the high-charged ship was replaced by the galleon as the principal warship of the sailing navies. The galleon was more maneuverable and less vulnerable to adverse weather conditions than the high-charged ship. The disappearance of the high-charged design also reflected a real change in the character of naval warfare with the cannon displacing earlier forms of combat at sea.

Robert Gardiner, ed., *Cogs, Caravels and Galleons: The Sailing Ship 1000–1650*, London, 1994.

High Seas Fleet

The main fleet of the GERMAN NAVY during WORLD WAR I, 1914–18, the High Seas Fleet was organized in three battle squadrons, with a separate battle cruiser squadron. In August 1914 it consisted of 15 dreadnoughts, four battle cruisers, 32 pre-dreadnoughts, nine armored cruisers, ten light cruisers and 88 destroyer/torpedo boats. Its strategy was severely constrained by the policies adopted by the British and by its own government. The British aimed to confine the High Seas Fleet to the North Sea by means of a distant BLOCKADE, while German policy was extremely cautious. The kaiser, who took a special interest in naval matters, had decided that it should not be risked unnecessarily. He expected the land war in Europe to be over quickly, and he wanted to use the intact fleet as a lever in negotiations with the Allies.

Although this expectation soon proved to be unrealistic, restrictions on the use of the High Seas Fleet continued indefinitely. Limited operations were, however, authorized after the Battle of HELIGOLAND BIGHT, August 28, 1914, in an effort to reduce the numerical superiority of the British GRAND FLEET. The High Seas Fleet sought to engage individual British squadrons rather than the British fleet as a whole, slowly reducing the power of Royal Navy. Only when parity between the two fleets had been achieved would a final engagement between opposing battleships be contemplated. Several towns on the east coast of Britain were bombarded in November–December 1914 with limited effect, but all operations were suspended after the narrow German escape at the Battle of the DOGGER BANK, January 24, 1915.

With Admiral Rheinhard SCHEER's appointment as commander of the fleet in January 1916, a more aggressive policy was pursued, leading to the Battle of JUTLAND, May 1916, when the main fleets of Britain and Germany clashed. Jutland confirmed British dominance of the North Sea, and as a result the High Seas Fleet ventured into the North Sea only three more times before the end of the war. Transfer of personnel to the expanding U-BOAT fleet and MUTINY undermined the fleet's efficiency. Unrest in 1917 was followed by open mutiny in October 1918 in response to Scheer's plans for a "death ride" into the North Sea, where a final battle with the British Grand Fleet would take place. The sailors' action marked the demise of the High Seas Fleet as a fighting force.

Richard Hough, *The Great War at Sea, 1914–1918*, Oxford, 1983; Dan van der Vat, *The Grand Scuttle: The Sinking of the German Fleet at Scapa Flow in 1919*, London, 1986.

Hipper, Franz von
1863–1932

German admiral who served with the main battle fleet for much of his career and, on the outbreak of WORLD WAR I, 1914–18, was in overall command of the scouting forces of the HIGH SEAS FLEET. Admiral Franz von Hipper held this post for virtually the entire war, until August 1918. He deployed his forces with initiative and skill within the narrow limits set by the German ADMIRALTY, leading two raids on the English coast in 1914. On November 2–3 he shelled Yarmouth and Lowestoft, causing light damage and a few casualties; on December 15–16 Hartlepool, Scarborough and Whitby received similar treatment. Early in 1915 a further sortie, this time to the Dogger

Franz Ritter von Hipper: commander of the German scouting forces at the Battle of Jutland, 1916   *(Copyright © Imperial War Museum, London)*

Bank, was intercepted by the stronger British battle cruiser force under the command of Admiral David BEATTY. (See Battle of the DOGGER BANK, 1915.) Hipper quickly withdrew but the battle cruiser SEYDLITZ, his FLAGSHIP, was severely damaged and the BLÜCHER, an armored cruiser, was lost.

Hipper supported the idea of a decisive encounter with the British GRAND FLEET, but it was not until the Battle of JUTLAND, May 1916, that the opportunity materialized. In the first phase of the battle he revealed his considerable tactical skill, outmaneuvering Beatty and destroying two British battle cruisers without sustaining any losses himself. As events turned against the Germans, Admiral Rheinhard SCHEER, the fleet commander, ordered Hipper to attack the enemy in order to facilitate the withdrawal of the main German force. Hipper threw his group against the entire Grand Fleet, but the attack lasted only four minutes before his orders were changed. During that brief period his flagship *Lützow* was lost and was replaced by the *Moltke*, the only German battle cruiser that was still functioning. Jutland enhanced Hipper's reputation considerably, and he was awarded the Pour Le Mérite.

On Scheer's elevation to the supreme command of the navy in August 1918, Hipper succeeded him as the last commander of the High Seas Fleet. He was unable to handle effectively the fleet mutinies of October–November, which were prompted in part by his own plan for a final attack on the Grand Fleet. Hipper retired from the navy in December 1918 after having witnessed the surrender of his fleet to the Royal Navy.

Tobias R. Philbin, *Admiral von Hipper, The Inconvenient Hero*, London, 1982.

Hiryu

Japanese AIRCRAFT CARRIER of WORLD WAR II, 1939–45. Completed in 1939, the *Hiryu* was involved in many of the early naval actions in the Pacific until her destruction at the Battle of MIDWAY, June 1942. The *Hiryu* had a displacement of 17,300 tons, a maximum speed in excess of 34 knots, making her one of the fastest carriers of the war, and was operated by a crew of 1,100. Her main armament consisted of 12 5-inch (13-cm) guns, and she had a navigating bridge on the portside. She could accommodate 64 aircraft, including Mitsubishi A6M Zero fighters. The Zeros were in use during the attack on PEARL HARBOR, December 1941, when the *Hiryu* and her sister ship the *Soryu* formed the second Carrier Division. More campaign successes followed, but she failed to survive the Battle of Midway. Before the end, she helped to immobilize the American carrier YORKTOWN but was herself set on fire by dive-bombers from the carrier ENTERPRISE. Two Japanese destroyers were forced to complete the task of sinking the *Hiryu* with torpedoes. The *Soryu* was also lost at Midway, being severely damaged by dive-bombers and finally sunk by the submarine *Nautilus*.

Hiyo

Japanese AIRCRAFT CARRIER of WORLD WAR II, 1939–45, one of two ships of the Junyo class. Like her sister ship *Junyo*, she was designed as a passenger liner but was converted during construction. Completed in 1942, the *Hiyo* had a displacement of 24,140 tons, a maximum speed of 22.5 knots and a length of 719 feet 6 inches (219.3 m). Operated by a crew of 1,224, she carried 53 aircraft and was armed with 36 antiaircraft guns. The two Junyo-class ships formed the Second Carrier Division of the Japanese navy. (This division had previously consisted of the aircraft carriers HIRYU and *Soryu*, both of which had been lost at the Battle of MIDWAY, June 1942.) The *Hiyo* saw action at GUADALCANAL, 1942–43, and at the Battle of the PHILIPPINE SEA, 1944, where she was sunk by two air-launched torpedoes. The *Junyo*, her sister ship, also was damaged in the same engagement; although repaired, she played no further part in the war.

H.L. Hunley

A Confederate SUBMARINE, the *H. L. Hunley* became the first submarine to sink a ship in wartime when she torpedoed the Union steam frigate *Housatonic* in 1864, during the AMERICAN CIVIL WAR, 1861–65. Built in 1863, this boat was made from a steel cylinder that was tapered at both ends. She was about 40 feet (12 m) long and was operated by a crew of nine: One man steered while the other eight turned a crankshaft that drove the propeller. She could obtain a maximum speed of about 4 knots. Her armament consisted of a single spar TORPEDO, which was fixed to a pole at the front of the boat.

The *H. L. Hunley*, a member of the DAVID class of Confederate boats, was named after her designer. Technically, she was a submersible or semisubmersible rather than a submarine in the modern sense, because she was unable to dive. Two ballast tanks enabled her to operate with only her hatchway above water. This provided air for the crew to breathe.

She had a brief operational career. Her first intended victim was to have been the Union warship *New Ironsides* off Charleston, but that ship was anchored in water that was too shallow for the *H. L. Hunley* to operate in. The *H. L. Hunley*'s opportunity came in February 1864 when she attacked the *Housatonic* off Charleston. The Northern ship's crew reacted too slowly to the submersible's approach, and the *Housatonic* was hit below the waterline by a spar torpedo. She sank rapidly, but not before taking the *H. L. Hunley*, which had been caught by the effects of the blast, with her.

Hobart-Hampden, Augustus Charles (Hobart Pasha)
1822–86

B ritish naval officer who became an admiral in the Turkish navy after a varied service career. The son of the Third Earl of Buckinghamshire, Hobart-Hampden entered the Royal Navy in 1835 and served in the CRIMEAN WAR, 1853–56. A few years later he exchanged the monotony of the peacetime navy for blockade-running in the American Civil War, 1861–1865. Using the name "Captain Roberts," he ran the Union blockade of Southern ports many times, delivering much-need military supplies to the hard-pressed Confederate forces. He recorded his adventures in the book *Never Caught*, published in 1867. His experiences in the United States proved invaluable when he joined the Turkish navy shortly afterward. This move was a wise one in terms of his naval career: Subsequently he played a major role in ending a Greek revolt in Crete in 1866–68 and was rewarded with the title of pasha and the rank of admiral. As "Hobart Pasha" he commanded Turkey's Black Sea Fleet during the Russo-

Turkish War, 1877–78, and successfully contained the enemy fleet. Later he was promoted to the rank of marshal in recognition of his services to the Turkish navy.

Hobson, Richmond Pearson
1870–1937

A merican naval officer. Born on August 17, 1870 in Greensboro, Alabama, Hobson graduated first in his class from the U.S. Naval Academy at ANNAPOLIS in 1889. Resigning his commission in the line to accept an appointment as a naval constructor, he completed graduate studies in naval construction and design in Paris. He returned to Annapolis in 1897 to organize and conduct the graduate course for officers entering the navy's Construction Corps.

Hobson's main contribution to the navy was his work in ship construction, but his greatest fame came during the SPANISH-AMERICAN WAR of 1898 when, on June 3, he and a volunteer crew took the explosive-filled collier *Merrimac* into Santiago Harbor, Cuba, attempting to blow it up at the channel's narrowest point and thus trap the Spanish fleet. Under enemy gunfire, several of the explosive charges failed, and the vessel was finally sunk in a harmless part of the channel. Hobson and his crew were rescued by Spanish troops and held captive in Morro Castle at the harbor entrance from June 3 to July 6.

Although he and his crew had failed in their attempt, after his release and return to the United States Hobson became a popular hero of the war. Resigning from the navy in 1903, he served as a member of Congress from Alabama for four consecutive terms from 1907 to 1915. During this time he assisted leading naval officers in expanding the navy and in creating the Office of Chief of Naval Operations in 1915. An avid writer on the need for American naval expansion and for American leadership in the international movement for peace, he also was an advocate for national and international prohibition. In 1934 Hobson was awarded the Congressional Medal of Honor and promoted to rear admiral on the retired list for his action in the Spanish-American War. He died in New York City in March 1937.

Elting E. Morison, "Richmond Pearson Hobson," *Dictionary of American Biography: Supplement 2*, Old Tappan, N.J., 1981, pp. 308–309.

Holland, John Philip
1840–1914

T he inventor of the first successful submarine, born in Liscanor, Ireland in 1840. Conceiving the idea that a submersible vessel would assist the Irish in gaining their independence, Holland emigrated to the United States in 1873. Holland's idea received support in 1881 from the

American Fenian Society to finance the construction of the *Fenian Ram*, "which embodied the chief principles of the modern submarine in balance, control, and compensation of weight loss in torpedo discharge." Until 1898, however, his designs for submarines constructed for the U.S. Navy were not adopted, principally because of the official emphasis on the BATTLESHIP as the chief vessel for construction. The value of submarines was clearly demonstrated in 1898 with the successful and hugely influential *HOLLAND* design, which provided the basis for all future developments. Built to John Holland's specifications, it was purchased by the Navy Department in 1900.

Richard K. Morris, *John P. Holland, 1840–1914, Inventor of the Modern Submarine*, Annapolis, 1966.

Holland, U.S.S.

This American design represented a major step forward in the development of the SUBMARINE and provided the basis for all subsequent models. Designed privately by John HOLLAND and built by the Electric Boat Company, the *Holland*, which had a surface displacement of 64 tons (submerged 74 tons) was launched in 1897 and completed the following year. It was the first submarine to use an electric motor for propulsion underwater and an internal combustion engine for power on the surface. (An earlier Holland design, the *Plunger*, had combined a steam engine and an electric motor.) The 45-horsepower gasoline engine powered the boat at 8 miles (13 km) per hour, while the electric motor produced a maximum speed of 5 miles per hour underwater. She had a length of 53 feet 11 inches (16.43 m) and a beam of 10 feet 3 inches (3.12 m). The *Holland* was also the first submarine to be equipped with horizontal rudders, which enabled it to dive rather than merely sink when it wished to submerge. The U.S. Navy purchased her after extensive trials and she entered the service in October 1900, the first submarine commissioned by the navy. Her armament was very limited, consisting of a single torpedo tube and a dynamite gun, and she was of little operational value. However, the *Holland* was a key influence on later submarine design.

Holmes, Sir Robert
1622–92

British admiral who captured the Dutch settlement of New Amsterdam in 1664. He renamed it New York—not after the city of York, England, but after JAMES, Duke of York, the Lord High Admiral. Holmes was heavily involved in the Second ANGLO-DUTCH WAR, 1665–67, which broke out shortly afterward. He fought with great success and was knighted. His greatest achievement was commanding the squadron that destroyed more than 160 enemy merchant ships on the Dutch coast on August 8, 1666 after the English victory at the Battle of ORFORDNESS, July 25–26, 1666. The action was known, appropriately, as "Holmes' Bonfire." Holmes went to sea again during the Third Anglo-Dutch War, 1672–74, and the Battle of SOLEBAY, May 28, 1672, was his final engagement.

R. Ollard, *Man of War: Sir Robert Holmes and the Restoration Navy*, London, 1969.

Holtzendorff, Grand Admiral Henning von
1853–1919

Chief of the German Admiralty Staff during WORLD WAR I, 1914–18, from the spring of 1915 until August 1918. Previously commander in chief of the HIGH SEAS FLEET, 1909–13, he had been forced into retirement because of disagreements over naval policy. During the world war he never expressed a consistent view on the question of unrestricted submarine warfare but was a significant influence in the decision to adopt it in 1917. The U-BOAT campaign would, in his optimistic view, bring the British to the conference table within a few months and certainly before American intervention could have made a decisive impact. Promoted to the rank of grand admiral in July 1918, he was succeeded almost at once by Admiral Reinhard SCHEER, who was appointed to run a new centralized naval headquarters.

Hood, H.M.S.

Named after Admiral Lord Samuel HOOD, this British BATTLE CRUISER had a displacement of 41,200 tons and a maximum speed of 32 knots. Operated by a crew of 1,420, its main armament consisted of eight 15-inch (38-cm) guns in twin turrets. It was 860 feet 6 inches (262 m) in length and had a beam of 105 feet (32 m). When the *Hood* was completed in 1923, she was the largest warship in the world, but her design was already dated: She had been laid down before the Battle of JUTLAND, 1916. As a result, her deck armor was inadequate, even though some corrective action had been taken once the ADMIRALTY absorbed the lessons of the Jutland action.

The *Hood* was not modernized before WORLD WAR II, 1939–45, and entered it in relatively poor condition. On May 24, 1941, she led the *PRINCE OF WALES*, a new BATTLE-SHIP, in an action against the *BISMARCK*—the world's most powerful warship—and the *PRINZ EUGEN* in the Denmark Strait off Greenland. With her thin armor, the *Hood* could not hope to withstand the German battleship's 15-inch shells. They soon found her main magazine, and the explosion that followed caused her to disintegrate: 1,416 men were lost, and only three survived. The *Hood*'s destruction was a considerable blow to British prestige, with Prime Minister Winston CHURCHILL even describing it as a "national calamity." However, the destruction of the *Bismarck* shortly afterward helped to restore British morale and removed a major threat to the Atlantic CONVOYS.

John Roberts, *The Battlecruiser Hood*, Greenwich, 1982.

Hood, Alexander, First Viscount Bridport
1726–1814

*E*nglish naval commander, the brother of Samuel, First Viscount HOOD, 1724–1816. Alexander Hood first saw service during the SEVEN YEARS' WAR, 1756–63, but was to establish his reputation during the AMERICAN WAR OF INDEPENDENCE, 1775–83, when he was appointed rear admiral. He served under Richard, First Earl HOWE, in the English Channel and in the Straits of Gibraltar during the American war, taking part in the relief of GIBRALTAR, 1782. During the FRENCH REVOLUTIONARY AND NAPOLEONIC WARS, 1792–1815, Hood again served again under Earl Howe at the Battle of the GLORIOUS FIRST OF JUNE, 1794, where his contribution was recognized by the award of a peerage. As First Viscount Bridport he was later appointed to the command of the Channel Fleet, 1797–1800, and in this capacity was caught up in the SPITHEAD mutiny, 1797. He finally left the service in 1800 following a period directing the BLOCKADE of BREST.

Dorothy Hood, *The Admirals Hood*, London, 1942.

Hood, Samuel, First Viscount Hood
1724–1816

*B*ritish naval commander, brother of Alexander HOOD, First Viscount Bridport, 1726–1814. Samuel Hood entered the Royal Navy in 1741. By the beginning of the SEVEN YEARS' WAR, 1756–63, he was a post-captain and, as commander of the frigate *Vestal*, he captured the French frigate *Bellona* in 1759. At the end of the war he was appointed to the command of the North American station, a post he held until 1767. During the AMERICAN WAR OF INDEPENDENCE, 1775–83, he served with distinction in the Caribbean as second in command to Admiral Sir George RODNEY in operations against French naval forces led by Vice Admiral the Comte de GRASSE. Hood's role in the decisive British victory off DOMINICA in 1782 was particularly notable.

On his return to England, Hood was raised to the peerage and became a Lord of the Admiralty. He was appointed vice admiral in 1787 and became a full admiral in 1794. In 1793, on the outbreak of war with France, Hood returned to sea even though by then he was nearly 70 years old. He was appointed to the command of British

naval forces in the Mediterranean. With assistance from the Spanish, he took Toulon and Corsica, although inevitably these conquests proved to be short-lived. Hood returned from the Mediterranean in 1794 at the end of a long and distinguished career.

Hood's cousin and namesake, Vice Admiral Sir Samuel Hood, 1762–1814, was one of Lord NELSON's "band of brothers." He served with Nelson in the French Revolutionary Wars, 1792–1802. After much distinguished service against the French, he died in 1814, as he arrived in India to take up the post of commander in chief.

Dorothy Hood, *The Admirals Hood*, London, 1942.

Hopkins, Esek
1718–1802

*A*merican merchant captain who commanded the Continental Navy from 1775 to 1777. Hopkins was born in Scituate, Rhode Island in 1718. He gained some naval command experience during the SEVEN YEARS' WAR, 1756–63. In 1775, largely through the political influence of his brother, Stephen, who sat on the Continental Congress's Marine Committee, Esek Hopkins was commissioned commander in chief of the almost nonexistent Continental Navy. Liberally interpreting Congress's orders to attack blockading British vessels off the Virginia and Carolina coasts, he took his small squadron to raid New Providence (Nassau) in the Bahamas. The attack was successful, and much-needed ordnance and powder were seized. Rather than taking the supplies to the Continental forces, he delivered them to his native Rhode Island, which was being blockaded in Narragansett Bay in late 1776 by British vessels. The following year Hopkins was suspended by the Continental Congress. He ended the war serving his native Rhode Island.

William M. Fowler, Jr., "Esek Hopkins: Commander-in-Chief of the Continental Navy," in *Command Under Sail. Makers of the American Naval Tradition, 1775–1850*, ed. James C. Bradford, Annapolis, 1985.

Hopsonn, Sir Thomas
1642–1717

*B*ritish vice admiral who was second in command of the Anglo-Dutch fleet under Sir George ROOKE during the opening stages of the War of the SPANISH SUCCESSION, 1701–14. In October 1702, following its failure at Cadiz, the English fleet was deployed against VIGO, where Spanish treasure galleons had just arrived under the protection of the French. Hopsonn led the attack in the *Torbay*, an 80-gun ship, but at first failed to break a boom that protected the inner harbor. A French FIRESHIP, which had been improvised from a merchantman, set the *Torbay* on fire, but she was saved by an extraordinary stroke of fate: As the fireship exploded she scattered her large cargo of snuff and extinguished the fire on the *Torbay*. Hopsonn could now enter Vigo harbor where the outnumbered French were setting fire to their own ships. On his return home, Hopsonn, who brought booty valued at some £2 million, was knighted for the much-needed victory on which his reputation now rests. The action at Vigo was the last of 42 naval engagements at which Hopsonn had been present since first entering the navy in 1662.

Horthy de Nagybanya, Miklós
1868–1957

*H*ungarian naval officer and ruler (as regent) of Hungary from 1920 until 1944. Vice Admiral Miklós Horthy served in the AUSTRO-HUNGARIAN NAVY during WORLD WAR I, 1914–18. Following a period of training at the Austro-Hungarian naval academy at Fiume (Rijecka), he first came to public attention in May 1915 when he commanded a squadron that attacked and sank 14 Italian merchant ships off Albania. He enjoyed other notable operational achievements in sorties against the Allied blockade before his appointment as commander of the Austro-Hungarian fleet early in 1918. At the end of the war he was responsible for the transfer of the Austro-Hungarian navy's ships to the new state of Yugoslavia. In 1919, he was Minister of War in the postwar counterrevolutionary government. Horthy suppressed the succeeding Communist regime in 1920 and became regent. He established an authoritarian regime that would support the Axis powers during WORLD WAR II, 1939–45. His leadership survived until 1944, when he was deposed by the Germans.

Horton, Sir Max
1883–1951

*B*ritish admiral who led the battle against the German U-BOAT as commander in chief of the Western Approaches (to the British Isles) during WORLD WAR II, 1939–45. Horton was a specialist submariner who first commanded a SUBMARINE in 1905. During WORLD WAR I, 1914–18, he gained notice as the first submarine commander to sink an enemy warship. His submarine *E.9* destroyed the German cruiser *Hela* in the Heligoland Bight on September 13, 1914. He followed up this early victory with a successful campaign in the Baltic in 1914–15, operating from Russian bases. Horton later promoted the development of MIDGET SUBMARINES and other improvements in this arm of the navy. In the period immediately before World War II, Horton, now a vice admiral, commanded the Reserve Fleet of the Royal Navy. As the war began he was appointed to the head of the Northern Patrol and then, in January 1940, he became Flag Officer, Submarines.

When Horton was appointed to the command of the Western Approaches in November 1942, he assumed responsibility for the security of the Allied CONVOYS making the hazardous Atlantic crossing. The Battle of the ATLANTIC, 1939–45, was at its most critical period, and Horton quickly adopted a variety of countermeasures. These included improvements in long-range air cover and the establishment of convoy support groups consisting of escort warships and escort carriers. These changes progressively reduced the tonnage lost to U-BOATS in this vital region. By May 1943, largely as a result of Horton's actions, the course of the battle had turned in the Allies' favor. Horton remained in this post until his retirement at the end of the war.

William S. Chalmers, *Max Horton and the Western Approaches*, London, 1954.

Hosho

*T*he first AIRCRAFT CARRIER to be built for the JAPANESE NAVY, the *Hosho* was completed in 1922. She had been laid down as a naval oiler and then converted as a carrier with British technical assistance. The *Hosho* had a displacement of 7,470 tons, a maximum speed of 25 knots and was operated by a crew of 550. The ship was equipped with a 430-foot (130-m) long, high-sided hangar, which supported the flight deck. She operated 21 aircraft at first but later, as larger machines appeared, the number was reduced to 12. The Japanese navy used the experience gained in operating the *Hosho* in designing other converted carriers.

The *Hosho* saw service off China during the 1930s and during WORLD WAR II, 1939–45, she formed Carrier Division 3 together with the *Zuiho*. At the Battle of MIDWAY, 1942, she was included in Admiral Isoroku YAMAMOTO's battleship group, where her Nakajima B5N aircraft provided long-range reconnaissance. However, for the rest of the war the now-obsolete carrier was used exclusively on training duties. One of the few Japanese carriers to survive the war, she finally was scrapped in 1947.

Hosier, Francis
1673–1727

*B*ritish admiral who was first appointed captain in 1696. In 1707, during the War of the SPANISH SUCCESSION, 1701–14, Hosier recovered the body of Admiral Sir Clowdisley SHOVELL who had been killed after his ship, the *ASSOCIATION,* was wrecked off the Scilly Isles. Hosier's career was interrupted between 1714 and 1717 when he was suspended for being a suspected Jacobite. He returned to the service in 1723 and was promoted to vice admiral. Three years later he was sent to the West Indies in command of a squadron of 16 ships. His orders prevented him from fighting the Spanish yet required him to prevent their treasure ships leaving for home. With this objective in mind, Hosier blockaded Porto Bello, a seaport of Panama, but yellow fever devastated his ships' crews. More them 4,000 men, including Hosier himself, died. A contemporary popular ballad, "Admiral Hosier's Ghost," written by Richard Glover, commemorated the blockade. Notable for its inaccuracy, it blamed the strain imposed by contradictory ADMIRALTY orders for Hosier's death.

Hoste, Sir William
1780–1828

*B*ritish naval commander whose career owed much to the influence of Admiral Lord NELSON. Born in Ingoldisthorpe, Norfolk, Hoste entered the Royal Navy at the beginning of the FRENCH REVOLUTIONARY AND NAPOLEONIC WARS, 1792–1815, and served with Nelson at the Battle of the NILE, 1798. He established his professional reputation during the Napoleonic Wars, 1803–15, when he commanded a squadron of frigates in the Adriatic Sea from 1808 to 1814. Operating against the French and Venetians, Hoste captured large numbers of enemy ships. His record year was 1808–9, when he seized some 200 vessels, followed by 46 in 1810.

Hoste's greatest achievement was his victory over the French in the engagement off the island of Lissa in 1811. (See the BATTLE OF LISSA.) His squadron of four frigates defeated a force of ten French and Venetian warships; the enemy commander, Admiral Dubourdieu, was killed. Hoste was injured during the battle but remained on duty during the subsequent mopping-up operations. He added to his battle honors in 1813–14 when he helped the Austrians capture Cattaro (Kotor) and Ragusa (Dubrovnik). Hoste was knighted for his naval services, which came to an end with the peace of 1815.

Hovercraft

A raftlike vehicle that rides on an enclosed cushion of air. A British invention that made its first successful flight in 1959, it is powered by four gas turbines that propel four variable-pitch airscrews. They also drive the centrifugal lift fans that create an air cushion, lifting the craft above the surface. The fact that no part of the hovercraft's structure is immersed in the water means that it cannot be attacked by torpedoes or by many types of mine. Typically a hovercraft is 131 feet (40 m) in length with a beam of 75 feet (23 m). Hovercraft, which can operate on land and sea, have been adapted for combat use, although their primary role has been commercial, as ferries. However, their ability to operate on land and at sea, combined with a maximum speed of some 65 knots, has persuaded several navies, including those of Britain and the United States, to deploy them. Often they can be used in areas where conventional patrol boats may be of limited use. The U.S. Navy used hovercraft as patrol craft during the VIETNAM WAR, 1964–75, and they also have been used to transport supplies in inaccessible areas. In addition, they have been used in the hunt for enemy mines and torpedoes.

Howard, Charles, Second Lord Howard of Effingham (later, Earl of Nottingham)
1536–1624

*C*ommander of the English fleet that defeated the SPANISH ARMADA, 1588, Lord Howard of Effingham was Lord

Lord Howard of Effingham: commander in chief of the English fleet that defeated the Spanish Armada, 1588 *(Copyright © National Maritime Museum, Greenwich, London)*

High Admiral of England—administrative head of the Royal Navy—for 33 years. His appointment to an active role in 1585 owed more to his position as a leading courtier than to his military record, which consisted of brief periods of command on land and at sea.

At the end of 1587, as the threat of an invasion developed, Howard was designated "lieutenant-general and commander in chief of the navy and army prepared to the seas against Spain." He raised his flag in the ARK ROYAL and personally supervised the preparation of the fleet and its supplies. In May 1588 he joined Sir Francis DRAKE, his vice admiral, and the main English force of 90 ships that had been assembled at Plymouth. His original aim had been to attack the Spanish fleet in its own bases but his plan was abandoned, partly because of the unfavorable weather conditions. As the Spanish advanced through the English Channel, Lord Howard adopted a cautious but ultimately successful strategy. Relying on long-range artillery, he refused to fight at close quarters because of the fear that enemy soldiers might overwhelm his ships.

It was not until the Armada had progressed to a critical point that Howard, reinforced by two squadrons, fought the decisive Battle of Gravelines. As a result four Spanish galleons were destroyed, and the survivors were forced to retreat into the North Sea. Howard discussed and agreed on tactics with his able senior commanders at regular meetings of the Council of War but was unable to exercise any control during an engagement because he had no means of communicating with them. The fact that his commanders continued to operate effectively together is a tribute to his powers of coordination and leadership.

Howard led only one other major naval expedition—the attack on Cadiz in 1596—in his later career, his responsibilities being largely administrative. He remained at the head of the navy well into old age, being compelled to retire in 1618 following the disclosure of unchecked fraud and other abuses within the service.

Robert W. Kenny, *Elizabeth's Admiral: The Political Career of Charles Howard, Earl of Nottingham, 1536–1624*, Baltimore, 1970.

Howe, Richard, First Earl
1726–99

*B*ritish naval commander, born in London; the brother of William, Fifth Viscount Howe, commander in chief of the British army during the AMERICAN WAR OF INDEPENDENCE, 1775–83. Noted for his mastery of tactics and his strong sense of responsibility, Richard Howe was one of the most distinguished officers of the period. He was also an innovator who introduced improved methods of signaling at sea. Howe entered the Royal Navy at the age of 13. His early service included a period under the

command of Admiral George ANSON fighting against the Spanish in the Pacific. He secured rapid promotion and by the age of 20 had reached the rank of post-captain, serving in the War of the AUSTRIAN SUCCESSION, 1740–48. In 1746 he was involved in operations against the supporters of Charles Edward Stuart, the Young Pretender, and intercepted two of his supply ships en route to Scotland.

Howe first came to prominence during the SEVEN YEARS' WAR, 1756–63, and as commander of the *Dunkirk* fired the first shot in that conflict. He played a leading role under Hawke at the Battle of QUIBERON BAY, 1759. As the war ended he was appointed a Lord of the Admiralty, and two years later he became Treasurer of the Navy. Returning to sea as a rear admiral at the beginning of the American War of Independence, as commander in chief of the British fleet he worked in close cooperation with his brother, William Howe, the head of British land forces. However, disagreements with his political masters led to Admiral Howe's resignation in 1778. He returned to sea in 1782 as commander of the Channel Fleet and was responsible for the relief of GIBRALTAR, which had been under siege for some time. At the end of the war he was appointed First Lord of the Admiralty, but he was replaced in 1788. Two years later he was reappointed to the command of the Channel Fleet, serving in this capacity during the opening stages of the FRENCH REVOLUTIONARY AND NAPOLEONIC WARS, 1792–1815. He ended his operational career in victory at the Battle of the GLORIOUS FIRST OF JUNE, 1794. In a final act at the end of a long career he helped to end the mutinies at SPITHEAD and Portsmouth in 1797.

Troyer S. Anderson, *The Command of the Howe Brothers During the American Revolution*, New York, 1936.

Huascar

A British-designed turret IRONCLAD dating from 1864, the *Huascar* served in the Peruvian navy until her crew mutinied early in 1877. Under the command of a rebel general, she was engaged in PIRACY off the western seaboard of South America and attacked British merchant shipping that happened to be in the area. Pursued by the ROYAL NAVY's Pacific Fleet, the *Huascar* was located by the *Shah* and the *Amethyst* off the Chilean port of Ilo on May 29, 1877. The rebel ship successfully withstood a volley of gunfire and managed to avoid a TORPEDO released at a range of 400 yards (366 m); the action was notable as the first time a self-propelled torpedo was fired against an enemy ship. The *Huascar* escaped from the British but was soon recaptured by the Peruvian navy. During Peru's war with Chile, 1879–84, she was overpowered by five enemy warships and forced to surrender to the Chilean navy.

Lord Howe, commander of the English Channel Fleet, at the Battle of the Glorious First of June, 1794 *(Copyright © National Maritime Museum, Greenwich, London)*

Hughes, Sir Edward

1720–94

British admiral of wide operational experience who commanded the fleet in the East Indies during the AMERICAN WAR OF INDEPENDENCE, 1775–83. Hughes had relatively little to do until Holland entered the war in December 1780. He responded, early in 1781, by taking the Dutch-held port of Trincomalee, on the island of Ceylon (Sri Lanka). Soon afterward a superior French fleet, commanded by Admiral Pierre de SUFFREN, appeared, and the struggle for control of the Indian Ocean began. Hughes and his French adversary fought a series of five battles in just over a year. Although Suffren recaptured Trincomalee, neither side gained a decisive strategic advantage. Suffren's inability to defeat the British may be attributed in part to the skill of Hughes and his comrades. The Treaty of Versailles, 1783, finally ended hostilities, and Hughes returned to England.

Hulk

The term "hulk" refers to the hull of an old or damaged sailing ship with its masts and rigging removed. During the 18th and 19th centuries it had naval and other uses that did not require it to move. Hulks were often employed as GUARDSHIPS to protect a naval installation or anchorage. In wartime they might be used as BLOCKSHIPS by sinking them to protect an anchorage to impede the enemy. Hulks also could be equipped with guns and used as floating batteries. Their most common use was as some form of storage vessel for such basic items as food or guns, or as a barracks or a prison. A hulk also was the final point of disembarkation for new naval recruits, including those who had been brought there against their will by the press gangs.

Hull, Isaac
1773–1843

*A*merican naval officer. Born in Connecticut, Isaac Hull was the nephew and adopted son of William Hull, who fought in the major campaigns of the AMERICAN WAR OF INDEPENDENCE, 1775–83, but who surrendered Fort Detroit to the British in the WAR OF 1812. Appointed a lieutenant in the navy in 1798, Isaac Hull saw action in the QUASI-WAR, 1798–1800, against France, in the attacks on Tripoli in 1804 and at Derne in the following year. Promoted to captain, he was given command of the U.S.S. *CONSTITUTION* in 1810 and was in command in August 1812 when that vessel fought one of its greatest actions, that against H.M.S. *Guerrière*. Following the war, Hull commanded several naval stations, retiring as a commodore in 1841. Hull died in Philadelphia in 1843.

Linda M. Maloney, "Isaac Hull: Bulwark of the Sailing Navy," in *Command Under Sail. Makers of the American Naval Tradition, 1775–1850*, ed. James C. Bradford, Annapolis, 1985.

Humphreys, Joshua
1751–1838

*A*merican shipbuilder, born in Haverford Township, Pennsylvania. Humphreys was instrumental as a shipbuilder and naval architect in designing and constructing the U.S. Navy's early FRIGATES. Considered one of the best shipbuilders by the time of the American Revolution, he fitted out at his Philadelphia shipyard vessels that sailed in the Continental Navy. When the United States decided to create a permanent navy and build six frigates, Humphreys was appointed the first U.S. Naval Constructor, a post he held from 1794 to 1801. As such he proposed a radical new design that was incorporated into the construction of these vessels—the *UNITED STATES, CONSTITUTION, CONSTELLATION, CHESAPEAKE, PRESIDENT* and *CONGRESS*. (The *United States* was built under his personal supervision.) These vessels were longer, broader, sat lower in the water and hoisted more canvas that any other vessel in their class of frigates. These specifications made Humphreys' frigates more powerful and faster than their rivals. The accomplishments of these vessels, which served with distinction in the WAR OF 1812, became legendary.

Henry H. Humphreys, *Who Built the First United States Navy?* . . . New York, 1916.

Hydrofoil

*T*he fastest vessel type in the modern postwar navy, the hydrofoil has a boat-shape hull equipped with planes or foils. As the boat's speed increases, the hull rises above the water and the foils skim the surface or, in some designs, remain submerged just below it. The main advantages of the design are greatly improved stability and a much higher potential maximum speed—up to 100 knots in some cases. Such characteristics suggested immediate naval applications, and the hydrofoil principle has been applied in the postwar period to some types of fast patrol boat—and patrol gunboat—in the service of the U.S. Navy and other naval powers. A typical hydrofoil is powered by a single gas turbine, with secondary diesel engines, and is equipped with eight missiles and a rapid-firing gun. It has a displacement of 250 tons, a length of 145 feet (44 m) and is operated by a crew of 25.

Hydrography

*T*he scientific study of the sea and other waters on the earth's surface, hydrography dates back to the earliest explorations of the oceans of the world. The Arabs, who invented the compass and astrolabe, were the first to record systematically the results of their surveys of coastlines, harbors, sea depths, currents and winds during the medieval period. Their charts and maps were made widely available to seafarers as they navigated the globe. The development of hydrography as a scientific study expanded as the oceans were explored and new instruments, including the sextant and quadrant, became available. The science gained further momentum during the 1500s through the 1800s—when the sailing navies required more accurate information that would enable them to navigate the oceans with much greater precision.

The hydrographic departments of most of the world's principal navies date from the 18th century. The French navy took an early lead, forming a hydrographic department in 1720, with the U.S. Navy following nearly 100 years later in 1830. Although the British equivalent was not formally established until 1795, the Royal Navy had played a key role in shaping knowledge about the world's oceans during the 18th century. During the 19th century it assembled comprehensive information on all aspects of the sea. Changes in the nature of naval warfare have made new demands on naval hydrographic departments. For example, submarine warfare has stimulated the need for improved SONAR-based information about sea depths. Another has been the growth in AMPHIBIOUS operations, which have required more data about coastlines and how they might best be approached. These gaps are increasingly filled by the use of satellite surveys, which often provide a cost-objective method of supplementary existing knowledge. See also Sir Francis BEAUFORT and Charles D. SIGSBEE.

G. S. Ritchie, *The Admiralty Chart: British Hydrography in the Nineteenth Century*, London, 1967.

Hyères, Battle of
July 13, 1795

Following their inconclusive engagement in the Gulf of Genoa, March 13–14, 1795, the British and French Mediterranean fleets met again some four months later off the southern coast of France. However, this later battle was to have no more effect on the initial course of the FRENCH REVOLUTIONARY AND NAPOLEONIC WARS, 1792–1815, than the first. Under the command of Vice Admiral William Hotham, the British fleet had increased in strength since the Gulf of Genoa battle with the arrival of additional ships from England. Hotham's 23 SHIPS OF THE LINE were ranged against 17 French equivalents, based at Toulon, under the command of Vice Admiral Pierre Martin.

When the two fleets met off the Hyères Islands on July 13, 1795, the weaker French squadron sought to withdraw. With the British quickly in full pursuit, the opposing fleets were soon spread over a wide area, and it proved impossible for Admiral Hotham to engage the enemy effectively. The French came under fire from the British van, which included the *Agamemnon* under Admiral Horatio NELSON's command, but when the wind changed direction Hotham ordered an immediate withdrawal. The British commander was concerned that his leading ships might be blown ashore and wrecked. Apart from the seizure of a single French ship, the 74-gun *Alcide*, the engagement produced no positive benefits for the British war effort. It came as no surprise when, in November, Hotham was replaced by Sir John JERVIS.

Île d'Aix, Battle of
April 4, 1758

An engagement between British and French naval squadrons near the naval base of Rochefort, southwest France, during the SEVEN YEARS' WAR, 1756–63. British Admiral Edward HAWKE, who commanded a squadron of seven ships of the line and three frigates, came across the French CONVOY at anchor off the Île d'Aix. Bound for North America, the convoy of 40 merchantmen was to be escorted by five ships of the line and some seven frigates. In a brief but confused battle the British gained the upper hand, and some of the French warships ran aground. Although some were later refloated, the planned convoy to North America had to be abandoned.

Île de Groix, Battle of the
June 23, 1795

In June 1795, during the FRENCH REVOLUTIONARY AND NAPOLEONIC WARS, 1792–1815, a British squadron, commanded by Commodore Warren, had escorted a group of returning French royalist exiles, landing them at Quiberon Bay in Brittany. Distant cover had been provided by the Channel Fleet headed by Admiral Alexander HOOD, Lord Bridport. On June 22, following the successful completion of this operation, the Channel Fleet sighted a French squadron of nine ships of the line under the command of Rear Admiral Louis VILLARET-JOYEUSE. The French retreated toward L'ORIENT in the face of the superior British force, but the gap between the two closed rapidly. By June 23 the British van had overtaken the enemy off the Île de Groix. The fight that followed, often known as "Bridport's action," produced confusion among the French. Three of the French rear ships surrendered. Fortunately for the French, the British did not press home their advantage, and Lord Bridport ended his attack rapidly without causing further damage. As the British removed their prizes, the French retreated in the direction of L'ORIENT.

Illustrious, H.M.S.

A British AIRCRAFT CARRIER of 23,000 tons that won eight battle honors during WORLD WAR II, 1939–45. The Illustrious, which was 753 feet 6 inches (229 m) in length and had a beam of 95 feet 9 inches (29.23 m), was also notable for her pioneering work in RADAR-controlled interceptions by carrier-based aircraft. She was operated by a crew of 1,392 and could accommodate 36 aircraft. Launched in 1939, she joined the British Mediterranean fleet in August 1940 and operated constantly against the Italian navy. On November 11–12, 1940, her Fairey Swordfish torpedo bombers attacked TARANTO, the enemy fleet's main base, firing 11 torpedoes and sinking an Italian battleship, the Conte di Cavour. Two other Italian battleships were badly damaged. This was the first time in naval history that a fleet was destroyed by enemy aircraft. Only two of the Illustrious's own aircraft (out of a total of 21 involved) were lost.

The Illustrious was herself severely damaged in retaliatory attacks carried out soon afterward by Luftwaffe dive bombers. Her heavy armor protection prevented her complete destruction, but she was put out of action for a year. Like her sister ships the Formidable and the Victorious (together with the Indomitable, Implacable and Indefatigable, which were modified designs), the Illustrious served for much of the rest of the war in the Pacific, remaining there until April 1945 when a KAMIKAZE attack finally forced her to return home. Before being scrapped in 1955, she was used for postwar jet aircraft trials.

Impressment

The forcible rounding up of men to serve as crew on warships in the absence of sufficient volunteers.

Impressment was a key method of recruiting qualified seamen during the era of the European sailing navies; the "pressed man" was forced to serve his country in wartime whether he wished to do so or not. A forerunner of compulsory national service or the draft, this power originally was exercised under the royal prerogative in England whenever there were insufficient volunteers to operate the king's ships. However, in Tudor times it was embodied in various Acts of Parliament, which specified the categories that were eligible for impressment and those that were exempt. Sailors who were impressed always received a lower rate of pay than volunteers, although some continued in the navy after a war on standard terms, and at least one "pressed man" became an admiral during the 18th century.

Impressment also became a convenient way of disposing of vagrants and petty criminals, who often found it difficult to escape the attention of the press gangs that operated in the main seaports and across the country. Press gangs were groups of sailors, under the command of an officer, whose function was to pick up men for service in the wartime navy. They would raid homes and taverns in their search for men. This technique also was employed at sea when a merchant ship could be stopped and a proportion of its crew removed for naval service. During the FRENCH REVOLUTIONARY AND NAPOLEONIC WARS, 1792–1815, the British extended this practice to American merchant ships on the grounds that they employed men who had deserted from the Royal Navy; it was to be a major cause of the WAR OF 1812. Impressment was widely used in England during the Napoleonic period but was not revived in subsequent wars. The power of impressment fell into disuse among other naval powers as well during the 19th century.

P. Kemp, *The British Sailor: A Social History of the Lower Deck*, London, 1970.

Inchon Landing
September 15–25, 1950

A large-scale AMPHIBIOUS landing by American forces at Inchon, Korea that proved to be a turning point in the KOREAN WAR, 1950–53, and saved United Nations forces headed by the United States from possible defeat. Code-named "Chromite," the plan was produced by General Douglas MacArthur and was feasible only because of the U.S. Navy's command of the sea. A substantial force of 261 ships, headed by Admiral Arthur Struble, was assembled. Two American divisions landed at the port of Inchon, where they cut enemy supply lines and advanced on Seoul. The North Korean forces then were caught in a dual movement by these forces and the American Eighth Army, which broke out from the Pusan perimeter to the south. The proposed landing area was particularly difficult, and landings could be made only for a few hours each day because of the tides. MacArthur persuaded a skeptical Joint Chiefs of Staff to approve his plan, and the amphibious force was assembled in less than a month. Following a naval bombardment, the landing of X Corps took place as planned. Opposition to it was limited and losses were light. Inchon was secured on September 15–16, 1950, and the invading forces advanced according to plan, with Seoul falling to the allies before the end of the month.

Max Hastings, *The Korean War*, London, 1987.

Indefatigable, H.M.S.

*T*he British Indefatigable-class BATTLE CRUISERS of WORLD WAR I, 1914–18, consisted of three vessels, including H.M.S. *Indefatigable*, which entered service in 1911. The Indefatigables were the cheapest CAPITAL SHIPS to be produced in recent times. Their main armament consisted of eight 50-caliber 12-inch (29-cm) guns, their maximum speed was 25 knots and they had a displacement of 18,800 tons. With a crew of 800, they were 590 feet (179 m) in length and had a beam of 80 feet (24 m).

The *Indefatigable* and her sister ships were based on the INVINCIBLE class and shared the same basic weaknesses—poor armor protection and vulnerable magazines. This fact was graphically illustrated at the Battle of JUTLAND, 1916: During the first phase of the battle cruiser action, the *Indefatigable* sank following a magazine explosion caused by 11-inch (26.4-cm) shell fire from the German warship VON DER TANN.

Notable among the other warships of the ROYAL NAVY named *Indefatigable* was the 44-gun vessel commanded by Sir Edward PELLEW, the distinguished FRIGATE captain, during the FRENCH REVOLUTIONARY AND NAPOLEONIC WARS, 1792–1815. Her greatest achievement was the destruction of the *Droits De L'Homme*, a French ship of the line, off the coast of France early in 1797.

Independence, U.S.S.

*T*he American Independence-class light AIRCRAFT CARRIERS of WORLD WAR II, 1939–45, consisted of nine vessels, including the U.S.S. *Independence*, which entered service in 1943. These ships used the incomplete hulls of the Cleveland-class light cruisers as the basis for their construction. The *Independence* herself had a displacement of 11,000 tons, an overall length of 622 feet 6 inches (189.74 m) and a beam of 71 feet 6 inches (21.79 m). With a maximum speed of 32 knots, she was equipped with four 5-inch (13-cm) antiaircraft guns and 66 smaller-caliber weapons. Normally she could carry 45 aircraft, although she could hold 90 when she was employed as an aircraft transport. The Independence-class carriers were an important addition to American naval strength during a critical period of the Pacific War. Only one Independence-class ship, the *PRINCETON,* was sunk during the war, although two others were damaged in KAMIKAZE attacks. The U.S.S. *Independence* survived the Pacific War, serving at the Battles of LEYTE GULF, 1944, and the PHILIPPINE SEA, 1944, and after the war acted as a target ship during the first nuclear tests at Bikini Atoll.

Indianapolis, U.S.S.

American heavy cruiser that served in the Pacific during WORLD WAR II, 1939–45. Commissioned in 1941, the *Indianapolis* had a displacement of 9,950 tons, a length of 610 feet 3 inches (186 m) and a beam of 66 feet (20 m). With a maximum speed of 32.75 knots, her main armament consisted of nine 8-inch (20-cm) guns and eight 5-inch (13-cm) antiaircraft guns. Together with her sister ship the *Portland,* she served in the Pacific from PEARL HARBOR to IWO JIMA. She was hit during a KAMIKAZE attack off Okinawa on March 31, 1945, but damage was relatively light and she soon was able to return to active service. She was less fortunate when the enemy struck for a second time. The Japanese submarine *I-58* torpedoed her as she was en route from Guam to Leyte on July 29, 1945. Although a large number survived this initial attack, many subsequently died in the water because of an 82-hour delay before help arrived. An electrical failure had prevented the *Indianapolis* from sending a distress signal, and it took some time before the navy realized that she was missing. Out of a total crew of 1,199, 883 men were lost.

Indomitable, H.M.S.

The name of several British warships including the ILLUSTRIOUS-class AIRCRAFT CARRIER of WORLD WAR II, 1939–45. In 1942 H.M.S. *Indomitable* formed part of FORCE H and was one of three carriers that protected the vital convoy route to Malta. In 1945 she joined the British Pacific Fleet and served as Sir Philip VIAN'S FLAGSHIP. At this late stage of the war, the Japanese launched their mass KAMIKAZE attacks against the Allied fleet. The *Indomitable* was hit by a kamikaze that bounced off the ship and exploded harmlessly.

An earlier *Indomitable,* sister ship of the *INVINCIBLE,* built in 1907, had the performance of a CRUISER (maximum speed 28 knots) and the heavy armament of a BATTLESHIP (eight 12-inch [30 cm] guns). She was a prototype BATTLE CRUISER, representing a considerable improvement over her predecessors. With a displacement of 17,250 tons and a crew of 784, she was powered by four steam turbines and had a range of 3,100 nautical miles. Her main weakness was her relatively poor armor protection. In 1915 she was involved in the sinking of the *BLÜCHER* and in the

bombardment of the Turkish forts protecting the DARDANELLES.

The latest *Indomitable* in British service is an antisubmarine cruiser, completed in 1980, with a displacement of 19,500 tons. With her sister ship the *Invincible,* she is the largest warship to have been built in Britain since World War II.

Inflexible, H.M.S.

The most remarkable of the various British warships named *Inflexible* was the heavily armed 19th-century BATTLESHIP that was laid down in 1876 and launched in 1881. She represented an important step in warship design for two main reasons. First, she was the first battleship to be equipped with underwater TORPEDO tubes, of which she had four. The *Inflexible* was also the most heavily armored British ship of the period, with armor 2 feet (61 cm) thick protecting the armament and the engines.

Another unusual feature of the *Inflexible* was the fact that she was built with two masts and sails, although these were later removed. Her 6,500-horsepower engines produced a maximum speed of about 15 knots. The *Inflexible* had a displacement of 11,800 tons, a length of 320 feet (97.5 m) and a beam of 75 feet (23 m). She was armed with four 16-inch (41-cm) muzzle-loading rifled guns mounted in two turrets, eight 4-inch (10-cm) breech-loaders and 21 antitorpedo-boat guns. The weight of a single discharge—6,800 pounds (3,084 kg)—was not to be exceeded for another 25 years.

Ingenohl, Friedrich von
1857–1933

German admiral who commanded the HIGH SEAS FLEET in the opening stages of WORLD WAR I, 1914–18. Although he had enjoyed the support of Alfred von TIRPITZ, the navy minister, Ingenohl's tenure at the head of the German fleet, which began in 1913, was brief and unsuccessful. Always a cautious commander, he failed to exploit Germany's relatively favorable position at the beginning of the war, when the difference in strength between the High Seas Fleet and the British GRAND FLEET was not too great. However, the balance of naval power soon altered decisively in Britain's favor and the Germans missed their opportunity. It was not until after Germany's defeat in the Battle of the FALKLAND ISLANDS, 1914, that Ingenohl ordered the High Seas Fleet into action. The fleet bombarded the east coast of Britain but was unable to lure the Grand Fleet out to sea. Following the Battle of the DOGGER BANK, January 24, 1915, Ingenohl was replaced by Hugo von Pohl as commander in chief of the High Seas Fleet.

Ingersoll, Royal Eason
1883–1976

American naval officer, born in Washington, D.C., on June 20, 1883, the son of Rear Admiral Royal Rodney Ingersoll, U.S.N., 1847–1931. Entering the service in 1901, Royal Ingersoll early and throughout his career demonstrated a gift for organization and logistics. During America's involvement in WORLD WAR I, 1914–18, he was attached to the office of the chief of naval operations, where he developed the communications office for the navy. From 1921 to 1923 he headed the branch of the Office of Naval Intelligence responsible for Japanese espionage; his branch was then working on the cryptographic program known as "Magic," which was to enable the Americans to read the JAPANESE NAVY's signals traffic and made an important contribution to victory in the Pacific war. In 1929 he served as chief of staff to Admiral William Veazie PRATT, commander of the U.S. Fleet. When Admiral Pratt became Chief of Naval Operations in 1930, Ingersoll served as head of the fleet training division.

Heading the war plans division of the Navy Department during the critical years from 1935 to 1938, Ingersoll worked on revising the navy's tactical and war preparations, especially "Plan Orange," the war plan against Japan. When the United States entered World War II, Ingersoll served as assistant to Admiral Harold STARK, Chief of Naval Operations. In early 1942 Ingersoll succeeded Admiral Earnest J. KING as commander of the Atlantic Fleet, with responsibility for protecting convoys, antisubmarine patrols, and the naval defense of the Western Approaches. Operating out of bases from Iceland to South America, his fleet conducted much of the navy's training work, and he held general authority for the North African landings in late 1942. In late 1944 he became commander of the Western Sea Frontier, based in San Francisco. With the task of overseeing all facets of the projected invasion of the Japanese home islands, Ingersoll became deputy chief of naval operations and deputy commander, U.S. Fleet, hence serving directly under Admiral King. He retired in August 1946. At the time of his death in Bethesda, Maryland in 1976, Admiral Ingersoll was the senior officer on the retired list. His son, Lieutenant R. R. Ingersoll II, U.S.N., was killed on the carrier HORNET during the Battle of MIDWAY in 1942.

James E. Sefton, "Royal Eason Ingersoll," *Dictionary of American Military Biography,* ed. Roger J. Spiller et al., Westport, Conn. 1984, pp. 509–512.

Intelligence

Naval forces always have made use of the intelligence gathered as a result of espionage activity or from more open sources, including photographic reconnaissance obtained by aircraft or satellite. High-quality intelligence collected, analyzed and distributed by specialist agencies has played a vital part in the outcome of several major naval battles of the 20th century. Equally, the absence of relevant intelligence—or the failure to interpret it correctly—also has had major consequences. The establishment of permanent national intelligence organizations is a relatively recent development, dating back to the late 19th century. Specialist naval intelligence services also originate from this time, although most remained underdeveloped and small scale until the outbreak of WORLD WAR I, 1914–18, forced expansion on them.

The ability to read encoded signals traffic has provided a valuable source of naval intelligence. A notable early example occurred during the RUSSO-JAPANESE WAR, 1904–5, when the Japanese intercepted and decoded the radio messages sent to the Russian fleet at the time of the Battle of TSUSHIMA, 1905. Early in World War I the British obtained a copy of the German navy's code book. Unknown to the Germans, they were able to decode intercepted radio messages for the rest of the war. The British also achieved remarkable success against the Germans in WORLD WAR II, 1939–45, as they were able to read messages encoded on the famous Enigma machine. As a result, British naval intelligence was able to produce valuable information bearing on, for example, the U-BOAT war and operations in the Mediterranean. A parallel American operation, code-named "Magic," involving army and navy personnel, was established in 1939 to break Japanese military codes. The team succeeded in breaking the main code in 1940 but it was ill-equipped to analyze the vast quantity of intercepted signals. Its single most important success was to uncover the Japanese attack plan for the Battle of MIDWAY, 1942, a decisive American victory and a turning point in the Pacific war.

Expert analysis of intelligence gathered from decoded messages or from any other source is required if the correct conclusions are to be drawn. It also needs to be communicated effectively within an appropriate time period to operational commanders. One of the most notable examples of an intelligence breakdown occurred at PEARL HARBOR. The Magic team had become aware of a possible Japanese attack but failed to predict precisely when and where it would occur. This shortcoming was compounded by the fact that increasingly explicit indications of Japanese action received in the days leading up to the attack were not passed on to naval headquarters at Pearl Harbor. It has been suggested, as an alternative explanation, that these intelligence warnings were deliberately withheld so that the Japanese attack would give the U.S. government a reason to enter the war. Another major example of a communications failure occurred at the Battle of JUTLAND, May 1916, when vital information about German fleet movements was not passed on to the British commander. Despite these shortcomings, the role played by naval intelligence in the two world wars ensured that there would be increased investment in such services in a postwar environment dominated by superpower rivalry between the United States and the Soviet Union. (See also COLD WAR.)

Patrick Beesly, *Room 40: British Naval Intelligence in World War I*, London, 1982; D. Kahn, *The Codebreakers*, London, 1966.

Invergordon Mutiny
1931

British naval MUTINY, triggered by an ADMIRALTY decision to cut pay rates in the Royal navy by ten percent as part of cost-cutting measures introduced during the Great Depression. The navy's announcement was made without prior warning and caused great resentment, particularly because the personnel of the other British armed services were not being asked to make similar sacrifices. Seamen serving with the Atlantic Fleet, which was based at Invergordon on the Cromarty Firth in the northeast of Scotland, seemed particularly incensed by the decision. Following a series of mass meetings to discuss the issue, the entire complement responded by refusing to weigh anchor and take the fleet to sea when ordered to do so. Faced with this overwhelming opposition, the Board of Admiralty decided to abandon the pay cut; the mutiny was ended within a few days. Some of the ringleaders were later court-martialed and dismissed from the service, but most mutineers escaped any punishment.

David Divine, *Mutiny at Invergordon*, London, 1970.

Invincible, H.M.S.

Developed by the ROYAL NAVY as the armored CRUISER equivalent of the dreadnought, the *Invincible* reflected Admiral Jackie FISHER's concern with speed and firepower rather than armor. With the performance of a cruiser (maximum speed 28 knots) and the heavy armament of a BATTLESHIP (eight 12-inch [30 cm] guns), she was a prototype BATTLE CRUISER, representing a considerable improvement over her predecessors. Completed in 1908, the *Invincible* had a displacement of 17,250 tons and a crew of 784. Powered by four steam turbines, she had a range of 3,100 nautical miles.

As a battle cruiser working with the GRAND FLEET during WORLD WAR I, 1914–18, the *Invincible*'s main weakness was the fact that her armor had been sacrificed in the interests of speed and was thus too thin to provide the protection she needed. This became clear at the Battle of JUTLAND, 1916, when one of her turrets was hit. The ensuing enormous explosion blew her in half; she sank immediately, and only three of her crew survived. The lessons of Jutland were quickly assimilated, and the armor of her two surviv-

ing sister ships (the INDOMITABLE and the *Inflexible*) was improved.

The first British vessel to be named the *Invincible* was a former French warship that had been captured at the Battle of CAPE FINISTERRE in 1747. A well-designed third rate (see RATING OF SHIPS) of 74 guns, she was to be used as a model for similar British-produced ships. The latest *Invincible* in Royal Navy service is an antisubmarine cruiser, completed in 1980, with a displacement of 19,500 tons. She and her sister ship, INDOMITABLE, are the largest warships to have been built in Britain since WORLD WAR II, 1939–45.

V. E. Tarrant, *Battlecruiser* Invincible: *The History of the First Battlecruiser, 1909–1919*, Annapolis, 1987.

Iowa, U.S.S.

American WORLD WAR II, 1939–45, battleship and name ship of a class that also included the MISSOURI, NEW JERSEY and WISCONSIN. The largest and fastest American battleships ever constructed, these four vessels were equipped with the biggest guns used in any U.S. Navy ship. Designed to protect fast U.S. carriers from an attack by enemy cruisers, the Iowa design emphasized speed rather than armor, although sufficient protection was provided. The *Iowa*, like her sister ships, was 887 feet (270 m) in length and had a displacement of 58,000 tons. She was armed with nine 16-inch (41-cm) guns, housed in triple turrets, that could fire a 27,000-pound (12,247-kg) shell over a distance of 23 miles (37 km). The *Iowa* was operated by a crew of 2,788.

Launched on August 27, 1942, the *Iowa* entered service in August 1943 as a convoy escort off Newfoundland. She later served in the Pacific as part of the Fifth Fleet and was slightly damaged by a Japanese shore battery in the Marshall Islands. During the Battle of LEYTE GULF, 1944, she served as part of Admiral William HALSEY's fast carrier force. In the closing stages of the war she participated in the Okinawa campaign and bombarded Hokkaido and Honshu. Decommissioned after the war, she was returned to service during the KOREAN WAR, 1950–53, but was then mothballed. Like her sister ships, she was modernized and recommissioned in the 1980s, her new cruise and antiship missiles giving her a new lease of life.

Malcolm Muir, *The Iowa Class Battleships*, Poole, Dorset, 1987.

Iquique, Battle of
May 21, 1879

An action in the early stages of the Pacific War, 1879–81, which was fought by Chile against Bolivia and Peru. The battle occurred during the Chilean navy's BLOCK-

The battleship U.S.S. *Iowa* during the Pacific War, 1941–45 *(Copyright © Imperial War Museum, London)*

ADE of the Peruvian port of Iquique. The blockading force, commanded by Admiral Rebolledo, was largely withdrawn in May when it was ordered to sea to attack a Peruvian convoy. Two Chilean ships were left to maintain the blockade, but because they consisted only of an aging sloop (the *Esmeralda*) and a gunboat (the *Covadonga*), a Peruvian response was almost inevitable. The Peruvian attack was mounted by two IRONCLAD RAMS—the *HUASCAR* and the *Independencia*—on May 21, 1879. In the unequal fight that followed, the Chileans fought with great courage and determination. The *Esmeralda* was rammed by the *Huascar* and capsized; her captain, Arturo Prat, was killed as he tried to board the *Huascar* and became the hero of the battle. The Chilean gunboat *Covadonga* was more fortunate and escaped southward. She was pursued by the *Independencia*, which was wrecked while attempting to ram her, and later by the *Huascar*, but managed to make good her escape. The Chilean navy was determined to track down the *Huascar* but did not do so until October 8, when she was forced to surrender after being surrounded and attacked by five Chilean warships. With the command of the sea in

her hands, Chile was able to mount a seaborne invasion of Bolivia and Peru. Her successful land-based operations were recognized in the Treaty of Ancón, October 1883, when she gained Bolivian and Peruvian Territory.

Iran-Iraq War
1980–88

This prolonged war of attrition, which resulted in heavy loss of life on both sides, began with Iraq's invasion of Iran and the capture of oil-rich Iranian territory near the border. Iraq's primary aims were to topple the regime of the Ayatollah Khomeini and secure a readjustment of its borders with Iran. The initial operations included successful attacks on Iranian gunboats in the Shatt-al-Arab River. A determined Iranian response in 1981 recaptured much of the lost territory, but neither side was able to muster sufficient strength to gain a decisive advantage during eight years of war. Regular Iranian offensives were repelled from strong Iraqi defensive positions.

During the prolonged stalemate on land, both parties turned their attention to the Persian Gulf, where their respective oil shipments were the target of frequent air attacks. An Iranian threat to close the Straits of Hormuz was a further dangerous escalation of the war and produced a firm response from the West. The United States and its allies dispatched naval patrols to the area to ensure that the straits remained open to international shipping. The maritime dimension had little real impact on the underlying course of events. Ultimately the Iranians recognized that a decisive land victory was beyond their powers and a cease-fire was finally agreed to in August 1988.

Ironclad

A term in use in the 19th century to describe both the wooden warships that were armored with iron plating and the first warships to be built of iron. The use of iron in the construction of warships was a direct result of the Battle of SINOPE, November 1853, when the Russian fleet conclusively demonstrated the vulnerability of wooden ships to modern shell projectiles by destroying a Turkish squadron. As a result, ship designs and production methods changed rapidly. The French launched the first iron ship, the frigate *LA GLOIRE,* in 1859. The British followed with their first iron warship, the *WARRIOR,* in 1860. During the AMERICAN CIVIL WAR, 1861–65, the appearance of the *MERRIMACK* and the *MONITOR,* and the first battle between opposing ironclads (in HAMPTON ROADS, Virginia), also confirmed that the era of the wooden warship was finally over. The word "ironclad" gradually fell into disuse in the latter part of the century and was superseded by the term "dreadnought" when this new BATTLESHIP type was launched in 1906.

William C. Davis, *Duel Between the First Ironclads,* Garden City, N.Y., 1975.

Iron Duke, H.M.S.

*N*amed after the first Duke of Wellington, the *Iron Duke* was a British super-DREADNOUGHT that served in the ROYAL NAVY throughout WORLD WAR I, 1914–18. She was completed in 1914 along with the three other ships of this class. With a displacement of over 30,000 tons, she was heavier and longer than her predecessors, the King George class. She also had improved secondary armament, with her 6-inch (15-cm) guns replacing the inadequate 4-inch (10-cm) variety of the earlier class. The *Iron Duke* and her sisters were also the first ships to be equipped with antiaircraft guns as a defense against airships.

The *Iron Duke* was Admiral John JELLICOE'S FLAGSHIP as commander in chief of the GRAND FLEET until November 1916. She then served with the Second Battle Squadron

of the Grand Fleet. Like her sister ships the *Benbow* and the *Emperor of India,* she was present at the Battle of JUTLAND, 1916, and avoided sustaining any damage. The *Marlborough*—the other ship of this class—was also at Jutland but was not so fortunate, being the only British dreadnought to be torpedoed during World War I. The damage she sustained there required major repairs, but the *Marlborough* eventually was able to resume her wartime service. The entire Iron Duke class, except for the *Iron Duke* herself, was scrapped during the 1930s. The *Iron Duke* survived first as a gunnery training ship and then, during WORLD WAR II, 1939–45, as a depot ship at SCAPA FLOW in the Orkney Islands. She was finally scrapped in 1946.

Ise

*T*he *Ise* and her sister ship, the *Hyuga,* were Japanese DREADNOUGHTs that were constructed in response to the pre-1914 naval building programs of the other major powers. Completed in 1917, the *Ise* had a displacement of 29,900 tons and a maximum speed of 23 knots. She was operated by a crew of 1,360. Her main armament consisted of 12 14-inch (36-cm) guns in six twin turrets. During the 1930s her tripod foremast was replaced by a towering bridge structure, and she was equipped to operate seaplanes. Her armament and command facilities also were updated in readiness for WORLD WAR II, 1939–45.

Following the heavy Japanese carrier losses at the Battle of MIDWAY, June 1942, both ships of the Ise class were converted as carrier BATTLESHIPS. A flight deck was added to the stern, a conversion that required the removal of the two after turrets (X and Y). The *Ise* now could accommodate 22 bomber seaplanes, which were to be used on fleet protection duties. These aircraft were launched by catapult and recovered from the sea by a crane. The only time the two Ise-class ships operated in their new role was when they sailed with the decoy force commanded by Admiral Jisaburo OZAWA at the Battle of LEYTE GULF, October 1944. Both ships were sunk by American naval aircraft during raids on Kure harbor in July 1945.

Isherwood, Benjamin Franklin
1822–1915

*O*ften considered the mid-19th century's leading American marine engineer, Isherwood was very actively involved in designing what would become the foundation of the steel navy of the United States. Born in New York City on October 6, 1822 and educated at the Albany (New York) Academy, famous for its scientific curriculum, he worked as a draftsman and civil engineer for railroads in New York before entering the U.S. Navy's new Engineering

Corps in 1844 as a first assistant engineer. He rose through the ranks to become Engineer-in-Chief just prior to the AMERICAN CIVIL WAR, 1861–65.

Promoted in July 1862 to head the newly formed Bureau of Steam Engineering with the rank of commodore, he served in this position until 1869. As chief engineer, he developed many revolutionary types of engines, propellers and vessels, contributing greatly to the North's war effort as well as to the advance of naval technology generally. He wrote prolifically on the experiments he conducted. Following a succession of duties, he served on the navy's first Naval Advisory Board from 1881 until his retirement in 1884. Promoted to rear admiral on the retired list in June 1906, he died in June 1915 in New York City.

Edward W. Sloan III, *Benjamin Franklin Isherwood, Naval Engineer,* Annapolis, 1965.

Italian Navy

Formed in 1861, following the creation of the Kingdom of Italy, the Italian navy has had a mixed wartime record. The new force was barely established when it was defeated by Austria at the Battle of LISSA, 1866. A period of rapid expansion in the 1870s and 1880s provided the Italian navy with a relatively modern fleet third in size to those of Britain and France. Italy took an initial lead in the development of the all-big-gun ship and, by 1915, was equipped with six DREADNOUGHTS and eight pre-dreadnoughts.

During WORLD WAR I, 1914–18, the Italian navy's principal role was to neutralize the numerically inferior Austrian fleet in the Adriatic. With the support of four British battleships, it was largely successful. Except for three limited sorties, Austria's CAPITAL SHIPS were to remain in port throughout the war. As a result, Italy's battleships were relatively inactive apart from shore bombardments and some patrol duties. Both sides concentrated on hit-and-run raids, with the Italians making heavy use of the high-speed MAS motor TORPEDO BOAT, of which almost 300 were built. The Italian navy also had to devote considerable resources to defend its bases at Brindisi and Venice, which were subject to regular air attack, and to the Otranto barrage, a minefield across the Otranto Straits that was subject to Austrian raids. Italian wartime losses included three battleships, two armored cruisers and two small cruisers. In compensation, much of the former Austrian fleet was transferred to the Italians at the end of the war.

In the interwar period the navy was weakened by political interference from the fascists, although the government invested substantial sums in reequipping it. Until the mid-1930s France was seen as the main adversary in a future naval war; thereafter, Britain replaced France as the focus of Italian naval concerns. By 1940 Italy had six battleships, seven heavy cruisers, 14 light cruisers and 119 submarines as well as support ships. However, it had no aircraft carriers,

the fleet lacked SONAR or RADAR, and there had been no practice in night fighting. The Italian navy was, therefore, ill-equipped to carry out its primary roles of controlling the Mediterranean and maintaining the country's supply routes to its territory in North Africa. Given these unfortunate weaknesses, it is not surprising that the Italian navy's record during WORLD WAR II, 1939–45, has little to commend it. The initiative was lost to the British early on and was never recovered due in part to the demoralizing effect on the Italian high command of successive defeats at TARANTO, 1940, CAPE MATAPAN, 1941, and elsewhere in the Mediterranean.

The only noteworthy victory against the British was the heavy damage caused to two battleships in Alexandria in December 1942 using a human torpedo (see MIDGET SUBMARINE), a successful Italian design, but this success was not followed up with effective surface action. During the 18 months preceding the Italian armistice in September 1943, the Italian navy was used largely defensively, particularly on convoy duty to North Africa, as British naval dominance in the Mediterranean had been established at this time. When Italy surrendered, part of the Italian fleet was handed over to the British in Malta, but many other naval units fell into German hands and were used against the Allies. Italy was a founding member of the North Atlantic Treaty Organization (NATO) in 1949; the Italian navy has since operated in the context of the alliance and has taken no active part in postwar naval operations.

James J. Sadkovich, *The Italian Navy in World War II,* Westport, Conn., 1994.

Ito, Sejichi
1890–1945

Japanese admiral who was centrally involved in planning the attack on the American fleet at PEARL HARBOR in 1941. As vice chief of the naval general staff, Ito played a major role in the formulation of Japanese naval strategy in WORLD WAR II, 1939–45. In the latter stages of the war he promoted the use of KAMIKAZE pilots. In April 1945 Ito commanded the super-battleship YAMATO and supporting ships on a mission to OKINAWA. His objective was to destroy the Allied invasion fleet, but he was killed when the *Yamato* was sunk well before she reached her intended destination.

Iwabuchi, Sanji
1893–1945

Japanese vice admiral. As commander of the battleship *Kirishima,* Iwabuchi was present at MIDWAY, 1942, and during the Battles of the SOLOMON ISLANDS, 1942–43. He established his reputation in the last few months of WORLD

WAR II, 1939–45. In February 1945 he commanded Japanese naval forces in Manila, which was about to fall to the Americans. Although originally ordered to withdraw by General Tomoyuki Yamashita, Iwabuchi did not abandon the city without a fight. Supported by only 4,000 soldiers, his determined resistance over nearly a month caused widespread destruction and heavy loss of life. Iwabuchi, who made a last stand at Intramuros, took over 100,000 Filipinos, 16,000 Japanese and 1,000 Americans with him. He was killed as the battle came to an end.

Iwo Jima, Battle of
February–March 1945

A major American amphibious operation in the Pacific theater during WORLD WAR II, 1939–45, to capture the small Japanese-occupied island of Iwo Jima. It was garrisoned by 21,000 troops who were protected by strong defenses. The U.S. military planned to use the captured island as a forward air base for future operations against Japan. The landing was preceded by a massive air and sea bombardment by the U.S. Fifth Fleet, commanded by Admiral Raymond SPRUANCE. On February 15 the navy landed some 30,000 troops. Despite the ferocity of the preliminary bombardment, the Japanese defensive positions had been largely unaffected. The Japanese pinned down the American 5th Marines as they landed and held them for a total of five weeks, despite heavy attacks from superior forces. The battle eventually moved inland; organized Japanese resistance did not end until March 26. One of the enduring images of World War II occurred when a small group of marines raised the American flag on top of Mount Suribachi toward the end of this, one of the bloodiest battles of the Pacific war. Some 20,000 Japanese troops—virtually the entire garrison—were killed, while the Americans sustained nearly 25,000 casualties (including almost 7,000 killed).

Iwo Jima, U.S.S.

Named for the hard-won American victory at the Battle of IWO JIMA, 1945, the American amphibious assault ship *Iwo Jima* was notable as the world's first ship to

U.S. Marines land on Iwo Jima, 1945, during the Pacific War, 1941–45   *(Copyright © Imperial War Museum, London)*

be designed and built specifically for helicopter operations. Completed in 1961, she had been requested in response to a need first identified during the SUEZ CRISIS, 1956, when helicopters used in carrying commandos were operated from two aircraft carriers. The *Iwo Jima*, which had a displacement of 17,000 tons, carried a marine battalion (1,724 troops) and its equipment as well as backup facili-ties, including a fully equipped hospital. She could carry some 20 helicopters, enough to provide transport for the entire battalion. Eventually a total of seven assault landing ships of the Iwo Jima class were built. One ship of this class was later reequipped with 12 Harrier V/STOL aircraft and several Sea King antisubmarine HELICOPTERS that were used for CONVOY escort work.

Jackson, Sir Henry
1855–1929

British admiral who was First Sea Lord during WORLD WAR I, 1914–18, succeeding Lord FISHER on his resignation in May 1915. Jackson was a surprising choice as a wartime leader of the ROYAL NAVY, as he was noted for his specialist scientific interests and achievements (in particular, his role in introducing radio telegraphy in the navy at the turn of the century) rather than his command experience or leadership qualities. In fact, with Arthur Balfour installed as First Lord of the Admiralty in succession to Winston CHURCHILL, a much less dynamic style was soon evident at the heart of British naval administration.

Jackson's tenure was not a success. He was incapable of delegating effectively and unable to establish close relations with his political masters. Late in 1916 mounting public concern at the scale of Allied shipping losses produced by the U-BOAT campaign brought his unhappy tenure at the ADMIRALTY to a close. He resigned in December 1916 and was replaced by Admiral John JELLICOE.

James II, Duke of York
1633–1701

Second son of Charles I and younger brother of Charles II; James II, King of England and James VII, King of Scotland, 1685–88. James' association with the ROYAL NAVY began at the Restoration, 1660, when he was appointed Lord High Admiral. As James, Duke of York, he had fled abroad during the English Civil War, 1642–51, and spent a period in the French army during 12 years in exile. As head of the Restoration navy, James restructured the Navy Board and made a major contribution to the reform of other aspects of central naval administration. He issued the official FIGHTING INSTRUCTIONS, which provided officers with orders and guidance on tactics and formations in naval warfare. James's role was not entirely desk-bound:

He went to sea as commander of the fleet when the Second ANGLO-DUTCH WAR, 1665–67, broke out. He defeated the Dutch at the Battle of LOWESTOFT, June 3, 1665, although he did not pursue the enemy effectively afterward. Forced to return home soon thereafter on the king's instructions because of concerns about his safety, he took no further part in operations at sea.

As Lord High Admiral he was criticized for disbanding the fleet before peace negotiations had been concluded, allowing the Dutch fleet under Admiral Michiel de RUYTER to enter the Medway River and attack British shipping at CHATHAM in June 1667. James returned to sea during the Third Anglo-Dutch War, 1672–74, and commanded the fleet at the Battle of SOLEBAY, May 28, 1672, flying his flag in the *Prince*. However, once more he was forced to withdraw prematurely from his command at sea—although this time the reason was very different. The Test Act, which banned all Catholics from public office, was passed early in 1673, forcing James—a Roman Catholic—to resign from his post as Lord High Admiral. He was able to return to office during the following year, and he retained it when he acceded to the throne in 1685. James's program of naval administrative reforms continued but his religious views, which were unpopular in the navy, led to his deposition in the Glorious Revolution of 1688. James escaped to France, where he enjoyed the hospitality and support of Louis XIV. In March 1689 he invaded Ireland with a contingent of French troops in an attempt to regain the throne, but he was defeated at the Battle of the Boyne.

F. C. Turner, *James II*, New York, 1948.

Japanese Navy

Following the restoration of imperial rule in 1867, Japan decided to become a major power capable of resisting the growing threat of Western imperialism. This strategy included the creation of a modern navy, which emerged rapidly with the advice and support of British naval officers. As a result, within little more than 30 years it had defeated its two principal opponents in the Far East. The Chinese navy was Japan's first victim in the war of 1894–95, closely followed by the Russian navy in the RUSSO-JAPANESE WAR, 1904–5. Russian expansionism in the Far East led to conflict with the Japanese, in which Russia suffered a series of naval reverses, culminating in the decisive defeat of the Russian Baltic fleet at the Battle of TSUSHIMA, May 1905. This engagement marked Japan's emergence as a significant world naval power, a position it was to sustain until the destruction of its fleet in the closing phases of the Pacific War in 1944–45. Japan had required external assistance to develop an oceangoing navy within a generation. Her British ally played a major role in the construction of the Japanese fleet and the training of her crews.

Britain had signed a defense treaty with Japan in 1902, and this alliance was maintained throughout WORLD WAR I, 1914–18. With British forces concentrated in home waters, Japan was the only Allied power with a strong naval presence in the Pacific. At the beginning of the war it occupied the German Pacific islands in order to prevent Admiral Maximilian von SPEE's East Asiatic Squadron using them. The German colony of Tsingtao on the Chinese mainland, which had been von Spee's base, fell to Japanese and British troops on November 7, 1914. In a major AMPHIBIOUS operation, the Japanese fleet landed nearly 25,000 men. The rest of the war was much less eventful for the Japanese navy. Its principal tasks included escorting Australian New Zealand Army Corps (ANZAC) troops to the Middle East and hunting down German commerce raiders. Japanese capital ships did not serve outside the Pacific during the war, but, at the request of the British, Japan did assign several destroyers to the Mediterranean in 1917–18.

Like the other major naval powers, Japan was subject to the restrictions imposed by the Washington Naval Treaty, 1922, which meant that it was permitted to build no more than three capital ships for every five produced by either the United States or Britain. (See WASHINGTON CONFERENCE.) Japan tried to narrow this gap because her territorial ambitions in Asia were likely to bring her into conflict with these major naval powers. In order to circumvent the aims of the treaty, she installed heavy armament on warships whose displacements conformed to the relatively low treaty limits. The treaty did not, however, prevent Japan from having the third largest navy or being the world leader in naval aviation by the beginning of WORLD WAR II, 1939–45. At that time, advanced naval aircraft operated from ten aircraft carriers, which were supported by 12 battleships, 18 heavy cruisers and 18 light cruisers. The navy also had a number of long-range submarines and 100 destroyers in commission.

In the opening phases of the PACIFIC WAR, 1941–45, the navy, which was headed by Admiral Isoroku YAMAMOTO until his death in 1943, enjoyed several major successes. These included the surprise attack on PEARL HARBOR (although the victory was far from complete), the destruction of British FORCE Z off Malaya and several key amphibious landings in support of the Japanese army, which soon had Southeast Asia under its control. However, the Japanese navy soon was forced onto the defensive as the Americans struck back. In June 1942, as the Japanese tried to extend their conquests, they were attacked and defeated by the Americans at the Battle of MIDWAY, with the loss of four carriers. Although these carriers could be replaced, the Japanese found it increasingly difficult to replace the experienced air crews who were lost in growing numbers as the war progressed. The use of submarines as an adjunct to the fleet also quickly ran into difficulties as the U.S. Navy's antisubmarine warfare capability was relatively highly developed. The Japanese navy was also ill-equipped to provide the necessary protection to its merchant fleet, and the escorts that were made available did not have effective antisubmarine defenses. Unsustainable losses resulted, with a third of the Japanese merchant fleet being destroyed in the first two years of the war. However, the underlying problem facing the Japanese navy was strategic: The territory captured by Japan was so extensive that it was to stretch its naval resources to the breaking point.

The Japanese defensive perimeter was first breached in August 1942 when the Americans launched a counteroffensive in the SOLOMON ISLANDS, 1942–43, followed by subsequent attacks on the Gilbert and the Marshall Islands. The Japanese navy was increasingly placed on the defensive and was further constrained by the fact that the Americans could read its secret codes. (See INTELLIGENCE.) In the last year of the war, the Japanese navy made increasingly desperate efforts to bring the U.S. Navy to a final decisive battle. It assembled most of its surviving ships for the Battle of LEYTE GULF, October 1944, when it was heavily defeated and lost most of its remaining air crews. The navy still was able to launch frequent KAMIKAZE raids, however, and at OKINAWA, April–May 1945, its surviving units, including the battleship *YAMATO*, the most powerful then afloat, led an unsuccessful suicide mission against the U.S. invasion force.

The destruction of these remaining warships by U.S. naval aircraft marked the effective end of the Japanese navy as a fighting force. The navy had been well served in terms of the quality of its leaders, the performance of its ships and the dedication of its crews. It was defeated by the daunting scale of the task it was allocated and the underlying strength of its main adversary. In the postwar period, the Japanese navy was reconstituted as part of the country's self-defense force. It is a medium-size fleet that reflects the country's reduced international role. See also SINO-JAPANESE WAR, 1894–95; RUSSO-JAPANESE WAR, 1904–5.

Stephen Howarth, *Morning Glory: A History of the Imperial Japanese Navy*, London, 1993.

Japan-Korea War
1592–93

*I*n pursuit of a plan developed by the Japanese dictator Hideyoshi to conquer Korea and then China, an expeditionary force landed at Fusan (Pusan) in southern Korea in May 1592. It reached Seoul some 18 days later. Once the Korean peninsula was in their hands, the Japanese gave priority to gaining control of the sea that separated Japan from Korea. However, at the Battle of the Yellow Sea, July 1592, they were heavily defeated by the Korean navy, which was far more powerful and effective than its Japanese opponent. The Koreans were equipped with a fleet of "tortoise" boats that had spike-studded iron roofs. These "ironclads" were powered with oars and were designed so that they could be rowed in either direction. They attacked the enemy vessels by ramming them. Japan's slow and unmaneuverable transports were no match for these boats; thus the Koreans had no difficulty in disrupting Japanese supplies and preventing reinforcements from reaching the peninsula.

By the beginning of 1593, extra Japanese troops were urgently needed because of large-scale Chinese intervention in support of the Koreans. Soon the Japanese were forced to agree to a truce, although peace negotiations continued for years. Peace finally was concluded in 1598, but not before the Japanese had fought a further campaign on the Korean peninsula. Japanese transports again proved to be vulnerable to the Korean "tortoise" boats, and heavy losses were sustained as troops were brought to and from Japan. At the Battle of Chinhae Bay, November 1598, Admiral YI SUNG SIN defeated the Japanese and destroyed more than half their ships.

Japan Sea, Battle of the
August 14, 1904

*A*n action during the RUSSO-JAPANESE WAR, 1904–5, in which the Vladivostock Squadron of the RUSSIAN NAVY was defeated by its better-equipped opponent. Commanded by Rear Admiral Yessen, the Russian squadron consisted of three armored cruisers. When news of the departure of the main Russian battle squadron from Port Arthur reached Yessen, he went to meet it in the Straits of Korea. By this time, however, the main fleet already had been defeated by the Japanese in the Battle of the YELLOW SEA, August 10, and was returning to Port Arthur. On

August 14 the Vladivostock Squadron, still unaware of their colleagues' defeat, met a Japanese squadron, commanded by Admiral Hikonojo Kamimura, some 36 miles northeast of Tsushima. Consisting of four armored cruisers, the Japanese force was soon in the ascendancy. The Russian armored cruiser *Rurik* was sunk and the other two ships under Yessen's command were badly damaged, although they managed to escape. Japan's success in this battle meant that its domination of the sea was now complete.

John N. Westwood, *Russia Against Japan, 1904–05. A New Look at the Russo-Japanese War*, Basingstoke, 1986.

Jasmund, Battle of
May 25–26, 1676

A naval engagement during the war between Denmark and Sweden, 1675–79, that resulted in a victory for the Danes and their Dutch allies. A joint Danish and Dutch fleet, consisting of 35 ships commanded by the Danish Admiral Niels Juel, met a much larger Swedish fleet, commanded by Admiral Lorens Creutz, some ten miles north of the Jasmund peninsula on the northeast coast of Rügen, a Baltic Sea island. The force was not at full strength—expected reinforcements from Holland under the command of Admiral Cornelis TROMP had not arrived. Undeterred by the fact that the Swedish fleet consisted of 59 ships, Juel attacked on May 25. He had the advantage of being a more experienced and effective commander than Creutz, who was unable to maintain his line of battle and lost five ships. A further engagement on a more limited scale took place the next day, but neither side gained the advantage. However, only a week later the Swedes were decisively defeated at the Battle of ÖLAND, June 1, 1676.

Java Sea, Battle of the
February 27, 1942

*B*attle between Allied and Japanese forces in the Pacific Theater during WORLD WAR II, 1939–45. By February 1942 Japanese plans for the invasion the Dutch East Indies island of Java were well advanced; and Allied naval units based at Soerabaja were the only real obstacle. This mixed force of American, British and Dutch warships, commanded by Dutch Rear Admiral Karel Doorman, included five cruisers and nine destroyers but had no air support. It had been operating against Japanese convoys off Sumatra and Java for some months. On the afternoon of February 27, 1942, at 2:27, Doorman was notified of the approach of an invasion force some 80 miles northeast of Soerabaja in the Makassar Straits. Soon after 4 P.M. he sighted the Japanese escort, commanded by Rear Admiral Takeo

Takagi, which consisted of two heavy and two light cruisers and 14 destroyers.

The engagement began at 4:20 when the Japanese heavy cruisers opened fire at a range of some 16 miles. The Allied force closed in so that its light cruisers could attack the enemy destroyers. During a Japanese torpedo attack, the British cruiser EXETER was soon badly damaged and withdrew together with three other ships. An Allied counterattack resulted in the loss of two more ships—the *Electra* and the *Kortenear*—and Doorman was forced to turn south to regroup. He was forced to go through a Dutch minefield off the coast of Java and lost the *Jupiter*, his last remaining destroyer. (Four American destroyers that had run out of torpedoes were sent back to port.) Later in the evening Doorman turned north again in a final bid to stop the invasion. By 11:00 P.M. he had made contact with two Japanese warships, which sunk two Dutch cruisers, including the *De Ruyter*, Doorman's FLAGSHIP. The Dutch commander and many of his men died. The cruisers *Perth* and *Houston* escaped but were sunk a few hours later in western Java, the final Allied losses in the abortive attempt to stop the Japanese invasion of the island.

F. C. van Oosten, *The Battle of the Java Sea*, London, 1976.

Jean Bart

*F*rench battleship of the WORLD WAR II, 1939–45, Richelieu class, launched at St.-Nazaire in March 1940, shortly before France surrendered to the Germans. She had a displacement of 35,000 tons with a length of 814 feet (248.1 m) and a beam of 108 feet 6 inches (33.07 m). She had a maximum speed of 35 knots, and her incomplete armament consisted of four 15-inch (38-cm) guns and four 35-mm antiaircraft guns. Like her sister ship *Richelieu*, the *Jean Bart* had not been completed by June 1940, but she escaped to Casablanca, where she was to be stored throughout the war. Her only operational use occurred during the Allied Torch landings, November 1942, when her guns fired on American troops landing at Casablanca. The American battleship *Massachusetts* quickly disabled her armament. The *Jean Bart* was returned to France for repairs at the end of the war. See also Jean DARLAN.

Jellicoe, John, Earl
1859–1935

*B*ritish naval officer who, on the outbreak of the WORLD WAR I, 1914–18, was appointed commander of the British GRAND FLEET, a post he held until 1916. Jellicoe, who entered the ROYAL NAVY in 1872, came into contact with Lord FISHER in the 1880s, and won rapid promotion as a gunnery specialist. After several periods of service at

sea, he was appointed director of naval ordnance at the ADMIRALTY in 1905. He was promoted again in 1908 and became Controller and Third Sea Lord. In these posts he worked closely with Fisher in his reforms of the Royal Navy and in organizing the dreadnought construction program. Command of the Atlantic Fleet and then of the second division, Home Fleet, followed. This enabled him to develop his knowledge of strategy and tactics, as much of his recent career had concentrated on matériel. In the immediate prewar period Jellicoe became Lord Fisher's preferred candidate for the crucial GRAND FLEET command in the event of a conflict with Germany. A further period at the Admiralty, as Second Sea Lord, ended as World War I was declared.

Jellicoe was appointed to the command of the Grand Fleet and flew his flag in the IRON DUKE, a super-dreadnought. The major sea battle with the German HIGH SEAS FLEET expected by Jellicoe and much of the Royal Navy did not materialize, as the Germans preferred to keep their fleet in harbor until a favorable moment arrived. The Grand Fleet operated a distant BLOCKADE and, apart from the isolated operations of the BATTLE CRUISER force, 20 months of inaction followed. Jellicoe was a popular leader, who maintained morale and established a high standard of training, even though he was too preoccupied with details and was unwilling to delegate his authority. He always had been noted for his caution and would avoid any risk that might reduce or destroy the superiority in numbers that was the main asset of the British fleet.

It was not until the Battle of JUTLAND, May 1916, that he was able to engage the High Seas Fleet. The result was a British strategic victory, but tactically Jellicoe could claim no more than a draw. British losses were heavier than those of the Germans, and there was great disappointment that Jellicoe had not been able to mount a decisive strike against them. Although he had placed his fleet between the enemy and its base with considerable skill, a number of failures occurred during the battle. Jellicoe's fear of torpedo and submarine attacks had led him to turn away rather than follow the enemy at two critical points, with the result that contact was lost. His unwillingness to risk the main battle fleet was, however, justified on the grounds that, as Winston Churchill suggested, "he could have lost the war in an afternoon." There were also reservations about his use of the single line-ahead battle formation, which did not offer sufficient flexibility in this kind of engagement. Moreover, he suffered from various signaling problems, in particular the Admiralty's failure to inform him of the Germans' course of retreat.

In December 1916 Jellicoe was moved to the Admiralty as First Sea Lord and replaced as commander of the Grand Fleet by Admiral David BEATTY. Jellicoe's new principal task was to deal with the German U-BOAT threat, which by this time had replaced the Grand Fleet as the main danger to British shipping. Although Jellicoe was a major opponent of the CONVOY system, he was responsible for its successful introduction in May 1917 after the intervention of Prime Minister David Lloyd George had secured a change of policy. His relations with Lloyd George were always tense, as the latter had little patience with a "tired, over-conscientious man who could not delegate business, constantly overworked and always saw the black side of things too clearly." It was no surprise when, in December 1917, Jellicoe was abruptly dismissed by the new First Lord of the Admiralty, Sir Eric Geddes, and his wartime career brought to an end. Early in 1918 he was raised to the peerage, and the next year he was promoted admiral of the fleet in recognition of his wartime service.

John Winton, *Jellicoe*, London, 1981.

Admiral Sir John Jellicoe, commander of the British Grand Fleet during World War I, was unable to secure a decisive victory at the Battle of Jutland, 1916   *(Copyright © National Maritime Museum, Greenwich, London)*

Jenkins, Robert
fl. 1731–45

*E*nglish merchant captain who was involved in an incident with Spanish coast guards that eventually led to the War of JENKINS' EAR, 1739–43. Jenkins had been trading in the West Indies in the BRIG *Rebecca* without incident until 1731, when he was stopped and boarded by the Spanish. Although they discovered no evidence of smuggling, the Spanish stole the *Rebecca*'s cargo and tortured Captain Jenkins, cutting off one of his ears. When he arrived in England, he presented his grievance to King George II, but it was not pursued at that time.

However, in 1738, when English feelings against the Spanish were running high, Jenkins raised the issue again in the House of Commons and produced his severed ear. This outburst eventually led Robert Walpole, the prime minister, into war with Spain in the following year. The War of Jenkins' Ear, which was fought largely in the waters off Florida and in the Caribbean, was to merge into the War of the AUSTRIAN SUCCESSION, 1740–48. Jenkins continued his career in the service of the East India Company although his time at sea was interrupted by a period as governor of the small South Atlantic island of St. Helena, a staging post on the route east to India.

Jenkins' Ear, War of
1739–43

*C*ontinuing friction between England and Spain led, on October 19, 1739, to an English declaration of war. The immediate cause of the conflict was the claim by a merchant captain, Robert JENKINS, that his ear had been cut off by Spanish officials some years earlier when he had been operating in the Caribbean. In Parliament, the opposition fully exploited the issue, and Prime Minister Sir Robert Walpole was reluctantly forced to go to war. The underlying causes of the war included disagreements over the boundaries of Florida and the creation of an English monopoly of the slave trade with the Spanish colonies. Operations began when Admiral Edward VERNON captured the Spanish fort of PORTO BELLO in 1739 and seized Chagres, Panama, in 1740. In the same year Vernon failed to capture Cartagena and James Oglethorpe, governor of Georgia, was unable to take St. Augustine, Florida. A Spanish counterattack on St. Simon's Island, 1742, was repulsed, but a second English attempt on St. Augustine failed and English troops withdrew from Florida. At this point this regional conflict merged with the much wider War of the AUSTRIAN SUCCESSION, which continued until 1748.

Michael Morpurgo, *The War of Jenkins' Ear*, London, 1993.

Jervis, John, Earl St. Vincent
1735–1823

British admiral. Born in Staffordshire, Jervis entered the Royal Navy at the age of 13. He served as a post-captain in the SEVEN YEARS' WAR, 1756–63, and was present at the capture of QUEBEC, 1759. He commanded the FOU-DROYANT in the latter stages of the AMERICAN WAR OF INDEPENDENCE, 1775–83. His notable capture of the *Pegase*, a French SHIP OF THE LINE, in 1782 was rewarded with a baronetcy. During the FRENCH REVOLUTIONARY AND NAPO-LEONIC WARS, 1792–1815, he led, as a vice admiral, an expedition to the West Indies, capturing the French possessions of Martinique, St. Lucia and Guadaloupe. In 1795 he was appointed commander in chief in the Mediterranean. He won a great victory against the Spanish, who were allied to France, at the Battle of CAPE ST. VINCENT, February 14, 1797. Later in the same year he was raised to the peerage as Earl St. Vincent.

Jervis followed this success with his victory over the

John Jervis, First Earl St. Vincent, British naval commander, won a series of major naval victories against the French during the French Revolutionary War, 1792–1802   *(Copyright © National Maritime Museum, Greenwich, London)*

French at the Battle of the NILE, 1798, when he gave Rear Admiral Horatio NELSON the key role. Following a period of ill health in 1799–1800 he abandoned his sea command for an office in Whitehall as First Lord of the Admiralty in Prime Minister Henry Addington's administration. With a seat in the Cabinet, he reformed abuses, increased naval hygiene and improved conditions belowdecks. When William Pitt the younger returned to power in 1804, he dispensed with Earl St. Vincent's services. He returned to sea some two years later as commander in chief of the Channel fleet, 1806–7, before finally retiring from the service.

B. Blackman, *Nelson's Dear Lord: A Portrait of St Vincent*, n.p., 1963; D. Smith Bonner, ed., *The Letters of Lord St Vincent*, 2 vols., London, 1922–27.

Jervis Bay

A British ARMED MERCHANT CRUISER that engaged the German POCKET-BATTLESHIP ADMIRAL SCHEER while on escort duty during WORLD WAR II, 1939–45. The *Jervis Bay*, a former passenger liner built in 1922–23, had a displacement of 14,000 tons and a maximum speed of about 15 knots. Armament consisted of seven 6-inch (15-cm) guns. Her fateful encounter with the *Admiral Scheer* occurred on November 5, 1940 when she was the only escort for 37 ships traveling across the Atlantic from the United States to Europe. During the evening of November 5 the convoy was intercepted by the German battleship, and Captain Edward FEGEN, commander of the *Jervis Bay*, launched what was in effect a suicide attack on her. The *Admiral Scheer* took some 30 minutes to destroy her gallant opponent, and the delay allowed all but six ships in the Allied convoy to escape into the darkness. Captain Fegen, who was posthumously awarded the Victoria Cross, was not so fortunate, but a number of survivors from the *Jervis Bay* were picked up.

Jones, Catesby ap Roger
1821–77

American naval officer, born in Fairfield, Virginia, who entered the naval service as a midshipman in 1836 and in the 1850s worked on experiments on the DAHLGREN GUN at Washington Navy Yard. A brief period as a captain in the Virginia navy followed Virginia's secession from the Union. In June 1861 he joined the CONFEDERATE NAVY as a lieutenant and had a varied career for the first two years of the AMERICAN CIVIL WAR, 1861–65. Jones was present during the notable engagement between the IRONCLADS *MERRIMACK* and *MONITOR* off HAMPTON ROADS, March 1862. When Franklin BUCHANAN, captain of the *Merri-mack*, was injured, Jones temporarily succeeded him. He later commanded his own ship, the *Chattahoochee*, before moving to head the works that produced much of the Confederate Navy's wartime ordnance.

Jones, John Paul
1747–92

The quintessential American naval hero, born John Paul in Kirkbean, Galloway, Scotland. Going to sea on a merchant ship, his career prospered and he soon became a captain. Events turned against him in 1773, when he killed a mutinous seaman in Tobago and was forced to flee to Virginia, where he changed his name to Jones. On the outbreak of the AMERICAN WAR OF INDEPENDENCE, 1775–83, he received a commission as a first lieutenant and served on the *Alfred*, a converted merchantman, the first vessel to fly the Continental flag. In 1776 he was present at the capture of New Providence (Nassau) by the squadron under Esek HOPKINS. Later the same year he commanded the *Providence*, capturing or destroying 16 prizes on one cruise. In 1777, as commander of the sloop *Ranger*, he was sent to France, where he began raiding English ports and merchant shipping using Brest as his base of operations. He received from the French an old EAST INDIAMAN he renamed the *BONHOMME RICHARD*, in honor of the Ameri-

John Paul Jones: an outstanding American naval captain during the American War of Independence, 1775–83 *(Copyright © National Maritime Museum, Greenwich, London)*

can commissioner in Paris, Benjamin Franklin; the name referred to Franklin's popular publication, *Poor Richard's Almanac*.

In the summer of 1779, Jones sailed with a small squadron around Britain taking many prizes. In September he fought the British warship SERAPIS off Flamborough Head in one of the most fiercely contested and desperate sea actions ever, defeating his opponent but receiving so much damage that he lost his own ship two days later. During this engagement, when all appeared hopeless and he was asked by the British captain to surrender his damaged ship, Jones defiantly replied, "I have not yet begun to fight." Becoming a popular hero in France and America, he saw relatively little action for the rest of the war, but was the only Continental naval officer presented by Congress with a gold medal commemorating his brilliant services.

Returning to Europe after the war, Jones served as a rear admiral in the Russian navy, commanding a squadron on the Black Sea in 1788 against the Turks. Political rivalries and jealousies caused Jones to leave the Russian service and return to Paris in 1790. Offered a commission in 1792 by the U.S. government to treat with Algiers for peace and the release of prisoners, he died before the commission reached him. His body was exhumed and returned to the United States in 1910. Entombed at the U.S. Naval Academy in ANNAPOLIS, Maryland, he has since by general popular consent been declared the father of the U.S. NAVY.

Samuel E. Morison, *John Paul Jones: A Sailor's Biography*, Boston, 1959.

Joy, Charles Turner
1895–

American naval officer who served as Allied commander during the KOREAN WAR, 1950–53. Joy was born on February 17, 1895 in St. Louis, Missouri. Commissioned as an ensign in 1916, he served on many types of vessels as an ordnance officer. In WORLD WAR II, 1939–45, he saw action in the Pacific as early as February and March, 1942, in the operations at Bougainville, Lae and Salamaua. As commander of the *Louisville* he participated in the engagements of the ALEUTIAN ISLANDS CAMPAIGN, 1942–43. In mid-1944 he was elevated to commander of a CRUISER division of the Pacific Fleet, participating in the actions of Saipan, the Marianas, the first and second Battle of the PHILIPPINE SEA, the landing at LEYTE GULF, IWO JIMA, and Okinawa. In 1949 he became commander of the U.S. Naval Forces, Far East, headquartered in Tokyo. With the outbreak of war in Korea in June 1950, he assumed command of all United Nations naval forces until June 1952, serving also as senior negotiator in the talks at Panmunjom. After serving as superintendent of the U.S. Naval Academy, he retired in 1954.

Clark G. Reynolds, *Famous American Admirals*, New York, 1978.

Juan of Austria, Don

1545–78

Spanish naval commander and general who defeated the Ottoman navy at the Battle of LEPANTO, 1571, the last major engagement to be fought by galleys. He was the illegitimate son of Charles V and half brother of Philip II, who recognized him on acceding to the throne in 1556. Having completed his education in Spain, Don Juan decided to pursue a military career that would include periods of active service at sea and on land. His first appointment, in 1568, was to the command of a GALLEY squadron operating against the pirates of Algeria. He turned to land warfare later in the same year, taking two years to suppress a revolt by Moors in Grenada.

Don Juan's limited experience at sea made him a surprising choice as commander of the Holy League's fleet of 300 ships that had been assembled at Messina, in September 1571, to bring the Turkish navy to battle. However, his appointment was soon justified. On October 7, 1571 the opposing forces met in the Gulf of Corinth, and during a confused battle the Allies' superior numbers and skills proved to be decisive. The Turks suffered severe losses and the Battle of Lepanto, as it was later called, marked the beginning of their decline in the central and western Mediterranean. Don Juan's reputation as a naval commander was now secure, but he had little further opportunity to demonstrate his abilities. Not long after the capture of Tunis in August 1572, the Holy League's naval operations in the Mediterranean were brought to an end and Don Juan returned to Italy.

During his last years, 1576–78, Don Juan was governor-general of the Netherlands. In this office he had little success in suppressing the revolt against Spanish rule, and his reputation suffered as a result.

Charles Petrie, *Don Juan of Austria*, New York, 1967.

Jutland, Battle of

May 31–June 1, 1916

The greatest naval battle of WORLD WAR I, 1914–18, Jutland was the only full-scale encounter of the British and German battle fleets. It originated in a plan developed by Admiral Reinhard SCHEER, commander of the HIGH SEAS FLEET since January 1916, to lure the British GRAND FLEET from its bases in order to bring it to battle. Early on May 31, 1916 the High Seas Fleet left the Jade Estuary and moved into the North Sea parallel to the west coast of Denmark. Admiral Franz von HIPPER, commander of the German scouting forces, led the way toward the Skaggerak with five battle cruisers and 35 other fast ships at his disposal. The main German fleet, consisting of 59 vessels, including 22 battleships (of which 16 were dreadnoughts), was a long way behind. Radio messages intercepted by the British ADMIRALTY had warned of the German sortie, and the Grand Fleet was ordered to sail immediately. The main British fleet, under Admiral John JELLICOE, left its base at SCAPA FLOW in the Orkney Islands on May 30. It comprised 99 ships, of which 24 were dreadnoughts. Sixty miles (96 km) ahead of Jellicoe was Admiral David BEATTY's scouting force, which had left the Firth of Forth on the same day. It consisted of 52 ships, including six battle cruisers and an associated squadron of four super-dreadnoughts.

As the two fleets moved across the North Sea, neither side had any clear information about the size of the opposing force or its whereabouts. Contact was made during the afternoon of May 31, when the British light cruiser *Galatea* sighted Hipper's force. Without waiting for his super-dreadnoughts, Beatty proceeded south at maximum speed on a course parallel to the German squadron, which was now moving in the same direction. Hipper had reversed course after having sighted Beatty in the hope that he would be able to draw him toward the main German fleet. The two scouting forces were soon in action, opening fire at 16,500 yards (15,088 m). More accurate German fire and faulty British ship design caused the loss of two of Beatty's battle cruisers—the *INDEFATIGABLE* and the *Queen Mary*. With four battle cruisers left to oppose Hipper, Beatty ordered his remaining ships to "engage the enemy closer." However, almost immediately Beatty, who had been informed that the main High Seas Fleet was still in harbor, found it steaming toward him. He changed course immediately, moving north to join Jellicoe in the hope of luring the enemy into the hands of the Grand Fleet. The Germans, who were still unaware of the Grand Fleet's presence in the area, chased Beatty north for two hours, with both sides inflicting heavy damage on the other.

As Beatty sighted Jellicoe's six divisions approaching from the northwest, he turned eastward in front of the Germans to position himself correctly. Jellicoe deployed his fleet into the line of battle on the port wing column, placing the Grand Fleet across Scheer's escape route to his bases in Germany. At about 6:30 P.M. the first British shells were fired. As all the ships of both fleets came into range, there was a heavy general engagement during which the British fleet in line crossed the German T. (See CROSSING THE T.) Realizing that he faced imminent destruction, Scheer suddenly reversed course in an 180-degree turn under cover of smoke and destroyer attacks. He headed west, and his ships were soon out of range, as Jellicoe continued south. Just before 7 P.M. Scheer turned back again toward the British, apparently because he believed, incorrectly, that Jellicoe had divided his fleet. The Germans again came under heavy attack from the Grand Fleet, and once more Scheer withdrew, ordering his four remaining battle cruisers against the British line to cover the retreat. Fearing repeated torpedo attacks, Jellicoe decided to turn away at 7 P.M., allowing the enemy to escape to the southwest.

H.M.S. *Invincible* was one of three British battle cruisers lost at the Battle of Jutland, 1916 *(Copyright © Imperial War Museum, London)*

The British commander positioned himself across one of the enemy's possible lines of escape in the hope of bringing Scheer to battle the next morning. However, Jellicoe chose the wrong route and the Germans were able to pass southeast through the rear of the British fleet during the night. Several small actions took place, but none affected the outcome of the battle. As soon as Jellicoe realized that Scheer had escaped, he arranged to return home. The last great battle fought solely with surface ships, Jutland (or the Skaggerak, as the Germans have called it) was a strategic victory for the British. The High Seas Fleet never again challenged British dominance in the North Sea, and in the future the German naval effort was to be concentrated on unrestricted submarine warfare. Tactically, however, the battle was a draw. The British were considerably disappointed that the enemy had not been decisively defeated. As Britain's losses were heavier than her opponent's, the battle was claimed to be a German victory. The British suffered 6,784 casualties and lost three battle cruisers, three cruisers and eight destroyers; German losses consisted of one old battleship, one battle cruiser, four light cruisers and five destroyers, as well as 3,099 casualties.

D. Macintyre, *Jutland*, London, 1957.

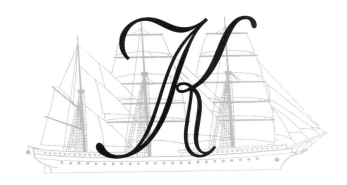

Kaga

*J*apanese AIRCRAFT CARRIER that had been laid down as a battleship in 1918. Destined to be one of the largest ships of her type then afloat, work on her was halted by the Washington Naval Treaty, 1922. (See WASHINGTON CONFERENCE.) She was rescued from the scrapyard because an earthquake had badly damaged a battle cruiser due to be converted as an aircraft carrier. The *Kaga* took her place, but the conversion was delayed and it was not until 1930 that she joined the Japanese fleet. She had a displacement of 29,000 tons, a length of 781.5 feet (238.2 m) and a maximum speed of just under 28 knots. Two hangars, over which a flush flight deck was constructed, provided accommodation for 60 aircraft. The ship was operated by 1,340 men. During modernization in 1935, her flight deck was extended to cover the full length of the ship, and aircraft accommodation was increased to 90.

The *Kaga* served off China from 1937 to 1940 and formed, with the *Akagi*, Carrier Division 1 for the attack on PEARL HARBOR in 1941. She launched the first wave of attacks by Nakajima B5N torpedo-bombers against the American fleet and participated in Admiral Chuichi NAGUMO's subsequent operations in the East Indies, South Pacific and Indian Ocean. During the Battle of MIDWAY, 1942, she sustained four hits at the hands of the U.S. Navy's Dauntless dive-bombers; she caught fire and eventually sank with the loss of 800 men.

Kaiten

*T*he JAPANESE NAVY'S principal torpedo of WORLD WAR II, 1939–45, the kaiten consisted of a 24-inch (60-cm) LONG LANCE torpedo with a single pilot's cockpit on top. Equipped with a compass and a small periscope, the cockpit was sealed once the pilot was in position. The torpedo carried a 3,418-pound (1,550-kg) impact-fused warhead.

The Japanese aircraft carrier *Kaga* in 1936 *(Copyright © Imperial War Museum, London)*

Developed as a last line of defense against the final Allied advance toward Japan, this suicide weapon first went into service against the United States Navy in late 1944. Some 150 were launched before the end of the war.

The kaiten had a range of up to 85,300 yards, or approximately 48 miles (78 km) at the minimum operating speed of 12 knots, and was brought within striking distance of its target by a host submarine or surface vessel. When the pilot had sighted the target through his periscope at some 200 yards (180 m), he submerged the kaiten. He then set the controls, which locked it on to the target. The kaiten secured a small number of successes; but it was always constrained by its limited range, which was reduced to 25,100 yards, or 14.25 miles (22,950 m) at its maximum speed of 30 knots, and the unreliability of its engines. Several improved engine designs were developed, and four different kaiten designs were produced, but the war ended before they could all enter service. See also MIDGET SUBMARINE.

Kamikaze

Japanese term meaning "divine wind." As the Allies pushed nearer Japan in the final year of WORLD WAR II, 1939–45, and Japanese defeat became inevitable, the Japanese began making suicide air attacks on Allied naval vessels. Pilots would deliberately crash their bomb-laden aircraft directly onto the warships. The idea had been briefly put into practice by pilots of the Special Attack Corps during the defense of the Philippines in 1944 but, as the United States Navy's armada neared Japan itself, more young Japanese pilots offered to sacrifice themselves in this fashion. A total of some 2,400 KAMIKAZE attacks were made on the Allies, resulting in the sinking of 26 warships and severe damage to 164 others (including the British carrier FORMIDABLE and the American carrier SARATOGA). During these attacks the advantage of the armored deck used in British carriers (but not employed by the carriers of the U.S. Navy) proved itself. For example, a

The aftermath of a kamikaze attack: burning debris and chemicals cover the deck of the American carrier *Saratoga* (Copyright © Imperial War Museum, London)

kamikaze struck the 32,000-ton H.M.S. *INDOMITABLE* but merely bounced off the deck into the sea. Although these kamikaze attacks failed to halt the Allied advance, they showed very plainly the sacrifices the Japanese were prepared to make to defend their homeland, and this had a considerable influence on the decision of American President Harry S Truman to use the atom bomb to bring the war to a swift conclusion. (See also Rear Admiral Masafuni ARIMA.)

Denis Warner and S. Seno, *Kamikaze. The Sacred Warriors, 1944–45,* Melbourne, 1983.

Kanaris, Constantine
1790–1877

*G*reek patriot, politician and naval commander, born on the island of Ipsara, northwest of Chios. Kanaris, who spent his early career at sea as a merchant captain, was one of many merchant seamen who joined the struggle against the Turks during the Greek War of Independence, 1821–28. He went into battle in his own, suitably modified merchant ship and fought with distinction and courage. Serving under Admiral Andreas MIAOULIS, he conducted a number of successful operations during the war, including the destruction of a Turkish flagship in the Straits of Chios in 1822, when he deployed several FIRESHIPS. Kanaris repeated this operation in Tenedos harbor and later was responsible for the loss of other Turkish ships. He became a senior officer in the navy of the new Greek state and held a succession of important commands. In later years he turned to politics, becoming a senator in 1847. The following year he became prime minister and held the post on three separate occasions between 1848 and 1877. In 1863 he was involved in the revolution that placed George I on the throne.

C. M. Woodhouse, *The Greek War of Independence,* London, 1952.

Kearsarge

A United States sloop of war notable for her destruction, in 1864, of the *ALABAMA,* the most successful commerce raider of the AMERICAN CIVIL WAR, 1861–65. A screw steamer with a displacement of 1,031 tons, the *Kearsarge* was one of a number of sloops of war constructed during the conflict. She was well armed with seven guns, including four 32-pounders (14.5 kg). Her most famous exploit was followed by a U.S. government claim for compensation for the damage caused by the *Alabama* and two other ships that had been built for the Confederacy at Birkenhead in northwest England. The settlement eventually cost the British government $15.5 million. The *Kearsarge* survived for another half century before being broken up. (See also COMMERCE RAIDING.)

Keats, Sir Richard Goodwin
1757–1834

*B*ritish naval commander, a close associate of Lord NELSON, who served throughout the FRENCH REVOLUTIONARY AND NAPOLEONIC WARS, 1792–1815. Appointed a captain in 1789, Keats had been caught up in the MUTINY of the Channel Fleet at SPITHEAD in 1797. During the French Revolutionary Wars he commanded the 74-gun *Superb,* which acted against French and Spanish naval forces in the Mediterranean. In 1801, operating in a squadron commanded by Sir James SAUMAREZ, Keats was responsible for the destruction of three enemy ships off Algeciras. Keats missed the Battle of TRAFALGAR, 1805, but he had learned of Nelson's plans for beating the French firsthand. Promoted to vice admiral in 1811, he returned to the Mediterranean, where the British fleet was under the command of Sir Edward PELLEW. Forced to resign his command the following year, Keats held a succession of shore appointments before being promoted to the rank of full admiral in 1825.

Kelly, H.M.S.

*T*he best-known British destroyer of the WORLD WAR II, 1939–45, the *Kelly* was commanded by Captain Lord Louis MOUNTBATTEN. As leader of the 5th Destroyer Flotilla, she rescued survivors from the British aircraft carrier *COURAGEOUS* when she was sunk off the west coast of Ireland early in the war. During the Norwegian campaign, 1940, she was seriously damaged on two occasions and had to be towed back to Britain for repairs. She later served with distinction in the Mediterranean, where she finally met her end during the Battle of Crete on May 23, 1941. A 1,000-pound (436-kg) bomb from a Stuka dive-bomber caused her to capsize and sink. The *Kelly* was one of seven K-class destroyers, which were launched in 1938–39 and completed in 1939–40. She had a displacement of 1,760 tons, a maximum speed of 36 knots and her armament included six 4.7-inch (12-cm) guns. Operated by a crew of 183, she was 356 feet 6 inches (108.7 m) in length and had a beam of 35 feet 9 inches (10.9 m).

Kenneth Poolman, *"The Kelly." HMS Kelly, the Story of Mountbatten's Warship,* London, 1980.

Kempenfelt, Richard
1718–82

*B*ritish rear admiral who was lost when the *ROYAL GEORGE* sank at Spithead in 1782. Richard Kempenfelt's wide naval experience included service in the SEVEN YEARS' WAR, 1756–63, and the AMERICAN WAR OF INDEPENDENCE, 1775–83, but his name is not associated with any great naval victory. Rather, he is best remembered as a professional officer who wrote widely on strategy and tactics. In particular, Kempenfelt's development of a new signal code of much greater scope and flexibility than the one then officially in use was an important practical contribution to the development of naval warfare. It was an innovation readily adopted by Admiral Lord HOWE, who first used it during the relief of GIBRALTAR, 1782.

Kentish Knock, Battle of
September 28, 1652

*T*he Battle of DOVER, May 19, 1652, marked the beginning of the First ANGLO-DUTCH WAR, 1652–54, but Kentish Knock was the first major engagement to follow the formal declaration of war in July. Late in September 1652 the 59 ships of the Dutch fleet, under the command of Vice Admiral Witte de WITT, left Calais and crossed the English Channel in search of the enemy. On September 28 the Dutch were lying by Kentish Knock sand in the southern North Sea, some 18 miles to the northeast of North Foreland, when they were sighted by the British fleet under Admiral Robert BLAKE.

The action, which involved 68 British ships, began at about 5 P.M. and lasted for three hours until nightfall brought it to an end. It started without warning as Blake attacked the Dutch van and center divisions; the action then became general. Two Dutch ships were captured and several others were damaged; the Dutch also suffered many casualties, but the British escaped relatively lightly. Dutch effectiveness was undermined partly because of discontent among their crews that kept some ships from participating in the action. However, within a few weeks the Dutch, under the command of Admiral Marten TROMP, were to reverse this outcome at the Battle of DUNGENESS.

Keppel, Augustus, First Viscount
1725–86

*B*ritish admiral who fought the French at the First Battle of USHANT, July 1778, and faced a court-martial shortly afterward. Keppel, who had joined the ROYAL NAVY at the age of ten, served with Admiral George ANSON during his circumnavigation of the globe, 1740–44. He gained most of his operational experience at sea during the SEVEN YEARS' WAR, 1756–63. As a Whig he had refused to fight when the AMERICAN WAR OF INDEPENDENCE, 1775–83, began, but later changed his position when France entered the war. The basis of his political creed was opposition to the tyranny of King George III and support for the movements—including the American colonies—that fought against him.

As commander in chief of the British Channel Fleet,

he had engaged the enemy at Ushant but without a decisive result. An acrimonious public debate with his second-in-command, Sir Hugh Palliser, about the conduct of the battle followed and led to his court-martial in 1779. Keppel was charged with attacking the enemy prematurely before properly forming a line of battle and with failing to do his utmost to take or destroy the enemy fleet. At the end of the hearing, the court dismissed these charges as "malicious and ill-founded." The trial had no long-term effect on Keppel's career; subsequently he was appointed First Lord of the Admiralty and raised to the peerage.

Keppel, Sir Henry
1809–1904

*B*ritish naval commander, the son of the Fourth Earl of Albemarle, who rose to the rank of admiral of the fleet in 1877. He was to spend much of his operational career in China and was engaged on active service there during the First and Second OPIUM WARS, 1839–42, 1856–60. Keppel returned to Chinese waters in 1867–69 as the commander of a seven-nation force charged with the suppressing pirates in the region. He was appointed admiral on the completion of this mission in 1869. Keppel's tours of duty in the Far East had been interspersed with service in the CRIMEAN WAR, 1853–56, where, in 1854, he served with distinction with the naval brigades during the attack on Sebastopol.

Kersaint, Armand, Comte de
1742–93

*F*rench admiral. The son of a distinguished naval officer, Kersaint entered the navy in 1755. In 1757, while serving in his father's ship during the SEVEN YEARS' WAR, 1756–63, he was promoted to ensign for bravery in action. He made steady but unspectacular progress, reaching the rank of captain in 1782. Despite his high birth, Kersaint supported the French Revolution and the creation of a republic. His active campaign for naval reform was facilitated by his election as a deputy to the Convention and his promotion to vice admiral. However, his republicanism did not extend as far as supporting the execution of Louis XVI, and he eventually was tried and executed for conspiring for the return of the monarchy.

Ketch

A two-masted sailing vessel used for coastal trading that originated in England during the mid-17th century. Initially, ketches were square-rigged on both masts and were similar to yawls although ketches had a larger mizzen;

later a fore and aft rig was adopted. The ketch, which normally had a displacement of 100 to 250 tons, soon acquired a naval role as a supply ship and tender to the battle fleets of northern Europe. This role disappeared when the age of the sailing navies came to an end, but for some 200 years the ketch had proved its worth by its ability to sail in almost any conditions.

It also acquired a more specialist combat function. The French developed the ketch as a BOMB VESSEL, as the clear deck space in front of the mainmast was an ideal platform for one or two large mortars. Design improvements, including increased size and strength, enhanced the ketch's speed and seaworthiness, and as a result, other navies also introduced ketches for bombing operations. The bomb ketch disappeared during the 19th century in response to the development of modern naval guns, but the basic design was to survive as a merchant ship. Ketches continued as coastal trading vessels for some years, and they are still used for yachting.

Keyes, Roger, First Baron
1872–1945

The youngest captain in the Royal Navy on his appointment in 1904, Keyes quickly made his mark and, in 1910, became head of the SUBMARINE service. During the first six months of WORLD WAR I, 1914–18, he was based at Harwich and was responsible for British submarine activity in the North Sea. He planned and took part in the HELIGOLAND BIGHT operation in August 1914, which resulted in the loss of three German cruisers and a destroyer. Early in 1915 he became chief of staff under Admiral Sir Sackville CARDEN, who was in command of the DARDANELLES operation. He continued under Carden's successor, Admiral Sir John de ROBECK. Keyes had a more optimistic view of the value of the navy in this theater than did de Robeck, and he even pressed for a further assault on Gallipoli after a complete withdrawal had been decided upon.

In October 1917, after a period of service with the GRAND FLEET, Keyes became director of plans at the ADMIRALTY and developed an imaginative proposal for a naval attack on the German U-BOAT bases at ZEEBRUGGE and Ostend. He soon was appointed to the command of the Dover Patrol with the aim of implementing this plan. The action on April 22, 1918 failed in its military objective of blocking the entrance to either harbor, although it had a considerable psychological impact. Knighted after the attack, Keyes remained in his command until the end of the war. He was a notable wartime naval leader who seized every opportunity to strike at the enemy.

C. F. Aspinall-Oglander, *Roger Keyes: Being the Biography of Admiral of the Fleet Lord Keyes of Zeebrugge and Dover*, London, 1951.

Kiev

Notable as the SOVIET NAVY's first AIRCRAFT CARRIER, the *Kiev* was launched in 1972 and was commissioned in 1975. She was a cruiser carrier with a long-range antisubmarine role rather than a conventional attack carrier. With a displacement of up to 37,000 tons at full load and a length of 899 feet (274 m), the *Kiev* was the largest ship ever produced for the Soviet Navy. She had a maximum speed of some 20 miles (32 km) per hour and was operated by a crew of 1,900. Her appearance reflected her dual cruiser and carrier functions: The construction of her bow and forecastle were influenced by earlier cruisers, while the design of the rest of the ship was determined by her carrier role. The *Kiev* carried some 25 helicopters and 20 fixed-wing V/STOL aircraft. She also was equipped with 12 SS-N-12 surface-to-surface missiles that could be used against long-range targets. Well equipped to deal with enemy submarines, her arsenal included antisubmarine mortars and missile launchers as well as ten twin torpedo tubes. The *Kiev* was withdrawn from service in 1993.

Kimmel, Husband Edward
1882–1968

American naval officer, commander of PEARL HARBOR on December 7, 1941, who received much criticism for the lack of naval preparation for the attack. Born on February 26, 1882, in Henderson, Kentucky, he entered the navy in 1900. Kimmel participated in the Cuban pacification campaign of 1906 and in the 1914 Mexican campaign, during which he was slightly wounded in the Battle of Vera Cruz. Advancing rapidly because of his skill as a gunnery officer and as a staff officer, he was involved in the development of new gunnery techniques. Kimmel was detached from the American squadron of battleships to the British GRAND FLEET once the United States had entered WORLD WAR I, 1914–18, in order to help instruct the British in new gunnery techniques. While doing so, he served as a naval observer at the action off HELIGOLAND BIGHT in November, 1917.

In February 1941 Kimmel, who was then a rear admiral, was advanced over 46 superior officers to assume command of the Pacific Fleet, raising his flag on the *PENNSYLVANIA*. He was in that post in December when the Japanese attacked the Pacific Fleet at Pearl Harbor, Hawaii. Along with the army's commander at Hawaii, General Walter C. Short, Kimmel received the blame for the lack of preparation for the attack and was relieved of his command shortly afterward. On March 1, 1942 he was retired from the navy at the suggestion of Admiral Ernest KING, Chief of Naval Operations, "for the benefit of the country." After many investigations, both military and civilian, into the circumstances at Pearl Harbor, the 1944 Naval Court of Inquiry concluded that "no blame or mistakes in judgment could be attached to Kimmel and that he had done everything possible under the circumstances." In 1945–46 Kimmel testified before a joint congressional committee that charged him with "errors of judgment and not with dereliction of duty." Yet from the time of the attack in late 1941 until his death in Groton, Connecticut, in May 1968, the stigma of responsibility for the Pearl Harbor disaster remained with him.

Donald G. Brownlow, *The Accused: The Ordeal of Rear-Admiral Husband Edward Kimmel, U.S.N.*, New York, 1968.

King, Ernest Joseph
1878–1956

The top-ranking American naval officer during WORLD WAR II, 1939–45, and one of four officers advanced to the rank of fleet admiral, King was born on November 23, 1878 in Lorain, Ohio. Appointed to the U.S. Naval

Admiral Ernest King: as commander in chief of the U.S. fleet and chief of naval operations during World War II he had a major influence on Allied strategy *(Copyright © Imperial War Museum, London)*

Academy in 1897, he graduated fourth in his class of 67, serving as battalion commander, the top leadership position there. A relatively routine career followed, until WORLD WAR I, 1914–18, when his professional life took a new turn.

With the postwar military reductions and few prospects for rapid advancement for surface line officers, King began his association with submarines and with naval aviation. He purposely sought as wide a range of experience as possible in nearly every type of vessel and base installation. Although he never qualified as a submariner, he did command submarine squadrons as well as the New London, Connecticut submarine base. He then took flight training and qualified as a pilot in 1927 at the advanced age of 48, before assuming command of the carrier *LEXINGTON* in 1930. Failing to succeed Admiral William D. Leahy as chief of naval operations in 1938, King settled to await his mandatory retirement in late 1942. World War II, however, interrupted his retirement plans, and he was pressed into service at the highest level.

As commander of the Atlantic Fleet in 1941, King was authorized by President Franklin ROOSEVELT "to conduct defensive operations against Axis surface and undersea raiders." Within two weeks of the PEARL HARBOR attack, King was elevated to the position of commander of the U.S. Fleet, and the following March he was made chief of Naval Operations, becoming the first officer to combine these two key positions. As such he was in charge of and exercised complete control over the navy, Marine Corps, and Coast Guard, not to mention coordinating the war effort with the army, the civilian sides, and America's war Allies. King served in this capacity throughout World War II and was thus second only to General George C. Marshall in the U.S. military hierarchy. His experience in submarine and aviation warfare "uniquely fitted him for the task of commanding a naval war on two oceans." Under his overall command, personnel increased from 420,000 in late 1941 to more than 4 million by the war's end in September 1945, while the number of U.S. navy ships of all types increased over the same period from about 4,500 to over 92,000, "comprising a fleet greater than the combined fleets of all the other nations in the world."

Besides his operational duties commanding this huge force, King also advised President Roosevelt at home as well as at important conferences such as those at Quebec, Casablanca, Cairo and Tehran. He continued to advise Roosevelt's successors as well as several secretaries of defense and secretaries of the navy between his retirement in late 1945 and his death at Portsmouth, New Hampshire in June 1956. The recipient of many awards, foreign and domestic, as well as honorary degrees, he was generally regarded as "brilliant, cantankerous, outspoken, blunt, cold arrogant, [and] rude."

Thomas B. Buell, *Master of Seapower: A Biography of Fleet Admiral Ernest J. King*, Boston, 1980.

King Edward VII

The British King Edward VII-class BATTLESHIPS of WORLD WAR I, 1914–18, consisted of eight vessels, including H.M.S. *King Edward VII*, which entered service in 1905. The King Edward VIII pre-dreadnoughts represented a distinct improvement on their predecessors, the London and Duncan classes. Their secondary armament was enhanced by the introduction of four 9.2-inch (23-cm) guns, and armor protection was increased. Maximum speed was a creditable 19 knots, and their displacement was 15,630 tons. Operated by a crew of 777, they each had a length of 453 feet 9 inches (138 m) and a beam of 78 feet (24 m).

During WORLD WAR I, 1914–18, the eight warships of the King Edward VII class formed the Third Battle Squadron of the GRAND FLEET, where they were known as the "Wobbly Eight." Two ships were lost during the war: The *King Edward VII* herself hit a mine and sank in January 1916, while the *Britannia* was even less fortunate, being torpedoed only two days before the end of the war. The remainder of the King Edward VII class—*Commonwealth*, *Zealandia*, *Dominion*, *Hindustan*, *Africa* and *Hibernia*—survived, only to be broken up shortly after the final conclusion of hostilities.

King George V

The British King George V-class BATTLESHIPS of WORLD WAR I, 1914–18, consisted of four vessels, including H.M.S. *King George V*, which entered service in 1912. This class was a modified version of the earlier Orions, the main differences being a slight increase in dimensions, the repositioning of the mast ahead of the two large funnels and changes to the armor. These warships had a displacement of 23,000 tons, a length of 597 feet 6 inches (182 m) and a beam of 89 feet (27 m). Operated by a crew of 782, their main armament consisted of ten 13.5-inch (34-cm) guns. A major weakness of the new class was its relatively poor secondary armament. Its 4-inch (10-cm) guns were inadequate to meet effectively the increasing threat posed by destroyers and torpedo boats.

The *King George V*, the *Centurion* and the *Ajax* served with the Second Battle Squadron, British GRAND FLEET, throughout WORLD WAR I, 1914–18, and all were present at the Battle of JUTLAND, 1916. The *Audacious*—the other member of this class—also joined the same unit of the Grand Fleet in August 1914, but on the following October 24 she sank after hitting a mine off the Irish coast. She was one of only two dreadnought battleships to be lost by the Royal Navy during World War I.

Kinkaid, Thomas Cassin
1888–1972

American naval officer who eventually was to command the Seventh Fleet in the Pacific theater of WORLD WAR II, 1939–45. Kincaid was born on April 3, 1888 and entered the navy in 1904. As a young midshipman he was on one part of the GREAT WHITE FLEET's circumnavigation in 1907–9. In late 1917 he saw service with the British ADMIRALTY and then as a gunnery officer on board the U.S.S. *Arizona*. In 1938 he became naval attaché in Rome,

British King Edward–class battleships at sea   *(Copyright © National Maritime Museum, Greenwich, London)*

followed by similar duty in Belgrade, Yugoslavia until March 1941. During the summer and autumn prior to America's entry into World War II, he commanded a squadron of destroyers on escort duty through the war zone of the eastern Atlantic.

Transferred to the Pacific and reaching flag rank in November 1941, he commanded a division of cruisers in the raids on Japanese-held islands as well as at the battles of the CORAL SEA and MIDWAY, 1942. Becoming commander of Task Force 16 in the carrier ENTERPRISE, he saw action in the GUADALCANAL campaign as well as in naval battles in the eastern SOLOMON ISLANDS. In January 1943 he led the forces in the northern Pacific, overseeing the recapture of the ALEUTIAN ISLANDS of Attu and Kiska from Japanese forces. By November 1943 he returned to the South Pacific as commander of the Seventh Fleet, supporting the army's operations against the Japanese in New Guinea and the Philippines, including the landings at LEYTE GULF. He retired in 1950 and died on November 17, 1972.

Gerald E. Wheeler, "Thomas Cassin Kinkaid," *Dictionary of American Military Biography, Vol. 2,* pp. 565–569, Westport, Conn., 1984.

Kirk, Alan Goodrich
1888–1963

The naval commander who oversaw American operations on D-Day, (See NORMANDY LANDINGS.) Kirk was born on October 30, 1888 in Pennsylvania. A surface warrior throughout most of his career, he served on many vessels as well as in important shore billets; in the 1920s he was an aide to Presidents Warren G. Harding and Calvin Coolidge. In the summer of 1939 he became naval attaché in London, remaining in that important assignment until March 1941. He then returned to the United States as director of the Office of Naval Intelligence and a division commander with the Atlantic Fleet, concentrating on amphibious operations. He returned to London in May 1942, again as naval attaché but also as chief of staff to Admiral Harold R. STARK, commander of American Naval Forces, Europe.

In February 1943 he headed the Atlantic Fleet's amphibious force, transporting and supporting the American forces's assault on SICILY. In November 1943 he became the senior American naval commander under British naval command that planned the Normandy landings, June 1944, participating in the assault as commander of Task Force 122. In the late summer of 1944 he became naval commander to General Dwight D. Eisenhower and commander, U.S. naval forces, France. Retiring from the service in 1945, he subsequently served as U.S. ambassador to Belgium, Luxembourg, the Soviet Union, Nationalist China and the Philippines. He died on October 15, 1963.

Karl Schuon, *U.S. Navy Biographical Dictionary,* New York, 1964, pp. 140–142.

Kjøge Bight, Battle of
June 30, 1677

The third naval defeat suffered by the Swedes in their war with Denmark, 1676–79, the Battle of Kjøge Bight followed earlier engagements at JASMUND, May 25, 1676, and ÖLAND, June 1, 1676. Although the Danes were to fare less well in the land battles of 1677 and 1678, they redeemed themselves at Kjøge Bight. Danish admiral Niels Juel, who flew his flag in the 84-gun *Christianus V,* had 25 SHIPS OF THE LINE at his command. He engaged a larger Swedish force, commanded by Admiral Evert Horn, in the Kjøge Bight, a bay near Copenhagen. After heavy fighting the Swedes, who lost eight ships of the line and three other ships, were forced to withdraw. This battle marked the end of any real threat to Danish seapower for the remainder of the war.

Knowles, Sir Charles
c. 1704–77

British admiral who served in the Royal Navy during the War of the AUSTRIAN SUCCESSION, 1740–48, and the SEVEN YEARS' WAR, 1756–63. Although Knowles reached the rank of admiral by 1758, his career had suffered because of his mixed reputation. In 1748, during the War of the Austrian Succession, he was court-martialed for failing to engage a Spanish squadron in the West Indies. He was reprimanded as a result.

A year earlier he had been promoted to the rank of rear admiral and appointed commander in chief at Jamaica. Knowles retained his link with Jamaica up to the outbreak of the Seven Years' War, when he returned home to England. Appointed vice admiral and second in command under Admiral Sir Edward HAWKE, his involvement in an abortive expedition to Rochefort marked the end of his active naval career in England. However, in 1770 he revived his career when he accepted the offer of an active command in the Russian navy, which was then involved in a war against Turkey, 1768–74.

Koga, Mineichi
1885–1944

Japanese admiral who was appointed commander in chief of the Japanese Combined Fleet in April 1943 on the death of Admiral Isoroku YAMAMOTO. Koga previously had been a vice chief of the naval general staff and also had commanded the Yokusuka Naval Station. Efficient but lacking any real flair, Koga was under constant pressure from American naval forces in 1943–44 as he sought to defend the Pacific Islands from the enemy counteroffensive. With WORLD WAR II, 1939–45, turning against the Japanese, he planned to seize the initiative in a final decisive naval battle, known as Plan Z, against U.S. forces that would be launched from a main base on Hollandia, New Guinea, in 1944. Koga, who was preoccupied with the plan even though its prospects were poor, was killed in an air crash on March 31, 1944 before Plan Z could be executed. The proposed Japanese initiative was finally abandoned when his chief of staff was captured and a copy of the plans was obtained by the Americans. Admiral Soemu TOYODA succeeded Koga as commander in chief of the combined fleet.

Kolchak, Aleksandr
1874–1920

One of Russia's finest naval leaders of WORLD WAR I, 1914–18, Kolchak established his reputation as an explorer on an expedition to the North Pole in 1900 and as the commander of a destroyer during the RUSSO-JAPANESE WAR, 1904–5. During the world war he greatly enhanced his standing as an energetic and resourceful sea captain while in service with the Baltic fleet. Supporting the aggressive strategy of the fleet commander, Admiral Nikolai von ESSEN, against the German navy, he won rapid promotion in a succession of staff and line appointments. In July 1916 he became commander of the Black Sea fleet, with the rank of vice admiral. Kolchak led many successful operations against Turkish and German naval forces, but in the aftermath of the March Revolution, 1917, he was forced to leave his command. When the Bolsheviks seized power in November 1917, Kolchak assumed the leadership of the White forces in Siberia during the Civil War, 1917–22. He enjoyed some initial success against the Reds, but these were soon reversed and, as the war drew to a close, he was captured by the Bolsheviks and executed by firing squad.

Kolombangara, Battle of
July 12–13, 1943

Shortly after the Battle of KULA GULF, July 6, 1943, in the Pacific theater of WORLD WAR II, 1939–45, the opposing American and Japanese navies were to fight again in the same area of the SOLOMON ISLANDS. The battle was a consequence of Japanese efforts to deliver further reinforcements to their garrison at Vilna on Kolombangara Island in four destroyer transports under the command of Rear Admiral Shunji Izaki. They had left Rabaul escorted by a light cruiser and four destroyers. The U.S. Navy soon became aware of their departure and Task Force 18, commanded by Rear Admiral W. T. Ainsworth, was dispatched from Tulagi. Consisting of two cruisers, a light cruiser and ten destroyers, it moved up the Slot (the sheltered strip of water inside the Solomon Islands group)

during the hours of darkness and was deployed off Kula Gulf.

The two forces met off the northwest coast of Kolombangara during the early hours of July 13; during the battle the Japanese once more were able to demonstrate their night-fighting skill and the effectiveness of their LONG LANCE torpedoes. Three American cruisers were hit and a destroyer was sunk. The Japanese light cruiser *Jintsu* was targeted by American radar-controlled guns. She was hit and blew up, taking Rear Admiral Izaki and many of the crew with her. Despite these American successes, the engagement failed in its objective of preventing the transports from reaching Kolombangara.

Komandorski Islands, Battle of the
March 26, 1943

Battle between U.S. and Japanese naval forces in the North Pacific during WORLD WAR II, 1939–45, in which the Americans fought with great skill against a more powerful enemy. In March 1943 a Japanese convoy was taking supplies and reinforcements to Attu, one of the islands in the Aleutian group that had been seized from the Americans earlier in the year. (See ALEUTIAN ISLANDS CAMPAIGN, 1942–43.) Two large transports were accompanied by two heavy cruisers—the *Nachi* and the *Maya*—two light cruisers and four destroyers, under the command of Vice Admiral Hoshiro Hosogaya. At dawn on March 26, an American squadron of lesser strength commanded by Rear Admiral Charles H. McMorris attacked the Japanese south of the Komandorski Islands. The American squadron consisted of two cruisers—the *Salt Lake City* and the *Richmond*—and four destroyers. This prolonged surface action, which lasted some 3½ hours, was fought without support from submarines or aircraft. The gun duel began at some 20,000 yards, or approximately 11⅓ miles (18,300 m), and both the *Salt Lake City* and the *Nachi* were badly damaged. The Japanese commander decided to reduce the range between the opposing squadrons, but a threatened American counteroffensive persuaded him to change his mind. The Japanese, who had already sent their transports away, were forced to withdraw without completing their mission. This engagement marked the end of Japan's attempts to resupply the troops occupying the Aleutians by sea.

Dan van der Vat, *The Pacific Campaign: World War II. The U.S.-Japanese Naval War*, London, 1992.

Kondo, Nobutake
1886–1953

Japanese vice admiral who commanded the Japanese Southern Force at the beginning of WORLD WAR II, 1939–45. During the Battle for Singapore, December 1941,

Kondo sank the British warships—the battle cruiser *Repulse* and the battleship PRINCE OF WALES—of FORCE Z off the Malayan coast. At the Battle of MIDWAY, June 1942, he was commander of the Main Support Force, but he had to abandon his objective of capturing Midway after the main Japanese carrier force was destroyed. Kondo soon transferred his activities to the Solomon Islands, where he played a key role in the struggle for GUADALCANAL, 1942–43. He was instructed to lure the American fleet into a trap, but at the Battle of the Eastern SOLOMON ISLANDS, August 24, 1942, he failed to do so. At the Battle of SANTA CRUZ, October 1942, he provided naval support in the operation to recapture Henderson Field, Guadalcanal. In the naval actions off GUADALCANAL, November 12–15, 1942, Kondo suffered a tactical defeat. In May 1945 he was appointed to the Supreme War Council in Tokyo.

König Class

The last German battleships to be completed before the outbreak of WORLD WAR I, 1914–18, the König class was similar in many respects to the earlier Kaiser class. A major change was in the location of all the turrets on the centerline: They were arranged in superfiring pairs fore and aft, with the fifth between the funnels. The last German warships to be equipped with 12-inch (30-cm) guns, the Königs had a displacement of 25,390 tons, excellent armor protection and a maximum speed of 21 knots. The Königs were 576 feet 6 inches (175.7 m) in length and had a beam of 96 feet 9 inches (29.5 m).

The *König, Grosser Kurfürst, Markgraf* and *Kronprinz* served with Battle Squadron III of the HIGH SEAS FLEET throughout the war. All were present at the Battle of JUTLAND, 1916, with only the *Kronprinz* escaping undamaged. After Jutland, the *Grosser Kurfürst* was torpedoed by a British submarine, in collision with the *Kronprinz* and then damaged by a mine. All the König-class ships surrendered to the British GRAND FLEET in November 1918 and were scuttled at SCAPA FLOW on June 21, 1919.

Königsberg

Notable as the first warship to be sunk by dive-bombing, the *Königsberg* was a German light CRUISER that served in WORLD WAR II, 1939–45. Launched in 1929, the *Königsberg* (and her sister ships the *Karlsruhe* and the *Köln*) were heavily armed but had limited armor protection. The armament of the Königsberg-class ships, which were built under the restrictions imposed by the Treaty of Versailles, 1919, included nine 5.9-inch (15-cm) guns and six 3.5-inch (9-cm) antiaircraft guns. With a displacement of 6,650 tons, they had a maximum speed of 30 knots and could operate at an extended range across the Atlantic.

The *Königsberg* was involved in the invasion of Norway, April 1940. While based at Bergen, British reconnaissance aircraft detected her presence. A group of 15 British Blackburn Skua dive-bombers, based in the Orkney Islands, were ordered to attack the *Königsberg*. Operating at the limit of their range, the Skuas took the German cruiser by surprise. Three 500-pound (227-kg) bombs were sufficient to sink the ship without difficulty. The *Karlsruhe* was also lost during the Norwegian campaign, but the *Köln* was to survive until almost the end of the war.

Kongo

Japanese BATTLE CRUISER, built in Britain by Vickers and completed in 1913. Similar in design to the TIGER, the *Kongo*'s main armament consisted of eight 14-inch (36-cm) guns in twin turrets. Displacing 27,500 tons, she had a maximum speed of 27.5 knots and was operated by a crew of 1,221. There were three other members of the Kongo class—*Hiei, Kirishima* and *Haruna*—all of which were built in Japan using materials shipped from England. All four ships were rebuilt during the 1930s to create fast BATTLESHIPS capable of escorting fleet AIRCRAFT CARRIERS. The changes included a remodeled superstructure, new secondary armament and replacement engines with twice the power of the originals.

The Kongo class saw much action in the Pacific during the WORLD WAR II, 1939–45. The *Kongo* herself fought at the Battle of the PHILIPPINE SEA, 1944, and subsequently at the Battle of LEYTE GULF, 1944. She survived these battles relatively unscathed but, in November 1944, she was torpedoed off Formosa by the U.S. submarine *Sealion*. Her three sister ships had little better fortune: All were lost as a result of enemy action during the war.

Korean War
1950–53

Following Japan's defeat at the end of WORLD WAR II, Korea was partitioned between the Communist north and the non-Communist south. A series of border clashes was followed by Communist forces invading South Korea from the north on June 25, 1950. A United Nations force commanded by General Douglas MacArthur intervened, and their success in pushing back the North Koreans resulted in Communist Chinese involvement in the war. With the balance of power turned in their favor, the Communist forces advanced southward and captured Seoul, the South Korean capital. UN forces counterattacked and were able to push the North Koreans back across the 38th parallel, and the war settled into a bloody stalemate. By the end of the war, in 1953, the UN force had restored the status quo ante.

Naval power made an important but indirect contribution to the war. Neither the North nor South Koreans had significant naval forces at their disposal. American control of the sea was maintained by the U.S. 7th Fleet supported by British, French and other naval units. This naval power was a vital factor in the outcome of the war; without it, providing UN ground forces with the necessary supplies would have been impossible. Moreover, this fleet prevented Communist forces from being resupplied by sea. The U.S. Navy regularly supported land operations with air strikes and heavy shore bombardments (led by the battleship MISSOURI), although its most visible contribution was in mounting AMPHIBIOUS operations. The most important was the INCHON landing, September 15–16, 1950, which saved the South from certain defeat. The navy also successfully evacuated 200,000 UN troops and civilians from the port of Hungnam in December 1950 in the face of Chinese offensive operations. The Korean War emphasized the key role of the navy in conventional warfare and ensured that it did not suffer drastic postwar reductions.

Max Hastings, *The Korean War*, London, 1987.

Krab

Laid down in 1908, the Russian-built *Krab* was the world's first submarine designed to lay mines. The *Krab* had a surface displacement of 560 tons (740 tons submerged) and was 173 feet 10 inches (53 m) in length, with a beam of 14 feet (4.3 m). Operated by a crew of 25, it had a surface speed of 11 knots, which was reduced to 7.5 knots when submerged. It was equipped with 60 mines and four 45-cm (17.7-inch) torpedo tubes. Mines were dropped over the *Krab*'s stern while the vessel was cruising on the surface using a chain-and-sprocket mechanism to carry them through two hatches aft.

Built at Nikolaiev on the Black Sea, the *Krab* took seven years to complete. By the time she appeared the German navy already had produced the first examples of its own UC-class minelaying submarines, and the *Krab* was no longer the revolutionary concept it had once seemed. The Russian submarine operated in the Black Sea during WORLD WAR I, 1914–18, laying mines off the Turkish coast. Her victims included a Turkish TORPEDO-BOAT and a German U-BOAT. In 1919 the *Krab* was captured by British forces during the Russian Civil War, 1917–22, and scuttled to prevent her falling into Bolshevik hands. In 1935 she was raised and scrapped.

Kretschmer, Otto

b. 1912

The leading German SUBMARINE commander of WORLD WAR II, 1939–45, Kretschmer sank over 350,000 tons of Allied shipping between 1939 and 1941. His success is attributable to his own distinctive style of attack, which involved firing his torpedoes at very short range, often moving his U-BOAT inside the surface escort. He usually operated at night and on the surface. Kretschmer's good fortune came to an end during a CONVOY battle in the Atlantic that extended over three days, March 15–17, 1941. Operating in *U-99*, he destroyed five enemy ships before his own boat was sunk by a British destroyer. Kretschmer and most of his crew were taken prisoner and spent the rest of the war in captivity.

Kronstadt Rebellion

1921

Kronstadt, a Russian Baltic naval base founded by Peter the Great in 1710 on the island of Kotlin in the Gulf of Finland, was the scene of two naval mutinies (see MUTINY) during the period of the Russian Revolution and Civil War, 1917–22. During the October Revolution, 1917, the Kronstadt base was the first to rise in support of the Bolsheviks. Soviets (workers' councils) were established on every warship as the officers' authority disappeared. In March 1921 the sailors of Kronstadt mutinied again, seizing the fortress and two warships. On this occasion the source of their discontent was the economic impact of Lenin's Bolshevik policy of "war communism." The mutineers demanded political and economic reforms and established a revolutionary commune. Red Army intervention led to heavy casualties. Following a lengthy bombardment of the base, the army made a successful night attack that finally brought the mutiny to an end. Later that same month the tenth Congress of the Communist Party adopted Lenin's New Economic Policy, which ameliorated some of the worst effects of war communism.

Kula Gulf, Battle of

July 6, 1943

A night action between American and Japanese naval forces during the SOLOMON ISLANDS campaign in WORLD WAR II, 1939–45. The action was triggered by a Japanese attempt to reinforce its garrison at Vila on the island of Kolombangara, which is separated from New Britain by Kula Gulf. (See Battle of KOLOMBANGARA.) During the night of July 5–6 a Japanese naval squadron consisting of three destroyers, commanded by Rear Admiral Teruo Akiyama, escorted seven destroyer transports toward Kolombangara. The U.S. Navy learned of the Japanese plan and deployed an interception force across the mouth of Kula Gulf. Commanded by Rear Admiral W. L. Ainsworth, it consisted of three cruisers and four destroyers. The Americans opened fire shortly before 1 A.M. on July

6. The *Nitzuki* was quickly sunk taking Admiral Akiyama down with her. However, the *Suzukaze* and the *Tanikaze* replied with their deadly LONG LANCE torpedoes. Sixteen were fired and their main target, the *Helena*, was sunk. Despite this American challenge, the Japanese were able to complete the reinforcement operation successfully before returning to base. They were forced to abandon the destroyer *Nagatsuki* when she ran aground on Kolombangara; she was destroyed by American aircraft. The Japanese lost 300 men and two ships; the Americans lost 168 men and one warship. This action was soon followed by the Battle of Kolombangara, July 12–13, 1943.

Kurita, Takeo
1889–1977

*J*apanese vice admiral who commanded the Close Support Force at the Battle of MIDWAY, June 1942, where he lost half his strength to American naval air power. At the Battle of LEYTE GULF, October 1944, he was commander of the First Striking Force, which included the battleships *YAMATO* and *Musashi*. His objective was to attack the 7th U.S. Fleet, commanded by Rear Admiral Thomas KINCAID, which was covering the American landings. Enemy action delayed Kurita's arrival at Leyte Gulf.

On October 23 two American submarines sank two of Kurita's heavy cruisers; on the following day he lost the battleship *Musashi* during an attack by aircraft from Task Force 38, commanded by Vice Admiral Marc MITSCHER. Arriving on October 25, some six hours late, Kurita surprised the American transports and their escorts. Four American warships were sunk but Kurita did not press home his advantage. Convinced that a trap had been set, he withdrew before attacking the transports. This turned out to be the last time during the war that the Japanese seriously challenged American naval power.

Kusaka, Ryunosuke
1893–1971

*J*apanese vice admiral and aircraft carrier specialist who was involved in the planning of key naval operations in the Pacific during WORLD WAR II, 1939–45. As chief of staff to Vice Admiral Chuichi NAGUMO, he played a key role in developing plans for the suprise attack on PEARL HARBOR, December 1941, and later at the Battle of MIDWAY, June 3–6, 1942. In 1944 Kusaka served as chief of staff to Admiral Soemu TOYODA who was commander of the Combined Fleet. Kusaka sought to give effect to Toyoda's aim of bringing the Americans to a decisive naval battle that would change the course of the war.

Kuznetsov, Nikolai G.
1902–74

*R*ussian admiral who was Chief of Naval Forces throughout WORLD WAR II, 1939–45. Appointed in 1939, a beneficiary of Joseph Stalin's prewar purges, Kuznetsov had a planning rather than an operational role and contributed to general strategy by means of his membership of *Stavka* (the High Command). The SOVIET NAVY's wartime contribution was relatively small, but Kuznetsov was able to persuade Stalin to equip the navy with an air arm. Involved in strategic planning meetings throughout the war, Kuznetsov attended the conferences at Potsdam and Yalta in 1945. He later was demoted as part of Stalin's postwar purge but was reinstated by Leonid Brezhnev.

La Bourdonnais, Bertrand François, Comte Mahé de
1699–1753

French naval commander, born in St. Malo. Beginning his career at sea in the service of the French East India Company, he distinguished himself at an early stage when, in 1723, he played a leading part in the capture of Mahé on the Malabar coast. After a brief period in Portuguese service, he was appointed governor of Madagascar and Mauritius in 1734. As the War of the AUSTRIAN SUCCESSION, 1740–48, began, La Bourdonnais returned to France and was given another sea command. His new fleet was ordered to India, where he scored several successes against the British. He prevented Mahé and Pondicherry from falling into enemy hands and, in 1746, blockaded and captured Madras. The English, anxious to recover the city, paid La Bourdonnais 9 million *livres* to relinquish control. His acceptance of this bribe led to a serious dispute with Joseph Dupleix, governor-general of the French Indies, with accusations and counteraccusations being made. On his return to Madagascar, he found that Dupleix had replaced him as governor. When he finally arrived in France, he was accused of failures in administration; after spending two years in prison awaiting trial, eventually he was acquitted.

La Galissonnière, Roland-Michel, Marquis de la
1693–1756

French admiral, the son of a naval lieutenant general. He studied at the College of Beauvais in Paris. In 1710 he entered the French navy as a midshipman and, in 1711, served on a ship taking supplies to Canada. This was the beginning of his long association with North America, which included a term as Governor of Canada (commandant-general of New France), 1747–49. Following active naval service in the West Indies, 1734–35, he was pro-

moted to the rank of post-captain. Regular advancement to the rank of commodore and then of rear admiral followed. In 1754 he commanded a squadron operating against Barbary pirates (see CORSAIRS) in the Mediterranean, where they posed a significant threat to French merchant shipping. In 1756, during the SEVEN YEARS' WAR, 1756–63, La Galissonnière commanded a French fleet with orders to land troops on the British-held island of MINORCA. He fought an inconclusive engagement against Admiral John BYNG, who failed to take any subsequent action against the French. As a result they had soon seized control of the island. La Galissonnière took no further part in the war and died soon afterward.

La Hogue, Battle of
May 22–24, 1692

Following the Battle of BARFLEUR, May 19, 1692, the second major naval engagement of the War of the GRAND ALLIANCE, 1688–97, the French fleet under Admiral the Comte de TOURVILLE withdrew toward the Channel Islands. In close pursuit of the 44 enemy ships of the line was the much more powerful Anglo-Dutch fleet of 96 warships commanded by Admiral Edward RUSSELL (later Earl of Orford). During a three-day chase some French ships managed to break away and return safely to their base at BREST. A further 22 French warships made for St. Malo, but the remainder—15 ships of the line—were unable to escape from the immediate area because they were swept eastward by the flood tide.

The French warships anchored in Cherbourg Bay off the northern coast of the Cotentin Peninsula where, on May 22, the English found them. Admiral Sir Ralph DELAVALL, leader of the English Red Squadron, attacked and sank three large enemy warships—the *Soleil Royal* (Tourville's flagship), *Admirable* and *Triomphant*. The remnants of the French force—12 warships—withdrew into the Baie de la Hogue, where the transports for JAMES's invasion of England where being prepared. Vice Admiral George ROOKE, leader of the Blue Squadron, was given responsibility for their destruction. During the night of May 23–24 all the surviving warships and many of the transports were destroyed by Anglo-Dutch FIRESHIPS. The allied victories against the French at Barfleur and La Hogue were major turning points in the War of the Grand Alliance.

P. Aubrey, *The Defeat of James Stuart's Armada, 1692*, Leicester, 1979.

Lagos, Battle of
August 18–19, 1759

A notable British naval victory against the French during the SEVEN YEARS' WAR, 1756–63. On August 16, 1759 Admiral Edward BOSCAWEN, British commander in the Mediterranean, whose fleet was undergoing a refit in GIBRALTAR, learned of the departure of a French squadron from Toulon. Under the command of Admiral de la CLUE SABRAN, who was not aware of the English presence, it consisted of ten ships of the line and five other warships. It was bound for the French port of BREST, where it was to join the main French fleet with the aim of mounting an invasion of England and Scotland. Boscawen's force of 15 ships of the line and several accompanying frigates left Gibraltar and turned west in pursuit of the enemy. By the time the French were sighted off the Portuguese coast on August 18, their numbers had been reduced by the departure of all but seven ships for the Spanish port of Cadiz.

The five-hour battle, which began in the early afternoon, resulted in the capture of a French 74-gun ship and in severe damage to Boscawen's flagship, the *Namur*. Operating from the *Newark*, Boscawen pursued the enemy during the night. Two French ships managed to escape, but the remaining six were driven into Lagos Bay, near the southwest tip of Portugal. On the following day two more French ships were captured, and two others, including the French flagship, the *Ocean*, were wrecked. The French commander was severely wounded and later died of his wounds at Lagos. The British had destroyed five French ships and had achieved a decisive tactical success.

Lake Champlain, Battle of
October 11–13, 1776

Toward the end of 1775, during the early stages of the AMERICAN WAR OF INDEPENDENCE, 1775–83, an American-led attack on British-held Quebec had ended in failure. By mid-1776 the Americans, who were commanded by Benedict ARNOLD, were forced to retreat to Lake Champlain where, in October, they were to fight two naval battles against the British. A small FLOTILLA had been assembled on this lake on George Washington's instructions, but Arnold spent the next four months constructing much-needed additional vessels. Despite these efforts, Arnold's force of 15 boats did not compare favorably with a British flotilla of 25 vessels commanded by Commodore Pringle, who attacked on October 11, 1776. The Americans were heavily defeated off Valcour Island and were forced to withdraw southward with the British in close pursuit. Two days later they suffered further heavy losses and were forced to beach the *Congress*, their flagship. Only four American boats managed to escape to Ticonderoga. Despite their clear tactical defeat, the American strategic objective—to delay a British invasion from Canada toward New York—had been achieved. It was now too late in the year for the British to mount a new offensive to the south.

Lake Champlain, Battle of
September 11, 1814

A decisive battle fought by the inland navies of the United States and Britain during the WAR OF 1812, 1812–15. In September 1814, as 11,000 British troops under Sir George Prevost advanced from Montreal, Canada toward the American town of Plattsburg (on Lake Champlain, in northern New York State), a parallel movement was made across Lake Champlain. A British FLOTILLA, under the command of Captain George Downie, was dispatched with the objective of engaging the American ships, led by Lieutenant Thomas MACDONOUGH, that were defending Plattsburg from the lake. The two sides were almost equally balanced, with four ships and 12 galleys each, although the Americans had a larger number of long guns. As the British land attack began, the Americans opened fire on Downie's flotilla as it approached the narrow channel where they were deployed.

During a two-hour battle, both sides sustained heavy losses, although the British ships suffered the greatest damage. In the closing stages of the battle the American flagship *Saratoga* turned at its anchorage to renew the attack on the *Confiance*, Downie's flagship, which soon struck its flag. Increasing destruction eventually compelled the entire British flotilla to surrender, leaving the Americans in control of the lake. There were some 300 British casualties, including Downie, who was killed early in the battle. American casualties of 200 were also high. At this point Prevost, who was making better progress on land, decided to abandon the invasion attempt and withdraw his forces to the north. This failure marked the end of the British threat to the United States from the north and was a positive influence at the Ghent Peace Conference, which was soon to agree to terms for ending the war.

Lake Erie, Battle of

September 10, 1813

A key battle between British and American naval forces as they fought for supremacy on Lake Erie during the WAR OF 1812, 1812–15. When the war began, the Americans had no naval capability on any of the Great Lakes, including Lake Erie, but this deficiency was soon rectified. Within a year two BRIGS, six schooners and a SLOOP had been constructed and were placed under the command of Captain Oliver Hazard PERRY. The British squadron, which also had been built on the lake, consisted of two ships, two brigs, a schooner and a sloop. It was commanded by Captain Robert Barclay who, at noon on September 10, 1813, moved against the American FLOTILLA near Bass Islands with the aim of maintaining Britain's dominant position on the lake.

Perry's FLAGSHIP, the *Lawrence*, a 20-gun ship, left its anchorage to meet the British force as it moved closer. It advanced ahead of the other American ships and was subject to the full force of British fire. The *Lawrence* was badly damaged, and Perry was forced to transfer by rowboat to the *Niagara*, which was undamaged. It was this ship that broke the British line and put three ships out of action, including the *Detroit*, Barclay's flagship. The remaining American vessels closed in, and after three hours the action came to an end. The entire British flotilla had been either destroyed or surrendered, and some 130 casualties had been sustained. This defeat strengthened the American position across the whole northeast and was to lead to the eventual withdrawal of British forces from Detroit.

Landing Craft

B oats used to land troops directly onto a beach during an attack or invasion from the sea. The large-scale production of specialist ships for use in AMPHIBIOUS landings against defended positions first occurred in WORLD WAR II, 1939–45, although the first specially-built landing craft appeared as early as the mid-18th century. These were English-designed flat-bottomed boats with ramps similar to models in use for over 100 years. Landing craft were often adaptations of other vessels; it was not until World War II that the scale of amphibious operations in Europe and the Pacific necessitated the development of a wide range of specialist types. Indeed, landing craft were to play a crucial role in many wartime operations, including North Africa, NORMANDY and the island-hopping campaigns in the Pacific. The first example widely in use from the beginning of the war—the Landing Ship Infantry (LSI)—was normally a conversion, typically based on a ferry. The Landing Ship Mechanized (LSM), a modified lighter, was used to deliver vehicles and supplies.

The first specially designed landing craft to be built in large numbers was the Landing Craft Personnel (LCP), constructed of wood, with a displacement of just under 5 tons and the ability to carry 20 troops. The Landing Craft Assault (LCA), which had a displacement of 12.8 tons, had a maximum speed of 10 knots. The much larger Landing Ship Infantry (LSI) of 378 tons could carry some 200 men. It was equipped with its own smaller landing craft that made the final stage of the approach to the beach. Tanks required their own landing craft, in the form

Landing craft in action on D-Day, Normandy, June 6, 1944   *(Copyright © National Maritime Museum, Greenwich, London)*

of the Landing Ship Tank (LST). When the LSTs arrived in the landing area, their cargo would be transferred individually to the smaller Landing Craft Tank (LCT), which were used at the heart of an amphibious operation. However, they were only partially armored; the development of amphibious tanks enabled them to keep well offshore. Other specialist types of the World War II period included, for example, Landing Ship Headquarters, Landing Craft Rocket and Landing Ship Dock.

In the postwar period, the design of landing craft has continued to evolve but amphibious vehicles, the HELICOPTER, the HOVERCRAFT and short-takeoff aircraft have tended to reduce the importance of specialist ships in present-day amphibious operations.

Langley, U.S.S.

The first American aircraft carrier, the *Langley* was converted from the fleet oiler U.S.S. *Jupiter,* which had been launched in 1912. The conversion, which involved dismantling the collier's superstructure, was completed early in 1922. A flush flight deck of 534 feet (162.8 m) was constructed over the upper deck, which gave access to the four holds where the aircraft were stored. Up to 33 aircraft could be accommodated. There were command positions at the side of the flight deck. The conversion did not provide for an island superstructure.

Named after the American aircraft pioneer Samuel Langley, the U.S.S. *Langley* had a displacement of 11,500 tons, a low maximum speed of 14 knots and was operated by a crew of 550 men. She was to be the United States Navy's only carrier for five years, until the LEXINGTON and the SARATOGA joined the fleet. In 1936 she was converted again and emerged as a seaplane carrier. The *Langley* served during WORLD WAR II, 1939–45, as an aircraft transport and was sunk off Java by Japanese aircraft in February 1942.

Launch

The main auxiliary boat of a warship in the age of the sailing navies. Replacing the smaller longboat, the launch typically had two masts and up to 16 oarsmen, although there were many different variants. The launch normally was stored near the pinnace (a smaller ship's boat) on the upper deck between the foremast and the mainmast. It was used primarily for taking officers and crew back and forth from shore when the ship was anchored in a harbor, for transporting supplies of fresh water and for carrying heaving anchors. The launch sometimes was used as a LANDING CRAFT and could be fitted with a small gun for defensive purposes. During the 19th century, relatively large steam- and motor-powered versions were developed;

in this form the launch was retained as the largest ship's boat to be carried by a battleship or armored cruiser. When these warships were withdrawn from the world's navies, the launch in this specific form also disappeared, although small auxiliary boats are still carried. In the Mediterranean, the launch was a flat-bottomed sailing gunboat that was widely used by the principal navies of the region during the 18th and 19th centuries.

Lawrence, James
1781–1813

American naval officer. Born in Burlington, New Jersey, Lawrence was commissioned a midshipman in 1798. He served with distinction in the Tripolitan War of 1801–5 and participated in the famous burning of the *Philadelphia* in Tripoli harbor. As commander of the *Hornet* in the WAR OF 1812, he sank the H.M.S. *Peacock* early in 1813. He was then given command of the frigate CHESAPEAKE blockaded by the British in Boston harbor. On June 1, 1813, ignoring orders to remain in port, and with an inexperienced crew, he set out to fight the H.M.S. SHANNON. In some 15 minutes, the *Chesapeake* was defeated with heavy casualties, including Lawrence, who uttered the famous words as he was taken below, mortally wounded: "Don't give up the ship." This motto was inscribed on a flag to inspire the American forces under the command of his friend, Oliver Hazard PERRY, at the decisive Battle of LAKE ERIE later in 1813.

Albert Gleaves, *James Lawrence, Captain, United States Navy, Commander of the Chesapeake*, New York, 1904.

Lawson, Sir John
c. 1605–65

British admiral who commanded the fleet that conveyed King Charles II from Holland to England at the time of the Restoration, 1660. Although Lawson supported the return of the monarchy, he had served in the navy of the Protectorate during the First ANGLO-DUTCH WAR, 1652–54. He was present at all the major engagements of the war, and by the time of the Battles of the GABBARD and SCHEVENINGEN in mid-1653 he was a rear admiral in command of the Blue Division. In the Restoration navy he went to the Mediterranean to fight the Algerine pirates before returning to engage the Dutch once more. In the Second Anglo-Dutch War, 1665–67, Lawson commanded the Red Division but died as a result of wounds received during the Battle of LOWESTOFT, June 3, 1665, the first engagement of the war.

Leahy, William Daniel
1875–1959

One of the longest-serving naval officers in American history, Leahy was also one of the most powerful, serving as chairman of the Joint Chiefs of Staff during WORLD WAR II, 1939–45. Born in Hampton, Iowa on May 6, 1875, he entered the navy in 1893. He was on the *Oregon* during her famous record-breaking journey around the Horn in order to participate in the Battle of SANTIAGO, July 1898, during the SPANISH-AMERICAN WAR. Commanding various ships and stations during the 1920s and 1930s, including a term as chief of the Bureau of Ordnance and later chief of the Bureau of Navigation, he served finally as chief of Naval Operations from 1937 to 1939, when he was required to take normal retirement. He remained an active administrator and diplomat, assuming the difficult and delicate position of U.S. ambassador to the Vichy government of France toward the end of 1940.

After the United States entered the war, he was restored to active duty, serving as President Franklin ROOSEVELT's chief of staff and as chairman of the Joint Chiefs of Staff. In this latter capacity he was a regular participant at the Allied conferences and thus a key player in Allied strategy. He received his fifth star (for the rare rank of Admiral of the Fleet) in December 1944. He remained on active duty as adviser to President Harry S Truman during the early years of the COLD WAR and during the difficult period of the unification of the services. He resigned his post in 1949 and died on July 20, 1959.

Henry H. Adams, *Witness to Power: The Life of Fleet Admiral William D. Leahy*, Annapolis, 1985.

Leake, Sir John
1656–1720

British admiral of the fleet and sometime commander in chief in the Mediterranean during the War of the SPANISH SUCCESSION, 1701–14. Appointed to his first command during the War of the GRAND ALLIANCE, 1688–97, Leake was present at the actions in BANTRY BAY and at LONDONDERRY in 1689. He commanded the *Eagle* at the Battle of BARFLEUR, 1692. Following a brief interlude as governor and commander in chief in Newfoundland, Leake served in the Mediterranean for much of the War of the Spanish Succession. He also was involved in the capture and subsequent defense of GIBRALTAR, 1704. Starting in 1708 he enjoyed a successful tenure as Sir Clowdisley SHOVELL's successor as commander in chief in the Mediterranean. Leake's achievements included the capture of Sardinia and Minorca during his first year in office. At the end of his appointment, he became a Lord of the ADMIRALTY.

Leghorn, Battle of
March 13, 1653

In the mid-17th century, England and Holland both maintained squadrons in the Mediterranean to protect their merchant shipping from Barbary pirates. It was inevitable that these forces would be drawn into the First ANGLO-DUTCH WAR, 1652–54, which was decided in northern waters. Part of the English Mediterranean squadron met the Dutch off ELBA on August 28, 1652. The English were defeated and then blockaded by the Dutch in Elba and Leghorn (present-day Livorno, on Italy's Tuscany coast). After some six months, on March 13, 1653, the Dutch succeeded in their aim of encouraging the English to leave the safety of their anchorage at Leghorn. In the engagement that followed, one English ship was destroyed and four others were captured, along with English commander himself. Only one English ship managed to escape to join the remainder of the squadron, which had left Elba too late to alter the outcome of the Battle of Leghorn.

Lend-Lease Agreement
1941

In the period shortly before the United States entered WORLD WAR II, 1939–45, the U.S. government instituted a major program of international military aid known as Lend-Lease. Primarily designed to provide much-needed support to beleaguered Britain, which was running short of cash to pay for war materials, it was later extended to other American allies. The Lend-Lease Act, which was authorized by Congress on March 11, 1941, permitted the U.S. President to lend or lease equipment to any country "whose defense the President deems vital to the defense of the United States." Payment could be made in "kind or property," although in practice much of the equipment was transferred without payment. As a result of this initiative, the United States supplied warships and other military equipment to Britain and later to the Soviet Union and China. As a major supplier of military equipment to its wartime allies, the United States was to enjoy a greater role in strategic decision making once it entered the war than it might otherwise have had. The Lend-Lease program was brought to an end at the conclusion of World War II. The total value of the aid given was $49 billion.

Lepanto, Battle of
October 7, 1571

A decisive naval engagement between the Ottoman Turks and the Christian Holy League, an alliance of Spain, Venice, Genoa and the Papal States in the Gulf of

The Battle of Lepanto, 1571: the decisive engagement between Christian forces and the Turks, which ended the latter's dominance in the eastern Mediterranean *(Copyright © National Maritime Museum, Greenwich, London)*

Corinth. The battle had its origins in the Turkish attack on Cyprus, which was then under Venetian rule, in the spring of 1570. A Venetian-led counterattack in the autumn was ineffective, and not until the following year did the Christians assemble an effective fighting force. Under the joint leadership of the papacy and Venice, some 300 ships and 50,000 men were earmarked for the operation. The fleet as actually assembled at Messina during August and September 1571 included more than 200 GALLEYS and over 75,000 men from many different nations, including Venice, Naples, Genoa and Sicily. DON JUAN of Austria was appointed as supreme commander. The Christian fleet left Messina on September 16 and arrived off the Curzolari Islands, some 36 miles (58 km) from Lepanto, three weeks later.

The Turkish fleet, commanded by Ali Pasha, had arrived at Lepanto on September 26. His force, which closely matched that of his opponents, consisted of 273 galleys, 40 GALIOTS and 20 other craft. It was operated by some 75,000 men, half of whom were rowers. On October 6 the Turks left Lepanto harbor and moved westward to meet the Christian fleet. Andrea DORIA, who commanded the Spanish on the Allied right, sighted the enemy early the following day south of Cape Scropha, near the Gulf of Patras. They approached each other in crescent-shape formations. Ali Pasha, in command of the center, was supported by Mahomet Scirocco and Uluch Ali on the right and left respectively. Don Juan formed the Christian forces into a line of battle that ran from left to right: the Venetians (Agostino Barbarigo); the center (Don Juan, Colonnia and Sebastiano Veniero); the reserve (Alvaro de BAZAN, Marquis of Santa Cruz); and the Spanish (Doria).

The first shots were fired from Venetian galiots at about 10 A.M., and the battle initially developed on the Turkish right. The Turks made little impact on the Christian left, and Barbarigo's squadron soon gained the upper hand, although Barbarigo himself was killed. Action flared in the center with fighting at close quarters. The Christian center soon ran into great difficulty and was saved only by the intervention of the reserve commanded by the Marquis of Santa Cruz. Don Juan eventually gained the upper hand, and, as a result, the Turkish FLAGSHIP was captured and

Ali Pasha, the Turkish commander, was killed. The Turks made more progress on their left, but Andrea Doria soon regained the lost ground in an effective counterattack.

With Ali Pasha's death, the Turkish fleet rapidly disintegrated and soon fled the battle area. The Turkish right, under the command of Uluch Ali, skillfully extricated itself with minimal losses, but elsewhere the cost of defeat was high. Don Juan had defeated the Turks and seized 170 ships and 7,000 prisoners. Many more Turks had been killed. The battle marked the end of Turkish naval dominance in the eastern Mediterranean and was notable as the last major engagement ever in which galleys manned by oarsmen were deployed.

Beeching, Jack, *The Galleys at Lepanto*, London, 1982

Lestock, Richard
c. 1679–1746

*B*ritish admiral who came to prominence during the War of the AUSTRIAN SUCCESSION, 1740–48, following service at the Battle of CAPE PASSARO, August 11, 1718, and in the West Indies. During this period he was serving as a rear admiral in the Mediterranean under Vice Admiral Thomas MATHEWS, the commander in chief, with whom his relations were strained. Matters came to a head on February 11, 1744 when Mathews fought a Franco-Spanish fleet off TOULON. The English commander in chief was unable to engage the enemy in accordance with the rigid provisions of the official *FIGHTING INSTRUCTIONS*, which required that the two sides fought van to van, center to center and rear to rear. Unable to form a regulation line, Mathews ordered his van to attack the French center. Lestock, who commanded the rear division, was not well positioned to engage the enemy and did not do so.

After the battle, Lestock was sent home to face a court-martial for failing to do his utmost to attack the enemy. Lestock was acquitted because he had obeyed the letter of the *Fighting Instructions* rather than the orders of his commander in chief, an outcome that tended to reinforce the natural conservatism of the Royal Navy. Mathews himself then faced trial for not conforming to the official instructions and was found guilty. Lestock returned to sea after the trial and was promoted to the rank of admiral.

Letter of Marque

*A*n official license, issued by most maritime nations during the age of the sailing navies, that gave a measure of protection to PRIVATEERS who operated against enemy merchant ships in wartime. The state provided privateer's with the legal backing that distinguished them from pirates. In practice, however, privateers might not necessarily restrict their activities to enemy ships, and in these circumstances there might be little or nothing to distinguish them from pirates. Like that of the pirate, the privateer's motive was solely financial gain; but in order to secure a degree of official endorsement, they had to agree to give a share to the government.

This latter element was to die out during the 18th and 19th centuries as the state abandoned its claim, increasing privateers' already large earnings potential. From the government's point of view, however, the letter of marque provided a cheap and useful way to supplement the naval resources of the state, and the basic elements of this arrangement remained in place from the 13th to the 19th centuries. The granting of letters of marque was finally abolished at the Convention of Paris, 1856, which ended the whole practice of privateering. The last major occasion when the system was still fully operational occurred during the FRENCH REVOLUTIONARY AND NAPOLEONIC WARS, 1792–1815, and WAR OF 1812, when several thousand letters of marque were issued by the British, French and American governments alike.

Lexington, U.S.S.

*T*he name *Lexington* has been given to several ships of the UNITED STATES NAVY; the two most notable of these were both AIRCRAFT CARRIERS that saw important action in the Pacific during WORLD WAR II, 1939–45. The first aircraft carrier *Lexington* was laid down as a BATTLE CRUISER soon after the end of WORLD WAR I, 1914–18. As a consequence of the provisions of the Washington Treaty, 1922 (see WASHINGTON CONFERENCE), the *Lexington* and the *SARATOGA*, her sister ship, could not be completed in their original form and they were converted into aircraft carriers.

The *Lexington*, which was known as *Lady Lex*, had a displacement of 33,000 tons, a maximum speed of over 34 knots and a flight deck that was over 900 feet (274.32 m) in length. She could carry 90 planes, had a crew of about 3,000 and was armed with eight 8-inch (20-cm) guns. At the time of their completion in 1927, the *Lexington* and the *Saratoga* were larger and faster than any other carriers in service at the time. The *Lexington* played an important role in operations in the Pacific during the initial stages of World War II and contributed to the development of carrier tactics, but her operational career was brought to a premature end on the second day of the Battle of the CORAL SEA, May 8, 1942. The FLAGSHIP of Task Force 11, the *Lexington* was attacked by Japanese bombers. She was devastated by fire, and an American destroyer subsequently torpedoed the wreck.

The name *Lexington* was given to a later American carrier that entered service in February 1943. She was one of the Essex class and won 11 battle stars in operations in the Pacific. Several other ships named *Lexington* have served in the U.S. Navy, the first being a brigantine that was acquired by Congress during the AMERICAN WAR OF INDEPENDENCE, 1775–83.

Leyte Gulf, Battle of
October 23–26, 1944

The final engagement between the American and Japanese surface fleets during WORLD WAR II, 1939–45, the Battle of Leyte Gulf was one of the great battles of naval history. It was triggered by the U.S. invasion of the Philippines, which the Japanese were determined to retain because it provided ready access to much-needed raw materials. The American landings at Leyte Gulf began on October 20, 1944 following the seizure of three islands at the entrance to the gulf three days earlier. The American Sixth Army, whose 200,000 troops were commanded by General Walter Kreuger, was brought to Leyte Gulf by the Seventh Fleet under Admiral Thomas KINCAID. Together with the Third Fleet, commanded by Admiral William HALSEY, it provided air cover for land operations on Leyte and had as many as 1,000 aircraft at its disposal.

The Japanese responded by assembling all their remaining naval units for a final battle with the Americans. Admiral Soemu TOYODA, the commander in chief, dispatched three separate fleets to the Philippines. The Northern Force, commanded by Admiral Jisaburo OZAWA, came from Japan. It included four carriers, two battleships, three cruisers and eight destroyers. Ozawa's orders were to approach the Philippines from the north and lure the American Third Fleet away from Leyte. This would enable two other Japanese naval groups to attack from the west. The Center Force, commanded by Vice Admiral Takeo KURITA, consisted of five battleships, ten heavy cruisers, two light cruisers and 15 destroyers. It would cross the Sibuyan Sea and the San Bernardino Strait and enter Leyte Gulf from the north. The Southern Force would approach from the south, having crossed the Sulu and Mindanao Seas. Its two divisions, commanded by Vice Admiral S. Nishimura and Vice Admiral K. Shima, included two battleships, four cruisers and eight destroyers.

Aerial view of the Japanese battleship *Musashi*, which was destroyed by American bombers during the Battle of Leyte Gulf, October 1944, the largest engagement in the history of naval warfare *(Copyright © Imperial War Museum, London)*

Due to arrive off Leyte in the early hours of October 25, these Japanese naval forces were attacked far from their planned destination. On October 23, Kurita's Center Force was attacked off Palawan by two American submarines, the *Darter* and the *Dace*, which sank two heavy cruisers and damaged a third that had to return to Singapore, where it was based. On the following day Vice Admiral Kurita, who was now in the Sibuyan Sea, was attacked by bombers from the Third Fleet carriers. The giant 64,000-ton battleship *Musashi* was sunk and two other capital ships were damaged. Kurita, who was without air cover, decided to withdraw temporarily. He would move toward Leyte only at night, when there was firm news of the progress of Vice Admiral Ozawa's Northern Force. Meanwhile, the Americans were increasingly aware of the apparent threat posed by Ozawa, who had been responsible for the destruction of the light carrier *Princeton*.

With the threat from Kurita evidently receding, Admiral Halsey decided to head north to engage Ozawa, leaving the San Bernardino Strait completely undefended. It was an action for which he later was heavily criticized. To the south, the Japanese Southern Force was approaching Leyte Gulf; and the American Seventh Fleet prepared to engage the enemy at the Surigao Straits. In the early hours of October 25, Rear Admiral Oldendorf, who commanded six battleships, eight cruisers and other lesser warships of the Seventh Fleet Support Force, ambushed Nishimura's Southern Force as it left the Surigao Strait, with devastating results. The battleship *Fuso* and three destroyers were sunk by American torpedoes in the first phase of the battle. The battleship *Yamashiro* was severely damaged and later sank after being torpedoed, taking Nishimura with her. The heavy cruiser *Mogami* withdrew and was able to warn Admiral Shima, commander of the rear division of the Southern Force, who was some 30 miles (55 km) behind, of the impending danger. He was able to reverse course before coming in range of Rear Admiral Oldendorf.

On the same day, October 25, Kurita's Center Force passed through the San Bernardino Strait without encountering the Americans. Kurita headed southeast for Leyte Gulf, passing the east coast of Samar Island, where he encountered a force of American escort carriers and destroyers under the command of Rear Admiral Clifton Sprague. During the three-hour Battle of Samar, the much stronger Japanese force sunk an escort carrier and three destroyers, but Kurita never capitalized on his advantageous position. He reversed course and reentered San Bernardino Strait. The reasons for his action remain obscure, but it is possible that he was unsure of the position of Halsey's carriers, which posed a considerable potential threat to him.

Halsey was in fact some 400 miles (644 km) to the north, where he engaged and defeated Ozawa's Northern Force off Cape Engano, the northeast point of Luzon, on

October 25. Before returning to San Bernardino Strait in search of Vice Admiral Kurita, who already had passed back through the straits, he sank four aircraft carriers and a light cruiser. Ozawa had acted as an effective decoy, but with the key Center Force already having decided to withdraw, it was a futile action.

This major Japanese defeat marked the effective end of Japanese naval power and sealed the fate of the Philippines. Their total losses amounted to three battleships, four carriers, ten cruisers, 11 destroyers and one submarine. Most of the surviving ships had been badly damaged, and 500 aircraft had been lost. There were 10,500 Japanese casualties. American losses consisted of three light carriers, two destroyers, one destroyer escort and about 200 aircraft.

St. L. Falk, *Decision at Leyte*, New York, 1966.

Liberty, U.S.S.

A name associated with the early naval history of the United States, the *Liberty* was originally a British-owned schooner that was operated on Lake Champlain. Seized in May 1775 during the AMERICAN WAR OF INDEPENDENCE, 1775–83, her captors appropriately renamed her the *Liberty*. She was used to facilitate the seizure of a second British ship at Fort Ticonderoga. These two vessels gave the Americans control of the entire lake and were used in support of land operations during the invasion of Canada. The *Liberty*, armed with four 4-pounders and four 2-pounders, survived a renewed British offensive but was lost during General Burgoyne's march south in 1776.

A more recent U.S.S. *Liberty* was the 7,725-ton technical research ship, completed in May 1945. Originally launched as the *Simmons Victory*, she was not renamed until 1963. Equipped with sophisticated surveillance and communications technology, she was stationed off Sinai in the eastern Mediterranean during the Arab-Israeli War, 1967. During this brief conflict, the *Liberty* was severely damaged when she was attacked first by Israeli fighter aircraft and then by three motor torpedo boats; 34 crewmen were killed. Despite her difficult predicament, the *Liberty* managed to withdraw without further incident. The Israelis later claimed that their action was a case of mistaken identity.

Liberty Ships

Mass-produced merchant ships constructed in various American shipyards during WORLD WAR II, 1939–45. A total of 2,770 Liberty ships were built as replacements for the tonnage sunk by the Axis powers, particularly during the Battle of the ATLANTIC, 1939–45. These prefabricated ships, which were based on an original British design dating back to 1879, could be built in less than five days. With a length of 441 feet 6 inches (134.5 m) and a beam of 56 feet 10 inches (17.3 m), they had a displacement of 10,500 tons deadweight and a maximum speed of 11 knots. Because every single turbine and diesel engine produced in the United States at the time was required for combat use, power was provided by triple-expansion steam engines.

Although most Liberty ships were used as general cargo carriers, some had a direct naval or military use. For example, they were used to transport aircraft and tanks, for supply purposes or as troop transports. They were widely used to resupply the American fleet operating in the Pacific. Some 200 Liberty ships were lost before the end of the war, but they had made an invaluable contribution to the Allied war effort.

L. Sawyer and W. Mitchell, *The Liberty Ships*, Newton Abbot, Devon, England, 1970.

Lightning

*B*uilt for the ROYAL NAVY in 1876, the *Lightning* was the first naval vessel that was equipped to fire a self-propelled TORPEDO. This fast steam launch had a maximum speed of 19 knots and a displacement of 34 tons; she was 75 feet (22.86 m) in length. Soon to be renamed *Torpedo Boat No. 1*, she had been built to carry a SPAR TORPEDO, an explosive charge that was fixed to a long pole over the bows and detonated by a contact pistol.

The spar torpedo was soon superseded by the locomotive torpedo, produced by Robert Whitehead, and, in 1879, the *Lightning* was adapted to use the more efficient weapon. She was fitted with two bow torpedo tubes above the waterline, which meant that they could be launched while the warship was in motion. Once the success of this modified TORPEDO BOAT had been demonstrated, others quickly followed, ordered by the Royal Navy and several other major fleets.

Lind, James
1716–94

*B*ritish naval surgeon who was responsible for major advances in hygiene at sea during the 18th century. Born in Edinburgh, Lind joined the Royal Navy in 1739 and qualified as a physician in 1748. His main contribution to the development of naval medicine was in finding a cure for scurvy, a major cause of death at sea. Lind's pioneering experiments on the human diet resulted in the discovery that the juice of lemons or oranges was effective in preventing the onset of scurvy. Despite Lind's advocacy of this treatment, there was a long delay while bureaucratic inertia was overcome and many more deaths occurred.

It was not until 1795, some 40 years after Lind's findings were first published, that the British ADMIRALTY issued an order on the supply of lemon juice to the navy. It proved effective in eradicating scurvy, a costly disease. Lind spent most of his naval career at the Haslar Naval Hospital, Portsmouth, where he was appointed surgeon in 1758. He continued his pioneering work, producing two more publications, including the first textbook on tropical medicine. Lind was succeeded by his son at Haslar Hospital in 1783.

Lion, H.M.S.

*A*lthough the name *Lion* has been used frequently by the ROYAL NAVY since the 16th century, it is associated most often with the WORLD WAR I, 1914–18, BATTLE CRUISER that joined the First Battle Cruiser Squadron as Admiral David BEATTY's flagship in 1913. The *Lion* and her sister ships the *Princess Royal* and the *Queen Mary*, the battle cruiser equivalents of the Orion-class super-dreadnoughts, were known as the "splendid cats" because of their speed and fine appearance.

Their maximum speed of 27 knots was significantly faster than that of the Orions, and in order to carry the very powerful machinery needed to propel them, they were substantially larger and had a greater displacement. They had a displacement of 26,270 tons, a length of 700 feet (213 m) and a beam of 88 feet 6 inches (27 m). Their eight 13.5-inch (34-cm) guns were housed in four twin turrets on the centerline, while secondary armament—16 4-inch (10-cm) guns—were located in casemates—armored enclosures—that ringed the ship. The arrangement of the main turrets was not particularly efficient, but the principal weakness of the Lion class was the inadequacy of its armor. Partial protection was provided, but the ends and upper decks of the ships were vulnerable to attack. As a result, the vessels of the Lion class are widely considered to be the least satisfactory warships built for the modern Royal Navy.

On the outbreak of World War I, in August 1914, the *Lion* formed part of the British GRAND FLEET and was soon in action at HELIGOLAND BIGHT, August 28, 1914. She was damaged at the DOGGER BANK action, January 1915, but at the Battle of JUTLAND, May 1916, she nearly sank: A shell almost penetrated one of her turrets and burst inside. Only the quick action of one of the crew prevented the magazine from blowing up. The *Princess Royal* also served with the First Battle Cruiser Squadron and fought in the Heligoland and Dogger Bank actions. She was not damaged until Jutland, but after repairs remained in service until the end of the war. The *Queen Mary*, which entered service in 1913, was lost at the Battle of Jutland.

Lissa, Battle of
March 13, 1811

A successful British naval action against a Franco-Venetian squadron in the Adriatic during the Napoleonic Wars, 1803–15. Early in 1811 a British squadron of four FRIGATES, commanded by Captain William HOSTE, was using Lissa Island off the Dalmatian Coast as a base for its operations against the enemy. In response, the French made plans to take the island. In March 1811 a joint Franco-Venetian force of six frigates and five lesser warships left Ancona under the command of Commodore Dubourdieu. The force carried 500 ground troops, who had orders to occupy the island. On March 13 the Franco-Venetian squadron arrived off the northern coast of Lissa and divided into two divisions. It quickly engaged the British. During a three-hour battle that lasted until noon, the smaller British force gradually gained the ascendancy. Four enemy frigates were captured or destroyed, including the French FLAGSHIP *Favorite*, which blew up after being driven on-shore. The loss of this ship, together with the death of the French commander, marked the end of the battle and of the French attempt to seize control of Lissa Island.

Lissa, Battle of
July 20, 1866

The only naval battle of the Austro-Italian War of 1866, Lissa was notable as the first encounter between IRONCLADS in the open sea. On July 16, 1866, nearly a month after the declaration of war, the Italian fleet under the command of Admiral Carlo di Persano left its base at Ancona. Its destination was Lissa Island (now known as Vis) off the Dalmatian coast. Persano's powerful force of 34 ships (12 ironclads, 14 wooden vessels, five scouts and three transports) was to be used to try to seize the island, which was held by an Austrian garrison. Their unsuccessful attempts to take the main harbor were interrupted, on July 20, by the approach of the Austrian fleet, under the

The Battle of Lissa, July 1866: notable as the first engagement between armored ships at sea   (*Copyright © National Maritime Museum, Greenwich, London*)

command of Admiral Wilhelm von TEGETTHOF, which had left its base at Pola during the previous day. Organized in three divisions, this less powerful force consisted of 27 ships, including seven wooden ships and four scouts but only seven ironclads.

As the Italians advanced northward in line-ahead formation, the Austrian fleet, which had adopted an arrowhead formation, was ordered to attack. "Ironclads will dash at the enemy and sink him!" was Tegetthof's dramatic signal. The battle began at 10:45 A.M. when they broke through the Italian line. It quickly became a mêlée, with the Austrians trying to ram or fire at their opponents at close range. Although the *Kaiser,* an Austrian wooden battleship, was severely damaged by the *Affondatore,* Persano's FLAGSHIP, the Italians' fortunes soon began to decline quickly. Tegetthof's flagship, the *Erzherzog Ferdinand Maximilian,* rammed the stationary *Re d'Italia* a large Italian frigate, which sank rapidly with the loss of 440 lives. The *Palestro,* an Italian ironclad, was set on fire and later sank. Admiral Persano tried to regroup his forces but by 2:30 P.M. he was forced to leave the battle area and return to base.

Weak leadership and poor tactics were the main reasons for the Italian navy's defeat in the first major fleet action in Europe since 1815. Although the battle had little political impact, it was to have a major influence on warship design for the rest of the century because Austrian ramming tactics were regarded as an important determinant of the outcome. The ram became a prominent feature of battleship design, and European navies were to become well versed in its use.

K. Gogg, *Österreichs Kreigsmarine, 1848–1918,* Salzburg, 1967.

Littorio

During the interwar period, the BATTLESHIP *Littorio* and her three sister ships were the ITALIAN NAVY's answer to the French BATTLE CRUISERS *Dunkerque* and *Strasbourg.* A naval disarmament conference held in Rome in 1931 had failed to halt a naval arms race between France and Italy; as a result, the construction of the first two Littorio-class ships went ahead. Completed in 1940, the *Littorio* had a displacement of 41,650 tons, main armament of nine 15-inch (38-cm) guns in three triple turrets and well-developed underwater protection. A catapult was installed on the quarterdeck, and three seaplanes could be carried. Operated by a crew of 1,872, she was 778 feet 9 inches (237.8 m) in length and had a beam of 107 feet 10 inches (32.9 m).

The *Littorio* was sunk by British aircraft during the raid on Taranto on November 12, 1940, but she was later raised and repaired. She was present at the First Battle of SIRTE, December 1941, and was torpedoed during the following year. In 1943, after Benito Mussolini was deposed, she was renamed *Italia* because the name *Littorio* had direct fascist connotations. She avoided falling into German hands and, after the surrender of Italy, September 1943, she was transferred to Malta. The *Littorio* then was interned together with her sister ship, the *Vittorio Veneto,* which also had had an eventful war and had been damaged at the Battle of CAPE MATAPAN, 1941, and on a later occasion. The other ships of the Littorio class made no contribution to the Italian war effort: The *Imperio* was destroyed before completion and the *Roma,* which saw no active service, was sunk in 1942.

Lockwood, Jr., Charles Andrew
1890–1967

American naval officer who became the leading SUBMARINE commander in the Pacific Theater in WORLD WAR II, 1939–45. Born in Virginia on May 6, 1890, Lockwood entered the U.S. Naval Academy in 1908. He began his long career in submarines in 1914, commanding the Asiatic Fleet's first submarine division three years later. Much of his career was spent in outfitting, commissioning and commanding new classes of submarines between the two world wars. His shore billets included submarine-related duty while at the office of Chief of Naval Operations.

With the United States' entry into World War II and after a short stint as naval attaché in London from January to March 1942, he became commander, Submarines Southwest Pacific, based at Fremantle, Australia. Under orders to try to stem the tide of the Japanese advance, he operated with limited resources. Early in February 1943 he was based at Pearl Harbor as the new commander of submarines for the Pacific Fleet. In this post he coordinated the destruction of Japan's merchant fleet and much of its navy during the American counteroffensive. He retired in 1947.

Clark G. Reynolds, *Famous American Admirals,* New York, 1978.

London, H.M.S.

A 40-gun English man-of-war built in King Charles I's reign was the first of nine warships named *London* to serve in the Royal Navy. One of the most notable of these ships was Admiral Sir Hyde *Parker*'s flagship at the Battle of COPENHAGEN, 1801, when he gave his famous order to disengage: Lord NELSON, who said he could not see the signal (he used his blind eye), disregarded the order.

Apart from a guided missile destroyer of that name, the most recent *London* was the 10,000-ton WORLD WAR II, 1939–45, cruiser that had a distinguished operational career. At the end of her service with the Eastern Fleet, she was the scene of a Japanese surrender in April 1945. Just before she was decommissioned in 1949, the *London* was one of the British ships that tried unsuccessfully to rescue the *AMETHYST* when that vessel became trapped in the Yangtze River during the Chinese Civil War, 1946–49. The *London* was badly damaged by Chinese shore batteries and was taken out of service later the same year.

Londonderry, Siege of
July 28, 1689

*F*ollowing the Glorious Revolution of 1688, JAMES II landed at Kinsale, Ireland, in March 1689, in an attempt to regain the English throne. Accompanied by a small French force, he moved northward with local Jacobites and surrounded Protestant-held Londonderry in April. A siege of over three months' duration followed that left the city facing imminent starvation. With no hope of immediate relief by land forces under the command of General Piercy Kirke, the only option for the hard-pressed Protestants was to bring supplies up the Foyle River. Two merchant ships, which had been supporting General Kirke's troops, were pressed into service and moved toward the city escorted by the English frigate *Dartmouth*, which was commanded by Captain John LEAKE. Their passage was blocked by a boom, which they eventually managed to cut, and the three vessels passed through. The *Dartmouth* engaged enemy shore batteries as the other two ships reached the city quay and began unloading the much-needed supplies. This marked the turning point in Londonderry's struggle; three days later the Jacobites were forced to raise the siege.

Long Beach, U.S.S.

*L*aunched at Quincy, Massachusetts in July 1959, the *Long Beach* was the world's first nuclear-powered surface warship. She was also the first ship to be armed with a main battery of guided missiles as well as the first American CRUISER of any kind to be built since the end of WORLD WAR II, 1939–45.

The *Long Beach* has a displacement of just over 14,000 tons and is 721 feet (220 m) in length; her twin nuclear-powered turbines produce a maximum speed of 30 knots. Her original armament included two Terrier twin missiles forward and a Talos twin missile launcher aft. She has a large boxlike bridge superstructure that supports the fixed radar panels. Following the updating of her missile system after some 20 years' service, the *Long Beach*'s operational life has been extended significantly.

Long Lance Torpedo

*T*he Japanese Long Lance TORPEDO was generally regarded as the most successful weapon of its kind in use in WORLD WAR II, 1939–45. This 24-inch (61-cm) weapon had a liquid-oxygen–powered engine and was equipped with a 1,000-pound (454-kg) warhead. Noted for its reliability, it had a maximum speed of 49 knots and a range of some 11 miles (20 km). (Alternatively, it could travel for 22 miles [41 km] at a lower speed of 36 knots.) The high-performance Long Lance torpedo first was used to great effect in the Battle of the JAVA SEA, February 1942, and in many subsequent surface engagements of the Pacific War. See also KAITEN.

Lord Clyde, H.M.S.

A British warship, launched in 1864, that was a curious mixture of old and new. She was the first ship in the ROYAL NAVY to mount an armor-plated bow battery on her main deck but was one of the last with an armor-plated wooden hull. A steam-powered frigate of 7,750 tons, she was equipped with the latest trunk-type engines, which were among the most powerful then available. She also was well protected: Her armor-clad plates were up to 5.5 inches (14 cm) thick. Her design weakness proved to be her timber structure, which began to rot relatively quickly. The *Lord Clyde* soon became obsolete and was decommissioned in 1875 after a fairly short period of service.

Lord Nelson, H.M.S.

*C*ompleted in 1908, a year after the *DREADNOUGHT*, the *Lord Nelson* and her sister ship the *AGAMEMNON* were in fact the last pre-DREADNOUGHTS to enter British service. However, some of the new ideas about battleship design were incorporated in their construction with the result that, for example, they did not carry any small-caliber secondary weapons. Instead, in their place were ten 9.2-inch (23-cm) guns (in one single and two twin turrets on each beam), as well as four 12-inch (30-cm) guns. With good armor protection, these ships had a displacement of 15,925 tons and a maximum speed of 18 knots. They had a length of 443 feet 6 inches (135 m) and a beam of 77 feet (23 m). The *Lord Nelson* and the *Agamemnon* both served in the English Channel after the outbreak of WORLD WAR I, 1914–18, and went together to the DARDANELLES in February 1915. They operated in the Eastern Mediterranean for the rest of the war. In November 1918 the Armistice with Turkey was signed aboard the *Agamemnon*.

L'Orient

A French naval base and port on the Bay of Biscay in the Morbihan Department of Brittany, northwestern France. It owes its early development—and its name—to the French East India Company, which established a base there in the first part of the 17th century. By the early years of the 19th century, it had become a major naval base; as a major shipbuilding center, it was to construct many major warships for the FRENCH NAVY. During their occupation of France in WORLD WAR II, 1939–45, the German navy used L'Orient as a base for the U-BOATS involved in the Battle of ATLANTIC, 1939–45. They were housed in concrete bunkers that helped to protect them from the worst effects of regular Allied bombing raids. The disadvantage of regular air attack was offset by the fact that the U-boats stationed at L'Orient avoided the long and potentially dangerous journey back to their home bases in Germany after seeking their prey in the Atlantic.

L'Orient

Flagship of Admiral François Paul BRUEYS D'AIGAILLIERS at the Battle of the NILE, August 1, 1798, L'Orient was one of 13 French ships lost as a result of this notable British victory. L'Orient was a French SHIP OF THE LINE armed with 120 guns and commanded by Captain Louis de Casabianca. He was one of the many casualties when the ship caught fire during the battle; among these were the French commander Admiral Brueys, who had little chance to escape. British guns had set fire to wet paint on board, quickly igniting L'Orient's magazine. The heroism of the captain's ten-year-old son, who refused to leave the ship and died at his father's side, was widely celebrated.

Louisburg, Capture of

1758

The British capture of LOUISBURG was an essential preliminary to the operations against the French in mainland Canada in 1759–60 during the SEVEN YEARS' WAR, 1756–63. This heavily fortified port on Cape Breton Island, off the east coast of Canada, had been an important factor in the 50-year-long struggle between the English and French for control of Canada. A combined English force of 41 warships and 11,600 troops, under the command of Admiral Edward BOSCAWEN and Major General Jeffrey Amherst, had left England in February 1758 with the objective of taking the port. It traveled via Halifax, Nova Scotia where, on May 28, 157 warships and supporting vessels left for Louisburg.

Delayed by bad weather, the first troops could not be disembarked until June 8. They came under heavy French attack but were able to start siege operations within a few days. However, adverse weather conditions caused considerable difficulties for Boscawen's force as they landed men and matériel over a few days; 100 boats were lost. Siege guns were landed on July 18, and within two days the defenses had been breached. Boscawen entered Louisburg Harbor on July 25–26 and neutralized the remaining French warships. With Louisburg cut off by land and sea, the French had little choice but to surrender the port and the whole island. French losses amounted to 1,200 deaths and 5,637 men taken prisoner. The English destroyed Louisburg's fortifications and moved its population elsewhere in order to remove a potential threat to future operations against the French in Canada.

Low-Charged Ship

The transition from the CARRACK to the GALLEON exemplified the disappearance of the HIGH-CHARGED ship during the 16th century. Its replacement, the low-charged ship, was introduced in the 1570s in England and slightly later elsewhere. By this time the unwieldy high-charged ship with its large castles fore and aft increasingly belonged to a period of naval warfare that had almost passed. The new naval CANNON had largely replaced the archers and musketeers who operated their weapons from these protected positions during fighting at close quarters, with the aim of boarding an enemy ship and setting it on fire.

The low-charged ship dispensed with these top-heavy structures and allowed the development of a much more seaworthy and maneuverable design. This new design typically would accommodate three rows of cannon for use in the low-charged ship's primary role of engaging enemy ships at a distance at sea. It was no longer necessary deliberately to distort the shape of the hull to make it difficult for the enemy to board, which had been the primary aim of naval warfare before the age of the cannon. The low-charged ship formed the basis for the design of the capital ships of the sailing navies for the next 250 years.

Robert Gardiner, ed., *Cogs, Caravels and Galleons: The Sailing Ship 1000–1650*, London, 1994.

Lowestoft, Battle of

June 3, 1665

The opening battle of the Second ANGLO-DUTCH WAR, 1665–67, which, like the first war, was the product of intense commercial rivalry between England and the Netherlands. The Dutch fleet of 103 ships under the command of Jacob Van WASSENAER arrived off the Suffolk coast at the end of May 1665. It already had seized some English merchant ships near the Dogger Bank and now waited for the ROYAL NAVY to arrive. A fleet of 109 ships under the command of JAMES II, Duke of York, had been warned of the enemy's arrival and proceeded to the area immediately.

After two day's maneuvering, the battle began at about 4 A.M. on June 3, some 40 miles (74 km) southeast of Lowestoft. Initially the fleets fought in opposing lines, but the battle quickly became a mêlée. At the center of the fighting were the opposing fleet commanders' FLAGSHIPS—the *Eendracht* and the *Royal Charles*—which were locked in a fierce struggle. The turning point came when the *Eendracht* suddenly blew up, killing all but five of her complement of 400 and undermining the morale of the rest of the Dutch fleet. By 7 P.M. the Dutch were in full retreat; in the confusion, seven of their ships collided and caught fire. Some semblance of order was maintained by Admiral Cornelis TROMP and Admiral Jan EVERTSEN, who withdrew their squadrons without further loss.

Dutch losses—more than 30 ships—were heavy, but the English only lost two vessels. English casualties—283 killed and 440 wounded—were also light compared with those of the Dutch, who lost 4,000 killed and wounded and 2,000 captured. The opposing navies did not meet again until the FOUR DAYS' BATTLE, June 1–4, 1666, by which time France had entered the war on the Dutch side.

Luce, Stephen Bleecker
1827–1917

American naval officer of great intelligence and of extreme importance and influence in officer training and education. Born on March 25, 1827 in Albany, New York, Luce received his appointment in 1841 and was one of the first to attend the new naval school at ANNAPOLIS, Maryland. His early career was characterized by sea duty followed by shore duty at the Naval Academy, either as an instructor of seamanship or as Commandant of Midshipmen in the years immediately following the AMERICAN CIVIL WAR, 1861–65. During that conflict he commanded an IRONCLAD in the actions against Charleston, South Carolina. In 1881 he commanded the Naval Training Squadron.

Luce's experiences at Annapolis and his observations during the Civil War on what he conceived to be principles of warfare led him to campaign vigorously and finally successfully to establish the Naval War College at Newport, Rhode Island in 1884. Along with other reform-minded naval officers, he was instrumental in founding the Naval Institute in 1873; he served as president of that body from 1887 to 1892. A consistent proponent of American naval

expansion, he authored numerous works on a variety of topics dealing with sea power and naval policy and strategy. Regularly attached to the Naval War College, he advised President Theodore ROOSEVELT on building the new battleship navy of the early 20th century. He died in Newport on July 28, 1917.

John B. Hattendorf, B. Mitchell Simpson III, and John R. Wadleigh, *Sailors and Scholars: The Centennial History of the U.S. Naval War College*, Newport, R.I., 1984.

Lusitania, R.M.S.

An early victim of the U-BOAT during WORLD WAR I, 1914–18, the *Lusitania*, a luxurious British (Cunard Lines) transatlantic liner of 31,500 tons, was sunk off the coast of southern Ireland on May 7, 1915 while en route from New York to Liverpool. Earlier German warnings that she would be attacked had been disregarded, and the *Lusitania* took no special precautions on her return journey from New York at the beginning of May. After being struck without warning by a single TORPEDO from the German submarine *U-20*, she sank in less than 20 minutes; 1,198 passengers and crew were lost.

Subsequent German claims that the *Lusitania* was an ARMED MERCHANT CRUISER and therefore a legitimate wartime target are completely untenable. The liner carried no troops or guns—in fact, nothing more suspect than a small cargo of ammunition. The action was vigorously denounced by the Americans, who lost 124 citizens when the liner went down. Public opinion in the then-neutral United States turned squarely against Germany, and in fact the incident probably contributed to the U.S. government's eventual decision to enter the war in April 1917.

Thomas A. Bailey and Paul B. Ryan, *The Lusitania Disaster: An Episode in Modern History and Diplomacy*, London, 1975.

Lynch, Patricio
1825–86

Chilean naval commander of Irish origin who served in the navy of his adopted country for most of his life, joining the service at the age of 12. He spent a brief period in the ROYAL NAVY during the Anglo-Chinese War of 1840. Lynch first rose to national prominence during the war with Spain in 1865, when he became Minister of Marine. In this post he modernized and expanded the navy and introduced an effective training program. His role was expanded during the war with Peru, 1879–82, when he fought on land as well as at sea. In recognition of Lynch's wartime services, he was appointed to head the Chilean army that occupied conquered Peruvian territory.

The destruction of the British transatlantic liner *Lusitania* brought American intervention in World War I, 1914–18, closer
(Copyright © Imperial War Museum, London)

Lyons, Edmund, First Baron
1790–1858

Successively second in command and commander in chief of the British Black Sea Fleet during the CRIMEAN WAR, 1853–56, Admiral Lyons' naval career began during the latter stages of the FRENCH REVOLUTIONARY AND NAPOLEONIC WARS, 1792–1815. He was present at the decisive Battle of NAVARINO, 1827, during the Greek War of Independence, 1821–32, but spent much of the postwar period in the diplomatic service. During the Crimean War he worked with Lord Raglan in planning the whole campaign but, initially, as second in command under Sir James Dundas, he retained a direct operational role. In October 1854, for example, his flagship, the *Agamemnon*, played a prominent part in the attack on the defenses of Sevastopol.

MacDonough, Thomas
1783–1825

American naval officer. MacDonough entered the navy as a midshipman in 1800 and served under Commodore Edward PREBLE in the efforts against Tripoli. He participated in the famous cutting-out operations of the captured warship *Philadelphia* in Tripoli harbor. In the WAR OF 1812, he was directed to command the naval forces on Lake CHAMPLAIN, a vital link in the strategic route between British Canada and the United States. Working against formidable odds to build a naval force to compete against his British opponent, by the summer of 1814 he had constructed a fleet of some 13 vessels, still inferior to the British force that was to accompany and support a powerful British army marching south on the western side of Lake Champlain toward Plattsburg.

Using the bold tactic of anchoring his fleet close to shore so that, using springs and cables to swing his vessels around quickly, he could use both BROADSIDES of his vessels, he defeated the British naval force on September 11, 1814. Without naval support, the British army was forced to retreat into Canada, thus ending this particular campaign. Macdonough's action proved to be not only decisive in the Lakes campaign of the war but decisive also in ending the conflict. Without control of Lake Champlain, any British attempt to invade the United States was futile, and negotiators in Europe quickly moved to conclude the war. Following a few more commands on shore and at sea, Macdonough's health deteriorated; he died at sea in 1825.

Fletcher Pratt, *Preble's Boys: Commodore Preble and the Birth of American Sea Power*, New York, 1950.

Macship

A British merchant ship type of WORLD WAR II, 1939–45, that was fitted with a temporary flying deck. The name was derived from the initial letters of the term "merchant aircraft carrier." Like the CAMSHIP, it was developed as a result of the heavy losses that British convoys crossing the Atlantic had suffered from 1940 at the hands of the Focke-Wulf FW 200 Condor, a long-range German bomber. Merchant aircraft carriers were vessels with long decks, such as oil tankers and grain ships, above whose superstructure a flying platform was fitted. Fighter aircraft operating from macships provided the Atlantic convoys with much-needed additional protection from enemy air attack. They later carried machines that operated in an antisubmarine role. Macships were much more efficient than camships because aircraft launched from them could return to them. Planes could not return to camships; normally the planes had to be ditched in the sea.

McCalla, Bowman Hendry
1844–1910

American admiral who frequently led troops into combat during his career, thereby gaining a reputation as a fighting admiral. Born in Camden, New Jersey on June 19, 1844, McCalla entered the naval service in 1861. In 1885 he led a landing party of bluejackets and marines that quickly occupied Panama City and helped quell trouble there. In 1890, while commanding the *Enterprise*, he struck a mutinous sailor, for which he was court-martialed and suspended for three years, a sentence that was reduced by his recall in 1891. As a captain during the SPANISH-AMERICAN WAR of 1898, he commanded the *Marblehead*, which participated in the action at Guantanamo Bay, Cuba, during which he led a force of marines and sailors, establishing and commanding a naval base there for the remainder of the war. (The Guantanamo base has remained in American hands ever since, even though the anti-American Communist regime of Fidel Castro.) McCalla later was advanced six ranks for his action and eventually received two congressional medals for action at Cienfuegos and at Guantanamo Bay and another congressional medal for "specially meritorious service other than in battle."

During the Boxer Rebellion in China of 1900, he commanded a landing party as part of the column the Royal Navy assembled to relieve the besieged Western legations in Peking (Beijing). Wounded three times during the expedition, he subsequently was advanced again three ranks. He was promoted to rear admiral in 1903 and retired in 1906. McCalla received the China War Medal from King Edward VII of Great Britain for his efforts as well as the Order of the Red Eagle from German Kaiser Wilhelm II. He died on May 6, 1910 in Santa Barbara, California.

Paolo E. Coletta, *Bowman Hendry McCalla: A Fighting Sailor*, Lanham, Md., 1979.

Madden, Sir Charles
1862–1935

British naval commander who spent much of his career at the ADMIRALTY, although he served at sea with the British GRAND FLEET during WORLD WAR I, 1914–18. From 1914 he was chief of staff to Sir John JELLICOE, his brother-in-law, who valued his tactical skills and organizational ability. When Sir David BEATTY succeeded Jellicoe as commander in chief of the Grand Fleet in 1916, Madden became second in command, with direct responsibility for the First Battle Squadron, where he remained for the rest of the war. In 1919 he was promoted to the rank of full admiral and given command of the new Atlantic Fleet. His career concluded with a three-year term as First Sea Lord, 1927–30.

Mahan, Alfred Thayer
1840–1914

Probably the best-known American naval figure of the period between the AMERICAN CIVIL WAR, 1861–65, and WORLD WAR I, 1914–18, Alfred Mahan's advocacy of sea power had a profound effect on naval strength and competition from 1890 until the present. Such was his influence that Mahan's name became synonymous with naval history and sea power. He was born in West Point, New York on September 27, 1840, the son of Dennis Hart Mahan, a professor of civil and military engineering at the U.S. Military Academy there. Alfred Thayer Mahan's early naval career could best be described as uneventful. Entering the navy in 1856, he served on various blockading squadrons during the Civil War, followed by a series of routine shore and sea tours during the postwar years, including several at the U.S. Naval Academy.

Mahan's career took a more promising turn when he was called to the newly established Naval War College to lecture in naval history, tactics and strategy. He subsequently served twice as the college's president (1886–88; 1892–93). From 1893 to 1895 he commanded the *Chi-*cago—the FLAGSHIP of the European Station and Naval Review Fleet. Retiring in 1896 with the rank of captain, he was called back in an advisory capacity on the Naval War Strategy Board during the SPANISH-AMERICAN WAR, 1898, and as a delegate to the Hague Peace Conference in 1899. Subsequently he was promoted to rear admiral on the retired list in 1906. Besides his seminal work, *The Influence of Sea Power upon History, 1660–1783*, 1890, he wrote numerous works on naval history, including over a dozen monographs and at least 50 articles in scholarly journals. He received several honorary degrees for his historical studies, including the D.C.L. from Oxford University and the L.L.D. from Cambridge, Harvard, Yale, McGill and Columbia universities. In 1902 he was elected president of the American Historical Association. He died on December 1, 1914 at the Naval Hospital in Washington, D.C.

Robert Seager II, *Alfred Thayer Mahan: The Man and His Letters*, Annapolis, 1977.

Maine, U.S.S.

An American armored CRUISER of 6,682 tons. In 1898 the *Maine* was destroyed in Havana, the capital of the Spanish colony of Cuba, in circumstances that were never fully explained at the time. She had been dispatched to Havana early in 1898 to protect U.S. citizens who were threatened by serious riots on the island. On February 15, 1898, while she was moored in Havana harbor, two explosions destroyed her and killed most of her crew—260 officers and men. An American inquiry concluded that a MINE or TORPEDO had set off the ship's magazines, while the Spanish authorities suggested that an accidental internal explosion had caused the sinking.

Popular opinion in the United States was clear about the cause, holding the Spanish government responsible for the deaths. There is no doubt that the incident helped to precipitate the SPANISH-AMERICAN WAR, 1898, which began only two months after the loss of the *Maine*. During the war, "Remember the *Maine*!" was a common American battle cry. A later investigation, in 1911, concluded that the loss of the *Maine* had been an accident, with unstable explosives in the ship's magazine being the most likely cause. A more recent inquiry has established that the explosion almost certainly was caused by a defective engine boiler.

G. J. A. O'Toole, *The Spanish War: An American Epic*, New York, 1984.

Mainwaring, Sir Henry
1587–1653

English vice admiral and pirate whose early combat experience was as a soldier in the Netherlands, 1608–

10. Mainwaring soon turned his attention to the sea and, in 1611, was authorized to act against the pirates who plied the Bristol Channel. Mainwaring soon broadened his horizons and obtained a LETTER OF MARQUE to act as a PRIVATEER against the Spanish. Operating from a base on the Barbary coast in the *Resistance*, a 160-ton ship, he soon established himself as a successful pirate. In 1618, having amassed a fortune at the expense of the Spanish, he returned to England, where he received a royal pardon for his acts of piracy and was knighted by King James I.

Mainwaring's standing in England rose further when his role in preventing a Spanish plot against Venice in 1618 became known. He was appointed Deputy Warden of the Cinque Ports and, in 1626–27, was a member of an inquiry into abuses in the navy. During this period he had also produced his *Seaman's Dictionary*, which eventually was published in 1644. It was the first manual of its kind and had a considerable influence on senior naval officers. In Charles I's reign he was involved in the reorganization of the navy and became a vice admiral. He served in the annual ship money fleets that were dispatched from 1636 to 1641 enforce British sovereignty of the English Channel and the adjoining North Sea. The cost of these fleets was met from the proceeds of the ship money tax. Mainwaring's naval career came to end with the English Civil War, 1642–51, in which he supported the losing royalist cause.

Majestic, H.M.S.

Comprising the largest class of BATTLESHIPS ever to be constructed in Britain or elsewhere, the *Majestic* and her eight sister ships were produced for the ROYAL NAVY between 1895 and 1898. Similar in appearance to the Royal Sovereign class, the Majestics carried four 12-inch (30-cm) main guns that were more than equal to the performance of earlier 13.5-inch weapons because of design improvements. Secondary armament was increased to 12 6-inch guns compared with the ten guns fitted to ships of the previous Royal Sovereign class. Greater protection was also provided because of the availability of lighter armor. The Majestics had a displacement of just under 15,000 tons, a length of 421 feet (128.3 m), a beam of 75 feet (22.9 m) and a maximum speed of 18 knots. In 1905–6, the *Mars* became the first battleship equipped to burn oil fuel, and all but two of the remaining Majestic-class ships were similarly converted.

During WORLD WAR I, 1914–18, three ships of the Majestic class—the *Mars*, the *Hannibal* and the *Victorious*—were used in supporting roles only, but the others were more actively employed by the Royal Navy. The *Majestic* and the *Prince George* both were sent to the DARDANELLES, where the former was sunk by a torpedo from a German submarine in May 1915. In January 1916 the *Prince George*

also was severely damaged in the same area but was to survive the war.

Makarov, Stepan Osipovich
1848–1904

A dynamic and effective Russian admiral who was appointed to the command of the Pacific Fleet at Port Arthur at the beginning of the RUSSO-JAPANESE WAR, 1904–5. Japanese naval forces quickly blockaded the base, and Makarov led a number of sorties against them. On his return from one such expedition, in April 1904, his flagship *Petropavlovsk* hit an enemy mine, and all on board were lost. Makarov's death was a considerable loss to the RUSSIAN NAVY at a critical period of the war, and from that point the fleet remained at Port Arthur, where it was soon to be destroyed by Japanese land artillery. Makarov also was noted as a successful inventor and tactician who had pioneered the use of torpedoes in his earlier naval career.

Málaga, Battle of
August 13, 1704

A naval battle during the War of the SPANISH SUCCESSION, 1701–14, some three weeks after a combined Anglo-Dutch fleet captured GIBRALTAR on July 23–24, 1704. In response to the British victory, King Louis XIV of France dispatched from Toulon a Franco-Spanish fleet of 50 ships of the line under Admiral the Comte de TOULOUSE with the aim of defeating the enemy fleet and retaking Gibraltar. On August 9 the Franco-Spanish fleet was first sighted a few miles east of Gibraltar, and the opposing fleets made contact off Málaga four days later.

The Comte de Toulouse positioned himself between the Rock of Gibraltar and the Anglo-Dutch fleet, which consisted of 53 ships of the line under the overall command of Admiral Sir George ROOKE. The van division was headed by Admiral Sir Clowdisley SHOVELL and the Dutch rear by Admiral Gerald Callenburgh. The exchange of gunfire between the two fleets lasted several hours, but as the British were unable to break through, no decisive result was achieved. Both fleets suffered heavy damage, and the French were unable to renew the fight. The Comte de Toulouse withdrew during the night and Rooke retired to Gibraltar. He later returned home to England for the winter.

The real significance of the Battle of Málaga was the fact that the Franco-Spanish fleet had been unable to dislodge the British from Gibraltar and were unable to make another successful attempt to do so before the war ended.

Malta Convoys

At the beginning of WORLD WAR II, 1939–45, Malta was the only British base in the Mediterranean. With Italy's entry into the war, holding the island (only 60 miles south of Sicily) was essential; it was a vital base for Allied operations against the Italian supply routes to North Africa. Allied submarine operations from Malta continued despite the fact that the island was under constant German and Italian air attack for nearly two years (January 1941–October 1942) and narrowly avoided an airborne invasion. Supplies had to be brought to the island by sea, and from January 1941 to December 1942 ten major CONVOYS were dispatched from either GIBRALTAR or Alexandria, Egypt. They were heavily protected by British warships, including those operating as FORCE H, but losses were high.

Four convoys arrived in 1941, but toward the end of the year German air and submarine activity was stepped up. In the first half of 1942 three convoys set out for Malta, but only five merchantmen reached their destination (three of which were sunk soon after arrival by bombing). Although Malta was still supplied by submarine, supplies were insufficient to meet the needs of the population, which, by April 1942, was suffering from starvation. Following the German decision to abandon plans to invade Malta, bombing activity eased during the summer and autumn. The "Pedestal convoy," which left Gibraltar on August 10, 1942, was the last to face strong enemy opposition. Five merchant ships arrived (out of a total of 14 in the convoy at the outset) but at the cost of the aircraft carrier EAGLE, two cruisers and a destroyer. With the Allied victories in North Africa and the end of German air superiority in the Mediterranean, the threat to Malta's security gradually eased further. The next convoy, "Stonehenge," left Alexandria on November 16 and suffered no more than light damage from German air attacks. In December the "Portcullis" convoy was to arrive completely unopposed, indicating that the siege of Malta had finally ended.

Peter Smith, *Pedestal: The Malta Convoy of August 1942*, London, 1971.

Manila Bay, Battle of
May 1, 1898

Shortly after the outbreak of the SPANISH-AMERICAN WAR of 1898 on April 25, the UNITED STATES NAVY's Asiatic Squadron left Chinese waters. Its destination was the Philippines, the Spanish colony it hoped to capture. Under the command of Commodore George DEWEY, the squadron consisted of five cruisers and two gunboats. Dewey disregarded the dangers of shore batteries and mines as the squadron entered Manila Bay on May 1. Anchored in the bay off the naval station at Cavite was a less powerful Spanish squadron of four cruisers, three gunboats and several other vessels under the command of Admiral Patricio Montojo.

The *Olympia*, Dewey's FLAGSHIP, led the four other American cruisers toward the Spanish squadron. The enemy opened fire first but Dewey did not return it until he was within a range of 5,000 yards (4,572 m). His ships went past the enemy five times, reducing the distance between them to 2,000 yards (1,829 m), before bringing the action to a temporary halt. When the ships were sent back independently, the success of the initial attack was immediately apparent. The Spanish squadron had been virtually destroyed, and the remaining ships were quickly finished off. By noon the battle was over with the Americans, who had been hit only 18 times, sustaining few casualties.

Dewey then silenced Cavite's shore batteries and began the BLOCKADE of Manila, waiting for the arrival of sufficient ground troops to take the capital. It finally fell after a combined sea-land attack on August 13; this event marked the end of Spanish colonial rule in the Philippines.

David F. Trask, *The War with Spain in 1898*, 1981.

Mansell, Sir Robert
1573–1656

British admiral and naval administrator who owed his rank and position to royal patronage rather than professional competence or service at sea. During his term as Treasurer of the Navy, 1604–18, corruption was rife, although there is no evidence that Mansell used his position to enhance his own personal fortune. By 1618 he had been appointed vice admiral of England, even though his command experience was relatively limited. Apart from his involvement in the expedition to CADIZ, 1596, his service had been confined to minor actions in the seas around Britain. In 1620 he ventured farther afield, leading an expedition against the Algerine pirates. It achieved little: An attack on the port of Algiers failed and pirate activity continued unabated. Mansell never served at sea again.

Marbella, Battle of
March 10, 1705

The failure of the Franco-Spanish fleet to defeat the British at the Battle of MALAGA, August 13, 1704, marked the first of several attempts to retake GIBRALTAR, which had fallen to the British on July 23–24, 1704, during the War of the SPANISH SUCCESSION, 1701–1714. French naval forces were deployed in support of the siege of Gibraltar but at first made little impact against the defending British squadron commanded by Admiral Sir John

LEAKE. In March 1705 the French squadron under Admiral de Pointis planned an amphibious landing with the aim of recapturing GIBRALTAR. Driven off the landing area by adverse weather conditions, most of his squadron were forced away to the northeast in the direction of Marbella, where the British under Admiral Leake lay in wait. The French were taken completely by surprise and were decisively defeated during a brief engagement on March 10. Three French ships of the line were captured and two more, including the *Magnanime*, the French squadron's FLAGSHIP, were driven ashore.

Marines

Soldiers who serve on board ship or who operate in close association with naval forces. Before the 16th century, soldiers were mainly responsible for fighting at sea. The HIGH-CHARGED medieval warship, equipped with fore- and aftercastles, was essentially a fighting platform that was used to board and capture an opponent. (See HIGH-CHARGED SHIP.) Soldiers were deployed to fire missiles and to engage in hand-to-hand fighting as they struggled to take an enemy ship or repel an attack. The nature of warfare at sea changed radically at the end of the medieval period, as the naval gun made its impact and hand-to-hand combat largely disappeared.

Despite this time of revolutionary change, navies continued to require the services of soldiers at sea. They operated guns, made up crew numbers and maintained discipline on board as well as led amphibious operations. These increasing demands eventually led to the formation of separate marine forces. France first took this step as early as 1627, although the new unit did not survive for long and had to be reconstituted later. The first English marine regiment was established in 1664, but it did not become a permanent force until 1755. It has been known as the Royal Marines since 1923, when two separate marine branches—the Royal Marine Light Infantry and the Royal Marine Artillery—were abolished. In the United States the first marine corps was created in 1775 at the beginning of the AMERICAN WAR OF INDEPENDENCE, 1775–83. The United States Marine Corps remains a separate organization managed by the Department of the Navy and is the largest service of its kind in the world, with just under 200,000 men and women under arms.

Other countries also developed separate marine services, but only in Britain and the United States did they come to play a wide variety of roles onboard ship. They acted as sharpshooters, served as sentries and made up landing and boarding parties and could constitute up to a quarter of the crew. The introduction of IRONCLAD warships prompted a change in their role because marksmen were no longer needed on board. Instead, now they were expected to man

English marines of the Napoleonic period, 1803–15 *(Copyright © National Maritime Museum, Greenwich, London)*

the gun turrets. Their most important contribution has been to take a leading role in AMPHIBIOUS operations, from the capture of GIBRALTAR in 1704 to the FALKLANDS WAR, 1982. During WORLD WAR I, 1914–18, this role was extended further when British and American marine units served on land in France. In a more traditional guise, they served in the landing parties during the raid on ZEEBRUGGE, April 1918.

History provided no real advance warning of the scale of amphibious warfare experienced during WORLD WAR II, 1939–45, when marine forces were forced to respond rapidly to events in the European and Pacific theaters. From the DIEPPE RAID, 1942, onward, marines have led most major amphibious operations and typically have assumed a commando role on each occasion. They played a key role in the U.S. island-hopping campaign in the Pacific theater, bearing the brunt of the fighting on Guadalcanal, Iwo Jima and the other islands. This commando function has continued in the postwar period when they have been regarded as an elite force that is highly selective in recruitment and undergoes particularly demanding training. Marines have been widely deployed in the conflicts of the Cold War period, from Korea to Vietnam and the Falklands, in a wide variety of contexts, reflecting their special skills and training in operating in diverse types of environment. Marine forces typically have a special esprit de corps and regard themselves as the toughest and proudest of all the armed services.

C. Field, *Britain's Sea Soldiers*, 2 vols., Liverpool, 1924. W. D. Parker, *A Concise History of the United Stated Marine Corps, 1775–1969*, Washington, D.C., 1970.

Marshall Islands, Occupation of
1944

*T*his island group in the central Pacific, which consists of thousands of islands, was occupied by the Japanese during WORLD WAR II, 1939–45, and was the site of several airfields and a fleet anchorage. By the latter part of 1943, the American central Pacific offensive was under way and plans for the invasion of the Marshall Islands, which were relatively lightly defended, were made. Their capture would put the U.S. Navy within striking distance of Truk, headquarters of the Japanese Combined Fleet, 1,000 miles (1,609 km) away.

Code-named "Operation Flintlock," the amphibious invasion of the Marshall Islands required the assemblage of a large force at Pearl Harbor. It was split into two and ordered to attack separate targets 300 miles (558 km) apart: The first group was to go to Roi and Namur while the second was to attack Kawajalein. Accompanying the amphibious units were four carrier task forces of the U.S. Fifth Fleet, which were to deal with any local opposition from adjoining islands and to meet any threat from the main Japanese fleet. Following three days' bombardment, landings began on January 31 and U.S. forces took Majuro, the first Japanese possession captured in the war. Other islands, including Kwajalein, fell after fierce fighting. Confident after the quick success of this operation, the Americans decided to bring forward the attack on Truk. On February 17–18 the Fifth Fleet attacked Truk and caused the loss of two enemy cruisers and four destroyers. By the end of February 1944, the Eniwetok island group had finally fallen, completing the U.S. occupation of the Marshall Islands.

Martinique, Battle of
April 29, 1781

*A*n engagement in the Caribbean during the AMERICAN WAR OF INDEPENDENCE, 1775–83, that followed the Battle of DOMINICA, April 17, 1780. After the earlier encounter, Admiral George RODNEY, the English commander in chief, departed for America, returning to the West Indies to capture the Dutch island of St. Eustatius, a wealthy trading center, in February 1781. Admiral Rodney, who expected the island to be a rich source of prize money,

had been reinforced by Admiral Sir Samuel HOOD and eight ships of the line. This established England as the predominant naval power in the Caribbean, although the English position was soon to be challenged when a French fleet under Admiral the Comte de GRASSE arrived from Brest. Rodney had received advance warning of these reinforcements and ordered Hood, who had 11 ships of the line, to blockade the French base at Fort Royal, Martinique, de Grasse's expected destination. He was to join a small English squadron under Rear Admiral Drake that was already present there. Rodney's squadron remained at St. Eustatius.

By dividing his forces in this way, Rodney missed an opportunity to strike a decisive blow at the French fleet before it reached Fort Royal. De Grasse's fleet consisted of 20 ships of the line and a convoy of 150 transport ships. With insufficient strength to attack the French at close quarters, Hood opened fire at long range as de Grasse arrived off Fort Royal. The French were reinforced by four warships that came out from Port Royal and they entered the port without damage. Four English ships were hit by French gunfire and Hood was forced to withdraw to St. Eustatius, while de Grasse went on to capture Tobago.

Mary Rose

*E*nglish warship, one of the "great ships" of King Henry VIII's navy, the *Mary Rose* was a high-charged CARRACK of 600 tons, constructed in 1509. (See HIGH-CHARGED ship.) Named after the king's sister, Mary Tudor, the new ship had a crew of 400 and was armed with 20 heavy and 60 light guns. These were a mixture of wrought-iron breech-loaders and the new one piece muzzle-loading CANNON manufactured in brass. A revolutionary feature of the *Mary Rose*'s design was the fact that her heavy guns were mounted on the lower deck and gun ports were cut in the sides. She was in fact the first BROADSIDE ship, and her appearance represented a major turning point in the development of naval warfare.

The *Mary Rose* was the FLAGSHIP of the English fleet during Henry VIII's first two wars against the French. During the course of the third, on July 19, 1545, she went to engage the French fleet off Portsmouth but was soon in difficulty. Water had entered her lower deck ports, and she sank quickly with the loss of almost all of her crew. Her hull was rediscovered in the Solent in 1968 and she was raised from the seabed 14 years later. She is now on display in a dry dock at Portsmouth. Three other ships in the ROYAL NAVY have been named the *Mary Rose*, including a 500-ton vessel that fought against the SPANISH ARMADA, 1588, and subsequently served as Sir John HAWKINS's flagship.

M. Rule, *The Mary Rose*, London, 1982.

Mathews, Thomas
1676–1751

British admiral whose service at the Battle of CAPE PASSARO, August 11, 1718, was followed by regular promotion during the long period of peace that followed. By the time of the War of the AUSTRIAN SUCCESSION, 1740–48, he had reached the rank of vice admiral and was appointed commander in chief in the Mediterranean. His predecessor, Rear Admiral Richard LESTOCK, remained as his second in command; not surprisingly, relations between the two men were strained. Matters came to a head in February 1744 when Mathews fought a combined Franco-Spanish fleet off Toulon. The commander in chief was unable to engage the enemy in accordance with the provisions of the official FIGHTING INSTRUCTIONS, which required the two sides to fight van to van, center to center and rear to rear.

Unable to form a regulation line, Mathews ordered his van to attack the French center. Lestock, who commanded the rear division, was not well positioned to engage the enemy, and, despite orders to attack, he did not do so. The less powerful enemy fleet was thus allowed to escape with very little damage. After the battle Lestock was sent home to face a court-martial for failing to do his utmost to attack the enemy. Lestock was acquitted because he had obeyed the letter of the *Fighting Instructions* rather than the orders of his commander in chief, an outcome that tended to reinforce the natural conservatism of the Royal Navy. Mathews himself then faced trial for not conforming to official instructions. He was found guilty of beginning the attack before forming the line of battle, even though there were sound practical reasons for doing so. Mathews was cashiered and never served at sea again.

Maury, Matthew Fontaine
1806–73

One of America's most famous oceanographers, Maury earned the nickname "Pathfinder of the Seas." Born near Fredericksburg, Virginia in 1806, he entered the navy as a midshipman in 1825. He saw various duties but concentrated on the studies of HYDROGRAPHY, publishing in 1836 a much-used text entitled *A New Theoretical and Practical Treatise on Navigation*.

As a critic of naval practices and an advocate of many reforms, he wrote a series of articles under the *nom-de-plume* "Harry Bluff." Beginning in 1842 as superintendent of the Depot of Charts and Instruments and from 1844 to 1861 as director of the U.S. Naval Observatory, he began a long period of research in oceanography, gathering data on winds, tides, temperatures and currents from merchant as well as naval officers throughout the world. This infor-

mation was published, and his books as well as his charts became standard navigation works that greatly reduced sailing times on many routes. His *Physical Geography of the Sea*, published in 1855, became the first classic work of modern oceanography.

As advocate for American expansion and the Southern states' commercial development in South America, he followed his native state at the outset of the AMERICAN CIVIL WAR, 1861–65, and was commissioned in the CONFEDERATE NAVY. His international reputation served him well as a Confederate agent in Britain, where he worked to secure warships for the Confederacy. He was also instrumental in developing new naval technologies, such as electric mines, to break the Union BLOCKADE of the Southern ports. A short period of service with Mexico after the war was followed by a professorship in meteorology at the Virginia Military Institute that lasted until his death in 1873.

Frances L. Williams, *Matthew Fontaine Maury: Scientist of the Sea*, New Brunswick, N.J., 1963.

Mayaguez Incident

On May 12, 1975 an American freighter, the *Mayaguez*, was seized by a Cambodian gunboat when it allegedly strayed into Cambodian territorial waters. The *Mayaguez* was taken into custody and her 39 crew members were imprisoned. The Communist Khmer Rouge government did not respond to American demands for the immediate return of the ship and its crew although there were informal indications that they might be released after further negotiations. Despite this possibility, U.S. President Gerald Ford ordered immediate military action to release the ship. On May 14, 200 MARINES launched a raid on Cambodian soil to secure the release of the crew, but the captives had been moved to a different location before the attack. The raid was accompanied by heavy air strikes and a naval operation in which the warship U.S.S. *Holt* freed the *Mayaguez*. This action resulted in 15 American dead and 50 wounded. Soon afterward, the Khmer Rouge freed the crew.

Mayo, Henry Thomas
1856–1937

American naval officer. Born in Burlington, Vermont on December 8, 1856, Mayo experienced a fairly routine early naval career. He served on the *Yantic* as part of the Greely Relief Expedition of 1883 to the Arctic. Commanding several divisions of the Atlantic Fleet from late 1913, he demanded, in April 1914, a public apology, disciplinary action against the citizens responsible, and a

21-gun salute to the American flag after Mexican officials seized a boat's crew in Tampico. This action and the Mexican government's refusal to comply prompted President Woodrow Wilson to seize the Mexican customs house at Vera Cruz, resulting in the U.S. occupation of that city. Appointed in 1916 to command the Atlantic Fleet with the rank of vice admiral, Mayo was thereby in charge of all U.S. naval forces in the Atlantic and Europe. He held this important position during WORLD WAR I, 1914–18, representing the U.S. at the Allied naval conference in London in September 1917. He chaired the navy's General Board until his retirement in late 1920. Among numerous American and foreign decorations, he was awarded the Distinguished Service Medal. He died in Portsmouth, New Hampshire on February 23, 1937.

James C. Bradford, "Henry T. Mayo: Last of the Independent Naval Diplomats," in *Admirals of the New Steel Navy: Makers of the American Naval Tradition, 1880–1930*, ed. James C. Bradford, Annapolis, 1990.

Medina Sidonia, Don Alonso Pérez de Guzmán El Bueno, Seventh Duke of

1550–1619

Spanish naval commander and captain-general of Andalusia who led the SPANISH ARMADA against England in 1588. The Duke of Medina Sidonia, a member of one of the wealthiest and most influential Spanish families, had great success in operations against Portugal and was an effective naval administrator. He enjoyed considerable royal influence, and there can have been little surprise when Philip II appointed him commander in chief of the Armada on the death of the Marquis of Santa Cruz (see Alvaro de BAZAN) early in 1588. Without experience at sea, Medina Sidonia was reluctant to accept the post, and his record as a naval commander proved to be one of consistent failure although there were often strong extenuating circumstances. He was always an effective organizer who maintained strong fleet discipline from his FLAGSHIP, the *San Martin*, throughout the operation against England.

Medina Sidonia never deviated from the main objective of linking up with the Duke of Parma. He always displayed great courage during operations against the English, but he was no real match for his opponents. Following his defeat at the Battle of Gravelines, he was forced to withdraw northward, returning to Spain via Scotland and Ireland. Despite the complete failure of the Armada, the king retained his full confidence in Medina Sidonia, who retained all his posts. However, he was widely unpopular in the country and his reputation was further damaged by the British attack on CADIZ in 1596 and by the defeat of his squadron at the hands of the Dutch in 1606.

Peter Pierson, *Commander of the Armada: The Seventh Duke of Medina Sidonia*, London, 1989.

The Spanish Armada departs for England under the command of the Duke of Medina Sidonia   (*Copyright © National Maritime Museum, Greenwich, London*)

Mediterranean, Naval War in the
1939–45

Italy's entry into WORLD WAR II, 1939–45, on June 10, 1940 marked the beginning of the naval war in the Mediterranean, which was to continue for some three years until the Axis powers had been defeated. With the fall of France ten days later, initially the battle for control in this theater was fought between the Italians and the British, although the Germans and the Americans were to intervene later. The Italian fleet was larger and more modern than the Royal Navy's Mediterranean Fleet but had few other advantages. (See ITALIAN NAVY.) The first task facing Admiral Andrew CUNNINGHAM, the British commander in chief, was to prevent French naval units from falling into German hands. Action at Alexandria, MERS-EL-KEBIR and elsewhere quickly achieved this objective. Early successes were also secured against the Italian surface fleet, which British naval forces first met at the Battle of CALABRIA, July 9, 1940. The notable night raid on TARANTO, November 11, resulted in heavy damage to the Italian surface fleet, including three battle cruisers and two cruisers. The Italians suffered further losses at the Battle of CAPE MATAPAN, March 1941.

With Italy's naval forces on the defensive, the British had relatively little difficulty in resupplying the strategically positioned island of Malta. They were assisted by the fact that Italian ground forces also were performing badly in North Africa and Greece. However, these more favorable circumstances did not long survive the arrival of the Germans in the Mediterranean early in 1941. Land-based Luftwaffe squadrons operating from bases on Sicily and elsewhere soon placed the Royal Navy under considerable pressure. Several British warships were lost during the Battle of Crete, May–June 1941, and in other air attacks across the Mediterranean. As the Luftwaffe increasingly dominated the skies, Malta, which came under sustained air attack, could be supplied only by heavily protected convoys, which were to suffer considerable losses. British military and naval resources came under further pressure with German successes in Greece and North Africa. During 1941 the submarine was of growing importance, although it too was vulnerable to air attack and the shallow waters of the Mediterranean made operations more difficult than they were elsewhere. Despite these dangers, the U-BOAT caused serious damage to several MALTA CONVOYS, while Italian human torpedoes sank two British battleships at Alexandria. With supplies disrupted, Malta was close to collapse in the first few months of 1942 and its own flotilla of submarines had to be withdrawn from the island.

The changing fortunes of the North African war eventually came to Malta's rescue, as Luftwaffe units were diverted in support of General Rommel's offensive, which had been brought to a halt at El Alamein in July 1942. With American support, Malta was resupplied with increasing regularity, and now Axis convoys were subject to frequent attack. Their positions was further weakened by the British victory at El Alamein, October 23–November 4, 1942, and the Torch landings, November 7–10, 1942, which disrupted Luftwaffe operations from bases on the North African coast. By the time the Axis forces in North Africa had been defeated in May 1943, the balance of air and naval power had moved clearly in favor of the Allies, who also had access to better intelligence, although German submarines and aircraft remained as a reduced threat for some time.

The Italian navy surrendered at Malta in September 1943, although this action had little direct effect on the balance of power in the area. By this time the Mediterranean had been the scene of major amphibious landings in Italy, with Allied surface units providing support in the form of shore bombardments. The invasion of the south of France followed in August 1944. From late 1943 the Mediterranean had returned to a semblance of normality with Allied shipping traveling east once more using the route through the Suez Canal in preference to the much longer, but previously safer, journey around the Cape of Good Hope.

Corelli Barnett, *Engage the Enemy More Closely: The Royal Navy in the Second World War*, London, 1991; Donald Macintyre, *The Battle for the Mediterranean*, London, 1964; S. E. Morison, *History of United States Naval Operations in World War II*, 15 vols., Boston, 1948–64.

Melville, George Wallace
1841–1912

American naval officer who was identified with Arctic exploration and naval engineering. Born on January 10, 1841 in New York City, Melville was educated in engineering institutions and eventually received honorary engineering and doctorate degrees from Stevens Institute and Georgetown and Columbia universities. He entered the service as a third assistant engineer in 1861. During the AMERICAN CIVIL WAR, 1861–65, while serving on the *Wachusett* with the West India Squadron in 1863–64, he participated in the destruction of the Confederate cruiser *Florida* in Brazil. He volunteered as chief engineer on the *Jeannette* that sailed in 1879 to reach the North Pole through the Bering Straits; the vessel became trapped in pack or drifting ice for nearly two years until she sank in 1881 in northern Siberia.

Three boats left the *Jeannette*; Melville commanded the only one that survived. He set out to save his companions but only found the frozen bodies of the expedition's commander and 14 crewmen. Congress commended his efforts to find the remaining crew members. In 1884 he served on the *Thetis*, which was part of the squadron searching for the missing expedition led by Adolphus Greely that had set out in 1881 to reach the North Pole. For all his efforts in Arctic exploration, Melville was promoted over 44 officers ahead of him to become engineer in chief and chief of the Bureau of Steam Engineering in 1887. Melville subsequently served in that capacity until his retirement in 1903. An innovative administrator, he was instrumental in the adoption of steam propulsion in the navy. He died in Philadelphia, Pennsylvania on March 17, 1912.

William L. Cathcart, "George Wallace Melville," *Journal of the American Society of Naval Engineers* 24 (May 1912), pp. 477–511.

Menéndez de Avilés, Pedro
1519–74

*S*panish naval officer, founder of St. Augustine, Florida. Born in Avilés, Spain on February 15, 1519, Menéndez ran away to sea at the age of 14. Although eventually he was to become an officer in the SPANISH NAVY, Menéndez served as a CORSAIR during his first 15 years at sea. In 1549 King Charles I recognized his abilities by commissioning him to rid the Spanish coast of pirates. In 1554 Menéndez was appointed to the command of the Spanish treasure fleet on its annual voyage across the Atlantic to Spain. He not only held this responsibility for several years and suffered few losses, but also served in the Valois-Hapsburg War, 1547–1559, against France.

In 1565 King Philip II ordered him to expel a French Huguenot settlement that had occupied land in Florida claimed by Spain. Menéndez, who was given the right to found a Spanish colony there, left Spain in July 1565 with 11 ships and a crew of 2,000. He established a fort at St. Augustine and massacred the French settlers. Three years later the Spanish garrison was hanged following the capture of St. Augustine by the French. Menéndez died before he could bring more settlers from Spain. Today St. Augustine remains the oldest continually inhabited city in the United States.

Mermaid, H.M.S.

*S*crew propulsion was to be a revolutionary influence on the development of naval warfare in the 19th century because it allowed warship design to combine speed and maneuverability with an uninterrupted field of fire. The first seagoing ship with screw propulsion was the British-built *Archimedes*, which was launched in 1839. At first the ROYAL NAVY was not very receptive to the new technology, but, in 1843, it acquired the *Mermaid*, a small iron vessel of 164 tons, notable as its first screw-propelled steamer.

Built at Blackwall, east London, in 1842, her trials were held in May of the following year. The single screw turned at up to 153 revolutions per minute, producing a maximum

speed of 10.5 knots, or some 12 miles per hour. The ADMIRALTY had agreed to take her over if she could reach this speed, and the *Mermaid* was duly commissioned in the Royal Navy, with her name changed to *Dwarf*. The *Mermaid*'s performance helped to change official attitudes, but not until the decisive trials between the RATTLER and the ALECTO were held in 1845 was the Royal Navy finally persuaded of the benefits of screw propulsion.

Merrimack

A CONFEDERATE NAVY warship that fought a notable duel with the the MONITOR, a Union armored ship, in the Battle of HAMPTON ROADS on March 9, 1862, during the AMERICAN CIVIL WAR, 1861–65. The battle was notable as the first engagement between IRONCLADS. The *Merrimack* was originally a wooden-hulled steam-powered FRIGATE, authorized by Congress in 1845, with a displacement of 4,650 tons. She was armed with 40 guns. During the Civil War she was scuttled by Union forces when they abandoned the U.S. naval base at Norfolk, Virginia in April 1861. The Confederates subsequently raised her and converted her into an ironclad by covering her entire deck with 4-inch (10-cm) armor plates. The *Merrimack*'s armament was increased to 100 guns, and she was fitted with an iron RAM.

Renamed the *Virginia*, she went into action on March 8, 1862, attacking a federal blockading force in Hampton Roads and destroying two ships—the *Cumberland* and the *CONGRESS*. Fighting was renewed there the next day following the arrival of the MONITOR, which the Union navy had commissioned in response to news of the refurbished *Merrimack*. This first battle of the ironclads, which lasted more than four hours, proved to be a disappointment to both sides from a tactical standpoint. Neither vessel was able to inflict serious damage on the other because of the limited power of contemporary projectiles. Nevertheless, the engagement marks an important turning point in naval history because it established the importance of armor and the turreted gun. The *Merrimack* returned to Hampton Roads a month later, but she never fought her Northern opponents again. When the Confederates evacuated Norfolk in May 1862, she was burned and scuttled by her own crew.

William C. Davis, *Duel Between the First Ironclads*, Garden City, N.Y., 1975.

Mers-el-Kebir, British Attack on
July 3, 1940

*F*ollowing the defeat of France in the opening stages of WORLD WAR II, 1939–45, the fate of the FRENCH NAVY became a critical issue for the British. There were real fears that it might be turned over to the Germans; consequently, the British took action at several French naval bases to prevent this. On July 3, 1940 a British naval force under the command of Admiral Sir James SOMERVILLE arrived at the French base at Mers-el-Kebir in Algeria. Known as FORCE H, it consisted of two battleships, a battle cruiser, an aircraft carrier and 11 destroyers. The French commander refused all the options offered to him by Admiral Somerville, including surrender or sailing to a neutral port.

The British reluctantly replied to the French refusal with a massive bombardment and aerial attacks from carrier-based aircraft. The French battleship *BRETAGNE* was sunk and three other warships—the *DUNKERQUE, Mogador* and *Provence*—were seriously damaged. The battle cruiser *Strasbourg* escaped to Toulon, along with several smaller ships. Some 1,300 French seamen were killed, and the incident caused great bitterness. In retaliation, French aircraft attacked GIBRALTAR twice, and the bombardment generally soured Anglo-French relations for a significant period. On the other hand, no French warships joined the Axis powers. To that extent, the attack on Mers-el-Kebir (together with actions at other French naval bases) was a success.

Arthur Marder, *From the Dardanelles to Oran: Studies of the Royal Navy in War and Peace, 1915–40,* Oxford, 1974.

Miaoulis, Andreas
1768–1835

Commander of Greek naval forces during the Greek War of Independence, 1821–32, Andreas Miaoulis previously had been a merchant captain operating from the island of Hydra. Vessels of many different types were assembled under his authority as *navarch,* or admiral, and deployed in operations against the Turkish fleet, which used bases on the Greek mainland. The Greeks' general objective was to expel the Turks from Greek soil. Although the odds were stacked heavily against the much weaker Greek forces, Miaoulis proved to be an effective naval commander. A notable example was his success, in 1822, in raising the siege of Missolonghi. He remained in command until British, French, and Russian naval assistance appeared and decisively defeated the Turkish navy at the Battle of NAVARINO, 1827, with the result that the Greek War of Independence was finally won. Miaoulis continued in the service of the newly independent Greek state and, in 1831, fought a naval engagement at Poros against an extremist group with Russian connections that was attempting to seize power. Miaoulis was a member of the delegation that went to invite King Otto to accept the Greek crown; he was rewarded with eventual promotion to rear admiral and then vice admiral.

Middleton, Charles, First Baron Barham
1726–1813

British admiral and naval administrator. Middleton's early years at sea were spent partly in the West Indies. It was not until he moved, in mid-career, into naval administration that he made a real contribution to the development of the ROYAL NAVY. In 1778 Middleton was appointed Comptroller of the Navy, a post he was to hold for 12 years. As a rear admiral, he had overall responsibility for ship design and construction during the critical period of the war with France and the years preceding it. He also became a member of Parliament during this period. In 1794 he became a member of the Board of Admiralty and was able to contribute to the development of wartime naval strategy.

Middleton's great opportunity came in 1805, during the NAPOLEONIC WARS, 1803–15, when he replaced Lord MELVILLE as First Sea Lord following the latter's impeachment for misappropriating naval funds. Raised to the peerage as Lord Barham, the new First Sea Lord was responsible for naval strategy in the critical period before the Battle of TRAFALGAR, October 1805. He gave priority to the defense of the English Channel and its entrances, and supported Admiral Lord NELSON in his preparations for Trafalgar. Once the French threat had receded, Lord Barham, who was now over 80 years old, retired with an exemplary record of naval service behind him.

Midget Submarines

Largely a creation of WORLD WAR II, 1939–45, the midget submarine was used by most of the principal naval powers for attacking ships in harbor. Naval interest initially had focused on the development of the human torpedo, with the midget submarine following later. The ITALIAN NAVY, which had first used the human torpedo against the Austrians in WORLD WAR I, 1914–18, had considerable success with a later design, nicknamed the *Maiale* or Pig, which was operated by a two-man crew and was armed with a detachable 500-pound (227-kg) warhead. In 1940–41 these devices operated successfully against enemy merchant shipping in the Bay of Gibraltar. On December 19, 1941 three Italian human torpedoes penetrated Alexandria harbor and caused heavy damage to the British battleships *QUEEN ELIZABETH* and *Valiant.*

The British also developed a strong interest in the human torpedo and developed the CHARIOT from an earlier Italian design that had been found after the attack on Alexandria. Operated by two men who rode astride the body on saddles, its main purpose was to penetrate harbor defenses and attack enemy warships. The body housed a battery-powered motor and a 700-pound (317-kg) detachable warhead in the nose-cone. The Chariots operated most effectively in warm Mediterranean waters and achieved a number of spectacular successes against the Italian navy, including the destruction of three cruisers. The ROYAL NAVY developed the human torpedo concept with the introduction, in January 1943, of the X-CRAFT, which was a true midget submarine. The X-craft was designed to attack enemy warships in heavily defended anchorages that were beyond the range of land-based aircraft. Operated by a crew of four, the X-craft was armed with 2.2-ton Amatol explosive charges that were released under the target; they were detonated by a timing device. A diving chamber enabled a diver to leave the submarine to attach the devices to the hull of an enemy warship. The X-craft were involved in a number of successful operations including, most notably, the attack on the *TIRPITZ* in September 1943, which caused severe damage to her machinery. In another important action two midget submarines immobilized the Japanese cruiser *Takao* in Singapore Harbor on July 31, 1945.

The German and Japanese navies also had an interest in the midget submarine, although generally they were less successful in operating them. In the interwar period the Japanese developed an A-type midget submarine, which was used in the attack at PEARL HARBOR, December 1941. Armed with two torpedoes, it was employed in the first few months of the Pacific War until it was superseded by larger, more seaworthy designs, including the five-man D-type. However, production was disrupted by American air attacks, and in the closing stages of the war the Japanese turned to the less complex human torpedo as a last line of defense against the final Allied advance toward Japan. The KAITEN was a suicide weapon that consisted of a 24-inch (61-cm) LONG LANCE TORPEDO with a single pilot's cockpit on top. It achieved several successes against the U.S. Navy but was not produced in sufficient quantity to have a real impact on the course of the war. The German investment in midget submarines was less significant but the *Biber*, which carried two torpedoes, had some impact in northern European waters in 1944–45.

R. O'Neill, *Suicide Squads*, London, 1981.

Midway, Battle of
June 3–6, 1942

*O*ne of the decisive naval battles of WORLD WAR II, 1939–45, the Battle of Midway destroyed Japanese naval air superiority and placed Japan's naval forces in the Pacific on the defensive. Fought entirely by naval aircraft, out of range of the opposing fleets' guns, the battle had its origins in a complex Japanese plan to attack and occupy Midway Island, 1,000 miles (1,609 km) west of Hawaii.

The Japanese fleet was divided into eight task forces.

The first two were earmarked for a diversionary operation to seize the islands of Attu and Kiska in the Aleutian group, far to the north of Midway. (See ALEUTIAN ISLANDS CAMPAIGN, 1942–43.) This operation was designed to divert the U.S. Pacific Fleet from the Midway area to the north, but it failed completely because the Americans could read the Japanese fleet's secret signals codes. Four battleships and a light carrier group were involved in this action. The Midway occupation group, accompanied by cruisers and destroyers, was dispatched from the Mariana Islands. The main naval forces were sent direct from Japan. The First Carrier Strike Force, commanded by Admiral Chuichi NAGUMO, consisted of four carriers—the *KAGA, AKAGI, SORYU* and *HIRYU*—and 250 aircraft. Admiral Isoroku YAMAMOTO's main battle fleet included the battleship *YAMATO,* two other battleships, two heavy cruisers and a destroyer screen.

Admiral Chester NIMITZ responded to signals intelligence about Japanese intentions by dispatching two task forces from Pearl Harbor under the command of Rear Admiral Raymond SPRUANCE and Rear Admiral Frank FLETCHER, respectively. They included the carriers *Hornet, YORKTOWN* and *ENTERPRISE*. On June 3 land-based American aircraft first sighted the Japanese fleet some 600 miles (966 km) west of Midway and successfully attacked several transports. The following day 108 Japanese planes were sent to bomb Midway in preparation for the invasion; they caused severe damage to American aircraft on the ground.

Successive waves of American fighters were dispatched to attack the enemy, but it was not until the fifth attack—by Dauntless dive-bombers—that the Japanese suffered fatal damage. The aircraft carrier *Kaga* was sunk and the *Akagi* and the *Soryu* had to be abandoned. The *Hiryu* was sunk during the afternoon of June 4, but not before her aircraft had severely damaged the *Yorktown*, which was later sunk. Without carriers or air support, Yamamoto was unable to engage the American fleet in direct combat and was forced to withdraw to the west. Spruance pursued the enemy and launched further air attacks on them.

By the time the two fleets had lost contact on June 6, the Japanese had lost three carriers, some 275 aircraft and 5,000 men. The Americans suffered the loss of a destroyer and the carrier *Yorktown* as well as 150 aircraft and some 300 men. The Battle of Midway represented a turning point in the Pacific War and provided the opportunity for the Americans to mount a major counteroffensive. (See also Battle of the CORAL SEA.)

A. J. Barker, *Midway: The Turning Point*, New York, 1971.

Mikasa

A Japanese pre-dreadnought BATTLESHIP of 15,200 tons, the *Mikasa* was Admiral Heihachiro TOGO's

A Japanese Mogami-class heavy cruiser severely damaged by U.S. naval aircraft during the Battle of Midway, 1942 *(Copyright © Imperial War Museum, London)*

flagship at the Battle of TSUSHIMA, May 1905, during the RUSSO-JAPANESE WAR, 1904–5. Like much of the Japanese fleet of that era, she was British-built and was launched at the Vickers Yard in Barrow in Furness, northwest England, in 1900 and completed in 1902. The *Mikasa* had a maximum speed of 18.5 knots; her main armament consisted of four 12-inch guns (30-cm) and 16 six-inch (15-cm) guns. She had a length of 432 feet (132 m), a beam of 76 feet (23 m) and was operated by a crew of 830. During Togo's encounter with the Russian Baltic Fleet, commanded by Admiral Zinovi ROZHESTVENSKY, at the Battle of Tsushima, 1905, his flagship was severely damaged.

In September 1905, while undergoing repairs, an accidental magazine explosion caused the *Mikasa* to sink, but she was raised and repaired. She continued in service until after WORLD WAR I, 1914–18, when she was retired. The *Mikasa*'s close association with Admiral Togo meant that she was preserved as a national monument at Yokosuka dockyard, where she still remains today.

Milne, Sir Archibald Berkeley

1855–1938

*A*ppointed commander in chief of Britain's Mediterranean fleet in 1912, Archibald Berkeley Milne owed his position to royal influence rather than professional ability. His lack of judgment and initiative were, in fact, clearly revealed almost as soon as WORLD WAR I, 1914–18, began. In a very confused political and military situation in the Mediterranean area, the forces under his command failed to intercept the German warships GOEBEN and *Breslau* as they escaped through the eastern Mediterranean to neutral Turkey, where they were to be an important influence on the course of events.

Returning home soon afterward, Milne blamed equally Sir Ernest TROUBRIDGE for failing to engage the ships with his cruiser squadron and the ADMIRALTY for its unclear and incomplete orders. In particular, he complained that he had never been given any indication that the Germans' intended destination might be neutral Turkey rather than the Atlantic. Although Milne escaped official censure while Troubridge was court-martialed, it was clear that the navy's most senior officers held him directly responsible for failing to stop the *Goeben* and *Breslau*. As a result Admiral Jackie FISHER always referred to him contemptuously as "Sir Berkeley Goeben," and he was never again employed by the Royal Navy.

Minelayer

A specially-built or modified warship used by the world's navies for laying mines. Mines were first used in the CRIMEAN WAR, 1853–56, and appeared in larger numbers during the RUSSO-JAPANESE WAR, 1904–5. However, it was not until WORLD WAR I, 1914–18, that mines were used in substantial numbers and minelayers were produced in quantity. Normally they were equipped with powerful engines to enable the difficult job of mine-sowing to be completed as quickly as possible during the hours of darkness. This activity was not confined to surface ships for very long: Minelaying submarines, which could operate in secret, soon made their appearance.

Most minelayers in use during World War I were converted passenger liners or warships (normally cruisers or destroyers), but during the interwar period specially designed vessels, which were capable of carrying several hundred mines, appeared. These custom-made ships had a high maximum speed and could lay mines quickly at night. They were, however, soon to be replaced by minelaying aircraft and submarines as new types of mine appeared. Using aircraft and submarines proved to be the quickest and cheapest method of laying mines without revealing their position to an enemy, although some modern warships also have this capability.

Mines

A cheap but nevertheless highly effective form of passive defense, naval mines were first used by the Russians in the Black Sea during the CRIMEAN WAR, 1854–56, and later during the AMERICAN CIVIL WAR, 1861–65. The explosive power of these early mines, however, was so small as to cause little real damage to a ship. By WORLD WAR I, 1914–18, two main types of mine were in use: observation mines, which were detonated from shore, and contact mines, moored just below the water's surface, that exploded when a ship struck one of the "horns" protruding from the mine's casing. The British contact mine Type H2 was laid in large quantities from 1916 onward in coastal waters; nearly a third of all U-BOAT losses were due to its effectiveness.

During the interwar years, improved electronics allowed the development of magnetic, acoustic and pressure mines, which were in production by the beginning of WORLD WAR II, 1939–45. German aircraft dropped the first type around British coasts in 1939. This led to the countermeasure of degaussing (counteracting a ship's magnetic field by installing a live wire around her hull) and the use of wooden (later replaced by fiberglass) hulled minesweeping vessels (See MINESWEEPER.) Acoustic mines were destroyed by simulating the noise of a ship's propeller, but pressure types were the most difficult to sweep; first they had to be detected by sonar and then removed by divers.

Although contact mines are still in use (and proved to be a hazard during the GULF WAR, 1990–1), today's mines are far more sophisticated and can be programed to activate themselves when certain types of vessels are in the area but to let others pass without exploding.

N. Friedman, *U.S. Naval Weapons. Every Gun, Missile, Mine and Torpedo Used by the U.S. Navy from 1883 to the Present Day*, Annapolis, 1982.

Minesweeper

A n essential component of the world's navies, the minesweeper encompasses a wide variety of vessels capable of sweeping or exploding mines laid in coastal waters or on the high seas. In the late 19th century, the first minesweepers often were converted fishing boats that had the task of disabling the contact mines in use at the time. The minesweeper would trail under water a long serrated cable that would catch the mine's anchor chain. This cable had cutters that severed the chain, with the result that the mine would float to the surface. The crew could then use rifles to shoot at the mine; when they hit one of its horns, it would explode. When two minesweepers operated together, with a cutting wire extended between them, a wider area of minefield could be cleared in a single operation. Shortly after the end of WORLD WAR I, 1914–18, a device (the Oropesa sweep) was invented to spread a wire net while in use at sea, enabling one minesweeper to do the work of two. As other types of mines were invented, the techniques to clear them became more complex and new minesweeper designs were called for.

The task became even more difficult when different types of mines were mixed in the same field and antisweeping devices were added to them. Pressure mines (which are activated by the pressure waves of a passing ship) are the most difficult to locate and deal with: Sonar equipment is needed to locate them and frogmen are required to disable them. Acoustic mines are detonated by simulating the sound of a ship's engine and propellers using underwater noise. Sweeping magnetic types requires the use of ships with wooden or fiberglass hulls—the magnetic field of a steel-hulled vessel would detonate the mine. To deal with magnetic mines, two minesweepers were normally used, with two electric cables, known as the LL sweep, stretched

A British World War II minesweeper at sea   (Copyright © National Maritime Museum, Greenwich, London)

between them. Electric current was passed along the cables, creating a series of magnetic fields that detonated any magnetic mines positioned between the two ships. A typical contemporary oceangoing minesweeper has a displacement of about 800 tons and is operated by a crew of 45. Minesweepers have played a crucial role in the naval wars of the 20th century. Nowhere was this more evident than in the NORMANDY LANDINGS, 1944, when British minesweepers led the invasion force across the English Channel on June 6, clearing any mines from its path and allowing it to land on the French coast.

Peter Elliot, *Allied Minesweeping in World War II*, London, 1979.

Minorca, Battle of

May 20, 1756

The loss of Minorca to the French represented a significant setback to the British position in the opening stages of the SEVEN YEARS' WAR, 1756–63. A French squadron of 12 ships of the line under Admiral Roland de La Galissonnière had escorted a CONVOY of 150 transports carrying 13,000 troops to Minorca in April 1756. The island was rapidly brought under French control, with the exception of Port Mahon, which the French soon blockaded. The British, who were under pressure elsewhere, could manage only a feeble response. A squadron of ten ships of the line commanded by Admiral John BYNG left England for Minorca early in April.

As Byng arrived off Port Mahon, the French came out to meet him and, on May 20, a limited engagement began. Byng attacked the French center at an angle, but Glassonnière took effective counter action. Both sides sustained damage, although the French received the worst of it. Instead of remaining in the area, Byng decided to withdraw to GIBRALTAR, allowing the French to force the surrender of the British garrison at Port Mahon on June 29. Unfavorable public reaction to the surrender compelled the British government to find a scapegoat, and on his return to England Admiral Byng was court-martialed for neglect of duty. He was found guilty and shot.

H. W. Richmond, ed., *Papers Relating to the Loss of Minorca in 1756*, London, 1913.

Mississippi, U.S.S.

An American BATTLESHIP of only 12,985 tons, the Mississippi was launched in 1905. Her construction on this small scale reflected the views of those admirals and politicians who wished to guard against the United States becoming an imperial power by preventing the creation of a powerful American battleship fleet. This unrealistic strategy meant that the Mississippi was obsolete even before she entered service following the launch of the British-built DREADNOUGHT in 1906. The Mississippi had a maximum speed of 17 knots, was operated by a crew of 736 and her main armament consisted of four 12-inch (30-cm) guns. She was only 382 feet (116.43 m) in length and had a beam of 77 feet (23.47 m).

Her brief career with the UNITED STATES NAVY was uneventful except for a period in 1914 when she was deployed at Vera Cruz during the dispute with Mexico. There she operated two seaplanes, which carried out what were among the first photographic reconnaissance missions in aviation history. Later the same year the outdated Mississippi, together with her sister ship the Idaho, was sold to the Greek navy. Shortly afterward the U.S. Navy again used the names Mississippi and Idaho for two battleships of the New Mexico class that appeared in the 1920s and served throughout WORLD WAR II, 1939–45.

Missouri, U.S.S.

The fourth American Iowa-class battleship, which had been authorized in 1940, the Missouri was the setting for the Japanese surrender in Tokyo Bay on September 2, 1945. Known as the Mighty Mo, she had been commissioned in mid-1944 and was the last battleship to enter the U.S. Navy during the war or after. The Missouri saw some action in the Pacific in the closing stages of WORLD WAR II, 1939–45. Along with her sister ships IOWA, NEW JERSEY and WISCONSIN, she also served in the KOREAN WAR, 1950–53, before being decommissioned. The Missouri and the three other Iowa-class battleships were modernized and recommissioned in the 1980s. The Missouri briefly returned to service during the GULF WAR, 1990–1. She was used to shell land-based targets on the Kuwaiti coast and as a CRUISE MISSILE platform for strikes against Iraq.

The Iowa-class vessels were the largest American warships ever built, the Missouri herself being 887 feet 6 inches (270 m) in length and having a displacement of 58,000 tons. Operated by a crew of 2,788, she was armed with nine 16-inch (41-cm) guns, housed in triple turrets, that could fire a 27,000-pound (12,247-kg) shell over a distance of 23 miles (37 km). Despite her great size, the Missouri had a maximum speed of 33 knots, which was sufficient to enable her to screen the fast American carriers operating in the Pacific during World War II.

The Missouri is to be given a permanent resting in Pearl Harbor, Hawaii, as a "Statue of Liberty of the West."

Malcolm Muir, *The Iowa Class Battleships*, Poole, Dorset, 1987.

Mitscher, Marc Andrew
1887–1947

One of the most popular and well-respected commanders in American naval aviation during WORLD WAR II, 1939–45, Mitscher was born in Hillsboro, Wisconsin, on January 26, 1887 and entered the U.S. Naval Academy in 1906. Joining the fledgling naval aviation program, he earned his wings in 1916 as naval aviator number 33, then engaged in early experiments in aircraft catapults aboard AIRCRAFT CARRIERS. Following WORLD WAR I, 1914–18, he piloted one of the three Navy-Curtiss planes that were attempting a transatlantic crossing. Although he was forced down, one plane completed the crossing from Newfoundland to Plymouth, England via the Azores and Lisbon, in May 1919. Soon afterward he served on the U.S.S. LANGLEY, the U.S. Navy's first aircraft carrier.

A central figure in the interwar years who advocated and worked to develop naval aviation and incorporate it with the fleet, he outfitted and commanded the carrier Hornet just before the Japanese attack on PEARL HARBOR, December 7, 1941. Mitscher commanded that vessel when she served as the takeoff point for the army bomber units of Lieutenant Colonel James Doolittle on the famous raid over TOKYO in April 1942. He continued to command the Hornet during decisive the Battle of MIDWAY, June 1942, before taking charge of all aircraft involved in the actions in the SOLOMON ISLANDS in 1943. He led the First Carrier Task Force and Task Force 58 during the Central Pacific drive, winning the Battle of the PHILIPPINE SEA in June 1944, which all but ended Japan's naval air power. As commander of First Fast Carrier Task Force, he participated in the Battle of LEYTE GULF in October 1944 as well as in the attacks on IWO JIMA, OKINAWA and on the Japanese home islands. In July 1945 he became Deputy Chief of Naval Operations for Air. He died on February 3, 1947 while serving as commander in chief of the Atlantic Fleet.

Theodore Taylor, *The Magnificent Mitscher*, Annapolis, 1991.

Mobile Bay, Battle of
August 5, 1864

Used as a base by Confederate BLOCKADE runners during the AMERICAN CIVIL WAR, 1861–65, Mobile Bay (at the mouth of the Mobile River, in Alabama, on the Gulf of Mexico) was closed by a successful action by the Union

Rear Admiral David Farragut defeats the Confederate Navy at the Battle of Mobile Bay, 1864 *(Copyright © National Maritime Museum, Greenwich, London)*

navy. On August 5 a Union squadron commanded by Rear Admiral David FARRAGUT entered the narrow channel that led from the Gulf of Mexico to Mobile Bay. The channel was mined and also protected by the guns of Fort Morgan. The squadron was organized in two columns: The first consisted of four IRONCLAD MONITORS and the second, 14 wooden steamers that were tied together in seven pairs.

The leading monitor, the *Tecumseh,* was destroyed by a mine (see MINES); the rest of the squadron hesitated until Farragut led the way in his FLAGSHIP, the *Hartford.* Several Union ships were hit by gunfire from Fort Morgan, but the minefield did not claim any more victims. As the squadron entered the bay, it encountered the Confederate ironclad *Tennessee* and three gunboats under the command of Admiral Franklin BUCHANAN. The stronger Union squadron overwhelmed the Confederate gunboats in fierce fighting and eventually forced the *Tennessee* to surrender. Resistance finally ended when Fort Morgan capitulated. Mobile Bay was firmly in Northern hands and one of the Confederacy's few remaining ports had been lost. As a result, blockade running in the Gulf of Mexico effectively came to an end.

J. T. Scharf, *History of the Confederate States Navy,* New York, 1887.

Mocenigo, Pietro
d. 1476

Venetian naval commander and Doge of Venice, 1474–76, a member of a noble Venetian family that produced several distinguished admirals. Pietro Mocenigo, one of the most accomplished of Venice's naval leaders, was responsible for the reconstruction of the Venetian navy after its defeat by the Turks at Negroponte in 1470. In its revitalized form, under Admiral Moncenigo's leadership, the navy achieved a series of victories against the Turks. In 1472 he captured Smyrna. The following year he placed Cyprus under his protection; by 1475 he had taken control of the island. Moncenigo's distinguished naval career concluded in 1476 with a spectacular victory over the Turks, who were besieging Scutari (Albania). During this campaign he contracted an illness from which he died.

Moewe

The most successful German COMMERCE RAIDER of WORLD WAR I, 1939–45, the *Moewe* was originally a banana carrier of 4,788 tons, launched in 1914. As a disguised ARMED MERCHANT CRUISER she was, in effect, the German equivalent of the British Q-SHIP. During her first voyage of just over two months, mainly in the Atlantic, she sank 15 Allied merchant ships before returning home in March 1916. On the *Moewe*'s second four-month sortie, which began late in November 1916, her activities resulted in the destruction of a further 27 ships and the disruption of Allied ship movements over a wide area. After returning to Germany unscathed, she was employed as an auxiliary MINELAYER for the remainder of the war.

Moffett, William Adger
1869–1933

Often termed the Father of American Naval Aviation, Moffet was born in October 1869 in South Carolina. He entered the U.S. Naval Academy in 1886. Following a routine career until 1898, he took part in the capture of Guam during the SPANISH-AMERICAN WAR as well as in the last bombardment of MANILA before the city surrendered. In 1914 he participated in the occupation of Vera Cruz, Mexico, while captaining the U.S.S. *Chester*, for which he was awarded the Congressional Medal of Honor. During WORLD WAR I, 1914–18, he was instrumental in establishing training procedures for new recruits.

In March 1921 Moffett was made director of naval aviation; he was elevated to chief of the newly created Bureau of Aeronautics in July of that year. As a rear admiral, he earned enough flying time to receive his naval aviation observer's qualifications. In an unusual procedure, he served as chief of the aeronautics bureau for three consecutive four-year tours, transforming the bureau—amid criticism both from within and without the navy—into a firmly established part of the navy's administration and policy. He died on April 4, 1933 in the crash of the airship *Akron* off Lakehurst, New Jersey.

Edward Arpee, *From Frigates to Flat-tops: The Story of the Life and Achievements of Rear-Admiral William Adger Moffett, U.S.N.*, Lake Forest, Ill., 1953.

Moltke

German BATTLE CRUISER OF WORLD WAR I, 1914–18. Although she did not have the impact of her identical sister ship the *GOEBEN*, she also had an eventful war, serving with the Scouting Group of the HIGH SEAS FLEET throughout. The *Moltke* was present at the Battle of the DOGGER BANK, 1915, and at the Battle of JUTLAND, 1916, where she was hit by four shells. In 1918 she was torpedoed by British submarines after she had stripped one of her turbines. Although seriously damaged, she managed to survive the war. The *Moltke* was surrendered to the Allies at the end of the war and was scuttled at SCAPA FLOW in June 1919.

Monarch, H.M.S.

The first British warship to be named *Monarch* was notable as the place of execution of Rear Admiral John BYNG on March 14, 1757. A third-rate (see RATING OF SHIPS) SHIP OF THE LINE, she had been seized from the French at the Battle of USHANT, 1747, during the WAR OF THE AUSTRIAN SUCCESSION, 1740–48.

Monarch was also the name of a second British warship that had a notable career lasting some 48 years. Launched in 1765, she served in the AMERICAN WAR OF INDEPENDENCE, 1775–83 and the FRENCH REVOLUTIONARY AND NAPOLEONIC WARS, 1792–1815. This *Monarch* played a leading role in the Battle of CAMPERDOWN, 1797, where she fired the opening shots, and in the first Battle of COPENHAGEN, 1801. She was finally broken up in 1813.

Monck, George, First Duke of Albemarle
1608–70

British naval commander and general, a member of an influential Devonshire family. Chosing the career of a soldier, Monck fought in the Low Countries for ten years, 1629–38. In the English Civil War, 1642–51, he fought on the royalist side until his capture at the Battle of Nantwich, 1644. During two years' imprisonment in the Tower of London, he switched sides, and on his release he fought for the Commonwealth in Ireland and then in Scotland, where he defeated opposition to Cromwell.

His command in Scotland was interrupted by the First ANGLO-DUTCH WAR, 1652–54, when he was asked to go to sea. Despite his lack of experience, he proved to be a bold and able naval commander, defeating the Dutch at the Battle of PORTLAND, February 18–20, 1653 and following it with victories at the GABBARD, June 2–3, and at Scheveningen, July 31. The period of relative instability that followed Cromwell's death convinced Monck of the need for the restoration of the monarchy, and he played a key role in ensuring its return in 1660.

Monck was ordered to return to sea in 1665 at the beginning of the Second Anglo-Dutch War, 1665–67, but he did not repeat the successes he achieved in the first war with the Dutch. He was defeated by Admiral Michiel de RUYTER at the FOUR DAYS' BATTLE, June 1–4, 1666, although the Battle of ORFORDNESS, July 1666, reversed England's fortunes. He could not prevent, but responded quickly to, the Dutch attack on CHATHAM in June 1667, organizing the defense of key positions on the Medway River. After the end of the war Monck increasingly withdrew from public life because of ill health.

Admiral George Monck was an outstanding naval commander during England's wars against the Dutch in the 17th century   *(Copyright © National Maritime Museum, Greenwich, London)*

Hugh C. B. Rogers, *Generals-at-sea. Naval Operations During the English Civil War and the Three Anglo-Dutch Wars*, Bromley, Kent, 1992; Oliver Warner, *Hero of the Restoration: A Life of General Monck, First Duke of Albemarle, KG*, London, 1938.

Monitor

𝒜 shallow-draft armored warship, introduced in the 1860s. With its origins in the earlier BOMB VESSEL, the first ship of this type actually was named the *MONITOR*. It was built for the Union navy during the AMERICAN CIVIL WAR, 1861–65. Equipped with two 11-inch (28-cm) guns mounted in a rotating gun tower positioned amidships, she was designed primarily for shore bombardment purposes. Several similar ships were built during the war, and the name "monitor" was used to describe an entire class of ship that continued in use in the UNITED STATES NAVY into the 20th century.

Monitors also were employed by the BRITISH NAVY in the two world wars, but elsewhere they often appeared in a reduced form as river GUNBOATS. Used in blockades and on river patrols, their low freeboard made them unsuitable for use on the open sea. In the period following WORLD WAR II, 1939–45, monitors disappeared because their armament became obsolete with the development of the GUIDED MISSILE. (See also IRONCLAD.)

Monitor

𝒯 he original *Monitor*, which gave her name to an entire class of ship, was a shallow-draft American IRONCLAD. She was designed by the Swedish engineer John ERICSSON for use by the Federal navy in the AMERICAN CIVIL WAR, 1861–65. A strange-looking vessel, described by a contemporary as a "cheesebox on a raft," the *Monitor* was produced in response to the news that the Confederates were converting the wooden ship *MERRIMACK* as an ironclad. Launched in 1862, she had a displacement of 1,200 tons and was armed with two 11-inch (28-cm) guns in a revolving turret protected by 8-inch (20-cm) plates. The *Monitor* was steam-powered and had a maximum speed of only four knots.

She went into action on March 9, 1862, when she fought the *Merrimack* in HAMPTON ROADS, notable as the first engagement between ironclads and a turning point in naval history. The battle was inconclusive because of the limited power of contemporary projectiles, but it clearly demonstrated the advantages of armored ships and revolving gun turrets. There were, however, doubts about the seaworthiness of this particular design: She was not very stable and was almost lost twice on her journey to the famous battle. These doubts were confirmed only a few months later when she sank in a gale on December 31, 1862.

In spite of the *Monitor*'s limitations, more shallow-draft ironclads were ordered during the American Civil War. Britain and the United States used MONITORS for shore bombardment and river duties until well into the 20th century.

William C. Davis, *Duel Between the First Ironclads*, Garden City, N.Y., 1975.

Monson, Sir William
1568–1643

𝓔 nglish admiral and author, Sir William Monson served throughout the war with Spain, 1585–1603. In 1581, he ran away to sea and was involved almost immediately in an engagement with an enemy ship that became the first Spanish prize ever brought to England. During the SPANISH ARMADA, 1588, he was a volunteer on the *Charles*, a royal ship. He served under the Earl of Cumberland in subsequent operations against the Spanish treasure fleets. During the second of these expeditions, in 1591, he was captured by Spanish forces and spent two years in captivity. Monson gained his revenge in 1596 when, as commander of the *Rainbow*, he participated in the successful CADIZ expedition. Operations against Spain were concluded in 1602 when Monson commanded the *Swiftsure*. He was part of the force that captured a valuable enemy CARRACK as well as the GALLEY in which he himself had been confined some 11 years earlier.

In 1604 Monson's services were rewarded by his appointment as Admiral of the Narrow Seas, a post that made him second in command under the Lord High Admiral. As commander of English home waters, his responsibilities included suppressing PIRACY and preventing incursions by Dutch and Spanish ships. His term of office ended in 1614 with his brief imprisonment in the Tower of London after evidence was discovered that he had received payments from Spain in return for turning a blind eye to the activities of Spanish ships. Monson returned to naval duty for a short period in 1635, but his later years were largely occupied in compiling six volumes of *Naval Tracts*, a detailed and valuable picture of 16th-century naval warfare based largely on his own experiences.

Montagu, Edward, First Earl of Sandwich
1625–72

*E*nglish admiral who first distinguished himself as a soldier fighting on the side of Parliament in the Civil War, 1642–51. In spite of his lack of naval experience, Montagu was made a general at sea in 1653 and served under Admiral Robert BLAKE. Initially he saw little action, and it was political influence rather than distinguished service that secured his appointment as commander of the fleet in the final months of the Protectorate. Samuel PEPYS was Montagu's secretary at this time, and there are frequent references to Montagu, in his diary.

Montagu's leading role in the restoration of the monarchy in 1660 was rewarded with a peerage. As the Earl of Sandwich he served with distinction in the Second and Third ANGLO-DUTCH WARS (1665–67, 1672–74) and was briefly, in 1665, commander in chief of the fleet. However, he was temporarily removed from the navy because of his involvement in the misappropriation of prize money and sent to Spain as ambassador extraordinary. He was killed during the Battle of SOLEBAY, May 28, 1672, when his ship, the *Royal James*, was blown up by the Dutch.

F. R. Harris, *The Life of Edward Montagu, KG, First Earl of Sandwich (1625–1672)*, 2 vols., London, 1912.

Montagu, John, Fourth Earl of Sandwich
1718–92

*B*ritish politician and naval administrator who held the office of First Lord of the Admiralty for three separate periods (1749–52, 1763, 1771–82) during the 18th century. Although his reputation was severely tarnished by

Britain's naval failures in the AMERICAN WAR OF INDEPENDENCE, 1775–83, when he served in Lord North's administration, Montagu was an able administrator by the standards of his age. He made a significant contribution to the modernization of the ROYAL NAVY by ending abuses and introducing much-needed reforms. He laid the foundations of Lord NELSON's navy and thus contributed to the victory at TRAFALGAR, 1805, which occurred some 13 years after his death. Sandwich's decision to give the fleet copper-bottomed hulls, enhancing their performance, is one major example. The improvement in the system of ship-to-ship signals is another. Sandwich also was responsible for the introduction of the CARRONADE, a short-barreled light gun, on British warships.

At the same time, Sandwich was not immune to the excesses of the period: Corruption, gambling and the Hellfire Club were inextricably linked to him, particularly in the early years of his career. During this period he gave his name to the "sandwich," a snack he created so that he could eat without leaving the gaming table. The Sandwich Islands, the Hawaiian group discovered by Captain James COOK, also were named for him: Sandwich was honored because of his active support for Cook's three voyages of exploration.

N. A. M. Rodger, *The Insatiable Earl: A Life of John Montagu, Fourth Earl of Sandwich, 1718–1792*, London, 1993.

Monte Christi, Battles of
March 20 and June 20, 1780

*T*wo naval engagements between British and French squadrons fought off the north coast of Santo Domingo in the West Indies during the AMERICAN WAR OF INDEPENDENCE, 1775–83. The first engagement occurred when Captain William CORNWALLIS, commander of a British squadron of three ships, intercepted a French CONVOY as he cruised off Monte Christi. The French merchantmen, on their way from Martinique to Cape François, were escorted by four ships of the line and a frigate under the command of La Motte-Picquet. A prolonged fight ensued; it continued until Cornwallis was reinforced and the French were compelled to withdraw. The British commander returned to battle at the same location three months later when he intercepted a French convoy escorted by Commodore de Ternay, who commanded a squadron of seven ships of the line. Despite his more powerful naval force, the French commander, who was reluctant to attack the British, made good his escape from the area.

Moorer, Thomas Hinman
1912–

*T*he youngest American naval officer to earn four stars (the rank of full admiral) in peacetime, Moorer served for two consecutive terms as Chief of Naval Operations. He was the highest-ranking naval officer in post during the VIETNAM WAR, 1964–75. Born in Mount Willing, Alabama on February 9, 1912, he entered the U.S. Naval Academy in 1929. As a young aviator at PEARL HARBOR in December 1941, he was one of the few pilots to get airborne in a vain search for the Japanese after their attack. Early in 1942 he was shot down north of Australia in his patrol plane. Wounded, he was able to land his craft in the water. He and his crew were rescued by a passing merchant vessel, only to be sunk by enemy planes on the same day as his rescue.

A series of shore and sea tours followed until 1964 when he received, at the age of 52, his fourth star as commander in chief of the Pacific Fleet. The following year he served as the supreme Allied Commander, Atlantic, of the North Atlantic Treaty Organization (NATO) and as commander in chief of the Atlantic Fleet. He was the only officer to have commanded both the Atlantic and Pacific fleets. Moorer became the Chief of Naval Operations in 1967 and was reappointed two years later. In 1970, President Richard M. Nixon named him chairman of the Joint Chiefs of Staff, the highest military office in the United States. Moorer retired in July 1974.

J. Kenneth McDonald, "Thomas Hinman Moorer," in *The Chiefs of Naval Operations*, ed. Robert W. Love, Jr., Annapolis, 1980.

Moreell, Ben
1892–1976

*A*merican naval engineer who became known as the King of the Seabees. Born on September 14, 1892 in Utah, Morrell received his civil engineering degree in 1913 and entered the navy's Civil Engineering Corps in 1917. Advancing through the ranks as public works officer as well as designer and builder of dockyards and repair facilities, he was promoted to rear admiral and appointed in December 1937 to be the navy's Chief Engineer as well as Chief, Bureau of Yards and Docks, positions he held throughout WORLD WAR II, 1939–45.

With the Japanese attack in December 1941, Moreell created the Naval Construction Battalion, nicknamed the "Seabees," consisting of engineers and construction workers who, unlike those on Guam and Wake Island, would be trained in the use of weapons in order to defend themselves. Assigned to build any type of advanced base, their numbers grew from about 3,000 early in 1942 to 250,000 by the war's end, and they oversaw the construction of roads, airstrips, bridges, docks and other facilities, many within range of hostile action. In February 1944 Moreell became the first Civil Engineering Corps officer to reach the rank of vice admiral. He remained instrumental in engineering operations after the war, becoming in June 1946 the first

U.S. Navy staff officer to reach the rank of admiral. He died on July 30, 1976.

Karl Schuon, *U.S. Navy Biographical Dictionary*, New York, 1964, pp. 178–180.

Morgan, Sir Henry
1635–88

*W*elsh-born buccaneer who operated against the Spanish in the Caribbean from 1655 to 1671. Morgan first arrived in Barbados as an indentured servant, but he later left to join a group of BUCCANEERS operating from St.-Domingue (Santo Domingo). In 1655 he took part in the capture of Jamaica and participated in a raid on Cuba. Morgan was later commissioned by the governor of Jamaica to attack and capture various Spanish settlements, including Puerto Bello, 1668, Maracaibo, 1669, and Panama, 1671. These operations were conducted during a period when England was at peace with Spain, and they caused

Henry Morgan, a notable buccaneer, at the storming of Panama in 1671 *(Copyright © National Maritime Museum, Greenwich, London)*

considerable irritation in London. Morgan was sent home with his future in considerable doubt, but a sharp deterioration in Anglo-Spanish relations saved him. Knighted by King Charles II, he continued in the service of the English crown on his return to Jamaica, holding the deputy governorship on two separate occasions.

D. Pope, *Harry Morgan: The Biography of Sir Henry Morgan, 1638–84*, London, 1977.

Morosini, Francesco
1618–94

Venetian admiral of noble birth who served the city-state of Venice and defended its imperial possessions with distinction in a series of campaigns against the Turks. His early career at sea concluded with his distinguished conduct at the Battle of Naxos in 1650. Soon afterward he was appointed commander in chief of the Venetian navy, and he continued naval operations against the Turks with renewed vigor. His operational career was interrupted by political intrigues that resulted in his temporary recall. Morosini was quickly restored to his command when the Turks laid siege to the fortress of Candia in an effort to extend their hold on Crete. Despite Morosini's courageous leadership, eventually the Venetians were forced to surrender. When war with the Turks was renewed in 1684, Morosini was again appointed commander in chief of the navy. Through a succession of naval victories, Morosini recaptured lost Venetian possessions in the Peloponnese and elsewhere on the Greek mainland. In 1688 he became doge of Venice; five years later he returned to sea for the last time, adding to his earlier victories against the Turks.

Motor Gunboat

A fast coastal motor boat used by the principal navies of WORLD WAR II, 1939–45, based on the designs successfully deployed in WORLD WAR I, 1914–18. Produced in large numbers, its main function was to attack enemy ships in coastal waters; its victims during World War II ranged from a cruiser to small merchantmen. After a period of neglect in the interwar period, the ROYAL NAVY led the way with a major construction program at the beginning of the war. Sharing the same basic design as the motor TORPEDO BOAT, the typical gunboat might have a displacement of 40 tons, a maximum speed of 40 knots and a crew of 12, although there was a wide variation in the detailed specifications. It was likely to be armed with a 2-pounder (.9 kg) gun, two 20-mm cannon and four 0.303-inch machine guns. One of the secondary tasks of the motor gunboat was to act in support of the torpedo boat, and as the war progressed a combined boat was produced. The motor torpedo boat was widely used in the main theaters of the war and produced an impressive toll of enemy ships. In the postwar period motor gunboats were succeeded by fast patrol boats as a generic type. Typically, they are powered by gas turbines; are armed with guns, torpedoes or guided missiles; and have a range of up to 100 miles (60 km). They have been used by major navies during the key conflicts of the Cold War period, including VIETNAM, as well as for regular coastal patrol and defense by countries that otherwise have few naval resources at their disposal.

Mountbatten, Louis, Prince Louis of Battenberg
1854–1921

British admiral of the fleet who was the eldest German-born son of Prince Alexander of Hesse and the Rhine. He went to England at an early age and was naturalized as a British subject. Admiral Prince Louis entered the ROYAL NAVY in 1868, and his early career progressed rapidly. In 1902 he was appointed director of naval intelligence and later served successfully as commander of the Atlantic Fleet and then as Second Sea Lord at the Admiralty. He made many contributions to the development of his profession, particularly in the areas of signals and gunnery.

Appointed First Sea Lord in 1912, Prince Louis's tenure at the British ADMIRALTY did not long survive the outbreak of WORLD WAR I, 1914–18. Attacks on his German origins soon began, and he resigned his office in October 1914, being succeeded by Admiral Jackie FISHER. Just prior to the declaration of war, Prince Louis had made the critically important decision to keep the reserve fleet in commission rather than disperse it after the completion of the general test mobilization in July. As a result, Britain's naval forces were in a high state of readiness. His second son, Louis MOUNTBATTEN, was a distinguished British naval officer and statesman.

Mark Kerr, *Prince Louis of Battenberg, Admiral of the Fleet*, London, 1934.

Mountbatten, Louis Francis Victor Albert Nicholas, First Earl Mountbatten of Burma
1900–79

British naval commander, statesman and confidant of leading members of the royal family, Mountbatten was the younger son of Prince Louis MOUNTBATTEN. Known as Prince Louis Francis of Battenberg until 1917, when the German family name was Anglicized, he followed his father's footsteps into the ROYAL NAVY. He was educated at the Royal Naval Colleges at Osborne and Dartmouth before joining the fleet in 1916 for operational service in WORLD WAR I, 1914–18. Mountbatten served successively

Lord Mountbatten, Admiral of the Fleet, played a critical role in planning many of the combined operations of World War II
(Copyright © Imperial War Museum, London)

in the battleships *LION* and *QUEEN ELIZABETH*, which formed part of the GRAND FLEET. During the interwar years he became a radio communications specialist and, in 1934, was appointed to his first command as captain of the *Darling*.

During the first two years of WORLD WAR II, 1939–45, Mountbatten, then a captain, commanded the Fifth Destroyer Squadron, which he led in the *KELLY*. He was involved in the evacuation of Allied troops from Norway, May 1940, but soon afterward the *Kelly* was torpedoed by the Germans off the Dutch coast. She escaped under Mountbatten's skillful leadership while under constant attack, and the episode added greatly to his reputation. The flotilla later was sent to the Mediterranean, where the *Kelly* was sunk off Crete in May 1941. Later that year Mountbatten was appointed as adviser on combined operations, where he was involved in the raids on ST. NAZAIRE and DIEPPE, the North African landings and advance planning of the NORMANDY invasion. In 1943 he moved to a wider stage as Supreme Allied Commander, Southeast

Asia, where his strategy was to focus on the reconquest of Burma from the Japanese; this was finally achieved in 1945.

At war's end he was raised to the peerage and was appointed, in 1947, as the last viceroy of India, overseeing the transition of the colony to independence. His naval career resumed in 1948 when he was appointed to the Mediterranean fleet, which he later commanded, 1953–54. In 1955 he became First Sea Lord and then, in 1959, chief of the defense staff, where he was heavily involved in the creation, in 1964, of a unified Ministry of Defence. He retired in 1965. Mountbatten was murdered by the Irish Republican Army in 1979 when a bomb planted in his boat blew up while he was vacationing in Ireland.

Malcolm H. Murfett, *The First Sea Lords: From Fisher to Mountbatten*, London, 1995; Philip Ziegler, *Mountbatten*, London, 1985.

Mulberry Harbor

When the Allied invasion of France was being planned during WORLD WAR II, 1939–45, it was obvious that a large port (such as CHERBOURG) would have to be captured initially in order to land sufficient supplies. However, the severe losses incurred during the DIEPPE RAID, August 1942, showed that this would be an impossible operation. As a result, it was decided to build an artificial harbor, code-named Mulberry, that could be towed across the English Channel in sections and sunk off the Normandy beaches.

A brilliant idea (that owed much to Winston Churchill's personal encouragement), the Mulberry harbor consisted of concrete cassions, code-named Phoenix, connected together by a series of causeways that rose and fell with the tide. To protect the Mulberry harbor, a row of old merchant ships would be sunk alongside the structure to provide a breakwater. During the NORMANDY landings, June 1944, a Mulberry harbor was used at Arromanches and another at Omaha Beach, although the latter was badly damaged in a storm on June 19–21. The idea of Mulberry harbor caught the Germans by surprise. After Dieppe they had heavily fortified all the main ports along the French coast but failed to anticipate the development of an artificial harbor.

G. Hartcup, *Codename Mulberry*, Newton Abbot, Devon, 1977.

Muller, Georg Von
1854–1920

Chief of the German Navy cabinet, 1908–18, Muller was at the center of naval policy-making throughout WORLD WAR I, 1914–18. His close working relationship with Kaiser Wilhelm II and his role in trying to reconcile the differing views of political and naval leaders on key

An artificial Mulberry Harbor at Arromanches on the Normandy coast in 1944 *(Copyright © National Maritime Museum, Greenwich, London)*

issues often brought him into conflict with his professional colleagues. His opposition to an all-out attack on the British GRAND FLEET and, during the first half of the war, to unrestricted SUBMARINE warfare also caused friction within the navy. Although he was a late convert to the benefits of a new U-BOAT campaign, he never regained the confidence of his naval critics. In fact, when Admiral Reinhard SCHEER assumed the supreme naval command in August 1918, plans were made to remove Muller from office, but the war ended before they could be implemented.

Murderer

Naval antipersonnel gun of the 17th and early 18th centuries. Constructed of brass or iron, this handgun fired iron balls or pieces. It was fitted with a pin that enabled the gun to be secured in a socket located at various key points on board ship. The ship's crew used the murderer to repel enemy boarding parties; it was an essential piece of naval equipment until MARINES became part of the crew of every English warship early in the 18th century. The murderer survived longer in the merchant service, where there was a continuing need for it in case of attack by privateers.

Mutiny

In a naval context, mutiny may be defined as a persistent refusal by one or more members of a ship's crew to obey legitimate orders issued by a superior officer. The term also describes a general uprising by the crew or a physical attack on an officer. Mutiny does not necessarily involve violence, although the threat of violence normally is present. By its very nature mutiny is an extreme act that has occurred irregularly in naval history. It has been prompted by a variety of motives, although in the days of the sailing navies mutinies often were organized to secure improvements in basic pay and conditions.

The British naval mutiny at SPITHEAD, April–May 1797, is an example of a case where mutinous crews sought and secured much-needed improvements in their terms of employment. There was general agreement that the crews' claims were justified, and those involved escaped punishment. In another case, the British INVERGORDON MUTINY, 1931, was triggered by a decision to reduce naval pay by 10%, and again the action produced a positive result: the withdrawal of the cut. Mutiny also can be used to remove an authoritarian captain from his command. The mutiny on the *BOUNTY* is a prime example of this type of action, which succeeded in ejecting Captain William BLIGH from his ship.

A third type of mutiny is more politically based and might seek to change the direction of government policy. The mutiny of the crews of the German HIGH SEAS FLEET at Wilhelmshaven and Kiel in October 1918 was designed to prevent the fleet's final death ride as planned by its commanders. As a result, the fleet disintegrated, and the mutinies were a factor in bringing World War I to an end. Yet another example is the KRONSTADT MUTINY in 1917, when Russian sailors threw their weight behind the revolution, although only four years later, in 1921, they were to rise against the new Soviet government. (See KRONSTADT REBELLION.)

Until relatively recently the penalty for mutiny in virtually all the world's navies was death by hanging at the yardarm. In practice only the ringleaders might suffer the extreme penalty, with the rank and file receiving a lesser punishment or none at all. Today mutiny would be rewarded with dismissal from the service and a period of imprisonment rather than death. The Spithead mutiny is a good example of an illegal act that the authorities came to regard as justified; as a result, those involved escaped punishment.

Myngs, Sir Christopher
1625–66

*B*ritish naval commander who served under both Oliver Cromwell and Charles II and whose career was unaffected by the Restoration of 1660. Myngs served in the First ANGLO-DUTCH WAR, 1652–54, and was appointed to his own ship, the *Elizabeth*, shortly before the war ended. Some months later, in October 1653, he captured a Dutch convoy and two escorts in the English Channel, an action that brought him wide recognition. Myngs spent several years in the West Indies before returning home to fight in the Second Anglo-Dutch War, 1665–67. At the Battle of LOWESTOFT, 1665, he was vice admiral of the white squadron and was knighted for his services there. Myngs was killed in the closing stages of the FOUR DAYS' BATTLE, 1666.

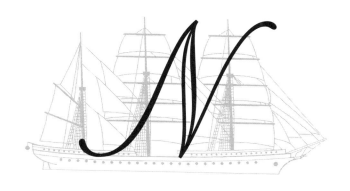

Nagano, Osami
1880–1947

Japanese naval commander, educated at Harvard University and the Japanese naval academy, Etajima, whose first major posting was as naval attaché to the Japanese Embassy in Washington, D.C., 1920–23. In 1928 he was promoted to the rank of rear admiral. Nagano's progress continued with his appointment as superintendent of the naval academy, 1928–29. In 1935–36, he headed the Japanese delegation to the second London naval conference, where he spoke in support of the development of Japanese naval power. He was JAPANESE NAVY minister, 1935–36, and commander in chief of the combined fleet, 1937. In April 1941, shortly before Japan's entry into WORLD WAR II, 1939–45, Nagano was appointed chief of the naval general staff and had a major influence on the strategic direction of the Pacific War. He held the post until February 1944. Initially an opponent of war with the United States on the grounds that it was potentially more powerful and therefore bound to prevail in the long run, he later supported the objective of securing a decisive blow against the American fleet at PEARL HARBOR. Nagano died in 1947 while awaiting trial for war crimes.

Nagato

The Japanese BATTLESHIP *Nagato*, which was completed in 1920, was the first to be armed with 16-inch (41-cm) guns. The guns were mounted in four twin turrets and had a maximum range of 17.5 miles (28 km). The *Nagato* had a maximum speed of 24.75 knots, a displacement of 33,800 tons and efficient armor protection, particularly below the waterline. She was 708 feet (216 m) in length and had a beam of 95 feet (29 m). During a major refit in 1934, the *Nagato*'s armor protection was further improved; the introduction of oil-fired boilers significantly increased her range. During WORLD WAR II, 1939–45, the *Nagato*

served in some of the major battles of the Pacific War, including MIDWAY, 1942, the PHILIPPINE SEA, 1944, and LEYTE GULF, 1944. She survived the war but was confiscated by the Americans and sunk at Bikini Atoll during an atomic bomb test in July 1946. The *Mutsu*, her sister ship, was lost when one of her magazines exploded in July 1943.

Nagumo, Chuichi
1887–1944

Japanese vice admiral and commander of the aircraft carrier force used in the attack on PEARL HARBOR, December 1941, in WORLD WAR II, 1939–45. His previous experience had been concentrated on cruisers, and he was a TORPEDO specialist. In view of inexperience with naval aviation and the fact that he was noted for being extremely cautious, Nagumo's wartime appointment is difficult to explain. He also was known to have little enthusiasm for underlying Pearl Harbor strategy. As commander of the First Air Fleet, Nagumo, in the flagship *AKAGI*, successfully launched a surprise air attack against Pearl Harbor from his carrier force. A second strike was completed successfully; despite professional advice to the contrary, Nagumo failed to order a third attack, which might have completed the destruction of the American base. In the months that followed, his carriers supported the conquest of the Dutch East Indies and were involved in successful raids on Darwin and Ceylon (Sri Lanka).

At the Battle of MIDWAY, June 1942, Nagumo suffered a serious blow. Dogged by bad luck and poor intelligence, he failed in his objectives of sinking the American carriers and destroying the islands' defenses. His failure to move decisively resulted in the loss of all four of his fleet carriers, and Nagumo's wartime career took a downward path from that point on. Lacking sufficient confidence in himself, he was unable fully to exploit tactical advantages at the Battle of the EASTERN SOLOMONS, August 1942, and the Battle of the SANTA CRUZ ISLANDS, October 1942. In November

1942 Nagumo was relieved of his command and replaced by Vice Admiral Jisaburo OZAWA. He was appointed to the command of the much less important Central Pacific Fleet. In 1944 he organized the defense of the Marianas Islands but, on July 6, he committed suicide when it became clear that the American invasion of Saipan would succeed.

Nakhimov, Paul
1803–55

Russian naval commander, a veteran of the Battle of NAVARINO, 1827, during the Greek War of Independence, 1821–32, who defeated a Turkish squadron under Vice Admiral Osman Pasha at SINOPE on November 30, 1853. The battle, a turning point in modern naval history, revealed the vulnerability of unprotected wooden ships to high-explosive shells. As a result, navies rapidly replaced their traditional ships with the IRONCLAD. Nakhimov continued to serve as head of the Russian Black Sea Fleet during the CRIMEAN WAR, 1853–56, which soon followed the initial conflict with Turkey. He was fatally wounded during the Anglo-French attack on Sebastopol that led to the port's capture in September 1855.

Napier, Sir Charles
1786–1860

British admiral and eccentric, widely known as Mad Charley, who lost substantial sums operating a steamboat service on the Seine River in Paris. His service on the side of the Portuguese monarchy in the Miguelite Wars, 1826–34, an extended struggle for control of the monarchy, was his greatest success. Napier had seen two earlier periods of service in the ROYAL NAVY and had reached the rank of post-captain during the Napoleonic Wars, 1803–15. During the postwar period he operated steam vessels on the Seine, and he financed the construction of the world's first iron steamship in 1821.

In 1833 Napier accepted command of Dom Pedro's "Liberation Squadron", which had been formed by the Brazilian emperor as part of the force attempting to recover the throne for his daughter, Queen Maria. She had lost her position in 1828 when Miguel, her former regent, seized it by force. Napier defeated the naval forces of Dom Pedro's opponents, the Miguelite Party, off Cape St. Vincent on July 5. During the civil war on land he commanded the forces that captured Lisbon on July 24 and then held it against the Miguelites until the latter were forced to surrender. Napier was created Count Cape St. Vincent by a grateful Dom Pedro.

Napier returned to the Royal Navy for a time for the Syrian campaign of 1840, where he damaged his reputation by disobeying orders and exceeding his authority. When the CRIMEAN WAR, 1853–56, began Napier was appointed to the command of the British Baltic Fleet, but he achieved virtually nothing at a time when public expectations of success were high. As an elderly commander out of touch with the requirements of modern naval warfare, he could offer little, and after his return home he was not sent to sea again, although he spent much energy in trivial disputes with the Admiralty.

Napoleonic Wars
1803–15 *See* FRENCH REVOLUTIONARY AND NAPOLEONIC WARS, 1792–1815.

Narborough, Sir John
1640–88

English naval commander who first saw service as a lieutenant in the Second ANGLO-DUTCH WAR, 1665–67; he was promoted to the rank of captain before the war had ended. Narborough commanded a ship in the West Indies before being appointed, in 1669, to command an expedition to the Pacific Ocean with the objective of undermining the Spanish trade monopoly there. The expedition had only limited success in unfavorable circumstances, but Narborough's reputation was unaffected by its indecisive outcome. He subsequently commanded the *Prince*, the FLAGSHIP of JAMES, Duke of York, at the Battle of SOLEBAY, 1672, during the Third Anglo-Dutch War, 1672–74.

After the war he was appointed commander in chief in the Mediterranean with the rank of rear admiral. During his three years in this post, 1674–77, he waged war against the pirates and was successful in securing the return of British property and slaves. When he arrived back in London he became a Lord Commissioner of the Admiralty, 1679–87, which proved to be his final naval appointment. He resigned from this office in order to recover gold from a wrecked Spanish treasure ship in the Caribbean but died on the outward journey.

Florence E. Dyer, *The Life of Admiral Sir John Narborough*, London, 1931.

Narvik, Battles of
April 1940

On April 9, 1940, during WORLD WAR II, 1939–45, the Germans invaded Norway at a several points, including a landing by sea at Narvik, a port in the north of the country at the head of the Ofot Fjord. Several German invasion transports, which were accompanied by ten destroyers, disembarked troops with orders to seize the port.

Narvik was of strategic importance because it handled shipments of Swedish iron ore bound for Germany.

The Second British Destroyer Flotilla, which was in the area, was ordered to attack the enemy naval force. Commanded by Captain B. Warburton-Lee, the British FLOTILLA consisted of five destroyers—*Hardy, Hunter, Havock, Hotspur* and *Hostile*. At first light on April 10, the British entered Ofot Fjord and moved eastward toward Narvik, where they entered the harbor and attacked the stronger German naval force. Initially the British action met with success: Two enemy destroyers—the *Wilhelm Heidkamp* and the *Anton Schmidt*—were sunk and three others damaged. However, a group of five German destroyers struck back with devastating effect. Two British ships were lost and Captain Warburton-Lee was fatally wounded. By 6:30 A.M. the action was over, and the British withdrew from the fjord. During the withdrawal the British hit and sank the transport ship *Rauenfels*, which carried most of the Germans' stock of ammunition.

The British made a second attempt to destroy the remaining German destroyers three days later in the second Battle of Narvik. A flotilla consisting of the battleship WAR-SPITE and nine destroyers, commanded by Vice Admiral W. Whitworth, entered the fjord. The first action occurred when the British discovered and sank the destroyer *Erich Koellner* in an inlet some distance from Narvik. The main engagement took place outside Narvik Harbor when three German destroyers were sunk. The surviving German warships were pursued farther east into Rombaks Fjord, where they all met their end. This second battle cost the German navy eight destroyers and a submarine. Combined German losses in the two battles amounted to about half of its entire destroyer capability. The British flotilla survived intact although two destroyers were damaged.

J. L. Moulton, *A Study of Warfare in Three Dimensions: The Norwegian Campaign of 1940*, Athens, Ohio, 1967.

Nassau

$\mathcal{G}$erman BATTLESHIP OF WORLD WAR I, 1914–1918, that was the namesake of a class. Germany's first dreadnoughts, the Nassau-class battleships were ordered in 1907 and produced quickly in response to the British lead in this new type. An enlarged version of the pre-dreadnought DEUTSCHLAND class, the *Nassau* had a displacement of 18,570 tons and a maximum speed of 18 knots. Main armament consisted of 12 11.1-inch (28-cm) guns; there were twin turrets fore and aft on the centerline and two on each beam. She also was well equipped with secondary armament. The relatively light main guns enabled the designers to give her additional armor protection, and in this respect the Nassau-class ships were superior to contemporary Allied ships. The *Nassau* had a length of 479 feet (146 m) and a beam of 88 feet (27 m).

Completed in 1909–10, the *Nassau, Posen, Rhineland* and *Westfalen* all served with Battle Squadron I of the HIGH SEAS FLEET from the beginning of World War I, 1914–18, and all were present at the Battle of JUTLAND, May 1916. Only the *Posen* was undamaged. The *Rhineland*, which ran aground in 1918, was the sole ship of this class not in service at the end of the war.

Nautilus, U.S.S.

$\mathcal{T}$he world's first nuclear SUBMARINE, the *Nautilus* entered service with the United States Navy in 1954 and marked the beginning of a revolution in submarine warfare. She was part of a plan to create a nuclear-powered U.S. fleet. Among the surface ships to follow the *Nautilus* were U.S.S. LONG BEACH, 1961, the first nuclear-powered CRUISER, and U.S.S. ENTERPRISE, 1961, the first nuclear-powered AIRCRAFT CARRIER.

Built in Groton, Connecticut by the General Dynamics (Electric Boat) Corporation, the *Nautilus* had a displacement of 4,040 tons, a length of 319 feet (97 m) and a beam of 28 feet (8.5 m). Her nuclear reactor powered two steam turbines that gave a record submerged speed of more than 20 knots; she could dive to a depth of 720 feet (219 m). The *Nautilus* was equipped with six torpedo tubes and was operated by a crew of 105, including ten officers.

She was capable of remaining underwater for long periods. An indication of her potential was given in 1958 when she became the first submarine to travel under the polar icecap from the Pacific to the Atlantic—a feat that had enormous strategic implications. The *Nautilus*'s naval career ended in 1980; and she has been preserved at the U.S. Navy submarine base at Groton.

The *Nautilus* was the name of three other submarines, including an early experimental craft built in France in 1801. It also was the name that French author Jules Verne gave to the submarine in his novel *Twenty Thousand Leagues under the Sea*, 1870.

Naval Aviation

$\mathcal{T}$he development of naval aviation began not long after the Wright brothers made the first powered and controlled flight in December 1903. At first it was believed that the main maritime role of aircraft would be reconnaissance patrols, but various experiments in the period before WORLD WAR I, 1914–18, confirmed that the potential of aircraft at sea was much wider. Early American bombing experiments included an aerial attack on a ship in June 1910. In Britain, the newly established Naval Wing of the Royal Flying Corps (soon to become the ROYAL NAVAL AIR SERVICE) also conducted some early bombing tests, dropping torpedoes from seaplanes. It soon became clear that

An American carrier packed with aircraft (including U.S. Navy Hellcats, Helldivers and Avengers) during the Pacific War, 1941–45 *(Copyright © Imperial War Museum, London)*

if naval aircraft were to be used effectively against enemy warships, they could not be based at coastal air stations but would have to operate from ships underway at sea. Experiments in the United States, Britain and other countries began in 1910 with American trials involving takeoffs from stationary ships that had been fitted with flying platforms. The first takeoff from a moving ship occurred in 1912, when a biplane took off from the British warship H.M.S. *Hibernia.*

The British devoted significant resources to the Royal Naval Air Service in the prewar period, and by the beginning of World War I, it had over 90 aircraft and seven airships. The GERMAN NAVY had devoted considerable effort to the development of large rigid airships (dirigibles), designed by Graf Ferdinand von Zeppelin, quantities of which were produced during the war. Zeppelin naval airships were used on reconnaissance duties in the North Sea and for bombing raids on England. The British and German navies used land-based naval aircraft—typically twin-engined flying boats—on reconnaissance duties and antisubmarine warfare. British naval aircraft patrolled the North Sea in a systematic spiderweb pattern. Ship-based aircraft also were widely used during the war, although at first the takeoff deck was no more than a simple platform fitted to a battleship or a converted merchant ship. Early ship-based aircraft were seaplanes that were forced to land in the water and were lifted on board by a crane. Not until August 1917 did an aircraft land on a moving ship: a British Sopwith Pup returned to the deck of H.M.S. *Furious.* This major step led to the development of new naval aircraft, such as the Sopwith Cuckoo, that were specifically designed for use on carriers. However, the revolutionary impact of these developments on naval warfare was not immediately accepted or understood.

Claims by General William (Billy) Mitchell, head of the U.S. Army Air Service, that air power had made the BATTLESHIP obsolete led to his court-martial and suspension from the service in 1925. Mitchell's views were based on his experiments in which a formation of bombers was used successfully to attack and sink several decommissioned battleships. Despite the strength of naval conservatism, the development of the AIRCRAFT CARRIER continued during the interwar period. The typical carrier aircraft of the period was a monoplane that was armed with bombs or torpedoes and equipped with folding wings, enabling it to be stored belowdecks. The PACIFIC WAR, 1941–45, demonstrated the importance of air power at sea, with dive-bombers determining the outcome of an engagement without the opposing surface fleets ever coming into contact. One of the finest naval aircraft of the Pacific War was the Mitsubishi A6M, known as the Zero by the Allies. The Japanese navy used it in KAMIKAZE attacks on Allied naval forces during the closing stages of the war.

In the postwar period, naval aviation has retained its key place in naval warfare. The role of carrier-based naval aircraft was extended during the Cold War period and afterward as major powers intervened in local wars. Carriers often provided the means for such intervention, with carrier-based aircraft being used against land targets. Carrier aircraft have been supplemented by the HELICOPTER, which has been deployed on a variety of different ships in an antisubmarine role. Maritime patrol aircraft also have played a major role in the detection of enemy submarines and in providing early warnings of impending attacks.

John W. R. Taylor, *A History of Aerial Warfare*, London, 1974.

Naval Warfare

*I*n the Middle Ages, fighting at sea was similar to warfare on land. The medieval HIGH-CHARGED SHIP was a fighting platform that carried soldiers as well as seamen to sail it. A fleet would close in on the enemy, who would be attacked by arrows or gunfire. The soldiers would seek to board an enemy vessel, overcome their opponents in hand-to-hand combat and then set fire to it. The Mediterranean GALLEY also carried soldiers for fighting, with slaves being used to man the oars. The general introduction of the naval CANNON in the early 16th century marked the end of the warship as a fighting platform. Gunports were cut in the sides of the warship, which became an instrument of war in its own right. Although soldiers were still carried on board for a while, the tactic of boarding as the primary objective of war soon disappeared. This transition was completed with the appearance of the GALLEON with two or three gundecks in the late 16th century.

At first the same lack of order was evident in these newly equipped naval forces as had been the case in the past, but discipline gradually improved during the 17th century. In England, the official *FIGHTING INSTRUCTIONS,* first issued in 1653, provided the basis for fighting in line-ahead formation, which enabled broadside guns to be used to their maximum effect. Coordination was further enhanced by the introduction of improved SIGNALING systems. Eventually the benefits of these changes were over-shadowed by the excessive rigidity in their application, enforced by official sanction, which made it difficult for individual captains to seize opportunities that might arise during battle. The only officially permitted flexibility in these rules was the provision for a general chase if the enemy started to withdraw. In these circumstances individual ships were permitted to leave the line and engage an enemy ship. The old rules broke down to some extent during the FRENCH REVOLUTIONARY AND NAPOLEONIC WARS, 1792–1815, as English captains, including Lord NELSON, developed innovative new tactics to defeat the French. Harnessing the power of new gun designs, the English fleet concentrated the fire of several ships on the center and rear, with the aim of breaking the enemy line before other warships had an opportunity to intervene.

The traditional tactics remained in place until armored ships, breechloading guns and explosive shells forced radical changes in naval warfare in the 1860s. (See GUNS AND GUNNERY.) The introduction of these more powerful guns meant that naval combat at close quarters came to an end, although the RAM made a brief but unsuccessful reappearance in the latter part of the 19th century. Exchanges of gunfire took place at increasingly long range as improvements in gunnery sought to keep pace with developments in armor protection and the risks of fighting in close proximity became ever more apparent. However, the prospects of hitting a ship on the horizon were always uncertain, and other means of attacking enemy ships, including TORPEDOES, destroyers and submarines, were soon to appear. During the first part of the 20th century, improvements were made in the gunnery and control systems of the new dreadnought BATTLESHIPS and BATTLE CRUISERS. At the same time, the introduction of the RADIO improved the control of ships during battle.

Despite these improvements, WORLD WAR I, 1914–18, provided strong indications that the days of the battleship—and of the big gun—were numbered as the MINE, aircraft and submarine made their impact. The full potential of the SUBMARINE as an instrument of economic warfare was felt in the Battle of the ATLANTIC, 1915–17, which almost brought Britain to its knees before the belated introduction of the CONVOY system. By WORLD WAR II, 1939–45, direct combat between large surface units was rare, and during the war only one battleship was sunk solely by gunfire. The main threat to surface ships came from the submarine and from the air, and the AIRCRAFT CARRIER was the capital ship of the World War II period. Protected by supporting ships, it did not normally see the target that its aircraft were attacking.

The submarine has been dominant naval unit of the postwar period, with the nuclear-armed types playing a major strategic role in nuclear deterrence. Much naval capability has been devoted to protecting and hunting these boats, using the GUIDED MISSILE warships that form the core of the modern navy. Despite their cost and potential vulnerability, the aircraft carrier has survived. It has provided the basis for great-power intervention in limited war and has given contemporary naval power the ability to influence the outcome of operations on the ground as well as at sea.

J. S. Corbett, ed., *Fighting Instructions, 1530–1816*, London, 1905; John Keegan, *The Price of Admiralty: The Evolution of Naval Warfare*, London, 1989; Brian Tunstall, *Naval Warfare in the Age of Sail: The Evolution of Fighting Tactics, 1680–1815*, London, 1990.

Navarino, Battle of

October 27, 1827

The decisive battle of the Greek War of Independence, 1821–32, Navarino had its origins in an agreement made by England, France and Russia in July 1827, known as the Treaty of London. The treaty aimed to secure an armistice between the Greeks and Turks as well as the withdrawal from Greece of the Egyptian forces that had been involved in the war since early in 1825. Turkey opposed these peace moves because it had not yet restored its control over the whole of Greece. By 1827, land operations were focused on the southwest Peloponnese. Supplies and reinforcements for the Turkish army were transported to Navarino Bay, where an Egyptian-Turkish fleet of 65 ships, under the command of Ibrahim Pasha, was based.

In September 1827, Sir Edward CODRINGTON, British commander in chief in the Mediterranean, was instructed to prevent further reinforcements from reaching the Turks. He was ordered to blockade Navarino but to avoid a battle. French and Russian squadrons soon joined the British off the Greek coast; the combined force consisted of 11 ships of the line and 16 other warships. Local efforts to negotiate a cease-fire with Ibrahim Pasha ended in failure, and, on October 20, having learned of new operations ashore, Codrington decided to increase pressure on the enemy. The allied ships entered Navarino Bay, where the enemy fleet was anchored in an extended horseshoe formation. Codrington's principal warships moved into the semicircle and anchored by 2:30 P.M. At this point a dispatch boat from the British frigate *Dartmouth* was attacked at close range; as the allies returned fire, the Egyptian warships responded with a BROADSIDE.

The action became general with a heavy bombardment that lasted for three hours. It was no more than a gun duel between floating batteries and the Turks, who had unwisely fired the opening shots, were defeated decisively. Heavily outgunned, even with supporting shore batteries, they lost one ship of the line, 34 other warships and a number of smaller vessels. With only 15 vessels left afloat and over 4,000 casualties, the Turkish navy sustained losses that were to have a long-term impact on its power. Many allied ships also were severely damaged, and 696 lives were lost.

Apart from its contribution to the struggle for Greek independence, Navarino was notable as the last major fleet action to be fought entirely under sail. Codrington himself was unable to celebrate his victory because he had been

British, French and Russian naval forces defeated the Turks at the Battle of Navarino, 1827, and brought the struggle for Greek independence to a successful conclusion   *(Copyright © National Maritime Museum, Greenwich, London)*

ordered to return to London, where he was charged with disobeying his orders not to engage the enemy. Eventually he was cleared of blame.

C. M. Woodhouse, *The Battle of Navarino*, London, 1965.

Nef

A type of fully rigged sailing merchantman and warship, developed in France, that was very similar in design and function to the COG. The medieval nef had a broad beam, was bulbous in appearance and its hull was carvel-built (i.e., with flush side planks). It was normally single-masted and had the typical fore- and aftcastles of the cog and other ROUND SHIPS. Usually, however, its stern was more rounded than that of the cog. Later 15th- and 16th-century versions were significantly larger (up to 400 tons) and had three masts. Like other medieval ships, the nef's naval function—to act as a fighting platform at sea—would remain essentially unchanged throughout its long life.

Negapatam, Battle of
June 25, 1746

*A*lso known as the Battle of Fort St. David, this action between French and English forces during the War of the AUSTRIAN SUCCESSION, 1739–48, took place between Negapatam and Fort St. David on the east coast of India. A small English squadron, commanded by Commodore Edward Peyton, was cruising off the Coromandel coast on June 25. It sighted a small enemy squadron commanded by Admiral the Comte Mahé de la Bourdonnais. The more powerful English force, which consisted of six ships, including the 60-gun *Medway*, seemed incapable of taking decisive action. The engagement, which began at 4 P.M. was constrained by a lack of wind, but the English commander proved ineffective. The French were able to withdraw from a potentially dangerous situation with less damage than their opponents. Peyton also withdrew from the area, and the French were able to capture the Indian city of Madras.

Negapatam, Battle of
August 3, 1758

*S*ome three months after their engagement in the Indian Ocean at CUDDALORE, in April 1758, the English and French fleets met again off Negapatam on the east coast of India. This second battle, on August 3, 1758, was as inconclusive as the first and had little or no impact on the course of the SEVEN YEARS' WAR, 1756–63. Vice Admiral Sir George Pocock, who had seven British ships of the line under his command, returned to the fight on July 27,

appearing off Pondicherry, which was held by the enemy. A French squadron of nine ships of the line, under the command of Admiral the Comte d'Aché, left Pondicherry the following day and was pursued southward for a few days. Eventually the French were brought to battle off Negapatam on August 3, and in fierce fighting they sustained particularly heavy casualties. The Comte d'Aché's tactics were wholly defensive, and the French squadron made good its escape to the north as soon as possible.

Negapatam, Battle of
July 6, 1782

*F*ollowing the Battles of SADRAS and PROVIDIEN, the naval engagement off Negapatam was the third battle between British and French naval forces in the Indian Ocean during the latter stages of the AMERICAN WAR OF INDEPENDENCE, 1775–83. After the Battle of PROVIDIEN, April 12, 1782, Admiral Sir Edward HUGHES and his squadron of 11 ships of the line had completed their voyage to Trincomalee in Ceylon, where he disembarked troop reinforcements. The French force, which also consisted of 11 ships of the line, commanded by Admiral Pierre de SUFFREN, had returned to the Coromandel coast near Madras. Suffren then landed troops at the coastal town of Cuddalore, with the objective of retaking Negapatam, some 60 miles away, which was held by the British. Hughes, who was aware of the enemy's intentions, sailed for Negapatam. The two opposing squadrons clashed on July 6. Fighting was intense but, like the two earlier engagements, did not produce a clear outcome. However, the French were unable to land at Negapatam and Suffren was forced to withdraw to the north while the British entered the city.

Nelson, Horatio, First Viscount
1758–1805

*B*ritain's greatest admiral, the hero of numerous naval battles, most notably that of Trafalgar. Born in Burnham Thorpe, Norfolk, on September 29, 1758, Horatio Nelson was the son of a parson. He entered the ROYAL NAVY in 1770 at the age of 12 and served under his uncle, Captain Maurice Suckling, in the West Indies and elsewhere. He became a captain in 1784 before spending five years on half pay. Returning to the service when war with France began in 1793, Nelson was appointed to the command of the 60-gun *AGAMEMNON* and ordered to serve under Rear Admiral Samuel HOOD in the Mediterranean. In 1794, during the campaign in Corsica, Nelson was blinded in the right eye while the siege of Calvi was under way. He recovered sufficiently to take command of an independent squadron, 1795–97, operating in the Mediterranean.

Lord Nelson as victor at the Battle of the Nile, 1798   *(Copyright © National Maritime Museum, Greenwich, London)*

Nelson served as a commodore under Admiral John JERVIS (later Earl St. Vincent) at the Battle of CAPE ST. VINCENT, February 13, 1797, and played a key role in the defeat of the Spanish fleet. His initiative and personal courage were much in evidence throughout the battle. He was knighted and promoted to rear admiral for his contribution to the victory. In further operations against the Spanish, he attempted to capture Santa Cruz, Tenerife, but was unsuccessful and lost his right arm as the result of a wound suffered in the fighting. He returned to service in 1798 as commander of the squadron blockading the French naval base at Toulon and raised his flag in the *Vanguard.* The French fleet, commanded by Admiral François Brueys, escaped during a storm, with Nelson, rapidly appointed to the command of a detached squadron, in pursuit. Nelson eventually concluded that Brueys's fleet was escorting Bonaparte's army across the Mediterranean for an invasion of Egypt. The fleet was discovered in Aboukir Bay and, on August 1, the Battle of the NILE ensued. In a famous victory Nelson mounted a high-risk attack from the shore side for which the French were completely unprepared. Due to his destruction of the enemy fleet, he was elevated to the peerage as Baron Nelson of the Nile. Nelson was based next at Naples, where he unsuccessfully involved himself in the king's affairs and began a celebrated liaison with Emma, Lady Hamilton, the wife of the British ambassador.

Returning to England in 1800, he fought as a vice admiral at the Battle of COPENHAGEN in 1801. In this expedition he served as second in command under Sir Hyde PARKER whose fleet was sent to Denmark to prevent the Danes from providing further economic aid to France. The British victory over the Danish fleet was achieved only because Nelson ignored Parker's ill-judged signal to withdraw at the height of the battle. Nelson raised a telescope to his blind eye and declared that he could not see the signal. For his contribution to the British victory, he was created Viscount Nelson. When war with France resumed in 1803, Nelson was appointed to the command of the British Mediterranean Fleet in his FLAGSHIP VICTORY. He was ordered to Toulon to blockade the French fleet but was unable to prevent Admiral the Comte de VILLENEUVE from eventually breaking out in April 1805 as part of Napoleon's plan to invade England. The French crossed the Atlantic before returning to unite with the Spanish fleet and taking shelter at Cadiz.

When the combined navies returned to sea under Napoleon's orders, they were intercepted by Lord Nelson and defeated at the Battle of TRAFALGAR, October 21, 1805, one of the last major actions to be fought under sail. The battle was notable for Nelson's unconventional tactics in breaking the enemy line, which led to Villeneuve's defeat. Although fatally wounded in the *Victory* by an enemy musket fired by a sharpshooter from the French warship *Redoutable,* Nelson survived long enough to be aware of the final outcome. His victory meant that Napoleon was unable to proceed with his invasion plans, and English seapower dominated the oceans for the remainder of the Napoleonic Wars. Nelson's four major victories—Cape St. Vincent, the Nile, Copenhagen and Trafalgar—established his reputation as one of the greatest of naval tacticians who was always receptive to new approaches. He also possessed outstanding leadership qualities and enjoyed particularly close working relations with his immediate subordinates who were always extremely loyal.

Christopher Hibbert, *Nelson. A Personal History,* London, 1994; Tom Pocock, *Horatio Nelson,* London, 1987; Oliver Warner, *A Portrait of Lord Nelson,* London, 1988.

Nelson, H.M.S.

A British BATTLESHIP of almost 34,000 tons built in accordance with the terms of the Treaty of WASHINGTON, 1922. (See WASHINGTON CONFERENCE.) Completed in 1927, the *Nelson* (named after Admiral Lord NELSON) and her sister ship, the *Rodney,* were the only British battleships to carry 16-inch (40-cm) guns, which were mounted in three triple turrets. These were all located forward of the tower bridge; as a result the ship had an unusual appearance. The *Nelson*, which had a relatively low maximum speed of 23 knots, was heavily protected by 14-inch (36-cm) armor in vital areas. She was 710 feet (217 m) in length, had a beam of 32 feet (9.6 m) and was operated by a crew of 1,314.

As WORLD WAR II, 1939–45, began, the *Nelson* and the *Rodney* were the only modern ships available to the ROYAL NAVY because ships of the King George V class were still under construction. The *Nelson* had a distinguished war record, spending much of her time in the Mediterranean. She participated in the SALERNO landings, 1943, and later the Italian surrender was signed on board. The *Nelson* was involved in the NORMANDY invasion, June 1944, before spending the rest of the war in the Far East. She was scrapped in 1949.

Nemesis, H.M.S.

The world's first iron warship, a British-built FRIGATE constructed by John Laird at Birkenhead, in northwest England. Launched in 1839, she was a paddle steamer with a displacement of 660 tons. The *Nemesis* was armed with two of the swivel guns that had been developed recently. The East India Company, not the Royal Navy, had commissioned this innovative design, and the *Nemesis* spent much of her operational career in the Far East. The soundness of her design was put to the test during the First OPIUM WAR, 1841–42, when she operated effectively against enemy war junks off the coast of China.

Neptune, H.M.S.

The name *Neptune* has been used regularly by the Royal Navy since the first *Neptune*, a 90-gun ship, was launched in 1683. A recent *Neptune* was the WORLD WAR II cruiser of 7,175 tons that was sunk by a MINE off Tripoli in December 1941 with the loss of 761 crew. The most famous British ship of this name was a 98-gun vessel, launched in 1797, that fought at the Battle of TRAFALGAR, 1805, under the command of Captain Thomas FREMANTLE. She was third in the weather column and suffered several hits, which caused 54 casualties. After the battle the *Neptune* towed the VICTORY, the fleet FLAGSHIP, into Gibraltar. The *Neptune* later was employed in operations in the West Indies and was finally broken up in 1818.

Nevada, U.S.S.

The name ship of the first class of American super-dreadnoughts, which, as completed in 1916, were the only WORLD WAR I, 1914–18, warships to be armored on the "all-or-nothing system." The key areas of the hull were enclosed with heavy armor, while the remainder was unprotected because lighter plate was of no value against large-caliber armor-piercing shells. Both Nevada-class ships had a displacement of 29,000 tons, an overall length of 583 feet (178 m) and a beam of 108 feet (33 m). Equipped with ten 14-inch (36-cm) guns, the *Nevada* and the *Oklahoma* were the first American warships to adopt triple turrets. They were easily recognizable because, unlike earlier American dreadnoughts, they had only a single funnel.

Both ships served with the Sixth Battle Squadron of the British GRAND FLEET, from August 1918 until the end of the war. Modernized in the interwar period, both were with the Pacific Fleet at PEARL HARBOR in December 1941 when the Japanese attacked. The *Oklahoma* was hit by bombs and torpedoes and capsized with the loss of 400 members of her crew. She was raised some two years later but was beyond repair. The *Nevada*, which was the only battleship to leave the harbor during the attack, also was hit and had to be beached to avoid causing an obstruction. She was repaired and returned to service in 1943, seeing action in the Pacific and in Europe. After the war she went to Bikini Atoll, where her structure survived two atomic bomb tests. The *Nevada* finally was torpedoed near Pearl Harbor in 1948.

New Ironsides, U.S.S.

One of the MONITOR's successors, the Union Navy ship *New Ironsides* was hurriedly constructed during the AMERICAN CIVIL WAR, 1861–65, and shared many of her design weaknesses. She was launched at Philadelphia in May 1862 and was ready for operational service early in the following year. In April 1863 she was involved in Admiral Samuel DU PONT's unsuccessful operation against Charleston, when she was hit by a torpedo fired by the Confederate submersible *DAVID*. She was in fact "the first ship to be damaged in a submarine attack." The *New Ironsides* survived and managed to return to her base; the shock waves produced by the explosion caused the sumbersible to sink.

New Jersey, U.S.S.

American BATTLESHIP, commissioned in May 1943, that served as the FLAGSHIP of the Third Fleet during the latter part of the PACIFIC WAR, 1941–45. She survived the conflict and was still in service in the 1980s when she was sent to the Lebanon, 1983–84. The second ship of the Iowa class (which also included the *IOWA*, *MISSOURI* and *WISCONSIN*), the *New Jersey* had a displacement of 58,000 tons and an overall length of 887 feet 6 inches (270 m). Operated by a crew of 2,788, her beam was 108 feet (33 m), and she had a maximum speed of 33 knots. She was equipped with nine 16-inch (41-cm) guns in three triple turrets, 20 5-inch (13-cm) dual-purpose guns and 64 40-mm antiaircraft guns.

The *New Jersey* served as the flagship of Admiral Raymond SPRUANCE, commander in chief of the Fifth Fleet, in February 1944, and took part in operations against the Carolines and off the Mariana Islands. In August 1944 she became the flagship of Admiral William HALSEY, commander in chief, Third Fleet, and was based at Ulithi. Transferred to Battleship Division 7, she was involved in the assaults on IWO JIMA and OKINAWA. She ended the war as Admiral Spruance's flagship for a second time. Soon decommissioned, the *New Jersey* was modernized during the 1980s and equipped with CRUISE MISSILES. She returned to active duty on several occasions in the postwar period and did not finally leave the U.S. Navy until 1991.

Malcolm Muir, *The Iowa Class Battleships*, Poole, Dorset, 1987.

New Mexico, U.S.S.

The American BATTLESHIP *New Mexico*, commissioned in 1918, was the first warship to use electric transmission. Her steam turbines drove the generators that provided the current for her four electric motors. The *New Mexico* also was notable in having a clipper bow, but in other respects she was a conventional battleship design of the period. She had a displacement of 32,000 tons, a crew of 1,080 and her main armament consisted of 12 14-inch (36-cm) guns.

The *New Mexico* and her sister ships, the *Mississippi* and the *Idaho*, which were refitted during the 1930s, saw much service during the WORLD WAR II, 1939–45, although as a type the battleship was already obsolete and had been displaced by the AIRCRAFT CARRIER. All three ships survived despite suffering serious KAMIKAZE and TORPEDO attacks. In a notable action on October 24–25, 1944 the *Mississippi* fought the Japanese warship *Yamashiro* in the Surigao Strait in a final contest between opposing battleships. The *Mississippi* was retained as an experimental gunnery ship in the postwar period, but her two sister ships were scrapped in 1947–48. She finally was scrapped in 1956.

New Orleans, Battle of
1862

During the second year of the AMERICAN CIVIL WAR, 1861–65, the Union government decided to split the Confederacy by taking control of the Mississippi River. A key objective was the city of New Orleans, Louisiana—the largest in the South—which occupied a controlling position on the river. This mission was entrusted to the West Gulf Blockading Squadron under the command of Captain David FARRAGUT, who had a total of 43 vessels at his disposal. Proceeding upstream from the river's mouth on the Gulf of Mexico, the main obstacle they had to overcome were the two forts, Fort Jackson and Fort St. Philip, to the south of the city, which were occupied by Confederate troops and protected by 115 heavy guns. Moreover, the river was blocked by a line of stationary HULKs and twelve assorted naval vessels, including two IRONCLADS.

On April 18, when Farragut arrived in the area, he launched a five-day bombardment using 13-inch (33-cm) mortars that could fire 200-pound (91-kg) shells. Two days later his gunboats broke through the hulks, and within 48 hours his main fleet fought its way through. The CONFEDERATE NAVY was defeated—nine gunboats were destroyed—and its forts, which had been designed to deal with sailing vessels, were unable to make much impact against steam-driven warships. Farragut advanced toward New Orleans, which surrendered on April 25, successfully completing this phase of the federal strategy. The two forts, which had been cut off by Farragut's decisive action, surrendered three days later.

Newport News, Virginia

American port and industrial city in southern Virginia, situated at the point where the James River enters Hampton Roads. During the AMERICAN CIVIL WAR, 1861–65, Union forces captured and fortified the city. The famous naval engagement between the two IRONCLAD ships, the *MONITOR* and the *MERRIMACK*—a turning point in naval history—took place off Newport News in March 1862. In the late 19th century the shipbuilding industry developed there, and it now has one of the world's largest shipyards, in which U.S. Navy and merchant ships are built. These yards have made or repaired some of the largest naval ships in the world, including the U.S.S. *ENTERPRISE,* the world's first nuclear-powered AIRCRAFT CARRIER. Hampton Roads also accommodates Norfolk Naval Base, the U.S. Navy's largest installation.

New York, U.S.S.

The first American BATTLESHIPs equipped with 14-inch (36-cm) armament, the *New York* and her sister ship *Texas* served during the WORLD WAR I, 1914–18. They were similar in appearance to the Wyoming class and had ten heavy guns mounted in twin turrets: two superfiring fore and aft and one in the center. Some of the 21 5-inch (13-cm) secondary guns were poorly positioned and unusable in bad weather; five were removed during the war. Completed in 1914, these ships had a maximum speed of 21 knots, a displacement of 27,000 tons and a complement of 864 men. They were 573 feet (175 m) in length and had a beam of 95 feet (29 m).

The *New York* served as FLAGSHIP, Sixth Battle Squadron, U.S. Atlantic Fleet, together with the *Texas* after they entered service in 1914. This squadron later became the 6th Battle Squadron of the British GRAND FLEET after the United States entered the war in April 1917 and close naval cooperation was agreed upon. Both were present at the surrender of the German HIGH SEAS FLEET in November 1918. Soon afterward the *Texas* was fitted with a flying-off platform for aircraft, although her first plane did not take off until March 1919. She was the first American battleship to be so converted. Reconstructed in the 1920s, both ships served in Europe and the Pacific during WORLD WAR II, 1939–45. The *New York* was finally scuttled off Pearl Harbor in 1948, while the *Texas* was allocated a permanent berth as a war memorial at San Jacinto, Texas.

Nile, Battle of the
August 1, 1798

On May 19, 1798, during the FRENCH REVOLUTIONARY AND NAPOLEONIC WARS, 1792–1815, Napoleon and his Army of the Orient left Toulon for Egypt with the aim of acquiring an empire in the East. The expeditionary force was transported there in a large CONVOY protected by the French fleet under the command of Admiral François BRUEYS D'AIGAILLIERS. The British had some information about the enemy's plans but did not know where a landing was to be made. Admiral Horatio NELSON was appointed to the command of a detached squadron that John JERVIS, Lord St. Vincent, commander of the English fleet, had sent from his base in the Tagus. At first they searched the Mediterranean for the French without success. On July 1 the French arrived undetected near Alexandria, having captured Malta en route. Napoleon's army was disembarked and the French fleet sheltered some 15 miles away in Aboukir Bay, which Brueys regarded as a safe anchorage. Having failed to intercept the French at sea, Nelson made for Egypt, which he believed to be their final destination. His search of the coast was unsuccessful at first, and he did not locate Brueys until a second search.

The French fleet, including 14 ships of the line, was finally sighted at anchor in line-ahead formation on August 1. Nelson's own squadron was similar in number, with 13 ships of the line, although his vessels were smaller and less well armed. The British, who had the advantage of surprise, entered Aboukir Bay shortly afterward, at about 6 P.M. on the same day. Nelson decided to strike from both sides. His four leading ships crossed the enemy van and attacked from the landward side, where the French guns were not prepared for action. Another difficulty for Brueys was the fact that many of his men were ashore when the British opened fire at about 6:30 P.M. During the two hours of daylight that remained, the first five ships in the French line were put out of action. As darkness fell, British fire was concentrated on the enemy center, where Brueys's most powerful ships, including *L'ORIENT,* his FLAGSHIP, were

deployed. The British sustained heavy damage, but the death of Brueys and the subsequent destruction of his flagship in a massive explosion represented the decisive phase of the battle. Fighting continued until dawn although there was now no doubt that the British would win.

The French lost 11 ships of the line and two frigates. Their remaining two ships of the line and two frigates under Rear Admiral the Comte de VILLENEUVE escaped, although they were all eventually to be captured by the British. The Battle of the Nile was a major British success that helped to boost morale in the long war with France. With this win, the balance of naval power in the Mediterranean shifted in favor of the British and the French army was stranded in Egypt. This was the first fleet action in which Nelson had been in command, and all the qualities that made him an outstanding naval commander were in evidence there. He was raised to the peerage in recognition of his great victory.

Oliver Warner, *The Battle of the Nile*, London, 1960,

Nimitz, Chester William
1885–1966

American naval commander who headed the Pacific Fleet from 1941 to 1945 and who thus directed the U.S. Navy's victory over the Japanese in WORLD WAR II, 1939–45. Born in Fredericksburg, Texas on February 24, 1885, Nimitz entered the U.S. Naval Academy in 1901. He spent most of his early career in submarines. During this service, two notable events occurred. The first was his court-martial and reprimand for running aground a destroyer in 1905; the second was the heroic rescue of a drowning sailor in 1912 while Nimitz was in command of the submarine *E-1.* Nimitz remained with submarines throughout WORLD WAR I, 1914–18. By 1929 Nimitz, then a captain, was given command of Submarine Division 20 as well as the Battle Fleet's Submarine Divisions at San Diego, California. Reaching flag rank in 1938, he became Chief of the Bureau of Navigation in 1939, the position he occupied on December 7, 1941.

Not having any connection with the debacle at PEARL HARBOR, Nimitz was raised over the heads of many superiors when he was appointed Commander in Chief, Pacific Fleet, and Commander in Chief, Pacific Ocean Areas, on December 31, 1941. Despite the devastation and the severe shortages due to the Japanese attack, Nimitz reorganized the Pacific forces and executed first a series of successful defensive measures to stop the Japanese advance, culminating six months after his appointment in the Battle of MIDWAY, which turned the tide of the Pacific war. He then directed the huge counteroffensive through the Central Pacific that ultimately resulted in the defeat of Japan and the end of the war. Promoted to fleet admiral (five stars) in 1944, he served as Chief of Naval Operations from 1945 to 1947, followed by a period as goodwill ambassador for

Admiral Chester Nimitz, commander of the U.S. Pacific Fleet, led the Americans to victory in the Pacific   (*Copyright © Imperial War Museum, London*)

the United Nations. The recipient of many medals and awards, foreign and domestic, and with a name synonymous with the naval victory in the Pacific theater of World War II, Nimitz died on February 20, 1966.

E. B. Potter, *Nimitz*, Annapolis, 1976.

Nimitz, U.S.S.

The world's first nuclear AIRCRAFT CARRIER, the U.S.S. *Enterprise*, launched in 1960, was followed in 1972 by the *Nimitz*, a slightly smaller but even more powerful warship. This was the name ship of a class that has set the pattern for contemporary American aircraft carrier design. The *Nimitz* is 1,092 feet (332 m) in length, 252 feet (77 m) at its widest point and displaces 81,600 tons. It is powered by two nuclear reactors that provide the equivalent of 280,000 horsepower and produce a maximum speed of more than 30 knots and a range of up to 1 million miles (1.6 million km). The *Nimitz* is operated by a crew of 3,000, with a further 3,000 to support the 100 fixed-wing aircraft that the ship can operate. It is equipped with four

steam catapults, and its angled flight deck enables aircraft to take off and land simultaneously. Armed with three missile launchers, the *Nimitz* also is equipped for antisubmarine warfare. The U.S. Navy now operates five Nimitz-class carriers, including the *Theodore Roosevelt*, which served in the GULF WAR, 1990–1.

Njegovan, Admiral Maximilian
1858–1930

Njegovan succeeded Anton Von HAUS as fleet commander of the AUSTRO-HUNGARIAN NAVY in February 1917 and subsequently was appointed commander in chief. Earlier in the war, as commander of the First Squadron of the Battle Fleet, he had been involved in the bombardment of the Italian coast. His term of office as commander in chief coincided with the growth of national and political tensions within the navy as WORLD WAR I, 1914–18, drew to a close. Following the serious MUTINY at Cattaro Bay in February 1918, he was quickly replaced. Rear-Admiral Miklós HORTHY became fleet commander and Vice Admiral Franz von Holub was appointed as head of the naval section of the War Ministry.

Noble, Admiral Sir Percy
1880–1955

British naval commander who served as commander in chief, Western Approaches, from February 1941 to November 1942, during WORLD WAR II, 1939–45. In his earlier naval career Noble served on cruisers during WORLD WAR I, 1914–18, and had commanded the China Station, 1937–40. In his principal World War II command he prepared the way for an eventual British victory in the Battle of the ATLANTIC, 1939–45, under his successor Admiral Sir Max HORTON. Noble believed that thorough training in ANTISUBMARINE WARFARE would be essential if the U-BOAT threat were to be overcome, and he established three schools for this purpose. He also improved the effectiveness of CONVOY escorts by constituting them as permanent groups. Some escorts were given the specific task of hunting U-boats that were detected as they approached the target ships. When he left the Western Approaches command, he was sent to Washington as head of the British ADMIRALTY delegation. In this capacity he was involved in maintaining Anglo-American naval cooperation for the remainder of the war.

Nore Mutiny
1797

An important anchorage of the British navy—a sandbank at the mouth of the River Thames—the Nore was the scene of a serious MUTINY in 1797. It followed an earlier mutiny over pay and conditions at SPITHEAD. Before the Spithead mutiny had run its course, it sparked a similar action in the warships at the Nore on May 12. Led by Richard PARKER, the mutineers controlled 13 ships of the line at the height of the mutiny. They also enjoyed the support of the English North Sea Fleet, which was lying up the coast at Yarmouth. However, when the Nore mutineers failed to acknowledge that most of their demands already had been achieved in the settlement of the Spithead mutiny, support for this second uprising soon began to falter.

When Parker suggested taking the warships under their control to Holland, further dissension—and fighting between the mutineers—resulted. The authorities stood firm; the mutineers began to surrender or, in a few cases, escape to Holland. Finally isolated on the *Sandwich,* Parker was forced to abandon the action on June 13. Along with 24 other ringleaders, Parker was tried and convicted. He was executed on June 30, 1797.

C. Gill, *The Naval Mutinies of 1797,* Manchester, 1913.

Normandy Landings
1944

The invasion of Normandy, France, June 6, 1944, Operation Overlord, under Supreme Allied Commander General Dwight D. Eisenhower, marked the long-expected opening of a second front in Europe during WORLD WAR II, 1939–45. The Allies planned to land five American, British and Canadian divisions between Cherbourg and Caen in the first phase of the operation. Preparations had begun more than a year earlier, and the lessons of earlier amphibious operations, including the disastrous DIEPPE RAID, 1942, were taken into account. The timing of the operation was affected by the moon and the tides, and was delayed by bad weather. British Admiral Sir Betram RAMSAY was appointed naval commander-in-chief with responsibility for planning and directing Operation Neptune, the successful naval dimension of Operation Overlord. New types of LANDING CRAFT were designed and produced in large quantities. By June 1944 almost 5,000 naval vessels of all kinds had been assembled for the invasion, which began with airborne landings to protect the flanks of the landing areas. Landing craft made the English Channel crossing from an assembly area south of the Isle of Wight. The landings took place across a 50-mile (80-km) stretch of the French coast, which was divided into five sectors: Omaha, Utah, Gold, Juno and Sword.

British forces landed in the east from a fleet commanded by Rear Admiral Philip VIAN. A group of British warships, which consisted of two battleships, 12 cruisers and 37 destroyers, bombarded the shore. The Americans landed to the west. Their landing fleet, which was commanded by Rear Admiral Alan Kirk, was supported by a bombardment

group consisting of three battleships, nine cruisers and 20 destroyers. With complete Allied dominance of the skies and the advantage of surprise, the landings made steady progress. Allied naval forces come under attack from German motor TORPEDO BOATS and destroyers, with one British and one German destroyer being sunk. Two other Allied destroyers were sunk by mines or coast artillery and four cruisers were damaged. In total, some 176,000 troops were landed by sea in some 4,000 ships and landing craft on the first day. To facilitate the buildup of forces and supplies as the invasion force advanced inland, it was planned to assemble two prefabricated harbors (known as MULBERRY HARBORS) at Arromanches and on Omaha Beach. Because the harbor on Omaha Beach was wrecked in a storm, the harbor at Arromanches had to bear all the heavy cross-Channel traffic that followed the initial landings.

Despite this serious supply bottleneck, the Allies made steady progress and, by August 21, in spite of several setbacks, the Battle of Normandy had been won. It was the largest and most complex amphibious operation ever undertaken and marked the beginning of the end of Nazi domination of Western Europe.

Max Hastings, *Overlord,* London, 1984.

Norris, Sir John
1660–1749

British naval commander who served with distinction during the War of the SPANISH SUCCESSION, 1701–14, and rose to be deputy to Sir Clowdisley SHOVELL as commander in chief of the Mediterranean fleet in operations against the enemy in 1706–7. Norris first made his mark in 1693 when, as a member of the ill-fated Smyrna CONVOY, he saved several ships from destruction at the hands of the French. Known for his volatile temperament, Norris was arrested after striking a senior officer during the expedition to Cadiz in 1702 but was quickly released when his victim died unexpectedly. He distinguished himself at the Battle of MÁLAGA, 1704; largely on the strength of this performance, subsequently he was appointed to serve as a rear admiral under Shovell. Although he served later in the Baltic, 1715–27, he had few further opportunities to demonstrate his qualities as a seaman.

North Cape, Battle of
December 26, 1943

A naval engagement fought off the North Cape of Norway between British and German naval forces during WORLD WAR II, 1939–45, which resulted in the loss of the German battle cruiser SCHARNHORST. The action had its origins in a German plan to attack one of the regular ARCTIC CONVOYS between Britain and the Soviet Union, which had been resumed in the autumn of 1943 following a reduction in hostile enemy naval activity. The target was convoy JW 55B, consisting of 19 ships, which left Loch Ewe, Scotland, for the Soviet Union with a DESTROYER escort and a covering force of three CRUISERS—the BELFAST, Norfolk and SHEFFIELD—commanded by Vice Admiral R. L. Burnett. Ships of the British Home Fleet, which included the battleship DUKE OF YORK (the flagship of Admiral Sir Bruce FRASER, the fleet commander in chief), the cruiser Jamaica and four destroyers, provided distant cover. The fleet had left Reykjavik, Iceland on December 23.

By this time convoy JW 55B, which was being shadowed by German long-range aircraft, was no more than a few hundred miles away from Alten Fjord, in the far north of Norway, where a German naval squadron, commanded by Rear Admiral Erich Bey, was lying in wait. It consisted of the Scharnhorst and five destroyers. In the early evening of December 25 Bey left the fjord and gave orders to attack the British convoy the next morning. However, he was never to reach his target, some 50 miles (80 km) south of Bear Island. By the early hours of December 26, Fraser was 200 miles (322 km) to the southwest and Burnett was some 150 miles (241 km) to the east. Burnett's squadron first picked up the Scharnhorst's signal, and soon it was in action against her. The Scharnhorst sustained some damage and was forced to withdraw to the south, but later she turned north in a second attempt to find the British convoy. Again she came into contact with Burnett's cruiser squadron; in a short action soon after midday, the Scharnhorst and the British cruiser Norfolk were slightly damaged.

Bey then decided to abandon his pursuit of the convoy and turned south for home at high speed. He could not have known that he was heading straight for Fraser's squadron, which opened fire as soon as it was within range. The Duke of York's main guns put the Scharnhorst's armament out of action and reduced her speed. Fraser's destroyers completed the task with four torpedo hits. At 7:45 P.M. the Scharnhorst sank with the loss of all but 36 of her complement of more than 1,800 men.

Michael Ogden, *The Battle of North Cape*, London, 1962.

North Carolina, U.S.S.

American BATTLESHIP OF WORLD WAR II, 1939–45, which, together with her sister ship *Washington*, formed the North Carolina class. Commissioned in 1941, the *North Carolina* was the first American battleship to enter the service in 18 years. With a maximum speed of only 28 knots, she was not particularly fast, but she was well armed and had good armor protection. The *North Carolina* had a displacement of 35,000 tons and was 728 feet 9 inches (222 m) in length, with a beam of 108 feet 3 inches (33 m). She was equipped with nine 16-inch (41-cm) guns in three triple turrets and 20 5-inch (13-cm) dual-purpose guns. She also was well equipped with antiaircraft guns and, as the war progressed, with RADAR.

After a brief period in the Atlantic, the *North Carolina* was transferred to the Pacific, where she spent the remainder of the war as a carrier escort. She survived a torpedo attack by a Japanese submarine off the East Solomon Islands on September 15, 1942; the *Washington* was responsible for the destruction of the Japanese battleship *Kirishima* during the naval Battle of GUADALCANAL, November 14–15, 1942. Both North Carolina–class ships survived the war and were taken out of service in 1947.

Northumberland, H.M.S.

The most distinguished *Northumberland* to have been commissioned in the British naval service was a 74-gun third-rate (see RATING OF SHIPS) SHIP OF THE LINE launched in 1798. This *Northumberland* is best known as the ship that carried Napoleon into exile on the island of St. Helena in October 1815. Following his defeat at the Battle of Waterloo and his escape from the battlefield, Napoleon surrendered aboard the *Bellerophon*, which brought him to the coast of England. There he was transferred to the *Northumberland*, which took him on his final journey. Her active service began with the expedition to Egypt in 1801 and continued throughout the war with France. She was finally broken up in 1850, although she had been decommissioned many years earlier.

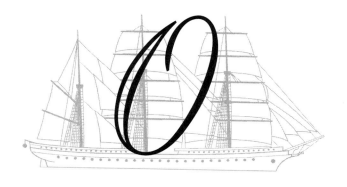

O'Kane, Richard Hetherington
1911–1994

The U.S. Navy's leading SUBMARINE commander in WORLD WAR II, 1939–45, with more sinkings than any other, Richard O'Kane was born on February 2, 1911 in New Hampshire and entered the U.S. Naval Academy in 1930. Beginning in the spring of 1942, he became executive officer of the submarine *Wahoo*, sinking some 16 Japanese vessels with a total of more than 45,000 tons by July 1943. Later that summer he reported to the submarine U.S.S. *Tang* and, as her commander, undertook five successful patrols, sinking the largest amount of enemy tonnage in the war: more than 31 ships and nearly 227,800 tons. He also rescued downed American and Allied aviators.

During the Battle of LEYTE GULF, October 1944, the *Tang* was sunk by one of her own TORPEDOES. Instead of hitting the target ship, it had circled out of control and returned to strike the *Tang*. O'Kane was injured but survived as a prisoner of the Japanese for the rest of the war. After the war he continued to command submarines as well as submarine squadrons. He retired as a rear admiral in 1957 and died on February 16, 1994.

Clark G. Reynolds, *Famous American Admirals*, New York, 1978, pp. 242–243.

Okinawa, Invasion of
March–June 1945

The massive American amphibious assault on Japanese-occupied Okinawa, an island in the Ryukyu group, south of Formosa, was designed to provide a forward base for the projected invasion of Japan in 1945 or 1946. The island was defended by 100,000 troops of the Japanese 32nd Army, which had constructed strong defensive positions with heavy artillery support. Code-named Operation Iceberg, the American plan involved landing 154,000 troops on the southwest of the island, using an invasion force of 1,300 ships. Air support was provided by Task Force 58 and a British carrier force commanded by Admiral H. B. Rawlings. These naval units, which were under constant attack from KAMIKAZE pilots, carried out a four-day bombardment of Japanese shore positions as well as launching air strikes on key enemy installations.

In the days following the first landing on April 1, heavy ground fighting was matched by further major action at sea. On April 6 some 700 Japanese aircraft mounted a kamikaze raid on the Allied fleet, resulting in damage to 13 American destroyers. The JAPANESE NAVY also mounted a suicide attack using its last remaining battle squadron. Commanded by Vice Admiral Sejichi ITO, who flew his flag in the super-battleship YAMATO, the remnants of the Japanese Combined Fleet made a final attempt to save the doomed island. The plan was destined to fail from the start: The Japanese fleet was sighted and destroyed by American aircraft a considerable distance from its intended destination. The destruction of the *Yamato* and its supporting units marked the effective end of the Japanese navy as a fighting force. Later stages of the battle to capture Okinawa focused on ground operations. The island finally fell to the Americans on June 21.

B. M. Frank, *Okinawa. The Great Island Battle*, New York, 1978.

Öland, Battle of
June 1, 1676

Only a week after their defeat at the Battle of JASMUND, May 25–26, 1676, the Swedes fought a combined Danish and Dutch fleet, commanded by Cornelis TROMP, one of Holland's greatest naval leaders, at the Battle of Öland. In this second key naval battle of the war between Denmark and Sweden, 1675–79, the Swedish fleet was commanded by Admiral Lorens Creutz. Before the fighting had even begun the Swedes suffered a misfortune that led directly to their defeat at the hands of the Dutch. The

American amphibious vehicles land on Okinawa, April 1945   (*Copyright © Imperial War Museum, London*)

Krona, the Swedish FLAGSHIP, took on water during a sudden storm and sank quickly. With the Swedish fleet in disarray, Admiral Tromp launched his attack with devastating consequences. During a battle lasting most of the day, the Swedes lost three large warships, including the *Svard*, the flagship of the Swedish second-in-command. The Danish army was to perform less well than its navy, and it was the balance of power on land that finally determined the outcome of the war in Sweden's favor.

Öland, Battle of
July 26, 1789

As the winter of 1788–89 set in, the opposing fleets of the RUSSO-SWEDISH WAR, 1788–90, were locked into their respective ports by ice in the Baltic. The RUSSIAN NAVY was divided among Copenhagen, Reval and Kronstadt, where it remained until July 1789. A squadron of 20 ships under the command of Admiral Vasili Tchitchagov then left Reval bound for the southern Baltic, where it

was to meet with the squadron commanded by Admiral Koslianinov, which had been based at Copenhagen. Before these two Russian squadrons could combine, the Swedish fleet, commanded by Duke Carl, had departed from its winter quarters at Karlskrona and had come in sight of Tchitchagov's squadron off Öland. On July 26 the two fleets fought a six-hour battle that did not produce a decisive result and caused only minor losses. As a result, Russia continued to be the dominant naval power in the Baltic. See also CHARLES XIII.

Onishi, Takijiro
1891–1945

Japanese vice admiral who helped to plan the attack on PEARL HARBOR, December 1941, even though he initially had opposed the concept. At that time he was serving under Admiral Isoroku YAMAMOTO as chief of staff of the 11th Air Fleet. He also led the successful air assault on the Philippines, 1941, but his subsequent career stalled for much of the rest of WORLD WAR II, 1939–45, because of his overly aggressive leadership style.

In October 1944 he was appointed to the command of the Fifth Base Air Force on Luzon in the Philippines. He was ordered to support Admiral Takeo KURITA's attack on the American invasion force at the Battle of LEYTE GULF, October 23–26, 1944. With only about 150 aircraft available to him, Onishi formed suicide units with pilots who were willing to sacrifice their lives. These operations began on October 25, 1944, and their initial successes led to the creation of other KAMIKAZE units, a strategy Japan pursued until the end of the war. In May 1945 Onishi was appointed vice chief of the Naval General Staff. Unable to live with the consequences of surrender, he committed ritual suicide at the end of the war.

Opium Wars
1839–1843, 1856–1860

The two Opium Wars were fought between British and Chinese forces (with the French participating in the Second Opium War) because of disagreements about foreign trading activities. The First Opium War, 1839–43, had its origins in sustained Chinese attempts to restrict foreign trade and in particular to prevent British merchants from illegally importing opium. The war was triggered when the Chinese government seized opium stored in British warehouses in Canton. The British responded by sending a naval force, with accompanying East India Company and ground troops, which seized several Chinese coastal cities. Canton fell after an amphibious assault in May 1841. Fighting was renewed in 1842 when a British naval FLOTILLA advanced up the Yangtze River. It led to the loss of Shanghai and then of Nanking in August 1842. The Chinese were forced to sue for peace. The terms of the Treaty of Nanking, 1842–43, acceded to most of the British objectives.

Despite this, tensions between the two countries were to revive in the 1850s, with the British, in company the French, demanding more trading concessions. Matters came to a head when the Chinese seized the *Arrow*, a British merchant ship engaged in the illegal opium trade, and the Second Opium War, 1856–60, began. In response, an Anglo-French naval force under Admiral Sir Michael Seymour seized Canton in December 1857, after having successfully attacked a fleet of Chinese junks at the Battle of FATSHAN CREEK in June of that year. Seymour then sailed north to occupy briefly the Taku forts near Tientsin, May 1858. China was forced to make further trading concessions, including the legalization of opium importation, which were embodied in the Treaty of Tientsin. However, China's refusal to admit foreign diplomats to Peking in 1859 brought a renewal of hostilities. In response, British naval forces attacked the Taku forts but were to accept American assistance to withdraw. A larger amphibious force was assembled in 1860, and the Taku forts and then Tientsin were finally taken. After further land-based operations, the allies entered Peking and the Chinese were forced to sign a new agreement—the Treaty of Peking—ending the war.

Orde, Sir John
1751–1824

British admiral who first made his mark in the AMERICAN WAR OF INDEPENDENCE, 1775–83, serving at Philadelphia in 1778 and Charleston in 1780. He was made governor of Dominica in 1783 and created a baronet. As a rear admiral he served as third in command under Admiral John JERVIS, Lord St. Vincent, during the FRENCH REVOLUTIONARY AND NAPOLEONIC WARS, 1792–1815. A difficult personality at the best of times, Orde came into conflict with his commanding officer in 1798 and was sent home as a result. (St. Vincent had disregarded the rules of seniority and had appointed Admiral Horatio NELSON rather than Orde to the command of a detached squadron operating in the Mediterranean.) In 1805 Orde returned to the sea in command of a squadron off Cadiz, but his target—the Franco-Spanish fleet under Admiral the Comte de VILLENEUVE—eluded him. Leaving his command at his own request, Orde later was promoted to the rank of admiral but saw no further sea service.

Oregon, U.S.S.

Authorized by Congress in 1890, the *Oregon* was one of the United States Navy's Indiana-class BATTLESHIPS. She was a compact, heavily armed vessel with a displacement of just over 10,000 tons. Her main armament consisted of four 13-inch (33-cm) guns in twin turrets fore and aft and eight 8-inch (20-cm) guns, also turret mounted. This arrangement allowed good all-round fire. The *Oregon* was 350 feet 11 inches (107 m) in length, had a beam of 68 feet 3 inches (21 m) and was operated by a crew of 636.

On the outbreak of the SPANISH-AMERICAN WAR of 1898, she left her Pacific station on the long journey to join the American squadron besieging Havana, the Cuban capital. She arrived in time to take part in the defeat of the Spanish squadron commanded by Admiral Pascual CERVERA at the Battle of SANTIAGO, July 3, 1898. The *Oregon*'s long voyage via Cape Horn strengthened the case for a more direct route from the Pacific by the construction of a PANAMA CANAL. The *Oregon*, which returned soon to the Pacific, remained there until she was employed in support of American intervention in Siberia, 1918–19, during the Russian Civil War.

Orfordness, Battle of
July 25–26, 1666

Following their defeat in the FOUR DAYS' BATTLE, June 1–4, 1666, the English did not have long to wait before redeeming their reputation. The third major engagement of the Second ANGLO-DUTCH WAR, 1665–67, the Battle of Orfordness—also known by its alternative names of the Battle of St. James's Day Fight or North Foreland—was occasioned by the arrival of the Dutch fleet off the Thames estuary on July 22, 1666. Commanded by Admiral Michiel de RUYTER, the Dutch fleet consisted of 88 ships, 20 FIRESHIPS and ten dispatch vessels. The English fleet of 89 ships, under the joint command of Prince RUPERT and George MONCK, Duke of Albemarle, was anchored some 18 miles away in the Gunfleet.

The opposing fleets maneuvered for two days before the engagement began at 10 A.M. on July 25, some 40 miles (64 km) southeast of Orfordness. The van and center divisions of the two fleets were locked in combat for several hours. The Dutch suffered the loss of three flag officers in the van division, which was forced to withdraw. The Dutch center also suffered badly; de Ruyter's FLAGSHIP, the *Zeven Provincien*, was dismasted. Despite this, the Dutch center retreated in good order in the late afternoon despite the heavy punishment it had sustained. Fortunately for the Dutch, the English did not have the strength to pursue them with any vigor. Some distance to the west, the two opposing rear divisions, headed by Admiral Cornelis TROMP and Admiral Jeremy Smyth, were engaged in a separate battle. Although events initially went in Tromp's favor, the English soon gained the advantage and pursued the enemy to the Dutch coast, where Tromp took shelter. The battle altered, at least temporarily, the balance of power at sea in favor of the English. The Dutch fleet lost 20 ships, and some 7,000 men were killed or injured. The English fleet, which suffered negligible losses, was to demonstrate its new dominance in an action known as Sir Robert HOLMES' Bonfire, August 8, 1666, when it destroyed more than 160 Dutch merchantmen in the Vlie River in the Netherlands.

Orion, H.M.S.

The name of five British warships, including a famous 74-gun SHIP OF THE LINE built on the Thames River in 1787 that served in the ROYAL NAVY for 26 years. She was present at many of the great battles of the war against France from the GLORIOUS FIRST OF JUNE, 1794, to the Baltic in 1808, including CAPE ST. VINCENT, 1797, the NILE, 1798, and TRAFALGAR, 1805, where she played a distinguished role. The *Orion* eventually was broken up at Plymouth in 1814, having gained five clasps to her war medal in commemoration of her key role in five critical battles.

A notable 20th-century *Orion* was the super-dreadnought that featured in the Royal Navy's 1909 building program. She had a displacement of 25,000 tons and was armed with powerful and accurate 13.5-inch (34-cm) guns. The *Orion* was the first dreadnought to have all her heavy armament in centerline turrets fore and aft. Her side armor was extended to upper deck level in contrast to earlier designs. She was 581 feet (177 m) in length, had a beam of 29 feet (8.7 m) and was operated by a crew of 752. With a maximum speed of 21 knots, the *Orion* was a powerful, elegant ship with low lines and provided a basis for a further five classes, its only weakness being the location of the tripod mast between the funnels. The *Orion* served with the GRAND FLEET during WORLD WAR I, 1914–18, and survived the Battle of JUTLAND, 1916, without damage.

Ozawa, Jisaburo
1886–1966

Japanese naval commander and highly regarded strategist who succeeded Admiral Chuichi NAGUMO as head of the Third Fleet (later known as the Mobile Fleet) in unfavorable circumstances in November 1942. Prior to WORLD WAR II, 1939–45, Ozawa had served as an instructor at the naval academy and as a battleship and cruiser commander. He argued for the creation of large carrier groups for offensive action. In 1937–38 he was chief of staff to the Combined Fleet and later commanded task forces during the conquest of the Dutch East Indies, Malaya and the Philippines. Ozawa commanded the fleet at the Battle of the PHILIPPINE SEA, June 1944, but his skillful tactics could not compensate for Japanese weaknesses in ships and aircraft. His lack of air cover was even more pronounced at the Battle of LEYTE GULF, October 1944, where his decoy force succeeded in luring Admiral William HALSEY away from the battle but without any effect on the outcome. Vice Admiral Ozawa was appointed vice chief of the naval general staff in November 1944 and replaced Admiral Soemu TOYODA as the last commander in chief of the Combined Fleet in May 1945. However, all hope had gone by this point and Ozawa presided over the final destruction of the Japanese navy.

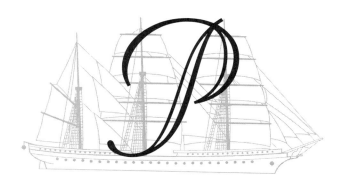

Pacific War

1941–45

The Pacific War was a key part of WORLD WAR II, 1939–45, although it was conducted largely independently of the other theaters. The Allies gave the highest priority to defeating Germany, Japan's principal ally, and the Pacific never had first claim on their resources. Japan supported Germany's war aims but had specific objectives of her own. The principal cause of the Pacific War was the Japanese ambition to dominate Southeast Asia for political and economic reasons. Control of the region would produce a "Greater East Asia Co-Prosperity Sphere." Japan's dependence on imported raw materials would end and the country would have a ready market for its manufactured goods. As the dominant power in the area, Japan's security would be enhanced at the expense of the European colonial powers. Japan put its plans to conquer China and Manchuria into effect before World War II, 1939–45, but the beginning of the European conflict in 1939 gave Japan the opportunity to extend its horizons. Japan's territorial ambitions included American possessions in the Pacific, but before it could act it needed an effective plan to neutralize U.S. naval power.

The Japanese naval high command formulated a plan for a preemptive strike against the U.S. fleet at PEARL HARBOR that would effectively knock America out of the war for an extended period. Japan would then be free to launch an offensive that would capture the whole of Southeast Asia, extending as far as the boundaries of India and Australia. This vast area then would be heavily defended against Allied counterattacks, which would be unable to dislodge the Japanese. Although some Japanese admirals were skeptical about these plans because of the United States' potential economic and military power, they were implemented with the surprise attack on Pearl Harbor on December 7, 1941.

This operation damaged the U.S. fleet only partially and missed three carriers that were at sea at the time, but it brought the United States immediately into the war. The Japanese launched seven other attacks at the same time, including the initial invasions of Malaya, Thailand and the Philippines. As British FORCE Z returned to base at Singapore after a search for Japanese landing forces off Malaya, the *PRINCE OF WALES* and the *Repulse* were sunk, a devastating blow to the ROYAL NAVY, which thereafter played only a limited role in the region until 1944. During the first part of 1942, territorial losses in Southwest Asia continued to mount as the Japanese maintained their advance. The fall of the Dutch East Indies early in March was a major setback and followed the Battle of the JAVA SEA, January 27, when Allied naval forces were defeated. The British suffered a further disaster in March when the Japanese navy entered the Indian Ocean and sank the British carrier *HERMES* and other warships. With the final American surrender in the Philippines early in May 1942, the Japanese had captured a vast area in a remarkably short period.

Further offensive operations were planned to strengthen the defensive perimeter against American attack and to disrupt communications between Hawaii and Australia. In the north the Japanese succeeded in capturing the ALEUTIAN ISLANDS, but elsewhere they ran into major difficulties. The Battle of the CORAL SEA, May 7–8, forced the Japanese to abandon a planned attack on Port Moresby, New Guinea. More serious was the outcome of the plan to take the Midway Islands and also to bring the U.S. Pacific fleet to a decisive battle. The Americans, armed with vital information from the Magic intelligence team, which decrypted Japanese codes, dealt the enemy a devastating defeat. During the Battle of MIDWAY, June 3–6, 1942, Japan lost four aircraft carriers and, consequently, its naval superiority in the Pacific. Although Japan extended its gains with landings in the Solomon Islands soon afterward, American plans for a counteroffensive, known as Operation Watchtower, were in preparation. It was decided to concentrate on the recapture of the SOLOMON ISLANDS and New Guinea, with a major priority being the isolation of the major Japanese base at Rabaul on New Britain. A series of American land and naval operations, which began in March 1942 and extended until the end of 1943, focused on the strongly contested island of GUADALCANAL but also resulted in the capture of other islands in the Solomons group.

Following the Japanese defeat at the Battle of the BISMARCK SEA, March 1943, which isolated New Guinea, American naval strategy was revised. The U.S. Third Fleet, commanded by Admiral Chester NIMITZ, was brought from the central Pacific to complete American operations in the Solomons. With Rabaul effectively bypassed, American naval operations in the south Pacific area came to an end. Naval resources were now concentrated in the central Pacific under the command of Admiral Nimitz. Together with the Seventh Air Force and 100,000 ground troops, they pressed on westward in 1943–44, taking Makin and Tawara in the Gilbert Islands before advancing on the Marshall Islands. The Japanese naval base at Truk in the Carolines held despite attacks from Admiral Marc MITSCHER's Fast Carrier Task Force. At the same time General Douglas MacArthur made progress with his capture of the Admiralty Islands early in 1944, followed by his advance through New Guinea. Faced with these two westward offensives, the Japanese fleet, commanded by Vice Admiral Jisaburo OZAWA, fought Nimitz's fleet at the Battle of the PHILIPPINE SEA, June 19–21, 1944, and suffered another heavy defeat, losing 346 aircraft and two carriers.

By September 1944 Nimitz had reached the Palau Islands; a decision was made to attack Luzon in the Philippines during the advance on Japan, rather than Formosa and China, as Nimitz had proposed. A landing began on October 20 and triggered the massive naval Battle of LEYTE GULF, which resulted in a decisive Japanese defeat. Their losses included four carriers, three battleships and ten cruisers as well as the destruction of much of their remaining naval air power. This did not prevent ground fighting from continuing in Luzon and the other Philippine islands until the end of the war. American forces advanced toward Japan with the assaults on IWO JIMA and OKINAWA, which were launched in January and April 1945, respectively. These operations provided a last opportunity for the Japanese navy, mainly in the form of KAMIKAZE attacks, to strike at the American fleet. Although these attacks caused considerable damage, they failed to stop the American advance. The capture of Okinawa brought the Japanese mainland within reach of American land-based bombers, and invasion plans were prepared by the U.S. Navy. The need for an invasion was averted when the Japanese capitulated after the destruction of the cities of Hiroshima and Nagasaki by atomic bombs. The official surrender took place on the U.S.S. MISSOURI, Nimitz's flagship, on September 2, 1945.

Richard Hough, *The Longest Battle: The War at Sea, 1939–45*, London, 1986; S. E. Morison, *History of United States Naval Operations in World War II*, 15 vols., Boston, 1948–64; Dan van der Vat, *The Pacific Campaign: World War II. The U.S.-Japanese Naval War*, London, 1992.

Paddle Steamers

During the early years of the steam-powered ship, the paddle wheel was the most common form of propulsion. Driven by reciprocating steam engines, a ship of this type would be equipped either with a single paddle wheel at the stern or with a pair of wheels amidships on a single shaft. The paddle wheels were enclosed in a protective paddle box. During the first half on the 19th century, the design of the paddle wheel floats underwent continuous improvements, resulting in increased power and reductions in the wheels' impact as they entered the water.

Although paddle steamers were adopted by the world's navies and played a prominent role in several wars, including the AMERICAN CIVIL WAR, 1861–65, their severe operational weaknesses meant that they could not replace the sailing warship. Soon the paddle wheel was found to be highly vulnerable to destruction by ramming or gunfire, leading naval authorities to consider the merits of the propeller as an alternative. In 1845 the British ADMIRALTY conducted trials using the RATTLER and the ALECTO that clearly demonstrated the superiority of the propeller over the paddle wheel. The adoption of the propeller enabled navies to exploit steam power fully for the first time, and the paddle wheel rapidly disappeared into naval history.

Pakenham, Sir Thomas
1757–1836

British admiral who first distinguished himself as a frigate captain during the AMERICAN WAR OF INDEPENDENCE, 1775–83. In May 1781, as commander of the 28-gun *Crescent*, he fought a prolonged duel with the *Briel*, a Dutch 36-gun ship, on his return from duty in the Mediterranean. Sustaining heavy losses, eventually he was forced to surrender, but the *Flora*, an accompanying British frigate, came to his rescue. Both British ships had been badly damaged and were captured by the French navy as they continued on their journey to England. The *Flora* managed to escape, but the *Crescent* was lost to the French. A court-martial inquiring into Pakenham's conduct honorably acquitted him. During the early stages of the FRENCH REVOLUTIONARY AND NAPOLEONIC WARS, 1792–1815, Pakenham played a key role in naval operations against France. He commanded the *Invincible*, a 74-gun SHIP OF THE LINE, under Admiral Lord HOWE at the Battle of the GLORIOUS FIRST OF JUNE, 1794. Pakenham fought with great flair and the British achieved a notable victory. During later wartime service against France he reached the rank of rear admiral in 1799 and admiral in 1810.

Panama Canal

Since 1914, the Atlantic and Pacific Oceans have been linked by a canal across the Isthmus of Panama, cutting thousands of miles from the previous route around the southern tip of South America. The canal, which is open to the largest oceangoing ships, runs from Cristóbal on Limón Bay, an extension of the Caribbean, to Balboa, on the Gulf of Panama. The canal is slightly more than 40 miles (64 km) long, with a minimum depth of 41 feet (12.5 m) and a minimum width of 300 feet (91.5 m). Differences in the levels of the two oceans meant that a series of locks had to be built, including a series of three that lifts ships by 85 feet (25.9 m) to the level of Gatun Lake.

Interest in linking the two oceans by canal dates back to the early years of the 16th century, but the idea was soon abandoned. It was revived in the 19th century by Vicomte Ferdinand de Lesseps, French builder of the Suez Canal, and construction work was under way from 1879 to 1888. The project then failed; it was not until the SPANISH-AMERICAN WAR of 1898 that the U.S. government developed a serious interest in it. The difficulty of moving American naval resources quickly from one ocean to the other in a crisis had been demonstrated during the war. A canal would give the U.S. Navy much more flexibility in a period when its role was rapidly expanding, and President Theodore ROOSEVELT strongly backed the project. The need to overcome this constraint was a powerful argument in persuading Congress to sanction the perpetual leasing of a 10-mile (16-km) strip for the canal—the Panama Canal Zone. Constructed by the U.S. Corps of Army Engineers, since its completion in 1914 the canal has helped the United States to exercise control more effectively over the two oceans it joined and facilitated the country's development as a world naval power. In 1979 the canal zone was returned to Panama and there are current plans to hand over control of canal operation by the year 2000.

Parker, Sir Hyde
1739–1807

British admiral. The son of Admiral Sir Hyde Parker, 1714–82, the younger Parker was notable as the commander in chief of the fleet that was sent to the Baltic in 1801. His orders on that occasion were to act against the armed coalition of Russia, Sweden, Denmark and Prussia that had formed in response to Britain's insistence on the right to search neutral shipping during the FRENCH REVOLUTIONARY AND NAPOLEONIC WARS, 1792–1815. During the first Battle of COPENHAGEN, April 2, 1801, Parker gave orders to withdraw in the face of continuing Danish resistance. In a celebrated response, Admiral Horatio Lord NELSON ignored this instruction and continued the action:

He viewed Parker's signal by raising a telescope to his blind eye. As a result, the British achieved an important victory. Parker was recalled to London, with Lord Nelson replacing him as fleet commander.

Earlier in his naval career Parker gave worthy if uneventful service in North America and the Mediterranean. His father was a distinguished naval officer who served in the West Indies and the North Sea during the AMERICAN WAR OF INDEPENDENCE, 1775–83. In 1782 the elder Parker was appointed as commander in chief in the East Indies, but en route to his new command he was shipwrecked and subsequently murdered by hostile natives.

Parker, Sir Peter
1721–1811

British admiral of the fleet who spent much of his long naval career off the shores of America and in the West Indies. During the first phase of the AMERICAN WAR OF INDEPENDENCE, 1775–83, he commanded a squadron that attacked Charleston, South Carolina in 1775. He was forced to retreat with the loss of three frigates. In 1777 he was appointed commander in chief in the West Indies, where he remained for the rest of the war. During his period in Jamaica he met the young Horatio NELSON, and he is best remembered as Nelson's early patron. Parker was chief mourner at Lord Nelson's funeral in 1806, although he was present as senior naval officer rather than as a personal friend.

Parker, Richard
1767–97

English seaman who led the NORE MUTINY, 1797. Parker volunteered for naval service in 1797 in order to secure his release from prison in Edinburgh, where he was serving a sentence for debt. He was posted to H.M.S. *Sandwich* in the Nore in March 1797 with the rank of able seaman. (He may have seen earlier service at sea.) Shortly after his arrival a MUTINY over pay and conditions occurred at SPITHEAD. Before it had run its course, it sparked a similar action in the warships at the NORE on May 12. Led by Parker, the mutineers, who controlled 13 ships of the line, failed at first to acknowledge that most of their demands already had been achieved in the settlement of the Spithead mutiny. As a result, support for the mutiny's leaders soon began to falter. When Parker suggested taking the warships under their control to Holland, further dissension resulted. The authorities stood firm and the mutineers began to surrender, until Parker was isolated on the *Sandwich* and finally forced to abandon the action on June 13. Parker and 24 other ringleaders were tried and convicted. He was executed on June 30, bringing his brief period of naval service to an untimely end.

Parsons, Sir Charles
1854–1931

British marine engineer. During the early part of his long and productive career, he worked for the Armstrong Company, Newcastle upon Tyne, which produced large guns. He later joined Clarke, Chapman and Co. as a junior partner and produced the world's first steam turbine dynamo, which was produced in quantity and used to power ships' lighting systems. Parsons subsequently founded his own company, the Parsons Marine Steam Turbine Company, to exploit the potential of the new power plant. This company produced the world's first turbine-powered ship, the *TURBINIA*, in 1894. An Admiralty order for the first two turbine-propelled DESTROYERS followed. These destroyers, which could reach a maximum speed of 37 knots, demonstrated the full potential of the new engines. Parsons's turbines soon were employed in a wide variety of naval vessels, including H.M.S. *DREADNOUGHT*. Parsons was undoubtedly one of the most creative marine engineers of the 19th century.

Rollo Appleyard, *Charles Parsons*, London, 1933.

Pasco, John
1774–1853

British rear admiral who was responsible for sending the most famous signal in British naval history as the fleet sailed into battle at TRAFALGAR, 1805. Employed as a

signal lieutenant on the *VICTORY*, Pasco contributed to the wording of Horatio, Lord NELSON's message, as his own account of a conversation with his commander makes clear. Nelson had wanted it to read, "England confides that every man will do his duty." He told Pasco to be quick because he wanted to send an order for close action shortly afterward. In response, Pasco said, "If your Lordship will permit me to substitute 'expects' for 'confides,' the signal will soon be completed, because the word 'expects' is in the vocabulary, and 'confides' must be spelt." According to Pasco, Nelson replied, "in haste, and with seeming satisfaction: 'That will do, Pasco, make it directly'." Pasco, who was severely wounded during the battle, was unemployed for many years but returned to the *Victory* as her commander toward the end of his life. (See also SIGNALING.)

Pearl, Harbor, Attack on
December 7, 1941

Surprise Japanese attack on the U.S. Pacific fleet at its base at Pearl Harbor, Oahu, Hawaii, that brought the United States into WORLD WAR II, 1939–45. At the time of the operation some 75 warships, including three aircraft carriers, were based there in case they were required to respond to any acts of Japanese aggression in the Pacific region. Planning for the operation had begun almost a year earlier under the direction of Admiral Isoroku YAMAMOTO, commander in chief of the JAPANESE NAVY. His objective was to destroy the bulk of the U.S. fleet in a single decisive

Japanese naval aircraft attack Pearl Harbor, December 1941 *(Copyright © National Maritime Museum, Greenwich, London)*

attack, leaving the Japanese free to extend their rule across large areas of Southeast Asia. The plan reflected the view of many senior Japanese naval officers that they did not have the resources to fight an extended war with the United States; they believed that an effective preemptive strike was the only real option for an expansionist Japan.

Once the plan had been approved in the autumn, a strike force under the command of Vice Admiral Chuichi NAGUMO was assembled. It consisted of six carriers, two battleships, three cruisers and nine destroyers. They carried 104 high-level bombers, 135 dive-bombers and 81 fighter aircraft. Leaving the Kurile Islands on November 26, the strike force moved into position during the night of December 6–7. By 6 A.M. on December 7, when the first attack was launched, it was some 275 miles north of Oahu Island. The first bombs were dropped on the U.S. fleet at 7:55 A.M., sinking three battleships—the ARIZONA, West Virginia and California—and badly damaging a fourth—the NEVADA. The Japanese attacked five airfields, destroying some 200 aircraft on the ground. There was a supporting operation by Japanese MIDGET SUBMARINES. A second wave of enemy aircraft followed some 45 minutes later and continued the destruction, although smoke rising from damaged warships impaired their visibility.

U.S. ground defenses, which were totally unprepared for the attack, offered little effective response, and Japanese losses were correspondingly small: 100 casualties, 29 aircraft and five midget submarines. By contrast, the Americans suffered heavy losses: 2,400 lives had been lost, 1,300 were wounded and another 1,000 were missing; 18 warships were hit. Despite this toll, however, the Japanese victory was far from complete. The most notable survivors were the U.S. fleet's three aircraft carriers—the ENTERPRISE, LEXINGTON and SARATOGA—which were at sea at the time of the attack. The harbor installations also escaped serious damage. In these circumstances it surprising that the Japanese failed to launch a third airborne attack, which might have achieved greater damage to the fleet and its base. American reaction to this Japanese betrayal—diplomatic negotiations on U.S.-Japanese relations had been in progress—was swift. The following day the United States declared war on Japan with the aim of securing its unconditional surrender.

Several official inquiries into the Pearl Harbor attack took place, concluding with a congressional investigation after the war. Admiral Husband KIMMEL, naval commander at Pearl Harbor, and his army equivalent, who had been relieved of their commands after the attack, were found guilty of errors of judgment rather than dereliction of duty. Responsibility for the failures on December 7 clearly go well beyond these two men, and evidence collected by the investigation pointed to a general breakdown in the government and military. In the weeks before the attack U.S. intelligence had become aware of the possibility of a Japanese attack, but it failed to identify Pearl Harbor as a probable target. Early in December clear warnings of the impending danger were received but were not effectively handled or passed on to the naval and military authorities at Pearl Harbor.

Whatever shortcomings the action on December 7 revealed in American preparedness for war, the Japanese decision to attack Pearl Harbor was a disastrous one. The U.S. fleet had not been destroyed and, as some Japanese admirals had predicted, Japan could not survive a prolonged war with the United States once its dominant economic power had been redirected to military purposes.

Henry C. Clausen and Bruce Lee, *Pearl Harbor: Final Judgement*, New York, 1992; John Toland, *Infamy: Pearl Harbor and Its Aftermath*, London, 1982.

Peary, Robert Edwin
1856—1920

*O*ne of America's foremost explorers. Peary was born in Cresson, Pennsylvania on May 6, 1856. He received a degree in civil engineering from Bowdoin College in 1877 and subsequently received the Sc.D. in 1894 and two L.L.D. degrees from the University of Edinburgh and Tufts University. Serving with the U.S. Coast and Geodetic Survey from 1879 to 1881, he entered the navy as a civil engineer with the rank equivalent to lieutenant in October 1881. Peary's career was more that of a privately financed explorer than of a conventional naval officer. Most of his service career was spent on leave, during which he made many remarkable explorations, including one in central Greenland from 1886 to 1887, another as engineer-in-chief of the Nicaraguan Survey Expedition from 1887 to 1888 and yet another in Greenland from 1891 to 1893.

Promoted to civil engineer with rank of captain in 1909, he officially retired from the navy in the same year. On April 6, 1909 he apparently became the first man to reach the North Pole although his claim has long been challenged by Dr. Frederick Cook, who said that he had achieved this goal almost a year earlier. Nonetheless, Peary was given the thanks of Congress and promoted to rear admiral on the retired list for his efforts. His later years were spent studying aviation. During WORLD WAR I, 1914–18, he founded the National Aerial Coast Patrol Commission and chaired the National Committee on Coast Defense by Air. A member of many international organizations and congresses, he was awarded numerous medals and citations. He died in Washington, D.C. on February 20, 1920.

John E. Weems, *Peary, The Explorer and the Man*, Boston, 1967.

Pellew, Sir Edward, Viscount Exmouth
1757–1833

*B*ritish admiral whose reputation was based on his courage as a FRIGATE captain. During the AMERICAN

WAR OF INDEPENDENCE, 1775–83, he was promoted three times as a reward for gallantry, and almost as soon as the FRENCH REVOLUTIONARY AND NAPOLEONIC WARS, 1792–1815, began he made his mark again. Commanding the *Nymphe*, Pellew seized the French frigate *Cléopâtre*, the first French vessel to be captured during the war. In 1796 he helped to save the passengers and crew of the *Dutton*, a troop transport that had run aground near Plymouth. For this action Pellew was rewarded with a baronetcy.

He then joined the frigate *INDEFATIGABLE* and soon achieved another success: the destruction of the *Droits de l'Homme*, a French SHIP OF THE LINE, off the coast of France in 1797. In 1804, on promotion to flag rank, he was appointed commander in chief in the East Indies, where he destroyed a local Dutch fleet. On his return home in 1809 Pellew was appointed commander in chief in the North Sea, but on Admiral Cuthbert COLLINGWOOD's death in 1810 he was given the Mediterranean command. He remained in this post until after the conclusion of the Napoleonic Wars, 1803–15, his active career ending in August 1816, following his successful action against the Dey of Algiers, who had refused to abolish the enslavement of Christians in the territory he ruled.

Pellew's brother, Sir Israel Pellew, 1758–1832, also rose to flag rank in the British naval service. At the Battle of TRAFALGAR, 1805, his ship, the *Conqueror*, was fourth in the windward column and captured the French flagship *Bucentaure*.

C. Northcote Parkinson, *Edward Pellew, Viscount Exmouth*, London, 1934.

Penelope, H.M.S.

The name of two successive British 19th-century warships that were closely associated with the ROYAL NAVY's earliest development of steam propulsion. The first *Penelope*, built as a sailing frigate of 46 guns, was launched in 1829 but radically remodeled in 1843, when she was cut in two and lengthened to house a 650-horsepower engine and 600 tons of coal. In her new form she was the world's first PADDLE STEAMER warship of conventional design. Despite her unconventional origins, she performed to the required standards although she was never used in action. Another British warship named *Penelope*, completed in 1867, was the Royal Navy's first twin-screw oceangoing IRONCLAD. She was armed with ten 12-inch (30-cm) guns.

Penn, Sir William
1621–70

British naval commander who fought on the side of Parliament during the English Civil War, 1642–51. He was appointed a rear admiral in 1648. During the First ANGLO-DUTCH WAR, 1652–54, he was second in command to Admiral Robert BLAKE and became, successively, vice

admiral and general-at-sea. Despite his rapid promotion during the Protectorate (1654–59), Penn was politically unreliable; he offered, in 1654, to deliver the fleet to the exiled King Charles II. Nothing came of the plan, and Penn led the expedition that captured Jamaica during the following year. The failure to take Santo Domingo—the original objective of the operation—led to his disgrace and brief imprisonment in the Tower of London on his return home.

Penn retained his loyalist connections and was to help in the Restoration of the monarchy in 1660. He was well rewarded for it, receiving a knighthood and appointment as a commissioner of the navy. He served at sea again during the Second Anglo-Dutch War, 1664–67, leading the fleet at the Battle of LOWESTOFT, 1665, but his main contribution during this period was the code of tactics that formed the basis of the official *FIGHTING INSTRUCTIONS* issued by JAMES, Duke of York, later King James II. Penn's son, William, 1644–1718, was a leading Quaker and the founder (1681) of Pennsylvania.

Pennsylvania, U.S.S.

American BATTLESHIP, commissioned in 1916. She and her sister ship, the *Arizona*, formed the Pennsylvania class. The *Pennsylvania* had a displacement of 33,100 tons and was 608 feet (185.3 m) in length. Her beam was 106 feet 3 inches (32.4 m), and she had a maximum speed of 21 knots. Armor protection of the main belt and turret was provided. She was armed with 12 14-inch (36-cm) guns in four triple turrets and 12 5-inch (13-cm) guns in single turrets. Equipped to carry three aircraft, she was operated by a crew of 2,290. The *Pennsylvania*, which served with the U.S. Atlantic Fleet during WORLD WAR I, 1914–18, was extensively modernized in 1929–31. She was damaged at PEARL HARBOR, December 7, 1941, and needed repair and improvement before she could begin operational service in WORLD WAR II, 1939–45. Recommissioned in August 1942, she served in the Pacific theater from the ALEUTIAN landings onward and won a total of eight battle honors. A notable point in her wartime career was her contribution to the destruction of the Japanese battleship *Yamashiro* on October 24, 1944. The *Pennsylvania* was torpedoed by an aircraft off Okinawa on August 12, 1945. She was undergoing repairs when the war ended and, in 1946, was used as a target during the atomic tests at Bikini Atoll.

Pensacola, U.S.S.

The *Pensacola* and her sister ship *Salt Lake City* were American heavy CRUISERS, completed in 1929–30, that served throughout WORLD WAR II, 1939–45. The first American vessels to be constructed within the restrictions imposed by the Washington Naval Treaty, 1922, the two

Pensacola-class ships had a displacement of 9,100 tons—900 tons within the limit. (See WASHINGTON CONFERENCE.) They were equipped with ten 8-inch (20-cm) guns—in mixed twin and triple turrets—as well as 18 antiaircraft guns of various specifications. With a maximum speed of 32.5 knots, they were 585 feet 9 inches (179 m) in length and had a beam of 65 feet 3 inches (19.8 m). During World War II, both ships served successfully in the Pacific from MIDWAY to OKINAWA and survived to be used as nuclear test targets in the postwar period.

Pepys, Samuel
1633–1703

*B*ritish naval administrator, diarist and member of Parliament whose early progress owes much to his patron, Edward MONTAGU, Earl of Sandwich, who was a cousin of Pepys's father. Montagu had been a general-at-sea during the Commonwealth and secured Pepys a post as a clerk in the Exchequer. Pepys later served at sea as Montagu's secretary. Montagu eventually transferred his loyalties to the crown and supported the Restoration of the monarchy in 1660; elevated to the peerage as the Earl of Sandwich, he was able to secure Pepys's appointment as Clerk of the Acts to the Navy Board, a senior post in which he acted as secretary to the board. The Navy Board

Samuel Pepys: England's greatest naval administrator and reformer   *(Copyright © National Maritime Museum, Greenwich, London)*

was responsible for the civilian administration of the navy, which was notoriously corrupt and inefficient during this period.

Pepys proved to be an able administrator who devoted much of his energy to improving the quality of naval administration. The fruits of his labors were first evident during the Second ANGLO-DUTCH WAR, 1665–67, when only his actions prevented a complete breakdown of the supply system. He successfully shielded the Navy Board from taking any blame for the disastrous Dutch BLOCKADE of London in 1667. Pepys continued this work as First Secretary to the Admiralty from his appointment in June 1673, and instigated further improvements in naval administration. In 1678 he was removed from office and thrown into prison on a false charge of being involved in the Popish plot, an imaginary conspiracy to assassinate King Charles II and place James, Duke of York (later JAMES II) on the throne. Following service under Lord Dartmouth in Tangier, Pepys returned to his old post in the Admiralty after a gap of five years.

There he remained until the Glorious Revolution, 1688, when once more he was removed from office, following accusations that he was a Jacobite (i.e., a partisan of King James II, who had been deposed). During this second term he continued his work in modernizing the navy. In 1686, a special commission had been established to produce an efficient fleet and, in 1690 Pepys produced an account of its work entitled *Memoires relating to the state of the Royal Navy*. Pepys's reputation as a man of letters rests on his *Diary*, 1660–69, which is the most complete contemporary account of the Restoration period. It also throws much light on the naval administration of these times.

R. Ollard, *Pepys: A Biography*, London, 1974.

Perier

A short-barreled naval gun of the 15th and 16th centuries, also known as the canon-perier. Specifications varied but typically a perier might be five feet (1.52 m) in length with an 8-inch (20-cm) caliber. A muzzle-loader, it fired a standard-size stone shot of 24 pounds (10.89 kg) over relatively short distances and could cause severe damage. The perier had a maximum range of some 1,600 yards (1,463 m)—significantly less than that of the CANON and the CULVERIN of the same period. It was a chambered gun, which meant that the powder chamber was of a different width from the ball.

Perry, Matthew Calbraith
1794–1858

*Y*ounger brother of Oliver Hazard PERRY (the hero of the Battle of LAKE ERIE) whose own considerable achievements included that of opening Japan to Western trade. Matthew Perry was born in South Kingstown, Rhode Island in 1794. As a midshipman he served in the WAR OF 1812 on the *President* and on the *United States*. Early duties included the taking of Black American settlers to Liberia and helping to rid the West Indies of pirates. (See PIRACY.) A vigorous proponent of reforms in the naval service, he argued successfully for an apprentice system for young recruits as well as organizing in 1833 the U.S. Naval Lyceum to promote learning among the officer corps. He served as a member on the Board of Examiners, which approved and established the first curriculum at the new Naval School in 1845 at ANNAPOLIS.

Perry's reform efforts also included the promotion of steam propulsion in the navy. He served as captain of the steam vessel *Fulton* and eventually created the navy's Engineering Corps. After a period commanding the squadron that tried to suppress the slave trade off West Africa, he commanded naval forces that assisted the army in capturing such key Mexican ports as Vera Cruz during the U.S. war against Mexico in 1846–48. His greatest fame, however, came when, as commodore, he commanded the squadron in 1852–54 assigned to negotiate an agreement with isolationist Japan and open that island nation to Western trade and influence. In 1853 he anchored his squadron of four U.S. Navy ships in lower Tokyo Bay. Through a combination of conciliation and force, the skilled diplomat Perry negotiated a treaty permitting American ships to use two Japanese ports. He died in 1858. Perry's Japanese feat had the unintended and ironic effect of stimulating Japan's transformation in a major industrial and naval power—a transformation that would have worldwide repercussions in the 20th century.

Samuel E. Morison, *"Old Bruin": Commodore Matthew C. Perry, 1794–1858*, Boston, 1967.

Perry, Oliver Hazard
1785–1819

*A*merican naval officer who won fame during the WAR OF 1812. Born in South Kingstown, Rhode Island in 1785, elder brother of Matthew C. PERRY, he entered the service in 1799, seeing action in the QUASI-WAR, 1798–1800, with France and in the Tripolitan War. During the War of 1812 he was given command to build a fleet on Lake Erie to reverse the British military advantage on the western Great Lakes. Hampered by the absence of materials and skilled shipwrights, he succeeded in creating a force of ten vessels, the largest being the *Niagara* and the *Lawrence*. (The latter was named after his friend, James LAWRENCE.) Making his base near Sandusky, Ohio, on September 10, 1813 he engaged the British force of roughly equal size, although Perry enjoyed a superiority of firepower. Perry flew a flag bearing Lawrence's final words: "Don't Give Up the Ship." The Battle of LAKE ERIE was a hotly contested one resulting in heavy casualties but an American victory. Perry relayed the result with more words that became famous: "We have met the enemy and they are ours." The Battle of Lake Erie secured the United States' claim to the Northwest Territories. Perry died in 1819 while commanding an expedition on the Orinoco River following negotiations with the new nation of Venezuela.

Richard Dillon, *We Have Met the Enemy: Oliver Hazard Perry, Wilderness Commodore*, New York, 1978.

Peter the Great
1672–1725

*R*ussian tsar (emperor), 1682–1725, notable for his efforts to modernize and westernize the giant Slavic nation. Among his accomplishments were the expansion of Russian territory and the building of a new Russian capital, St. Petersburg. The creator of the Russian army, he is also known as the father of the RUSSIAN NAVY. Central to Peter's expansionist policy was his plan to secure outlets in the Black Sea and the Baltic. Control of the Black Sea, including the Dardanelles, would give Russian merchant ships access to the Mediterranean and beyond. In order to accomplish this, however, Russia first would have to defeat the Turks, the controlling power, on land and at sea—and it would have to build a fleet to do so. In

Peter the Great: the father of the Russian navy   *(Copyright © National Maritime Museum, Greenwich, London)*

1695 the Russians sailed down the Don River; by 1696 they had taken the Turkish fortress at Azov. Peter's first naval base was established at Taganrog on the Sea of Azov. Peter had participated in these operations as an ordinary bombadier and sought to broaden his military and naval knowledge during a tour of Europe in 1697. During this tour he worked as a shipwright in the Netherlands and DEPTFORD, England.

Peter also sought to establish a Russian naval presence in the Baltic and to defeat Sweden, which maintained a powerful naval force in the area. A Swedish fort captured in 1703 was used as the first Russian naval base in the Baltic, and soon a fleet was under construction at the newly designated capital of St. Petersburg. The main naval base was established on Kronstadt Island. In the early 18th century, Peter achieved further Russian land and sea victories in the Baltic area, although these came at the expense of earlier gains against the Turks on the Sea of Azov, which he was forced to abandon. Russia's Baltic victories included the Battle of Gangut, August 1714, when a fleet of Russian galleys decisively defeated the Swedes.

By the end of the Great Northern War, 1700–21, the Russian navy had been established as a major power in the Baltic, with a fleet of some 180 warships. Peter had firmly lain the foundations of Russian naval power, and the gains he made were to be extended by his successors. However, his successes were achieved at a great human cost, reflecting the fact that he was a traditional despot as well as modernizer who had established Russia as an effective European power for the first time.

M. S. Anderson, *Peter the Great*, London, 1978, Robert K. Massie, *Peter the Great: His Life and World*, London, 1982.

Pett, Peter
fl. 1560

The first member of a dynasty of English shipbuilders. Master shipwright at DEPTFORD during the reign of King Edward VI, and England's leading shipbuilder, Peter Pett was responsible for the construction of most of the warships added to the English fleet during this period. The galleon *Elizabeth Jonas*, one of the largest warships to fight against the SPANISH ARMADA in 1588, was a good example of his output.

Pett, who died in 1589, was succeeded by his son Phineas, 1570–1647, who became master shipwright in 1605. Phineas Pett's most notable achievement was the construction of the 1,500-ton SOVEREIGN OF THE SEAS, which was then the largest ship in the world. He also built the slightly smaller (1,200-ton) *Royal Prince*. Several close relations followed in his footsteps, and all became master shipwrights. Phineas Pett's son, Peter, 1610–72, who had worked on the *Sovereign of the Seas*, was appointed master shipwright at Woolwich and later became a commissioner of the navy at Chatham. He was removed following the Dutch attack on the English fleet in the Medway in 1667 during the Second ANGLO-DUTCH WAR, 1665–67.

William G. Perrin, ed., *The Autobiography of Phineas Pett*, London, 1918.

Philippine Sea, Battle of the
June 19–21, 1944

The surprise American invasion of the Marianas Islands in the central Pacific, which began on June 11, 1944 during WORLD WAR II, 1939–45, provoked a strong Japanese reaction. If the American thrust in the central Pacific could be defeated decisively, it would reverse the course of the war, which was moving strongly in the Americans' favor. The Japanese Mobile Fleet, commanded by Vice Admiral Jisaburo OZAWA, which included nine aircraft carriers in two groups, supported by land-based planes from Guam and Truk, would seek to defeat the American Fifth Fleet, headed by Admiral Raymond SPRUANCE, which had protected the Marianas landings. Vice Admiral Marc MITSCHER's Task Group 58, consisting of seven fleet and eight light carriers as well as 956 aircraft, was part of the Fifth Fleet.

Spruance was well aware of the possibility of enemy action from intelligence reports, and he remained close to the invasion force. The Japanese struck on June 19 with wave after wave of shore- and carrier-based aircraft attacking the American task force. During the eight-hour battle that followed, some three-quarters of the attacking force—300 aircraft—were shot down, while the Americans suffered relatively little damage. This action was to be known as the Great Marianas Turkey Shoot and reflected the poor quality of Japanese crews and aircraft. At the same time the U.S. submarines *Albacore* and *Cavalla* torpedoed and sank the two largest Japanese carriers, the *Taiho* and the *Shokaku*. The following day some units of Task Force 58 left in pursuit of the Japanese carrier force as it withdrew from the area. The Americans did not locate these carriers until the late afternoon and had the opportunity for only one strike before nightfall. Another Japanese carrier, the *Hiyo*, was sunk, along with two other ships, but the Americans also suffered losses because numerous aircraft were unable to return to their carriers in the hours of darkness. The remnants of the Japanese force were able to escape while valuable time was lost rescuing air crews from the sea, where they had ditched their planes.

Although Japanese losses might have been even higher. Japan could not replace the great many carriers, aircraft and air crews destroyed during the battle. There is no doubt that the Battle of the Philippines was a key engagement of the Pacific theater: It removed the Japanese carrier fleet,

American dive-bombers attack a Japanese heavy cruiser during the Battle of the Philippine Sea, 1944 *(Copyright © Imperial War Museum, London)*

which now had insufficient aircraft and crews, as a major threat for the duration of the war.

W. Y'Blood, *Red Sun Setting*, Annapolis, 1980.

Phillip, Arthur
1738–1814

British vice admiral who founded Sydney, Australia in 1788 and was the first governor of New South Wales. Phillip was born in London and trained at Greenwich before joining the navy in 1755. During the SEVEN YEARS' WAR, 1756–63, he first served under Admiral John BYNG in the Mediterranean and then went to the West Indies. He returned to active service during the AMERICAN WAR OF INDEPENDENCE, 1775–83, rising to the rank of post-captain. In 1787 he was appointed to command the "First Fleet" (which consisted of the frigate *Sirius* and ten other ships) carrying convicts to Australia. He established a penal colony at the landing point he named Sydney (in honor of Viscount Sydney, English Under-Secretary of State for Home Affairs) and served as governor of New South Wales until 1792. Phillip was promoted to vice admiral in 1810.

Phillips, Sir Tom
1888–1941

British vice admiral who was killed in action off the coast of Malaya in 1941. Phillips was vice chief of the naval staff at the outbreak of WORLD WAR II, 1939–45, but failed to establish effective working relations with Winston CHURCHILL, who was First Lord of the Admiralty in Neville Chamberlain's wartime government. In late 1941 Phillips was appointed commander in chief of the Eastern Fleet and sailed for Singapore with the battleship *PRINCE OF WALES* and the battle cruiser *Repulse*. When news arrived of an impending Japanese invasion of Malaya, he set off to find the enemy naval force. The mission was unsuccessful, and as the *Prince of Wales* and the *Repulse* returned to Singapore they were attacked by Japanese bombers. On December 10, 1941 both capital ships were sunk and the British commander in chief was killed on one of the blackest days in the history of the ROYAL NAVY.

Pinnace

A small three-masted ship of about 20 tons that was employed as a FRIGATE by the navies of England,

France and Holland during the 16th and 17th centuries. Its two forward masts each had two square sails; the mizzen mast had a lateen sail with a square topsail. The pinnace had a flat stern, two full-length decks, a forecastle and a half deck aft. Armed with up to 30 guns, pinnaces were employed primarily as scouts and naval tenders. They also were widely used for trading purposes and, despite their small size, on the voyages of discovery.

Piracy

$\mathcal{A}$ feature of life at sea from ancient times to the present, piracy is the unlawful seizure and plundering of ships for personal gain. Pirates were the individuals responsible for such attacks. Although the dividing line was not always clear, pirates may be distinguished from a BUCCANEERS, because the latter did not normally prey on ships of their own country of origin. There is a clearer dividing line between pirates and privateers, with the latter being licensed by the state to take prizes in time of war. Like buccaneers, CORSAIRS and others involved in illegal attacks at sea, pirates had the greatest freedom of action in the days before the formation of national navies. Without regular national patrols, every ocean of the world was subject to frequent acts of piracy. Pirates normally operated from fast, well-armed vessels and captured their victim by boarding the ship and overpowering the crew. In more recent times, pirates have boarded a ship disguised as passengers and have seized control of it at sea. In the 16th and 17th centuries, major concentrations of pirates were to be found on the SPANISH MAIN—particularly the Caribbean, off Japan and in the Mediterranean. The normal punishment for piracy—if the felon could be caught—was death by hanging.

The Mediterranean has perhaps the longest continuous record of piracy, which persisted there until well into the 19th century. The Barbary corsairs, who operated mainly from Algiers and Tunis on the coast of North Africa, attacked shipping and coastal settlements in their search for booty and for captives who could be sold as slaves. Dating back to the Middle Ages, the Barbary corsairs were at their most powerful prior to the 18th century, when national naval power began to affect their activities. However, they remained a potent force, extending their activities to include ships of the United States once it had gained its independence. The United States concluded agreements with Algiers and the other Barbary states to ensure that its shipping was immune from attack in return for money payments. These agreements soon broke down and led to U.S. naval action against Tripoli in 1801–5 and against Algiers in 1815. An Anglo-Dutch fleet returned to Algiers in 1816 and destroyed several pirate ships. Even so, the pirates' activities were not finally curtailed until the French occupied Algeria in 1830. In the 20th century piracy has become a rarity, although it is not unknown, particularly in the Far East, where merchant ships have been attacked in the South China Sea and the waters of Malaysia and Indonesia.

Plymouth, Battle of
August 16, 1652

$\mathcal{S}$ ome three months after the Battle of DOVER, the opening engagement of the First ANGLO-DUTCH WAR, 1652–54, the English and Dutch fleets met again off Plymouth. Nearly two weeks earlier a Dutch naval force of some 30 warships under the command of Admiral Michiel de RUYTER had arrived off Calais. Their task was to escort a merchant CONVOY through the English Channel. Departing on August 13, the Dutch meet an English force of Plymouth under the command of Admiral Sir George AYSCUE that consisted of 38 men-of-war.

The battle, which was fiercely fought, lasted most of the afternoon and evening of August 16. Despite claims of victory from both sides, the outcome was indecisive, perhaps partly because the Dutch were unable to deploy their FIRESHIPS. (The wind was not in their favor.) The Dutch convoy proceeded down the English Channel. The two fleets were not to meet off the English coast again until the next month, at the Battle of KENTISH KNOCK, September 28.

Pocket-Battleship

$\mathcal{T}$ he term "pocket-battleship" is used specifically to describe three German warships—the DEUTSCHLAND (later renamed *Lutzow*), the ADMIRAL GRAF SPEE and the ADMIRAL SCHEER—constructed in the 1930s under the terms of the Treaty of Versailles, 1919. This treaty prevented Germany from building warships in excess of 10,000 tons; the pocket-battleship was designed specially to get around these constraints. In essence, these scaled-down BATTLESHIPS were heavily armored CRUISERS, but with much larger main armament than was normally associated with cruisers. They were equipped with six 11-inch (28-cm) guns, arranged in two triple turrets, that fired 700-pound (317-kg) shells. Supplementary armament consisted of eight 5.9- inch (15-cm) guns and several antiaircraft guns. These ships were nominally 10,000 tons, in accordance with treaty requirements, but were in fact larger than this on completion and had a displacement of 11,750 tons. They were 610 feet 3 inches (186 m) in length, had a beam of 67 feet 6 inches (21 m) and were operated by a crew of 619.

This class was designed for long-range COMMERCE-RAIDING activities of up to 20,000 miles (32,186 km), and their relatively small scale and powerful diesel engines reflected this intention. They were the first warships to be propelled by diesel drive only. The *Admiral Graf Spee's* WORLD WAR II, 1939–45, career came to an abrupt end when she was scuttled off Montevideo on December 17, 1939 after the Battle of the RIVER PLATE. Her sister ships survived until the closing stages of the war, when they were destroyed by British bombers at anchor at different locations on the German coast.

Polaris

*A*merican submarine-launched ballistic missile, first used in operational service in November 1960 when the *U.S.S. George Washington* was commissioned and equipped with it. Three versions of the Polaris missile, with a range of up to 2,780 miles (4,635 km), were produced. The original design was 31 feet (9.4 m) in length and 4.5 feet (1.4 m) in diameter and was powered by two solid-fuel rocket stages. The first two types carried single nuclear warheads of up to 800 kilotons, but the final version embodied three 200-kiloton nuclear warheads. The latter was adopted by the British, who added decoy warheads to enable it to penetrate Moscow's missile defenses. Designed to be launched underwater from submarines that were very difficult to detect, Polaris missiles were a major element in the COLD WAR strategy of nuclear deterrence. A total of 41 submarines in the United States navy were equipped with the Polaris. Each submarine normally carried 16 missiles. These remained in service until they were finally phased out in 1981, although most had been replaced by POSEIDON missiles some three years earlier. Britain also commissioned four Polaris-equipped submarines, which, following modernization, remained in service until they were replaced by the new TRIDENT weapons system in the mid-1990s.

Graham Spinardi, *From Polaris to Trident: The Development of U.S. Fleet Ballistic Technology,* Cambridge, Mass., 1994.

Polyphemus, H.M.S.

*A*n experimental British warship, completed in 1881, that was designed to demonstrate the potential of the RAM (as opposed to the gun) as an effective offensive weapon. The *Polyphemus* originally was designed to carry the ram, which projected forward 12 feet (3.65 m) from the bow of the ship, as her only armament, but light guns and six 14-inch (36-cm) TORPEDO tubes were added during construction. The ram was removable and was designed to strike an enemy ship well below the waterline, where the hull would be unprotected by armor. The *Polyphemus* had a displacement of 2,640 tons, a maximum speed of 18 knots and was provided with some armor protection. A very low profile in the water reduced her vulnerability to enemy attack, but she proved to be insufficiently seaworthy to accompany the fleet, as had been intended. Like several

other rams of the period, including the five units of the French Taureau class, the *Polyphemus's* design had little to commend it apart from relative cheapness. The increasing efficiency of long-range naval weapons quickly made it obsolete.

Pondicherry, Battle of
September 10, 1759

*F*ollowing the Battles of CUDDALORE and NEGAPATAM in 1758, British and French naval forces met in the Indian Ocean off Pondicherry, India, in a third and final action during the SEVEN YEARS' WAR, 1756–63, on September 10, 1759. The French squadron, which was under the command of the Comte d'Aché, had been reinforced at Mauritius and now consisted of 11 ships of the line and two frigates. It was responsible for the defense of the French base at Pondicherry, on the Coromandel coast (the east coast of southern India), which was coming under increasing pressure from the British.

On his return journey to Pondicherry, the Comte d'Aché was intercepted on September 10 by a British squadron under Admiral Thomas Pocock, which had been cruising off the coast. The opposing squadrons formed into line-ahead on a parallel course. In a fierce running battle, the British, who were outnumbered, inflicted heavy damage on the French and wounded the Comte d'Aché. Altogether the French sustained some 1,500 casualties. The British also suffered some damage and were unable to prevent the French squadron entering Pondicherry, although the Comte d'Aché soon was compelled to take his squadron back to France. Thus, the battle marked the end of a French presence in India.

Popham, Sir Home Riggs
1762–1820

*B*ritish admiral who made a major contribution to the development of naval SIGNALING. Popham, who entered the Royal Navy in 1778, had an eventful career. It included his prosecution for participating, in 1806, in an unsuccessful attack on Buenos Aires without proper authorization after he had captured the Cape of Good Hope from the Dutch in a combined operation with General Sir David Baird.

The signaling code for which Popham is best remembered first appeared in 1800. A vocabulary code consisting initially of 1,000 words, it later was greatly enlarged, enabling many thousands of different signals to be sent using a four-flag hoist. Adopted by the British ADMIRALTY in 1803, it greatly improved communications between warships of the ROYAL NAVY, and remained in use throughout the 19th century. Popham's code was used to send Lord

NELSON's famous signal—"England expects that every man will do his duty"—at the Battle of TRAFALGAR, October 1805.

Porter, David
1780–1843

*A*merican naval officer. He was the father of Admiral David Dixon PORTER, foster father of Admiral David Glasgow FARRAGUT and the son of a naval officer who served in the AMERICAN WAR OF INDEPENDENCE, 1775–83. Born in Boston, Massachusetts in 1780, Porter saw service during the QUASI-WAR, 1798–1800, with France. He was imprisoned by Tripolitans while on board the *Philadelphia* under William BAINBRIDGE in Tripoli harbor when that vessel ran aground and was captured. Commanding the *Essex* in the period leading up the WAR OF 1812, he conducted a raiding campaign against British commerce in the Pacific before being defeated after a stalwart defense at Valparaiso, Chile. After another brief period of imprisonment, he was paroled and saw further action on the Potomac River during the British invasion of the middle-Atlantic region in 1814.

After the war and the navy's reorganization, Porter served as one of the navy commissioners until 1823, then as commander of the West India Squadron, where he was engaged in suppressing PIRACY. In 1825 he was court-martialed for the severity of his response to the mistreatment of one of his officers by Puerto Rican authorities. Porter resigned his commission and served until 1829 as commander of the new Mexican navy. Returning to the United States, but suffering from financial losses and declining health, he was given minor diplomatic responsibilities abroad and died near Constantinople in 1843.

David F. Long, "David Porter: Pacific Ocean Gadfly," in *Command Under Sail. Makers of the American Naval Tradition, 1775–1850*, ed. James C. Bradford, Annapolis, 1985.

Porter, David Dixon
1813–91

*D*avid Dixon Porter was born on June 8, 1813 in Chester, Pennsylvania, into a famous American naval family. His father was Commodore David PORTER, and his adopted brother was future Admiral David Glasgow FARRAGUT. At the age of ten he joined his father in an expedition to suppress PIRACY in the West Indies. When his father resigned from the U.S. Navy and became an admiral in the Mexican navy, young David received his first commission as a midshipman in the Mexican navy. Seeing considerable action, he was taken prisoner by the Spanish in Cuba in 1828. He was later released and entered the U.S. Navy in early 1829. During the Mexican War,

1846–48, he commanded 70 men against the town of Tabasco and succeeded in capturing the town's main fort.

With the outbreak of the AMERICAN CIVIL WAR in 1861, the then rather senior Lieutenant Porter was consulted by President Lincoln on the relief of Fort Pickens in Florida, an offshore fortress, and against which he led the relief expedition. Quickly promoted to commander and then to acting rear admiral, he recommended and helped plan and execute the attack on the Lower Mississippi, receiving the surrender of Fort Jackson and Fort St. Philip. His mortar FLOTILLA was used against Vicksburg in 1862. As commander of the Mississippi River Squadron with the rank of permanent rear admiral, he cooperated with the army on campaigns to take the region, including Vicksburg in July 1863. Then he was transferred to command the North Atlantic Blockading Squadron when the last major Confederate strongholds on the Atlantic—Fort Fisher and Wilmington, North Carolina—were taken. For his effort and success during the war, he received three different votes of thanks from the Congress.

In August 1865, he became superintendent of the U.S. Naval Academy, instituting numerous reforms and changes in curriculum and the academy's physical size. He was the founding president of the Naval Institute in 1873 and contributed many articles on naval subjects. Advanced to vice admiral in 1866 and then to admiral in 1870, he became the highest-ranking American naval officer. During the administration of President Ulysses S. Grant, he was a special adviser to the secretary of the navy—making him not only a powerful political and military figure but de facto head of the navy. He died in Washington, D.C. on February 13, 1891.

Richard S. West, Jr., *The Second Admiral: A Life of David Dixon Porter, 1813–1891*, New York, 1937.

Portland, Battle of
February 18–20, 1653

*F*ollowing the English fleet's defeat at the Battle of DUNGENESS, November 30, 1652, during the early stages of the First ANGLO-DUTCH WAR, 1652–54, its tactics and performance were thoroughly reviewed. One result was the publication, in March 1653, of the first official *FIGHTING INSTRUCTIONS*, which provided for line-ahead formations to make maximum use of the BROADSIDE. The English fleet also was strengthened, and by the beginning of 1653 some 80 ships had been gathered at Portsmouth under the joint command of Admiral Robert BLAKE and Admiral Richard DEANE. On February 18, 1653 they intercepted a large Dutch convoy in the English Channel some 20 miles south of Portland Bill. About 80 Dutch men-of-war, commanded by Admiral Marten TROMP, were escorting 200 merchant ships on their way back to Holland.

Tromp attacked before the British fleet was completely

in place. As the first shots were fired the White Squadron, under General George Monck, was five miles (8 km) away. The Battle of Portland, or the Three Days' Battle as it is sometimes known, had begun. On the first day the main engagement lasted until about 4 P.M. although sporadic fighting continued until nightfall. Tromp had achieved his main objective of keeping the CONVOY intact and moving up the Channel, but doing so had constrained him during the battle. A lack of wind prevented the British from pursuing the Dutch immediately, and they did not make contact with them again until the following afternoon. During a running battle on February 19 the Dutch fleet, which acted as a rear guard to the convoy, successfully fought off the British. However, Tromp's ammunition was running low and he was fortunate that dusk brought the short engagement to an end.

Fighting was renewed on February 20 off Beachy Head when the English fleet finally penetrated the escort and attacked the Dutch merchantmen. As darkness brought operations to a close Blake anchored for the night, intending to return to the attack in the morning. However, the Dutch, who were positioned off Calais, left undetected before morning, and with great skill Tromp brought his fleet and the remainder of the convoy back to home waters. Dutch losses—eight warships and up to 50 merchant ships—were heavy, and the Battle of Portland represented a turning point in the war, with the English Channel now being closed to all Dutch seaborne trade.

Porto Bello, Capture of
November 22, 1739

The first engagement of the War of JENKINS' EAR, 1739–43, between Britain and Spain. The immediate cause of the war, which began in 1739 and soon became part of the wider War of the AUSTRIAN SUCCESSION, 1740–48, was the claim of a British merchant captain that the Spanish had cut off his ear. A British squadron of six ships of the line, commanded by Vice Admiral Edward VERNON, had been sent to the West Indies in July 1739 to capture a Spanish treasure ship. The ship would almost certainly load its precious cargo at Porto Bello, an important harbor on the Caribbean coast of the Isthmus of Panama. Following a sustained bombardment of the Spanish defenses, landing parties were put ashore, and within a day the town had fallen. The British seized all the public money they could find and destroyed the remaining Spanish defenses at virtually no cost to themselves.

Porto Farina, Battle of
April 4, 1655

In October 1654 the English government ordered Admiral Robert BLAKE to the Mediterranean for an opera-

tion against Tunisian CORSAIRS. Launched in response to the damage caused by the corsairs to English shipping, Blake's mission went ahead when demands for compensation were refused. With a force of 24 warships, Blake located a corsair squadron at anchor in the harbor of Porto Farina, some 20 miles east of Bizerta, Tunisia. On April 4 Blake entered the harbor firing on the shore batteries that protected the corsairs. When these batteries were silenced, Blake turned his attention to the nine enemy ships and ordered his men to board them. Each one was burned in turn. Although there were some 65 British casualties, the corsairs failed to make an effective response to the attack. Blake was able to withdraw without sustaining any losses to his fleet. It was a brilliant victory for the British and for a period reduced the corsairs' capacity to attack merchant shipping on the Mediterranean trade routes.

Porto Praya, Battle of
April 16, 1781

An engagement between British and French naval forces off the Cape Verde Islands during the AMERICAN WAR OF INDEPENDENCE, 1775–1783. A French squadron consisting of five SHIPS OF THE LINE under the command of Admiral Pierre Andre de SUFFREN left BREST for the Cape Verde Islands en route to the Cape of Good Hope. His objective was to defend the Dutch colony from British attack. On April 16 he came across a larger British squadron off the south coast of St. Jago, one of the islands of the Cape Verde group. The British squadron, anchored in Porto Praya roads, consisted of five ships of the line and several other smaller warships. Commanded by Commodore George Johnstone, the squadron was escorting a number of troop transports that were to be used in the capture of the Cape of Good Hope. When Suffren launched his attack, the British were unprepared, with many of the crew onshore. Some British ships were damaged in the attack but the French operation, which only involved two ships of the line, did not make as much impact as it might have done. However, the British were forced to remain at their anchorage while essential repairs were carried out, and eventually they abandoned their expedition. This enabled Admiral Suffren to leave for the Cape of Good Hope without further delay.

Poseidon

An American nuclear weapons system developed in the 1960s as a successor to the POLARIS missile. (See GUIDED MISSILE.) First deployed in 1970, this long-range underwater launched ballistic missile was installed in modified Polaris submarines. By 1976 about 20 American nuclear submarines were equipped with Poseidon missiles. Up to 14 nuclear warheads of 40 kilotons could be accommodated, although the normal configuration was ten. The warheads could be targeted independently and represented a substantial enhancement of the nuclear arsenal of the United States. The Poseidon had a range of up to 3,120 miles (5,200 km), and 16 were installed in each submarine without destabilizing the nuclear balance between the superpowers. The missile has been phased out of the American service with the arrival of the TRIDENT.

Graham Spinardi, *From Polaris to Trident: The Development of U.S. Fleet Ballistic Technology*, Cambridge, Mass., 1994.

Potemkin, Grigori Aleksandrovich, Prince
1739–91

Russian naval administrator, field marshal and statesman. Potemkin was born in Smolensk and educated at Moscow State University. He established his military reputation in the Russo-Turkish War, 1768–74, and was appointed governor-general of the Ukraine and became a count. He was also the lover of Empress Catherine II and one of the most influential Russians of his time. He added to his military reputation by playing a key part in the Russian capture of the Crimea in 1783. Following this victory, Potemkin, by then a prince and a field marshal, was responsible for the construction of a Russian Black Sea fleet of 40 vessels, including 15 ships of the line. He also created several ports and an arsenal at Kherson and founded a naval dockyard at Sevastopol. In 1787 Catherine's tour of the Crimea, which he organized, led directly a second war with Turkey in 1787–92. Potemkin served in the war as army commander in chief but died on his way to the peace negotiations.

Potemkin

Completed in 1904, this famous pre-dreadnought BATTLESHIP—named after the famed Prince Grigori Aleksandrovich POTEMKIN—became the FLAGSHIP of the Russian Black Sea Fleet. The *Kniaz Potemkin Tavritcheski*—to give it its full name—was relatively slow (16 knots), had limited armor protection and was equipped with only four 12-inch (30-cm) guns in fore and aft twin turrets. However, the *Potemkin*'s performance compared favorably with that of Turkish warships of the period. Her crew mutinied during the Revolution of 1905 and she put to sea, but she later surrendered to representatives of the Romanian government. The events of this period were recreated in Sergei Einstein's classic film *Potemkin*, which appeared in 1926. She was renamed the *Panteleimon* on her return to the Black Sea Fleet.

During WORLD WAR I, 1914–18, the *Potemkin*, like other old Russian battleships, was used principally for shore bombardment, although in April 1915 she scored two hits on the German battle cruiser *GOEBEN*. Named *Potemkin* again by the Provisional Government of March 1917 and then finally the *Fighter for Liberty* by the Bolsheviks in May 1918, she was abandoned by her crew after the Russo-German armistice of December 1917. Later captured by the Germans, she was surrendered to the Allies in November 1918; her engines subsequently were removed to prevent her operational used by the Bolsheviks during the Civil War, 1917–22. She finally was scrapped in 1922.

Richard Hough, *The Potemkin Mutiny*, London, 1960.

Pound, Sir Dudley
1877–1943

British naval commander who was promoted captain at the beginning of WORLD WAR I, 1914–18, and commanded the BATTLESHIP *Colossus* at the Battle of JUTLAND, May 1916. During the final two years of the war he was employed at the ADMIRALTY but returned to sea in the 1920s in command of the *Repulse* in the Atlantic fleet. By 1936 he was commander in chief of the Mediterranean Fleet with the rank of admiral. In 1939 he was appointed Chief of the Naval Staff and First Sea Lord following the death of Sir Roger Backhouse; he held office for the first four years of WORLD WAR II, 1939–45. He also served, until March 1942, as chairman of the British chief of staffs committee and was a member of the Anglo-U.S. chiefs of staff committee.

In these posts, Pound maintained positive relations with Sir Winston CHURCHILL, then First Lord of the Admiralty, and was able to suppress some of his less firmly based ideas. He established a formidable reputation as an administrator, but his intervention in operational matters was not always so successful. The main example was his order to CONVOY PQ-17, which was bound for the Soviet Union, to scatter, in the face of objections from Sir John TOVEY, commander in chief of the Home Fleet. The ill-advised order led to the convoy's destruction. By this time Pound was seriously ill; he was forced to resign from the navy in October 1943, shortly before he died.

Pratt, William Veazie
1869–1957

American naval officer. Born in Maine on February 28, 1869, Pratt entered to U.S. Naval Academy in 1885, just as the navy modernized and began to compete as a worldwide naval power. His earliest tours were on vessels of the squadron of evolution (a special unit of new ships that operated in close tactical coordination). Service at sea was interspersed with shore tours that included teaching at the Naval Academy and at the Naval War College, during which he became closely associated with such other leading naval figures as William S. SIMS, under whom he served as aide in 1913. By June 1917 he was Assistant Chief of Naval Operations, closely working with Admiral Sims and with the Allies to help shape naval policy during WORLD WAR I, 1914–18. Reaching flag rank in June 1921, he served as president of the Naval War College during the mid-1920s, greatly improving the curriculum there. He spent most of that decade commanding successive battleship divisions and finally became commander in chief of the U.S. Fleet. In September 1930 he achieved the highest naval position, Chief of Naval Operations, which he held during the difficult times of the depression until his retirement in 1933. He died on November 25, 1957.

Gerald E. Wheeler, *Admiral William Veazie Pratt, U.S. Navy: A Sailor's Life*, Washington, D.C., 1974.

Preble, Edward
1761–1807

*A*merican naval officer. Born in Portland, Maine (then part of Massachusetts) in 1761, Preble served as a PRIVATEER during the early stages of the AMERICAN WAR OF INDEPENDENCE, 1775–83. He later became a midshipman in the Massachusetts state navy in 1779. A merchant captain between the War of Independence and the creation of the permanent U.S. Navy, he was commissioned a captain in 1799. He commanded the *Essex* during the QUASI-WAR, 1798–1800, with France. It was during the war against the Barbary states that he achieved fame and made his greatest contribution to American naval heritage. While on the *CONSTITUTION* as commodore of the squadron blockading Tripoli from 1803 to 1804, he had under his command—and thus instilled a strong sense of discipline and professional duty into—young officers such as Stephen DECATUR and others who would lead the U.S. Navy in the WAR OF 1812 and later.

Christopher McKee. *Edward Preble: A Naval Biography, 1761–1807*, Annapolis, 1972; reprint, New York, 1980.

President, U.S.S.

*A*n American FRIGATE of 52 guns, launched in April 1800, that was one of the first ships to be commissioned in the newly constituted United States Navy. She entered service under the command of Thomas TRUXTON only a few weeks before the QUASI-WAR, 1798–1800, was finally brought to an end. The *President* did not secure her place in history until 1811, during a period of increasing tension between the United States and Britain. She was then under the command of John RODGERS who fought the

smaller British warship *Little Belt* off the coast of Virginia in May 1811. The American ship, which may have precipitated the action by an accidental shot, was relatively unscathed, but the *Little Belt* sustained severe damage. The incident was a contributory factor in the outbreak of the WAR OF 1812. During the war the *President* played a valuable role in tying down British naval forces until her capture early in 1815.

Price, David
1790–1854

*B*ritish rear admiral who was commander in chief in the Pacific when the CRIMEAN WAR, 1853–56, began. In August 1854 he planned, in cooperation with the French, an attack on Russian warships at Petropavlosk on the Kamchatka peninsula. However, shortly before the operation began, he shot and killed himself with a pistol, an action that has never been explained satisfactorily. His apparent "dread of the responsibilities of his position" has been given as the reason for his suicide, but this seems unlikely. Although he had never commanded a squadron in action, he had served in the Royal Navy since 1801 and had fought the enemy on many occasions.

Prien, Gunther
1908–41

*O*ne of Germany's most successful U-BOAT commanders of WORLD WAR II, 1939–45, during a short-lived career. Prien secured an early victory on October 14, 1939 when he entered the fleet anchorage in SCAPA FLOW and torpedoed the British battleship *ROYAL OAK* with the loss of most of her crew. He went on to sink a total of 28 Allied merchant ships with a combined displacement of over 164,000 tons. On March 7, 1941 Prien, who had become a war hero, and his crew were lost when their boat (*U-47*) was sunk by the British destroyer *Wolverine* and the British corvettes *Arbutus* and *Camellia*.

Prince of Wales, H.M.S.

*F*amous British WORLD WAR II, 1934–45, BATTLESHIP, a member of the KING GEORGE V class, that was sunk off the east coast of Malaya by Japanese aircraft on December 10, 1941, after a very brief operational career. The *Prince of Wales* had only entered service early in 1941 with the British Home Fleet at SCAPA FLOW. She had a displacement of some 36,000 tons, main armament of ten 14-inch (36-cm) guns, a maximum speed of 28 knots and was operated by a crew of about 1,600 men. The *Prince of Wales* was

745 feet (227.1 m) in length and had a beam of 103 feet (31.4 m).

Some months earlier, on May 24, 1941, the *Prince of Wales* had sustained serious damage when, together with the battle cruiser HOOD, she engaged the German battleship BISMARCK and the cruiser PRINZ EUGEN in the Atlantic. Although she was hit seven times, the damage was not serious enough to endanger her World War II career. At the same time she also inflicted damage on the *Bismarck* even though some of the guns on this newly commissioned ship were not operating properly. However, she was compelled to withdraw when the *Hood* sank.

Following repairs she was sent to Singapore with the BATTLE CRUISER *Repulse* to form the core of FORCE Z. Their aim was to deter Japanese attacks against British and Dutch possessions in the East Indies. On their arrival, they were dispatched immediately to intercept an enemy invasion force heading for Malaya. The search was unsuccessful and, on December 10, 1941, as she returned to Singapore, the *Prince of Wales* was attacked by bombers and torpedo-bombers of the Japanese Twenty-second Air Flotilla. A single torpedo destroyed her steering and began a chain of events that caused her to sink. Her destruction provided further evidence of the vulnerability of unprotected battleships to air attack and the need for effective air cover if they were to survive.

Martin Middlebrook and P. Mahoney, *Battleship: The Loss of the* Prince of Wales *and the* Repulse, London, 1977.

Princeton, U.S.S.

The completion of the U.S.S. *Princeton* in 1844 represented an important step in the development of the modern warship and, in the words of an American, "dictated the reconstruction of the navies of the world." Designed by John ERICSSON, who later built the MONITOR, it embodied two important new features. Apart from being the U.S. Navy's first screw-propelled man-of-war, she was the first warship in the world to have her machinery located completely below the waterline. This meant that the *Princeton*'s engines, which were based on an original design by James Watt, could not be destroyed by a direct hit from enemy guns. This innovation was to influence on all future ship design. The *Princeton* had a displacement of 954 tons, a length of 164 feet (50 m) and a maximum speed of 7 knots. She was armed with two 12-inch (30-cm) guns named "Peacemaker" and "Oregon". Her short career ended in 1849 when she was broken up. The name *Princeton* was revived by the U.S. Navy for a light AIRCRAFT CARRIER of the Independence class that was commissioned during WORLD WAR II, 1939–45. This *Princeton*'s short operational career was brought to an end at the Battle of LEYTE GULF, October 1944, when she was destroyed by a single bomb.

Prinz Eugen

A German heavy CRUISER of the Admiral Hipper class. The *Prinz Eugen* was launched in August 1938 and entered service late in 1940. She had a displacement of 14,800 tons, a maximum speed of 32 knots and was operated by a crew of 1,599 men. The Prinz Eugen was 690 feet 4 inches (210.4 m) in length and had a beam of 71 feet 10 inches (21.8 m). Her armament included eight 8-inch (20-cm) and 12 4.1-inch (11-cm) guns. Among her distinctive features were a raked bow and a prominent funnel cap.

During an active WORLD WAR II, 1939–45, career, she accompanied the *BISMARCK* in her operations against Allied shipping in the Atlantic and took part in the engagement against the British warships HOOD and PRINCE OF WALES on May 24, 1941. Her 8-inch guns may have been responsible for the fires that destroyed the *Hood*. The *Prinz Eugen* ran short of fuel in the chase that followed and was forced to leave the *Bismarck*. She headed for the French port of Brest, thus escaping the fate that awaited the *Bismarck*. On February 12, 1942 she eventually broke out of Brest in a successful daylight dash through the English Channel known as Operation Cerberus. (See CHANNEL DASH.) She was accompanied by the battle cruisers *SCHARNHORST* and *GNEISENAU*.

In the latter part of the war she served on training duties in the Baltic but also was involved in supporting operations against the Soviets as they advanced through Poland and East Prussia. One of the few German warships to survive the war intact, the *Prinz Eugen* surrendered to the Allies at Copenhagen in 1945. She was allocated to the Americans, who used her as a target in the atomic test at Bikini Atoll, and finally sank in 1947.

Privateer

An armed merchant ship that was commissioned by the state to attack enemy ships during wartime, with the aim of undermining the opponent's trading relationships. The same term also describes the captain and men who operated these ships. Their activities were authorized by an official LETTER OF MARQUE, which in England dated back to the late 13th century. The letter referred to the privateer's right to take prizes and to receive a proportion of the cash proceeds. The prize money was divided unequally between the privateer and the crown, with the latter taking no more than 10 percent of the profits.

Privateers were widely employed during the age of sail even after permanent naval forces had been widely established, because they were a convenient method of rapidly expanding naval power in wartime. Britain, France and the United States were among the nations that used privateers most extensively until their abolition by international agreement in 1856. After this date armed merchant ships continued to be used in wartime, but they were operated as warships under naval direction rather than civilian vessels under the control of private individuals whose only concern was to maximize their profits. (See also ARMED MERCHANT CRUISER.)

Prize Money

Term used to refer to the proceeds of sale of a captured enemy ship and its cargo in England, America and other maritime powers. Prize money was regarded as a legitimate dividend of war and was distinct from the booty seized illegally by pirates. In England prize money originally was paid direct to the crown but, in 1708, the crown waived its rights and the entire amount was paid to the captors. Once the value of the prize had been assessed by the High Court of Admiralty, it was divided into eighths and distributed among the officers and crew of the ship responsible for the capture, according to a standard formula. The captain received three-eighths and the officers shared a further three-eights. The remainder was divided equally among the crew. A third of the captain's share went to his flag officer even if the latter had played no direct part in the action. Although the formula was later modified, the basic principles remained the same. While the prize money received by an individual crew typically was small, the possibility of receiving a substantial amount could not be ruled out. It was, therefore, always a strong inducement to enlist in the navy. Prizes for officers, and particularly for a captain, often were large and could amount to tens of thousands of pounds. The distribution of prize money continued in Britain until the end of WORLD WAR II, 1939–45, although since 1914 the beneficiaries were the whole naval service rather than the ship's captors alone.

Providien, Battle of
April 12, 1782

Following the Anglo-French naval engagement at SADRAS near Madras, February 17, 1782, in the Indian Ocean, the two opposing squadrons met again in April off Providien, on the northwest coast of Ceylon (Sri Lanka). It was the second of five naval battles fought off the coast of India and Ceylon in 1782–83 as both sides tried to establish their superiority in the final phase of the AMERICAN WAR OF INDEPENDENCE, 1775–83. The British squadron of 11 ships, under the command of Admiral Sir Edward HUGHES, had been refitted after the Battle of Sadras and was then ordered to Trincomalee in Ceylon with a detachment of troops. This port had been captured by the British

early in 1782 but was not adequately protected against a possible French attack.

Distinguished French Admiral Pierre de SUFFREN, who was anchored at Cuddalore, on the Coromandel coast of India, learned of the British movement and followed Hughes as he sailed southward. On April 12 the two squadrons met off Providien. Fierce fighting soon broke out and the British, who were forced against the shore, had little room to maneuver. The French concentrated on the British center and several ships, including Hughes' FLAGSHIP, the Superb, and the Monmouth, sustained heavy damage. The French also had exhausted themselves, and by the end of the day the fighting had died out. After carrying out emergency repairs, the French withdrew back to the north. Hughes was then able to continue his mission, reaching Trincomalee on April 22 with much-needed troop reinforcements. The opposing fleets were to meet again at the Battle of NEGAPATAM, July 1782.

PT Boat

A high-speed torpedo boat used by the U.S. Navy from 1938 to 1968. Developed from British designs, the 80-foot (24-m) PT (patrol-torpedo) boat of WORLD WAR II, 1939–45, typically had a displacement of 34 to 38 tons, a maximum speed of about 40 knots and a cruising range of 550 miles (880 km). It was powered by a three-shaft gasoline engine that produced 4,050 shp (shaft horse power). Operated by a crew of 14, the PT boat was armed with four 18-inch (46-cm) or 21-inch (53-cm) torpedo tubes as well as a 20- or 40-mm gun. Sometimes it was equipped with two 20-mm guns rather than a single 40-mm one. This armament was supplemented by .50-inch (1.27-cm) heavy machine guns. The PT-boat was designed to operate against enemy shipping in coastal waters.

Operating in squadrons of 12 to 17, PT boats served in every major naval theater of World War II. They were heavily involved in the fighting in the SOLOMON ISLANDS, 1942–43, when PT-109, captained by Lieutenant John F. Kennedy, was rammed by a Japanese destroyer. PTs also took part in later operations in the Pacific, including the recapture of the Philippines. In April 1943, the first PT boats arrived in the Mediterranean, and some PT squadrons were later sent to England for the Allied invasion of NORMANDY, June 1944. In operations off the coast of southern Italy in 1944, PT boats (together with other similar craft) sank at least 76 German ships. In this and other theaters, PT boats proved to be a useful ancillary naval weapon, although experience confirmed that there were limits to their ability to operate against conventional warships. A small number of modified PT boats—their torpedoes were removed to increase speed—were used dur-

An American PT boat   *(Copyright © Imperial War Museum, London)*

ing the VIETNAM WAR but subsequently were withdrawn from service. (See also MOTOR GUNBOAT.)

Frank Johnson, *United States PT Boats of World War II in Action*, Poole, Dorset, 1980.

Pueblo, U.S.S.

An American electronic surveillance ship of 906 tons. Manned by a crew of 83 and commanded by Lloyd Bucher, the *Pueblo* was captured by four North Korean patrol boats during the night of January 22–23, 1968 while operating off the coast of North Korea. The Koreans killed one member of the crew and wounded four others. The *Pueblo* was taken to the port of Wonsan, where the crew was accused of violating North Korea's territorial waters. The Americans remained in captivity for the best part of a year. The crew but not the ship were released in December 1968 following an admission by the United States that the *Pueblo* had violated North Korean waters. Although this statement was later repudiated, the Americans gave a firm assurance that there would be no repetition of the alleged incursion. The *Pueblo* was notable as the first American naval vessel to have been seized on the high seas since the WAR OF 1812.

E. Brandt, *The Lost Voyage of the Pueblo*, New York, 1969.

Q-Ship

The most notable decoy ships of WORLD WAR I, 1914–18, British Q-ships were used by the Royal Navy in an attempt to combat the U-BOAT threat. They seemed to be genuine merchant ships but were equipped with concealed guns and torpedoes, and sometimes with the false colors of noncombatants. Many different types of vessel were converted—from small sailing ships to 4,000-ton tramp steamers—and a small number were built specially for this purpose. Q-ships operated on the assumption that U-Boats would not normally use a torpedo to sink a small vessel of this kind, but would surface and destroy it more economically by gunfire. As the German submarine appeared on the surface, the Q-ship would uncover its weapons and open fire.

The first decoy vessels appeared in November 1914, but the first successful use of a Q-ship operating alone did not occur until July 1915, when the British collier *Prince Charles* sank the German submarine *U-36* off the Orkney Islands. A month earlier the armed trawler *Taranaki* had been involved in the destruction of *U-40* off the coast of Aberdeen: It towed the British submarine C24, which was directed on to its target by a telephone link. Although

these "mystery ships" may have had some romantic appeal, in practice they were not a great success. At the beginning of the war they were not available in sufficient numbers to make a real impact, but as the Q-ship fleet expanded the Germans became aware of their activities and adjusted their tactics accordingly. Submerged U-boats became much more likely to torpedo merchant ships without warning. Almost 200 Q-ships were produced; 31 were sunk. They were responsible for the destruction of 11 U-boats, with their last victim sinking in the autumn of 1917, when they were finally withdrawn.

The Royal Navy also used Q-ships in the early stages of WORLD WAR II, 1939–45, but on a much more limited scale. They were all withdrawn early in 1941 when it became clear that their impact on the course of the Battle of the ATLANTIC, 1939–45, was minimal.

A. Coles, *Slaughter at Sea: The Truth Behind a Naval War Crime*, London, 1986.

The British Q-ship *Hyderabad* was a specially constructed decoy vessel rather than a conversion *(Copyright © Imperial War Museum, London)*

Quasi-War
1798–1800

This Franco-American naval war had its origins in the FRENCH REVOLUTIONARY AND NAPOLEONIC WARS, 1792–1815, when French naval activity against the British in the West Indies produced conflict and clear examples of interference with American merchant ships. As tension between the two former allies grew during 1798, the French began to take more direct action against American ships even though France had not formally declared war on the United States. The Americans tried without success to find a diplomatic solution to the problem. In response, Congress authorized the commissioning of PRIVATEERS and instructed the fledgling U.S. Navy to seize any French naval vessels found in American coastal waters. George Washington was brought back from retirement to head the army. A Navy

Department was established, and the navy soon had 55 ships (compared to three when the war started).

When the French captured an American schooner off Guadeloupe on November 20, 1798, U.S. warships were sent to the Caribbean. Despite this action, the war was characterized by a large number of engagements between opposing privateers, with few direct fights between the two navies. This partly reflected the French view that there was no need to commit SHIPS OF THE LINE to defeat a weak and inexperienced opponent, particularly when these ships were urgently needed elsewhere. A few FRIGATES dispatched across the Atlantic would be sufficient. Despite its limitations, the U.S. Navy, which concentrated on protecting the main trade routes and CONVOYS, performed well. The frigate U.S.S. *CONSTELLATION,* commanded by Thomas TRUXTON, was able to defeat the French frigates *Insurgente* and *Vengeance* in separate engagements. In total, some 85 French vessels were captured before a peace convention covering trade and navigation issues was signed in September 1800. The French navy achieved a significantly higher number of American merchant victims before hostilities ceased.

H. P. Nash, Jr., *The Forgotten Wars: The Role of the U.S. Navy in the Quasi-War with France and the Barbary Wars, 1794–1805,* New York, 1968.

Quebec, Capture of

September 1759

*T*he French-held city of Quebec was captured by the British in 1759 in a joint naval and military operation during the SEVEN YEARS' WAR, 1756–63. Commanded by Vice Admiral Charles SAUNDERS and Major General James Wolfe, the British force left England on February 16, 1759, arriving off Orléans Island in the St. Lawrence River on June 26. English troops were landed from the transports and advanced on Quebec. For two months they had no success against a well-defended fortress. An alternative indirect approach was needed. Wolfe identified a new approach to the north of the city that involved climbing the cliffs in the Anse de Foulon. On September 12 some 5,000 English troops were moved upstream to the base of the cliffs and scaled them successfully. A decisive battle occurred on the Plains of Abraham on September 13; the French were defeated and both the opposing commanders—Wolfe and Louis Joseph, Marquis de Montcalm—were killed. The city surrendered shortly afterward. This is a key example of a successful AMPHIBIOUS operation in which the navy and army worked together effectively during the age of sail.

C. P. Stacey, *Quebec,* Toronto, 1959.

The capture of Quebec, 1759, by combined English land and naval forces   *(Copyright © National Maritime Museum, Greenwich, London)*

Queen Elizabeth, H.M.S.

*B*ritish super-dreadnought BATTLESHIP that gave outstanding service with the Royal Navy in both world wars. The *Queen Elizabeth* (not to be confused with the Cunard passenger liner of the same name) represented a considerable advance in design when she appeared in 1915.

All oil-fired, the *Queen Elizabeth* and her sister ships were equipped with additional boilers to produce an increased maximum speed (compared with the previous Iron Duke class) of 24–25 knots. They were intended to form a "fast squadron" that would perform a role similar to that allocated to the much-less-well protected BATTLE CRUISERS. In particular, they would improve tactical flexibility and help to frustrate enemy withdrawal. Additional space for the extra propulsion machinery was found by removing one of the turrets and the associated shell rooms from the original design. Eight new 15-inch (38-cm) guns, which could fire a 1,920-pound (871-kg) shell over 35,000 yards (32,004 m), were installed. They provided a greater weight of broadside than ten 13.5-inch (34-cm) guns. The *Queen Elizabeth* was 646 feet 1 inch (196.9 m) in length, had a beam of 90 feet 6 inches (27.6 m) and was operated by a crew of 925.

The *Queen Elizabeth* and her sister ships—the WARSPITE, *Valiant*, *Barham*, *Malaysia*—formed the Fifth Battle Squadron of the GRAND FLEET. All except the *Queen Elizabeth* were present at the Battle of JUTLAND, May 1916, where they played a valuable role, but only the *Valiant* was undamaged. The *Queen Elizabeth* also was involved in the DARDANELLES operation in 1915, and, in 1917–18, was Admiral Sir David BEATTY's flagship. She was also the ship in which the formal instrument of internment of the German HIGH SEAS FLEET was signed in November 1918.

Between the wars the *Queen Elizabeth* underwent considerable modifications to her armor, armament and machinery. Following this overhaul, early in 1941 she joined the Mediterranean Fleet. She was badly damaged by an Italian human torpedo attack in Alexandria harbor before the end of the year, and she was forced to retire to Norfolk, Virginia for repairs. During the latter part of the war she served as flagship of the Eastern Fleet and operated along the Burmese and Malayan coasts. The *Queen Elizabeth* was scrapped after the war. For the passenger liner *Queen Elizabeth*, see QUEEN MARY.

Queen Mary, R.M.S.

*B*ritish transatlantic passenger liner and WORLD WAR II, 1939–45, TROOPSHIP. Built for the Cunard Company, the *Queen Mary*, which was launched in September 1934, had a displacement of 81,237 tons and a maximum speed of over 30 knots. The *Queen Mary* entered commer-

cial service in June 1936; with her excellent performance characteristics, she held the record for the fastest transatlantic return journey for a period before the war. When World War II began, the *Queen Mary* was in New York and, after requisitioning by the British government, she was sent to Australia for conversion as a troopship. After modifications were completed she had the capacity to carry more than 8,000 troops, and she was used intensively on various transport missions until early in 1943. From this period she was used exclusively to transport troops across the Atlantic; in this role she could accommodate as many as 15,000 troops. Her sister ship, the R.M.S. *Queen Elizabeth*, an 82,998-ton passenger liner, was also converted as a troopship and saw a similar pattern of wartime service to the *Queen Mary*. The two ships carried a total of 320,000 American troops across the Atlantic during World War II. After the war, both ships served as transatlantic passenger liners for over 20 years. The *Queen Mary* was finally withdrawn from service in 1967; the *Queen Elizabeth* was withdrawn two years later.

Quiberon Bay, Battle of
November 20, 1759

*D*uring the SEVEN YEARS' WAR, 1756–63, British fears of a French invasion of England led, in 1759, to the maintenance of a close BLOCKADE against the enemy fleet at BREST. The Royal Navy's Western Squadron, commanded by Admiral Sir Edward HAWKE, had remained on station during the summer and autumn but, on November 9, poor weather forced Hawke to shelter in Torbay, Devon. By the time Hawke returned to sea some five days later, a French squadron had entered Brest on its return from the West Indies; much more seriously, the French fleet, which included 21 SHIPS OF THE LINE and several FRIGATES, had escaped. Under the command of Admiral Hubert de CONFLANS, they made for Vannes, where the French invasion fleet was being prepared. During the journey to Vannes, severe gales forced Conflans on November 20, to take shelter west of Belle Isle off the Breton coast.

Hawke, who had 23 ships of the line under his command, set off in pursuit of the French. The British were first sighted by Conflans' rear division in the early hours of November 20; by noon the opposing fleets were in close proximity. The French, who were outnumbered, proceeded into Quiberon Bay through a narrow channel that was particularly dangerous to negotiate in such bad weather. Although Conflans assumed that he was now relatively safe from immediate attack, Hawke was not afraid to launch an engagement in such a confined space. In the early afternoon Hawke, who had been joined by a British inshore squadron that had been monitoring French invasion preparations, began an attack on the French rear division. As a result, three enemy ships of the line were destroyed with heavy loss of life. Conflans decided that his best hope was to change direction and make for the open sea again. He was unsuccessful; Hawke, in the *Royal George,* drove him back. Fighting continued until nightfall in very poor conditions.

As Hawke anchored off Dumet Island some of the French fleet managed to escape south to Rochefort. Other French ships were less fortunate. Seven of Conflans's ships headed for the Vilaine estuary, where they ran aground or were trapped. Conflans's FLAGSHIP, the *Soleil,* and another French ship of the line subsequently were lost as a result of the poor weather. In total, the French lost seven ships of the line and sustained some 2,500 casualties. English losses were light in a major victory that ended the French invasion plans and significantly weakened their naval power for the remainder of the Seven Years' War.

G. J. Marcus, *Quiberon Bay*, London, 1960.

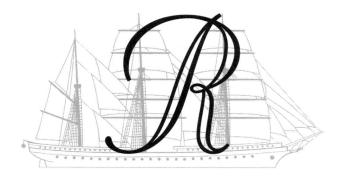

Radar

The use of radio waves to detect a metallic object beyond the range of vision by reflecting them back to their source. It dates back to experiments conducted by the Germans well before WORLD WAR I, 1914–18. During the 1930s the German navy took the lead in developing this technology, which was originally known as RDF (radio direction finding). They were closely followed by the French, the Americans and others. It was, however, the British, in 1939, who first produced radar—radio detecting and ranging—in a practical form when they established a chain of radar stations along the south-east coast. This was soon followed by the invention of the magnetron, a device that produced short radio waves and provided the basis for the development of modern radar. When a transmitted signal was reflected back to its source, information on a ship's range and direction would be shown on a cathode-ray oscilloscope. The ship's transmitting radar aerial revolves so that the whole of the surrounding area—a full 360 degrees—is scanned. The range of modern radar is some 25 miles (40 km).

Radar has several important naval applications, including detection of enemy ships and submarines. The latter do not need to be on the surface to be detected: Radar will pick up even a protruding periscope without any difficulty. Radar also was used to establish the range for naval guns and soon became an important element in antiaircraft defense. The British (and American) lead in radar development was maintained during WORLD WAR II, 1939–45, even though the Germans had their own systems. The Allies gradually overcame the technical problems of using radar in wartime, which include countermeasures and the identification of signals. Since World War II, radar systems have been further developed and have a wide variety of naval functions, from navigation to missile control. A warship can call on the support of aircraft equipped with radar to monitor the movements of enemy naval units. (See also SONAR.)

John Monsarrat, *Angel on the Yardarm: The Beginning of Fleet Radar Defense and the Kamikaze Threat*, Newport, R. I., 1985.

Radford, Arthur William
1896–1973

American naval officer. Born on February 27, 1896, Arthur William Radford entered the navy in 1912. He trained as a naval aviator in 1920 and remained in that service for most of his career. In late 1941 he became director of Aviation Training for the Bureau of Aeronautics. By July 1943 he was promoted to rear admiral and headed a carrier division, even though he had not yet commanded a ship. Training light carrier crews in the waters around Pearl Harbor, he led carrier forces against the Japanese on Wake Island and on the Gilbert Islands in late 1943, before becoming chief of staff to Admiral John H. TOWERS, commander of the Pacific Fleet Air Force. A short tour as Assistant Chief of Naval Operations for Air was followed by his return to the Pacific. With his flag on the YORKTOWN, he commanded Task Group 58.1 in the operations against IWO JIMA and OKINAWA. He completed the summer of 1945 as commander of Task Group 38.

After the war ended, he served as Deputy Chief of Naval Operations for Air as a vice admiral and then as Vice Chief of Naval Operations with the rank of admiral from 1948 to mid-1949. Just prior to the KOREAN WAR, 1950–53, he was promoted to Commander in Chief of the Pacific Fleet as well as High Commissioner of the Pacific Islands Trust Territory. As such he administered the U.S. Navy's operations during the Korean War. In June 1953 he was appointed chairman of the Joint Chiefs of Staff by President Dwight D. Eisenhower; reappointment for another two-year term followed in 1959. Throughout the postwar period he was a strong supporter of nuclear weapons and of a significant naval role in nuclear deterrence. (See COLD WAR.) He retired in August 1957 and died on August 18, 1973.

Arthur W. Radford, *From Pearl Harbor to Vietnam: The Memoirs of Admiral Arthur W. Radford*, ed. Stephen Jurika, Jr., Stanford, Calif., 1980.

Radio

$\mathcal{T}$he transmission of electromagnetic energy through space as a means of communication—known as radio or wireless telegraphy—was first achieved in 1892. Three years later Guglielmo Marconi carried out experimental transmissions using a telegraph key to send messages in Morse code. From as early as 1901, Marconi was able to send messages to ships at sea, often over considerable distances. Radio's naval applications were quickly appreciated and were facilitated by rapid improvements in electronics. During the RUSSO-JAPANESE WAR, 1904–5, the opposing fleets were in radio contact with their respective headquarters, enabling the headquarters commanders to exercise a degree of control and coordination impossible before the invention of the radio.

Radio technology also provided the basis for a direction finder that established a ship's bearing using the signal transmitted by a shore-based radio beacon. Radio communication developed rapidly during WORLD WAR I, 1914–18, and was extended to submarines when they were on the surface. During WORLD WAR II, 1939–45, it often was used for the transmission of false messages. At the Battle of the RIVER PLATE, 1939, for example, false radio messages convinced the commander of the *ADMIRAL GRAF SPEE* that he faced defeat at the hands of a larger British force. At the same time, however, the limitations of this form of communication also were evident. The interception of a warship's messages would be sufficient to reveal her position. Monitoring stations were established to pick up and decipher an enemy's radio signals, which had to be transmitted in code. In the 1930s voice transmission was introduced; the adoption of the radio telephone further enhanced the potential of this medium of communication. Progressive improvements in technology, including the introduction of satellite communications, has enhanced radio's potential. However, its basic role in naval warfare remains unchanged except for the invention of RADAR— "Radio Detecting and Ranging"—in 1940, which has had far-reaching consequences.

Raeder, Erich

1876–1960

$\mathcal{G}$erman naval commander who served during both world wars, most notably as grand admiral of the Third Reich during World War II. Erich Raeder entered the navy in 1894. During WORLD WAR I, 1914–18, he served as chief of staff to Admiral Franz von HIPPER, who was flag officer commanding the scouting forces of the German HIGH SEAS

Admiral Eric Raeder was commander in chief of the German navy during World War II until his replacement in 1943, after he lost the confidence of Adolf Hitler following the failure of the German surface fleet   *(Copyright © Imperial War Museum, London)*

FLEET. In the final days of the war he was appointed to a post at the German Admiralty, where he remained for some years. He rose steadily and, in 1928, was promoted to the rank of admiral and made chief of naval staff. In 1935 Adolf Hitler appointed him as commander in chief of the navy. He was responsible for the reconstruction of the German navy, drawing up a long-term "Z-plan," which included the provision of new battleships, pocket- battleships, battle cruisers, submarines and other ships. This would provide a naval force capable of challenging the ROYAL NAVY by 1944.

In 1939 he was rewarded with promotion to grand admiral although his work was far from complete. As WORLD WAR II, 1939–45, began, U-BOATs in particular were in short supply, and land operations were used to compensate for these deficiencies. Raeder planned the invasion of Norway, 1940, and managed a successful U-boat campaign against British shipping using captured French bases. Apart from these operations, however, German naval successes were few and far between. The escape of the *SCHARNHORST,* the *GNEISENAU* and the *PRINZ EUGEN* from BREST in the CHANNEL DASH of February 1942 was one example of German naval success; the destruction of convoy *PQ-17* was another. But the German failure to halt the Allies' ARCTIC CONVOYS to the Soviet Union and their defeat in the Battle of the BARENTS SEA, December 30, 1942, completed Hitler's disillusionment with his surface navy.

Raeder resigned shortly afterward following disagreements with Hitler over strategy and was replaced by Admiral Karl DÖNITZ. In 1946 he was prosecuted at the Nuremburg trials for his contribution to the preparations for a war of aggression. He was sentenced to life imprisonment but was released in 1955.

Erich Raeder, *My Life*, Annapolis, 1960.

Raleigh, Sir Walter
c. 1552–1618

*E*nglish naval commander, soldier, courtier and man of letters who was a favorite of Queen Elizabeth I. Born near Budleigh Salterton, Devon, Raleigh was educated at Oxford and took part in military operations in France in 1569. In 1578 he joined a voyage of exploration under command of his half brother, Sir Humphrey Gilbert, which turned out to be a series of engagements against the Spanish in the North Atlantic. It was abandoned after a disastrous engagement with Spanish warships in the Atlantic. After the failure of a second expedition, Raleigh returned to London, where he became an important influence at court. He was to be a favorite of Elizabeth for some 20 years before her death in 1603. She knighted him in 1584 and accompanied the honor with grants of land that made him extremely wealthy. From 1583 to 1589, he sponsored six expeditions to North America with the stated aim of forming a colony in Virginia, but they did not lead to the creation of a permanent settlement. Raleigh's real purpose in financing the expeditions was to look for gold and silver in North America, but he was unsuccessful.

Although Sir Walter Raleigh was appointed vice admiral of Devon in 1588, he played no active part in the operations against the SPANISH ARMADA (unlike his close colleagues, Francis DRAKE and John HAWKINS). He participated in an expedition to Portugal in 1589 that failed in its objective of stimulating a revolt against Philip II of Spain. In 1591 he joined an expedition against the Spanish treasure fleet but was recalled by the queen when she discovered his involvement with one of her maids of honor. He soon returned to royal favor and in 1595 led an expedition to search for gold in South America. In 1596 he commanded a successful combined operation against Cadiz. When James I became king in 1603, Raleigh's political enemies moved against him. He was found guilty of conspiracy against the new king; although he was condemned to death, he was imprisoned in the Tower of

Sir Walter Raleigh: Elizabethan explorer and adventurer   *(Copyright © National Maritime Museum, Greenwich, London)*

London for the next 13 years. In 1616 James agreed that he could undertake another expedition to search for gold in South America. The expedition failed and on Raleigh's return, the Spanish ambassador demanded his execution because he had sacked a Spanish settlement in Guiana. His execution was finally carried out on October 29, 1618, marking the end of a true Renaissance man who successfully combined the roles of sailor, explorer, poet and essayist.

Sinclair, Andrew, *Sir Walter Raleigh and the Age of Discovery*, London, 1984.

Ram

A sharp spike or armored projectile that could form part of the design of a ship's bows as an important offensive weapon. Dating back to the ancient world and the GALLEY warfare of the Mediterranean, the ram found no place in the warships of the age of the sailing navies. However, the ram was unexpectedly reintroduced when steam-powered warships made their appearance, even though the new weapons technology of the 19th century—particularly the long-range gun and the torpedo—made fighting at close quarters an unlikely scenario.

A major exception to this general rule occurred at the Battle of LISSA, 1866, when the *Ferdinand Maximilian*, an Austro-Hungarian IRONCLAD, was rammed by the *Re d'Italia*, an Italian battleship. Other examples of the successful use of the ram during this period are few and far between, although there were some spectacular accidents involving its use. A notable example involving two British warships occurred in the Mediterranean in 1910 when the *VICTORIA* was sunk by the *CAMPERDOWN*. The ram featured in new warship design until about 1910, but was then abandoned as it was believed that it had no useful role in modern naval warfare. Despite this, there have been occasions, during the 20th century, when ships have been rammed and sunk after other methods of attack had failed or could not be used.

Ramillies, H.M.S.

The name *Ramillies* has been given to four British warships, including Admiral John BYNG's flagship in his action off MINORCA, May 1756, during the SEVEN YEARS' WAR, 1756–63. The name Ramillies refers to the great victory won by the Duke of Marlborough over Louis XIV during the War of the Spanish succession in 1706. The third *Ramillies*, a third-rate (see RATING OF SHIPS) of 74 guns, was launched in 1785. She served throughout the wars against France, 1792–1815, and was present at the Battle of the GLORIOUS FIRST OF JUNE, 1794, and the Battle of COPENHAGEN, 1801. During the WAR OF 1812, the UNITED STATES NAVY tried to fix a MINE to the *Ramillies*'s hull in Chesapeake Bay, but abandoned the attempt when the British commander announced that there were American prisoners on board. This *Ramillies* served until 1850, when she finally was dismantled. *Ramillies* also was the name of battleship of WORLD WAR I, 1914–18, a 28,000-ton member of the Revenge class.

Ramsay, Sir Bertram Home
1883–1945

British admiral responsible for planning many of the AMPHIBIOUS operations of WORLD WAR II, 1939–45. Brought back from retirement as the war began, he served as flag officer in charge at Dover, where he organized

Operation Dynamo, the DUNKIRK evacuation, May 26–June 4, 1940. Ramsay subsequently was involved in the planning of the North Africa, SICILY, D-Day NORMANDY LANDINGS and Walcheren landings. He was mentioned twice in dispatches and during the Normandy invasion, 1944, the largest amphibious operation in history, he served as naval commander in chief under General Dwight D. Eisenhower. Early in 1945 he was killed while flying to a meeting with General Bernard Montgomery in Brussels during the Ardennes offensive.

William S. Chalmers, *Full Cycle: The Biography of Sir Bertram Home Ramsay*, London, 1959.

Ranger, U.S.S.

The name *Ranger* has been given to several American naval vessels. The sloop *Ranger* was notable as the first American warship to defeat a British naval vessel. Under the command of Captain John Paul JONES, the *Ranger* was employed in operations off the British coast in 1777 during the AMERICAN WAR OF INDEPENDENCE, 1775–83. Following a raid on the Cumberland coast (northwest England) on April 22–23, 1777, Jones crossed the Irish Sea and engaged the British warship *Drake* off Carrickfergus. During an hour-long duel, the Americans gradually gained the upper hand. With her rigging destroyed and her commander killed, the *Drake* was forced to surrender. Jones took her to France, where her crew was exchanged for American prisoners held by the British.

A more recent *Ranger* was a WORLD WAR II, 1939–45, AIRCRAFT CARRIER launched in 1933. The first American ship to be laid down as an aircraft carrier, this *Ranger* had a displacement of only 14,500 tons, which was significantly below contemporary standards, and was 769 feet (234 m) in length. She had been designed as a small carrier with the aim of establishing the feasibility of the design. The *Ranger* was able to accommodate as many as 86 aircraft only because of its minimal armament (eight 5-inch antiaircraft guns) and armor protection. With a maximum speed of 29.5 knots and a complement of 2,000 men, the *Ranger* served in the Atlantic during World War II; her aircraft provided air cover during the North African landings. In latter part of the war, as her combat limitations became increasingly evident, she was used in a training role.

Rating of Ships

During the age of the sailing navies, warships were classified according to the number of guns they carried. The original classification arrangement was a British creation and was introduced by Admiral George, Lord

ANSON during his first term as First Lord of the Admiralty, 1751–56. The ratings broke down as follows:

First rate	100 guns or more
Second rate	84–100 guns
Third rate	70–84 guns
Fourth rate	50–70 guns
Fifth rate	32–50 guns
Sixth rate	up to 32 guns

Other navies soon adopted this classification system; sometimes a displacement figure for each rate was included. By 1810, with the size and complexity of warships increasing, the Royal Navy modified all but one of the ratings:

First rate	110 guns or more
Second rate	90–110 guns
Third rate	80–90 guns
Fourth rate	60–80 guns
Fifth rate	32–60 guns
Sixth rate	up to 32 guns

An important operational distinction was drawn between the first three rates and the rest. Only the warships in the first three categories were considered suitable to take their place in the line of battle in a fleet action. Fourth- and fifth-rate ships were classified as FRIGATES with other duties to perform. Several smaller naval ships, including sloops and cutters, were completely excluded from this classification system. The ratings did not necessarily take account of all guns carried by a ship, and when new weapons were introduced it might be years before they were included in the official calculations. Lord Anson's classification, which provided a useful basis for comparing naval power, survived until the sailing warship was replaced by the IRONCLAD during the mid-19th century.

Rattler, H.M.S.

A British paddle sloop of 880 tons that was converted to screw propulsion following the invention of the propeller and the success of the first experiments. Equipped with a 220-horsepower engine, the *Rattler* was put through extensive trials in 1845. She was set against the paddle ship *Alecto*, her sister ship, which had a similar capacity engine, in two competitions—a 100-mile (160-km) race and a tug-of-war where the two ships were fastened stern to stern. Both events ended in a convincing victory for the new technology: The *Rattler* easily outperformed her opponent.

Apart from increased speed and power, the main advantages of screw propulsion were the fact that it was less vulnerable to enemy attack and that the absence of side paddles gave a ship's guns an uninterrupted line of fire along both sides of the ship. The Admiralty had already anticipated the *Rattler*'s victory over the *Alecto* by ordering several screw frigates; the general introduction of screw propulsion in the Royal Navy and other navies soon followed. (See also PADDLE STEAMER.)

Rawalpindi

British P & O liner of 16,697 tons that was converted as an ARMED MERCHANT CRUISER for service in WORLD WAR II, 1939–45. In her wartime role, the *Rawalpindi* was armed with eight 6-inch (15-cm) guns. The *Rawalpindi* was on patrol between the Faroe Islands and Iceland on November 23, 1939 when she was intercepted by the German battle cruisers SCHARNHORST and GNEISENAU, who were intending to break out into the Atlantic. The British ship was able to radio details of the enemy ships to Home Fleet headquarters before the *Scharnhorst* opened fire. The *Rawalpindi* returned fire, but within 12 minutes this unequal contest was over: The former passenger liner had caught fire and was sinking. The German ships started to pick up British survivors but withdrew from the area as soon as the British cruiser *Newcastle* appeared. The Germans returned to their base without engaging the *Newcastle*, and the German commander, Admiral Marschall, was criticized for his caution.

Razée

A term used in the days of the sailing navies to describe a vessel whose original structure had been modified by the reduction of one or more decks. Derived from the French verb *raser*, "to cut," the process typically might involve reducing a SHIP OF THE LINE by one deck to produce a FRIGATE. One example occurred in 1831, when the British 74-gun ship *EAGLE* was razéed to form a 50-gun frigate. There was no standard format for these modifications, which could be a cost-effective way of meeting changing naval needs. Such changes had varying degrees of success.

Recruitment

Many contemporary naval forces, including the Royal Navy and the United States Navy, are able to meet their manpower needs through the voluntary recruitment of men and women, although some services still depend on conscription. For much of their history, naval forces have found it difficult to attract significant numbers of recruits and have had to rely on various forms of compulsion.

The reluctance of men to serve in the sailing navies is explained largely by the difficulties and dangers of serving at sea. The long list of disincentives included severe discipline, poor living conditions, the risk of illness, long absences from home and uncertainties about pay. In these circumstances the major navies were forced to introduce some form of conscription, although this did not in itself provide any guarantee that sufficient manpower would be found. Impressment was an arbitrary but long-established form of conscription adopted by Britain, which did not fall into disuse until after 1815. It was a system of limited effectiveness that produced general public opposition and damaged the Royal Navy's image. As a result various expedients had to be adopted, including the use of soldiers on ships, to ensure that manning levels were maintained.

Growing resistance to impressment and its equivalents forced 19th-century navies to look increasingly to volunteers rather than conscripts. The need for greater numbers of trained specialists to operate the new steam ironclads and their successors pointed in the same direction. At the same time, conditions on board ship improved greatly and the disciplinary regime became much less harsh. For these reasons, naval forces have tended to attract a higher proportion of volunteers than the other services during periods of wartime conscription. These trends have continued since 1945, when further improvements in life on board ship, together with greatly improved training opportunities, have occurred. As a result, a naval career has become a serious option for sufficiently large numbers of men—and, increasingly, women—to meet the manpower needs of peacetime navies. Indeed as a result of cutbacks in naval forces, competition for places has intensified and entry standards have risen.

P. Kemp, *The British Sailor: A Social History of the Lower Deck*, London, 1970; C. Lloyd, *The British Seaman*, London, 1969.

Redoubtable, H.M.S.

Notable as the first BATTLESHIP to be fitted with external bulges (additional compartments added to the hull below the waterline) as a protection against TORPEDOES, the *Redoubtable* began life as the *Revenge*, which was completed in 1894. This British Royal Sovereign–class predreadnought battleship had a displacement of 14,635 tons, was 410 feet 6 inches (125.12 m) in length and had a beam of 75 feet (22.86 m). She was equipped with four 13.5-inch (34-cm) and ten 6-inch (15-cm) guns. The class represented a marked improvement over its predecessors, particularly in terms of its high freeboard, increased displacement, improved seaworthiness and enhanced armor protection. After service in the Mediterranean and home waters, the *Revenge* became a gunnery training ship in 1906. She was the only member of the class still in existence when WORLD WAR I, 1914–18, broke out and, fitted with protective bulges, was used to bombard German positions on the Belgian coast. In 1915 she was renamed *Redoubtable* to release her original name for a new battleship that had just been completed.

Reeves, Joseph Mason
1872–1948

American naval officer who was a key proponent of NAVAL AVIATION between the two world wars. Reeves was born on November 20, 1872, entering the U.S. Naval Academy in 1890. As a young assistant engineer he was part of the first crew of the U.S.S. OREGON. As such he was instrumental in that vessel's famous dash around Cape Horn from the Pacific in order to participate in the Battle of SANTIAGO Bay, Cuba, in July 1898 during the SPANISH-AMERICAN WAR. The voyage greatly dramatized the need for a transisthmian canal. (See PANAMA CANAL.) Reeves returned to the Naval Academy from 1906 to 1908 to instruct in physics and chemistry as well as serve as the school's football coach. During WORLD WAR I, 1914–18, he captained two of U.S. battleships but was restricted to training missions. Shortly after the war he became naval attaché to Italy.

In 1925 his career took an important turn when he reported to the air training station at Pensacola, Florida and qualified at age 53 as a naval aviation observer. He then took command of the Battle Fleet's Aircraft Squadrons, based aboard the U.S. Navy's first aircraft carrier, the *LANGLEY,* which had been converted from the collier *Jupiter.* In this position he began to develop the navy's first tactical doctrines for aircraft. His theories and efforts were realized when, in 1929, he conducted a successful mock raid on the Panama Canal by airplanes launched from carriers. He continued to refine fleet air tactics as he advanced in rank and responsibilities, becoming a four-star admiral while Commander, Battle Force, then as Commander in Chief, U.S. Fleet, from 1934 to 1936. He was brought back from retirement in 1940 and became the chief liaison officer for the LEND-LEASE program, a duty that he continued to execute until, at age 74 in late 1945, he was released from active duty. Reeves died on March 25, 1948.

Adolphus Andres, "Admiral with Wings: The Career of Joseph Mason Reeves," Ph.D. thesis, Princeton University, 1943.

Regent, H.M.S.

The first four-masted ship to be built in England, the *Regent* was a high-charged CARRACK of about 1,000 tons. (See HIGH-CHARGED SHIP.) Constructed at Portsmouth in 1487, during the reign of Henry VII, this "great ship" was operated by a crew of about 800 and was armed with at least 180 guns. The *Regent* was destroyed in action during King Henry VIII's first war against the French. On August 10, 1512 she engaged Louis XII's most formidable warship, the *Marie la Cordelière*, off Camaret at the entrance to BREST Harbor. The English boarded her but a French gunner started a fire that destroyed both ships and resulted in the loss of their entire crews.

Renown, H.M.S.

*C*ompleted in 1916, the *Renown* and the *Repulse* were BATTLE CRUISERS authorized by the British government in response to a request from Lord FISHER. His enthusiasm for fast, lightly armored warships of this kind had been strengthened by the success of the *Inflexible* and the *Invincible* in pursuing the enemy during the Battle of the FALKLAND ISLANDS, 1914, in the opening stages of WORLD WAR I, 1914–18.

The *Renown* and her sister ship were long, elegant ships with a displacement of 26,500 tons and a maximum speed of 32 knots. Their draft was limited because they had been designed with Fisher's projected AMPHIBIOUS landings on the northern coast of Germany in mind. Only six 15-inch (38-cm) guns (instead of Fisher's planned 12) could be provided for each ship within the limited construction time available. Secondary armament consisted of 17 4-inch (10-cm) guns in five triple and two single mountings. The *Renown* and the *Repulse* were the first ships to have antitorpedo bulge protection designed as an integral part of the hull. Armor was, however, rather limited for ships of this size, and by the time they were commissioned the fatal weakness of the battle cruiser design—inadequate armor protection—had been revealed at the Battle of JUTLAND, May 1916. As an interim measure, at Admiral John JELLICOE's request, further armor was added to the decks of both ships during 1916–17.

The *Renown* and the *Repulse* joined the First Battlecruiser Squadron of the British GRAND FLEET in the summer of 1916 and served with it for the remainder of World War I. The *Repulse* was in action against German light cruisers on November 17, 1917 in the Battle of HELIGOLAND BIGHT, but otherwise they saw no action. Both ships were further modified between the wars and saw service in WORLD WAR II, 1939–45. The *Repulse* began her final mission on December 8, 1941 when she left Singapore with the *PRINCE OF WALES* and an escort of destroyers. They were to attack a Japanese invasion force that was approaching the eastern coast of Malaya. Only two days later she was attacked by waves of Japanese bombers. The torpedoes did their work quickly but most of the crew was rescued. The *Renown* was more fortunate and survived a grueling war in many different theaters.

P. C. Smith, *Hit First, Hit Hard: The Story of H.M.S. Renown 1916–48,* London, 1979.

Resolution, H.M.S.

*T*he name of several notable British warships including a first rate (see RATING OF SHIPS) of 80 guns, launched in 1610, and the Royal Navy's first POLARIS SUBMARINE. The most famous *Resolution* was a Whitby collier, launched in 1770, that was purchased by the ADMIRALTY and used by Captain James COOK from 1771 until 1779. She was one of the ships that participated in his second and third voyages around the world. This *Resolution* later served as an armed transport during the AMERICAN WAR OF INDEPENDENCE, 1775–83, and, in 1781, was captured by the French in the East Indies. *Resolution* was also the name of two British battleships, including a vessel of 25,750 tons, launched in 1915, that served in both world wars. In 1966 the Royal Navy used the name *Resolution* for Britain's first *Polaris* submarine and for a class that included three other boats. This *Resolution* carried 16 Polaris A-3 missiles with a range of 2,300 nautical miles (4,255 km).

Reuben James, U.S.S.

*A*n American four-stack flush-deck destroyer of the WORLD WAR I Clemson class, the *Reuben James* was the first American warship to be lost during WORLD WAR II, 1939–45. She had been completed in 1920. With a displacement of 1,190 tons, she had a maximum speed of 35 knots and her principal armament consisted of four 4-inch (10-cm) guns. She was torpedoed and sunk by a German U-BOAT (*U-562*) on October 31, 1941 while escorting a CONVOY southwest of Iceland as part of the American effort in support of Great Britain during the Battle of the ATLANTIC, 1939–45. There was heavy loss of life. The incident, which caused considerable public disquiet, occurred five weeks before war between Germany and the United States was officially declared.

Reuter, Ludwig von
1869–1943

*A*ppointed commander of the scouting forces of the German HIGH SEAS FLEET in August 1918, Admiral Ludwig von Reuter had been captain of the *Derfflinger* at the beginning of WORLD WAR I, 1914–18, and was present at the Battle of the DOGGER BANK, 1914. At the Battle of JUTLAND, 1916, he commanded the Fourth Scouting Group of light cruisers. On the conclusion of the war he was charged with the task of taking to Britain the German ships that were to be interned at SCAPA FLOW under the terms of the Armistice. There they were to remain, under Reuter's command, until formal peace terms (which would involve their surrender) had been agreed on. When, in mid-1919, it became clear that a peace treaty (the Versailles Treaty) was to be signed, he ordered all his ships to be scuttled. Reuter said later that "it was unthinkable to surrender defenceless ships to the enemy." The scuttling took place on June 21, 1919 and Reuter, along with his colleagues, was held as a prisoner of war until January 1920.

Revenge, H.M.S.

Sir Francis DRAKE's flagship in the battle against the SPANISH ARMADA, 1588, the *Revenge* was among the first English GALLEONS and certainly one of the most famous. Produced under Sir John HAWKINS's major ship building program, this LOW-CHARGED SHIP, which had a displacement of 410 tons, was launched at Deptford in 1577. She was armed with 34 guns that were positioned on their own gundeck, another recent innovation in ship design.

In the year after the Armada, Drake again commanded the *Revenge* in an abortive expedition against the Spaniards in Portugal. In 1590 she was Sir Martin FROBISHER's flagship during an attempt to intercept treasure ships off the coast of Spain. The *Revenge*'s short operational career in the Royal Navy came to an abrupt end in 1591. As the flagship of Sir Richard GRENVILLE, second-in-command to Lord Thomas Howard, the *Revenge* left for the Azores in the summer of 1591 to await the Spanish treasure fleet. Surprised by the arrival of a large Spanish naval force on escort duty, the *Revenge* was soon trapped although the rest of the British squadron managed to escape.

Despite these very unfavorable circumstances, Grenville was determined to fight. In an epic 15-hour action on August 31–September 1, 1591, commemorated in Tennyson's poem "The Last Fight of the *Revenge*," he held off 15 Spanish galleons, sinking one and badly damaging another. At the end of this single-handed action, the *Revenge* was severely damaged and Grenville was mortally wounded. She was lost in a storm only five days after her surrender, taking her new Spanish crew of 200 with her.

Revenge was also the name of seven other ships in the Royal Navy. Among these was the first battleship to be fitted with antitorpedo bulges, which was completed in 1894. (See REDOUBTABLE.) It was also the name of a super-dreadnought that served in both world wars, and latterly, of a POLARIS submarine.

Revolutionary War

See AMERICAN WAR OF INDEPENDENCE.

Richelieu

French battleship (and battleship class) of WORLD WAR II, 1939–45, launched in 1939. The *Richelieu* was near-ing completion at the time of the fall of France, June 1940. Like her sister ship the JEAN BART, she had a displacement of 35 tons, an overall length of 814 feet (248.1 m) and a beam of 108 feet 6 inches (33.07 m). She had a maximum speed of 30 knots and her armament included eight 15-inch (38-cm) guns and 12 4-inch (10-cm) guns. In mid-1940 the *Richelieu* went to Dakar and, beginning in July, was involved in defending the port from British attack. Soon she was damaged by torpedo aircraft from the *Hermes*, but she continued to operate against British and Free French forces. Following the Allied Torch landings in North Africa in late 1942, Dakar and the rest of French West Africa agreed to peace terms with the Americans. Following a period in the United States for refitting, the *Richelieu* served in the Royal Navy, where she operated initially with the Home Fleet and then with the Pacific Fleet, 1944–45. She was returned to France in 1946 and was not scrapped finally until 1968.

Rickover, Hyman George
1900–86

American naval officer whose name became synonymous with the U.S. Navy's nuclear-propulsion program following WORLD WAR II, 1939–45, and thus with the country's nuclear-deterrent policy during the COLD WAR. Born on January 27, 1900 in Russia, he emigrated to the United States at an early age. Overcoming anti-Semitism, he graduated from the U.S. Naval Academy in 1922, earning an advanced degree in electrical engineering in 1929 before beginning his long association with submarines. From late 1937 he focused entirely on engineering duties. During WORLD WAR II, 1939–45, he headed the electrical section of the Bureau of Ships, thus overseeing the implementation of ships' electrical systems in the war.

Becoming involved with nuclear energy immediately after the war, he was connected with the Atomic Energy Commission, the successor to the wartime Manhattan Project. With an increasingly cantankerous and unorthodox manner that made him widely unpopular with other officers, he began a vigorous campaign to develop nuclear-powered submarines. As head of the Bureau of Ship's nuclear power division—a position he assumed in 1948—his efforts resulted in the launching in 1954 of the first nuclear-powered craft, the attack submarine NAUTILUS. Facing mandatory retirement by reason of age, he used political connections to remain on active duty, during which time he also worked on the POLARIS missile system for submarines and served as assistant chief of the Bureau of Ships and on the Atomic Energy Commission. Still on active duty but transferred to the retired list by President Lyndon Johnson in 1964, Rickover remained as such until 1981 when, at the age of 81, and as deputy commander for nuclear propulsion, naval sea system command, he was retired after 64 years on active duty, the longest in the history of the U.S. Navy. He remained controversial and outspoken to his death on July 8, 1986.

Theodore Rockwell, *The Rickover Effect: How One Man Made a Difference,* Annapolis, 1994.

Riou, Edward
c. 1758–1801

*B*ritish frigate captain—widely considered the best of his kind—who was killed at the Battle of COPENHAGEN, 1801, during the FRENCH REVOLUTIONARY AND NAPOLEONIC WARS, 1792–1815. Edward Riou, who was in command of the *Amazon,* worked closely with Admiral Lord Horato *Nelson,* and was put in charge of all the frigates and other small warships present at Copenhagen. When the battle was at its height, Admiral Sir Hyde PARKER, who was some distance away, ordered Nelson to discontinue the action. It was an order that was to cost Riou his life. With good reason Nelson ignored the command, putting his telescope to his blind eye. Riou, who had come under heavy fire from the Trekroner battery, did not appreciate that Nelson had decided to disregard the order. As he turned his ship to withdraw, he was killed by a shot from the Trekroner shore battery.

River Plate, Battle of the
December 13, 1939

*T*he first major naval engagement of WORLD WAR II, 1939–45. The Battle of the River Plate began when a British cruiser squadron sighted the German POCKET-BATTLESHIP ADMIRAL GRAF SPEE. Cruising near the mouth of the Plate River on the east coast of South America, the *Graf Spee* had been engaged in commerce-raiding in the Indian Ocean and South Atlantic since September 1939, with the ROYAL NAVY in close pursuit. After the *Graf Spee* attacked merchant ships off St. Helena, the commander of the British squadron, Commodore Henry HARWOOD (later Admiral Sir Henry Harwood) predicted that she would make for the Plate, where a good many similar victims usually could be found. His own ship, the light cruiser AJAX, her sister ship ACHILLES and the heavy cruiser EXETER arrived there a few hours before the *Graf Spee.* The enemy ship was first sighted at dawn on December 13, 1939.

As the *Graf Spee* approached at full speed, Harwood split his force: The *Ajax* and the *Achilles* were positioned to starboard and *Exeter* to port of the *Graf Spee.* Captain Hans Langsdorff, the German commander, concentrated fire from his 11-inch (28-cm) guns on the *Exeter.* She was badly damaged even though many of the German shells proved to be faulty. At the same time the *Ajax* and the *Achilles* hit their opponent several times, with the result that the *Graf Spee* was unable to complete the destruction of the *Exeter.* The British heavy cruiser eventually withdrew, but not before she had inflicted some damage on the *Graf Spee.* The remaining British ships now came under attack from the *Graf Spee*'s heavy guns. The *Ajax* suffered badly, forcing the British, who had maneuvered much more skillfully than their opponent, to break off the engagement.

The *Graf Spee* then made for the neutral port of Montevideo, Uruguay, where she arrived on December 14—Langsdorff having been compelled to carry out essential repairs rather than pursue his opponents. False information supplied by British intelligence convinced the German commander that a large Allied naval force had arrived off the River Plate and that certain defeat awaited him when he went back to sea. Unwilling to accept the ignominy of surrender to the British, Langsdorff scuttled his ship off the coast of Uruguay on the evening of December 17, having first consulted the naval high command in Berlin. Langsdorff himself committed suicide shortly afterward.

The destruction of the *Admiral Graf Spee* was a major boost to British morale during a particularly bleak period of the war. As far as Germany was concerned, it was one of the naval setbacks that helped to undermine Adolf Hitler's confidence in his surface fleet and raised major doubts about the pocket-battleship concept.

Robinet

A small naval gun of the 15th and 16th centuries that was intended for use exclusively against the crew of an enemy ship. With a caliber of 1 inch (3 cm), it normally fired a ball of eight ounces (0.23 kg), although the ball could weigh as much as 1 pound (0.45 kg). A matching half-pound charge typically was used to fire the shot over a maximum range of 1,000 yards (914 m), but the effective range was much shorter. A hand weapon, normally fired from the upper deck, the robinet was deployed at close quarters. The serpentine was another antipersonnel weapon of the same period. It had a larger caliber of 1.5 inches (4 cm) and a greater maximum range.

Rocket

*I*nvented in the 13th century, possibly in China, the rocket was originally developed for modern combat use by the British scientist Sir William Congreve in the early years of the 19th century. In essence it consisted of a warhead attached to a long stick, which gave it stability. Early versions, which had a range of several thousand yards, were used in naval operations against the French during the FRENCH REVOLUTIONARY AND NAPOLEONIC WARS, 1792–1815. It had a checkered history in the late 19th and 20th centuries but was given a new lease on life when multiple-

An American rocket ship in action in the Pacific *(Copyright ©
Imperial War Museum, London)*

launched rocket systems were developed intensively during
WORLD WAR II, 1939–45, by the American, Soviet and
other major navies. Multiple launching was intended to
compensate for the rocket's lack of accuracy and could be
particularly useful during amphibious operations to relieve
the pressure on the troops as they advanced under fire.
Landing craft often were fitted with multiple launchers for
this purpose. Rockets also were used by naval forces for
land bombardment and for antiaircraft defense. Fighter
aircraft also were equipped with rockets for antisubmarine
operations. In addition, rockets have played a role in safety
at sea. They are used to send distress signals and to carry
a line to a ship in difficulty.

Rodgers, John, Sr.
1773–1838

*A*merican naval officer who served with distinction in
the early years of the United States Navy. A member
of a large and influential family that has since been connected for several generations with the U.S. Navy, John

Rodgers was born near Havre de Grace, Maryland in 1773.
Initially entering the merchant service, he was commissioned as an officer in the young American navy in 1798,
serving under Thomas TRUXTON in the *CONSTELLATION*.
He was then appointed captain of the captured French
Insurgente and later the *Maryland* during the QUASI-WAR,
1798–1800, with France. Recalled to the navy during
the Barbary states conflict, he eventually commanded the
squadron blockading Tripoli and played a key role in the
negotiations for peace between the United States and the
Barbary states of Tripoli, Tunis, and Morocco.

As tension between the United States and Britain increased, Rodgers commanded the frigate *PRESIDENT* during
its action with the *Little Belt* in May 1811 off the coast of
Virginia. During the WAR OF 1812, he engaged mostly in
attacks on British commerce. Although these were not as
momentous as the single-ship actions and the battles on
the Great Lakes, they nevertheless contributed to the war's
conclusion. In 1814 he was active in defending both
Washington, D.C. and Baltimore. After the war Rodgers
served a brief term as secretary of the navy in 1823. He
died in Philadelphia in 1838. He was the father of John
RODGERS, Jr., who also followed a naval career.

K. Jack Bauer, "John Rodgers: The Stalwart Conservative," in *Command
Under Sail. Makers of the American Naval Tradition, 1775–1850*, ed.
James C. Bradford, Annapolis, 1985.

Rodgers, John, Jr.
1812–82

*B*orn near Havre de Grace, Maryland on August 8,
1812, John Rodgers, Jr. was the son of Commodore
John RODGERS. Appointed a midshipman in 1828, he assumed command of the exploring and survey expedition
of the North Pacific of 1852–56 when the expedition's
commander became ill. At the start of the AMERICAN CIVIL
WAR, 1861–65, he participated in the unsuccessful attempt
to destroy the dry dock at Norfolk, Virginia in April 1861,
before it fell into Confederate hands. Captured by rebel
forces, he was paroled and became aide to Rear Admiral
Samuel Francis DU PONT in the taking of Port Royal,
South Carolina, the logistical center for the Union navy's
BLOCKADE of the Confederate Atlantic coastline. Captaining an IRONCLAD during the unsuccessful attempt to
ascend the James River and take the Confederate capital,
Richmond, Virginia in May 1862, he would later command
the ironclad *Weehawken*, which forced the large Confederate ironclad *Atlanta* to surrender. Rising to become the
navy's senior officer as a rear admiral, he served as president
of the Naval Institute and of the navy's first Advisory
Board in 1881. He died in Washington, D.C. on May 5,
1882.

Robert E. Johnson, *Rear-Admiral John Rodgers, 1812–1882*, Annapolis,
1967.

Rodney, George Brydges, First Baron
1719–92

*B*ritish naval commander who made a notable contribution to naval operations during the latter stages of the AMERICAN WAR OF INDEPENDENCE, 1775–83. Rodney entered the Royal Navy in 1732 and had reached the rank of post-captain only ten years later, at the early age of 23. Although he may have owed his rapid rise to family connections, he soon was to justify his rank. During the War of the AUSTRIAN SUCCESSION, 1740–48, Rodney commanded the *Eagle* and was present at the Battle of CAPE FINISTERRE, 1747, when Sir Edward HAWKE was victorious against the French. A period as Governor of Newfoundland followed, 1748–52.

In 1759, during the SEVEN YEARS' WAR, 1756–63, Rodney, by now a rear admiral, commanded a squadron that blockaded the French port of Le Havre. He destroyed the FLOTILLA that was to have been used in an attempted invasion of England. In 1761 he was appointed to the command of the Leeward Islands station in the West Indies, and the following year he captured Martinique, St. Lucia, Grenada and St. Vincent from the French. In 1765 he was appointed governor of Greenwich but was recalled to operational service as commander in chief in Jamaica, 1771–74. On his return home severe financial problems obliged him to escape to Paris, where he lived until 1779.

When his debts were settled, Rodney returned to England, where he was required for active duty in the American War of Independence. He quickly made an impact by his relief of GIBRALTAR, which was then under siege. His defeat of a Spanish squadron in the "Moonlight battle" at CAPE ST. VINCENT, January 1780, was rewarded with a knighthood. Sent to the West Indies as commander in chief, he successfully interrupted trade between America and the Dutch trading stations in the Caribbean and established British naval supremacy in the area. After he returned to the West Indies the following year, 1781, Rodney secured a decisive victory over Admiral the Comte de GRASSE and the French fleet off Dominica at the Battle of the SAINTS. For this achievement he war raised to the peerage in 1782.

D. Spinney, *Rodney*, London, 1969.

Rodney, H.M.S.

*B*ritish BATTLESHIP of 33,730 tons that was built between 1922–27 under the terms of the Washington Navy Treaty, 1922. (See WASHINGTON CONFERENCE.) The *Rodney*'s main armament consisted of three triple 16-inch (40-cm) gun mountings concentrated amidships, with the superstructure aft. The *Rodney* and her sister, the *Nelson*,

Lord Rodney: English naval commander who decisively defeated the French at the Battle of the Saints, 1782, during the American War of Independence, 1775–83 *(Copyright © National Maritime Museum, Greenwich, London)*

the name ship of the class, were the only British battleships to be equipped with 16-inch guns and the first to have triple turrets. Armor was provided on the "all-or-nothing principle," with protection being provided in vital areas only. Her 16-inch guns never proved to be entirely satisfactory because they could not be fired aft of the beam due to damage that their blast pattern would have caused. On the other hand, her secondary armament of 12 6-inch (15-cm) guns, mounted in twin turrets worked normally. The *Rodney* was operated by a crew of 1,314 and had a maximum speed of 23 knots. She was 710 feet (216.8 m) in length and had a beam of 106 feet (32.4 m).

The *Rodney* and her sister ship served successively with the British Atlantic Fleet and the Home Fleet from 1932 to 1942. By the time of WORLD WAR II, 1939–45, the *Rodney* was in need of a refurbishment, but she did not sail to the United States for this purpose until May 1941. However, during her Atlantic crossing she was recalled to join the hunt for the German battleship BISMARCK, which had been responsible for the destruction of the battle cruiser HOOD on May 24. The *Rodney* fought in concert with the battleship KING GEORGE V during the final battle against the *Bismarck* on July 27. She hit the *Bismarck* several times and made a significant contribution to the German battleship's final destruction. After the completion of her refit, the *Rodney* joined FORCE H in the Mediterranean, but by 1944 her useful active service was over. She became FLAGSHIP of the Home Fleet at SCAPA FLOW but saw no further operational service, being scrapped in 1949.

Rooke, Sir George
1650–1709

Commander in chief of the Anglo-Dutch fleet during the War of the SPANISH SUCCESSION, 1701–14. Sir George Rooke first saw action during the Second ANGLO-DUTCH WAR, 1665–67, and established his reputation during the War of the GRAND ALLIANCE, 1688–97. Rooke was present at the Battle of BANTRY BAY, May 1689, and also at the relief of LONDONDERRY, where his inaction did little to help the beleaguered garrison. Subsequently he was appointed rear admiral and, in 1690, participated in the Battles of BEACHY HEAD and BARFLEUR.

The Battle of LA HOGUE, May 1692, which followed, was Rooke's first major success, and he received a knighthood for it. As commander of the British fleet, he destroyed several of the French warships that were to have joined the French expedition to restore JAMES II to the English throne. However, Rooke's moment of glory was to be overshadowed, in 1693, by the partial loss of the Smyrna convoy that ships under his command were escorting to the Levant. The French intercepted them and heavy losses were sustained, although Rooke himself was fortunate in not being blamed for the disaster.

Failure also marked the first two years of his command during the War of the Spanish Succession. His inability to capture Cadiz in September 1702 was only partially redeemed by a successful attack on Vigo (see the Battle of VIGO BAY, October 12) on the homeward journey. Two years later he was unable to seize Barcelona, but on his way back to England he took the opportunity to capture GIBRALTAR, which fell on July 23–24, 1704. Rooke successfully defended his conquest three weeks later when he fought the French fleet at the Battle of VELEZ MALAGA, and it has remained in English hands ever since. Strangely enough, Rooke's greatest victory brought about the abrupt end to his career. His Tory allies in Parliament used it as an occasion to attack the Whig government and their colleague the Duke of Marlborough, whose achievements on the battlefield were compared unfavorably with those of Rooke, who has been described as the "greatest seamen of his age," although he adhered rigidly to the tactical rules of the period. The Whigs responded accordingly and Rooke never went to sea again.

Theodore Roosevelt: 26th U.S. President and effective advocate of the United States as a global naval power *(Copyright © Imperial War Museum, London)*

Roosevelt, Franklin Delano
1882–1945

American politician, wartime leader and 32nd President who was unique in winning election to four terms of office. Born in Hyde Park, New York, Roosevelt trained as a lawyer and married Eleanor Roosevelt, a distant cousin who was a niece of President Theodore ROOSEVELT. He entered politics at an early age and was a Democrat State Senator in the period immediately before WORLD WAR I, 1914–18. Roosevelt served in the administration of President Woodrow Wilson as wartime Assistant Secretary of the Navy, 1913–20, and developed a strong interest in naval issues. Subsequently stricken by polio and paralyzed from the waist down, illness forced his temporary withdrawal from politics in the 1920s, although he returned as Governor of New York in 1929. He ran against President Herbert Hoover in the 1932 presidential elections and won a clear victory for the Democrats.

For the next six years President Roosevelt was preoccupied with domestic issues, introducing the New Deal, a package of public works initiatives to counter the effects of the Great Depression. This preoccupation did not prevent him from authorizing a major new naval construction program in 1933, intended to provide the navy with 32 new warships after a long period of postwar neglect. In the late 1930s growing international tension compelled him to turn his attention to foreign affairs, and he gradually brought the country out of a period of isolationism. Aware of the dangers posed by the Axis powers, he oversaw a massive expansion of the army and navy. In 1940 Congress passed the "Two-Ocean Navy" Acts, which doubled the size of the fleet. Roosevelt arranged urgently needed support to Britain in the form of the LEND-LEASE AGREEMENT, 1941, as that nation stood alone in the fight against Nazi Germany.

After the United States entered the war on December 8, 1941, following the Japanese attack on PEARL HARBOR, Roosevelt developed close working links with British Prime Minister Winston CHURCHILL. They agreed on a statement of peace aims, the Atlantic Charter, during a meeting at sea, although they often argued over tactics. Roosevelt's relations with the other Allied leaders were less satisfactory. Tensions were often evident during the series of wartime strategy conferences, particularly when Roosevelt and Soviet leader Joseph Stalin came to discuss the shape of the postwar world at the Yalta Conference early in 1945. Roosevelt was a firm advocate of the unconditional surrender of the Axis powers. His first priority was the defeat of Germany, and he was a strong advocate of the NORMANDY LANDINGS, 1944. Roosevelt died suddenly on April 12, 1945, a few weeks before the German surrender, and was succeeded by his vice president, Harry Truman.

Kenneth S. Davis, *FDR*, 3 vols., New York, 1985–86.

Roosevelt, Theodore
1858–1919

*A*merican soldier, conservationist, author and political leader who became the twenty-sixth president of the United States following the assassination of President William McKinley in 1901. Theodore Roosevelt was a Republican who developed strong naval interests. Following graduation from Harvard University in 1880, Roosevelt pursued a political career but also devoted some time to writing. His first substantial work was a *Naval History of the War of 1812*, which was published in 1882. After a period in the New York State legislature, he entered national politics in 1889 and, some eight years later, in 1897, was appointed assistant secretary of the navy under President McKinley. During a brief term of office Roosevelt, who advocated American expansionism, prepared the navy for its successful war with Spain. When the SPANISH-AMERICAN WAR of 1898 was declared, he resigned from office and organized and led a regiment, the Rough Riders, that fought Spanish ground troops in Cuba.

As vice president, 1901, and then president, 1901–9, Roosevelt demonstrated a continuing interest in naval issues. He was a strong advocate of an enhanced American role in international relations and, as such, supported the development of the U.S. Navy as a global force capable of intervening to protect U.S. interests. In 1908 he dispatched the GREAT WHITE FLEET on its round-the-world cruise.

The construction of the PANAMA CANAL, which helped to enhance American naval power, owes much to his action in negotiating a treaty with Panama, 1903. Roosevelt was also the moving force behind the conference that ended the RUSSO-JAPANESE WAR, 1904–5. For his work in mediating the peace settlement, embodied in the Treaty of Portsmouth (New Hampshire), he was awarded the Nobel Peace Prize, 1906. In his final years Roosevelt was heavily preoccupied with domestic politics, but his continued advocacy of the imperial role of the United States helped to underpin support for a powerful U.S. Navy.

Nathan Miller, *Theodore Roosevelt: A Life*, New York, 1992.

Rostislav

*T*he world's first oil-fired BATTLESHIP, the *Rostislav* served with the Russian Black Sea Fleet during WORLD WAR I, 1914–18. Launched in 1896, she had a displacement of 8,880 tons and four 10-inch (25-cm) and eight 6-inch (15-cm) guns. The secondary armament, unusually, was housed in four armored twin turrets. Two turrets were located on each beam amidships. The *Rostislav* was 351 feet 10 inches (107.24 m) in length, had a beam of 68 feet (20.73 m) and was operated by a crew of 650. She had a maximum speed of 15.6 knots. Used extensively during the war in operations in the Black Sea against Turkey, she was operated by the independent Ukraine after April 1918. The *Rostislav* later passed through German and British hands but was scuttled in 1920 to prevent her seizure by the Bolsheviks during the Russian Civil War, 1917–22.

Round Ship

*G*eneral term for the broad-beamed medieval ships used for trade, transport and warfare. The round ship's most distinctive feature was the fact that it had a length-to-beam ratio of three, two and a half or even two-to-one, giving it a round appearance. It was normally single-masted or square-rigged. The COG was a typical round-ship design: It had a large cargo-carrying capacity but was slow and cumbersome. It was equipped with a substantial castlelike structure fore and aft from which archers could defend the ship if an enemy tried to capture it. During the 15th century the round ship finally disappeared, replaced by the CARRACK and other more effective designs. The term excludes the other two principal designs of the ancient and medieval periods—the GALLEY and the longship—that were used for fighting at sea.

Robert Gardiner, ed., *Cogs, Caravels and Galleons: The Sailing Ship 1000–1650*, London, 1994.

Royal George, H.M.S.

The name of several British warships during the age of the sailing navy. The most notable *Royal George*, launched at Woolwich in 1756, during the reign of George II, was a first-rate (see RATING OF SHIPS) ship of 100 guns. Some 178 feet (54.25 m) long, with a beam of 68 feet (20.73 m), she had, at over 113 feet (34.44 m), the tallest masts of any English ship of the period. She served in the SEVEN YEARS' WAR, 1756–63, acting as Sir Edward HAWKE's flagship at the Battle of QUIBERON BAY, 1759, but was lost while the AMERICAN WAR OF INDEPENDENCE, 1775–83, was in progress.

Flying the flag of Admiral Richard KEMPENFELT, the *Royal George* was moored at Spithead undergoing repairs when, on August 29, 1782, she capsized and sank rapidly. Kempenfelt was among the 900 who lost their lives as a result of the disaster. Although the exact cause remains uncertain, the *Royal George* was heeled over for cleaning. Water may have entered her because she was leaning over too far, or some of the ship's decayed timbers may have collapsed. Although no other *Royal George* could have hoped to match this dramatic finale, her immediate successor, another 100-gun ship of the line, gave reliable service throughout the wars with France, 1793–1815.

Royal Naval Air Service

Naval aviation in Britain dates back to 1908, when the ROYAL NAVY became involved in the development of rigid airships. Experiments with heavier-than-air machines followed, and in 1912 the Royal Flying Corps (RFC), with separate naval and military wings, was created. With a proper organizational basis for the first time, British naval aviation began to develop more rapidly; by the summer of 1914 it had 31 seaplanes, seven airships and 40 landplanes. In July 1914 its progress was acknowledged when it was reconstituted as an independent force—the Royal Naval Air Service (RNAS)—under the ADMIRALTY.

At the beginning of WORLD WAR I, 1914–18, the service was primarily concerned with patrolling the North Sea, but its duties soon were expanded. A wing was sent to Ostend at the end of August with the aim of establishing control over a wide area of Belgium and northern France and preventing airship raids on Britain. This group made the first British raid on German territory, attacking the Zeppelin sheds at Dusseldorf on September 22, 1914. The RNAS was in fact the true pioneer of strategic bombing and the techniques associated with it; the service also promoted the development of specialist bomber aircraft. Bombing operations as well as reconnaissance also formed part of its work in the DARDANELLES.

One of the principal responsibilities of RNAS squadrons based at home was the air defense of Great Britain, a task that the RFC was unable to take over until March 1916. Antisubmarine and anti-Zeppelin patrols over home waters were another major responsibility, carried out mainly by aircraft operating from coastal air stations. These operations were expanded as U-BOAT activity increased and long-range flying boats became available.

During the second half of the war, the RNAS systematically patrolled the North Sea using a spider web search pattern, which enabled it to check on an area of 4,000

The *Campania*, a converted British seaplane carrier, was fitted with a flight deck in 1915 *(Copyright © Imperial War Museum, London)*

square miles (6,437 square km). The RNAS was also engaged in some notable dogfights with enemy seaplanes over the North Sea. Naval aircraft operated from ships as well as from coastal air stations, but on a much smaller scale. The aircraft carrier, equipped with special decks, appeared in 1917–18, but had very limited operational use during World War I. Takeoff platforms were fitted to some warships or towed by them, and in the closing stages of the war more than 100 aircraft were being carried by the GRAND FLEET.

In April 1918 the separate existence of the RNAS came to an end when the two different British air services were brought together once more as the Royal Air Force. With 2,900 aircraft, 103 airships, 126 air stations, and 55,000 officers and men, British naval aviation early in 1918 bore little resemblance to the embryonic force with which the country had entered the war. However, it soon became clear that a unified service did not provide an appropriate framework for the development of British naval aviation and, in 1924, a separate FLEET AIR ARM was created.

Geoffrey Till, *Air Power and the Royal Navy, 1914–45*, London, 1979.

Royal Navy

The origins of the English navy as a permanent organized force date back to the early 16th century, when England was facing a growing threat at sea from France and Spain as it extended its maritime interests across the globe. From this time onward, England typically invested more resources in the navy than in the army, reflecting its favorable position as an island nation. King Henry VIII, 1491–1547, had a strong interest in naval affairs and was responsible for the construction of several royal ships that operated in continuous service to the crown. In wartime these ships were supplemented by a much larger number of merchantmen, which were armed for the duration of the conflict. This period also witnessed the creation of royal dockyards at Deptford, Woolwich and Plymouth as well as the development of a central naval administration overseen by a body of commissioners appointed by the crown.

A notable commissioner of the Elizabethan period was Sir John HAWKINS, a celebrated naval commander, who was responsible for the development of the GALLEON, which formed the basis of warship design for the next 300 years. The quality of English warships partly explains its defeat of the SPANISH ARMADA in 1588. Further English attacks on the enemy fleet as well as privateer operations helped to undermine Spanish power, and war between the two countries eventually came to an end in 1603. In the early 17th century the navy was relatively neglected, and in the absence of an effective service Barbary pirates were able to operate regularly in the English Channel. King Charles I, 1600–49, tried to restore English naval power and was responsible for the construction of some fine ships, including the famous SOVEREIGN OF THE SEAS. His plan to levy ship money, a tax to raise funds for the navy, was one of the points of conflict between crown and Parliament that led to the Civil War, 1642–48. Most ships declared for Parliament when the war began, and the remaining royalist units were systematically eliminated.

The Parliamentary navy consisting of 154 warships at its peak, fought wars against the French, Spanish and Dutch. There were three 17th-century wars against the Dutch, whose merchant fleet was badly affected by the Navigation Act, 1651, which excluded the involvement of third parties in carrying foreign goods to England. Conflict with the Dutch continued after the Restoration of the monarchy in 1660, as Charles II was equally concerned to defend English trade. Samuel PEPYS, as a senior Admiralty official, provided the professional officers who could complete the task. Anglo-Dutch ties eventually were restored when William of Orange acceded to the English throne in 1688, and the two countries were united in resisting the expansionist aims of King Louis XIV of France.

During the War of the SPANISH SUCCESSION, 1701–14, the Royal Navy fought the combined fleets of France and Spain. Its most notable achievement was the capture of GIBRALTAR in 1704, which has remained a British colony ever since. For much of the 18th century the English fleet was to control the seas; it scored some notable successes against the French during the War of the AUSTRIAN SUCCESSION, 1740–48, and the SEVEN YEARS' WAR, 1756–63. During the AMERICAN WAR OF INDEPENDENCE, 1775–83, it was overstretched for a period; its failure at the Battle of Chesapeake, September 1781, led directly to the final surrender of the British army at Yorktown, 1781, and the achievement of American independence. The naval war with France continued until 1783; in the end, the Royal Navy was able to reassert its traditional supremacy. During the FRENCH REVOLUTIONARY AND NAPOLEONIC WARS, 1792–1815, the navy suffered some early reverses, although Admiral Horatio NELSON soon reestablished English naval dominance in the Mediterranean at the Battle of the NILE, 1798. French naval power was finally destroyed at the Battle of TRAFALGAR, October 1805, the Royal Navy's greatest victory. Nelson's tactical skills, superior guns and better morale were all part of the explanation for the French defeat. The navy suffered heavily in the postwar reductions, although it was to play a creditable role at the Battle of NAVARINO, 1827, and during the CRIMEAN WAR, 1853–56. The second half of the 19th century is associated more with rapid technological innovation—the evolution from sailing ship to dreadnought battleship taking less than 50 years—than with major naval battles. The navy established a clear lead over its rivals and played a key role in maintaining British trade routes and preserving the security of the empire.

At the beginning of WORLD WAR I, 1914–18, the Royal

Navy was the largest in the world, with a clear lead over its German rival in dreadnought battleships and in battle cruisers. She could not, however, maintain the "two-power standard" by which the Royal Navy's strength was to be greater than the next two strongest navies. The Grand Fleet, the navy's principal battle fleet, operated a policy of containing the German High Seas Fleet in the North Sea by means of a distant blockade. The Battle of JUTLAND, 1916, was the only time the main battle fleets fought each other during the war. Although the Royal Navy was unable to achieve anything more than a draw, the Germans realized that they would never be able to defeat their stronger opponent. Unwilling to risk its main battle fleet, Germany turned to the submarine as its main naval weapon. In 1917 it came close to success until the Royal Navy belatedly introduced the convoy system and the tide was turned. The pattern in other parts of the globe was different. The Royal Navy had been able to deal with the German cruiser threat more rapidly, and this threat had disappeared within a few months. It had less initial success in the Mediterranean, where the escape of the German warships GOEBEN and *Breslau* led directly to Turkey's entry into the war. In general, British naval forces succeeded in maintaining control of the seas throughout the war. They sustained heavy losses in capital ships but their operational effectiveness was little affected.

Although the Royal Navy maintained its position as the world's largest naval force during the interwar years, American and Japanese naval forces were expanding rapidly during this period. Moreover, Britain's ships were aging, and it had lost ground in the key area of NAVAL AVIATION. During WORLD WAR II, 1939–45, the British sought to blockade Germany while protecting their trade routes across the globe. However, Britain soon was forced on the defensive as the German navy stepped up the U-boat war, operating from bases in occupied France. Losses of Allied merchant shipping mounted partly because the Royal Navy's antisubmarine capability was inadequate and also because naval units had to be diverted to meet other potential threats, such as the German naval units based in Norway and the expected German invasion of England. The sinking of the BISMARCK, which curtailed the activities of the German surface fleet in the Atlantic, was a rare success. The Royal Navy was also under heavy pressure in the Mediterranean, where the main adversary was the Luftwaffe rather than the Italian navy. The convoy runs to Malta and North Africa resulted in heavy losses, as they did elsewhere. The Royal Navy's fortunes began to improve early in 1943 following American involvement, and the loss of German air supremacy changed the course of events.

There was also a reversal of fortunes in the Battle of the ATLANTIC in mid-1943, due in part to the arrival of more escort ships and aircraft. The Germans were never able to regain the initiative in this theater, and the Royal Navy's primary role in Europe in the latter part of the war

consisted of amphibious operations and shore bombardment. At this point some ships were transferred to the Far East, where the British had played only a limited role in the Indian Ocean following the destruction of FORCE Z off Malaya in December 1941. From late 1944 Britain operated with American naval units in the final operations against Japan.

In the postwar period, the Royal Navy has been scaled down as Britain's relative economic position declined and the process of decolonization was completed. Britain still has some overseas commitments, and it has sought to maintain the capability to operate on a global scale. Equipped with light aircraft carriers, destroyers, frigates and corvettes, it demonstrated its ability to operate effectively at long distance during the FALKLANDS WAR, 1982. The Royal Navy also maintains Britain's nuclear deterrent, which is based on the submarine-launched ballistic missile.

C. Barnett, *Engage the Enemy More Closely: The Royal Navy in the Second World War*, London, 1991; P. M. Kennedy, *The Rise and Fall of British Naval Mastery*, London, 1983; *The Oxford Illustrated History of the Royal Navy*, London, 1995.

Royal Oak, H.M.S.

The name of several British warships, including a 74-gun ship that served with distinction at the Battle of the SAINTS, 1782, during the AMERICAN WAR OF INDEPENDENCE, 1775–83. It was also the name of a super-dreadnought of 29,500 tons, completed in 1916, which served during WORLD WAR I, 1914–18. A member of the Royal Sovereign class, this 20th-century *Royal Oak* survived the conflict and was still in service at the beginning of WORLD WAR II, 1939–45. Shortly after the start of the war, on October 14, 1939, this elderly battleship was torpedoed at SCAPA FLOW by the German submarine *U-47* captained by Gunther PRIEN, one of Germany's most successful U-Boat commanders. He had managed to penetrate Scapa Flow's defenses by following another ship into the sheltered anchorage. Three torpedoes detonated the *Royal Oak*'s magazine and she sank, taking 833 crew with her. (See also SOVEREIGN OF THE SEAS.)

Gerald S. Snyder, *The Royal Oak Disaster*, London, 1976.

Rozhestvensky, Zinovi
1848–1909

Russian naval commander who was decisively defeated by the JAPANESE NAVY at the Battle of TSUSHIMA, May 27–28, 1905. Following a series of setbacks during the early stages of the RUSSO-JAPANESE WAR, 1904–5, Zinov Rozhestvensky, the former chief of the Russian naval staff, was appointed to take the Baltic Fleet on a voyage of 20,000 miles (32,187 km) to Port Arthur, the Manchurian

Seaport where the Russian Pacific Fleet was being blockaded. Leaving Labiau, its Baltic Sea base, on October 15, 1904, the fleet soon ran into difficulties. Its unprovoked attack on unarmed British trawlers in the North Sea—the DOGGER BANK incident—led to tension between Britain and Russia. The Russians had believed, quite wrongly, that the trawlers were shielding a fleet of Japanese torpedo boats. Rozhestvensky later faced severe problems in replacing supplies en route because several ports denied him their facilities.

Following the loss of Port Arthur to the Japanese early in 1905, the Russian commander decided to make for Vladivostock, a destination that forced him to pass uncomfortably close to Japan. The enemy fleet under Admiral Heihachiro TOGO was in fact waiting for him as he entered the Straits of Tsushima on 27 May. The better-equipped and trained Japanese outmaneuvered the obsolete Russian fleet, which was soon encircled and largely destroyed. Rozhestvensky himself was badly injured in the opening stages of the battle, and Rear Admiral Nikolai Nebogatoff assumed command before the end of the first day. Rozhestvensky was later captured by the Japanese and became a prisoner of war. Although Rozhestvensky's personal conduct during the battle could not be faulted, the RUSSIAN NAVY had suffered one of the most decisive defeats in naval history.

Richard Hough, *The Fleet That Had to Die*, London, 1958.

Rupert, Prince Palatine: English naval commander during the Anglo-Dutch Wars of the 17th century   *(Copyright © National Maritime Museum, Greenwich, London)*

Rupert, Prince Palatine
1619–82

*E*nglish prince and royalist cavalry commander, the third son of Elizabeth, Queen of Bohemia, and Frederick V, Elector of Palatine, and grandson of King James I. Rupert achieved some notable successes in the major land engagements of the Civil Wars, 1642–48, before his defeat at the Battle of Marston Moor, 1644. After the fall of Bristol he was abruptly dismissed by Charles I and was forced to take to the sea as commander of a small royalist fleet. In 1650 he was compelled to withdraw from European waters by a more powerful parliamentary fleet under the command of Admiral Robert BLAKE. He escaped to the West Indies but returned to Europe in 1653, living in Germany until the restoration of the English monarchy in 1660.

On his return to England, Charles II gave him the opportunity to renew his interest in naval affairs, appointing him admiral of the White Fleet at the Battle of LOWESTOFT, 1665, the opening engagement of the Second ANGLO-DUTCH WAR, 1665-67, during which he shared command with George MONCK, Duke of Albemarle. At the FOUR DAYS' BATTLE, 1666, he minimized the effects of a Dutch victory and, a month later, defeated Admiral Mi-

chiel de RUYTER at the Battle of ORFORDNESS. Rupert returned to sea during the Third Dutch War, 1672–74, succeeding JAMES II, DUKE OF YORK as First Lord of the Admiralty in 1673. He was unable to repeat his earlier success against the Dutch, but this was due more to the weakness of his French allies than any shortcomings on his part. He remained at the head of the ADMIRALTY until 1679.

P. Morrah, *Rupert of the Rhine*, London, 1976.

Russell, Edward, Earl of Orford
1653–1727

*E*nglish naval commander who won a notable victory over the French at the Battle of LA HOGUE, 1692, during the War of the GRAND ALLIANCE, 1688–97. Early in his naval career Russell served in the Third ANGLO-DUTCH WAR, 1672–74, but he first came to notice when he accompanied William of Orange to England during the Glorious Revolution of 1688. His career prospered under the new king, and, in 1689, he was appointed to flag rank under Admiral Arthur HERBERT, Earl of Torrington.

Edward Russell soon replaced Torrington and, in 1692, commanded an Anglo-Dutch fleet that defeated the French at the Battles of BARFLEUR and LA HOGUE. Despite this achievement Russell was relieved of his command because of his alleged failure to complete the destruction of the French fleet. He was reinstated during the following year. Raised to the peerage as the Earl of Orford, he devoted much of the rest of his career to naval administration. He held the office of first Lord of the Admiralty for three separate terms from 1694 to 1717.

Russian Navy

The origins of the Russian navy may be found at the end of the 17th century in the expansionist plans of Tsar PETER THE GREAT, who aimed to secure outlets for Russia in the Black Sea and the Baltic. Control of the Black Sea, including the Dardanelles, would give Russian merchant ships access to the Mediterranean and beyond. However, it would first require defeating the Turks, the controlling power, on land and at sea, and building a fleet to do so. By 1696 Russia had taken the Turkish fortress at Azov and established its first Black Sea base. In the Baltic Peter sought to defeat Sweden, the dominant sea power, and establish a Russian naval presence. A Swedish fort captured in 1703 was used as the first Russian naval base in the Baltic, and soon a fleet was under construction at the newly designated capital of St. Petersburg. These gains were extended in further Russian land and sea victories, including the Battle of Gangut, 1714, when a fleet of Russian galleys decisively defeated the Swedes. By the end of the Great Northern War, 1700–21, the Russian navy was established as a major power in the Baltic.

The struggle for supremacy in both the Baltic and the Black Sea continued for the rest of the 18th century in a series of wars with Sweden and Turkey respectively. The course of events sometimes favored one side and sometimes the other, but the long-term growth in Russian power in both theaters was clearly evident. After three Russo-Turkish Wars the Russians had established command of the northern part of the Black Sea. In the Baltic Sweden continued to challenge Russian power and secured a remarkable victory against Russia at the Battle of SVENSKUND, July 9, 1790, when the Russian navy was heavily defeated. Generally, however, the RUSSO-SWEDISH WAR, 1788–90, confirmed that Russia was the predominant power in the Baltic, and the Swedes never again challenged their old adversary. The struggle between Russia and Turkey continued during the 19th century and was never finally resolved. Russia gave its support to Greece in its struggle for independence against Turkey, and an Anglo-Russian fleet decisively defeated the Turks at the Battle of NAVARINO, 1827. Russia never abandoned its aim of eradicating Turkish

power and controlling the Bosphorus. In 1853 it precipitated the CRIMEAN WAR, 1853–56, by a ground attack on Turkish-held territory. The opposing fleets meet at the Battle of SINOPE, November 30, 1853, and the superior Russian navy, which was equipped with new explosive shells, decisively defeated the Turks. Both France and Britain intervened to thwart Russia's expansionist plans and decided to attack the source of its power in the Black Sea—the naval base at Sevastopol—which was besieged for a year before it capitulated.

By the terms of the Treaty of Paris, 1856, which ended the war, the Russians were prevented from maintaining a fleet in the Black Sea. These terms did not apply to the Baltic fleet, however, which was expanded and modernized over a 20-year period when naval technology was changing rapidly. Russia eventually renounced the offending treaty and built a new Black Sea fleet. However, in 1877, before this construction program had been completed, Russia went to war with Turkey once more. This was primarily a land war, but the Russian navy made a number of successful torpedo-boat attacks on the larger Turkish fleet.

From 1880, the Russian navy embarked on a 20-year building program that was designed to turn Russia into a world naval power. It included the formation of a large fleet in the Far East, based at Vladivostok and Port Arthur; by the beginning of the 20th century, the Russian Pacific Fleet matched the entire Japanese navy in terms of firepower. Tension between these two powers led to war in 1904. (See RUSSO-JAPANESE WAR, 1904–5.) The Japanese navy, which was led and trained more effectively than its opponent, soon had achieved its objective of neutralizing the Russian Pacific Fleet by blockading it in Port Arthur, where it was destroyed by besieging land forces. In a final attempt to reverse its fortunes at sea, the Russian Baltic Fleet was dispatched to the Far East. It was intercepted and decisively defeated by superior Japanese guns at the Battle of TSUSHIMA, May 1905. This disastrous outcome damaged the morale of the entire nation and led directly to the abortive revolution of 1905, in which there was a significant movement by mutinous naval crews.

A period of renewal followed, but progress was slow and the navy, the sixth largest in the world, still had many obsolete ships in service when WORLD WAR I began in 1914. It decided therefore to adopt a cautious, defensive strategy in the Baltic and the Black Sea, although it secured a number of successes against the German and Turkish navies and effectively disrupted enemy merchant shipping. Its mine-laying activities were particularly effective, and early in the war it captured the German navy's secret codebook. The Imperial Russian navy ceased to exist after the February 1917 Revolution, although its warships continued to fight the Germans until Russia left the war after the October Revolution. The Bolsheviks soon laid the foundations of Soviet naval power and created a new navy that ultimately would operate on a global scale. (See also SOVIET NAVY.)

David Woodward, *Russians at Sea*, London, 1965.

Russo-Japanese War
1904–5

The war between Russia and Japan in 1904–5 was a product of the two nations' conflicting territorial ambitions in east Asia. Russian plans for expansion had led to the acquisition of Port Arthur from China in 1898 and the arrival of Russian troops in Manchuria during the Boxer Rebellion, 1900. Under Anglo-Japanese pressure Russia promised to withdraw from China but never actually did so. Talks between Russia and Japan broke up on February 6, 1904; less than three days later the Japanese navy launched a surprise attack on the main Russian fleet at Port Arthur and then blockaded it. At the same time two Russian warships were sunk at the Battle of CHEMULPO (Inchon) Korea, February 9. With the rest of the Russian fleet trapped in icebound Vladivostok, the Japanese had temporary naval superiority. Land operations in Korea and Manchuria followed, while an attempted naval breakout from Port Arthur ended in failure at the Battle of the YELLOW SEA, August 10. At the Battle of the JAPANESE SEA, August 14, the remnants of the Vladivostok squadron were defeated, giving the Japanese command of the seas. The Japanese made equally rapid progress in Korea and advanced steadily northward across Manchuria. Two Russian counteroffensives failed and, on January 2, 1905, Port Arthur fell.

The Japanese victory at the Battle of Miction, February 21–March 10, effectively marked the end of the operations on land. However, the Russian navy remained a potential threat, a fact that was confirmed by the arrival of its Baltic Fleet in Far Eastern waters early in May 1905 on its way to Vladivostok. But the Russians were intercepted by the Japanese navy, under Admiral Heihachiro TOGO, between Korea and Japan. The destruction of the Russian fleet at the decisive Battle of TSUSHIMA, May 27–28, 1905, was followed by an offer of mediation by the American president, Theodore ROOSEVELT. The Treaty of Portsmouth, September 1905, recognized Japan's victory by acknowledging Japanese interests in Korea and forcing Russia to abandon various territorial gains in China.

Chronological List of Naval Events

1904

February 8–9	Japanese navy launches surprise attack on Port Arthur, base of the Russian Far East Fleet; ten destroyers hit two Russian battleships and a cruiser
	Two Russian warships sunk at Chemulpo, Korea
February 10	War is formally declared
April	Japanese naval support for land-based operations against Port Arthur begins
August 10	Battle of the Yellow Sea
August 14	Battle of the Japanese Sea (or the Battle of Oilstone)
October 15	Russian naval reinforcements leave the Baltic for the Far East

1905

January 2	Port Arthur surrenders
May 27–28	Admiral Togo defeats the Russian navy at Tsushima.
September 6	Treaty of Portsmouth ends hostilities

John N. Westwood, *Russia Against Japan, 1904–05. A New Look at the Russo-Japanese War*, Basingstoke, 1986.

Russo-Swedish War
1788–90

The Russo-Swedish War began when Swedish King Gustavus III mounted an invasion of Russian Finland in June 1788 to preempt possible future Russian or Prussian action against Sweden. It was timed to occur when Catherine the Great and her court were fully preoccupied with a war with Turkey, 1787–92. The land and sea offensives were successful at first but they soon lost momentum; moreover, they also brought Denmark into the war on the Russian side. The Swedish navy suffered a severe reverse at the first Battle of SVENSKUND, August 24, 1789, when it lost 33 ships. Thereupon Gustavus devoted his energies to building up Swedish naval strength, and his fortunes improved when campaigning resumed in 1790.

Swedish naval units under Gustavus III and Prince Carl set out from Karlskrona with the aim of entering Fredikshamn Harbor and destroying the arsenal. However, the Swedes had to fight their way out of the harbor and escaped to VIBORG, where they were blockaded. On July 3 they broke out, and Gustavus reached Svenskund. The second Battle of SVENSKUND began when the Russian fleet under Prince Nassau-Siegen made a reckless attack on the enemy fleet. Sweden's greatest naval battle resulted in the defeat of the Russian navy, which lost 53 warships. A truce was soon arranged and, on August 15, 1790, the Russian and Swedish governments signed the Treaty of Wereloe, which restored the status quo ante. Despite this victory, the Swedish never again mounted a serious challenge to the Russians, who became the dominant Baltic naval power. See also CHARLES XIII.

Oliver Warner, *The Sea and the Sword. The Baltic 1630–1945*, London, 1965.

Ruyter, Michiel Adriaanszoon de
1607–76

*D*utch admiral, born in Flushing, who gave distinguished service in the ANGLO-DUTCH WARS during the 17th century. Holland's greatest naval leader, Michiel de Ruyter was a courageous seaman, a fine leader and a skilled tactician. De Ruyter began his career at sea as a cabin boy, but he soon gained rapid promotion in the Dutch navy. Promoted to the rank of captain in 1635 and rear admiral in 1641, he served under Witte de WITH and Maarten TROMP during the First Anglo-Dutch War, 1652–54, against the naval forces of England commanded by George MONCK and Robert BLAKE. De Ruyter saw much action throughout the war, and his squadron played a prominent part in the Battle of PORTLAND, February 1653. In the years that followed he spent much of his time in the Mediterranean, where he was involved in the suppression of PIRACY.

Admiral Michiel de Ruyter was the Dutch navy's greatest admiral   *(Copyright © National Maritime Museum, Greenwich, London)*

During the Second Anglo-Dutch War, 1665–67, as fleet commander, he won notable victories in the FOUR DAYS' BATTLE, 1666, and in the raid on CHATHAM, 1667. In the Third Anglo-Dutch War, 1672–74, he achieved victory against a combined Anglo-French fleet at the Battle of SOLEBAY, May 1672. In 1673 a series of successful engagements, including his victory over Prince RUPERT at the Battle of the TEXEL, August 11, prevented a seaborne invasion of Holland. The Third Dutch War ended in 1674, but the conflict between the Dutch and French was to continue. De Ruyter sailed for the Mediterranean in support of the Spanish, who had sought Dutch assistance in their fight against rebellious Sicily (then a Spanish possession) and their French allies. He blockaded Messina, which was in French hands, for several months. When he met the French under Admiral the Marquis DUQUESNE off Augusta, in April 1676, the result was a Dutch victory; but de Ruyter himself was mortally wounded.

P. J. Blok, *The Life of Admiral de Ruyter*, London, 1933.

Ryujo

*J*apanese light AIRCRAFT CARRIER that saw much action in the first few months of WORLD WAR II, 1939–45, in the Pacific. Completed in 1932, the *Ryujo* had a displacement of 10,600 tons and was equipped to carry 48 aircraft. She had an overall length of more than 590 feet (179.83 m) and a beam in excess of 68 feet (20.72 m). In modified form, from 1934–35, she was equipped with eight 5-inch (13-cm) and 28 smaller-caliber antiaircraft guns. Following her completion, the *Ryujo* was found to be top-heavy at sea; within two years major modifications were made to her. Her four 12.5-inch guns were removed, a heavier keel was fitted and several changes were made to her superstructure. The *Ryujo* was involved in the first attack on the Philippines on December 8, 1941 and later served at the Battle of MIDWAY, June 1942. At the Battle of the EASTERN SOLOMONS, August 24, 1942, she was sunk by aircraft from the U.S.S. SARATOGA and the U.S.S. ENTERPRISE.

Sadras, Battle of
February 17, 1782

The Indian Ocean was one of the focal points of Anglo-French naval rivalry during the AMERICAN WAR OF INDEPENDENCE, 1775–83. With the arrival, in February 1782, of an able new French naval commander, Admiral Pierre Andre de SUFFREN, the conflict between the British and French was renewed. Suffren had succeeded the late Comte d'Orves as commander of the French squadron on the Coromandel coast (the southeastern coast of India). He had 11 ships of the line at his disposal. Vice Admiral Sir Edward HUGHES, his British counterpart, had nine ships of the line under his command. The opposing squadrons first made contact off Madras only a week after Suffren's arrival, but the French failed to take their opponent by surprise. The British were well protected by land-based guns, and the French were forced to withdraw.

As Suffren moved south from Madras toward Pondicherry, the British followed. During the night of February 15–16, Hughes managed to capture six of the transport ships sailing with Suffren's squadron. The following morning the two evenly matched squadrons fought off Sadras. With the wind in his favor, Suffren inflicted heavy damage on the British, with Hughes's FLAGSHIP, the *Superb,* and the *Exeter* being the main victims. During the late afternoon the wind changed to the advantage of the British, which gave them the opportunity to recover the *Exeter.* Suffren, who did not receive the full support of his captains, had been unable to press home his advantage, and the engagement ended without a clear conclusion.

St. Kitts, Battle of
January 25–26, 1782

The West Indies was the scene of a prolonged naval struggle between British and French naval forces during the AMERICAN WAR OF INDEPENDENCE, 1775–83, that con-

tinued until its closing stages. At the end of 1781, the French increased their pressure on British possessions in the West Indies, launching an attack on the island of St. Kitts on January 9, 1782. Some 8,000 troops were landed at Basseterre, the island's capital, from a naval force consisting of 24 ships of the line and several transport ships. They were under the command of Admiral the Comte de GRASSE. British naval forces, which were commanded by Admiral Sir Samuel HOOD in Admiral George RODNEY's absence in England, responded quickly.

Leaving their anchorage in St. John's, Antigua, 22 ships of the line made for St. Kitts. As soon as the French detected the approaching British squadron, they ordered their ships to sea. During the afternoon of January 25, the British rear was attacked, but Admiral Hood pressed on with his objective of seizing the Basseterre anchorage. In this he succeeded. Several French attacks were repelled, and de Grasse eventually withdrew. Hood's skill as a commander during this action was overshadowed, however, by the fact that the French regained control of St. Kitts some three weeks later.

St. Lucia, Capture of
December 15, 1778

Within months of France's entry into the AMERICAN WAR OF INDEPENDENCE, 1775–83, in 1778, it took advantage of the vulnerability of Britain's possessions in the West Indies. At that time British naval protection in the area consisted of no more than two ships of the line and 13 smaller warships. Following the French capture of Dominica in September 1778, the British naval forces in the West Indies, which were commanded by Rear Admiral Samuel Barrington, were reinforced from North America. However, during this same period the French naval presence in the area also was greatly strengthened by the arrival of 12 ships of the line under the command of Admiral Jean-Baptiste d'ESTAING.

The French moved into action as a British expeditionary force, with naval support provided by Admiral Barrington, landed at Castries, St. Lucia, on December 14 with the aim of securing the island for Britain. As d'Estaing approached the entrance to Carenage Bay, British batteries at Castries opened fire, and he was forced to withdraw. Barrington's squadron, which had anchored in the Bay of Grand Cul de Sac, to the south of Carenage Bay, was the next subject of d'Estaing's attentions. On December 15 the British repelled two French attacks and they were forced to move northward. Some 7,000 French troops were landed at Anse du Choc Bay, but their presence on the island was short-lived. They departed within a few days and the British were able to establish control over the whole island.

St.-Nazaire Raid
1942

The French port of St.-Nazaire, on the Bay of Biscay some 150 miles south of BREST, was used as a German naval base and U-BOAT depot for much of WORLD WAR II, 1939–45. On March 27–28, 1942 a combined operation was mounted by British forces with the objective of destroying the lock gates at St.-Nazaire. These gates protected St.-Nazaire's docks from the sea, and their destruction would mean that its extensive dry-dock facilities, which could accommodate the largest battleships, would no longer be available to the Germans. An obsolescent U.S. Navy flush-deck destroyer, the *Campbeltown*, packed with three tons of explosives, rammed the lock gates. She blew up the following day and wrecked the gates, putting the dock facility out of action for much of the rest of the war. The lock gates of the St.-Nazaire basin also were destroyed by another delayed explosion using a motor torpedo boat. The *Campbeltown* was accompanied by some 260 commandos and 18 small coastal assault craft. During the raid, which included an unsuccessful attack on the U-boat pens, 16 assault craft were destroyed and 170 commandos killed or captured.

Saints, Battle of the
April 12, 1782

Following the inconclusive Anglo-French action at the island of DOMINICA, April 9, 1782, during the AMERICAN WAR OF INDEPENDENCE, 1775–83, the Royal Navy pursued the enemy through the Caribbean for three days. The English squadron, consisting of 34 ships of the line, was commanded by Admiral George RODNEY; the French, who had 29 ships, were commanded by Admiral the Comte de GRASSE. Slowed down by the large CONVOY needed for their expedition to Jamaica, they were brought to battle by the British on April 12 near the Saints, a group of islands in the channel between Dominica and Guadeloupe.

In its early stages the engagement was fought by the two sides moving in parallel lines and exchanging BROADSIDES. As the wind dropped, de Grasse's ability to maneuver was reduced and the French formation began to break down. Rodney used the opportunity presented to him to great effect, and three British ships, including the *Formidable*, his FLAGSHIP, pierced the French line in two places. The rear division, under the command of Admiral Sir Samuel HOOD, followed. This operation completed the disorganization of the French line, which came under attack from both sides. The British inflicted severe damage on three French ships. De Grasse had no choice but to withdraw, and as the wind picked up he sought to escape westward.

The English managed to capture four more enemy ships, including the *Ville de Paris*, the fleet flagship, and the French commander. The remainder of the French fleet, now under the command of Admiral de Vaudreuil, managed to evade the British and leave the area. Rodney pursued them for a while but without result. The battle had been an important British victory in which they had broken the enemy line for the first time during the War of Independence. However, it came too late to affect the outcome of the war.

George B. Mundy, *The Life and Correspondence of the Late Admiral Rodney*, 2 vols., London, 1830.

Salerno Landings
September 9–17, 1943

The Allied invasion of Italy during WORLD WAR II, 1939–45 (code-named Avalanche) began with landings at the port of Salerno, south of Naples, in September 1943. There were to be other Allied landings at Reggio de Calabria and Taranto. An Allied naval task force, commanded by U.S. Vice Admiral Kent HEWITT, transported the American Fifth Army under General Mark Clark to the Salerno landing site. Although land-based air cover could be provided, Salerno was a poor location for the operation because surprise could not be achieved. As a result, the initial landings were heavily opposed and led to strong German counterattacks. Reinforcements were landed, and naval bombardments from the British battleships WARSPITE and *Valiant* were stepped up. The effectiveness of the naval bombardment eventually repelled the Germans and enabled the Americans to link up with other invading Allied forces. The Allies took their first key objective, Naples, on October 1. Several Allied warships were hit by the German Fritz-X guided bomb during the course of this operation. Used for the first time at Salerno, these 3,900- pound (1,769-kg) armor-piercing bombs damaged the British warship *Warspite* and the cruiser *Uganda* as well as the American cruiser *Savannah*.

David Mason, *Salerno. Foothold in Europe*, London, 1972.

Sampson, William Thomas
1840–1902

$\mathcal{A}$merican naval officer. Born in Palmyra, New York on February 9, 1840, William Thomas Sampson entered the navy in 1857, graduating top of his class at the U.S. Naval Academy in 1861. He saw service in the AMERICAN CIVIL WAR, 1861–65, with the Potomac Flotilla and the East Gulf Blockading Squadron. Over the next couple of decades, he became a familiar face at the naval academy, serving as an instructor of its training ship, later as chair of the department of natural philosophy and subsequently heading the department of physics and chemistry. From 1886 to 1890 he was the academy's thirteenth superintendent. A student of science and an advocate of reforms in the naval service, he was instrumental in advances in naval ordnance as a member of the International Prime Meridian and Time Conference in 1884 and an American delegate to the International Maritime Conference in 1887.

One of the founders of the Naval Institute in 1873, he contributed to that forum's publications as well as serving as the institute's president from 1898 to 1902. While commanding the Naval Torpedo Station at Newport, Rhode Island, Sampson played a very important part in the creation of the Naval War College there in 1884. While he was extremely influential, by far the most famous part of his career came in 1898, when he headed the commission that investigated the explosion of the U.S.S. MAINE in Havana harbor that helped propel the United States to declare war against Spain. He was then given command of the North Atlantic Squadron in 1898 during that war, imposing a BLOCKADE around Cuba. He received much of the credit for the decisive Battle of SANTIAGO on July 3, 1898, in which the Spanish fleet was destroyed. A bitter controversy over credit for the battle subsequently arose between himself and Commodore Winfield Scott SCHLEY although the weight of evidence strongly favors the former. Rear admiral Sampson died on May 6, 1902 in Washington, D.C.

Richard S. West, Jr., *Admirals of the American Empire*, Indianapolis, 1948.

San Domingo, Battle of
February 6, 1806

$\mathcal{D}$uring the latter stages of the FRENCH REVOLUTIONARY AND NAPOLEONIC WARS, 1792–1815, in December 1805, a French squadron escaped from Brest into the Atlantic some two months after the British victory at TRAFALGAR. Consisting of four ships of the line and two frigates commanded by Rear Admiral Leissègues, its destination was the West Indies. A British force under the command of Rear Admiral Sir John Duckworth learned of the French movement as it was cruising off Cadiz and

pursued the enemy squadron across the Atlantic, reaching Barbados on January 12, 1806.

There Duckworth was reinforced by Rear Admiral Thomas COCHRANE, commander in chief of the Leeward Islands station. On February 6 the British squadron—five ships of the line and two frigates—made contact with the French in Occa Bay off the eastern end of San Domingo, where they were unloading supplies. The French were trapped, and during an action lasting 90 minutes, all four French ships of the line were either captured or destroyed. Only the escape of the two French frigates slightly tarnished this successful British operation.

Santa Cruz, Battle of
April 20, 1657

$\mathcal{I}$n 1656 England joined France in an effort to challenge Spanish hegemony over the West Indies. England's first victory was the capture of the Spanish treasure fleet off Cadiz in September 1656. During the winter of 1656–57, Admiral Robert BLAKE imposed an extensive naval blockade on Cadiz and the adjoining coast. In the spring he learned that another Spanish treasure fleet had arrived in the Canary Islands from the West Indies. He quickly left his blockade at Cadiz and, on April 20, arrived off Santa Cruz de Tenerife with 25 warships. At anchor within the well-protected harbor were 16 Spanish galleons and their escorts.

In a well-conceived and executed operation, a detachment of 12 English ships, under the command of Rear Admiral Richard Stanyer, entered the harbor and began attacking the treasure galleons. Blake followed with the remainder of the fleet, which concentrated on the destruction of the shore forts. Within a few hours the entire Spanish fleet had been burned or blown up. English casualties of 170 were relatively light compared to those of the Spanish; only one of Blake's ships, the *Speaker*, was badly damaged, but she was still capable of returning home. The Battle of Santa Cruz was to be Admiral Blake's last action: He died before his squadron reached Plymouth on the return voyage.

Santa Cruz Islands, Battle of
October 26, 1942

$\mathcal{T}$he fourth in a series of naval engagements between the Americans and Japanese as they struggled for control of the SOLOMON ISLANDS during WORLD WAR II, 1939–45. (See also the Battles of EASTERN SOLOMONS; CAPE ESPERANCE; SAVO ISLAND). The focus of this conflict was the ground battle for GUADALCANAL. The Americans were on constant alert for Japanese attempts to resupply their units by sea: A Japanese force of four aircraft carriers under Vice Admiral

Nobutake KONDO was waiting off the Santa Cruz Islands for precisely this purpose. On October 24, 1942 Admiral William HALSEY ordered Task Forces 16 and 17 to search the sea surrounding the Santa Cruz Islands, some 250 miles (402 km) east of the Lower Solomons.

On October 26 the Americans discovered Kondo's squadron, and dive-bombers from the carrier ENTERPRISE were dispatched. At more or less the same time the Japanese located the Americans, and 65 Japanese bombers took off in the direction of the American fleet. When the opposing air squadrons met midway between the fleets, the Japanese fighters heavily damaged the American aircraft. The *Enterprise* herself escaped the first wave of air attacks as the weather closed in but was badly damaged later. The full weight of the Japanese onslaught fell on the carrier *Hornet*, which suffered torpedo and suicide attacks before eventually sinking. Meanwhile, simultaneous American attacks on the Japanese fleet caused heavy damage to the carriers *Zuiho* and *Shokaku*. Although the Japanese had suffered heavy aircrew losses they would find difficult to replace, they had won a tactical victory against the Americans, who were left for a while without any fully operational carriers in the Pacific. This did not, however, delay operations, and the *Enterprise* was used in the Battle of Guadalcanal while undergoing repairs.

Santa Marta, Battle of
August 20–24, 1702

A naval engagement in the West Indies between English and French squadrons in the opening stages of the War of the SPANISH SUCCESSION, 1701–13. The action began as six English ships of the line, under the command of Admiral John BENBOW, met a smaller French force off the SPANISH MAIN. Despite the favorable odds for the English, the engagement was notable for the remarkable conduct of four of Benbow's captains, who ignored Benbow's commands to join the battle. As a result, four ships—the *Defiance*, *Greenwich*, *Pendennis*, and *Windsor*—played no part in the battle.

Supported only by the *Ruby* and the *Falmouth*, Benbow, who flew his flag in the *Breda*, was under considerable pressure from the enemy during a running battle that lasted four days. He abandoned the action only after his ship sustained serious damage and he was injured by a CHAIN-SHOT. Benbow then made for Jamaica, where the four captains who had failed to support him were tried for cowardice; two received the death penalty. This trial and its outcome had the full support of the French commander, who was so incensed at the contemptible behavior of Benbow's captains that he wrote to Benbow: " . . . as for those cowardly captains who deserted you, hang them up; for, by God, they deserve it." Benbow himself was casualty of the battle; soon afterward he died from his wounds.

Santiago, Battle of
July 3, 1898

T he decisive battle of the SPANISH-AMERICAN WAR of 1898 and Spain's second naval defeat in that war. Within days following the American declaration of war, April 25, 1898, a Spanish squadron under Admiral Pascual CERVERA had left for Cuba. Outdated and ill-equipped, its four cruisers and two destroyers were no match for the much more powerful U.S. fleet. On its arrival at Santiago on May 19, it was subject to a BLOCKADE by American ships under the command of Rear Admiral William SAMPSON, lasting for weeks. Following the American invasion of Cuba on June 22, it seemed likely that Santiago would soon fall. Admiral Cervera decided to break out.

At 9:30 A.M. on July 3, he left the safety of Santiago harbor and was soon engaged by four American battleships and a cruiser. Within minutes the cruisers *Infanta Maria Teresa*, Cervera's flagship, and *Almirante Oquendo* were set on fire and run aground. As Cervera proceeded westward the *Vizcaya* became the third Spanish cruiser to meet the same end. His two destroyers had already been badly damaged. Only the *Cristóbal Colón*, the fastest Spanish ship, seemed to have a chance of survival, but she was caught after a 50-mile (80-km) chase. By the end of this brief battle the entire Spanish squadron had been destroyed and 1,800 survivors, including Cervera himself, had been taken prisoner. The Americans, on the other hand, sustained only superficial damage and virtually no casualties.

The decisive defeat at Santiago brought Spain quickly to the negotiating table. An armistice was a signed on August 12 and was followed, in December, by a peace treaty that gave the Americans substantial territorial gains.

David F. Trask, *The War with Spain in 1898*, New York, 1981.

Santissima Trinidad

A n 18th-century Spanish SHIP OF THE LINE, notable as the only four-deck sailing man-of-war ever produced. The *Santissima Trinidad* began life as a three-decker but was modified substantially when her original forecastle and quarterdeck were linked by a flush upper deck. The main advantage of these four decks was that they could accommodate 136 guns. In her new form she was then the largest ship in the world and saw service during the FRENCH REVOLUTIONARY AND NAPOLEONIC WARS, 1792–1815. She fought against the British without success at the Battle of CAPE ST. VINCENT, February 1797, and was sunk at the Battle of TRAFALGAR, 1805.

Saratoga, U.S.S.

F ive American warships have been named *Saratoga*, in memory of the American land victory at Saratoga,

New York during the AMERICAN WAR OF INDEPENDENCE, 1775–83. The most notable ship of this name to serve in the United States Navy was an AIRCRAFT CARRIER of WORLD WAR II, 1939–45. Like her sister ship the *LEXINGTON,* the *Saratoga* began life as a BATTLE CRUISER but was completed as a carrier due to the provisions of the Treaty of Westminster, 1922. Launched in 1927, she was only the second American carrier to be completed and was, with the *Lexington,* the largest and fastest ship of her type. Designed to accommodate 90 aircraft, she had a displacement of 33,000 tons and was 888 feet (270.66 m) long, with a beam of 130 feet (39.62 m). Her armament included eight 8-inch (20-cm) guns, and she had a maximum speed of over 33 knots. The *Saratoga* served in the Pacific throughout the war, although she was out of action for long periods, being damaged once by KAMIKAZE pilots and twice by torpedoes. After the war she met her end as a target in an atomic bomb test off Bikini Atoll in 1946.

Saumarez, James, Baron de
1757–1836

*B*ritish naval commander, one of Horatio NELSON's "band of brothers" who served with distinction during a long career of some 60 years extending from the AMERICAN WAR OF INDEPENDENCE, 1775–83, to a period of shore command at Plymouth, 1824–27. Saumarez, whose family originated in the Channel Islands, first came to notice during the FRENCH REVOLUTIONARY AND NAPOLEONIC WARS, 1792–1815, when he captured a French frigate off Cherbourg at the beginning of the conflict—an achievement for which he was knighted. As captain of the *ORION,* a 74-gun ship, he distinguished himself at the Battles of the ÎLE DE GROIX, 1795, and CAPE ST. VINCENT, 1797. He fought as Lord Nelson's second-in-command at the Battle of the NILE, 1798.

Rewarded with a baronetcy and flag rank, he quickly justified his new status, defeating a Franco-Spanish force off Cadiz in 1801. During the Napoleonic Wars, 1803–15, Saumarez at first operated in the English Channel but later was appointed to the command of the British Baltic fleet, 1809–13. Flying his flag in the *VICTORY,* he operated in support of Sweden and the protection of that country's trading links. In the closing stages of the war Saumarez was promoted to the rank of full admiral; he remained in the service during the years of peace that followed.

A. N. Ryan ed., *The Saumarez Papers,* London, 1968.

Saunders, Sir Charles
1713–75

*B*ritish naval commander who served with distinction as naval commander in chief of the expedition to capture QUEBEC, 1759, from the French during the SEVEN YEARS' WAR, 1756–63. Saunders gained promotion early in his career as commander of a BRIG in the expedition around the world led by Commodore George ANSON in 1740–44. Anson advanced him to the rank of post-captain in command of one of the ships captured during the expedition. He gained combat experience during the War of the AUSTRIAN SUCCESSION, 1740–48, commanding the *Yarmouth* at the second battle of CAPE FINISTERRE, October 1747. In the opening phase of the Seven Years' War he served in the Mediterranean as a rear admiral under Admiral Edward HAWKE. When Hawke returned to London in 1756 after the loss of Minorca, Saunders succeeded him as commander in chief in the Mediterranean.

With Lord Anson as First Lord of the Admiralty, Saunders's wartime career was almost certain to prosper, and in 1759 he was selected to lead the naval element of the expedition to capture Quebec. Although his role was not as prominent as that played by General James Wolfe, the army commander, Saunders made a major contribution to the success of the operation by bringing large ships up the hazardous St. Lawrence River to Quebec for the first time. With his ships moored off Quebec, he was able to operate in support of the British ground forces that eventually seized Quebec and paved the way for the capture of Canada. In his later career Saunders served at the ADMIRALTY and, in 1766, was briefly First Lord.

Savo Island, Battle of
August 9, 1942

*T*he first of several naval engagements fought off GUADALCANAL during the struggle for control of the SOLOMON ISLANDS in the Pacific during WORLD WAR II, 1939–45. American landings on Guadalcanal had begun on August 7, 1942; only a few hours later, during the night of August 8–9, a Japanese cruiser squadron responded by seeking to destroy the transports that were unloading off the island. The Japanese force, commanded by Vice-Admiral Gunichi Mikawa, consisted of seven cruisers and a destroyer. The American transports were protected by an Allied cruiser force under the command of British Rear Admiral Sir Victor CRUTCHLEY, who left to attend a conference before the battle began. The cruiser force was divided into two groups to protect the two approaches to the transports, which ran north or south of Savo Island. The northern group consisted of three cruisers and one destroyer; the southern group included three cruisers and two destroyers.

Two destroyers were deployed beyond the two groups as scouts, but despite this the Allies were taken by surprise. Mikawa attacked the southern group at night and hit the cruisers *Canberra* and *Chicago* before turning his attention northward. He sunk two more cruisers—the *Vincennes* and

Quincy—and damaged a third (the *Astoria*), which sank the following day. By this time Mikawa was could have ordered an attack on the American transports, but he also was concerned about his own vulnerability to air attack. Unaware that Rear Admiral Frank FLETCHER's carrier force already had left the area, and fearing an air attack, he decided to withdraw. Mikawa's incomplete Japanese victory was subject to much criticism within the navy despite the fact that four Allied cruisers and a destroyer had been sunk in an action lasting some 30 minutes. The only Japanese loss was the cruiser *Kako*, which was torpedoed by an American submarine as she left the area. Although Savo Island was a serious tactical failure, the Allies learned the lessons of defeat, particularly the need for improved communications. The survival of the American transport fleet would be critical in determining the outcome of the entire Guadalcanal campaign.

Scapa Flow

$\mathcal{A}$ large area of enclosed water in the Orkney Islands, to the north of Scotland, that was an important anchorage for the British GRAND FLEET during WORLD WAR I, 1914–18. It was from here that the fleet left for the Battle of JUTLAND in May 1916. At the end of the war, the German HIGH SEAS FLEET, under the command of Admiral Ludwig von REUTER, was interned at Scapa Flow, pending the negotiation of a peace treaty. When their surrender was imminent, the Germans successfully scuttled the ships on June 21, 1919 rather than turn them over to Britain. The ships later were raised and towed away for breaking. Scapa Flow also served as an anchorage for the British Home Fleet during WORLD WAR II, 1939–45.

Although it was generally a secure base, the defenses of Scapa Flow were breached early in the war with devastating results. On October 14, 1939 the elderly super-dreadnought *ROYAL OAK* was torpedoed by the German U-boat *U-47*, which had managed to penetrate Scapa Flow's defenses by following another ship into the sheltered anchorage. Three torpedoes detonated the *Royal Oak*'s magazine and she sank, taking 833 crew with her. The disaster led to the construction of improved defenses. Scapa Flow survived as a naval base until 1956.

Dan van der Vat, *The Grand Scuttle: The Sinking of the German Fleet at Scapa Flow in 1919*, Annapolis, 1985.

Scharnhorst (1)

$\mathcal{G}$erman armored CRUISER of WORLD WAR I, 1914–18, launched in 1906. With a displacement of more than 12,000 tons, the *Scharnhorst* was equipped with 6.7-inch (17-cm) main armament. Like other German ships of this type during the pre-1914 period, the *Scharnhorst* and her sister ship, the *GNEISENAU*, were designed to act as station ships in the German colonies abroad rather than serve with the main battle fleet. Both ships were stationed at Tsingtao, the German colony in China, on the outbreak of World War I, and were the principal units of Vice Admiral Maximilian Graf von SPEE's East Asiatic Squadron.

In August 1914 von Spee's force started to move east across the Pacific with the objective of disrupting British trade with South America before turning for home. The *Scharnhorst* and the *Gneisenau*, together with three light cruisers, successfully engaged a force under the command of Rear Admiral Sir Christopher CRADOCK at the Battle of

The British fleet anchorage at Scapa Flow in the Orkney Islands   *(Copyright © National Maritime Museum, Greenwich, London)*

Survivors from the German cruiser *Gneisenau* being picked up by the British battle cruiser *Invincible* after the Battle of the Falkland Islands, 1914   *(Copyright © Imperial War Museum, London)*

CORONEL, off the coast of Chile, on November 1, 1914. The British suffered a severe defeat but an opportunity for revenge soon appeared. Von Spee's force entered the South Atlantic but its objective of attacking the Falklands was abandoned when it encountered Sir Doveton STURDEE's much more powerful force there on December 8. During the Battle of the FALKLAND ISLANDS, both the *Scharnhorst* and the *Gneisenau* were sunk after a long pursuit, both ships maintaining a determined resistance to the end. The *Scharnhorst* went down taking all her crew with her, but there were some 200 survivors from the *Gneisenau.*

Scharnhorst (2)

German BATTLE CRUISER of WORLD WAR II, 1939–45, launched in 1936. Constructed in secret in violation of the terms of the Treaty of Versailles, 1919, the *Scharnhorst* had a displacement of 31,800 tons. Her steam turbine engines gave her a maximum speed of 32 knots and a range of 10,000 miles (16,093 km). The *Scharnhorst*'s main armament consisted of nine 11-inch (28-cm) guns in three triple turrets. She also had 12 5.9-inch (15-cm) guns in six twin turret and 14 4.1-inch (10-cm) guns in twin turrets. The *Scharnhorst* was given greater armor protection than many comparable ships of the period, and her defensive armament—26 antiaircraft guns—was generous. Operated by a crew of 1,840, she also was equipped to carry four aircraft. When World War II began she operated against British merchant shipping in the Atlantic in company with her sister ship the *Gneisenau*, which was constructed to similar specifications.

During two Atlantic cruises, in 1940–41, the two ships sank 22 ships of 115,622 tons, including the ARMED MERCHANT CRUISER *RAWALPINDI.* They also participated in the Norwegian campaign, 1940, when they sank the British aircraft carrier *GLORIOUS* and two destroyers. At the end of their second Atlantic cruise they returned to Brest, where they came under frequent attack from the Royal Air Force. On February 12, 1942 the two ships broke out from Brest in the CHANNEL DASH; both managed to reach home with relatively little damage. The *Gneisenau* subsequently was

The German battle cruiser *Scharnhorst* under aerial attack in 1941   *(Copyright © National Maritime Museum, Greenwich, London)*

damaged in an air raid, and the *Scharnhorst* returned to sea once minor repairs had been completed. She operated with the battleship TIRPITZ against the Allied ARCTIC CONVOYS. On September 6, 1943 she bombarded Spitzbergen but finally met her end at the Battle of NORTH CAPE, December 26. Badly damaged by gunfire from the *DUKE OF YORK,* a British battleship, she was sunk by a torpedo from a cruiser with the loss of 1,864 men.

Richard Garrett, *Scharnhorst and Gneisenau,* London, 1979.

Scheer, Reinhard
1863–1928

Commander in chief of the German HIGH SEAS FLEET at the Battle of JUTLAND, May 1916, Reinhard Scheer headed the Second Battle Squadron, which was composed of pre-dreadnought battleships, at the beginning of the war. Scheer had been a torpedo specialist in his earlier naval career and, in 1912, had been appointed chief of staff to the commander in chief. He moved to the command of the Third Battle Squadron, which operated dreadnoughts, in December 1914. When Hugo von Pohl left the command of the High Seas Fleet because of ill health, Scheer was appointed in his place in January 1916.

Scheer raised his flag in the battleship *Friedrich der Grosse*. He proved to be an outstanding fleet commander who recognized the importance of training and of maintaining the morale of his officers and men. Scheer planned a more active role for the main battle fleet than his predecessor had, with the aim of turning the balance of naval power in Germany's favor. U-boats would play an important part in this new offensive, but the surface fleet, assisted by aerial reconnaissance, would seek out isolated British squadrons.

At the Battle of Jutland, he used Admiral Franz von HIPPER's scouting force to entice Admiral Sir David BEATTY's Battlecruiser Force from its base and draw it toward the main German fleet. During the course of the battle

Admiral Reinhard Scheer: commander of the German High Seas Fleet at the Battle of Jutland, 1916 *(Copyright © Imperial War Museum, London)*

do to influence the course of events. He retired from the navy soon after the Armistice.

Richard Hough, *The Great War at Sea, 1914–1918*, Oxford, 1983.

Schepke, Joachim
1912–41

German U-BOAT ace of WORLD WAR II, 1939–45, responsible for the destruction of 39 enemy ships with a total displacement of 159,130 tons. Schepke, who took part in the Battle of the ATLANTIC, 1939–45, with other U-boats in WOLF PACKS, preferred to attack at night with his boat on the surface. At first he proved to be difficult to detect and was able to move freely among the ships of a CONVOY inflicting heavy losses. On one notable occasion, in September 1940, Schepke sank seven merchant ships of 50,340 tons from a single convoy. His favored tactics were, however, potentially very risky, particularly once more effective methods of detection had appeared. This was the case on March 15, 1941 when *U-100*, which Schepke commanded, was identified by RADAR as she surfaced at full speed to attack an Allied convoy. The British destroyer *Vanoc* rammed and sank her before she could move into action. Schepke, one of Germany's leading U-boat aces, lost his life; only seven members of his crew survived.

Scheveningen, Battle of
July 31, 1653

The final engagement of the First ANGLO-DUTCH WAR, 1652–54, the Battle of Scheveningen (or the Texel, as it is sometimes known) was the result of a Dutch attempt to break the blockade imposed by the English following their victory at the GABBARD, June 2–3, 1653.

On July 24 Admiral Marten TROMP's fleet of 100 ships left its base on the Maas River for the island of Texel, where an English presence offshore had imprisoned a smaller squadron of 37 ships (including ten FIRESHIPS) under Admiral Witte de WITT. General George MONCK, who commanded the blockading fleet of about 100 men-of-war, first sighted Tromp's squadron off the Texel on July 29. He was lured southward in pursuit of the Dutch, making contact with them some five hours later off Katwijk. About 30 ships eventually were involved in this partial engagement, but the main purpose of the operation—to enable de With to leave the Texel—already had been achieved. Delayed by storms, the two Dutch squadrons met off Scheveningen during the afternoon of the next day, giving Tromp a superiority of about 30 ships.

The two fleets met off Scheveningen at 7 A.M. on July 31. The Dutch suffered a major setback during the first

Scheer was himself lured toward the GRAND FLEET, unaware of its presence in the area. Cut off from his base by Admiral Sir John JELLICOE, Scheer tried twice to find a way around the British fleet. Pounded by superior forces, he extricated himself with great skill on both occasions, aided by poor visibility that hampered the British. During the night he finally managed to pass behind the Grand Fleet, which was hindered by a lack of intelligence, and made for home. On his return home Scheer presented Jutland as a victory, but although his forces had sunk more ships than had the Grand Fleet, his claim was an empty one. Strategically Jutland was a British victory, and Germany was compelled to return to unrestricted submarine warfare to strike effectively at England.

Apart from an abortive sortie in April 1918, Scheer kept the High Seas Fleet in port for the rest of the war. In August 1918 the German naval high command was reorganized and Scheer was appointed to the head of the new supreme command. Beyond authorizing a massive new submarine construction program, there was little he could

English and Dutch naval forces both suffered heavy losses at the Battle of Scheveningen, 1653, the last engagement of the first Anglo-Dutch War, 1652–54 *(Copyright © National Maritime Museum, Greenwich, London)*

stages of the battle when Tromp was killed by a musket ball as his flagship led the attack on the English fleet. Vice Admiral Jan EVERTSEN assumed command, with Tromp's death being concealed for many hours to avoid undermining Dutch morale. The heaviest fighting took place in the morning, when neither side seemed to be in the ascendant, but during the afternoon the Dutch gradually conceded. By 8 P.M. they had retreated north toward the Texel, having suffered many casualties and the destruction of up to 30 men-of-war. English losses were less, although still considerable—1,000 killed or wounded. With the death of their greatest admiral and a much-reduced fleet, the Dutch lost the will to continue to fight. The Treaty of Westminster, April 5, 1654, finally brought the war to an end on terms favorable to England.

Schley, Winfield Scott
1839–1911

*A*merican naval officer, active in the latter half of the 19th century. Born near Frederick, Maryland on October 9, 1839, Schley entered the navy in 1856. In the AMERICAN CIVIL WAR, 1861–65, he gained distinction for dangerous volunteer duty in small boats against enemy fire while on BLOCKADE duty off Mobile Bay in 1861–62. He also participated in nearly all the engagements during the spring and summer of 1863 leading up to the capture of Port Hudson, the last Confederate stronghold on the Mississippi River to fall to Union forces. Between tours as an instructor at the U.S. Naval Academy, he served with the Asiatic Squadron in 1871 and took part in the American attack on the Salee River forts in Korea in an unsuccessful attempt to open the area to foreign trade. In 1884 he headed the Greely Relief Expedition, rescuing army Lieutenant Adolphus Greely and six other survivors who had encountered difficulties during their attempt to reach the North Pole.

It was during the SPANISH-AMERICAN WAR of 1898 that Schley gained his greatest notoriety. He was given command of the "Flying Squadron," designed to defend the eastern seaboard of the United States from any possible attack by Spanish naval forces. When the contest focused on Cuba, Schley led the American forces in the decisive action at SANTIAGO, July 3, 1898, that destroyed the Spanish fleet. Sadly, he and Rear Admiral William T. SAMPSON became embroiled in a controversy over who should receive the credit for the victory. It began when Sampson publicly criticized Schley on the grounds that his conduct in the action lacked energy. The accusations were without substance, made by a man who was terminally ill with Alzheimer's disease, but they did little to enhance Schley's reputation. Retiring in 1901, he died in New York City on October 2, 1911.

Richard S. West, Jr., *Admirals of the American Empire*, Indianapolis, 1948.

Schnellboote

The German Schnellboote (fast boat) was one of the most successful motor TORPEDO BOAT designs of WORLD WAR II, 1939–45. Produced in several variants, the S-boats (known as E-boats by the British and Americans) were first developed in the 1930s. They had a displacement of just over 100 tons and were 106 feet (32 m) in length. Powered by three-shaft Daimler-Benz diesel engines, they had a maximum speed of 42 knots, which exceeded the performance of their English counterparts. The S-boats typically were equipped with two torpedo tubes and two ANTIAIRCRAFT GUNS. Larger versions, produced from 1944, carried up to six antiaircraft guns as well as replacement torpedo tubes or a supply of mines. They were operated by a crew of 23. The GERMAN NAVY used these fast and maneuverable boats with great success. They represented a serious threat to British shipping in the English Channel and along the east coast of Britain until they were constrained by Allied air power and the use of RADAR. The S-boat also was successfully deployed in operations against the SOVIET NAVY in the Baltic and the Black Sea.

Bryan Cooper, *The E-boat Threat*, London, 1976.

Schooneveld, Battles of
May 28 and June 4, 1673

The opening battles of the second year of the Third ANGLO-DUTCH War, 1672–74, took place in the long, narrow basin guarding the entrance to the Scheldt Estuary, where the Dutch fleet under Admiral Michiel de RUYTER had its anchorage. Ranged against the 52 Dutch ships were the combined naval forces of the English and French, which amounted to some 80 SHIPS OF THE LINE. The British fleet was commanded by Prince RUPERT, who raised his flag in the *Royal Charles*; Sir Edward SPRAGGE was his second-in-command. The French were commanded by Admiral Louis d'Estrées. The combined force moved across the English Channel with the aim of defeating the smaller Dutch fleet and then landing ground troops.

With the Dutch fleet positioned among the sandbanks of the estuary, Prince Rupert hesitated for three days without taking any action. Before he could attack, de Ruyter seized the initiative when a favorable wind developed. The battle, which began at noon on May 28, lasted for some nine hours. The allied force never managed to gain the advantage, and they eventually withdrew with the loss of two French ships. The Dutch also lost a 70-gun ship. The allies anchored off the Oster Bank and carried out emergency repairs. De Ruyter returned to the attack on June 4, some seven days later, when the wind was again in his favor. The outcome was again indecisive, although the allies were forced to withdraw from the Dutch coast to carry out further repairs. It was not until the Battle of the TEXEL, August 11, 1673, that an allied invasion was once more threatened.

Sciré

Italian SUBMARINE of World War II, a member of the 17-strong Adua class that was completed in 1936–38. These 600-ton submarines were 197 feet 5 inch (125.2 m) in length and had a beam of 21 feet 2 inches (6.45 m). Operated by a crew of 46, they had a surface speed of 14 knots, which reduced to 7½ knots when submerged. The *Sciré* was one of two Adua-class boats—the other was the *Gondar*—that was modified to transport human torpedoes to within range of their intended targets. To accommodate these weapons, which were nicknamed *Maiale* (or Pig), the standard 100-mm gun was removed and three cylinders were welded to the deck casing. In 1940–41 the *Sciré* delivered human torpedoes to the Bay of Gibraltar, where they operated successfully against enemy merchant shipping. On December 19, 1941 three Italian human torpedoes penetrated Alexandria harbor and caused heavy damage to the British battleships QUEEN ELIZABETH and *Valiant*. In August 1942 the *Sciré* was sunk off Haifa, Palestine, while unloading her cargo of human torpedoes. See also MIDGET SUBMARINE.

Scott, Sir Percy Moreton
1853–1924

British admiral and leading naval gunnery expert who correctly assessed the impact of air power and the submarine on war at sea. Joining the Royal Navy in 1866, he quickly established himself as a gunnery specialist and, by 1890, had been appointed to the command of the gunnery school H.M.S. EXCELLENT. In this and later posts he made significant improvements in gunnery drill and pioneered the use of telescopic sights; as a result, much more accurate fire became the norm in the Royal Navy. In the latter part of his career he worked on the centralized control of gunnery. He produced a director sight that enabled a battleship's guns to be aimed and fired by means of a telescopic sight and an electrical control system (see DIRECTOR FIRE CONTROL SYSTEM). Scott had to overcome official reservations about the new system, but eventually it was adopted just before WORLD WAR I, 1914–18, giving the Royal Navy the edge over its opponents. In retirement he campaigned against the construction of new battleships on the grounds that their central role in naval warfare was coming to an end as the aircraft and submarine grew in importance.

Scott, Robert Falcon
1868–1912

British naval officer and explorer who commanded two Antarctic expeditions in 1901–4 and 1910–12. Born in Devonport of a seafaring family, he joined the Royal Navy at an early age. His naval career made steady progress and, in 1899, as a lieutenant commander, he was appointed to the command of the national Antarctic expedition. In August 1901 he left for Antarctica in the DISCOVERY with the aim of carrying out a scientific expedition in part of the New Zealand sector of the continent. The expedition, which lasted until 1904, was successful. During the course of this Antarctic journey, Scott traveled farther south than anyone before him. On his return to England Scott resumed his naval duties with the rank of captain. In 1909 he decided to return to Antarctica with the dual aim of reaching the South Pole and continuing the scientific work he began on the first expedition.

In June 1910 Scott left England in the *Terra Nova*. On his arrival in New Zealand he learned of a rival Norwegian expedition, led by Roald Amundsen, that was also aiming to reach the South Pole. Scott left on the 800-mile (1,287-km) journey in November 1911 and achieved his goal on January 18, 1912, but he was beaten by the rival Norwegian expedition, which had arrived there first. On the return journey, Scott and his party ran into severe difficulties, including poor weather conditions and insufficient supplies. Two members of the party had died by the time the rest, including Scott, perished in a severe blizzard only 11 miles (18 km) from the safety of their base camp. Captain Scott was an outstanding explorer and leader who made a major contribution to the world's knowledge about Antarctica.

Apsley Cherry-Garrard, *The Worst Journey in the World*, London, 1922.

Sea Beggars

The origins of the Dutch navy, which was formed in the 17th century, are to be found in the Sea Beggars, the nickname for a group of Dutch exiles that had been formed during the previous century. Operating mainly from the French Huguenot port of La Rochelle, they were issued LETTERS OF MARQUE by William the Silent, who led the revolt of the Netherlands against the Spanish occupation of the country. They raised funds for the cause by acts of PIRACY. Under the leadership of Guillaume de la Marck, the Sea Beggars, with 25 ships, captured the Dutch port of Brill in Zeeland in 1572.

This initial gain was followed by the capture of Flushing a week later, and soon was extended to cover most of the provinces of Holland and Zeeland. A year later the Sea Beggars defeated a larger Spanish FLOTILLA on the Zuider Zee. Seven ships were captured and the Count of Bossu was taken prisoner. In another operation the Sea Beggars, who by now dominated the sea off the Netherlands' coast, successfully engaged the Spaniards in Haarlem Lake. The Sea Beggars, who were soon to lose their character as PRIVATEERS, had made an important contribution to the Dutch revolt against Spain. They also provided the nucleus of the new national navy and served as a valuable training ground for Dutch naval leaders.

Jaap R. Bruijn, *The Dutch Navy of the Seventeenth and Eighteenth Centuries*, Columbia, S.C., 1993.

Seal

An elite American amphibious force, the SEAL (sea, air, land) teams originated in 1942, soon after the United States entered WORLD WAR II, 1939–45. The force was first known as the Navy Combat Demolition Unit and was responsible for clearing beaches and harbor installations in advance of major amphibious landings, although it was later to acquire wider combat functions. Underwater demolition teams (UDTs) were established to undertake specific operations in North Africa, NORMANDY and the PACIFIC. Although these units were scaled down at the end of the war, they returned to service in the KOREAN WAR, 1950–53 and have been heavily employed ever since, including VIETNAM, 1964–75, the GRENADA INVASION, 1983, and the GULF WAR, 1991. In the latter conflict, the SEALs were the first Allied troops to enter Kuwait City as the Iraqi army retreated.

The UDTs were reconstituted as the SEALs from 1962; today the force consists of about 2,000 men. Its functions are similar to those of other elite amphibious forces, including reconnaissance, sabotage, demolition and combat. A separate SEAL unit has specialist antiterrorist responsibilities. Entry standards to the SEALs are necessarily high, and the training is extremely demanding. The U.S. Navy has also established Special Boat Units responsible for delivering SEAL teams as close as possible to their objective and for recovering them once their mission has been completed. (See also AMPHIBIOUS WARFARE.)

Hans Halberstadt, *U.S. Navy SEALS,* Osceola, Wis., 1993.

Seeadler

The only square-rigged ship to be used as a commerce raider during WORLD WAR I, 1914–18, the *Seeadler* was the former merchant vessel the *Pass of Balmaha.* She had a displacement of 1,571 tons and an auxiliary diesel engine. In July 1915, while in British custody, this American-owned ship was seized by a German U-BOAT while cruising in the North Sea. The German Admiralty was persuaded to use her as a commerce raider, and she left base on December 21, 1916 under the command of Count Felix von Luckner. The idea proved to be sound: Cruising the Atlantic and Pacific Oceans, she was responsible for the destruction of as many as 16 Allied merchant vessels. Early in August 1917 her career came to an abrupt end when she was wrecked in the Society Islands. (See also COMMERCE RAIDING.)

Semmes, Raphael
1809–77

American naval officer. Born in Charles County, Maryland in 1809, Raphael Semmes entered the navy as a midshipman in 1826. A routine career followed until 1846, when, as commander of the brig *Somers* on blockade duty during the Mexican-American War, he lost his ship in a storm. Exonerated of any blame, he continued to serve during the war with Mexico, receiving gallantry citations for his actions. Semmes's real place in naval history came during the AMERICAN CIVIL WAR, 1861–65, when he became a commerce raider for the Confederacy, first on the *Sumter* then on the most famous of all Confederate raiders, the C.S.S. ALABAMA. Capturing over 80 vessels, he commanded the *Alabama* over vast areas ranging from the Atlantic to the Indian Oceans. His elusive efforts created havoc with northern shipping routes and insurance fares, forcing many vessels to change from American to foreign registry. Planning an overhaul in Cherbourg, France, in June 1864, he was challenged by the U.S.S. KEARSARGE as he approached the French 3-mile (4.8-km) limit. Accepting the challenge by the more powerful and cleaner Union ship, the *Alabama* received the worst of the exchange and sank. Semmes was rescued by an English pleasure boat that took him to England. Eventually he returned to the Confederacy and commanded the naval squadron on Virginia's James River. Destroying his command as Richmond fell, he served a brief spell in prison before being pardoned. He later prac-

ticed law in Mobile, Alabama until his death in 1877. (See also CONFEDERATE NAVY.)

Warren F. Spencer, "Raphael Semmes: Confederate Raider," in *Captains of the Old Steam Navy: Makers of the American Naval Tradition, 1840–1880,* ed. James C. Bradford, Annapolis, 1986.

Seven Years' War
1756–63

A global war involving a coalition of France, Austria, Russia, Sweden and Saxony opposed to Great Britain and Prussia. The wide-scale conflict had three major linked elements: the war in Europe, in which Prussia's enemies sought to contain its expansionist ambitions; the colonial struggle in which the British and French fought for control of North America (where it was known as the French and Indian War), India, the West Indies and Africa; and the Anglo-French struggle for control of the seas. British naval operations began badly when MINORCA was lost to the French in June 1756. It was a disaster for which Admiral John BYNG was held responsible and later executed. Later British naval operations in Europe focused on the need to increase pressure on France, and, in 1757–58, a series of raids was mounted on the French coast from Rochefort to St. Malo. It is, however, unclear how much real impact these raids had on the course of events.

Conflict between the French and English in Canada had continued since the end of the War of the AUSTRIAN SUCCESSION, 1740–48, but soon intensified as the Seven Years' War began. In 1757 Britain launched a major offensive designed to remove the French from Canada. An early key success was the capture of LOUISBOURG in 1758 by a combined force under General Jeffrey Amherst and Admiral Edward BOSCAWEN. The capture of QUEBEC by British land and naval forces in 1759 was a decisive blow against the French, and soon the entire country was in English hands. These critical events had a direct impact on the naval aspect of the war in Europe, with France developing plans to invade England in order to reduce growing British military pressure in Europe and elsewhere. However, after two notable British naval victories, France soon was forced to abandon these plans. In the first, Admiral Boscawen destroyed the Toulon Fleet off LAGOS Bay, August 1759; three months later Admiral Edward HAWKE defeated the French off QUIBERON BAY, November 1759.

These victories had a direct impact on French ability to sustain operations in the West Indies, where, in 1762, the British secured a long list of gains. Following Spain's entry into the war in April 1762, Britain captured the Spanish possessions of Havana, Cuba and Manila in the Philippines. Hostilities ended with the Treaty of Paris, 1763, in which Britain secured Canada and retained the gains the Royal Navy had won in the West Indies. In the

Mediterranean the retention of Minorca, which had been taken by the French in 1756, was a further benefit.

Chronological List of Naval Events

Europe

1756

April 12	French troops land on Minorca and besiege British naval base at Port Mahon
May 17	Britain declares war on France
May 20	Battle of Minorca; British failure to defeat the French fleet and thus save Port Mahon results in the trial and execution of Admiral Byng

1758

August–September	British operations against the French coast

1759

August 18–19	Battle of Lagos; the French lose much of their Mediterranean fleet as Boscawen attacks
November 20	Battle of Quiberon Bay; Admiral Hawke defeats the French and removes the long-threatened invasion of Britain
1760–63	Britain dominates the seas

Indian Ocean

1757

January 2	Joint British expedition recaptures Calcutta

1758

April 29	Battle of the Bay of Bengal; British engage French in an inconclusive action
August 3	Battle of Negapatam; Admiral Pocock, the British commander, renews operation against the French

1759

September 10	Battle of Pondicherry, the third decisive engagement between Britain and France. Damage to the French squadron and the lack of local bases end France's hopes of a breakthrough in India

North America and the Pacific

1755

	Franco-British rivalry in North America leads to undeclared war
June 8	Action of the Strait of Belle Isle (Canada). Boscawen's blockade fails to prevent French reinforcements from reaching Quebec

1757

June–September	Combined operation against Louisbourg (Canada) abandoned

1758

May 30–July 27	Wolfe and Boscawen capture Louisbourg. The French lose six ships of the line as well as their naval base

1759

June–September	A combined British force takes Quebec

1760

April	The arrival of a British naval squadron breaks the French siege of Quebec
September 8	French dominion of Canada ends

1761

August	Spain rejoins the war in April 1762 but its fleet is powerless to intervene

1762

January 4	British operations against Martinique and other French possessions in the West Indies begin
June 20–August 10	British squadron captures Havana
October 5	British capture Manila and much of the Philippines

1763

February 10	Treaty of Paris

J. S. Corbett, *England in the Seven Years' War*, London, 1907.

Seydlitz

Flagship of the scouting force of the German HIGH SEAS FLEET during WORLD WAR I, 1914–18, the BATTLE CRUISER *Seydlitz* sustained serious damage at the Battles of DOGGER BANK, 1915, and JUTLAND, 1916. Hit as many as 25 times on the second occasion and badly flooded, she was the most severely damaged German ship to survive the battle. The British interned her at SCAPA FLOW at the end of the war, where she was scuttled on June 21, 1919. She was raised and scrapped in 1928.

Based on the Moltke class, the *Seydlitz*, which was completed in 1913, had an additional weather deck, a longer hull and a displacement of 24,610 tons. Armor and armament remained unchanged, but she had an increased speed of 26.5 knots. The *Seydlitz* was equipped with ten 11-inch (28-cm) main guns, twelve 5.9-inch (15-cm) secondary guns and four torpedo tubes. She was operated by a crew of 1,068.

Shannon, H.M.S.

A British FRIGATE of 52 guns, launched in 1806, that won a notable victory in the WAR OF 1812. Under the command of Captain (later Rear Admiral Sir) Philip BROKE, a noted gunnery officer, the *Shannon* was widely regarded as one of the best-trained and most efficient ships in the service. The power of her guns and the professionalism of her crew were evident when she engaged the *CHESAPEAKE,* an American 50-gun frigate, commanded by James LAWRENCE, off Boston on June 1, 1813. After an intense struggle lasting no more than 15 minutes, the *Chesapeake* surrendered, her crew having suffered 146 casualties. The victorious *Shannon* remained in ROYAL NAVY service in various roles until 1859.

Peter Padfield, *Broke and the Shannon,* London, 1968.

Sheffield, H.M.S.

*T*wo notable British warships have been named *Sheffield.* The earlier of these was a CRUISER of WORLD WAR II, 1939–45. The third member of the Town class, the *Sheffield* and her seven sister ships were constructed during the late 1930s in response to the appearance of similar ships in other navies, particularly the Japanese Navy. Conforming to the restrictions imposed on the construction of heavy cruisers by the London Naval Treaty, 1930, the *Sheffield* had a displacement of 9,100 tons and was armed with six 12-inch (30-cm) guns. Secondary armament included eight 4-inch (10-cm) antiaircraft guns, eight 2-pound (0.9-kg) antiaircraft guns and six 21-inch (53-cm) torpedo tubes.

The *Sheffield* served off Norway in 1940 before moving to the Mediterranean, where she operated with the RENOWN and the ARK ROYAL as part of FORCE H. She was involved in the bombardment of Italian defensive positions and in the pursuit of the BISMARCK in May 1941. Later she went north again, acting in support of the ARCTIC CONVOYS. On one notable occasion, on December 31, 1942, she repelled an attack on a CONVOY by the German heavy cruisers LÜTZOW and ADMIRAL HIPPER and sank the destroyer *Friedrich Eckholdt.* Almost exactly a year later, in December 1943, she was involved in the destruction of the SCHARNHORST.

The second notable *Sheffield* was the Type-42 destroyer of 4,100 tons that served in the FALKLANDS WAR, 1982. On May 4, 1982 she was hit by an EXOCET missile fired from an Argentine air force Super Étendard and sank with the loss of 21 lives. She was the first British warship to have been lost since World War II.

Shepard, Alan Bartlett
1923–

*A*merican naval officer, test pilot and the first American to go into space. Born on November 18, 1923, Alan Shepard graduated from the U.S. Naval Academy in 1944. Assigned to destroyers during the final stages of WORLD WAR II, 1939–45, he served on picket duty off Okinawa and the Japanese home islands. Qualifying as a pilot shortly after the war, he spent most of the 1950s as a test pilot on such procedures as aircraft carrier operations and altitude experiments. In 1959, he was one of seven pilots selected for the new astronaut training program—specifically, the National Aeronautics and Space Administration's (NASA) Project Mercury. (The definitive popular account of this project may be found in Tom Wolfe, *The Right Stuff.*)

Less than a month after the Soviet Union launched the first man (Yuri Gagarin) into space in 1961, Shepard rode a rocket to an altitude over 100 miles (160 km) and more than 300 miles' distance downrange from the launch site at Cape Canaveral, Florida. Taking part in the successive Gemini and Apollo space programs, he headed the Astronaut Office beginning in 1969. Early in 1971 he piloted *Apollo 14* to the Moon and back, spending several hours walking on the Moon. The first astronaut to reach flag rank, Admiral Shepard retired from the navy in 1974.

Clark G. Reynolds, *Famous American Admirals,* New York, 1978, pp. 305–306.

Sherman, Forrest Percival
1896–1951

*A*merican naval officer, a central figure behind Pacific Theater strategy in WORLD WAR II and in the postwar interservice rivalries that preceded the creation of the Department of Defense in 1949. Sherman was born on October 30, 1896 in Merrimack, New Hampshire. Graduating from the U.S. Naval Academy in the accelerated Class of 1918 (accelerated because of WORLD WAR I, 1914–18), he saw wartime escort duty on destroyers. He qualified as a pilot in 1922 and became a flight instructor in the mid-1920s. Sherman's keen mind and opinions on strategy and policy direction became evident through publications in the U.S. Naval Institute's *Proceedings.* Remaining very active in naval aviation, he headed the War Plans Division of the Office of Chief of Naval Operations beginning in 1940. He also served on the American-Canadian Joint Board for Defense and as an adviser to President Franklin ROOSEVELT at the secret conference with British Prime Minister Winston CHURCHILL in August 1941 at Argentia, Newfoundland, which issued the Atlantic Charter.

In these roles, Sherman played a pivotal part in the strategic planning for U.S. involvement in World War II.

Given command of the carrier *Wasp* in 1942, he lost his ship to enemy submarine action while supporting the operations on GUADALCANAL. In late 1943, as a rear admiral, he became Deputy Chief of Staff for Plans and head of Admiral Chester NIMITZ's War Plans Division, advising on strategic matters through the end of the war. As Deputy Chief of Naval Operations, he forged the navy's position on the post-war reorganization of the military. In late 1949 he became the youngest Chief of Naval Operations ever and was given the responsibility to restore the navy's sunken morale, the result of fallout from the struggles over the reorganization of the armed forces and the creation of a single Department of Defense. Overseeing the navy's role during the first few months of the KOREAN WAR, 1950–53, and supporting President Harry Truman's decision to oust General Douglas MacArthur from command, he died on July 22, 1951 while on a diplomatic mission to Spain.

Clark G. Reynolds, "Forrest Percival Sherman" in *The Chiefs Of Naval Operations*, ed. Robert W. Love, Jr., Annapolis, 1980.

Shinano

*J*apanese naval air support ship, originally intended as the third Yamato-class BATTLESHIP. Construction began in 1940 but was suspended when the Pacific war started in December 1941. Following heavy Japanese carrier losses at the Battle of MIDWAY, June 1942, the scope of the warship construction program was redirected with the aim of replacing the lost ships. The *Shinano* was redesigned as a floating airbase where aircraft from other carriers would be repaired and maintained. She also could carry a small number of aircraft of her own. With a displacement of 64,800 tons, she was 872 feet 9 inches (266 m) in length and had a beam of 119 feet 3 inches (36.3 m). Her flight deck was armored and she was equipped with 16 5-inch (13-cm) and 145 25-mm guns. Launched in 1944, she was sunk by torpedoes from the American submarine *Archerfish* during her maiden voyage from Yokosuka to Matsuyama, where the final fitting-out was to have been completed.

Shinyo

A wooden-hulled motor boat type of basic design that was used by the Japanese navy for suicide missions during WORLD WAR II, 1939–45. Although they did not all conform to a standard design, shinyo boats normally were powered by one or two engines and had a maximum speed of between 25 and 30 knots. They carried some 4,400 pounds (2,000 kg) of TNT packed into the bows. The explosive was designed to detonate when the boat came into contact with an enemy warship. A single pilot steered the suicide boat toward its target; he then suffered the same fate as his air force KAMIKAZE equivalent. Although some 6,000 shinyo boats were constructed, they were no more effective than KAITEN suicide submarines in altering the course of the naval war in the Pacific.

Shinyo

*J*apanese escort carrier that was converted from the former German passenger liner *Scharnhorst*, which had taken refuge at Yokohama at the beginning of WORLD WAR II, 1939–45. Purchased by the JAPANESE NAVY in 1942, this 17,500-ton ship became the largest merchant vessel ever to be converted as a fleet auxiliary. A hangar was erected in place of the original upper deck, and it was topped by a flush flight deck that was 590 feet (179.8 m) in length. A navigating bridge was positioned at the forward end of the hangar structure under the flight deck overhang. The *Shinyo* could carry 33 aircraft, had a maximum speed of 23 knots and was operated by a crew of 942.

The *Shinyo* was commissioned late in 1943 and was used primarily as an aircraft transport and deck landing training ship. This carrier also was used on escort duties. While accompanying a convoy taking troops and aircraft from Japan to Manila, in November 1944, she was sunk in the South Yellow Sea by torpedoes from an American submarine.

Ship of the Line

A term used to describe the CAPITAL SHIPS of navies during the age of sail. A ship of the line was one that was capable, in terms of the number of guns carried, of lying in the line of battle. The concept of the "line of battle" was unknown before the mid-17th century, when fighting at sea was based exclusively on engagements between individual ships. However, during the ANGLO-DUTCH WARS of the 17th century, a greater degree of order was gradually imposed on the opposing fleets. The line-ahead formation, with one vessel following another, was adopted. This formation enabled each ship to fire at right angles to the line. This was soon formalized in official naval tactics, with the ships that could participate in the line being specified. By the late 17th and 18th centuries this was defined in England as ships with more than 70 guns, corresponding to the ROYAL NAVY's first three rates. (See RATING OF SHIPS.) Less well armed vessels sometimes served in the line but were not formally regarded as ships of the line.

Brian Lavery, *The Ship of the Line: The Development of the Battlefleet, 1650–1850*, 2 vols., London, 1983–84.

Shoho

*J*apanese light AIRCRAFT CARRIER of WORLD WAR II, 1939–45, launched in 1935. Constructed as a submarine tender because of international restrictions on the production of certain types of naval vessels, it was designed so that it could be converted as an aircraft carrier. Commissioned as the tender *Tsurugizaki* in 1939, she was refitted as an aircraft carrier less than two years later, in 1941. The *Shoho* had a displacement of 11,262 tons, an overall length of 712 feet (217 m) and a beam of 59 feet (17.8 m). Lacking armor protection, she was armed with eight 5-inch (13-cm) antiaircraft guns and 15 25-mm guns and could carry 30 aircraft.

Her operational career during the PACIFIC WAR, 1941–45, was short. She joined the Fourth Carrier Division in 1942, and later the same year was sunk by aircraft from the *LEXINGTON* and the *YORKTOWN* during the Battle of the CORAL SEA, May 1942. A second member of the Shoho class, the *Zuiho*, also began life as a submarine tender but was completed as an aircraft carrier. She served in the Pacific war for almost three years before being sunk at the Battle of LEYTE GULF, October 1944.

Shovell, Sir Clowdisley
1650–1707

*E*nglish admiral who commanded the fleet during the War of the SPANISH SUCCESSION, 1701–13. Shovell went to sea at an early age and spent much of his youth in operations against the Barbary pirates. He returned home not long before the Revolution of 1688 and served in the War of the GRAND ALLIANCE, 1688–97, that followed it. After the Battle of BANTRY BAY, 1689, he was knighted and promoted to the rank of rear admiral. He was present at the Battle of BARFLEUR, 1692, where he made an important contribution toward the victory against the French. In 1696 he was promoted to the rank of admiral and appointed to the command of the Channel Fleet.

On the outbreak of the War of the Spanish Succession, Shovell served under Admiral Sir George ROOKE during the capture of GIBRALTAR and in the subsequent Battle of VELEZ MALAGA, 1704, when the new colonial acquisition was defended successfully. He succeeded Rooke as commander in chief of English forces in the Mediterranean in 1705, when played a major role in the combined operation to capture Barcelona. During the summer of 1707 he operated in support of Prince Eugene's campaign in southern France by blockading Toulon, an action that impelled the French, who feared the imminent capture of the port, to sink their fleet.

Shovell's distinguished career was cut short by his untimely death in October 1707. As he was returning to England his flagship, the *ASSOCIATION,* and three other ships were wrecked off the Scilly Isles during a storm. One of the few survivors, Shovell managed to reach the shore semiconscious only to be murdered there by a local.

Shufeldt, Robert Wilson
1822–95

*C*ommander of the first U.S. steam-powered vessel to circumnavigate the globe and a pioneer in establishing commercial treaties between the United States and the Far East. Robert Wilson Shufeldt was born in Red Hook, New York, on February 21, 1822 and entered the navy as a midshipman in 1839, seeing regular duty until 1854, when he resigned from the service. He then became active in organizing and operating steamships between New York and Liverpool as well as between New Orleans and Havana. He also worked to open a trade route across the Tehauntepec region of Mexico. With the outbreak of AMERICAN CIVIL WAR in 1861, he was appointed by President Abraham Lincoln as consul-general to the Spanish colony of Cuba and thus served in a key role against Confederate raiders and privateers. He was recommissioned in the navy as a commander.

After the war he organized and initially commanded the Nicaraguan surveying expedition in 1870–71. As chief of the Bureau of Equipment and Recruiting, he served in 1878 on a special commercial and diplomatic mission for the U.S. State Department and as arbitrator of both American and British governments in a boundary settlement with Liberia in Africa. From late 1878 until 1880 he sailed on the *Ticonderoga* around the globe, returning to the Far East as naval attaché to China, where, in May 1882, he successfully negotiated the first treaty between Korea and a western nation. As president of the Naval Advisory Board in 1883–84, he was instrumental in the new design of steel cruisers and the foundation of the "New Navy" of the United States.

Following service as superintendent of the Naval Observatory and as president of the Naval Academy's Board of Visitors, he retired in 1884, having reached the rank of rear admiral. He died in Washington, D.C. on November 6, 1895.

Frederick C. Drake, *The Empire of the Seas: A Biography of Rear-Admiral Robert Wilson Shufeldt, U.S.N.*, Honolulu, 1984.

Sicily Landings
1943

*T*he largest amphibious landing operation of WORLD WAR II, 1939–45, the Allied invasion of Sicily was launched during the night of July 10, 1943, under the supreme command of General Dwight D. Eisenhower. Given the code-name Operation Husky, it was designed to

Allied landing craft en route to Sicily, 1943   *(Copyright © Imperial War Museum, London)*

secure Italy's withdrawal from the war and to relieve German pressure on the Eastern front. British Admiral Sir Andrew CUNNINGHAM, who was placed in charge of the naval operations, had the formidable task of transporting some 500,000 men to the southeast coast of Sicily and landing them on two 40-mile (64-km) strips of coast.

Cunningham constituted two formidable naval task forces—the Eastern Naval Task Force under British Vice Admiral Bertram RAMSAY and the Western Naval Task Force commanded by American Vice Admiral Kent HEWITT, who later commanded the naval task force at Salerno. The task forces assembled east and west of Malta before leaving for Sicily with full air cover. Despite poor weather conditions, the landings went according to plan. The only significant enemy counterattack was defeated with the help of Allied naval units, which at one point fired at German tanks above a landing beach. Further amphibious assaults to try to prevent the evacuation of German forces from Sicily to mainland Italy were unsuccessful. However, in just over a month Sicily fell to the Allies, and the eventual surrender of Italy was already in sight.

S. W. C. Pack, *Operation Husky: The Allied Invasion of Sicily*, Newton Abbot, 1977.

Signaling

Before the mid-17th century, communications between warships was limited to direct conversation or messages sent by boat. The introduction of a system of signaling by flags in the English naval service represented a significant step forward. At first only five different flags were used; although their meaning varied according to their position, the number of messages that could be conveyed was limited. This basic system was developed further during the 17th and 18th centuries. In time a large number of additional flags, including those that were partly colored, were added. Used in combination, they were sufficient to cover most needs and were employed to give orders and directions to an individual ship or an entire squadron. The introduction of numbered flags in England in the latter part of the 18th century provided the basis for a signal book, issued in 1799, in which a combination of three or four flags denoted a particular word or phrase. These numerical flags were later superseded by—or used in combination with—alphabetical designs.

Flags obviously could not be used at night or in fog; therefore, alternative arrangements had to be made. At night a combination of up to four lanterns was used, while guns were employed when fog affected visibility. An alternative to the flag that dated back to the late 18th century was the shutter telegraph, which consisted of a board with six holes in it. These holes could be opened or closed, revealing or concealing the light. The semaphore, which was fitted with two mechanical arms, was an alternative that was adopted by the British and French navies. At about the same time, the Morse code was successfully applied in a naval context. Short and long flashes from a lantern could be used to transmit the code. With the arrival of electricity, these signals could be sent from a ship by a high-powered flashing light operating in any direction. It could be used during the day as well as at night. In the early years of the 20th century, communications at sea were revolutionized with the invention of the RADIO. It was accompanied by the use of appropriate codes and ciphers because an enemy always could intercept messages. This was no guarantee of security; and the Royal Navy was able to read German naval codes in both world wars. Equally important, the U.S. Navy was able to intercept and read Japanese naval codes during WORLD WAR II, 1939–45, as a result of the Magic intelligence team, which had been specially created for this purpose. Warships are also vulnerable to detection from direction-finding equipment when they use their radio systems.

Sigsbee, Charles D.
1845–1923

*A*merican naval officer who served in the latter stages of the AMERICAN CIVIL WAR, 1861–65. Born in Albany, New York, Sigsbee was a graduate of the United States Naval Academy. He was present at the Battle of MOBILE BAY, August 5, 1864, where his courageous conduct was noted. Following the end of the war, Sigsbee devoted much effort to deep-sea exploration, particularly in the Gulf of Mexico. He invented various pieces of equipment, including a deep-sea sounding machine, which transformed the task of exploring the sea. Sigsbee was chief hydrographer of the Navy Department, 1893–97. (See HYDROGRAPHY.) In 1897 he was appointed to the command of the battleship *MAINE* and remained in that post until she was destroyed in Havana harbor on February 5, 1898. Sigsbee and his crew were cleared of any blame for the disaster. During the SPANISH-AMERICAN WAR, 1898, which quickly followed the incident, his successes included the destruction of two Spanish warships off San Juan, Puerto Rico. Sigsbee had

reached the rank of rear admiral in command of the second squadron of the U.S. Atlantic Fleet when he retired in 1907.

Sims, William Sowden
1858–1936

*O*ne of the great reformers and innovators in the U.S. Navy during the first part of the 20th century, William Sowden Sims was born in Port Hope, Ontario, Canada on October 15, 1858. His family returned to the United States, settling in Pennsylvania. Sims entered the naval service in 1876 and served as naval attaché at the U.S. embassies in Paris, St. Petersburg and Madrid successively from 1897 to 1900. He served in Spain during the SPANISH-AMERICAN WAR of 1898. Outspoken and determined, he recognized the poor state of American naval gunnery, as evidenced in its performance during the war with Spain. As Inspector of Target Practice from 1902 to 1909, he made great advances in the areas of naval gunfire. He also served additional duty as naval aide to President Theodore ROOSEVELT. While commanding the Atlantic Torpedo Flotilla, he developed a tactical doctrine for the new naval destroyers.

As a rear admiral, his tenure as president of the Naval War College was cut short by the entry of the United States into WORLD WAR I in 1917. He was dispatched to London for discussions with the British ADMIRALTY. As commander of U.S. Forces, European Waters, from May 1917 to March 1919 with the temporary rank of vice admiral and then of admiral, he created the CONVOY system that greatly assisted the Allied cause. He also served additional duty as naval attaché in London from late 1917 until March 1919. From then to his retirement in 1922 he resumed the duty of president of the Naval War College, where he continued to advocate reforms and to urge the development of NAVAL AVIATION. He received numerous American and foreign decorations as well as many honorary degrees. The author of numerous articles on technical, strategic and administrative topics, his book, *The Victory at Sea*, 1920, won the Pulitzer Prize for history. Sims died in Boston on September 28, 1936.

Elting E. Morison, *Admiral Sims and the Modern American Navy*, Boston, 1942.

Sino-Japanese War
1894–95

*F*ollowing an internal revolt designed to overthrow the established order, the Korean government appealed for help from China in June 1894. As troops were dispatched from China, the Japanese responded by sending their own forces to Korea, but neither side would leave once they had succeeded in restoring order. Both China and Japan had long-established plans to dominate the area and both had intervened in Korea on previous occasions. Japan acted quickly and, on July 20, 1894, in a preemptive strike, they established a puppet Korean government that ordered the Chinese to leave the country. Initial military and naval engagements were followed, on August 1, 1894, by a formal declaration of war between the two countries. The rapid defeat of the Chinese army on the Korean peninsula was matched by the successive reverses of its navy at sea.

The Japanese navy under Admiral Yuko Ito defeated Admiral Ting Ju-ch'ang at the Battle of the YALU RIVER, September 17, 1894. The Chinese fleet sustained heavy losses although the Japanese fleet also suffered some losses. The Chinese suffered further with the capture of Port Arthur, Manchuria, November 21, 1894, although Admiral Ting escaped to Weihaiwei. At the Battle of Weihaiwei, February 2–12, 1895, the Chinese fleet was destroyed and Admiral Ting committed suicide. With the enemy advancing across Manchuria, the Chinese were compelled to seek peace, which was concluded on terms favorable to the Japanese by the Treaty of Shimonoseki, April 17, 1895. China was forced to recognize Korean independence and to cede territory to Japan, which was now established as a major regional naval and military power. This did not, however, prevent the Russians from forcing the Japanese from Port Arthur and the Liaotung Peninsula. At the same time, Britain and Germany secured valuable territorial concessions from a severely weakened China.

Sinope, Battle of
November 30, 1853

Following the outbreak of war between Turkey and Russia on October 4, 1853, a Russian squadron detected an enemy fleet anchored in the Turkish port of Sinope on the southern coast of the Black Sea. Commanded by Vice Admiral Osman Pasha, the Turkish fleet included seven frigates, two corvettes, two transports and two wooden steamships. The Russians began a BLOCKADE until reinforcements arrived from Sebastopol.

Commanded by Admiral Paul NAKHIMOV, the enlarged Russian force included six ships of the line, three frigates and several smaller vessels. His capital ships were armed with a new type of naval gun—68-pounders firing smoothbore explosive shells—that made its first appearance at Sinope. The attack began on the afternoon of November 30; after they refused to surrender the Turks, who were outnumbered and outgunned, were subjected to heavy shelling. Russian projectiles quickly set Osman Pasha's ships on fire, and within two hours his entire squadron had been virtually destroyed. Nearly 3,000 Turks were lost, while Russian casualties were minimal.

The Battle of Sinope marked a turning point in the history of warship design because it demonstrated the extreme vulnerability of wooden ships to the new explosive shell and rendered them obsolete. In the future, iron would be used in the construction of warships. Before the end of the decade the first real IRONCLAD, the French frigate LA GLOIRE, appeared, with the Warrior, the British equivalent, following shortly afterward. A further consequence of the action was the entry of Britain and France into the CRIMEAN WAR, 1853–56, on the Turkish side.

Sirte, First Battle of
December 17, 1941

A battle between British and Italian naval units in the Mediterranean during WORLD WAR II, 1939–45, that ended inconclusively. Rear Admiral Philip VIAN, who was escorting the transport ship Breconshire from Alexandria, Egypt to Malta, had four cruisers and 12 destroyers at his disposal as he passed westward through the Mediterranean. As he approached the Gulf of Sirte on the coast of Libya, he faced attacks from German and Italian aircraft and learned that the ITALIAN NAVY was approaching from the north. This much larger CONVOY was being escorted from Taranto to Tripoli under the command of Admiral Angelo Iachino. The Italian force consisted of four battleships, five cruisers and 21 destroyers.

The two navies met in the Gulf of Sirte late in the afternoon of December 17. The Breconshire was sent ahead with two destroyers to act as escorts. As the Italians opened fire, Vian turned to make a simulated attack on the enemy, hoping that the use of smoke would conceal his real strength. The Italians already had been misled by faulty intelligence suggesting that the Breconshire was a battleship. As a result, both sides disengaged and escorted their convoys safely to their respective destinations. In a tragic postscript to the battle, the Royal Navy's Force K, which had been dispatched from Malta to search for the convoy, ran into a minefield some 17 miles (27 km) off Tripoli. A cruiser and a destroyer were lost and two cruisers sustained major damage. Admiral Vian would again encounter the Italian navy in the Second Battle of SIRTE, March 22, 1942.

Sirte, Second Battle of
March 22, 1942

The second engagement between British and Italian naval force off the Gulf of Sirte, Libya, during WORLD WAR II, 1939–45, arose from the requirement to resupply Malta in the spring of 1942. With a force of four cruisers and 11 destroyers under his command, Rear Admiral Philip VIAN left Alexandria, Egypt on March 20 with four merchantmen bound for Malta. When the Italians received intelligence of the passage of the British convoy, naval forces under the command of Admiral Angelo Iachino were dispatched from Taranto and Messina just after midnight on March 22 with orders to intercept it. Iachino's force consisted of the battleship *Littorio*, three cruisers and four destroyers. The British first sighted the greatly superior enemy fleet at 2:27 on the afternoon of March 22, although they had suffered German and Italian air attacks earlier in the day. Vian ordered the convoy to turn away to the southeast accompanied by its close escort.

Between 2:30 and 7:00 P.M. four separate engagements took place. By means of skillful counterattacks, involving the extensive use of torpedoes and smokescreens, the British held the Italians at bay while the convoy escaped. Enemy gunfire damaged a British cruiser and two destroyers. When dusk fell the Italians, who were reluctant to fight at night, withdrew to the north in deteriorating conditions. An Italian cruiser was damaged and two destroyers foundered in gale-force conditions on the way back to base. The British convoy also fared badly. Enemy air attacks continued during the final stages of its journey to Malta, and only two of the four merchantmen reached their destination. The outcome of the engagement was a tribute to the great skill of the British commander in unfavorable circumstances when he was heavily outgunned by the enemy.

Stanley W. C. Pack, *The Battle of Sirte*, London, 1975.

Sivertsen, Kurt
1622–75

*N*orwegian naval commander who served in three foreign navies during a long and distinguished career. Sivertsen's early naval experience, from 1639, was gained in the DUTCH NAVY, when he served under Admiral Cornelis TROMP. In 1642 he transferred his allegiance to the Venetian navy, where he remained until 1661. Sivertsen established his reputation in a series of remarkable victories against the Turks, ending in their final defeat in the Dardanelles in 1654. Rewarded with rapid promotion, he reached the rank of admiral-lieutenant in the Venetian navy. Sivertsen returned briefly to Holland in 1661, but two years later he was appointed to the command of the Danish navy. Given the title Count Adelaer ("Eagle"), he remained in this post until his death.

Skram, Peder
c. 1500–81

*D*anish naval hero and senator who first saw service in the war against the Swedes following the collapse of the union between the two countries early in the 16th century. He fought at the Battle of Brannkyrka, 1518, and at the battle of Uppsala two years later, and was awarded an estate in Norway for his services. During the Counts' War, 1533–36, the Danish government forged an alliance with the Swedes under Gustav I Vasa. It sent Skram to Sweden to help to organize the Swedish fleet. He commanded it successfully in actions against the Hanseatic fleets operating in support of Christian II, the deposed king of Denmark and Norway, 1512–23, and of Sweden, 1520–33. Christian and his Catholic supporters failed in their attempts to regain the Danish throne. They were opposed by Christian III, who emerged victorious in 1536. In recognition of his services, Skram was knighted by the new king at his coronation in 1534. Skram returned from retirement to serve as commander in chief of the Danish fleet during the Scandinavian Seven Years' War, 1563–70. He gained one significant victory against the Swedes before being superseded by Herluf TROLLE at the end of 1563.

Sloat, John D.
1781–1867

*A*merican naval officer who claimed California for the United States. Born near Goshen, New York, Sloat joined the navy as a midshipman in 1800. Forced to leave the service when the QUASI-WAR, 1798–1800, with France ended a few months later, he served in the merchant fleet until the WAR OF 1812, when he reentered the navy. He served under Stephen DECATUR in the frigate *UNITED STATES*. During the postwar period, Sloat's career made steady progress, and by 1844 he was appointed to the command of the U.S. Pacific squadron and raised his flag in the *Savannah*. This was a sensitive appointment because of the rapid deterioration in relations between the United States and Mexico. When the Mexican-American War began soon afterward, in May 1846, Sloat landed a detachment of marines at Monterey and, without clear authority, also issued a proclamation that he was taking possession of California on behalf of the United States. Shortly afterward, he handed over his command to Commodore Robert STOCKTON, who completed the conquest, using force wherever necessary to bring Mexican rule to an end. San Francisco was occupied soon afterward, and soon most of California was in American hands. George BANCROFT, Secretary of the Navy, described Sloat's actions as "ably conceived and brilliantly executed." Sloat reached the rank of rear admiral in retirement and died at Staten Island, New York in November 1867.

Sloop

A generic term used to describe the small sailing ships that ranked next after sixth-rate warships. (See RATING OF SHIPS.) The sloop was a fore-and-aft-rigged ship with a single mast, but in a naval context this term also encompassed several other designs. Some sloops of war were rigged as brigantines, ketches or snows. In use since the 17th century, sloops were equipped with up to 12 six-pounder cannon and were used primarily as naval auxiliaries. By the latter part of the 18th century the sloop had been grouped into two classes—the ship sloop and the brig sloop—although both were square-rigged on all masts. The ship sloop, which normally carried 16 guns, had three masts while the brig sloop had two. The sloop survived the introduction of steam power and continued throughout the 19th century in a training role. In Britain, sloops served until as late as 1904, being the final link with the age of the sailing navies.

Smalls, Robert
1839–1915

*A*frican American, born in Beaufort, South Carolina, who was impressed into service at sea during the AMERICAN CIVIL WAR, 1861–65 and who later served as a congressman. In 1861 he became a member of the crew of the *Planter*, a Confederate steamer that served on dispatch and transport duties in Charleston harbor. During an evening in May 1862, when the officers were on shore, Smalls took charge of the ship and managed to reach the Union squadron that was blockading the harbor. He was rewarded with a share of the PRIZE MONEY, an appointment as a pilot in the U.S. Navy and national fame. Smalls was able to provide the navy with valuable information about the harbor and its fortifications. In a second act of courage, he again took command of the *Planter* when its commander deserted his post as the vessel came under enemy attack. Smalls was rewarded with promotion to the rank of captain and appointment to the command of the *Planter*. Soon after the end of the war he retired from the navy and, turning to a political career, was elected to the U.S. House of Representatives.

Smith, Sir William Sydney
1764–1840

*B*ritish naval commander who was nicknamed the "Swedish knight" in reference to his service as a naval adviser to King Gustavus III during the RUSSO-SWEDISH WAR, 1788–90, and after. Sydney Smith had entered the Royal Navy in 1777 and made his mark rapidly, fighting with great courage under Admiral Sir George RODNEY at the Battle of CAPE ST. VINCENT, 1780, during the AMERICAN WAR OF INDEPENDENCE, 1775–83. He received relatively rapid promotion and became a post-captain in 1782. Following his later service in Sweden, he returned to the Royal Navy as volunteer during the opening stages of the FRENCH REVOLUTIONARY AND NAPOLEONIC WARS, 1792–1815. Smith arrived in the Mediterranean in his own small

ship and took part in the occupation of Toulon under Samuel, Viscount HOOD (1724–1816), in 1793.

His naval service was interrupted in 1796 when he was captured by the French during an attack on Le Havre; he spent the next two years in prison before managing to escape. Much of the remainder of Smith's naval career was spent in the Mediterranean—apart from an unhappy interlude, in 1808, as the commander of an obscure squadron operating off the Brazilian coast. Among several notable actions against the French in the Mediterranean, his amphibious operations to raise Napoleon's siege of Acre in 1799 stand out. In 1810 he was appointed vice-admiral of the blue squadron and second-in-command of the British Mediterranean fleet under Sir Edward PELLEW. Smith's naval career finally came to an end on his retirement in 1814.

Solebay, Battle of
May 28, 1672

*T*he opening battle of the Third ANGLO-DUTCH WAR, 1672–74. The Battle of Solebay began with a surprise attack by Admiral Michiel de RUYTER, the Dutch commander in chief. The opposing Anglo-French naval forces, which were commanded by JAMES, Duke of York and Admiral Jean d'Estrées respectively, had been at anchor in Southwold Bay where they were resupplying. The battle began at about 3 P.M. with the allies at a disadvantage because they had been caught unaware. The French division, cut off by the Zeeland squadron under Vice-Admiral Adriaen Banckert, played no part in the main battle. The main Dutch attack fell on the English center, under the Duke of York, and the rear, under Edward MONTAGU, Earl of Sandwich. Fierce fighting lasted until nightfall.

The Earl of Sandwich's flagship, the *Royal James,* was the victim of a concerted attack by three Dutch flagships despite considerable efforts to save her. The Earl of Sandwich himself died soon afterward when the rescue boat carrying the crew of the *Royal James* was lost. Although the Duke of York escaped injury he was forced to transfer his flag three times during the battle. The Dutch, who lost three ships, left the battle in the knowledge that the Anglo-French fleet would not be able to mount an immediate attack on Holland, as it had to return to port for a refit and would not be ready to return to the attack for several weeks. In fact, significant action against the Dutch was delayed until the following year, when the opening shots were fired at the Battle of SCHOONEVELDT.

Solomon Islands, Battles of the
1942–43

A series of battles between American and Japanese forces for control of the SOLOMON ISLANDS, a group of Pacific islands to the east of New Guinea, during WORLD WAR II, 1939–45. The islands had been occupied by the Japanese as they advanced southward during the opening stages of the PACIFIC WAR, 1941–45. The struggle by the United States to gain possession of the islands was part of its strategic objective of taking Rabaul, the major Japanese military base on New Britain. Operations began in August 1942, when the Americans landed on GUADALCANAL and established a beachhead. Japanese ships made regular supply runs (the "Tokyo Express") from Rabaul to Guadalcanal through the channel ("the Slot") between the Eastern and Western Solomons. These produced a regular American response.

The opposing navies met on six separate occasions—SAVO ISLAND, EASTERN SOLOMONS, CAPE ESPERANCE, SANTA CRUZ ISLANDS, GUADALCANAL and TASSAFARONGA—before the issue was resolved after six months. In total, both sides lost 24 warships; the Japanese also had to replace some 600 naval pilots. As the disputed possession of Guadalcanal was resolved in Americans' favor, the Americans turned their attention to the remaining islands in the group. In a further series of seven naval battles they progressively seized more territory: Rennell Island, KULA GULF, KOLOMBANGARA, VELLA GULF, VELLA LAVELLA, EMPRESS AUGUSTA BAY and CAPE ST. GEORGE. Operations in the Solomons were completed with the capture of Bougainville on November 1, 1943.

S. B. Griffith, *The Battle for Guadalcanal*, New York, 1980.

Somerville, Sir James
1882–1949

*B*ritish naval commander who gave distinguished service in both world wars. During WORLD WAR I, 1914–18, Somerville served as a radio communications specialist in the GRAND FLEET, 1915–18, following service in the DARDANELLES. During the interwar period he spent much time on battleships and was, in 1933, promoted to rear admiral. Following a period as commander in chief of the East Indies station, ill health forced his premature retirement in 1938. However, Somerville returned to the active list at the time of the DUNKIRK evacuation. In June 1940, as a vice admiral, he was appointed to the command of FORCE H, which was based at GIBRALTAR. His Mediterranean operations included the task of neutralizing French naval units at MERS-EL-KEBIR and Oran, but his principal activity was the provision of escorts for the MALTA CONVOYS. Force H also played an important role in tracking down the *BISMARCK* and disabling her. In 1942, following Japanese entry into World War II, Somerville was appointed commander in chief of the British Eastern Fleet based in Ceylon (Sri Lanka). He became head of the British naval delegation to Washington in 1944 and was appointed admiral of the fleet in 1945.

Donald Macintyre, *Fighting Admiral: The Life of Admiral of the Fleet Sir James Somerville*, London, 1961.

Sonar

*U*nderwater device that uses ultrasonic waves to detect the position and range of submerged submarines. SONAR came into general operational use during WORLD WAR II, 1939–45. It was originally known as ASDIC (Allied Submarine Detection Investigation Committee), after the committee established jointly by the British and French at the end of WORLD WAR I, 1914–18, that oversaw its development. The French played a leading role during the interwar years.

SONAR (Sound Navigation and Ranging) is similar to the commercial echo-sounder. A transducer, using a quartz crystal vibrator, emits a high-frequency sound wave that passes through the water and is reflected back by any solid object it encounters. As sound travels at a known speed through water, the depth of an object (or of the seabed) can be calculated from the time it takes the sound pulse to travel from the ship's transmitter and back to the receiver. If the submarine is moving a bearing can be obtained by measuring the change of pulse (known as the Doppler effect).

Early ASDIC sets projected a narrow beam ahead of the ship; but, as the final attack was made, the signal was lost when the ship passed over the target. The first solution to this problem was to devise ahead-firing weapons, such as the SQUID and the HEDGEHOG, that could be programmed while ASDIC was still in contact. More advanced ASDIC units overcame this problem. Today buoys containing sonar (Sonobuoys) are dropped into the water above the suspected target and relay their findings back to the antisubmarine warfare aircraft or helicopter.

Souchon, Admiral Wilhelm
1864–1946

*C*ommander of the German Navy's Mediterranean Squadron on the outbreak of WORLD WAR I, 1914–18. An experienced naval officer with a high professional reputation, Souchon had entered the service in 1881. He had served in the Pacific and, prior to the war, had been chief of staff of the Baltic Sea naval station.

Confirmation of his professional skills was soon provided when the ships under his command in the Mediterranean—the battle cruiser *GOEBEN* and the light cruiser *Breslau*—made their dramatic escape to Constantinople in August 1914. Soon both ships were formally transferred to the Turkish navy, and Souchon himself became its supreme commander. Under German influence Turkey rapidly joined the war, and Souchon was involved in operations against the Russian fleet in the Black Sea. By the time he returned to Germany in September 1917, Souchon had been promoted to the rank of vice admiral and had been awarded the medal *Pour Le Mérite*.

Souchon commanded the Fourth Squadron of the HIGH SEAS FLEET for much of the remainder of the war. After a brief appearance on the Retired List during the closing months of the war, he was appointed chief of the Baltic Sea naval station. His arrival in Kiel on October 30, 1918, coincided with the MUTINY organized in protest at the planned "death ride" against the British High Seas Fleet. Eventually order was restored, and Souchon finally retired from the navy a few months later.

Dan van der Vat, *The Ship That Changed the World: The Escape of the Goeben to the Dardanelles in 1914*, London, 1985.

Sound, Battle of the

October 29, 1658

Battle between the Swedish and Dutch navies that had its origins in the plan of Charles X, king of Sweden, to dominate the Baltic. As part of this strategy, Charles sought to defeat the Danes in the First Northern War of 1655–60 and tried to force them to close the Sound, the channel that leads from the Kattegat (an arm of the North Sea bounded by the east coast of Jutland and the west coast of Sweden) into the Baltic, to all foreign merchant ships. The Danes refused to comply, and the Swedes seized several key Danish coastal towns and besieged Copenhagen. The Dutch, who had vital trading links with the area, already had allied themselves with the Danes. They responded quickly to the Swedish aggression. In October 1638 a force of 35 warships, under the command of Admiral Jacob van WASSENAER, Lord of Obdam, left Holland. Carrying some 4,000 ground troops, it had orders to relieve Copenhagen and drive the Swedes from Denmark.

On October 29 the opposing navies met at the northern entrance to the Sound. A larger Swedish force under Count Wrangel fought with determination, but in the end the Dutch gained the upper hand although they sustained serious losses. Vice Admiral Witte de WITT was killed and his flagship the *Brederode* was boarded and sunk. The *Eendracht*, the Dutch commander's flagship, was also under heavy attack for a while. Swedish losses were even heavier, with five ships destroyed or captured. At the end of the battle Admiral Obdam was able to land his troops at Copenhagen without interference from the defeated Swedes.

South Carolina, U.S.S.

The first American all-big-gun BATTLESHIP, the *South Carolina* was in fact designed before the British-built DREADNOUGHT, although her period of construction was longer and she did not appear until 1908. She was armed with eight 12-inch (30-cm) guns mounted in twin superfiring turrets positioned fore and aft on the centerline. This unusual arrangement was influenced by the need to limit, for financial reasons, the *South Carolina*'s displacement to 16,000 tons. She had a length of 452 feet 9 inches (138.2 m), a beam of 80 feet 3 inches (24.5 m) and a crew of 869. With a maximum speed of no more than 18 knots, the *South Carolina* and her sister ship *Michigan* could not be used operationally with subsequent dreadnought designs, which were much faster. As a result they were employed as CONVOY escorts after the United States entered WORLD WAR I in 1917. Both ships were scrapped in 1924.

South Dakota, U.S.S.

American battleship of WORLD WAR II, 1939–45, which gave its name to a class consisting of the *Indiana*, *Massachusetts* and *Alabama* as well as the *South Dakota*. Commissioned in 1942, the *South Dakota*—the last CAPITAL SHIP to be designed within the limitations imposed by prewar naval treaties—had a displacement of 35,000 tons. Her overall length was 680 feet (207.2 m), and she had a beam of 108 feet 3 inches (32.99 m). She had good armor protection and was equipped with nine 16-inch (41-cm) and 16 5-inch (13-cm) guns. Operated by a crew of 2,354, she had a maximum speed of 28 knots and could carry three aircraft.

The quality of her design was to be demonstrated during her early service in the PACIFIC WAR, 1941–45, when she survived successive attacks at the Battle of SANTA CRUZ ISLANDS, October 1942, and at the naval Battle of GUADALCANAL, November 1942. Following the completion of repairs and a brief interlude attached to the Royal Navy, she returned to the Pacific in 1943, serving with carrier task forces for the remainder of the war.

Sovereign of the Seas, H.M.S.

Designed by the British master shipwright Phineas Pett, *Sovereign of the Seas* was a first-rate (see RATING OF SHIPS) SHIP OF THE LINE that served in the ROYAL NAVY for almost 60 years. She was laid down at Woolwich by Phineas's son, Peter PETT, in 1636 and was launched in October 1637. The largest warship in the world at that time, she had a displacement of 1,500 tons, an overall length of 232 feet (70.71 m) and a breadth of over 46 feet (14.02 m). Her gun deck extended for more than 172 feet (52.43 m). The *Sovereign of the Seas* also was notable as the first warship with three covered gun decks, which accommodated more than 100 guns, including demi-CANNON and demi-CULVERINS. She had three masts instead of the normal four, and her magnificent gilded decoration was unique.

During the Commonwealth period, when her name was shortened to *Sovereign*, she was present at the Battle of KENTISH KNOCK, 1652, during the First ANGLO-DUTCH WAR, 1652–54. Completely rebuilt at Chatham in 1659–60, she rejoined the Restoration navy as the *Royal Sovereign*. She served in the Second and Third Dutch Wars (1665–67; 1672–74) and for a time was the FLAGSHIP of Prince RUPERT, admiral of the fleet. Rebuilt again in 1684, the *Royal Sovereign* was present at the Battles of BEACHY HEAD, 1690, and BARFLEUR, 1692, during the War of the GRAND ALLIANCE, 1688–97. Early in 1696, while laid up at Chatham, she was accidentally destroyed by fire that started when a candle was left burning in a cabin.

The *Royal Sovereign* was also the name of another British first-rate ship, launched in 1786, which was the first vessel in action at the Battle of TRAFALGAR, 1805. A super-dreadnought BATTLESHIP that served in both world wars was the third British CAPITAL SHIP to share the distinguished name of *Royal Sovereign*.

Soviet Navy

*F*ollowing the effective collapse of the Russian navy during the revolutions of 1917, the Bolsheviks formally established the Red Navy early in the following year. In these difficult circumstances, the new navy was able only to play a small role in the Civil War, 1917–22. Some of its inherited warships were destroyed as the Allies intervened against the Bolsheviks; those that survived often were in a poor state of repair, with spare parts being in short supply. The navy did, however, carry out some effective defensive action, including the laying of large quantities of mines. The period following the war was difficult for the fleet: Its reconstruction could not begin on a large scale until the 1930s when the Soviet shipbuilding industry had developed the required capacity. With priority being given to coastal defense and the development of close operating links with ground forces, the construction program focused on submarines and torpedo boats, although there was increasing support for the creation of an oceangoing navy.

Under Admiral Nikolai KUZNETSOV, who became commissar of the navy in 1939, an ambitious naval construction program was approved. A modern surface fleet, which included three new battleships and two battle cruisers, was to be developed. Construction was abruptly halted in late 1940 as war with Germany approached. An early test of the Soviet navy had been provided by the Russo-Finnish War, 1939–40, when it performed badly, partly because its leadership had been undermined by Joseph Stalin's purges of senior officers the 1930s. Following the German invasion of the Soviet Union in June 1941, intensive air attacks by the Luftwaffe, which quickly dominated the skies, caused great damage to Soviet naval forces in the Baltic and the Black Sea. Many major surface units were put out of action as a result. Because the Soviets had no means of replacing them, the naval war with Germany was fought mainly by submarines and smaller surface units, including motor torpedo boats. The Soviet navy claimed a heavy toll of enemy warships and merchantmen, but independent estimates suggest that the total was 130 or so at most. In the Baltic, where the fleet had little room to maneuver, Soviet naval units used their guns in defense of the besieged city of Leningrad.

In the immediate postwar period, Stalin revived plans for a traditional oceangoing fleet, but severe economic constraints meant that again priority was given to the more modest requirements of coastal defense. Once more construction focused on submarines, small surface ships and naval aircraft. Following Stalin's death in 1953, the role of the Soviet navy was subject to a fundamental review in the light of the rapid development of American strategic nuclear weapons systems and other challenges of the COLD WAR. The eventual outcome was a decision to introduce nuclear weapons in the navy, and major priority was given to the development of submarine-launched ballistic missile systems. First entering in service in the 1960s, this strategic nuclear force would be capable of surviving an American first strike and would thus be a credible and effective deterrent. This objective was to remain at the heart of Soviet naval developments until the 1990s.

At the same time, the Soviet navy needed to develop the capacity to defend these submarines while posing a real threat to their American and British equivalents. The increasing distance at which Western submarines could operate meant that the Soviet navy also extended its own area of operations to include, for example, the Mediterranean Sea and the Indian Ocean. Although high priority was given to the development of an effective antisubmarine warfare capability across the globe, the traditional role of the Soviet navy in coastal defense and in supporting the army was not neglected. It developed the world's largest surface fleet, which consisted mainly of smaller warships but included some major new designs, including, for example, large general-purpose cruisers and Kiev-class carriers of advanced specification. Although the U.S. Navy was to retain its technological lead, the Soviet navy had developed the capability to participate in a third world war and to make its presence felt in every ocean. Since the breakup of the Soviet Union in 1991, the momentum of these strategic developments has been lost, although the fleet has largely been preserved as a coherent whole in Russian hands. However, continuing economic problems have led to serious maintenance problems and disaffected personnel, reducing the effectiveness of the Russian fleet as a fighting force. See also RUSSIAN NAVY.

Norman Polmar, *Guide to the Soviet Navy*, 5th ed., London, 1991.

The *Arkhangelsk* (formerly the British battleship *Royal Sovereign*) was transferred to the Russian navy in 1944   *(Copyright © Imperial War Museum, London)*

Spanish-American War
1898

Toward the end of the 19th century, there was growing concern in the United States (fanned by sensational reports in the newspapers of William Randolph Hearst) at the widespread violation of human rights in the Spanish colony of Cuba. Anti-Spanish feeling in the United States was greatly increased when the battleship U.S.S. MAINE exploded and sank in Havana harbor on February 15, 1898, with the loss of 260 crew. Spain was blamed for this disaster (although later inquiries concluded that a faulty boiler was responsible). In response to this incident, the United States increased its support for dissident Cubans and, on April 25, 1898, declared war on Spain. The U.S. Navy, unlike American ground forces, was prepared for war and went into action immediately. In the Pacific, the U.S. Asiatic Squadron, commanded by Commodore George DEWEY, entered MANILA BAY in the Philippines, a Spanish colonial possession, and, on May 1, attacked a larger

enemy squadron, commanded by Admiral Patricio Montojo. Dewey, who completely destroyed the Spanish fleet, blockaded the city of Manila until August 13, when sufficient American troops had arrived to capture it.

In the Atlantic, the U.S. Atlantic Fleet, commanded by Rear Admiral William T. SAMPSON, had been blockading Havana until it was learned that the main Spanish fleet, commanded by Admiral Pascual CERVERA, was on its way to Cuba from the Cape Verde Islands. Sampson was unable to intercept the Spanish fleet before it entered the relative safety of the fortified harbor at Santiago de Cuba. However, Sampson then blockaded the harbor from May to July, waiting for the American ground troops that had landed at Daiquirí on June 14 to force Cervera to move. By July 1 the U.S. forces dominated the area around Santiago. With the town likely to fall soon, Cervera decided to try to break through the American blockade. However, as the Spanish left Santiago they came under heavy fire from superior American naval forces, and at the Battle of SANTI-

AGO BAY, July 3, 1898, they were totally defeated. Santiago finally fell on July 17; following an American AMPHIBIOUS landing on Puerto Rico, an armistice was agreed. By the terms of the Treaty of Paris, December 10, 1898, Spain relinquished control of Cuba and ceded Puerto Rico, Guam and the Philippines to the United States. The outcome of the war recognized the emergence of the United States as a world power and the increasingly global role of its navy.

David F. Trask, *The War with Spain in 1898*, New York, 1981.

Spanish Armada

1588

*P*lans developed by Philip II, king of Spain, to invade England came to a head when a Spanish fleet under the command of the Duke of MEDINA SIDONIA left Lisbon in May 1588. It was to rendezvous with Spanish land forces operating under the command of the Duke of Parma in Flanders and then mount an invasion of England, landing on the coast between Dover and Margate. The operation was launched for several reasons, including retaliation for English support for the Protestant opposition to Spanish rule in the Netherlands and the execution of the Roman Catholic Mary, Queen of Scots. The frequent raids by English PRIVATEERS on Spanish possessions and treasure ships was a further contributory factor.

The Armada as originally planned by Don Alvaro de BAZAN, Marquis of Santa Cruz, would have involved some 556 ships and over 94,000 ground troops. This plan had to be modified following a raid on CADIZ, 1587, by English naval forces under the command of Sir Francis DRAKE, which resulted in the destruction of a significant number of Spanish warships. The sudden death of the Marquis of Santa Cruz in January 1588 was another complication. He was replaced by the Duke of Medina Sidonia, who was a much less experienced naval commander.

The Spanish Armada arrives off Calais and Gravelines in 1588   *(Copyright © National Maritime Museum, Greenwich, London)*

The Spanish fleet, which consisted of 130 ships, left Lisbon on May 28, 1588 but was delayed by bad weather. Forced to take shelter at Corunna, in northwest Spain, it was another month before it resumed its journey to England. It was not sighted in the English Channel until July 19, when it appeared off The Lizard, Cornwall. An English fleet consisting of 129 ships was organized in two commands: Lord HOWARD of Effingham commanded 94 ships based at Plymouth, while Lord Henry Seymour headed a squadron of 35 ships that was waiting off Calais for the arrival of the Duke of Parma's army. Lord Howard's squadron left Plymouth as soon as the Spanish were sighted, and the first shots were fired off the Eddystone, in the waters south of Plymouth, on July 21. The Armada was under continuous long-range fire from more maneuverable English warships as it moved up the Channel in a strong crescent-shape formation. Although it suffered a few losses during a series of running engagements, it remained in formation until it reached Calais, where it anchored on the evening of July 27.

At this point the entire English fleet arrived in the same area and decided to act to prevent the embarkation of enemy troops. The following night it attacked the enemy fleet with eight FIRESHIPS. The Spanish, who faced rapid destruction, were forced to abandon their anchorage, pursued by the English fleet. The opposing fleets came to battle off Gravelines, France, and the English quickly gained the dominant position. Three Spanish ships were lost and the entire fleet nearly ran aground off the Flemish coast. Medina Sidonia, who had been unable to board the Duke of Parma's troops and was running short of ammunition, was forced to abandon the expedition. Unable to retrace his original route because it was cut off by the English, he was forced to sail around the north of Scotland and the west of Ireland. Lord Howard pursued them northward for three days but eventually abandoned the chase. Severe weather conditions during this part of the journey wrecked many Spanish ships; only 67 of the original 130 vessels eventually returned to Spain. Despite the failure of the Armada, the war between the countries continued until 1604. The defeat of the Spanish Armada stands as a defining moment in English naval (and national) history. It marks the beginning of Spain's imperial decline and England's rise as a world power.

Garret Mattingly, *The Defeat of the Spanish Armada*, Boston, 1984.

Spanish Main

The term "Spanish Main" originally referred to Spain's extensive possessions on the northern coast of South America, covering the area from the Orinoco River to the Isthmus of Panama, which conquistadors had seized in the first part of the 16th century. However, by the late 17th century its meaning had changed radically. By this time the "Spanish Main" described the sea area of the Caribbean; the original meaning fell into disuse. The Spanish Main became notorious as a major hunting ground for European BUCCANEERS and PRIVATEERS in the 17th and 18th centuries. Acts of PIRACY in the Caribbean were commonplace until the efforts of national navies eventually extinguished them.

Spanish Navy

During the 16th century the Spanish navy had a wide range of functions, which included the protection of Spain's widely scattered overseas possessions in the Americas, Africa and the Far East. During the reign of Philip II, 1556–98, Spain's empire increased dramatically when it absorbed Portugal and its colonies. Spain also held the Netherlands, and its garrisons there were supplied by sea. In the Mediterranean, where the GALLEY rather than the sailing ship was the dominant type, the Spanish navy was engaged in constraining the Moors of North Africa and the Turks who were advancing steadily westward during this period.

The defeat of the Turks required the resources of more than one maritime power, and the Spanish fleet formed part of the Holy Alliance that Pope Pius V had organized for this purpose. Commanded by the Spaniard Don JUAN OF AUSTRIA, the combined fleet included a strong Spanish contingent headed by the Marquis of Santa Cruz (see Alvaro de BAZAN). They formed the fleet reserve, although Spanish seamen also manned some of the Venetian ships on the extreme left wing when the opposing forces met at the Battle of LEPANTO on October 7, 1571. The Spanish were at the center of the battle, which quickly became a mêlée in which they played a prominent part.

The greatest Spanish naval victory was soon to be followed by its greatest defeat. Philip's ill-conceived plan to invade England and return it to the Roman Catholic faith was always a high-risk enterprise, but the death of Don Juan and then of Santa Cruz, which deprived the navy of two of its most able commanders, reduced the prospects of success still further. The Duke of MEDINA SIDONIA, who was appointed to command the Armada, was not a professional naval officer and was ill-equipped to meet determined English resistance. The decisive English victory at the Battle of Gravelines and the rapid abandonment of the Armada marked a turning point in the history of the Spanish navy. It was a defeat from which it was never fully to recover. The navy's primary function in the centuries that followed—apart from local defense—was the protection of Spain's extensive and widely dispersed colonial empire. It was a duty that, in the long run, the Spanish navy was unable to sustain as more powerful and effective maritime powers (notably England, France and Holland) emerged.

The French, English and Dutch were able, over time, to seize control of the most valuable Spanish colonies while Spain, whether acting alone or in concert with other powers, proved to be powerless to prevent these losses. In alliance with France during the American Revolution and the FRENCH REVOLUTIONARY AND NAPOLEONIC WARS, 1792–1815, the Spanish navy proved to be no match for the ROYAL NAVY and was defeated at the Battle of TRAFALGAR, October 1805, leaving Britain in command of the seas. At the end of the 19th century, the remnants of Spain's once-extensive empire were transferred to the United States as the result of Spain's defeat in the SPANISH-AMERICAN WAR of 1898. This disastrous war for Spain was precipitated by the destruction of an American warship in Havana Harbor, Cuba. The brief conflict was decided at sea, with the U.S. Navy decisively defeating the modern Spanish fleet in the Pacific and the Caribbean. It marked both the end of Spain's long-held aspiration to maintain a powerful naval force as well as the emergence of the U.S. Navy as a global power. During the 20th century Spain has maintained a small defensive navy that today contributes to European defense through the country's involvement in the North Atlantic Treaty Organization (NATO).

John D. Harbron, *Trafalgar and the Spanish Navy,* London, 1988.

Spanish Succession, War of the

1701–14

At the beginning of the 18th century, England, Holland and Austria were united in seeking to prevent Spain from establishing a union with France. King Charles II of Spain was childless, and Louis XIV of France claimed the Spanish throne for his second grandson, Philip of Anjou. On Charles' death, on November 1, 1701, Philip was proclaimed Philip V of Spain. These events sparked a general European war, with the decisive battles being fought by ground forces in Italy, Germany, Spain and the Spanish Netherlands. English operations at sea were designed to underpin ground operations by weakening Franco-Spanish naval and economic power. On October 12, 1702, for example, Admiral Sir George ROOKE captured the Spanish treasure fleet in VIGO BAY and seized booty to the value of £2 million. Nearly two years later, on July 23–24, 1704, an English fleet under George BYNG, Viscount Torrington, captured GIBRALTAR from the Spanish and held it against determined enemy counterattacks.

The English fleet also operated in support of ground operations in Spain and Portugal, with naval units under Admiral Sir Clowdisley SHOVELL landing Lord Peterborough and his army in Catalonia in June 1705, where they enjoyed some initial successes. The Royal Navy secured a number of other gains at Spain's expense, including Alicante in August 24, 1706, before it turned its attention to the French naval base at Toulon. In July–August 1707, it mounted a BLOCKADE of the port while an allied invasion of France was in progress. The French, who were expecting to lose Toulon, already had sunk 50 warships to prevent them from falling into enemy hands, giving the English effective control of the Mediterranean for the rest of the war. The English navy also operated against French possessions in North America, where the conflict was known as Queen Anne's War, and secured a number of territorial gains. The war was largely brought to an end by the Treaty of Utrecht, 1713, which produced terms generally favorable to Britain and its allies. Although Philip remained king of Spain, the kingdoms of Spain and Portugal were to remain separate.

Chronological List of Naval Events

1702	
August 29–September 3	Action off Cartagena; English attack on a French squadron is repelled
August–September	Anglo-Dutch force under Admiral Sir George Rooke lands at Cadiz but is unable to capture the city
October 12	Rooke attacks the Spanish treasure fleet at Vigo Bay
1704	
July 24	English fleet seizes Gibraltar
August 13	Battle of Malaga; failure of French fleet secures British control of Gibraltar
1705	
March 10	Battle of Marbella; English fleet attacks French ships blockading Gibraltar
June	Combined operation under Admiral Shovell lands in Catalonia; Barcelona falls in October
1706	
June 1	English fleet captures Cartagena; Alicante follows in August and Mallorca in September
1707	
July–August	Allied fleet blockades Toulon as an invasion of France is attempted
1708	
August	British Mediterranean fleet captures Sardinia; Minorca falls in September
1713	Peace of Utrecht

A. D. Francis, *The First Peninsular War, 1702–13,* London, 1975.

Spar Torpedo

An early, primitive version of a weapon that was soon superseded by more elaborate, self-propelled models. Developed in the 1860s, the spar torpedo had no means of propulsion; rather, it was little more than an explosive charge that was detonated on contact. This weapon was carried on the end of a long spar projecting from the bows of a small warship. If the attack was to have any real chance of success, the spar torpedo had to be positioned under the hull of the target ship. Widely used during the AMERICAN CIVIL WAR, 1861–65, the spar torpedo was rapidly superseded by Robert Whitehead's locomotive torpedo, which, as the name suggests, was self-propelled. Widely adopted by the world's navies in the 1870s, it marked a major stage in the development of the TORPEDO. (See also SUBMARINE.)

Special Boat Squadron

British elite unit that was formed during WORLD WAR II, 1939–45, with the aim of carrying out clandestine amphibious raids in occupied Europe. The Special Boat Squadron (SBS) was responsible for attacking and destroying German installations and for gathering intelligence. In a typical major raid, SBS commandos (an SBS group) laid charges on German ships in the Gironde River, France, having reached their targets in kayaks. The SBS survived the end of the war and is now an established specialist unit within the Royal Marines. It has seen service in several conflicts since then, including, most recently, the GULF WAR, 1991, and seeks to operate in complete secrecy. Together with the Special Air Squadron (SAS) it was heavily involved on the FALKLANDS WAR, 1982, and it may have operated on the Argentine mainland as well as on the Falklands and South Georgia, where it was delivered by submarine and prepared the ground for invasion.

In addition to its sabotage and reconnaissance objectives, the SBS has been given responsibility for the security of Britain's offshore oil rigs. As an elite within an elite, admission standards to the SBS are high, and only successful Royal Marine commandos are considered. The training program for new entrants is rigorous and includes seamanship and demolition techniques. Organized in four-man patrols, the SBS commando might be equipped with an Armalite rifle or a Sterling submachine gun and have access to a paddle board or collapsible boat.

J. D. Ladd, *SBS: The Invisible Raiders. The History of the Special Boat Squadron, World War II to the Present*, London, 1983.

Spee, Maximilian Reichsgraf von
1861–1914

At the beginning of WORLD WAR I, 1914–18, Vice Admiral Maximilian von Spee, who had gained much of his naval experience in colonial operations, was commander of the German East Asiatic Squadron. His force consisted of two armored cruisers, the SCHARNHORST and the GNEISENAU, and three light cruisers, the EMDEN, the *Leipzig* and the *Nürnberg*. As a result of Japan's entry into the war on the side of the Allies, von Spee was unable to remain in the China Seas where he had planned to attack British merchant shipping. He moved to the west coast of South America. When he arrived off Chile, near the port of CORONEL, on November 1, 1914, he met and defeated a British squadron under the command of Sir Christopher CRADOCK.

Von Spee then decided to make for Germany, with the aim of attacking Port Stanley in the FALKLAND ISLANDS on the way. However, the squadron was sighted as it approached the British colony, and a powerful British naval force, assembled there especially for the purpose of intercepting von Spee, gave chase. Four of the five German ships were sunk during the battle on December 8, and von Spee, along with 2,000 of his officers and men, was lost. Von Spee enjoyed a high professional reputation in the GERMAN NAVY, and had he returned home as planned, he would have been appointed commander in chief of the HIGH SEAS FLEET. The celebrated but short-lived German World War II POCKET-BATTLESHIP *ADMIRAL GRAF SPEE* was named after him.

Richard Hough, *The Pursuit of Admiral von Spee: A Study in Loneliness and Bravery*, London, 1969.

Spithead

An expanse of water in the east Solent between Portsmouth, a key naval base, and the Isle of Wight in the south of England. It is some 14 miles (23 km) long by about 4 miles (6 km) wide on average and is well protected from all winds. Sometimes known as the Queen's Chamber because of its sheltered position, it was used heavily as a fleet anchorage and assembly point by the British navy during much of its long history, particularly in the era of the sailing navies. Spithead's other, less glorious, association with the history of the ROYAL NAVY was the MUTINY of the Channel Fleet in April–May 1797, during the FRENCH REVOLUTIONARY AND NAPOLEONIC WARS, 1792–1815. It began in a single ship, the *Queen Charlotte*, as a protest about a whole list of grievances, from low pay to poor food, but quickly spread to other Channel Fleet crews at Spithead. They all refused to set sail for operations against the French. Protracted negotiations between the mutineers and the authorities took place, and the mutiny spread to the Nore (a sandbank in the center of the river Thames estuary) before it could be resolved, when the main complaints had been addressed and a commitment was given not to punish the offenders. (See also NORE MUTINY.)

C. Gill, *The Naval Mutinies of 1797*, Manchester, 1913.

Spragge, Sir Edward

c. 1620–73

*E*nglish soldier and naval commander who turned to the sea after the restoration of the monarchy in 1660. Spragge rose quickly in the service and established his reputation during the Second ANGLO-DUTCH WAR, 1665–67. As captain of the *Triumph,* he fought the Dutch effectively and with great bravery at the Battle of LOWESTOFT, 1665, and later at the FOUR DAYS' BATTLE, 1666, and the Battle of ORFORDNESS, 1666. Spragge's reward was rapid promotion to rear admiral and then to vice admiral. He received further recognition with his appointment, following the war, as commander in chief in the Mediterranean, where he was engaged in operations against North African pirates.

Returning home before war was renewed with the Dutch, 1672–74, he played a leading role in tackling the enemy fleet, which turned into a series of personal duels with Dutch commander Admiral Cornelis TROMP. In 1673 he was promoted to the rank of admiral and commanded the rear division of the British fleet at the Battle of the TEXEL. On August 11 the *Prince Royal,* Spragge's flagship, was badly damaged in a fight with Tromp; the unlucky commander was drowned as the boat in which he was transferring was hit and sank.

Spruance, Raymond Ames

1886–1969

*A*merican naval officer, the commander of American naval forces at the decisive Battle of MIDWAY, June 1942, during the Pacific War, 1941–45. Raymond Spruance was born in Baltimore, Maryland on July 3, 1886. He graduated from the U.S. Naval Academy in 1907 in time to join the GREAT WHITE FLEET in its circumnavigation of the globe. Serving mostly in engineering duties both at sea and at shore billets, his quiet manner but bright intellect stood him in good stead, and he served as instructor in strategy at the Naval War College as well as having a tour at the Office of Naval Intelligence. When the United States entered WORLD WAR II, 1939–1945, in December 1941, he was commander of a cruiser division, participating in the early 1942 raids on the Marshall and Gilbert Islands and in the famous Doolittle Raid on Tokyo in April.

Relieving Admiral William HALSEY, who was ill, Spruance assumed command of Task Force 16 on board the U.S.S. ENTERPRISE and was thus subordinate to Admiral Frank J. FLETCHER in reacting to the Japanese advance toward Midway. However, the events of the battle were such that Spruance, a nonaviator, became the real hero of the navy's decisive victory over the Japanese at Midway. Appointed as Admiral Chester NIMITZ's chief of staff, Spruance helped coordinate and plan the central Pacific drive. In 1943 he commanded that campaign, then headed the Central Pacific Force. Promoted to the rank of full admiral in March 1944 and designated commander, Fifth Fleet, his forces conducted the invasions of the Marianas and engaged the Japanese navy at the Battle of the PHILIPPINE SEA, June 1944. Continuing to be involved with the planning and execution of the war, he participated in the campaigns against IWO JIMA, OKINAWA and the Japanese Home Islands. At the end of the war he briefly commanded the Pacific Fleet before serving as president of the U.S. Naval War College. Retiring in 1948, he served as U.S. Ambassador to the Philippines in the early 1950s. Spruance died in California on December 13, 1969, with his reputation secure as one of the key architects of Allied victory in the Pacific. He was a master of amphibious warfare and ranks as one of the great American naval leaders of World War II.

Thomas B. Buell, *The Quiet Warrior: A Biography of Admiral Raymond A. Spruance,* Annapolis, 1970.

Squadron

A naval term used by the world's navies whose precise meaning has varied over the centuries, "squadron" essentially describes a group of warships under a single command. The English fleet was first organized into three squadrons around the 1580s, a pattern that prevailed until 1864, when the age of the sailing navy had almost ended. These three squadrons were identified by a red, white or blue flag and were headed by an admiral, vice admiral and rear admiral respectively. As the fleet expanded, a single admiral could no longer lead it, and a more elaborate structure was needed. The Red, White and Blue Squadrons were each subdivided into three divisions—the van, middle and rear. Each squadron was headed by an admiral, with a vice admiral and rear admiral as his subordinate commanders. The squadrons were ranked in the following order— red, white, blue—and promotions also were made on the same hierarchical basis. A vice admiral of the white would, therefore, become admiral of the blue. By the early 19th century, the U.S. Navy also was organized in three squadrons, but on a very different basis from the Royal Navy. These three squadrons—the Pacific, Mediterranean and the West Indies—reflected the global interests of the United States. The ships in each squadron were widely dispersed or parted and were normally subject only to loose control by their commanding officer. This pattern of organization had no place in a mechanized navy but the term squadron has lived on into the 20th century in the world's naval forces. It now refers to any small group of warships, sometimes eight, operating together.

Squid

*B*ritish antisubmarine mortar, the successor to the HEDGEHOG, which entered service during WORLD WAR

II, 1939–45. The Hedgehog was the first mortar capable of firing ahead of a ship, thus allowing the SONAR to remain in contact with the target submarine during the final stages of an attack. The Hedgehog's main weakness was that its bombs had impact fuses and were much less likely to sink an enemy submarine than a depth charge with a hydrostatic (water pressure) fuse. The squid, which used the latter fuse, was developed as triple-barreled mortar that fired bombs carrying 100 pounds (45.3 kg) of explosive. The mortar swung down to the horizontal, enabling the bombs to be muzzle-loaded. The squid was first fitted to a ship in August 1943, but the new weapon's first victim, U-boat *U-736*, was not sunk until August 1944. Used by the UNITED STATES NAVY and other Allied services as well as the ROYAL NAVY, it proved to be a successful and long-lived design that was to remain in service for much of the postwar period.

Stark, Harold Raynsford
1880–1972

U.S. Chief of Naval Operations during the period up to and including the entry of the United States into WORLD WAR II, 1939–1945, and thus responsible for the navy's preparations for the war. Stark was born in Wilkes-Barre, Pennsylvania on November 12, 1880. Graduating from the U.S. Naval Academy in 1903, he embarked on a career that saw wide and diverse duties. He served on the battleship *Minnesota* as part of the circumnavigation by the GREAT WHITE FLEET from 1907 to 1909. With considerable experience as a commander of ships and stations as well as in staff positions, he served as chief of the Bureau of Ordnance from 1934 to 1937, then as Chief of Naval Operations from 1939 until March 1942. He successfully oversaw the rapid buildup of American naval forces during this period as the country prepared for war. He was replaced following criticism of his failure to warn Admiral Husband KIMMEL, naval commander at Pearl Harbor, of the impending Japanese attack in December 1941. In April 1942 he became commander of American naval forces in Europe, followed by the additional command of the Twelfth Fleet in the autumn of 1943. He relinquished both these positions at the end of the war and retired with the rank of admiral in April 1946, dying on August 20, 1972.

B. Mitchell Simpson III, *Admiral Harold R. Stark: Architect of Victory, 1939–1945*, Columbia, S.C., 1989.

Stark, U.S.S.

A United States frigate (named after Admiral Harold STARK) that was engaged in escorting Kuwaiti tankers through the Persian Gulf during the IRAN-IRAQ WAR, 1980–88. On May 17, 1987, as she passed through international waters near the coast of Bahrain, the *Stark* was attacked by an Iraqi jet. The Iraqi plane fired two EXOCET missiles at the *Stark* and badly damaged her. Her crew suffered heavy casualties: 37 men were killed and 21 injured. Iraq later apologized for this accident and offered compensation. The United States Navy censured the captain of the *Stark* for failing to respond more rapidly and effectively to this attack. This incident may have contributed to another accident just over a year later: There was no danger of the captain of the U.S.S. *Vincennes*, which was on patrol in the Gulf, being taken by surprise when it mistook an Iranian Airbus passenger jet for an attacking military aircraft and launched a surface-to-air missile at the jet. As a result 290 passengers and crew lost their lives.

Stewart, Charles
1778–1869

*O*ne of the longest-serving naval officers in American history. Charles Stewart was born in Philadelphia, Pennsylvania in 1778. Entering the merchant service at age 13, he was commissioned a lieutenant in the new U.S. Navy in 1798, just prior to the QUASI-WAR, 1798–1800, with France. Attached to the frigate *UNITED STATES*, he was involved in taking four French PRIVATEERS in the Caribbean. Remaining in the West Indies as commander of the *Experiment*, he seized two French merchantmen and a privateer. During the war with the North African states he saw service as the *CONSTELLATION*'s first lieutenant in the BLOCKADE of Tripoli, then as commander of the *Syren* participating in the famous burning of the *Philadelphia* in February 1804.

During the WAR OF 1812 Stewart commanded the *Constitution*, capturing several prizes, and on February 20, 1815—unaware that the war had been formally concluded—defeating the British frigate *Cyane* and the sloop *Levant*. He subsequently received the thanks of Congress. Service as commander of the Mediterranean Squadron, Pacific Squadron and as one of the Navy Commissioners followed, as did command of the navy yard in Philadelphia. Placed on the reserve list in 1855, he was honored by a special act of Congress by being designated senior flag officer, the navy's then highest-ranking officer. Consulted by President Abraham Lincoln on the relief of Fort Sumter at the beginning of the AMERICAN CIVIL WAR, 1861–65, in April 1861, he declined active service and retired that year at the age of 83. He had been a senior officer for about 17 years and in service for a total of 71 years. He died on November 6, 1869 in Bordentown, New Jersey. Stewart was the grandfather of the Irish statesman and advocate for home rule, Charles Stewart Parnell.

William B. Cogar, *Dictionary of Admirals of the U.S. Navy, Vol. 1, 1862–1900*, Annapolis, 1989.

Stockton, Robert Field
1795–1866

American naval officer and conqueror of California, born in Princeton, New Jersey in 1795, the son of U.S. Senator Richard Stockton. As a young midshipman, Robert Stockton served under John RODGERS in the WAR OF 1812 as well as in the forces against the Barbary states after 1815. A pioneering figure in the introduction of steam power for the U.S. Navy, he organized the construction of the *PRINCETON,* the first screw-propeller vessel, and commanded her during the 1840s. He had a long-standing feud with inventor John ERICSSON.

During the Mexican-American War, 1846–48, he reinforced a small naval squadron off Monterey, California in July 1846 and replaced Commodore John D. SLOAT as commander of the Pacific Squadron. Sloat had announced the American annexation of California but Stockton began land operations to eject the Mexican administration. In Los Angeles, he proclaimed the territory a part of the United States and established a civil and military government, taking for himself the function of governor-general and commander in chief. His efforts were premature, however, as Mexican forces temporarily retook Los Angeles, until the U.S. Army ended the war in California, which had been brought under control in only six months.

Stockton resigned his commission in 1850 and served from 1851 to 1853 as U.S. Senator from his native New Jersey. During this period he was a fervent reformer for such things as the abolition of flogging in the navy.

Harold D. Langley, "Robert F. Stockton: Naval Officer and Reformer," in *Command Under Sail. Makers of the American Naval Tradition, 1775–1850,* ed. James C. Bradford, Annapolis, 1985.

Stoddert, Benjamin
1751–1813

First United States Secretary of the Navy, born in Charles County, Maryland. Stoddert served as a Revolutionary war soldier and was a partner in a shipping company before entering politics. A Federalist, he became the first Secretary of the Navy when the Navy Department was created in 1798. As such, he oversaw the earliest legislation and procedures to launch the fledgling U.S. Navy during the period of the undeclared naval war—the QUASI-WAR, 1798–1800—against France. A believer that the future of the United States rested with commerce, he was a fervent supporter of a blue-water fleet, overseeing the construction of the first FRIGATES as well as the first navy yards. He left the post of Secretary of the Navy in 1801 after the Federalists lost to the Democratic-Republicans in the 1800 election.

John Joseph Carrigg, "Benjamin Stoddert," in *American Secretaries of the Navy,* ed. Paolo E. Coletta, Vol. 1, pp. 59–75, Annapolis, 1980.

Strachan, Sir Richard
1760–1828

British admiral who was notable as the naval commander in chief of the disastrous WALCHEREN expedition, 1809. Strachan entered the Royal Navy in 1772 and saw much service in the FRENCH REVOLUTIONARY AND NAPOLEONIC WARS, 1792–1815. He gained prominence during the Napoleonic Wars, 1803–15, when he was responsible for the close BLOCKADE of Cadiz at the beginning of the war. His greatest success was the capture of four French ships of the line that had escaped from the Battle of TRAFALGAR, October 1805. Strachan intercepted them in the Bay of Biscay; after a short action, all four surrendered. He gained several honors, including promotion to the rank of rear admiral, as a result of this action. Less fortunate was his involvement in the Walcheren expedition, which flowed from his appointment as commander of the British North Sea fleet. The failed operation, which was so costly in British lives, cast a shadow over Strachan's future career. He was never employed again although he was promoted to the rank of vice admiral and of admiral by seniority alone.

Sturdee, Sir Doveton
1859–1925

British admiral who gained distinction in the opening stages of WORLD WAR I, 1914–18. Following the disastrous British defeat in the Battle of CORONEL, November 1, 1914, at the hands of Vice Admiral Maximilian von SPEE, Sturdee was sent to the South Atlantic with two battle cruisers under his command. His orders were to locate and destroy von Spee's flotilla—a task he achieved with great success at the Battle of the FALKLAND ISLANDS on December 8, 1914.

In recognition of his victory, Sturdee, who had served as chief of naval war staff during the first few months of the war, was given command of the Fourth Battle Squadron of the GRAND FLEET, where he remained until 1918. Although he failed to secure command of the fleet on Admiral John JELLICOE's departure to the Admiralty, he was promoted full admiral in 1917 and ended his naval career as commander in chief at the Nore.

Styrsudden, Battle of
June 3–4, 1790

In the final phase of the RUSSO-SWEDISH WAR, 1788–90, Sweden made a major thrust against the Russian capital, St. Petersburg. In a combined operation the Swedish fleet, commanded by Carl, Duke of Södermanland (later King CHARLES XIII), moved across the Gulf of Finland in support of movements by the army and coastal flotilla. The

Russians responded to the Swedish action by dispatching a squadron under the command of Vice Admiral Alexander Kruse from its base at Kronstadt. Under Kruse's command were 17 ships of the line and 19 frigates. The two fleets met toward the eastern end of the gulf off Styrsudden, a cape on the southern coast of Finland, on June 3. They clashed twice on two succeeding days, exchanging fire at long range without a clear outcome. With the arrival of the Russian Reval (Tallinn) squadron, Duke Carl was forced to abandon the fight and postpone his planned action against St. Petersburg. Before the two Russian squadrons could join forces, he moved northwest and entered VIBORG BAY, where the Swedish galley fleet was anchored. The Russian fleet blockaded the Swedes almost immediately, and the Swedes remained there until July 3. Their breakout attempt led to the Battle of SVENSKUND, July 9–10, 1790.

Submarine

*E*xperiments with submersible vessels date back to the early 17th century but the first operational example was the screw-propelled *TURTLE*, designed by David BUSHNELL,

which was used unsuccessfully against a British warship in September 1776, during the AMERICAN WAR OF INDEPENDENCE, 1775–83. The first successful attack by a semisubmersible occurred in October 1863, during the AMERICAN CIVIL WAR, 1861–65, when the Confederate boat *DAVID* damaged a Union IRONCLAD using a SPAR TORPEDO. During the late 19th century, the development of electric and fuel oil motors, together with the self-propelled TORPEDO, made possible the production of a fully submersible boat that could travel a reasonable distance under its own power.

The first designs appeared in the 1880s, but it was the pioneering work of American engineer John HOLLAND that marked the beginning of the modern submarine. His streamlined gasoline-driven boat, which was equipped with electric motors for used when submerged, appeared in 1900. She had a conning tower, ballast tanks to enable her to float or submerge and horizontal rudders to control her depth underwater. Holland's basic design was refined by the use of safer diesel engines in place of gasoline versions and improved depth control. Surface and submerged speeds gradually increased and, by 1914, 16 and 10 knots respectively could be achieved. A typical submarine of this period had four torpedo tubes and a displacement of about 700 tons.

The German minelaying submarine *UC5*, which entered service in 1915   (*Copyright © Imperial War Museum, London*)

At the beginning of WORLD WAR I, Britain and France possessed about half of the submarines then in existence. The submarine arm of the GERMAN NAVY had only 20 operational boats available, but an urgent construction program was introduced as soon as war was declared. The Germans took the lead in the development of longer range and more specialist types, including MINELAYERS and large submarine cruisers, the latter having displacements of up to 3,000 tons. The number of operational U-BOATS reached its peak in October 1917, when 140 units were in service. British submarines were largely small coastal types, reflecting an early Admiralty view that they were useful mainly for harbor defense.

U-boats played the dominant part in German naval strategy, particularly in the period after the Battle of JUTLAND, May 1916, when Germany's dreadnoughts were effectively confined to port. Operating on the surface and below, and equipped with both guns and torpedoes, German submarines sank over 11 million tons of Allied shipping during the war, of which the great proportion (8 million tons) was British. During the first few months of 1917, Britain was brought close to defeat as Germany's second period of unrestricted submarine warfare exacted a heavy toll. However, the long-overdue introduction of the convoy system, assisted by new techniques of antisubmarine warfare, transformed the situation. German U-boat losses began to rise; by the end of the war, 178 had been sunk by the British.

Submarine design progressed so rapidly during the war that few major changes were introduced in the interwar period. The success of the convoy system and the introduction of SONAR discouraged major new development work, although the Germans produced the concept of the WOLF PACK, with several U-boats operating together in the hunt for enemy targets. During WORLD WAR II, 1939–45, the submarine was deployed on a much larger scale than during World War I. The advantage was at first held by the attacking submarine until Allied countermeasures swung the pendulum in the opposite direction. This enabled the Allies eventually to win the critical Battle of the ATLANTIC, 1939–45. Toward the end of the war, the Germans developed the snorkel tube, which allowed the U-boat's diesel engines to work at periscope depth. Batteries therefore could be charged more frequently, and the boat's submerged range was extended. The Germans also introduced faster boats with improved diving capability. These changes suggested that the balance was swinging in favor of the attack, but they came too late to affect the outcome.

Since the end of the war, the submarine has emerged as the CAPITAL SHIP of the modern navy, and both the Americans and the Soviets have built them in quantity. About 700 submarines, both conventional and nuclear-powered, currently are in service. The first nuclear-powered submarine, the U.S.S. *Nautilus*, appeared in 1955 and they are now operated by Russia, Britain, France and China as well as the United States. Equipped with torpedoes and guided missiles the nuclear submarine has become a formidable weapon that is capable of traveling underwater for long periods at maximum speed. Some submarines have been equipped with guided missiles with nuclear warheads, such as POLARIS and TRIDENT. The difficulty of detecting these submarines meant that they were an integral part of the superpowers' deterrent force during the Cold War.

Hashimoto Mochitsura, *Sunk. The Story of the Japanese Submarine Fleet, 1943–45*, London, 1945; Anthony Preston, *Submarines*, London, 1983; Dan van der Vat, *Stealth at Sea. The History of the Submarine*, London, 1994.

Submarine, British A-class

The first British-designed SUBMARINE, the 15 A-class boats were based on the experimental Holland types that had been produced under license by Vickers of Barrow in Furness in 1901–3. Built in 1902–5, they had twin torpedo tubes in the bow (with seven torpedoes carried) and the first real conning tower (the structure that connected the bridge with the hull and was sealed at both ends by watertight hatches). Operated by a crew of 11, they were 103 feet 3 inches (31.47 m) in length and had a beam of 11 feet 9 inches (3.58 m). Power was provided by a 16-cylinder Wolseley gasoline engine that gave a maximum speed of approximately 11.5 knots on the surface. All but one of these submarines were in service by the autumn of 1905.

Although the A-class boats—together with the improved B and C classes—were dismissed by conservative naval officers as "Fisher's toys" (see Admiral Lord FISHER), the quality of their design helped to ensure their acceptance as an important element in the naval armory. Surviving A-class units were still in Royal Navy use during WORLD WAR I, 1914–18, mainly in a training role. (See also SUBMARINE, BRITISH C-CLASS; SUBMARINE, BRITISH D-CLASS.)

Submarine, British C-class

The first British submarine to the produced in quantity—38 were built between 1906 and 1910—the C type was similar to its predecessors in appearance and performance. Operated by a crew of 16, it had a surface displacement of 286 tons, a length of 142 feet (44 m) and a surface speed of 12 knots. Like the B class, it had a proper deck fitted along the hull. In spite of its small size and limited range, which kept it confined to coastal waters, it played a useful role during WORLD WAR I, 1914–18. Four examples were transported by ship and rail to the Gulf of Finland (via Archangel), where they were used against

German shipping. These boats were scuttled in April 1918 to avoid capture. The C type often was used in conjunction with a trawler that acted as a decoy ship to lure German U-BOATS into its torpedo range, a tactic that had only limited success.

Submarine, British D-class

The first British submarine capable of patrolling the open oceans, the D class appeared shortly before WORLD WAR I, 1914–18. It was much larger than its B and C CLASS predecessors, with a length of 163 feet 7 inches (50 m), a surface displacement of just under 500 tons and a crew of 20. Power was provided by two diesel-driven screws that gave it a range of 2,500 nautical miles at a surface speed of 10 knots. The D class submarines were equipped with three 18-inch (46-cm) torpedo tubes (two bow, one stern). One member of this class—D4—also was the first submarine to carry a gun (a 12-pounder) mounted on the deck. Eight D-class boats were built between 1908 and 1911; three were lost during World War I, including one sunk in error by a French airship. The successful development of these boats led directly to the British E CLASS, the most important Allied submarines of the war.

Submarine, British E-class

The most advanced submarine in British service at the beginning of WORLD WAR I, 1914–18, the E class, of which 56 were built between 1912 and 1916, incorporated some important design modifications. It had a larger and stronger hull than its predecessors (see SUBMARINE, BRITISH A-CLASS, C-CLASS, D-CLASS) and was constructed with two watertight bulkheads. Operated by a crew of 30, it had a surface displacement of 660 tons and a length of 177 feet (54 m). There were a pair of beam torpedo tubes as well as one at the bow and another at the stern. Some E-class boats were fitted with a second torpedo tube in the bow and a third bulkhead. A 12-pounder gun was mounted on the deck as standard following successful trials of this design with a British D-class boat. Twin 800-horsepower diesel engines gave the boat a range of 3,000 nautical miles at a surface speed of 15 knots. Underwater it could travel for about 120 miles at low speed before the electric power failed. Six E-class boats were modified as minelayers, the first of their kind, and could hold 20 mines each. The E-22 became the world's first aircraft-carrying submarine when, early in 1916, it was fitted with a launching ramp.

The E-class boats were at the forefront of the Allied submarine offensive during World War I and achieved

A British E-class submarine of World War I, 1914–18 (Copyright © Imperial War Museum, London)

some notable successes in the Baltic and in the Sea of Marmara in southeast Europe. The *E-9* in fact became the first British submarine to score a victory when she sank the German cruiser *Hela* in the Baltic on September 13, 1914. Their service in the Sea of Marmara was dominated by the exploits of *E-11*, commanded by Lieutenant Commander Martin Nasmith. During the course of his two missions against the Turks, which amounted to a total of 96 days in the area, he destroyed 101 enemy ships. The cost of such operations was, however, very high. Almost half of the E-class submarines were lost by the end of the war.

Submarine, British K-class

Like the earlier British J-class, 1916–17, the Ks represented another ADMIRALTY attempt to produce a fast submarine that was capable of operating with the main battle fleet—traveling with it on the surface and submerging when the enemy was engaged. Developed in 1915, the K-class submarine was the largest submarine yet produced.

Operated by a crew of 50, it was 330 feet (100.5 m) in length, had a displacement of 1,980 tons on the surface and a distinctive swan-shaped bow. The design of the main power plant was based on the experience of the *Swordfish*, Britain's first steam-driven submarine. The oil-fired steam turbines with which the K class was equipped provided the only means of reaching the target speed—24 knots—needed to maintain contact with the battle fleet.

Batteries powered the boat underwater at a maximum speed of 9 knots, while a third power source—an 800-horsepower diesel engine—was used while steam was being built up after surfacing or while maneuvering in harbor. Although the Ks were technically advanced, they were relatively slow in diving because of the need to seal their funnels first. They were heavily armed with ten 18-inch (46-cm) torpedo tubes, including a revolving twin tube located in the superstructure. The Ks also were equipped with two 4-inch (10-cm) and one 3-inch high-angle guns.

The K submarines, of which 17 were produced, had a disastrous operational record in WORLD WAR I, 1914–18, and only once was the enemy engaged. They were, however, involved in a large number of accidents, the most serious

The British World War I steam submarine *K6*   *(Copyright © Imperial War Museum, London)*

being a notorious incident in January 1918. A flotilla of submarines and other ships was involved in a series of surface collisions as ten K-class submarines joined the GRAND FLEET. Two Ks were sunk and four others damaged. A jammed helm was the immediate cause but the incident raised wider questions about the suitability of operating submarines, with their limited bridge facilities, as part of the battle fleet.

Submarine-Launched Ballistic Missile

Since the appearance of the American POLARIS in 1960, submarine-launched ballistic missiles (SLBMs) have been an increasingly important part of the world's armory of nuclear weapons. Deployed by the United States, the Soviet Union, China, France and Britain, they are much more difficult to identify and destroy than other nuclear weapons. They were a key element in maintaining the "balance of terror" between the two superpowers during the latter stages of the COLD WAR in the 1970s and 1980s. The introduction of Polaris stimulated a technological race between the United States and the Soviet Union in the further development of SLBMs.

It took the Soviet Union some seven years to match the Polaris with the introduction of the SS-N-6 missile, which was launched from Yankee-class submarines. The American POSEIDON, which appeared in the 1970s, was equipped with multiple guided missile warheads, which marked a massive increase in its nuclear capability. The Soviets also developed a multiple warhead variant, the SS-N-18, which was introduced in 1977. This missile had a longer range (4,800 miles; 8,000 km) than its American equivalent, although by the 1980s the new TRIDENT missile could travel a similar distance. During the 1980s the two superpowers' SLBM designs tended to converge, and the disparities in absolute performance evident in earlier periods disappeared. Planned increases in strategic nuclear arsenals have been abandoned following the demise of the Soviet Union and the end of the Cold War.

Graham Spinardi, *From Polaris to Trident: The Development of U.S. Fleet Ballistic Technology*, Cambridge, Mass., 1994.

Sueter, Sir Murray
1872–1960

The first director of the air department of the British Admiralty, 1912–15, Rear Admiral Sir Murray Sueter was largely responsible for the creation of the ROYAL NAVAL AIR SERVICE (RNAS), which broke away from the Royal Flying Corps in 1914.

In his earlier naval career Sueter was associated with the development of radio telegraphy and with the introduction of submarines. A powerful advocate of naval air power,

he was to be an innovative head of the RNAS. He presided over the rapid expansion of the service on the outbreak of WORLD WAR I, 1914–18, and was an important influence on the adoption of the seaplane for naval use. Sueter was also among the first to see the potential of torpedo-carrying aircraft. He encouraged the development of naval airships and was responsible as well for the RNAS's pioneering use of armored cars on the Western Front.

In 1915–17 he oversaw naval aircraft production, which was followed by a period in command of RNAS units in southern Italy. As a result of differences with the Admiralty, Sueter was unemployed for the last few months of the war, bringing his distinguished naval career to an end.

Suez Crisis
1956

Following his failure to secure financing from Britain and the United States for the Aswan Dam project on the Nile, Egyptian President Gamal Abdel Nasser decided to nationalize the Suez Canal Company on July 26, 1956. Dues collected by the company, whose shares were largely owned by the British government and French private investors, would be used to finance the Nile project. This action coincided with increasing tension between Egypt and Israel. Nasser soon banned Israeli ships from the canal and denied them access to the port of Eilat. British Prime Minister Anthony Eden, whose judgment was colored by a strong personal antipathy to President Nasser, favored military action against Egypt. At the same time the Israelis were planning a preemptive strike against Egypt and secretly coordinated their plans with the British. In August military preparations began in England with the call-up of reservists in all three services. The French, who also favored direct action, joined with the British to form a joint command structure for the planned task force. The naval component of the expeditionary force was to consist of 130 warships as well as 79,000 men, 21,000 vehicles and 500 aircraft.

The Israelis made their move on October 29 as the expeditionary force left from several ports in Britain and France as well as from Malta, Algiers and Cyprus. On November 1 Allied air attacks on Egyptian military targets began and some carrier-based aircraft were involved. The Egyptians responded by using large numbers of BLOCKSHIPS to effectively seal the canal. On November 5 the first Allied paratroopers landed at El Gamil airfield and at Port Fouad. Port Said was the initial target of the Allied fleet, and the first units arrived there on November 6. After a short bombardment, landing craft were dispatched and the first ever AMPHIBIOUS attack using HELICOPTERS had begun. Once Port Said had been taken, British paratroopers advanced 15 miles toward Suez. Within a few days the remainder of the expeditionary force had arrived from

Blockships close the Suez Canal during the 1956 crisis   *(Copyright © Imperial War Museum, London)*

England. However, international political pressure led by the United States ensured that this Anglo-French operation went no further, and before the end of the year the whole expeditionary force had withdrawn in favor of a United Nations peacekeeping force. Although the naval and military forces performed their initial tasks according to plan with few casualties, the expedition had been a political disaster that undermined Britain's position in the Middle East and severely tested Anglo-American relations.

Roy Fullick and Geoffrey Powell, *Suez: The Double War*, London, 1979.

Suffren

Launched in 1899, this French BATTLESHIP had turreted secondary guns, an advanced arrangement that was not to be introduced in the warships of other navies for some time. The *Suffren* also had the main armament of four 12-inch (30-cm) guns, a maximum speed of almost 18 knots and a complement of 714. She was 411 feet 9 inch (125.5 m) in length and had a beam of 70 feet 2 inches (21.39 m). During WORLD WAR I, 1914–18, she participated in the DARDANELLES operations, 1915, sustaining some damage. In November 1916 she was torpedoed by the German submarine *U52* while traveling unescorted off Lisbon, and sank with the loss of all her crew.

Suffren de Saint Tropez, Pierre André de
1729–88

One of France's greatest naval commanders, Admiral Suffren gained his formative experience during the War of the AUSTRIAN SUCCESSION, 1740–48, entering as a *garde de la marine*, or midshipman. After fighting off Toulon in 1744 and at Cape Breton in 1746, he was captured by British Admiral Edward HAWKE in 1747. Released at the end of the war, Suffren spent some time in the service of the Knights Hospitallers of Malta. He continued in membership of this order throughout his career and gradually progressed up its ranks. During the SEVEN YEARS' WAR, 1756–63, Suffren was captured once more by the British when the *Ocean*, the ship in which he was serving, was seized off Lagos, Portugal, by Admiral Edward BOSCAWEN in 1759. During the AMERICAN WAR OF INDEPENDENCE, 1775–83, he first saw service in North America and the West Indies, where he commanded a French squadron that fought Admiral John BYRON at GRENADA in 1779.

In 1781 Suffren was dispatched to the Indian Ocean in command of a squadron of five ships that was to operate against the British fleet in the East Indies. En route he attacked a British squadron anchored off the Cape Verde Islands and thus neutralized a potential threat to the Dutch colony of the Cape of Good Hope. Suffren's squadron was enlarged to 11 ships of the line when he arrived at Mauritius because of the death of Admiral d'Orves, who commanded a force of six ships also operating in the area. With a strengthened fleet Suffren began an epic 18-month struggle against larger forces under the command of Admiral Sir Edward HUGHES off the coast of India and Ceylon (Sri Lanka). With great skill and determination, but with no permanent base, he engaged the British in five separate battles from SADRAS, February 17, 1782, to CUDDALORE, June 20, 1783. His greatest achievement was the capture of the British base of TRINCOMALEE, Ceylon, on August 22, 1782, with the loss of only one ship of the line throughout the entire campaign. Suffren returned home as a hero but died shortly afterward, possibly as the result of a duel.

Superb, H.M.S.

Superb was a frequently used name in the British navy and was applied to a wide variety of warships from the early 18th century until 1960. An interesting 19th-century *Superb* was an IRONCLAD of 9,710 tons, launched in 1875, with excellent armor protection. Although she was equipped with full barque-rigging, she proved to be virtually impossible to sail. The rigging was removed and she was propelled by her steam engines alone at a speed of just over 13 knots an hour.

A later *Superb* was a Bellerophon-class dreadnought battleship, launched in 1907, which had a displacement of 18,800 tons. She served throughout WORLD WAR I, 1914–18, as part of the GRAND FLEET and was present at the Battle of JUTLAND, May 1916. The name had first been used in the English service in 1710 when the *Superbe*, a French 60-gun ship, was captured during the War of the SPANISH SUCCESSION, 1701–14, and commissioned by the Royal Navy. Another 18th-century *Superb*, a 74-gun third-rate (see RATING OF SHIPS) ship, had served as Sir Edward

HUGHES's flagship during his five remarkable engagements against the French in the Indian Ocean, 1782–83, during the AMERICAN WAR OF INDEPENDENCE, 1775–83.

Surcouf

French submarine cruiser, launched in 1929, that had a displacement of 4,218 tons and a range of up to 10,000 miles (16,000 km) at 8.5 knots submerged (18 knots on the surface). At the time of her construction she was the largest submarine in the world. Operated by a crew of 118, she was 361 feet (110 m) long and had a beam of 29.5 feet (9 m). Armament included ten torpedo tubes, twin 8-inch (20-cm) guns and two 37-mm antiaircraft guns. She carried a small spotting aircraft in a hangar.

In June 1940, during WORLD WAR II, 1939–45, the *Surcouf* escaped from Brest to England when the French surrendered to the Germans. She became part of the Free French Naval Force on August 27, 1940 and, beginning in February 1941, was used as a convoy escort in the North Atlantic. Later that year the *Surcouf* was refitted for service in the Pacific, but she sank in the Gulf of Mexico in mysterious circumstances during the night of February 18, 1942. She had apparently been accidentally rammed by the American freighter *Thomson Lykes* as she made her way to the Panama Canal.

James Rusbridger, *Who Sank Surcouf? The Truth About the Disappearance of the Pride of the French Navy*, London, 1991.

Svenskund, Battle of
July 9–10, 1790

After its well-planned escape from VIBORG Bay on July 3, 1790, the Swedish fleet fought the Russians once more before the RUSSO-SWEDISH WAR, 1788–90, came to an end. The Swedes had entered Svensksund Fjord, where they were reinforced. Some 200 ships, anchored in an L-shape formation, were now at the disposal of Duke Carl (the future King CHARLES XIII), who trained their guns on the fjord entrance in expectation of a Russian attack. This materialized during the morning of July 9, when the Russian inshore fleet of 140 ships, commanded by Vice-Admiral Prince Charles Nassau-Siegen, approached the fjord from the south. The Russians came under concentrated Swedish fire, and ten hours' fierce fighting ensued. Eventually Prince Nassau-Siegen was forced to withdraw with heavy losses.

The following day, July 10, the Swedish fleet counterattacked, forcing the Russians to withdraw toward Aspo. The Russians suffered heavy losses, including 64 ships and more than 7,000 men, compared with the destruction of only four Swedish ships. Empress Catherine of Russia was now persuaded to make peace, which was concluded shortly afterward with the Treaty of Verela. Nonetheless, despite their defeat, the Russians had become the dominant Baltic power, while the Swedes entered a period of relative decline from which they never recovered.

Swedish Navy

*G*ustavus Adolphus, king of Sweden, 1611–32, was a great military commander who also developed the country's naval power. The navy was the means by which Sweden, at this time a significant European power, could send an army across the Baltic to Germany in support of the Protestants during the Thirty Years' War, 1618–48. Gustavus also used it to establish and preserve Sweden's position as the dominant Baltic power and to resist successfully Danish attempts to challenge it. The navy's role expanded as it was required to protect the extensive territorial gains that Sweden secured at the end of the Thirty Years' War. These gains extended as far as the archbishopric Bremen and were subject to regular challenge by the Danes. The Dutch defeated the Swedes' ill-conceived attempt to increase them further at the Battle of the SOUND, 1658.

Not until the early 18th century did the Swedes embark on major new military activity, with operations against Poland and Russia. Following Sweden's defeat at the land Battle of Poltava, 1709, Tsar PETER THE GREAT of Russia decided to develop a Russian Baltic fleet that would alter the balance of power in the area permanently. During the Great Northern War, 1700–21, the Russians exercised their new power at the Battle of Gangut, 1714, defeating the Swedish navy. Further Russo-Swedish naval wars followed during the 18th century, with the outcome sometimes favoring one side, sometimes the other. The RUSSO-SWEDISH WAR of 1788–90 produced a clearcut result when, on July 9, 1790, the Swedish fleet, under the command of King Gustavus III, soundly defeated the Russian navy at the second Battle of SVENSKUND, July 9, 1790. Notable as the last occasion in which a European monarch personally commanded a fleet in wartime, it was one of the greatest victories in the history of the Swedish navy. It was also to be its last.

Despite this victory, the outcome of the war had been far from certain and it gave a clear indication of the potential dangers of engaging an increasingly powerful Russian empire. Never again was the Swedish navy used for offensive purposes; instead, it has developed a key role in home defense in support of the country's policy of neutrality, which has been maintained until the present day.

Swiftsure, H.M.S.

*T*he name of several distinguished British warships including a 74-gun ship, the fifth *Swiftsure* in Royal Navy service, that served at the Battle of TRAFALGAR, October 1805. An earlier *Swiftsure,* under the command of Benjamin HALLOWELL, had played a leading part in the Battle of the NILE, August 1, 1798, during the FRENCH REVOLUTIONARY AND NAPOLEONIC WARS, 1792–1815. The first *Swiftsure* was a 400-ton ship of 41 guns that was launched in 1573. She saw action against the SPANISH ARMADA, 1588, and in the operation against Lisbon and Corunna the following year.

There also have been three 20th-century British warships of this name. In 1903, a pre-dreadnought BATTLESHIP of 11,800 tons was launched as the *Swiftsure*. She served for much of her active career in the Mediterranean and participated in the operation against the DARDANELLES, 1915, during WORLD WAR I, 1914–18. *Swiftsure* also was the name of a WORLD WAR II, 1939–45, CRUISER of 8,000 tons, launched in 1943, that served with the British Pacific fleet in last year of the war and survived until 1962. The most recent use of the name *Swiftsure* was for a class of six nuclear-powered hunter-killer submarines with an underwater displacement of 4,429 tons. Typically armed with five heavyweight torpedo tubes, these Swiftsure class submarines were capable of remaining underwater for extended periods. The *Swiftsure* has been decommissioned, but other members of the class remain in service.

Sydney

A British-produced light cruiser, one of three members of the Amphion class, which appeared in 1935–37. The *Sydney* was notable as the only regular warship to have been sunk by an ARMED MERCHANT CRUISER. The *Sydney* had a displacement of 6,830 tons, an overall length of 555 feet (169.16 m) and a beam of 56 feet 8 inches (17.2 m). She had a maximum speed of 32.5 knots, and her armament included eight 6-inch (15-cm) guns and four 8-inch (20-cm) antiaircraft guns. Like the *Hobart* and the *Perth*, her sister ships, the *Sydney* was transferred to the Royal Australian Navy on completion. During the early stages of WORLD WAR II, 1939–45, the *Sydney* served in the Mediterranean and, on July 19, 1940, she sank an Italian cruiser off Cape Spada, Crete. However, in November 1941, she suffered the same fate when she was torpedoed in the southwestern Pacific by the German auxiliary cruiser *Kormoran*. The *Perth* met a similar end at the hands of the Japanese, but the *Hobart* survived the Pacific war and was not scrapped until 1962.

Sydney Harbor Raid

1942

A key example of the use of MIDGET SUBMARINES during WORLD WAR II, 1939–45, this Japanese attack on Sydney, Australia, achieved virtually no success. At the beginning of the operation, three Type-A midget submarines were launched from three standard Japanese submarines some 23 miles (37 km) east of Sydney harbor in the early evening of May 31, 1942. They entered the harbor during the hours of darkness, but a patrol boat detected one midget almost immediately. The crew destroyed it before the Australians could act. As the second midget was located and pursued by the enemy, the Japanese crew committed suicide. The sole remaining midget submarine succeeded in reaching the anchorage, where several large warships were located. It midget surfaced to attack but came under heavy fire and was forced to dive. When it resurfaced its only victim was a barracks ship, although it had only narrowly missed an American heavy cruiser. The surviving midget crew were forced to scuttle their boat.

Taiho

Japanese AIRCRAFT CARRIER of WORLD WAR II, 1939–45, the *Taiho* was sunk during her first engagement in the PACIFIC WAR, 1941–45. Laid down in July 1941 and completed in March 1944 with a displacement of 29,300 tons, the *Taiho* had an overall length of 852 feet (259.7 m) and a beam of 90 feet 9 inches (27.66 m). Her maximum speed was 33 knots, she could carry 53 aircraft, and her main armament consisted of 12 3.9-inch (10-cm) antiaircraft guns. She was fitted with an armored flight deck, engine room and magazine. The *Taiho* served as Vice Admiral Jisaburo OZAWA's flagship of the First Carrier Strike Force for some three months before the Battle of the PHILIPPINE SEA, June 1944, when she was torpedoed by the American submarine *Albacore*. She survived this attack but caught fire a few hours later when concentrated oil vapor from her aircraft ignited in the hangar.

Taiyo

One of the first Japanese merchant ships to be converted as an AIRCRAFT CARRIER. The *Taiyo* and her sister ships, the *Chuyo* and the *Unyo*, were completed in 1941–42 as Japan entered WORLD WAR II, 1939–45. It soon became evident that they were unsuited for their intended role as fleet carriers, particularly because they lacked the necessary catapults and arrestor gear. However, they were larger and faster than their American equivalents and were used to deliver aircraft to remote locations; they also played a role in pilot training. The *Taiyo* had a displacement of 17,830 tons, was 591 feet 6 inches (180.29 m) in length and had a beam of 73 feet 9 inches (22.48 m). She had a maximum speed of 21 knots, eight 4.7-inch (12-cm) antiaircraft guns and a crew of 850. A total of 27 aircraft could be carried. All three Taiyo-class carriers were lost to American submarines during the PACIFIC WAR, 1941–45. The *Taiyo* and the *Unyo* were sunk within a few weeks of each other in

1944, while the *Chuyo* fell victim to the enemy at the end of 1943.

Takagi, Takeo
1892–1944

Japanese naval commander of WORLD WAR II, 1939–45, who established a solid reputation during service in the Pacific prior to his death in action in 1944. Takagi commanded carrier forces in a succession of early actions, from the invasion of the Philippines to the Battle of MIDWAY, June 1942. At the Battle of the JAVA SEA, January 27, 1942, he led powerful supporting forces that contributed to the elimination of the American presence in the East Indies. At the Battle of the CORAL SEA, May 7–8, 1942, Takagi commanded a fleet carrier squadron that consisted of the *Shokaku* and the *Zuikaku*. Although the *Shokaku* was badly damaged, aircraft under Takagi's command hit the carrier *LEXINGTON*. As a result, the Americans were forced to abandon and sink her. In the year before his death in action in July 1944, Takagi was in command of the Sixth Submarine Fleet based at Saipan in the Marianas.

Takao

The Japanese heavy CRUISER *Takao* and her three sister ships—the *Atago*, *Chokai* and *Mayo*—formed the Fourth Cruiser Squadron at the beginning of the PACIFIC WAR, 1941–45. The *Takao* had a displacement of 13,160 tons, was 663 feet 9 inches (202.3 m) in length and had a beam of 68 feet (21 m). Operated by a crew of 773, she had a maximum speed of 34.25 knots and her armament included ten 8-inch (20-cm) guns and 16 24-inch (61-cm) torpedo tubes. Armor protection was improved compared with previous Japanese cruiser designs and covered the main belt (hull), the deck and turrets and the magazine. Under the command of Vice Admiral Nobutake KONDO, the four Takao-class ships served at the Battle of GUADAL-CANAL, November 12–13, 1942, and in many other major engagements of the war in the Pacific. At the Battle of LEYTE GULF, October 1944, three members of the class were destroyed and only the *Takao* survived. She returned to Singapore where, on July 31, 1945, she was badly damaged by limpet mines laid by two British MIDGET SUBMARINES.

Tanaka, Raizo
1892–1969

*J*apanese rear admiral who commanded the reinforcement force—also known as the "Tokyo Express"—that resupplied GUADALCANAL in 1942. Tanaka had been the highly successful commander of a destroyer flotilla in the opening stages of the WORLD WAR II, 1939–45, and participated in the Philippines and Dutch East Indies campaigns.

He had been present in this capacity at the Battle of the JAVA SEA, February 1942, and at the Battle of MIDWAY, June 1942. It was, however, at Guadalcanal, August 1942–January 1943, that he made his mark, particularly in demonstrating his great skill in night fighting. At the same time, because of powerful attacks from enemy aircraft, he could not land enough men and matériel to bring the operation to a successful conclusion. In time, Tanaka's own destroyer, the *Teruzuki*, was torpedoed and sunk by the Americans. Tanaka survived but his opposition to a continuation of the campaign in the SOLOMON ISLANDS resulted in the loss of his command early in 1943.

Taranto, Attack on
November 11, 1940

A night attack by British naval aircraft on the Italian battle fleet at Taranto naval base in southern Italy

Fairey Swordfish torpedo aircraft were used with great success during the attack on Taranto, November 1940 *(Copyright © Imperial War Museum, London)*

during WORLD WAR II, 1939–45. The Italian navy's growing threat to British supply lines between Alexandria and Greece had dictated the timing of the raid. The operation was planned by Admiral Andrew CUNNINGHAM, commander in chief of the British Mediterranean fleet, who moved the aircraft carrier H.M.S. ILLUSTRIOUS to a position some 180 miles (290 km) southeast of Taranto. On November 11, 1940 a squadron of 21 single-engine Swordfish biplanes took off in two waves from the carrier. The squadron divided as it approached Taranto harbor, with ten aircraft dropping flares, bombing oil storage tanks and carrying out diversionary attacks on shipping in the harbor.

The remaining 11 aircraft, which were equipped with torpedoes, attacked the enemy battle fleet at anchor in the harbor. The raid achieved complete surprise. Eleven torpedoes were fired, destroying three Italian battleships— the *LITTORIO,* a new type, the *Conte di Cavour* and the *Caio Duilio*. In addition, two cruisers were badly damaged and two fleet auxiliaries sunk. Ony two British aircraft were lost. The Italians later retrieved the ships from the shallow waters of Taranto Harbor, but the raid permanently altered the balance of naval power in the Mediterranean in favor of the British. It also underlined the fact that the battleship was now obsolete.

Brian B. Schofield, *The Attack on Taranto,* London, 1973.

Tassafaronga, Battle of
November 30, 1942

*F*ought not long after the key Battle of GUADALCANAL, November 12–15, 1942 during WORLD WAR II, 1939–45, Tassafaronga was the last major battle of the entire SOLOMON ISLANDS campaign. During the night of November 30, Admiral Raizo TANAKA's Second Destroyer Flotilla, which consisted of six destroyers, left Buin to resupply Japanese troops on Guadalcanal using drums that would float ashore at Tassafaronga on the northeast coast. The Americans soon detected this movement and dispatched a more powerful squadron consisting of five cruisers and six destroyers under the command of Rear Admiral Carleton Wright to the expected landing area.

The opposing squadrons made contact at about 11:20 P.M., when the Americans opened fire. A Japanese destroyer was severely damaged and Tanaka regrouped his forces. They responded with their superior LONG LANCE torpedoes, severely damaging all four heavy cruisers, one of which— the *Northampton*—sank the next day. Before rapidly withdrawing from the area at midnight with relatively little damage, the Japanese were able to drop their drums into the sea (although only 20 percent of the drums reached their intended destination).

Taylor, David Watson
1864–1940

*A*merican naval officer, one of the most intelligent and influential figures in naval and marine science. Born in Louisa County, Virginia on March 4, 1864, David Watson Taylor attended Randolph-Macon College from 1877 to 1881, when he received an appointment to the U.S Naval Academy. He graduated from the academy at the top of his class, recording the highest marks then achieved. In 1885 he was sent to study on an advanced course of naval construction and marine engineering at Britain's Royal Naval College, from which he graduated again top of his class and with the highest record achieved there. Commissioned in the U.S. Navy's Constructor Corps, he played a pivotal role in the design of modern warships.

Primarily through his efforts in designing some of the U.S. Navy's new ships of the 1880s and 1890s, Taylor became aware of the lack of proper scientific experimentation in ship design and construction. He thus spent many years advocating the development of an experimental program to provide the much-needed scientific data to design and construct better vessels. It was through his efforts that the navy developed a testing basin for ship models in 1899 at Carderock, Maryland, a facility that Taylor remained in charge of until 1914. (It was renamed the David W. Taylor Model Basin in 1937.) He served two consecutive terms as Naval Constructor and Chief of the Bureau of Construction and Repair, overseeing the design and construction of nearly 900 vessels for the navy, plus many for foreign nations. He was also the first recipient of a medal created in his honor in 1936 for notable achievements in the field of naval architecture and marine engineering. While Chief Constructor, and until the Bureau of Aeronautics was created in 1921, he was in charge of design and construction of aircraft and submarines. He retired in 1925 but continued to serve as president of the Society of Naval Architects and Marine Engineers to 1927. The recipient of many medals, awards and honorary degrees, he was the author of books and a contributor to numerous learned journals. He died in Washington, D.C., on July 28, 1940.

William B. Cogar, *Dictionary of Admirals of the U.S. Navy, Vol. 2, 1901–1918,* Annapolis, 1991.

Taylor, Henry Clay
1845–1904

*A*merican naval officer. Born in Washington, D.C., on March 4, 1845, Henry Clay Taylor entered the service in 1860. A fairly routine career followed, but his appointment as president of the Naval War College from 1893 to 1896 was indicative of his administrative and intellectual abilities. He commanded the *Indiana* during the SPANISH-

AMERICAN WAR of 1898 and was involved in the bombardment of San Juan, Puerto Rico, in May. He also commanded the convoy that transported the army from Tampa, Florida to Santiago, Cuba in June and participated in the destruction of the Spanish fleet at SANTIAGO on July 3, 1898.

Taylor was subsequently advanced in seniority in rank for conspicuous conduct in battle. He twice served as Admiral George DEWEY's chief of staff. Best known as a naval philosopher and administrative reformer, he oversaw the creation of the navy's General Board in order to advise the Secretary of the Navy, contributing much on naval tactics and other subjects. Promoted to rear admiral in 1901, he died in Ontario, Canada on July 26, 1904 while serving as Chief of the Bureau of Navigation. An author of repute, Taylor wrote (with William Walton and Asa Bird Gardiner), *The Army and Navy of the United States from the Period of the Revolution to the Present*, 2 vols., 1889–95.

William B. Cogar, *Dictionary of Admirals of the U.S. Navy, Vol. 2, 1901–1918*, Annapolis, 1991.

Tchesme, Battle of
July 5–6, 1770

A major battle of the Russo-Turkish War, 1768–74, that resulted in the destruction of the Turkish fleet. During the war a Russian fleet under the command of Admiral Aleksei Orlov had established a presence in the Mediterranean. In June 1770 the Russians received intelligence that the Turkish fleet was positioned off the Aegean island of Chios and they went to intercept it. Admiral Orlov had a force of 12 ships, consisting of nine ships of the line and three frigates. Admiral Samuel GREIG, a Scottish officer in the Russian navy, served under Orlov and made a major contribution to victory.

The opposing fleet, under the command of Hosameddin Pasha, was considerably larger, with 20 ships of the line and three frigates. It was anchored off Tchesme, a port on the coast of Asia Minor opposite Chios. During the first phase of the battle, both sides lost a ship of the line, and the Turks were forced to withdraw into Tchesme harbor. With the entrance securely blockaded by the Russian fleet, the next day Admiral Orlov sent a squadron into the harbor. The accompanying FIRESHIPS proved to be very effective and resulted in the virtual destruction of the Turkish fleet.

Tegetthof, Baron Wilhelm von
1827–71

A ustrian vice admiral who led the AUSTRO-HUNGARIAN fleet to victory against the Italians at the Battle of

Lissa, July 20, 1866, in the Adriatic. Responding to an attack on the island by the ITALIAN NAVY, Tegetthof left his base at Pola in his flagship, the *Ferdinand Magellan*, on July 19. Outnumbered by 34 ships to 27, the Austrian navy had fewer IRONCLADS or long-range guns. Adopting an unconventional arrowhead formation, Tegetthof attacked the Italians north of Lissa; in the mêlée that followed, Tegetthof's ramming tactics were responsible for the sinking of a large Italian frigate. This proved to be the turning point in the battle, which ended in an Italian withdrawal.

Tegetthof's arrowhead formation and his ramming tactics were to be major influences on the development of naval warfare for the rest of the 19th century. In recognition of his victory at Lissa, the Austro-Hungarian navy decided that the fleet always should have an armored ship bearing his name. It was a fitting tribute to a distinguished career that also had included his involvement in the Schleswig-Holstein War of 1864, during which, as commander of an Austrian squadron, he had broken a Danish blockade of the Elbe and Weser Rivers.

Temeraire, H.M.S.

T he name *Temeraire*, which originated in France in the 17th century, was given to three French warships, including the 74-gun vessel launched in 1748. Captured by Admiral Edward BOSCAWEN at LAGOS, Portugal, in 1759, during the SEVEN YEARS' WAR, 1756–63, this *Temeraire* was then commissioned by the Royal Navy in 1760 and remained in service until 1784.

The most notable British vessel of this name, recorded in J. M. W. Turner's famous painting, "The Fighting Temeraire" was a 98-gun second-rate (see RATING OF SHIPS) ship launched at Chatham in 1798. She served in the Royal Navy for some 40 years, but the Battle of TRAFALGAR, 1805, was her single moment of glory. She was the second ship in the weather line (i.e., ships in line of battle on the windward side) immediately behind the *VICTORY*, Horatio NELSON's flagship. The *Temeraire* was responsible for the capture of two French warships—the *Redoubtable* and the *Fougueux*—after they had been shattered by heavy gunfire. She was sold for scrap in 1838.

Texel, Battle of the
August 11, 1673

T he concluding battle of the Third ANGLO-DUTCH WAR, 1672–74, the Texel represented the final effort by the Anglo-French fleet to defeat the Dutch navy and invade Holland. Following the fiercely fought but inconclusive Battles of SCHOONEVELDT on May 28 and June 4, 1673, the allied fleet retired to carry out essential repairs. When they were completed in mid-July, the English fleet under the command of Prince RUPERT put to sea again. They met the French, who were under the command of Admiral Jean d'Estrées, and the joint fleet of 92 men of war sailed for Scheveningen. Three days later the smaller Dutch fleet, under the command of Admiral Michiel de RUYTER left Schooneveldt; its presence was sufficient to deter an allied landing at Scheveningen.

Further action was delayed by poor weather, but the opposing fleets eventually met off the small coastal island of Texel on August 11. A fierce struggle quickly developed as de Ruyter deployed his smaller fleet to great effect. With d'Estreés's fleet of 30 ships, which formed the allied van, effectively neutralized by Admiral Adriaen Banckerts's squadron, the main Dutch attack was concentrated on the English. Prince Rupert's center suffered badly, but the heaviest fighting developed between the rear divisions. The two opposing divisional commanders, Cornelis TROMP and Sir Edward SPRAGGE, were forced to move ship three times. The *Prince Royal*, Spragge's flagship, was badly damaged, and the commander was drowned as the boat in which he was transferring was hit and sank. Admiral de Ruyter withdrew under cover of darkness after it was clear that the allied invasion attempt had failed. There were heavy casualties on both sides but, remarkably, not a single ship of the line had been lost.

Hugh C. B. Rogers, *Generals-at-Sea. Naval Operations During the English Civil War and the Three Anglo-Dutch Wars*, Bromley, Kent, 1992.

Thaon di Revel, Paolo
1859–1948

*I*talian admiral. Di Revel, who entered the service in 1877, was appointed chief of staff of the ITALIAN NAVY in 1913 and held the post throughout WORLD WAR I, 1914–18. He was responsible for the expansion of Italian naval power and built up the fleet of destroyers and submarines. In February 1917, following the retirement of the Duca di Abruzzi, he also became naval commander in chief. Di Revel, who had made a substantial contribution to the modernization of the navy before the war, was particularly concerned to preserve its operational independence from Allied control from 1915 onward. He successfully maintained this position, although he was compelled to contribute several warships in support of Allied efforts to guard against a possible German sortie from the Dardanelles. Promoted to admiral in 1918, he served as Mussolini's minister of marine, 1922–24, before retiring.

Thetis, H.M.S.

*B*ritish submarine that was the victim of one of the worst accidents of its kind in maritime history when it sank off the Lancashire coast on June 1, 1939. The *Thetis*

had been undertaking underwater trials and failed to surface on schedule. Although its position was quickly established, it proved impossible to raise her in time. With her escape hatch malfunctioning, only four crew members were able to escape; the remaining 99 men were trapped on board and died. This remained the world's worst submarine disaster until the loss of the U.S. nuclear submarine *THRESHER* (also during trials) in April 1963, when 129 crew members were killed. The *Thetis* eventually was brought to the surface in April 1940 and refitted. As the *Thunderbolt*, she served in the Mediterranean and was torpedoed by an Italian corvette in March 1943.

Thornycroft, Sir John Isaacs
1843–1928

*B*ritish naval architect who specialized in the construction of small, high-speed launches and who established, in 1866, John I. Thornycroft and Company for this purpose. In 1871 he completed a vessel of this kind with a light steel hull with a maximum speed of over 16 knots. This was followed, in 1873, by the *Gitana*, the world's first TORPEDO BOAT, which was armed with a SPAR TORPEDO. Produced for Norway, this boat had a maximum speed of over 20 knots. The *Gitana* provided the basic design for H.M.S. LIGHTNING, which was itself the prototype of the modern torpedo boat. Armed with a Whitehead torpedo in a revolving torpedo tube, it had a maximum speed of 18 knots.

The Thornycroft Company produced a whole series of torpedo boats and destroyers, equipping them with the most modern engines then available. These included water-tube boilers that had been designed by the company. Thornycroft himself continued to undertake research into hull design, and his stepped hulls were used in the construction of racing boats, seaplane floats and, during WORLD WAR I, 1914–18, coastal motor boats. He was also employed by the ADMIRALTY in an advisory capacity and was an important influence on the design of H.M.S. DREADNOUGHT.

Thresher, U.S.S.

*T*he name vessel of a class of 14 U.S. nuclear-powered hunter-killer SUBMARINES built between 1959 and 1968. The *Thresher* was laid down in May 1959 and completed in July 1960. She had a surface displacement of 3,750 tons, was 278 feet 6 inches (84.9 m) in length and was operated by a crew of 103. The *Thresher* had a surface speed of 20 knots and was armed with four 21-inch (53-cm) torpedo tubes as well as sub-Harpoon and Tomahawk missiles. Less than two years after she entered service, the *Thresher* was given an extensive refit. On April 9, 1963, in the trials in the Atlantic that followed these works, she quickly ran into difficulties. As she performed a test dive, she sent an incomprehensible final message before contact was lost. She failed to resurface and later was located lying in 8,400 feet (2,650 m) of water some 200 miles (322 km) off the coast of New England. Her crew of 107 officers and men, together with 17 civilian observers, were lost in this costly accident that has never been fully explained.

Tiger, H.M.S.

The British warship *Tiger* was the BATTLE CRUISER equivalent of the IRON DUKE class. Completed in October 1914, she was an improved version of the BATTLESHIP *Queen Mary*. The *Tiger* was elegant in appearance and was the fastest CAPITAL SHIP of her time, with a maximum speed of 29 knots. She was also the largest, with a displacement of 28,430 tons, because of the great space needed for the operating machinery. Her length was 704 feet (214.6 m), and she had a beam of 90 feet 6 inches (27.6 m). The *Tiger* was also notable as the last coal-burning capital ship built for the Royal Navy. Operated by a crew of 1,121, she was armed with eight 13.5-inch (34-cm) guns; secondary armament consisted of 12 6-inch (15-cm) guns, six to each side, and two 3-inch (8-cm) antiaircraft guns.

Entering service shortly after the beginning of WORLD WAR I, 1914–18, the *Tiger* joined the GRAND FLEET. She was soon in action with the First Battlecruiser Squadron at the Battle of the DOGGER BANK, January 1915. At the Battle of JUTLAND, May 1916, she sustained 15 hits, and it was a tribute to the quality of her construction and her more extensive armor protection that repairs took no more than a month to complete. She remained in service with the Grand Fleet for the rest of the war and survived on the active list until 1931, when she was scrapped.

Tinclads

Converted river steamboats used extensively by U.S. naval forces during the AMERICAN CIVIL WAR, 1861–65. Produced in response to regular riverbank attacks from Confederate forces on the Mississippi and other Southern rivers, some 60 boats, which were powered by stern or side paddle wheels, were modified by the addition of iron plates up to three-quarters of an inch (2 cm) thick to their exposed hulls. They were armed with howitzers of varying sizes. Despite their name, tin was not used in the conversion. Because the tinclads operated in the often-shallow rivers of the South and west of the United States, there was a limit to how much additional weight they could carry. This meant that a draft of no more than three feet (0.91 m) needed to be preserved. The tinclads proved to be a cost-effective conversion that were able to withstand

Confederate small arms and artillery fire without real difficulty during river operations in the South in 1863–64. They were an important instrument in the Union victory in the river war that gave it control of the Mississippi by May 1863. See also IRONCLAD.

Tirpitz, Alfred von
1849–1930

German grand admiral who, as Secretary of State of the Ministry of Marine, 1897–1916, played a key role in the dramatic growth of the GERMAN NAVY in the pre-WORLD WAR I, 1914–18, period. Indeed, he was given the title of "Father of the German navy." The naval race between Germany and Britain intensified after the appearance of the DREADNOUGHT, but, by 1914, Tirpitz's navy had almost as many battleships and battle cruisers as its principal maritime opponent. As State Secretary, Tirpitz's powers were confined to matériel, but on the outbreak of World War I, he argued for his own appointment as naval commander in chief, to resolve the problem of divided responsibilities in wartime.

The proposal was rejected and Tirpitz found that he was increasingly excluded from discussions on wartime strategy. In any case, his own views were often widely at variance with the official line. For example, he was disappointed that his own major creation—the battle fleet—was destined to have a passive role and would not be risked at sea. He wrote subsequently that "it only needed the right command to bring out all its qualities and lead the fleet to victory." As an alternative Tirpitz was a strong advocate of unrestricted submarine warfare on Allied shipping. Not unexpectedly, he objected strongly to the constraints associated with the reintroduction of U-BOAT attacks early in 1916. Frustrated by his inability to influence the direction of policy, Tirpitz resigned in March 1916 from the post he had held for almost 19 years.

Jonathan Steinberg, *Yesterday's Deterrent: Tirpitz and the Birth of the German Battlefleet*, London, 1965.

Tirpitz

Almost identical to the BISMARCK, her sister ship, the *Tirpitz* was a 42,500-ton German BATTLESHIP that was completed in 1941. Her WORLD WAR II service, which began early in 1942, was spent exclusively in Norwegian waters, where she was a constant threat to armed convoys en route to northern Russia. On one notable occasion, in July 1942, the British Admiralty responded to a false report that she had left her berth by ordering the CONVOY PQ-17 to scatter, with disastrous results. In practice, however, she was never involved in a surface action and made few trips to sea, partly because of fuel shortages and a reluctance to

Alfred von Tirpitz (fourth from left): creator of the modern Germany navy   *(Copyright © Imperial War Museum, London)*

risk her to Allied attack. A rare exception was the *Tirpitz*'s bombardment of Spitsbergen, part of the Norwegian archipelago, September 1943, remarkable as the only occasion on which she had an opportunity to fire her heavy guns.

Hidden deep in a Norwegian fjord, she was a difficult target for a conventional air attack. It was, in fact, MIDGET SUBMARINES rather than aircraft that reached her first. On September 22, 1943 two British X-CRAFT laid four delayed-action mines beneath her, causing so much damage that she never went to sea again. Temporary repairs had only just been completed, in April 1944, when she was attacked by the British FLEET AIR ARM and again put out of action. She was damaged on several other occasions before finally being sunk, on November 12, 1944, by three 12,000-pound (5443-kg) "tallboy" bombs carried by a force of Royal Air Force Lancasters.

Gervis Frere-Cook, *The Attacks on the Tirpitz*, London, 1973.

Togo, Heihachiro
1847–1934

Japanese admiral of the fleet who won a decisive victory against the RUSSIAN NAVY at the Battle of TSUSHIMA in May 1905. His service began during the earliest days of the JAPANESE NAVY in the 1860s. Togo spent three years training in England during the following decade, benefit-

ting from the close naval links between the two countries. On his return to Japan his career made steady progress, and by 1879 he was a lieutenant-commander with his own ship. However, it was not until the SINO-JAPANESE WAR, 1894–95, when he commanded the *Naniwa*, a British-built protected cruiser, that Togo had a sustained period of operational service. As part of the Japanese Flying Squadron, the *Naniwa* participated in the destruction of two Chinese warships on their return from Korea and also sank a British merchant ship that was carrying Chinese troops. Togo was then involved in the Battle of the YALU RIVER, September 1894, and in the capture of Port Arthur. Subsequently promoted to rear admiral, he commanded the Japanese naval contingent during the Boxer Rising, 1900.

Four years later, shortly before the outbreak of the RUSSO-JAPANESE WAR, 1904–5, he was appointed commander in chief of the combined fleet. He directed the BLOCKADE of Port Arthur, where the Russian Pacific Squadron was trapped, from his flagship, the MIKASA. An attempted enemy breakout ended in Togo's victory at the Battle of the YELLOW SEA, August 1904, where his flagship sustained heavy damage. The *Mikasa* was hit again during the Battle of Tsushima, the decisive engagement of the war on which Togo's reputation is based. On May 27, 1905 Togo intercepted the Russian Baltic Fleet in the Straits of Tsushima near the end of its long journey to Vladivostok. It was being sent there to provide much-needed reinforcements. Although the elderly Russian fleet was constrained by its convoy of auxiliaries, it fought vigorously at first. The outcome of the Battle of Tsushima was, however, never really in doubt, and within hours the Russian fleet had been encircled and almost totally destroyed. Togo's tactical skills and the superior gunnery of the Japanese warships had produced the most destructive naval battle for a century, and the result soon brought the Russian government to the negotiating table.

Togo became a national hero after Tsushima and subsequently was promoted to the highest rank, admiral of the fleet. He was appointed chief of the naval staff and remained a major influence on Japanese naval policy making until his death in 1934.

R. Butow, *Togo and the Coming of War*, Princeton, N.J., 1961.

Tokyo Raid
April 1942

"First Special Aviation Project" was the cover name for the famous American long-distance B-25 bomber raid against Japan on April 18, 1942. Commanded by Lieutenant-Colonel James H. Doolittle, 16 bombers were equipped with additional fuel tanks and were stripped of as much equipment as possible in order to extend their range. They took off from the aircraft carrier *Hornet*, which was some 600 miles (1,000 km) away from the target. The aircraft came in low over Tokyo, Yokohama, Yokosuka, Kobe and Nagoya and, not surprisingly, caught the Japanese by surprise. With their minds on victory, the Japanese had not contemplated the air defense of the homeland, and not a single fighter squadron was devoted to it. Although the material damage caused by the raid was relatively unimportant, the psychological impact was enormous, while Americans (although not told the precise details) saw it as a great victory and a boost to Allied morale.

Much more important, the raid caused great loss of face among the Japanese military leaders, especially Admiral Isoroku YAMAMOTO. He now realized the failure of his PEARL HARBOR attack and was forced to send his fleet out to secure Japan's defenses by attacking MIDWAY Island. The battle that resulted was a further disaster and turned the tide of war (just as Yamamoto had feared) irrevocably against Japan so that, less than a year after hostilities began, defeat loomed on the horizon. Of the 16 American planes that took part in the first Tokyo raid, some landed safely in China and eventually were repatriated, while other air crews were forced to bail out. Eight crew members were captured by the occupying Japanese forces: Of these, three were executed and the remainder imprisoned. One aircraft landed in the Soviet Union, where the crew were imprisoned until they escaped.

Tonkin Gulf Incident
August 2, 1964

This incident off the coast of North Vietnam led to direct American military intervention in the VIETNAM WAR. On August 2, 1964 the U.S.S. *Maddox*, a destroyer, was attacked by three North Vietnamese patrol boats as it engaged in secret intelligence work in the Gulf of Tonkin. One patrol boat was reported sunk and another damaged. It was forced to withdraw from the area but returned the following day accompanied by the U.S.S. *C Turner Joy*, another destroyer. During the night of August 4, the *C Turner Joy* reported a further attack by North Vietnamese patrol boats. The details of this second attack were confused, and the North Vietnamese later denied that it had ever taken place.

Despite this uncertainty, the U.S. government ordered, on August 5, the bombing of North Vietnamese naval installations and moved fighter and bomber aircraft from Japan and the Philippines to forward bases in South Vietnam. Two days later the U.S. Congress passed the Gulf of Tonkin Resolution, which gave the President the authority to "take all necessary precautions to repel any armed attack against the forces of the United States and to prevent further aggression." The resolution provided the legal basis for American military involvement in Vietnam, although the official account of events in the Gulf of Tonkin on which was it was based later was called into serious question. Eventually the resolution was repealed.

Tordenskjold, Peder
1691–1720

Danish naval hero of the Great Northern War, 1700–21, born as Peder Wessel, who went to sea at an early age. In July 1711 Wessel joined the royal marines and gained rapid promotion, Within a year he was placed in command of a 20-gun frigate and fought effectively and audaciously against his Swedish opponents in several different engagements. Promoted to captain in 1714, he won further victories before his ennoblement as Tordenskjold ("thundershield") in 1716. In the same year he added to his achievements when he forced King Charles XII of Sweden to abandon his invasion of Norway by destroying his transport fleet.

Tordenskjold was promoted to the rank of commander for this success and, early in 1717, was placed in command of a squadron with orders to destroy the Swedish Gothenburg fleet, which had disrupted communications between Denmark and Norway. Largely because of the disloyalty of some of his subordinates, the operation was no more than a partial success; only through the intervention of a powerful patron did he avoid a court martial. In 1718, when he brought news of the death of Charles XII to Denmark, he was promoted to rear admiral. In a final operation at sea he captured the Swedish fortress of Marstrand and seized or destroyed much of the Gothenburg fleet. He was promoted to the rank of vice admiral before being killed in a duel in 1720.

Torpedo

A self-propelled, cigar-shape projectile launched from a ship, SUBMARINE or aircraft that travels just under the water's surface. Its explosive charge is detonated on contact with the side of an enemy ship. The term originally was used to describe various types of sea MINE, including the SPAR TORPEDO, which consisted of an explosive device attached to a spar that extended over the bows of a ship and detonated on contact. The first self-propelled torpedo, which was developed by the British engineer Robert Whitehead for the Austrian navy, appeared in 1866. Propelled by a compressed air engine, it was equipped with devices to control its depth and balance in the water. This torpedo was 14 feet (4.27 m) long, had at a speed of about 7 knots, a range of 1,968 feet (600 m) and carried a 18-pound (8.16-kg) charge of guncotton. The Whitehead torpedo was adopted by the Royal Navy in the 1870s and other navies soon followed. In 1895, an effective directional control was invented which meant that torpedoes could be fired at targets that were not directly in line with the launch.

The development of this new weapon led to the creation of a new vessel—the TORPEDO BOAT—designed to launch it. This in turn led to the arrival of the DESTROYER, whose function was locate and attack the torpedo boat. However, the submarine would use the weapon to the greatest effect, and during WORLD WAR I, 1914–18, it sunk more ships than mines or gunfire. The first successful launching of a torpedo from an aircraft occurred in 1911. When Britain matched this achievement in 1914, it led to the development of the Short 184, the first torpedo-carrying seaplane to be specially designed for the purpose. Despite operating difficulties, the Short became the first aircraft to sink an enemy ship by means of an air-launched torpedo, on August 12, 1915. WORLD WAR II, 1939–45, was to demonstrate the potential of air-launched torpedoes, with PEARL HARBOR, December 1941, and the British attack on TARANTO, November 1940, being among the most notable examples. This war also saw the development of new torpedo designs, including a German weapon with an acoustic homing device that detected the sound of the target ship's propellers. The pace of development has intensified in the postwar period. New guidance and homing systems have been developed, and the torpedo's power plant—whether steam or electric—has been improved. A modern torpedo can have a speed of up to 45 knots, a maximum range of 25,000 yards (22,860 m) and a warhead with up to 800 pounds (362.8 kg) of explosive.

N. Friedman, *U.S. Naval Weapons. Every Gun, Missile, Mine and Torpedo Used by the U.S. Navy from 1883 to the Present Day.* Annapolis, 1982; L. Gerken, *Torpedo Technology.* Chula Vista, Calif., 1989.

Torpedo Boat

T he invention of the TORPEDO in 1866 led rapidly to the development of new types of ship from which torpedoes could be fired. Various experimental designs, including H.M.S. *LIGHTNING*, an 1876 construction that was fitted with torpedo tubes, followed. From these early designs emerged the basic concept of a fast boat of modest dimensions that was well armed but with very limited armored protection. Early experience suggested that the torpedo boat seemed most effective when operating as part of a FLOTILLA during the hours of darkness, although it was vulnerable to attack from larger warships. These included torpedo boat DESTROYERS, which were developed specifically in response to the torpedo boat threat. Torpedo boats were produced in large numbers during WORLD WAR I, 1914–18, and, powered by the internal combustion engine, were capable of 35 knots or even more. They were used primarily against SUBMARINES and surface ships in coastal waters, although they also were employed on escort and raiding duties. Their performance was disappointing when compared with that of destroyers, which were faster, better armed and had a longer range. Destroyers were widely used as seagoing torpedo boats.

After a postwar interregnum, large-scale production of torpedo boats resumed in the 1930s, with smaller and faster designs appearing from each of the major naval powers as WORLD WAR II, 1939–45, approached. The German SCHNELLBOOTE (or E-boat) was perhaps the most successful torpedo boat of the period and certainly outperformed the British Motor Torpedo Boat (MTB), which first appeared in the mid-1930s. The MTB typically was 70 feet (21.35 m) in length and had a maximum speed of some 40 knots. The Italian MAS boats were also fine examples of this class of warship. American PT BOATS were based on an improved version of the British MTB and proved to be of great value during the PACIFIC WAR, 1941–45. The Soviet Navy's surface fleet was virtually restricted to small craft, of which the torpedo boat was the most important element. The torpedo boat has a continuing place in the modern navy, performing much the same roles as in the past, although typically it is equipped with guided MISSILES as well as torpedo tubes. (See also MOTOR GUNBOAT.)

Toulon, Battle of
February 11, 1744

A battle during the War of the AUSTRIAN SUCCESSION, 1740–48, that had its origins in the English BLOCKADE of the French port of Toulon. Even though England and

A British motor torpedo boat in action in 1940 *(Copyright © National Maritime Museum, Greenwich, London)*

France were not yet formally at war, a loose blockade had been maintained there since 1742 with the aim of preventing Spain from using Toulon as a staging post for its convoys. These were involved in resupplying Spanish land forces operating in Italy. Toward the end of 1743 the English Mediterranean fleet, commanded by Admiral Thomas MATHEWS, pursued a Spanish squadron of 12 ships of the line into Toulon. Commanded by Don José Navarro, it remained there until February 8, 1744, when it reemerged in company with a French squadron of 15 ships of the line under the command of Admiral de la Bruyère de Court.

The British fleet, which consisted of 29 ships of the line, was positioned off Hyères. Admiral Mathews, who remained in command, headed the center division. The van was led by Rear Admiral William Rowley and the rear by Vice Admiral Richard LESTOCK. The two opposing forces were almost equally balanced. The British pursued the Franco-Spanish fleet for three days after it departed from Toulon. The British commander brought the enemy to battle on the morning of February 11, although the action seems to have been premature. With the rear squadron under Lestock a considerable distance behind, the fleet had not been formed into line ahead, as required by the official *FIGHTING INSTRUCTIONS*. Admiral Mathews attacked the enemy's rear in his flagship *Namur* and was actively sup-

ported by some English ships, which inflicted serious damage on the Spanish squadron. However, much of the British fleet failed to fight effectively during a confused battle. Sporadic fighting continued over the next two days before Mathews abandoned the chase and returned to Port Mahon. Mathews, Lestock and a number of subordinate commanders were held accountable for the failed action when they returned to England. In a verdict that had little logic to it, Mathews was found guilty of neglect of duty for having failed to adhere to the *Fighting Instructions* and was dismissed from the service, while Lestock was acquitted.

Toulouse, Louis Alexandre de Bourbon, Comte de

1678–1737

*F*rench naval commander—the third son of King Louis XIV and his mistress Madame de Montespan—noted for his courage in action. Made an admiral at the age of five, Toulouse was first wounded in action when he was only 12, having accompanied his father to Flanders during the War of the GRAND ALLIANCE, 1688–97. He returned to the sea when he was old enough to choose a profession for himself and commanded the French fleet during the War of the SPANISH SUCCESSION, 1701–14.

His most notable wartime encounter was the Battle of VELEZ MALAGA, August 1704, although tactically the outcome was inconclusive—he had withdrawn abruptly after inflicting heavy damage on the English fleet. Strategically it was a major setback because the undefeated English fleet was able to hold on to GIBRALTAR, which it had taken three weeks earlier. After the end of the War of the Spanish Succession, Toulouse became a member of the Council of Regency and secured funding for the reconstruction of the French navy.

Tourville, Anne-Hilarion de Contentin, Comte de
1642–1701

*F*rench admiral who was one of the key figures in King Louis XIV's navy in the late 17th century. Tourville served his apprenticeship on a Maltese frigate in operations against the Barbary pirates, entering the French navy in 1666. He participated in the Third ANGLO-DUTCH WAR, 1672–74, and at the Battle of SOLEBAY, 1672, he commanded a 50-gun ship against the Dutch. Tourville was also present at the Battle of the TEXEL, 1673. Promoted to rear admiral in 1683, he was heavily involved in the administration of the navy, although he again went to sea in operations against the Barbary pirates. He also may have been a major contributor to the works on naval tactics published by his secretary, the Abbé Hoste.

On the outbreak of the War of the GRAND ALLIANCE, 1688–97, Tourville was appointed commander in chief of the French fleet with the rank of vice admiral. In July 1690 he defeated the Anglo-Dutch fleet at BEACHY HEAD, but, partly because of Tourville's personal caution, the victory was not followed up. He led an effective naval campaign during the following year but, in 1692, he was ordered to participate in an ill-planned landing in England. Despite his great fighting skill, Tourville was heavily defeated at the Battle of BARFLEUR and his ships were then destroyed at the Battle of LA HOGUE, May 1692. He partially redeemed his reputation at the Battle of Lagos, June 27–28, 1693, when he intercepted an Anglo-Dutch convoy bound for Smyrna. Tourville defeated the naval escort and destroyed nearly 100 of the 400 transport ships. His mixed record at sea did little to undermine his close relationship with the king, and in the same year he was made a marshal of France. He did not return to sea after the Battle of Lagos, and he left the French navy at the end of the war.

Tovey, John Cronyn, Baron
1886–1971

*B*ritish naval commander who headed the Home Fleet, 1940–43, during the critical years of WORLD WAR II,

1939–45. Tovey originally made his mark as a DESTROYER captain during WORLD WAR I, 1914–18, and was present at the Battle of JUTLAND, May 1916, where he distinguished himself in the *Onslow*. By 1935 he had risen to the rank of rear admiral and, in 1939, was appointed second-in-command in the Mediterranean fleet on the outbreak of World War II. He was then appointed commander in chief, British Home Fleet, where his primary wartime duty was to prevent a German invasion. However, as the threat of German landings receded, Tovey gave priority to the protection of Allied convoys. In May 1941 he was in overall command of the operation to hunt and sink the battleship BISMARCK, which involved FORCE H as well as the Home Fleet.

The destruction of the *Bismarck* was the high point of Tovey's career even though it involved the loss of the battle cruiser HOOD. Friction with the ADMIRALTY was another aspect of his post. It came to a head in July 1942 when he objected to Admiralty orders to scatter the Arctic CONVOY PQ-17 when it faced an attack from the battleship TIRPITZ. Tovey realized that the unprotected convoy would suffer heavy losses as a result of this instruction, as indeed proved to be the case. In 1943 Tovey was moved to the NORE command, where he was heavily involved in the preparations for the NORMANDY LANDINGS, 1944. He retired from the navy soon after the end of the war.

Towers, John Henry
1885–1955

*O*ne of the early pioneers in American NAVAL AVIATION. Towers was instrumental in preparing the United States for the air war in the Pacific, 1941–45. Born on January 30, 1885, he graduated from the U.S. Naval Academy in 1906. He cruised on the battleship *Kentucky* as part of the 1907–9 circumnavigation of the GREAT WHITE FLEET. In 1911 he began his long career in naval aviation when he learned to fly the Curtiss A-1, the U.S. Navy's first aircraft. Designated Naval Aviator Number 3, he helped establish the first naval air base on the Severn River across from the Naval Academy in ANNAPOLIS, Maryland. After various duties with air squadrons and bases, he became assistant naval attaché in London during WORLD WAR I, 1914–18, before the United States entered the conflict. In this post he had the opportunity closely to observe the development of naval aviation by European nations.

From 1916 through the end of the war, he was connected with the naval aviation branch of the office of the chief of naval operations, assuming the lead role in preparing and managing the U.S. Navy's aviation role in the war. Shortly after the war, he commanded the small squadron of Navy-Curtiss Flying boats that attempted to fly across the Atlantic in 1919. Only one plane successfully made the crossing; the plane that Towers piloted was forced to ditch in the water but, rigging a sail, he managed to sail the craft to the Azores. After a stint in the mid-1920s as assistant naval attaché to various European nations, he rose to become chief of the Bureau of Aeronautics in June 1939 and was once again in a position to prepare the nation's naval aviation forces for possible war. With the rank of vice admiral he became Commander, Air Force Pacific, in October 1942, advising Admiral Chester NIMITZ on aviation matters and thereby overseeing the planning and execution of the offensive strikes by naval air units throughout the Central Pacific. From February to July 1944 Towers was Deputy Commander in Chief Pacific Fleet and Pacific Ocean Area; then, as commander of Task Force 38, he arrived off Japan too late to see any significant action. As full admiral in late 1945 he assumed command of the Fifth Fleet and then served as Commander, Pacific Fleet, from 1946 to 1947. Retiring in December 1947, Towers died on April 30, 1955.

Clark G. Reynolds, *Admiral John H. Towers: The Struggle for Naval Air Supremacy*, Annapolis, 1991.

Toyoda, Soemu
1885–1957

*J*apanese admiral who was commander of the Yokusa Naval Base for much of WORLD WAR II, 1939–45. In April 1944 Toyoda became commander in chief of the Combined Fleet, succeeding Admiral Mineichi KOGA. By this time the war in the Pacific had turned in favor of the United States, but Toyoda's strategy sought to lure the enemy's Central Pacific Fleet into a decisive battle. However, at the Battle of the PHILIPPINE SEA, June 1944, Japanese naval air power suffered further irreparable damage, and at the Battle of LEYTE GULF, October 1944, the Japanese navy itself suffered unsustainable losses. By April 1945 he was forced to take desperate measures in a vain attempt to save OKINAWA. However, neither the sacrifice of the battleship *YAMATO*, which was sent on a suicide mission to Okinawa, nor large-scale KAMIKAZE attacks could change the course of events. In May 1945 Toyoda was replaced by Admiral Jisaburo OZAWA and became naval chief of staff, a post he held after the end of the war. He opposed Japan's final surrender and later was tried and acquitted of war crimes.

Tracy, Benjamin Franklin
1830–1915

*B*orn near Owego in New York's Tioga County in 1830, Benjamin Tracy served as Secretary of the Navy from 1889 to 1893 in the administration of President Benjamin Harrison. He was therefore instrumental in moving the United States to commit itself to a powerful steel blue-water navy that would reflect and help implement the nation's increasing international involvement. A lawyer by training, he served in the New York legislature before the AMERICAN CIVIL WAR, 1861–65. During the war he was a brevet brigadier-general for the Union. He resumed his successful legal career in the 1860s and 1870s as U.S. Attorney for New York and then was judge of the New York Court of Appeals. He died on August 6, 1915.

Walter R. Herrick, "Benjamin F. Tracy," in *American Secretaries of the Navy*, ed. Paolo E. Coletta, Vol. 1, pp. 415–422, Annapolis, 1980.

Trafalgar, Battle of
October 21, 1805

*D*ecisive naval engagement between British and Franco-Spanish naval forces during the Napoleonic Wars, 1803–15. When Napoleon decided to invade England in the summer of 1805, he needed to secure control of the English Channel to enable his Grande Armée to cross from Boulogne, where it was camped. The three French squadrons blockaded at Brest, Toulon and other ports in the southwest were ordered to break out and make for the West Indies. They would then return as a combined fleet that would take control of the Channel and allow the invasion force to cross.

The Toulon squadron, which consisted of 11 ships of the line under the command of Admiral the Comte de VILLENEUVE, escaped in March. Villeneuve headed for Cadiz, where he combined with a Spanish squadron of six ships under Admiral Don F. Gravina, but the other blockaded French squadrons were unable to escape. The joint force arrived at Martinique on May 14 with Admiral Lord NELSON and the British fleet in pursuit. When Villeneuve learned of Nelson's arrival in the West Indies, he quickly returned to European waters. At the Battle of CAPE FINISTERRE, July 22, he was challenged by an English squadron commanded by Admiral Sir Robert CALDER, who failed to bring him to a decisive action. Villeneuve made for Cadiz and then Ferrol, where he joined another Spanish squadron. The Franco-Spanish fleet now consisted of 29 ships, but it was insufficient to activate Napoleon's invasion plans, which were abandoned for this and for other reasons.

However, Villeneuve's naval forces still posed a threat to the Royal Navy. Nelson was appointed head of the British Mediterranean fleet with orders to neutralize them. Flying his flag in the 100-gun *Victory*, Nelson joined his fleet off Cadiz at the end of September. He had a total of 27 ships under his command compared with Villeneuve's 33. Ordered to leave Cadiz for the Mediterranean, the French squadron departed on a southerly course on October 19, in sight of a British frigate. Following two days of maneuvering, at daybreak on October 21 the two fleets came in sight of one another off Cape Trafalgar. At about 6 A.M. Nelson divided his forces into two columns. He led the van or weather column of 12 ships of the line, while

H.M.S. *Belleisle* breaks the enemy line at the Battle of Trafalgar, 1805 *(Copyright © National Maritime Museum, Greenwhich, London)*

Vice Admiral Cuthbert COLLINGWOOD, who flew his flag in the *ROYAL SOVEREIGN,* led the rear or lee column of 15 ships. When Villeneuve realized the potential danger he faced, he reversed course with the aim of returning to Cadiz to the north. It was, however, too late, and by 11 A.M. the British were closing quickly on the enemy line. The Franco-Spanish van was commanded by Rear Admiral Dumanoir, while Gravina led the rear and commanded the Spanish squadron.

Following Nelson's famous signal, "England expects that every man will do his duty," the battle began at noon. The lee column came under fire first with the flagship *Royal Sovereign* coming under heavy attack before she broke the enemy line. The rest of the column followed, and during fighting at close quarters, three British ships were badly damaged. Nelson's weather column aimed for Villeneuve's flagship, the *Bucentaure,* and after surviving heavy enemy gunfire broke the enemy line. The *Victory* fought intensively with the *TÉMÉRAIRE,* the *Bucentaure* and the *Redoubtable*; during this part of the battle, at 1:15 P.M., Nelson was shot and fatally wounded. As the battle progressed powerful British BROADSIDES took their toll, and by 1:45 P.M. Villeneuve had surrendered. Collingwood, who now assumed overall command of the British fleet, also was making

considerable progress in fighting the Spanish squadron to the rear. By 4:30 P.M. the battle was effectively over, despite the efforts of the Franco-Spanish van, under Dumanoir, to rekindle it.

The remnants of the French van division managed to retreat toward Cadiz, where they were blockaded. Total French losses amounted to 18 ships captured or destroyed, 2,600 men killed or wounded and another 7,000 prisoners held on prizes in British hands. The British suffered 1,700 casualties; about half their ships were damaged, but none was lost in battle, although five vessels did sink in a subsequent storm. This decisive victory marked the beginning of a long period of British naval dominance in European waters.

Alan Schom, *Trafalgar: Countdown to Battle, 1803–05*, London, 1990.

Trent

A British mail steamer that was stopped off Cuba by the Union warship *San Jacinto* during the AMERICAN CIVIL WAR, 1861–65. On November 8, 1861 Captain Charles WILKES, acting without orders, boarded the *Trent*

Lord Nelson falls mortally wounded at the Battle of Trafalgar, 1805   *(Copyright © National Maritime Museum, Greenwich, London)*

and removed the Confederate envoys to Britain and France who were traveling to Europe to represent President Jefferson Davis. The Union action and the subsequent internment of the envoys in Boston produced strong British protests. At one stage war seemed possible between the two countries, but eventually the dispute was resolved by diplomatic means. Early in 1862 the envoys were released and continued their voyage to Europe on board a British warship.

Trident

The American Trident nuclear missile, a long-range SUBMARINE-LAUNCHED BALLISTIC MISSILE (SLBM), was the first to match the performance of a land-based intercontinental ballistic missile (ICBM). It was capable of hitting a target up to 4,600 miles (7,400 km) away. Each Trident C-4 missile, which is 34 feet (10.4 m) long, consists of eight 100-kiloton warheads that can be targeted independently. Since 1979 these missiles have been deployed in modified POSEIDON submarines. From 1982 they were deployed in Ohio-class submarines, which were designed for this specific purpose. By 1997, 18 Ohio-class submarines were operational. Carrying 24 missiles each, these submarines will hold half of the total strategic nuclear power of the United States. They are among the quietest submarines ever built and will prove difficult to detect. These submarines also will accommodate a larger version of the Trident (the D-5) that has been developed. This later type has been supplied to the British and will be carried in the new Vanguard-class submarines. It carries eight separate 335-kiloton warheads.

Graham Spinardi, *From Polaris to Trident: The Development of U.S. Fleet Ballistic Technology*, Cambridge, Mass., 1994.

Trincomalee, Battle of
September 3, 1782

The fourth naval engagement between the British and French forces in the Indian Ocean during the AMERICAN WAR OF INDEPENDENCE, 1775–83, the Battle of Trincomalee followed some two months after the inconclusive fight at NEGAPATAM. The French squadron, commanded by Admiral Pierre de SUFFREN, left Cuddalore, India on August 22, 1782, with the objective of taking the British base at Trincomalee, Ceylon (Sri Lanka). The French, who had 12 ships of the line available, achieved their goal on August 28. British reinforcements, in the form of Admiral Sir Edward HUGHES's squadron of 14 ships of the line, arrived from Madras on September 2, but were too late: By this time Trincomalee was securely in French hands.

Admiral Suffren emerged from Trincomalee harbor on the following day. Fighting began some 25 miles (40 km) southeast of Trincomalee in the early afternoon and continued for about three hours. The action focused on the British center and Suffren's flagship *Hermes* and two other French ships of the line. It ended inconclusively as darkness fell. The British were forced to return to Madras, while the French withdrew to their new possession. As Suffren entered Trincomalee Harbor, one of his ships, *L'Orient*, was wrecked on a reef at the entrance. It was the only ship to have been lost during the day's operations.

Triumph, H.M.S.

There have been several English warships named *Triumph* during the past 400 years, but the first was perhaps the most impressive. Launched in 1561, this *Triumph* had a displacement of 1,100 tons. At the time of the SPANISH ARMADA, 1588, when she served as Sir Martin FROBISHER's flagship, the *Triumph* was the largest ship in the English fleet. She served Frobisher well, and he was knighted at sea for his contribution to the fight against the Spanish. The second *Triumph*, a 42-gun second-rate (see RATING OF SHIPS) ship, fought equally well against the Dutch in the following century. The name was revived in the 19th century for one of the British Audacious-class battleships that appeared from 1870. These ships had a displacement of 6,010 tons and a central battery of ten 9-inch (23-cm) guns. They had the largest sail area in proportion to their displacement of any capital ships of the period. *Triumph* was also the name of a WORLD WAR I, 1914–18, pre-dreadnought battleship and a WORLD WAR II, 1939–45, submarine.

Trolle, Herluf
1516–65

Danish naval commander and diplomat who married into a wealthy family and became a member of the Senate. In 1559 Trolle was appointed admiral and inspector of the fleet and within four years had succeeded Peder SKRAM as admiral in chief. His tenure of office was dominated by war with Sweden. In May 1563 he fought a larger Swedish squadron under the command of Admiral Jacob Bragge. Following an engagement stretching over two days, the *Makalös*, the Swedish flagship, was captured but blew up soon afterward. Although Trolle's fleet was damaged in the battle, he fought against a second Swedish squadron commanded by Admiral Kas Horn only three months later. This proved to be indecisive, and both fleets returned to the fight during the following year. In a further inconclusive battle, on June 1, 1565, Trolle received injuries from which he died soon afterward.

Tromp, Cornelis Maartenszoon
1629–91

Dutch naval commander, born at Rotterdam, the second son of the more distinguished Maarten TROMP, 1597–1653. Cornelis Tromp's early service was based in the Mediterranean. In 1650 he led an expedition to Morocco, where he fought the Barbary pirates. Tromp then turned his attention to the English, first engaging them off LEGHORN on March 13, 1653, during the First ANGLO-DUTCH WAR, 1652–54, when he was in command of the *Maan*. He received early promotion to flag rank and was a vice admiral before the start of the Second Anglo-Dutch War, 1665–67. Serving under Admiral Michiel de RUYTER, he was present at every major engagement of the war, including the Battle of ORFORDNESS, July 25–26, 1666. In this concluding battle Tromp operated independently without de Ruyter's agreement, and his failure to cooperate with his commander contributed to the Dutch defeat. Tromp's conduct led to his dismissal from his command.

Tromp remained in the wilderness for some time and he was not reinstated until William of Orange became Stadtholder during the Third Anglo-Dutch War, 1672–74. Tromp's rehabilitation did not come too late for him to make a real contribution to the Dutch war effort, particularly at the concluding Battle of the TEXEL, August 11, 1673, where he distinguished himself. In 1676, when war broke out between Sweden and Denmark, Tromp was appointed to the command of the Danish navy. He was victorious against the Swedes at the Battle of ÖLAND, June 1, 1676, and became a noble of Denmark. Tromp was appointed to the command of a Dutch fleet during the War of the GRAND ALLIANCE, 1688–97, but did not see action against the French before his death in 1691.

Tromp, Maarten Harpertszoon
1597–1653

Dutch admiral who commanded the fleet during the First ANGLO-DUTCH WAR, 1652–54. Maarten Tromp entered the navy in 1622, but he had first been to sea at a much earlier age and had already experienced many adventures. At the age of twelve he was taken prisoner during an engagement with an English PRIVATEER and was held as a slave in North Africa for three years. He was later involved in operations against the Barbary pirates. In the DUTCH NAVY he obtained promotion to the rank of captain quickly, but his criticisms of naval administration won him a period of unemployment. In 1637 he was restored to favor as Lieutenant Admiral of Holland and became involved in much-needed naval reforms. Two years later he distinguished himself at sea, launching a successful attack on the privateers of Dunkirk and engaging the Spanish in the Battle of the DOWNS, October 21, 1639. His decisive victory marked the demise of Spanish sea power in northern waters.

With the outbreak of the First Anglo-Dutch War, Tromp met a more formidable opponent in Admiral Robert BLAKE, the English commander. The fleets clashed at the Battle of DOVER, May 19, 1652, in an engagement that marked the beginning of the war. The Dutch were forced to retreat, but Tromp returned in August to search out his opponent. He met with no success and, on his return home, he was relieved of his command. His successor, Admiral Witte de WITT, was defeated by the English at the Battle of KENTISH KNOCK in September and Tromp was rapidly reinstated. He succeeded in defeating Blake at the Battle of DUNGENESS, November 30, but Dutch naval supremacy was short-lived. During the three-day action known as the Battle of PORTLAND, February 18–20, 1653, a reinforced English fleet attacked Tromp while he was escorting a large convoy back to Holland. He was defeated with heavy losses. English superiority was confirmed at the Battle of the GABBARD, June 2–3, 1653, when Tromp lost another 20 ships.

Defeat was followed by a BLOCKADE of the Dutch coast. With commendable skill, Tromp managed to draw off the English fleet blockading the Texel, enabling a squadron under Admiral de With to escape to the open sea. It combined with Tromp's ships off SCHEVENINGEN and a final attack on the English was launched on July 31, 1653. During an intense struggle Tromp was killed and his fleet decisively defeated. He was buried with full honors. Tromp was one of Holland's greatest admirals. Although a courageous and skillful seaman, he was unable to overcome the more powerful and better equipped English fleet. His son, Admiral Cornelis TROMP, 1629–91, was also a key figure in the 17th-century Dutch navy who served in the Second and Third Anglo-Dutch Wars (1665–67; 1672–74).

Hugh C. B. Rogers, *Generals-at-Sea. Naval Operations During the English Civil War and the Three Anglo-Dutch Wars*, Bromley, Kent, 1992.

Troopship

A ship used to convey troops to a war zone or to an overseas garrison. The term "transport" also is used to describe any vessel used for carrying armed forces and their equipment. The transportation of troops was a traditional naval responsibility, although the use of warships for this purpose often caused friction on board because of the inherent rivalry between the two services. In the 1860s in Britain this led to the creation of a specific transport service operated by five ships that could carry an army battalion. By the late 19th century the British government increasingly turned to the merchant service to provide its major troop transportation needs. The manpower needs of British India alone required the regular use of several chartered passenger liners.

Liners were used extensively in the two world wars, with the British ships *Queen Elizabeth* and QUEEN MARY being the largest examples in use. Ships of this kind could carry large numbers of troops in relative safety without an escort because of their high cruising speeds. The safe movement of 2 million American troops to Europe during WORLD WAR I, 1914–18, was the largest operation of its kind ever mounted. Typically some 40 troopships (requisitioned merchant ships) would travel in convoy across the Atlantic protected by a single U.S. cruiser. A more recent example of the use of troopships was the requisitioning of the British passenger liners CANBERRA and QE2 for transport duties during the FALKLANDS WAR, 1982. Generally, however, the troopship has been effectively superseded by the jet aircraft as the main method of conveying troops to the battlefield.

Roland W. Charles, *Troopships of World War II*, Washington, D.C., 1947.

Trotha, Adolf von
1868–1940

German admiral who commanded the dreadnought BATTLESHIP *Kaiser* during WORLD WAR I, 1914–18, until his appointment, in 1916, as chief of staff to Vice Admiral Reinhard SCHEER, head of the HIGH SEAS FLEET. Trotha, who was awarded the Pour Le Mérite for his service at the Battle of JUTLAND, May 1916, remained in this post after the appointment of Admiral Franz von HIPPER as Scheer's successor in August 1918. Together they devised the abortive Plan 19, by which the High Seas Fleet was to launch an all-out attack on the British on October 30, 1918, in order to salvage the German navy's honor. Trotha's naval career continued after the war when he became deeply embroiled in right-wing politics.

Troubridge, Admiral Sir Ernest
1862–1926

English naval commander who was the subject of a famous court-martial during the opening stages of WORLD WAR I, 1914–18, Admiral Troubridge's career in the Royal Navy dated back to 1875. Much of his service had been spent onshore and included periods as naval attaché in Tokyo and chief of the naval war staff. When war broke out, in August 1914, he was a rear admiral in command of the cruiser squadron of the British Mediterranean fleet, whose commander in chief was Sir Archibald MILNE. Almost immediately after war had been declared, Troubridge was involved in the pursuit of the German warships GOEBEN and *Breslau.* He failed to engage them south of Greece as they moved into the eastern Mediterranean because he adhered strictly to orders that instructed him not to engage a stronger enemy force. The arrival of these warships in the Dardanelles facilitated Turkey's entry into the war on the German side, with disastrous long-term consequences for the Allies.

A court of inquiry described Troubridge's action as "deplorable and contrary to the traditions of the British navy," although there was no suggestion of cowardice. In the court-martial that followed, in November 1914, his successful defense to the charge of negligence was based on the argument that the Admiralty had specifically ordered him not to engage a superior force. Following his acquittal, Troubridge never again served at sea but, unlike his commanding officer, Sir Archibald Milne, he continued to be employed for the rest of the war—first as head of a naval mission to Serbia and then on the Prince of Serbia's personal staff.

Troubridge, Sir Thomas
1758–1807

*B*ritish naval commander, one of Admiral Lord NELSON's "band of brothers." Admiral Sir Thomas Troubridge served in the Royal Navy in the wars against France from 1793. Troubridge, who had entered the navy in 1773, distinguished himself at the Battle of CAPE ST. VINCENT, 1797, in command of the *Culloden,* a third-rate (see RATING OF SHIPS) SHIP OF THE LINE. His conduct was commended by Sir John JERVIS, First Earl St. Vincent, the British commander. Troubridge had served with Nelson in the East Indies at the beginning of his career, and after the Battle of Cape St. Vincent he joined him again in the attack on Santa Cruz, July 1797. He was with Nelson again at the Battle of the NILE, 1798, but the *Culloden* grounded and he did not take part in the action. Afterward he commanded the siege of Malta. Following his promotion to rear admiral, Troubridge was appointed to the command of the Cape of Good Hope naval station, but he was lost when his ship went down on her way to South Africa.

Truxton, Thomas
1755–1822

*A*merican naval officer. Born near Hempstead, New York in 1755, Truxton served in the merchant naval service until the outbreak of the AMERICAN WAR OF INDEPENDENCE, 1775–83, when he became a successful PRIVATEER. Following the war, he commanded the *Canton,* a merchantman, on a voyage from Philadelphia to China in 1786. Returning to the service in 1794 with the establishment of the U.S. Navy, he was commissioned a captain and served as commodore of a small squadron in the West Indies during the QUASI-WAR, 1798–1800, with France. While serving on the CONSTELLATION, Truxton won notable victories over the French frigates *L'Insurgente* and *La Vengeance,* in 1799 and 1800 respectively. A commander who insisted on rigorous discipline for his crews, he was thus instrumental in establishing professional standards and practices for the young American naval service. He died in Philadelphia in 1822.

Eugene S. Ferguson, *Truxton of the Constellation. The Life of Commodore Thomas Truxton, U.S. Navy, 1755–1822,* Annapolis, Md., 1982.

Tryon, Sir George
1832–1893

*B*ritish vice admiral who lost his life on June 22, 1893 in a major Victorian naval disaster that occurred during training maneuvers in the Mediterranean. Tryon was directly responsible for the incident, which caused heavy loss of life. A former captain of the WARRIOR, the Royal Navy's first IRONCLAD, and high-ranking staff officer at the Admiralty, Tryon was appointed commander in chief of the Mediterranean Fleet in 1893. He was noteworthy for the emphasis he placed on training and had a substantial reputation as a tactician.

The maneuver that cost him his life and reputation involved the VICTORIA, his own flagship, and the CAMPERDOWN, which headed two columns some 1,200 yards (1,097 m) apart. Tryon ordered the fleet to reverse courses by turning inward in succession, but at this point the two columns were clearly too close together for the maneuver to be completed successfully. As a result, the leading ships collided and sank with the loss of 359 officers and men, including the fleet commander. It was the heaviest loss ever sustained by the Royal Navy in peacetime. No satisfactory explanation of Tryon's bizarre conduct has ever been given.

Richard Hough, *Admirals in Collision,* London, 1959.

Tsushima, Battle of
May 27–28, 1905

*F*ollowing a series of Russian naval setbacks during the RUSSO-JAPANESE WAR, 1904–5, its Baltic Fleet was dispatched on a 17,000-mile (27,359-km) journey to the Far East. Its objective was to reinforce the few remaining operational Russian naval units. Under the command of Admiral Zinovi ROZHESTVENSKY, it consisted of eight battleships, eight cruisers, nine destroyers and several auxiliaries. They left Reval (Tallinn) and Libau (Liepaja) on October 15, 1904, but were soon, unexpectedly, involved in the bizarre DOGGER BANK incident. This did not delay their progress for long.

The main Russian force went around the Cape of Good Hope while a support squadron of two battleships and three cruisers, under the command of Rear Admiral Nikolai Nebogatoff, passed through the Suez Canal. After long delays the two groups rendezvoused at Madagascar, where they learned of the fall of Port Arthur, their intended destination, on January 12, 1905. Undeterred, Rozhestvensky continued his journey, making a final stop in French Indo-China before proceeding north to the Straits of Tsushima. This was on the route to Vladivostok, which became his new intended destination. Waiting for the approaching Russians was the Japanese fleet under Admiral Heihachiro TOGO. Togo had sent scouts to patrol the straits where he was certain the Russians would eventually appear. The main Japanese fleet, which was waiting in Masampo Bay on the south coast of Korea, consisted of four battleships, eight cruisers, 21 destroyers and 60 torpedo boats. It was much more powerful and modern than its opponent. On May 27 the Russians were first sighted as they approached the straits in line-ahead formation on a northeasterly course.

Togo put out to sea and first sighted the Russians at 1:40 P.M. Leading in the MISAKA, he crossed the Russian line of advance and turned again to bring his ships on a parallel course. At about 2:10, as the two leading ships closed to within 7,000 yards (6,300 m), both sides opened fire. The Japanese ships escaped serious damage from heavy enemy fire but Rozhestvensky's flagship, the *Suvorov*, was badly affected. The battleship *Osliabya* was attacked by Japanese cruisers and by 2:30 P.M. had been severely damaged. It sank 30 minutes later. By this time the faster Japanese ships had headed off the Russian line and forced it to turn southeast. The Russian flagship was disabled, and Rozhestvensky, who was badly injured, was taken off in the destroyer *Biedovy*. The *Suvorov* finally sank at about 7:30 P.M. The Russians, now led by Admiral Nebogatoff, turned north again, but Togo forced them back once more. The opposing cruiser squadrons fought to the south of the main battle area.

As the Russian fleet regrouped, Nebogatoff pushed north again, but heavy Japanese fire resulted in further losses. At about 8:30 P.M. Togo withdrew his heavy units, but Japanese destroyers and torpedo boats maintained the attack. Nebogatoff continued to head north with two battleships and three other vessels, but they were unable to break out. Fighting extended into the following day (May 28). In the final stages of the battle, the Japanese captured the destroyer with Rozhestvensky aboard and took him prisoner of war. At 10:00 A.M. Nebogatoff and the remaining Russian ships surrendered. Only six of their ships had escaped destruction or capture: three reached Vladivostok while the remainder were interned at Manila. Russian casualties

were heavy (4,830) but the Japanese (117) were remarkably light. The victory brought both sides to the negotiating table; the Treaty of Paris, September 6, 1905, marked the final end of the war. The terms were humiliating for the Russians and reflected their shattering defeat at Tsushima. It had been the first great battle of armored battleships and the only great engagement of pre-dreadnoughts.

Richard Hough, *The Fleet That Had to Die*, London, 1958.

Turbinia, H.M.S.

The British experimental ship *Turbinia* was the first vessel to be powered by a turbine engine. Built in 1894, she had a displacement of 44.5 tons and was 100 feet (30.48 m) long. Her steam turbine power plant, designed by Sir Charles PARSONS, had several advantages over the conventional steam reciprocating engine: It was lighter, more powerful and occupied less space. However, the performance of this original engine proved to be disappointing and it was replaced, in 1896, by three parallel-flow Parson engines that drove three separate shafts. These produced a maximum speed of 34.5 knots, which no other ship of the day could equal.

The *Turbinia* made her first public appearance at the Spithead naval review in 1897, which marked Queen Victoria's diamond jubilee. She steamed from one end of the British fleet to the other, and her impressive performance overcame earlier official indifference. It led to the rapid introduction of the turbine engine in the warships and merchant ships of the world. The Royal Navy soon installed it on several small TORPEDO BOATS and, in 1903, on the cruiser *Amethyst*.

Turner, Richmond Kelly
1885–1961

The man most closely connected with amphibious operations by the U.S. Navy in the Pacific theater of WORLD WAR II, 1939–45. Richmond Turner was born on May 27, 1885 and graduated from the U.S. Naval Academy with the Class of 1908. During the 1920s his career was closely connected with naval ordnance; he served as gunnery officer in various ships, including the battleship *Michigan* during the United States' involvement in WORLD WAR I, 1914–18. He then made a career change by qualifying as a pilot in 1927 at the rather senior age of 42. He headed the Plans Division of the Bureau of Ordnance and acted as an adviser at the 1932 disarmament conference in Geneva. Returning to the navy's line after heading the Strategic Section of the Naval War College, he served as director of the War Plans Division in 1940 after commanding the cruiser *Astoria*.

With the country's entry into World War II, Turner

immediately became assistant chief of staff to Admiral Ernest J. KING and was thus a key figure in Pacific theater strategy and particularly the amphibious aspect of the campaigns. In July 1942 he was appointed Commander, Amphibious Force, South Pacific, thereby leading the first major amphibious operations on GUADALCANAL in August. With that campaign secured early the following year, he went on to become Commander, Task Force 51, and therefore led the amphibious operations as part of the Central Pacific offensive. These included the landings on the Gilbert, Marshall, and Marianas Islands. Retaining his command of Task Force 51 but assuming additional duties as Commander, Amphibious Forces, Pacific, he led the landing forces against IWO JIMA and OKINAWA in 1945. Prior to his retirement in 1947 he served as the U.S. Navy's representative on the United Nations' Military Staff Committee. Admiral Turner died on February 12, 1961 in Monterey, California. (See also AMPHIBIOUS WARFARE.)

George C. Dyer, *The Amphibious Came to Conquer: The Story of Admiral Richmond Kelly Turner*, Washington, D.C., 1972.

Turner, Stansfield
1923–

One of the brightest and most influential American naval officers in the post–WORLD WAR II, 1939–45, period. Stansfield Turner was born on December 1, 1923 in Illinois. A member of the accelerated Class of 1947, he graduated in 1946. After a short period of sea duty, he became a Rhodes Scholar, studying politics at Oxford University before returning to naval duty on the command staff at Naples, Italy. Selected early on as a future policy leader, he served in the mid-1950s at the policy division of the Office of the Chief of Naval Operations. Following command of several vessels to the early 1960s, he became systems analyst in the Office of the Assistant Secretary of Defense. As commander of the guided missile frigate HORNE he saw action off VIETNAM while escorting the carriers of Task Force 77.

Returning to staff duties, Turner served as aide and executive assistant to two Secretaries of the Navy from 1968 to 1970, when he was promoted to flag rank and given command of the flotilla that maintained surveillance of the Soviet Union's Mediterranean squadron in the early 1970s. From 1972 to 1974 he was president of the Naval War College, implementing considerable changes in strategy to meet the threat of the Soviet Union's commitment to a blue-water navy. From 1975 to 1977, with the rank of admiral, he commanded forces of the North Atlantic Treaty Organization (NATO) in southern Europe. In 1977 Turner was appointed director of the Central Intelligence Agency by President Jimmy Carter. He retired on January 1, 1979.

Clark G. Reynolds, *Famous American Admirals*, New York, 1978, pp. 364–365.

Turtle

A small, hand-powered SUBMARINE, built in 1775, that was notable as the first vessel of its kind to attack an enemy ship in wartime. Designed by David BUSHNELL, c. 1742–1824, the *Turtle* floated upright in the water and could be partially submerged when two internal water tanks were filled. Strictly speaking, therefore, she was neither a submarine nor a submersible. Power was provided by a hand-cranked propeller. She was armed with a detachable explosive charge that could be fitted to the hull of an enemy warship.

The first ever submarine attack took place on September 6–7, 1776 during the AMERICAN WAR OF INDEPENDENCE, 1775–83. The *Turtle*'s target was Admiral Lord HOWE's flagship, the *Eagle*, which was blockading the Hudson River. The attack failed because her explosive charge could not be attached to the *Eagle*'s copper hull. Although the *Eagle* was untouched, the operation marked an important preliminary stage in the evolution of submarine design.

Tyrwhitt, Sir Reginald
1870–1951

Commander of the ROYAL NAVY's Harwich Force throughout WORLD WAR I, 1914–18, Sir Reginald Tyrwhitt was an outstanding naval leader who displayed great initiative and courage. His force of light cruisers and destroyers, which was used very intensively and suffered heavy losses, was first in action at the Battle of HELIGOLAND BIGHT, August 1914, in an operation he planned jointly with Commodore Roger KEYES. Tyrwhitt was present at the Battle of the DOGGER BANK, 1914, but, much to his regret, the Harwich Force missed the Battle of JUTLAND, 1916, because of ADMIRALTY orders.

An important function of Tyrwhitt's force was to counter the regular bombardments of the east coast of England by German battle cruisers: On April 25, 1916, for example, a powerful enemy force was turned back off Lowestoft. Tyrwhitt was a powerful advocate of NAVAL AVIATION, and many seaplane raids against German land targets were launched from his ships. His successful wartime career concluded with the surrender of German U-boats to the Harwich Force after the Armistice in November 1918. Tyrwhitt's naval career prospered in the postwar period, and he reached the rank of admiral of the fleet in 1934, shortly after leaving his final post as commander in chief at the Nore.

A. Temple Patterson, *Tyrwhitt of the Harwich Force*, London, 1973.

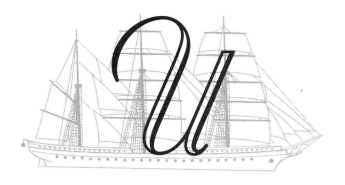

U-Boat

German SUBMARINE or *Unterseeboot*. See also U-BOAT *U-47*; U-BOAT *U-48*; U-BOAT *U-110*.

Norman Friedman, *Submarine Design and Development*, London, 1984.

U-boat *U-47*

German U-boat of World War II, 1939–45, commanded by the submarine ace Gunther PRIEN who achieved many notable victories against the Allies in this type VIIB boat. (See U-BOAT *U-48*.) His most important achievement was the sinking of the British battleship *ROYAL OAK* during the night of October 13–14, 1939. Prien's remarkable success in penetrating in the Royal Navy's defenses at SCAPA FLOW made him a popular hero in Germany. His wartime career was brought to an end on March 7, 1941

when the *U-47* was sunk in the Atlantic by the British corvettes *Arbutus* and *Camellia*. (See also Battle of the ATLANTIC, 1939–45.)

U-Boat *U-48*

The highest-scoring U-Boat of WORLD WAR II, 1939–45, the *U-48* was responsible for the destruction of 51 enemy ships (totaling 310,407 tons) during the period from September 1939 to June 1941. Following her sustained period of success, the *U-48* was transferred to training duties and survived to be scuttled at the end of the war. This type VIIB boat was one of the standard, mass-produced boats used by the German navy throughout the war. An oceangoing design built within the constraints of prewar naval restrictions, it had a surface displacement of 753 tons, was 218 feet 3 inches (66.52 m) in length and had a

A Deutschland-class U-boat arrives in London after surrender in December 1918   *(Copyright © National Maritime Museum, Greenwich, London)*

beam of 20 feet 3 inches (6.17 m). With a maximum speed of 17.25 knots on the surface and 7.25 knots submerged, the type VIIB U-boat was armed with one 3.5-inch gun, one 20-mm antiaircraft gun and five 21-inch (53-cm) torpedo tubes. The type VIIB boat had a range of 6,500 miles (10,400 km) at 12 knots. (See also Battle of the ATLANTIC, 1939–45.)

U-Boat *U-110*

During WORLD WAR II, 1939–45, this type IXB long-range U-boat was attacked by three British warships southwest of Ireland on March 9, 1941. Depth charges damaged the U-boat, and she was forced to the surface. As they abandoned the submarine, the crew set scuttling charges but they failed to detonate. Before the *U-110* sank under tow, she was boarded by British naval personnel who discovered and seized intact an Enigma coding machine. This discovery, which was to remain a secret for some 20 years, gave the British greatly improved access to German naval codes and was to have a major impact on the course of events during the Battle of the ATLANTIC, 1939–45.

Ugaki, Matome
1890–1945

Japanese vice admiral who died in one of the last KAMIKAZE actions of WORLD WAR II, 1939–45. At the beginning of the war Ugaki was appointed chief of staff of the Combined Fleet and had a key role in operational planning. He survived the attack by U.S. naval aircraft on April 18, 1943 that killed Admiral Isoroku YAMAMOTO even though his own aircraft also was shot down. Ukagi then served under Admiral Jisaburo OZAWA as commander of the First Battleship Squadron.

Flying his flag in the battleship *Yamato*, Ugaki fought at the Battle of the PHILIPPINE SEA, June 19–21, 1944. He later served at the Battle of LEYTE GULF, October 23–26, 1944, under Admiral Takeo KURITA. As the war drew to a close, Ugaki was appointed commander of the Fifth Air Fleet, which was based at Kyushu. In this post he was involved in the direction of KAMIKAZE operations at Okinawa. Following the announcement of the Japanese surrender, on August 15, 1945, Ugaki personally joined a final suicide operation against the Allied fleet off Okinawa as his last act.

Matome Ugaki, *Fading Victory: The Diary of Admiral Matome Ukagi, 1941–45*, London, 1991.

United States, U.S.S.

This 44-gun frigate, launched in May 1797, was the first ship to enter service with the newly constituted UNITED STATES NAVY. Its commissioning was timely because the country's naval war with France, the QUASI-WAR, 1798–1800, was just about to begin. The *United States*, which served as Captain John BARRY's flagship during the war, captured seven enemy ships and also conveyed the American peace commissioners to Europe in 1800. Laid up until the beginning of the WAR OF 1812, she had a brief moment of glory when, under the command of Stephen DECATUR, she captured the *Macedonian*, a 38-gun British frigate, in October 1812, but was otherwise blockaded in port for much of the conflict. She continued in service for many years and finally was destroyed at Norfolk Navy Yard during the AMERICAN CIVIL WAR, 1861–65.

United States Coast Guard

Formed in August 1790, the United States Coast Guard originally was known as the Revenue Marine and had a fleet of ten CUTTERS to prevent smuggling. It was given its present name in 1915 and now operates as a part of the Department of the Treasury except in time of war (or when the President so directs), when it serves as part of the U.S. Navy. Its temporary integration into the armed services is facilitated by the fact that it uses naval ranks and is headed by a full admiral. He is supported by two vice admirals who have responsibility for operations in the Atlantic and Pacific respectively. The Coast Guard's main peacetime function is the enforcement of maritime laws and treaties on the high seas and in American territorial waters.

Other major functions include the protection of life and property, offshore rescue, the suppression of smuggling and illicit drug traffic, the enforcement of safety standards for merchant ships and ship navigation. The Coast Guard also has played an active part in every major war in which the United States has participated. It has been involved in patrols, convoy escorts and amphibious landing operations, among other things. The current peacetime strength of the service is about 38,000 military members and some 6,000 civilian support staff. As well as a variety of ships, the Coast Guard operates aircraft, research facilities and shore installations on the Atlantic and the Pacific. Education and training facilities are provided by the United States Coast Guard Academy at New London, Connecticut, and the Coast Guard's three-masted training ship *Bark Eagle*.

R. E. Johnson, *Guardians of the Sea: A History of the U.S. Coast Guard, 1915 to the Present*, Annapolis, Md., 1987; I. H. King, *The Coast Guard Under Sail*. London, 1989.

United States Naval Academy

An institution of higher education, based at ANNAPOLIS, Maryland, for the education and training of young men and women who aim to become officers in the UNITED

STATES NAVY or U.S. Marine Corps. A counterpart to the U.S. Military Academy at West Point, New York, it was founded in October 1845 by George BANCROFT, Secretary of the Navy in President James Polk's administration. Some of America's most distinguished naval officers have been graduates of the Academy. Originally established as a naval school with a five-year course of training, its primary purpose was to improve the professional education of mid-shipmen, who previously had received little effective instruction. Only five years after its creation, the school was reconstituted at the U.S. Naval Academy and a four-year course, combined with training at sea during the summer, was introduced. The work of the academy has been much affected by the navy's wartime requirements, and the standard length of the course could be reduced if more officers were needed. The navy's combat experiences have helped to ensure that the academy's curriculum and organization have kept pace with rapid changes in naval warfare.

In recent years there has been an enrollment of some 4,400, and the highly qualified candidates, ages between 17 and 22, are drawn mainly from leading secondary schools. Cadets are drawn from several other smaller categories, including a small group of enlisted men who enter on a competitive basis. Women were first admitted to the academy as midshipmen in 1976. Apart from a sound academic record, cadets also must meet high physical standards. The academy combines professional training with degree-level study in engineering and the physical sciences as well as supporting courses in the social sciences. The greatest priority is given to academic study, and all successful cadets graduate with a Bachelor of Science (B.S.) degree, which is the only degree offered. There is a separate naval post-graduate school at Monterey, California. When cadets graduate from Annapolis, they receive a commission in the navy or the marines.

United States Navy

During the early stages of the AMERICAN WAR OF INDE-PENDENCE, 1775–83, the fight against the British at sea was conducted by PRIVATEERS. The Continental navy was founded on October 13, 1775 and, under the command of Esek HOPKINS, operated successfully against the British merchant fleet, producing some notable commanders, including John Paul JONES. It was supported by the individual naval units of 11 colonies, although these forces combined were not sufficiently strong to challenge the ROYAL NAVY's dominance. That task was left to the French navy, which fought the British in various locations across the globe and was for a time successful in seizing the initiative from the Royal Navy. The French victory at the second Battle of CHESAPEAKE, September 5, 1781, was decisive as it led to the surrender of the British army at Yorktown and the final achievement of American independence.

The Continental navy disappeared at the end of the war, and for a few years the United States survived without a permanent naval force. However, it soon became clear that this position was not sustainable. One problem was the activities of the Barbary pirates (see CORSAIRS) who regularly intercepted American merchant shipping in the Mediterranean. American trade also was badly affected by the naval conflict between Britain and France during the FRENCH REVOLUTIONARY AND NAPOLEONIC WARS, 1792–1815. As a result, on March 27, 1794, Congress approved the construction of six frigates—the UNITED STATES, CONSTITUTION, PRESIDENT, CHESAPEAKE, CONGRESS and CONSTELLATION—as the basis of a new American naval force. The latter was formally created on April 30, 1798, when Congress established the Department of the Navy with Benjamin STODDERT as its first Secretary. The new navy was soon in action during the QUASI-WAR, 1798–1800, with France and fought several successful duels with enemy warships. It then turned its attention to the Barbary pirates during the Tripolitan War, 1801–5, which started the process of bringing their activities under control; this process continued when the U.S. Navy returned to Algiers in 1815. During the WAR OF 1812 against Britain, fighting took place both on the high seas and on inland waterways. Despite the small size of its fleet, the U.S. Navy could claim some creditable successes, particularly in individual actions against British warships. A notable example was the famous victory of the *Constitution* over the British frigate *Guerrière*.

The period preceding the AMERICAN CIVIL WAR, 1861–65, was one of relative stagnation for the U.S. Navy, which, in 1861, could muster only 42 warships. Its key achievements during this time included its extensive involvement in exploration, particularly of Antarctica, its role in the Mexican War, 1846–48, and the founding of the UNITED STATES NAVAL ACADEMY at Annapolis in 1843. The Civil War brought a rapid expansion of the Union Navy, which was involved in blockading the South, seizing control of the Mississippi and New Orleans and capturing blockade runners. By contrast, the CONFEDERATE NAVY made relatively little impact except in the interception of enemy merchant shipping and in technological innovation, of which the IRONCLAD MERRIMACK is a notable example.

A long period of postwar retrenchment followed, and it was not until 1883 that the Congress authorized the modernization and expansion of the fleet. Rapid success in the SPANISH-AMERICAN WAR of 1898, when the U.S. Navy won major victories in the Philippines and Cuba, ensured that it enjoyed continued popular and political support. The navy's position was reinforced by Theodore ROOSE-VELT's arrival in the White House in 1901, and a further period of construction followed. In 1907–9, the world cruise of the GREAT WHITE FLEET provided solid evidence of the growth of American naval power and an expansionist foreign policy. During WORLD WAR I, 1914–18, a new shipbuilding program was in progress, providing a sound basis of the U.S. Navy's wartime role after the United States intervened in April 1917. It made a major contribution to defeating the U-BOAT threat during the Battle of the ATLANTIC, 1915–17, although it did not fight any surface engagements against the Germans. The navy also was responsible for transporting some 2 million ground troops to Europe without a single loss of life.

During WORLD WAR II, 1939–45, American naval operations were mounted on a scale that would have been unimaginable only 25 years earlier. In 1941 it had 16 battleships, seven aircraft carriers, 37 cruisers and 114 submarines as well as a large number of smaller warships. Following the surprise attack on the U.S. Pacific fleet at PEARL HARBOR, December 1941, American naval activity was focused on the struggle against Japan in the Pacific, with the Battle of MIDWAY, 1942, being the turning point. American offensive operations began in the SOLOMON IS-LANDS in 1942–43 and eventually moved forward across the Pacific. Occupied territory was reclaimed in a series of major combined operations using carrier strike forces. The American carrier and submarine had brought the Japanese navy to the point of extinction by the time of the Battle of LEYTE GULF, October 1944. In the final stages of the PACIFIC WAR, the navy was heavily involved in planning the invasion of Japan, but the bombing of Hiroshima and Nagasaki rendered this unnecessary. The U.S. fleet also played a vital role in the Battle of the ATLANTIC, 1939–45, and in the major amphibious operations in Europe, including the NORMANDY LANDINGS, 1944, in the latter part of the war.

For much of the postwar period, the U.S. Navy was the largest naval power in the world, although it was eventually overtaken by the former SOVIET NAVY. The U.S. Navy has maintained a full range of naval vessels and weapons systems, enabling it to operate in strength in any part of the world. Its naval units have intervened in a variety of conflicts during the COLD WAR. More recently they have been involved, under the United Nations banner, in the Gulf War, 1990–01, and the recent conflict in the former Yugoslavia. The navy has also made a key contribution to American strategic defense, and SUBMARINE-LAUNCHED BALLISTIC MISSILES from POLARIS to TRIDENT have underpinned the nuclear balance between the two superpowers over the last 35 years. The U.S. fleet includes some 127 nuclear-powered submarines, 14 aircraft carriers, four battleships, 31 cruisers and 135 antisubmarine vessels as well as numerous other specialist craft.

Stephen Howarth, *To the Shining Sea: A History of the United States Navy, 1775–1991*, London, 1991; John Sweetman, *American Naval History*, London, 1984.

Unryu

One of three completed Japanese AIRCRAFT CARRIERS of the Unryu class, which also included the *Amagi* and the *Katsuragi*. All three ships served in the Pacific in WORLD WAR II, 1939–45. The *Unryu* had a displacement of 17,150 tons, a complement of 1,450 men and could accommodate 64 aircraft. Equipped with 63 antiaircraft guns, she was 741 feet 6 inches (226 m) in length and had a maximum speed of 34 knots. The *Unryu* was launched in September 1943 and was sunk in the East China Sea by the U.S.S. *Redfish* in December 1944. The *Amagi*, her sister ship, fared little better: Launched in October 1943, she was sunk by an air attack on Kobe dockyard in July 1945. Three other ships of this class were under construction as the war ended but were not completed in time for operational service.

Urca

The name of two very different types of Spanish ship. The first was a sailing vessel that served as a naval auxiliary during the 16th century. A reduced version of the GALLEON in terms of her rigging, she had some armament and was used primarily for moving naval stores.

A later flat-bottomed craft (or fly-boat) with a high stern and a square or lateen rig was also given the name urca. Employed as a dispatch boat by the Spanish battle fleets during the 17th and 18th centuries, this urca was armed with a small number of guns and had a displacement of about 300 tons.

Ushant, First Battle of
July 27, 1778

Some three months after France had entered the AMERI-CAN WAR OF INDEPENDENCE, 1775–83, the French and English navies met for the first time in a fleet action. The English Channel Fleet, commanded by Admiral Augustus KEPPEL, left Portsmouth on July 9, 1778 in search of the enemy fleet. Keppel was a popular commander who had refused a command at the beginning of the war but was eager to fight the French. Consisting of 26 ships of the line, the English force sighted the French near Ushant, an island off the northwest coast of France, on July 23. The French force, which was commanded by Vice-Admiral the Comte d'Orvilliers, consisted of 32 ships of the line.

Four days of maneuvering followed before the opposing fleets came to battle on July 27, some 70 miles west of Ushant. During the inconclusive battle that followed, both sides sustained some damage. Keppel also was weakened by the lack of support he received from Vice Admiral Hugh Palliser, the commander of the rear division. Palliser had fallen behind the rest of the English fleet and did not respond rapidly to signals ordering him to close up. As darkness fell, the Comte d'Orvilliers made good his withdrawal and returned to BREST without further action. Palliser's apparent failures as a commander led to an acrimonious dispute with Keppel. As a result Palliser called for Keppel's court-martial. The charges against him were dismissed and Palliser himself was then tried and acquitted.

Ushant, Second Battle of
December 12, 1781

An Anglo-French naval engagement during the AMERICAN WAR OF INDEPENDENCE, 1775–83, that resulted in a partial victory for the Royal Navy. The events leading to the battle began when a major French convoy left BREST on December 10, 1781 bound for the West Indies. It was protected by 19 ships of the line under the command of Admiral Luc Urbain de GUICHEN. The convoy did not long escape the attentions of the Royal Navy; two days after it left Brest it was detected by the English Channel Fleet some 150 miles (241 km) west of Ushant, an island off the northwest coast of France. A squadron of 12 ships of the line under Admiral Richard KEMPENFELT was ordered to chase the French but was not sufficiently powerful to mount a direct attack. Kempenfelt did, however, manage to position himself between the French squadron and its convoy. Displaying great skill, he managed to seize 20 French merchantmen but could not achieve more without a much stronger force.

Vanguard, H.M.S.

Notable as the largest British-built BATTLESHIP, the *Vanguard* displaced over 50,000 tons and was completed in 1946 at a cost of £9 million. Ordered in March 1941, she had been due for completion in 1943 in time for service in World War II, but other priorities meant that her construction period was extended. She had an overall length of 814 feet (248 m), was armed with eight 15-inch (38-cm) and 16 5.25-inch (13-cm) guns and was capable of 29 knots. Operated by a crew of 1,893, the *Vanguard* never had a chance to use her formidable armament in action and, after extended service as a training ship, she finally was scrapped in 1960, the last battleship to serve in the Royal Navy.

The *Vanguard* was the name of eight previous British warships, the earliest being a GALLEON that served during the SPANISH ARMADA, 1588. A late 18th-century *Vanguard*, a third rate (see RATING OF SHIPS) of 74 guns, was Admiral Lord NELSON's flagship at the Battle of the NILE, 1798. The unluckiest vessel of this name was a Victorian battleship of 6,010 tons, launched in 1869. During maneuvers in the Irish Sea in 1875, she was accidentally rammed by her sister ship, the *Iron Duke*, and sank, although her entire crew survived.

Vasa

A large Swedish warship of 1,279 tons launched at Stockholm in 1627, the *Vasa* was armed with 64 guns mounted on two decks. She was some 170 feet (51.8 m) in length and 38 feet (11.58 m) in the beam. On August 10, 1628 she left Stockholm Harbor on her maiden voyage but was overwhelmed almost immediately by a sudden storm and sank rapidly. The ship's design rather than human error seems to have been to blame: the *Vasa* was top-heavy because the keel was much too small for such a large vessel. Buried in mud in Stockholm Harbor, she remained undisturbed until 1956, when she was rediscovered. In 1961 she was raised and found to be in such good condition that she could float unaided. The ship has since been placed on permanent exhibition at the Vasa Museum in Stockholm. She is the only surviving example of an intact hull of a 17th-century warship.

Velez Malaga, Battle of

August 13, 1704

The British capture of GIBRALTAR, in July 1704, during the War of the SPANISH SUCCESSION, 1701–14, prompted an immediate French reaction. The French Mediterranean fleet, commanded by Admiral the Comte de TOULOUSE, was sent out from Toulon. It included 50 ships of the line and 24 Spanish galleys. The defense of Gibraltar was organized by Sir George ROOKE, who had seized it with the 53 ships of the Anglo-Dutch fleet under his command. The Allied van was led by Admiral Sir Clowdisley SHOVELL and the rear by Admiral Gerald Callenburgh.

The two fleets met on August 13 some 25 miles (40 km) southeast of Marbella, Spain. The battle between these roughly equal naval forces began at about 10:30 A.M. and lasted all day. Intense exchanges of fire produced heavy damage and many casualties, including over 2,000 dead and 5,000 wounded. Three ships were lost but neither side captured any. Although the French were far from beaten, they left the area during the night; tactically the battle was a draw. However, it was a strategic victory for the British, who kept a precarious hold on Gibraltar, where Rooke returned to carry out repairs.

French and Spanish efforts to recapture the new British possession continued for many months but ended in defeat at the Battle of MARBELLA, March 10, 1705. The allies maintained dominance of the seas was until the end of the war, and the British have retained Gibraltar ever since.

Vella Gulf, Battle of
August 5–6, 1943

Following the Battle of KOLOMBANGARA, July 6, 1943, the Japanese continued to reinforce their garrison on the island by sea as the struggle for the SOLOMON ISLANDS continued. The Japanese had been largely successful in maintaining supplies, but the Battle of Vella Gulf would change that. Six American destroyers commanded by Commander F. Moosebrugger intercepted a Japanese squadron consisting of four destroyers in Vella Gulf. During this nightime action, American gunfire and torpedoes had a deadly effect: Three of the four enemy destroyers were sunk and over 1,500 Japanese soldiers were drowned. The Japanese had been unprepared for the attack, and none of their torpedoes hit an American target. Operations in the Solomons were to continue for another three months and included the Battle of VELLA LAVELLA, October 6–7, and the American capture of Bougainville on November 1, 1943.

Vella Lavella, Battle of
October 6–7, 1943

As the struggle for the SOLOMON ISLANDS during WORLD WAR II, 1939–45, neared its conclusion in the latter part of 1943, the Americans and Japanese fought another naval engagement at Vella Lavella in October 1943. A group of nine Japanese destroyers, commanded by Rear Admiral Matsuji Ijuin, were involved in evacuating troops from Vella Lavella, New Georgia, when they were intercepted by the U.S. Navy. Six destroyers, commanded by Captain F. R. Walker, opened fire. In view of the imbalance of strength, it is not surprising that the Americans sustained more damage than the Japanese: One ship was lost and two were damaged. The Japanese lost just one destroyer and were able to complete their evacuation during the following day. Operations in the Solomons were soon to be completed with the American capture of Bougainville on November 1, 1943.

Vernon, Edward
1684–1757

British admiral noted for the capture of Porto Bello, Panama, during the War of JENKINS' EAR, 1739–43, but best known for the introduction of "grog" in the Royal Navy. Vernon himself had been nicknamed "Old Grog" because he normally wore a grogram coat—a silk and wool mixture—when on board ship. In 1740 he issued an order that the seaman's daily mixture of rum should be watered down, and this drink has been known as grog ever since.

Vernon also was noted for his interest in the development of the naval profession, and he paid particular attention to training and tactics.

Vernon's first period of active service was during the War of the SPANISH SUCCESSION, 1701–14, and he was present at the capture of GIBRALTAR in 1704. During the long years of peace following the Treaty of Utrecht, 1713, Vernon served as a member of Parliament, where he took a special interest in naval matters. A strong advocate of war with Spain during the 1730s, he commanded, as a vice admiral, the squadron that captured PORTO BELLO, November 22, 1739, an achievement that greatly enhanced his public reputation. However, Vernon suffered a significant reverse later in the War of Jenkins' Ear when he failed to take Cartagena during a combined operation in 1741. Part of the explanation was Vernon's inability to work with the commander of the land troops.

In 1745 Vernon was appointed to the command of the North Sea fleet but quickly resigned when the Admiralty failed to accord him the title of commander in chief. Vernon's subsequent pamphlet attacks on the Admiralty led to his removal from the list of admirals and an inglorious end to a mixed but not undistinguished career.

B. M. Ranft ed., *The Vernon Papers*, London, 1958.

Vian, Sir Philip
1894–1968

British naval commander who established his high reputation during the early stages of WORLD WAR II, 1939–45, and later added greatly to it during the war in the Mediterranean. In February 1940, as captain of H.M.S. COSSACK, Vian led the Fourth Destroyer Flotilla into Norwegian territorial waters in a successful mission to rescue 299 British seamen who were imprisoned on the ALTMARK, a German supply ship returning from South America. Vian's flotilla later played a key role in the destruction of the German battleship BISMARCK, scoring several torpedo hits during the night of May 26–27, 1940. Later that year he was promoted to the rank of rear admiral and appointed commander of the 15th Cruiser Squadron in Admiral Andrew CUNNINGHAM's Mediterranean fleet. He was employed on convoy escort duties in support of Malta.

Vian fought the Battle of SIRTE, March 21, 1942, against a larger Italian force as he successfully battled his way through to Malta—an achievement for which he was knighted. As commander of an aircraft carrier force, he was later involved in covering the landings in SICILY, July 1943, and at SALERNO in September. In June 1944 he was successful as naval commander of the Eastern Task Force during the Allied landings in NORMANDY. Vian's final wartime role was as commander of the Pacific Fleet's carrier

Sir Philip Vian: an outstanding British naval commander during World War II   *(Copyright © National Maritime Museum, Greenwich, London)*

group, which participated in the operations that led to the capture of OKINAWA, 1945. In 1946 he was appointed Fifth Sea Lord and was later promoted to the rank of admiral of the fleet.

Viborg Bay, Battle of
July 3–4, 1790

During the final phase of the RUSSO-SWEDISH WAR, 1788–90, the opposing fleets clashed at the Battle of STYRSUDDEN, June 3–4, 1790, as the SWEDISH NAVY moved up the Gulf of Finland in support of the land forces moving against St. Petersburg. As a result of this battle the Swedish fleet, which was commanded by Carl Duke of Södermanland (later King CHARLES XIII), moved northwest into Viborg Bay on the south coast of Finland. The Swedish force, consisting of 280 GALLEYS, transports and gunboats, was blockaded by the Russians for a month. The need to strike against St. Petersburg and deteriorating supplies forced the Swedes to move. In the early hours of July 3, Duke Carl weighed anchor and moved toward the Russian

fleet. Although three Swedish FIRESHIPS blew up prematurely, causing some Swedish losses, the remaining ships managed to penetrate the Russian line and escape in a well-planned and executed operation. The Russian fleet came under heavy fire and its losses were high—11 ships of the line and 7,000 men. The Swedes made for Svenskund Fjord, where the final engagement of the war (the Battle of SVENSKUND) was to be fought.

Victoria, H.M.S.

The last wooden BATTLESHIP to be built for the ROYAL NAVY, the *Victoria* was launched in 1859. She carried 121 guns and was commissioned in 1864, being sent to Malta as FLAGSHIP of the British Mediterranean fleet. With the IRONCLAD already firmly established as the replacement for the wooden warship, the *Victoria* was an anachronism and was withdrawn from active service after only three years.

A second ship of this name was the single-turreted British battleship launched in 1867. Protected by steel armor, her armament included two 16.25-inch (41-cm) guns, which were among the heaviest ever produced for the Royal Navy. The *Victoria* was sunk in a collision with the *CAMPERDOWN* during naval maneuvers in the Mediterranean in 1893, the result of a signaling error by Sir George TRYON, the commander in chief of the British Mediterranean fleet—an incident that has never been explained satisfactorily.

Richard Hough, *Admirals in Collision*, London, 1959.

Victory, H.M.S.

The most famous ship in British naval history, the *Victory* was Admiral Lord NELSON's flagship at the Battle of TRAFALGAR, October 1805. Work on the fifth and last *Victory* to serve in the ROYAL NAVY began at Chatham in 1759. Designed by Sir Thomas Slade, a leading naval architect, she was a 100-gun first-rate (see RATING OF SHIPS) SHIP OF THE LINE, with three decks and a displacement of 2,162 tons. The *Victory*, the largest British warship of the period, was 186 feet (56.69 m) in length and 52 feet (15.8 m) in the beam. She was operated by a crew of 850 men. The conclusion of the SEVEN YEARS' WAR, 1756–63, brought construction to a halt for a time, and she was not launched until May 1765. Further work on her was postponed and was not to be resumed until the AMERICAN WAR OF INDEPENDENCE, 1775–83, began. The *Victory* was finally completed in 1778, and she served successively as the flagship of Admiral Augustus KEPPEL and Admiral Richard KEMPENFELT.

When the French Revolutionary Wars broke out in 1793 she became Admiral Lord HOWE's flagship and served as part of the English Channel fleet. Her most memorable

H.M.S. *Victory:* Lord Nelson's flagship   *(Copyright © National Maritime Museum, Greenwich, London)*

period was the Napoleonic Wars, 1803–15, when she served as Lord Nelson's flagship during his operations against the French fleet, 1803–5. When the fleets met at the Battle of TRAFALGAR, October 1805, the *Victory* headed the weather column (those in the line of battle on the windward side). Nelson was killed on the quarterdeck of his flagship just over an hour after the battle began. The *Victory* brought Nelson's body home for a state funeral. Her seagoing service came to an end in 1835, when she became the flagship of the commander in chief, Portsmouth, and remained at permanent moorings there. In 1922, after a long period of decline, the *Victory* was fully restored as she was in Nelson's time. She was moved to a dry dock in Portsmouth Harbor, where she remains as a permanent memorial.

Vietnam War

1964–75

The first postwar involvement of the U.S. Navy in Vietnam dated back to the period immediately following the final defeat of the French by the Viet Minh in the Indo-China War, 1946–54. In August 1954 a large American amphibious force started the process of evacuating some 300,000 refugees from the new Communist regime to South Vietnam. In the period that followed, the fighting was renewed and American support for South Vietnam gradually increased in an effort to halt the spread of communism. Initially this took the form of general aid, although growing numbers of American military advisers were also dispatched to South Vietnam. These included

U.S. naval officers who helped to train the embryonic South Vietnamese navy. One of the navy's main functions was to patrol near the seventh parallel with the aim of intercepting fishing vessels carrying Vietcong guerillas from their northern bases to the south. In 1961, when the first American warships arrived in Vietnam, they were used in support of these surveillance operations.

American involvement in the war escalated dramatically after Congress passed the Gulf of Tonkin resolution in 1964. President Lyndon Johnson had asked Congress to authorize the escalation following a reported attack on two U.S. destroyers by North Vietnamese torpedo boats, the TONKIN GULF INCIDENT. In 1965 anti-infiltration operations were stepped up. U.S. Naval Task Force 115 maintained radar coverage at sensitive points along the coast and directed high-speed patrol boats to intercept possible infiltrators. This blockade was maintained until American withdrawal, although the task force had other duties, including shore bombardment. Carrier-based aircraft from the *Constitution* and the *Ticonderoga* were first used against targets in the North in August 1964, and naval air missions continued throughout the war. U.S. naval aircraft also were to be used to mine the major harbors of North Vietnam to deny their use by munitions ships from the Soviet Union and China. The navy also soon turned its attention to the Mekong River and its numerous outlets. A large force of boats, some of which were armored and heavily armed, operated against the Vietcong. Despite the massive American military deployment, conventional forces were ill-equipped to defeat a guerilla force, and the U.S. Navy could only have a marginal impact on the course of events. The continuation of the war created serious internal divisions in the United States and led to the beginning of peace talks with North Vietnam. It was not until 1973 that a cease-fire agreement was reached and the Americans finally withdrew. The war continued for another two years and ended with the defeat of South Vietnam.

Phillip B. Davidson, *Vietnam at War: The History, 1946–1975*, New York, 1988; G. Kolko, *Vietnam: Anatomy of a War, 1940–75*, London, 1986.

Vigo Bay, Battle of
October 12, 1702

Allied (English, Dutch and Austrian) naval operations during the early stages of the War of the SPANISH SUCCESSION, 1701–14, suffered a setback when an Anglo-Dutch fleet of 50 ships under the command of Sir George ROOKE was repulsed at Cadiz in September 1702. On his return home to England, Rooke learned of an opportunity to restore his reputation even though a successful outcome might be very difficult to achieve. His target was the Spanish treasure fleet, which had recently arrived in VIGO BAY, a port in the northwest of Spain. It was still under the protection of the French squadron, commanded by Admiral the Marquis de CHÂTEAU-RENAULT, that had escorted the Spanish ships on their return journey from Havana. On the treasure fleet's arrival, Vigo Bay's defenses had been strengthened and a boom was laid across the entrance of the inner harbor.

Treasure was still being unloaded when the allies attacked on October 12. They deployed only part of their force because there was insufficient space in Vigo Bay for the whole fleet to operate effectively. The operation was led by British Vice Admiral Thomas HOPSONN in his 80-gun ship the *Torbay*, which broke the boom, allowing entrance to the harbor, with considerable difficulty. The rest of the allied squadron followed and soon unloaded the troops that were ordered to destroy the shore batteries without delay. Château-Renault, aware that he was facing certain defeat, ordered his captains to destroy their ships. Before his instructions could be carried out, the allies had captured 13 French ships of the line. Eleven Spanish treasure ships also were seized, and booty valued at over £2 million was removed and taken back to England. It may have been the largest amount ever seized in a single naval action. See also PRIZE MONEY.

Villaret de Joyeuse, Louis Thomas
1750–1812

French fleet commander during the FRENCH REVOLUTIONARY AND NAPOLEONIC WARS, 1793–1815, Admiral Villaret de Joyeuse first went to sea in 1765. He served under Admiral Pierre de SUFFREN during the AMERICAN WAR OF INDEPENDENCE, 1775–83, and was briefly held captive by the British at Madras, India. Villaret rose rapidly in the French navy, becoming a post-captain in 1793 and a rear admiral in 1796. Without experience of high command, his abilities were to be severely tested during the French Revolutionary Wars, 1792–1802. Failure at the Battle of the GLORIOUS FIRST OF JUNE, 1794, when he commanded the French fleet, did not prevent his promotion to vice admiral, but after a further setback at the Battle of the ÎLE DE GROIX, June 23, 1795, in an engagement with Admiral Alexander HOOD, Lord Bridport, he left the navy for a political career.

Villaret served in the Council of the Five Hundred but was forced to flee in 1797 when he was denounced as a crypto-royalist. In 1800 he was reemployed by the navy at Brest and two years later was dispatched to the West Indies with an expedition to Santo Domingo. Villaret stayed on as captain-general of Martinique and St. Lucia, a post he held until 1809, when he was ejected by the British. His reputation was called into question, but a committee of inquiry eventually exonerated him. As a result, in 1811,

Louis Villaret de Joyeuse: commander of the French fleet at the Battle of the Glorious First of June, 1794 *(Copyright © National Maritime Museum, Greenwich, London)*

he was reemployed as governor-general of Venice but saw no further naval service.

Villeneuve, Pierre Jean Pierre Baptiste Silvestre, Comte de

1763–1806

French admiral who commanded the fleet at the Battle of TRAFALGAR, 1805, during the FRENCH REVOLUTIONARY AND NAPOLEONIC WARS, 1792–1815. Villeneuve entered the navy in 1778 and served under Admiral François de GRASSE in the West Indies in 1781–82, during the AMERICAN WAR OF INDEPENDENCE, 1775–83. Early in 1793 he was promoted to *captaine de vaisseau* but was suspended shortly afterward because he was a former aristocrat. He returned to active service some two years later, becoming chief of staff at Toulon and, in 1796, a rear admiral. In 1798 he served under Admiral François BRUEYS D'AIGAILLIERS as he escorted the Napoleon's army to Egypt and was commander of the right wing at the Battle of the NILE, August 1, 1798. Brueys was killed during the battle but Villeneuve managed to escape to Malta in his flagship, the *Guillaume,*

accompanied by three other ships. When the British captured the island in September 1800, he was held as a prisoner of war for a short period.

On his return to France, Villeneuve's naval career continued to prosper, and, by 1804, he was promoted to the rank of vice admiral. In March 1805 he left for the West Indies with the objective of drawing British warships away from the English Channel while Napoleon's invasion plans were implemented. However, Admiral Lord NELSON was in pursuit and Villeneuve was compelled to return to European waters. On July 22 he was intercepted off CAPE FINISTERRE by a squadron of the Royal Navy under the command of Vice Admiral Sir Robert CALDER. After a short engagement, Villeneuve decided to take refuge at Ferrol. He later moved south to Cadiz because he believed his route home was blocked. Villeneuve left on October 19 when he had been effectively compelled to do so by Napoleon. Shortly afterward he was decisively defeated by Nelson at the Battle of Trafalgar and was taken prisoner. Released during the following year, he returned home. Unable to live with the consequences of his failure in battle, he committed suicide soon thereafter.

Vindictive

British Arrogant-class CRUISER of 5,750 tons, used in the operations against ZEEBRUGGE and Ostend, 1918, during WORLD WAR I, 1914–18. Commissioned in 1897, by the time of the war the *Vindictive* had long been obsolete, but nonetheless she had an active wartime career with the 9th Cruiser Squadron, including service off the American coast and in the White Sea. At the beginning of 1918 she was converted as an assault ship for use in the Zeebrugge raid. The main modifications were the creation of a new deck amidships and the removal of much of the original armament, which was replaced by two flamethrowers, eight mortars, 16 machine guns, three howitzers and three pompoms (automatic rapid-firing guns). During this largely unsuccessful raid, the *Vindictive* suffered heavy damage and many casualties, she but managed to return home. Beyond economic repair, she was used as a BLOCKSHIP when a second attempt was made to block the canal entrance at Ostend on May 10. Unfortunately, she was not positioned correctly and the channel remained open to enemy shipping.

Virginius

A former Confederate BLOCKADE runner, the steamer *Virginius* was operated by Cuban rebels during the Ten Years' War against Spain, 1868–78. She was still flying the American flag when she was intercepted by the Spanish navy in international waters off Jamaica on October 31, 1873. The *Virginius* was taken to Santiago de Cuba, where the four rebel leaders on board were tried and executed. Some of her crew, many of whom were British or American, suffered the same fate shortly afterward. The arrival of a British warship from Jamaica prevented further bloodshed, but the heavy loss of life almost led to war between the United States and Spain.

Viribus Unitis

The AUSTRO-HUNGARIAN NAVY's first dreadnought BAT-TLESHIP, the *Viribus Unitis* was ordered in 1910 in response to Italy's program of naval construction; she and her sister ships comprised the new Viribus Unitis class. Based on the pre-dreadnought Radetzky class, these compact ships had a displacement of just over 20,000 tons and a maximum speed of 20 knots. They were 499 feet 3 inch (152.18 m) in length, had a beam of 89 feet 8 inches (27.34 m) and were each operated by a crew of 1,050. Armament was much improved compared with her predecessor and consisted of 12 12-inch (30-cm) guns mounted in triple turrets in the centerline, producing a weight of broadside of 11,904 pounds (5,400 kg). The *Viribus Unitis*'s armor protection was less satisfactory, with her underwater coverage being particularly poor.

Completed between 1912–15, the *Viribus Unitis*, *Tegett-hoff*, *Prinz Eugen* and *Szent István* formed the first division of the First Battle Squadron of the Austro-Hungarian navy during WORLD WAR I, 1914–18. The *Szent István* was torpedoed by the Italians in June 1918 while serving with a force sent to attack the Otranto barrage. The *Viribus Unitis*, the fleet FLAGSHIP, was sunk by an Italian manned torpedo on November 1, 1918, shortly after it had been handed over to Yugoslavia. The *Tegetthoff* and the *Prinz Eugen* were to survive the war unscathed.

Von Der Tann

The first German BATTLE CRUISER. The *Von Der Tann* was launched in 1909 and demonstrated the superiority of her design over her British counterparts during WORLD WAR I, 1914–18. At the Battle of JUTLAND, May 1916, she sank the *Indefatigable*, a British battle cruiser, after hitting her fore and aft magazines during the opening minutes of the engagement. The *Von Der Tann* herself was hit more than 50 times by British shells but she survived, a tribute to the quality of her design and construction. The armor of the German ship provided much better protection than that of her English equivalent, and her lower superstructure meant that she was a much less easily identifiable target.

The *Von Der Tann*'s armament consisted of eight 11-inch (28-cm) guns in four twin turrets: two on the centerline fore and aft and two in wing positions, with sufficiently wide arcs to provide an eight-gun broadside. She had a displacement of 19,064 tons and a maximum speed of 24.75 knots. The *Von Der Tann* served with the HIGH SEAS FLEET throughout World War I and was interned at SCAPA FLOW after the Armistice. She was scuttled there on June 21, 1919.

Waddell, James I.
1824–86

Confederate naval officer. A graduate of the U.S. Naval Academy, Annapolis, Waddell was born in Pittsboro, North Carolina on July 13, 1824. The only notable feature of his early naval career was a duel with a fellow midshipman that left him with serious injuries and a permanent disability. Early in 1862 Waddell joined the CONFEDERATE NAVY as a lieutenant, but his first two years of service in the AMERICAN CIVIL WAR, 1861–65, were largely uneventful. It was not until September 1864 that Waddell, now a lieutenant commander, was given his chance. He was appointed to the command of the raider C.S.S. *Shenandoah,* a converted transport acquired in England, and given orders to destroy the North's whaling fleet. Eventually he located the fleet in the Bering Sea and captured 32 ships. He destroyed 27 whalers and sent the remainder to San Francisco, much of the action taking place between April and June 1865. Only later did Waddell learn, from a British ship, that the war had officially ended on May 29, 1865; he had destroyed eight Northern ships after that time. Fearing that he might be prosecuted as a war criminal if he returned to the United States, Waddell headed for exile in England, sailing 17,000 miles (27,359 km) without stopping, disguised as a merchant ship. Eventually he returned to the United States and died in Annapolis in 1886.

Wainwright, Richard
1849–1926

American naval officer. Born in Washington, D.C. on December 17, 1849, into a family long established in the military, Wainwright received his appointment into the navy in 1864. He served as executive officer on board the *MAINE* when she blew up in Havana Harbor on February 15, 1898, an event that led to the SPANISH-AMERICAN WAR of 1898. He subsequently directed the preliminary investigation of the wreckage. Commander of the gunboat *Gloucester* in the Battle of SANTIAGO on July 3, 1898, his ship silenced the Spanish destroyer *Furor.* He then participated in the capture of Guánica, Puerto Rico. After serving as Superintendent of the Naval Academy and as aide to the Secretary of the Navy, he commanded a division in the GREAT WHITE FLEET. Wainwright served his last assignment before his retirement in 1911 as aide for operations to the Secretary of the Navy, the highest naval position at that time. A naval reformer and regular writer on naval topics, he died in Washington, D.C. on March 6, 1926.

Damon E. Cummings, *Admiral Richard Wainwright and the United States Fleet,* Washington, D.C., 1962.

Walcheren Expedition
1809

An important example of a combined operation by British land and naval forces during the FRENCH REVOLUTIONARY AND NAPOLEONIC WARS, 1792–1815, that ended in disaster. Its objective was to divert French troops away from the Danube valley following the renewal of hostilities between France and Austria by means of a landing on the Dutch island of Walcheren. Commanded by the second Earl of Chatham, some 40,000 troops left England in 200 transports escorted by a large naval force of 58 warships (including 35 ships of the line) led by Sir Richard STRACHAN. The operation, which began in July, soon ran into difficulties, although the Dutch port of Vlissingen (Flushing) was taken without difficulty on August 16. Chatham failed to open a second front by moving forward to Antwerp before the French had an opportunity to reinforce it. With no sign of an expected rising against the French in the Netherlands and Germany, it was clear that the whole operation was doomed. The British suffered severe losses from a malaria epidemic, and after seven weeks in Vlissingen the expeditionary force withdrew with naval support. The operation had achieved nothing except heavy casualties and the loss of the reputations of those who had led it.

Gordon C. Bond, *The Grand Expedition: The British Invasion of Holland in 1809*, Athens, Ga., 1979.

War of 1812

1812–15

War between Britain and the United States that was fought in part to defend the doctrine of the freedom of the seas. During the FRENCH REVOLUTIONARY AND NAPOLEONIC WARS, 1793–1815, the English and French navies regularly violated the maritime rights of neutral nations. Merchant ships flying the U.S. flag were frequently seized, particularly by the English, who impressed thousands of American seamen into the wartime Royal Navy. (See IMPRESSMENT.) Both sides imposed economic blockades, which severely disrupted trade across the Atlantic and led to the seizure of some 1,500 American merchant ships. The United States responded by imposing its own restrictions on trade with France and England but lifted them with the former when Napoleon agreed to respect the rights of neutral shipping. No such undertaking was forthcoming from Britain, whose relations with the United States also were strained because of friction between the latter and Canada. On June 19, 1812, Congress declared war.

The war opened with an unsuccessful American invasion of Canada, which was followed by the loss of Detroit during a British counteroffensive. The Americans recaptured Detroit in 1813 after Captain Oliver Hazard PERRY's defeat of a British fleet on LAKE ERIE. At sea the war was characterized by individual duels between American and British warships; despite its small size, the U.S. Navy achieved good results in its campaign against enemy merchant ships, deploying its FRIGATES, the main American ship type, to good effect. A notable example was the cruise of U.S.S. *ESSEX* in the Pacific during which it captured or destroyed 40 merchantmen. However, the Royal Navy imposed a BLOCKADE on the eastern ports of the United States that badly affected trade, although many PRIVATEERS successfully evaded it. In 1814, fighting continued along the Canadian border until the war escalated with the

American naval forces defeat the British at the Battle of Lake Erie, 1813, during the War of 1812   *(Copyright © National Maritime Museum, Greenwich, London)*

arrival of more British troops from Europe. Combined British naval and land forces took the offensive on LAKE CHAMPLAIN and in Chesapeake Bay. In the north they eventually retreated to Canada following the decisive Battle of Lake Champlain, September 11, 1814, but farther south the British captured Washington, D.C. and burned the White House. The combined force advanced toward Baltimore, which British troops attacked on September 12–14, while the naval force attacked Fort McHenry. The operation failed, inspiring Francis Scott Key to write "The Star-Spangled Banner." Operations continued in the New Orleans area, but a combined British naval and land force was defeated there early in January 1815, some two weeks after the war had been formally ended by the Treaty of Ghent.

Kate Caffrey, *Twilight's Last Gleaming: British vs. America, 1812–15,* London, 1977.

Warren, Sir John Borlase
1753–1822

*B*ritish admiral whose reputation was based on his activities as a FRIGATE captain during the FRENCH REVOLUTIONARY AND NAPOLEONIC WARS, 1792–1815. In 1794 Warren captured three French frigates; two years later he attacked 220 ships, 37 of which were armed. He played a major role in defeating the French fleet that was planning to land an army in DONEGAL Bay in Ireland in 1798. Following his promotion to vice admiral in 1805, he raised his flag in the *FOUDROYANT,* which he used for his remaining service during the Napoleonic Wars, 1803–15. His final post was as commander in chief in North America, which he took up in 1813. A contemporary assessed Warren as "more an active and a brave man than an officer of any great professional knowledge."

Warrior, H.M.S.

*T*he forerunner of the modern BATTLESHIP, the *Warrior* was the first IRONCLAD to be built for the British navy. She was launched in 1860 in response to the French navy's *LA GLOIRE,* the world's first ironclad, which had appeared a year earlier.

The *Warrior* was the more advanced design: The French ship still had a wooden hull, but her rival was the first CAPITAL SHIP to be constructed of iron throughout. She

H.M.S. *Warrior:* the first British ironclad *(Copyright © National Maritime Museum, Greenwich, London)*

was also much larger, being 380 feet (115.82 m) in length (6.5 times the beam) and having a displacement of 9,000 tons. Other new features included internal subdivisions to prevent her sinking if she were damaged and armor that was an integral part of her construction. The *Warrior*'s protection was, however, limited to 4.5-inch (11.4-cm) plating amidships, with some 80 feet (24.38 m) of hull at each end remaining unprotected.

She had a single gun deck on which were mounted 26 68-pounder (31-kg) muzzle-loaders as well as ten 110-pounder (50-kg) and four 70-pounder (32-kg) breech-loaders. Operated by a crew of 707, she was screw-propelled with a maximum speed of 14 knots. She was, however, a fully rigged sailing ship capable of a similar speed under canvas. Her clipper bows and long black hull contributed to her elegant appearance.

After 30 years' uneventful service, she became part of the former Vernon Torpedo School, Portsmouth, and was renamed the *Vernon III*. Following her removal from the navy list in 1923, she was used as a pier in South Wales, where she was rediscovered in the 1960s. Recognized as a major step in the creation of the modern warship, the *Warrior* has now been restored to her former state and is on permanent public display at Portsmouth.

A. D. Lambert, *The Warrior*, London, 1986.

Warship Design

During the earliest period of the sailing navies, the typical warship would have been a merchant vessel that was hired or requisitioned for war service. These were HIGH-CHARGED SHIPS with substantial fore- and aftercastles that were manned by soldiers who would seek to board an enemy vessel, engage in close combat and then destroy it. The introduction of gunpowder marked the end of the merchant ship as a fighting platform in time of war. For much of the 16th century, guns were positioned on the castles of specially built warships, which now would engage directly with an enemy ship with the aim of destroying her. These warships at first followed the pattern of the medieval high-charged ships—the CARRACK is a major example—but a new, more seaworthy design was required before guns could be carried in quantity and deployed effectively.

The GALLEON, a LOW-CHARGED SHIP that dispensed with high fore- and aftercastles, was first developed in England in 1570 to meet this need. In this design, good performance and safety could be combined with the need to mount broadside guns in rows, together with sufficient space for ammunition magazines belowdecks. The three-masted galleon provided the basis for warship design that was to survive with remarkably little change for nearly 300 years until it was superseded by the IRONCLAD in the mid-19th century. This general trend did not apply in the Mediterranean, where the GALLEY remained the dominant form until the 18th century. Universally adopted elsewhere, the sailing warship varied widely in terms of its displacement and the number of guns carried, although its basic structure was similar. A standard classification, known as rating (see RATING OF SHIPS), was adopted generally, with only the more heavily armed vessels being recognized as SHIPS OF THE LINE.

The sailing warship did not disappear until long after the first steam engine made its appearance. The inherent conservatism of naval thinking was part of the explanation, as was the fact that the propeller was not invented until the 1840s. The paddle wheel was already long established by this time, but its vulnerability to attack meant that it was of limited value for naval purposes. (See PADDLE STEAMERS.) Other mid-19th century developments also pointed to the demise of the wooden sailing warship. The invention of the explosive shell, which had been used to considerable effect at the Battle of SINOPE, 1853, meant that iron would be needed to protect the external surface of warships. The French responded in 1859 with the frigate *LA GLOIRE*, the first IRONCLAD warship; she had a wooden frame and was powered by steam and sail. The parallel development of heavy breech-loading guns mounted in turrets also spelled the end of the traditional sailing warship. (See GUNS AND GUNNERY.)

Iron was to survive for only a few years as a shipbuilding material until its replacement by steel. Rapid changes in naval technology, including the development of the torpedo and the mine, led to the development of several specialist warships. These included the CRUISER and the DESTROYER, which operated in support of the BATTLESHIP, the capital ship of the period. The battleship concept was extended with the appearance, in 1906, of the *DREADNOUGHT*, the first all-big-gun ship. The SUBMARINE dated back to the 18th century—it was first used operationally during the AMERICAN WAR OF INDEPENDENCE, 1775–83—but was not feasible as a modern weapon of war until the diesel engine had been invented in the period before World War I. NAVAL AVIATION, bringing with it the AIRCRAFT CARRIER, also would soon make an impact.

The relative importance of these naval ships has changed during the course of the 20th century, principally because of the increasing impact of the aircraft on the conduct of modern naval warfare. The battleship was obsolete by the end of World War I and had virtually disappeared during World War II, with the aircraft carrier briefly replacing it as the capital ship of the main navies. This was clearly in evidence during the PACIFIC WAR, 1941–45, when American carrier strike forces were to dominate combat and landing operations from 1942.

The carrier has in turn given way to the nuclear submarine as the capital ship of the modern navy. Equipped with ballistic missiles armed with nuclear warheads, it played a key role in the deterrence strategy of the superpowers during the COLD WAR. In the recent past, the distinction between other types of warship has become increasing blurred as shipbuilders deploy advanced technologies to combat the threats from aircraft, missiles and submarines. With the disappearance of the big naval gun, warships have become more compact and more flexible, with heavily overlapping roles. The missile has become the principal weapon of the modern warship. The large warship, which had become increasingly vulnerable, has largely disappeared, although some navies still retain the aircraft carrier. Due to the high cost of the new naval technologies, only the largest navies can afford to equip themselves with the full range of equipment now available.

E. H. H. Archibald, *The Fighting Ship of the Royal Navy, 897–1984*, Poole, 1984; W. H. Garzke and Robert O. Dulin, *United States Battleships in World War II*, London, 1976. *Jane's Fighting Ships*, London, published annually since 1898.

Warspite, H.M.S.

The name of several notable British warships, beginning with the 36-gun ship of 648 tons built during Queen Elizabeth I's reign. Launched in 1596, she participated in several operations against Spain, including the Earl of Essex's expedition to CADIZ during her first year of service. (See Robert DEVEREUX, Earl of Essex.) Another *Warspite*, launched in 1666, served in the Second and Third ANGLO-DUTCH WARS (1665–67; 1672–74).

The most recent *Warspite* was a British nuclear submarine, but the best remembered 20th-century *Warspite* was one of the Queen Elizabeth–class BATTLESHIPS, probably the finest series ever produced. Completed in 1915, this *Warspite* was a super-dreadnought of 27,500 tons equipped with armor up to 13 inches (33 cm) thick. She was armed with eight accurate and powerful 15-inch (38-cm) guns and her oil-burning boilers produced a maximum speed of 23 knots. The *Warspite* had a length of 646 feet 1 inch (196.9 m), a beam of 90 feet 6 inches (27.6 m) and was operated by a crew of 925. Like her sister ships, the *Warspite* served in the Royal Navy in both world wars, having undergone major modifications in the 1930s. During WORLD WAR I, 1914–18, she served with the GRAND FLEET and was present at the Battle of JUTLAND, May 1916, where she sustained 13 hits.

The *Warspite*'s WORLD WAR II, 1939–45, operations were concentrated on the Mediterranean, where she was the fleet flagship and won many battle honors. She sustained serious damage on several occasions, including the SALERNO landings, September 1943, when she was hit by two glider bombs. The *Warspite* took part in bombardment operations in support of the NORMANDY landings in June 1944 even though her repairs had not been completed. Following further bombardment operations along the French coast later in the year, her wartime service came to an end. This *Warspite* ended her days in 1947 when she ran aground near St. Michael's Mount, in Mount's Bay, Cornwall, en route to the scrapyard.

Ross Watton, *The Battleship* Warspite, Annapolis, 1986.

Washington Conference
1921–22

Organized due to an initiative by the United States government, the Washington Conference had the dual aim of reducing international tension in the Far East and Pacific and imposing limits on the production of naval armaments. Designed to avoid another costly naval arms race of the pre–World War I type, this conference took place in Washington, D.C. from November 12, 1921 to February 6, 1922 and involved representatives of Belgium, China, France, Great Britain, Italy, Japan, the Netherlands, Portugal and the United States. The discussions produced seven treaties, of which the following agreements related to naval issues.

The British and Americans agreed not to strengthen the fortifications of their naval bases in an area extending from Singapore to Hawaii. All nine participants agreed that they would not build any new CAPITAL SHIPS—BATTLESHIPS and AIRCRAFT CARRIERS—for a period of ten years. The five major naval powers also agreed that the total tonnage of their capital ships (those of more than 10,000 tons displacement) should not exceed the following limits: United States: 525,000 tons; Great Britain: 525,000 tons; Japan: 315,000 tons; France: 175,000 tons; and Italy: 175,000 tons. It was agreed that existing capital ships exceeding these limits would be scrapped. The conference participants failed to extend these limits to other warships, although they agreed that submarines should follow the same rules of warfare as surface ships. The naval limitation treaty was signed by the five powers on February 6, 1922, but had a limited life. It was not difficult for these powers to work around these provisions if they wished to do so. A key example is the POCKET-BATTLESHIP concept, which was developed by the German navy, although this was a response to the restrictions imposed by the Treaty of Versailles, 1919, rather than the Washington Treaty. Generally, the treaty did not survive the rise of the dictators in Europe or Japan's aspiration to build a powerful navy in the 1930s.

Wasp, U.S.S.

American AIRCRAFT CARRIER that served in both the Atlantic and Pacific during WORLD WAR II, 1939–45. Completed in 1940, she was constructed within the terms of the WASHINGTON Naval Treaty, 1922, which imposed overall limits on American carrier construction. Similar in design to the earlier Yorktown class but built to a smaller scale, the *Wasp* had a displacement of 14,700 tons. She was 741 feet 3 inches (226 m) in length and had a beam of 80 feet 9 inches (25 m). The *Wasp*, which was operated by a crew of 1,800, had a maximum speed of 29.5 knots and could accommodate 84 aircraft. Defensive armament consisted of eight 5-inch (13-cm), 16 1.1-inch (2.6-cm) and 24 0.5-inch antiaircraft guns.

In December 1941 the *Wasp* joined the Atlantic fleet and was involved in transporting much-needed Royal Air Force Spitfires to Malta, which was under the constant threat of air attack. The operation was completed successfully and the *Wasp*'s crew were personally commended by Winston CHURCHILL, the British prime minister. In mid-1942 she was transferred to the Pacific theater and was involved in covering the landings at GUADALCANAL in August. On September 15, while on escort duty south of Guadalcanal, she was torpedoed by the Japanese submarine *I-19*. She was damaged beyond repair and was later sunk by torpedoes from an American destroyer. The name *Wasp* was transferred to an Essex-class carrier, launched on August 17, 1943, which previously had been known as the *Oriskany*. This new *Wasp* also served in the Pacific until she suffered bomb damage in March 1945.

Wassenaer, Jacob Van, Lord of Obdam
1610–65

*D*utch naval commander who was killed in action during the Second ANGLO-DUTCH WAR, 1665–67. Wassenaer had served in the Dutch army during his early career but later transferred to the navy. During the First Anglo-Dutch War, 1652–54, he replaced Admiral Marten TROMP, who had been killed at the Battle of SCHEVENINGEN, 1653, as commander of the Dutch fleet. He was notably successful in the war against Portugal, 1657–61, and during Holland's intervention in the First Northern War, 1655–60, when he defeated a Swedish force at the Battle of the SOUND, October 29, 1658. After a period of inaction he resumed command of the fleet when the Second Anglo-Dutch War broke out. He was killed during the Battle of LOWESTOFT, June 3, 1665, the opening engagement of the war, when his flagship, the *Eendracht*, blew up.

Watson, Charles
1714–57

*B*ritish vice admiral, one of the founders of British India, who rose rapidly in the Royal Navy and, in 1754, became commander in chief in the East Indies. An energetic and able leader, he supported Robert Clive in his operations against the French in India. In 1756, when news of the fall of Calcutta and the imprisonment of British subjects in the "Black Hole"—a small, badly ventilated room in which many died—reached Watson in Ma-

dras, he ignored recent orders to return home to England. Instead he participated in the expedition to recapture Calcutta from the Nawab of Bengal in January 1757.

Joint sea and land operations continued with the seizure of Chandernagore, March 23, and ended in June with Clive's victory at Plassey, where some of Watson's men were involved in the fighting. Throughout the campaign the effective use of naval force was critical; without it, Clive would have been unable to make progress in his land campaign. Watson died of fever soon after Plassey, and a memorial to his services was erected in Westminster Abbey. Despite this tribute, his contribution to the establishment of British control in India has not always been fully acknowledged.

WAVES

*T*he acronym for Women Accepted for Volunteer Emergency Service in the U.S. Navy in WORLD WAR II, 1939–45. By 1942 the navy was facing a severe RECRUITMENT crisis; it was clear that women would need to be enrolled to serve alongside men if the problem was to be resolved. In July 1942 Congress passed the legislation authorizing the recruitment of women in the naval reserve. Women had also been employed in the U.S. navy during WORLD WAR I, 1914–18, but their services had not been required in peacetime, and they had all left the service by 1919. The recruitment of women in the navy in World War II greatly exceeded expectations; by 1945 there were some 78,000 WAVES in the navy, of whom 8,000 were officers. Their work was entirely shore-based and included communications, air traffic control and administration. The employment of women made a significant contribution to U.S. naval strength in World War II, as a substantial number of men were released for service at sea. This contribution was recognized by the enactment in 1948 of the Women's Armed Service Integration Act, which aimed to give women a place in the regular peacetime navy as well as in the reserve. The term WAVES officially disappeared although it was retained as a nickname for female naval personnel. Despite these far-reaching changes, women's career progression in the U.S. Navy has been slow, and it was not until 1972 that a woman reached the rank of rear admiral.

Welles, Gideon
1802–78

*A*merican political leader who served as Secretary of the Navy and was one of the key figures in the Lincoln administration during the AMERICAN CIVIL WAR, 1861–65. Born in Glasonbury, Connecticut in 1802, Welles was a journalist by training. He entered politics as a Jacksonian Democrat and, as a member of the Connecticut state legislature, strongly advocated reforms to voting qualifications based on property and religion. His connection with the navy began when he became chief of the Bureau of Provisions and Clothing, a post he held from 1846 to 1849. Breaking with the Democratic party over the issue of slavery, he helped to organize the new Republican party and was a Connecticut delegate to that party's convention in 1860, when Abraham Lincoln was nominated as the Republican presidential candidate.

From 1861 to 1869 Welles served as Secretary of the Navy, reorganizing in a very short time what had been a small and inefficient department to one that contributed greatly to the Union victory in the war. Maintaining a vigorous eye over his department to prevent corruption and keep political favoritism to a minimum, Welles was instrumental in adopting such technological changes as IRONCLAD ships, heavy ordnance and steam propulsion. After the war he was a strong supporter of President Andrew Johnson's Reconstruction policy. Welles died in 1878.

John Niven, "Gideon Welles," in *American Secretaries of the Navy*, ed. Paolo E. Coletta, Vol. 1, pp. 321–361, Annapolis, 1980.

Wemyss, Rosslyn, Baron Wester Wemyss
1864–1933

British admiral who was First Sea Lord in the final year of WORLD WAR I, 1914–18. In August 1914 Wemyss was a rear admiral in command of the Royal Navy's 12th Cruiser Squadron. The dull routine of escort duties in the Atlantic and the English Channel was succeeded by his appointment, in February 1915, as governor of Lemnos Island, which served as the base for the Gallipoli operations. When Vice Admiral Sir Sackville CARDEN became ill after the failure of the assault on the DARDANELLES, March 1915, Wemyss was appointed second in command to Vice Admiral Sir John de ROBECK, the new commander in chief. He took an active part in the landing operations in April 1915, commanding the First Naval Squadron.

After the Allied evacuation from Gallipoli, Wemyss was appointed commander in chief of the East Indies and Egypt station. Returning to England in mid-1917, he was appointed Deputy Sea Lord, with responsibility for expanding the naval war staff. Upon Earl JELLICOE's dismissal in December 1917 he became First Sea Lord and worked closely with Sir Eric Geddes, the political head of the navy. He was fully involved in the planning of the ZEEBRUGGE raid, April 1918, and helped to deal with the residual U-boat threat. Wemyss represented the interests of the Allied naval powers at the final Armistice negotiations and played a major role in preparing the naval clauses of the Treaty of Versailles, 1919.

Lady Wester Wemyss, *The Life and Letters of Lord Wester Wemyss*, London, 1935.

Wickes, Lambert
c. 1735–77

One of the first American naval officers to serve in the AMERICAN WAR OF INDEPENDENCE, 1775–83. Wickes was born in Kent County, Maryland in about 1735. Entering the merchant service, he threw his hat into the struggle for independence when he refused to carry tea from London in his ships. In April 1776 he was given command of the armed ship *Reprisal*, seeing several victorious actions against British ships and capturing several prizes. Later that year he took Benjamin Franklin to France; hence, the *Reprisal* was the first American warship to receive a salute by a foreign country and Wickes was the first serving American naval officer to visit Europe following the Declaration of Independence. In September 1777, the *Reprisal* foundered in a gale off the Newfoundland Banks and the entire crew, including Lambert Wickes, was lost.

William B. Clark, *Lambert Wickes, Sea Raider and Diplomat; The Story of a Captain of the Revolution*, New Haven, Conn., 1932.

Wilkes, Charles
1798–1877

American naval officer who was a leading explorer as well as the figure at the center of the famous TRENT affair. He was born in New York City in 1798, great-nephew of the celebrated British politician John Wilkes. Entering the navy in 1818, he saw routine duty until on furlough he studied under Ferdinand R. Hassler, founder of the U.S. Coast Survey. Fascinated by exploration and the surveying of uncharted areas, in 1833 he was put in charge of the new Depot of Charts and Instruments. Obtaining his own instruments for survey work, he commanded the brig *Porpoise*, which, besides chasing pirates, surveyed the rivers of the southern U.S. coast.

In 1838 he set out as commander of a six-vessel surveying and exploration expedition, later referred to as the Wilkes Expedition. Ordered to survey areas of the Pacific and to explore the south polar regions, this was the first major expedition of its kind undertaken by the U.S. Navy. Lasting nearly four years and traveling over 80,000 miles (128,748 km), his command charted nearly 300 islands and collected thousands of artifacts. During his Antarctic cruise he aimed to sail as far south as possible. In January 1840 Wilkes's expedition sighted Antarctica only a day before a competing French expedition reached the continent. He moved along the coast for some 1,500 miles (2,400 km), through an area to be designated Wilkes Land, and gave the whole region the name Antarctica. Wilkes spent the next 18 years preparing various narratives and accounts of the expedition.

With the outbreak of the AMERICAN CIVIL WAR, 1861–65, Wilkes was given command of the Federal CRUISER *San*

Jacinto. Cruising the West Indies in search of Confederate raiders, he intercepted the British mail packet *Trent*, removing two Confederate emissaries and sending them to the United States for imprisonment. This clear violation of British neutrality resulted in strong protests by the British government and strained Anglo-American relations. The U.S. was compelled to apologize and release the Confederates. His later commands of the James and Potomac River flotillas and then of the West India Squadron led to further breaches of neutrality laws. Temperamental, outspoken, controversial and often at odds with Secretary of the Navy Gideon WELLES to the point of disobedience, Wilkes was court-martialed and suspended for a year. He died on February 8, 1877 in Washington, D.C.

Daniel MacIntyre Henderson, *The Hidden Coasts: A Biography of Admiral Charles Wilkes*, Westport, Conn., 1971.

William IV
1765–1837

*K*ing of Great Britain from 1830 until his death, the third son of George III. He was known as the "sailor king" although his active sea service was quite limited. William entered the Royal Navy in 1779 with the rank of midshipman and lieutenant and saw service in the United

William IV: "the sailor king"   *(Copyright © National Maritime Museum, Greenwich, London)*

States and the West Indies. In 1786 he was made a post-captain and commanded the frigate *Pegasus* in the Carribean. He soon established a reputation for being a difficult character who did not readily establish good working relations with his colleagues.

Although he did not serve at sea again after 1790, his naval promotions continued and by 1811 he was made admiral of the fleet. In 1827 William was appointed to the revived office of Lord High Admiral in recognition of his position as heir to the throne. There was no expectation that William would play any active part in the day-to-day management of the navy although in practice he did so. In 1828 William assumed command of the Channel Fleet during maneuvers and was accused of promoting his friends. Following protests from senior naval officers, William was persuaded to sever his connections with the Royal Navy.

Wilson, Henry Braid
1861–1954

*O*ne of the American naval leaders of WORLD WAR I, 1914–18. Wilson was born in Camden, New Jersey on February 23, 1861. He entered the service in 1876, in the period before the U.S. Navy embarked upon a program of modernization with the aim of becoming a global naval power. An able administrator as well as commander at sea, he served as officer in charge of the Bureau of Navigation's enlisted personnel section from 1904 to 1908, then as assistant chief of that bureau. Becoming a captain in 1911, he took command of the Atlantic Fleet's flagship *PENNSYLVANIA* in 1916.

With the United States' entry into World War I in April 1917, he was promoted to the rank of rear admiral and commanded the Atlantic Patrol Force, which escorted troop and supply ships and convoys to Europe. Promoted in 1918 to the rank of temporary vice admiral, he commanded all American naval forces on the French coast and then all of U.S. naval forces in France. Following the war, Admiral Wilson was Superintendent of the U.S. Naval Academy at ANNAPOLIS, Maryland, 1921–25, and helped to transform the academy from a training school to a university authorized to award a Bachelor of Science degree. Retiring in 1925, Admiral Wilson died in New York City on January 30, 1954.

William B. Cogar, *Dictionary of Admirals of the U.S. Navy, Vol. 2, 1901–1918*, Annapolis, 1991.

Winslow, John Ancrum
1811–73

*A*merican naval officer. Born in Wilmington, North Carolina, in 1811, Winslow entered the navy in 1827, rising through the ranks. In 1841 he helped fight a fire in the hold of a British Cunard liner in Boston Harbor, receiving from Queen Victoria a decoration for his bravery. In the Mexican-American War, 1846–48, he distinguished himself by gallantly leading a landing party at Tabasco and at Frontera. Although born a southerner, he was a fervent abolitionist and, regarding the AMERICAN CIVIL WAR, 1861–65, as a holy struggle, he served in the Union Navy. Beginning in 1863 he was given command of the KEARSARGE, patrolling the waters of the eastern Atlantic for Confederate cruisers. Finding the C.S.S. ALABAMA under Raphael SEMMES in CHERBOURG harbor, he defeated the Confederate cruiser in a short engagement on June 19, 1864. Subsequently he was promoted to commodore and commanded the Pacific Fleet after the war. He died on September 29, 1873.

John Mellicott, *The Life of John Ancrum Winslow, U.S. Navy*, New York, 1902.

Winter, Jan Willem de
1750–1812

*D*utch admiral and commander in chief during the FRENCH REVOLUTIONARY AND NAPOLEONIC WARS, 1792–1815. Winter reached the rank of lieutenant in the Dutch navy before his career was interrupted by civil war in the Netherlands in 1787. De Winter sought refuge in France and subsequently served in the revolutionary army, which later occupied Holland. Returning home in 1795, he was appointed head of the Dutch navy as a vice admiral shortly afterward. He commanded a fleet destined for the invasion of Ireland at the Battle of CAMPERDOWN, October 1787, off the Dutch coast. The Dutch were decisively defeated by a British naval force commanded by Admiral Adam DUNCAN. De Winter surrendered his flagship, the *Vrijheid*, which had been dismasted, and was briefly held as a prisoner of war in England. His later naval service was interrupted by a period as ambassador in Paris, but eventually he returned to the sea. His final appointment, shortly before his death, was as commander of a naval force assembled at the Texel on Napoleon's orders.

C. C. Lloyd, *St. Vincent and Camperdown*, London, 1963.

Wisconsin, U.S.S.

*T*he fourth American Iowa-class battleship, which had been authorized in 1940, the *Wisconsin* (B.B.64) was commissioned in mid-1944. She was the last battleship to enter the U.S. Navy. The *Wisconsin* saw some action with the Third Fleet in the Pacific in the closing stages of the WORLD WAR II, 1939–45. Along with her sister ships *IOWA*, *MISSOURI* and *NEW JERSEY*, she also served in the KOREAN WAR, 1950–53, before being de-commissioned in 1958. All four ships were modernized and recommissioned during the 1980s. The *Wisconsin* briefly returned to active service during the GULF WAR, 1991, where she was used to shell

The battleship U.S.S. *Wisconsin* firing her main armament during fire support operations in the Gulf War, 1991   (Copyright © *Imperial War Museum, London*)

land-based targets on the Kuwaiti coast and as a CRUISE MISSILE launching platform for strikes against Iraq.

The ships of the Iowa class were the largest American warships ever built, the *Wisconsin* being 887 feet 6 inches (270 m) in length and having a displacement of 58,000 tons. Operated by a crew of 2,788, she was armed with nine 16-inch (41-cm) guns, housed in triple turrets, that could fire a 27,000-pound (12,247-kg) shell over a distance of 23 miles (37 km). She also was equipped with 20 5-inch (13-cm) dual-purpose guns and 64 40-mm antiaircraft guns. The *Wisconsin's* size and high maximum speed of 33 knots had given her a distinct advantage when on carrier escort duty in the Pacific during World War II.

Malcolm Muir, *The Iowa Class Battleships*, Poole, Dorset, 1987.

Witt, Witte Corneliszoon de
1599–1658

*D*utch naval commander who joined the navy in 1620 and rose rapidly in the service. Promoted to the rank of vice admiral in 1637, he replaced Admiral Maarten

TROMP as commander of the Dutch fleet shortly after the beginning of the First ANGLO-DUTCH WAR, 1652–54. During his brief tenure in command he fought the British at the Battle of KENTISH KNOCK, September 28, 1652, but was defeated. Tromp was reinstated soon afterward and de With served under him for the rest of the war. Witte de With played a key role in the Battle of SCHEVENINGEN, July 31, 1653, when Tromp was killed in the early stages of the engagement. In June 1658 the Dutch navy intervened in the First Northern War, 1655–60, in support of the Danes in their fight against Sweden. Admiral de Witt was appointed second in command under Jacob Van WASSENAER. At the Battle of the SOUND, October 29, 1658, his ship was boarded and he was mortally wounded.

Hugh C. B. Rogers, *Generals-at-Sea. Naval Operations During the English Civil War and the Three Anglo-Dutch Wars*, Bromley, Kent, 1992.

Wolf

The former merchant ship *Wachtfels* of 5,890 tons, the *Wolf* was commissioned as a German ARMED MERCHANT CRUISER during WORLD WAR I, 1914–18. Leaving Germany in her new capacity for the first time in November 1916, her primary task was to lay MINES in Allied shipping lanes, the first batch being positioned off Cape Town, South Africa. After her supply of mines had been exhausted she moved through the Pacific searching for Allied merchant ships and sank a total of 12. The *Wolf* also captured a British vessel that was used to mine the Red Sea port of Aden until it was intercepted and scuttled by the ROYAL NAVY. In spite of intensive efforts by British warships, the *Wolf* evaded capture and returned to Germany unscathed in February 1918.

Edwin P. Hoyt, *The Raider Wolf*, London, 1975.

Wolf Pack

Name for a group of U-BOATS operating together against enemy CONVOYS during WORLD WAR II, 1939–45. The concept was developed by Admiral Karl DÖNITZ before the war. As head of the U-boat arm of the Germany navy, he put it into wartime operation. During the Battle of the ATLANTIC, 1939–45, a lone submarine on patrol might make little impact on a large convoy with a powerful escort, but coordinated wolf pack tactics sought to redress the balance.

A group of submarines, perhaps as many as 20 although normally much less, supported by aerial reconnaissance, would patrol the main convoy routes until the enemy ships were found. The submarine that made contact would radio the information back to the operational headquarters in Germany while continuing to shadow the convoy. Other U-boats then would be directed to the area, and a coordinated attack would be made on the enemy escort. Wolf packs usually made surface night attacks at close range. These tactics resulted in mounting losses for Allied merchant ships, and it was not until 1943 that effective counter-measures—including RADAR, improved air support and faster escorts—were introduced. Their introduction rapidly turned the Battle of the Atlantic in the Allies' favor, with the wolf packs facing fewer opportunities to attack and greater losses when they did so.

John Terraine, *Business in Great Waters: The U-boat Wars, 1916–45*, London, 1989.

Worden, John Lorimer
1818–97

American naval officer. Born in Sing Sing, Westchester County, New York on March 12, 1818, Worden entered the navy in 1834. Until the outbreak of the AMERICAN CIVIL WAR in 1861, his career was a routine one, with service on shore at the Naval Observatory and elsewhere being followed by service in one of the overseas squadrons. Just prior to the outset of war, Worden, who was then a lieutenant, was sent with secret, memorized dispatches to the naval squadron reinforcing Fort Pickens, Florida, then besieged by secessionist forces. He was captured while returning, remaining a prisoner of the Confederates until November 1861.

In January 1862 he was given command of the revolutionary MONITOR warship being built in New York; the ship was designed and built in response to the Confederate's IRONCLAD *Virginia* (formerly U.S.S. MERRIMACK). Worden took the unproven craft to HAMPTON ROADS, Virginia, where on March 9 the nature of naval warfare was changed forever by the famous battle that ensued. Temporary blindness caused by an exploding shell forced him to relinquish command late in the engagement. Given a vote of thanks by the Congress, he commanded another monitor in the ironclad attack against Charleston, South Carolina in July 1863, for which he was again given the thanks of Congress. He spent the remainder of the war overseeing the construction of ironclad vessels. From 1869 to 1874 he served as superintendent of the U.S. Naval Academy and was instrumental in the founding of the Naval Institute in 1873. He died in Washington, D.C. on October 18, 1897.

William B. Cogar, *Dictionary of Admirals of the U.S. Navy, Vol. 1, 1862–1900*, Annapolis, 1989.

World War I
1914–18

Although primarily a land war, World War I had an important naval dimension that, at a crucial stage in 1917, would directly affect the final outcome. Naval operations were widely dispersed, with the Baltic, Black Sea, Adriatic and other areas all seeing action. However, the key struggle between the two major naval powers was fought in the North Sea and the Atlantic.

In 1914 the ROYAL NAVY was still the world's most powerful navy, although the gap between it and other powers, particularly Germany, was closing. The arrival of the new DREADNOUGHT battleship in 1906 rendered all existing capital ships obsolete. Germany responded with its own program of battleship construction, making maintenance of its lead much more difficult for Britain. Despite this, the Royal Navy had 29 dreadnoughts compared with Germany's 13 at the war's outbreak. Another 17 British dreadnoughts were under construction against Germany's seven; its superiority in pre-dreadnoughts was even more marked. The Royal Navy's principal battle fleet, the GRAND FLEET, operated a wartime policy of containing the German HIGH SEAS FLEET in the North Sea by means of a distant BLOCKADE. A close blockade of the German coast was ruled out because it would have resulted in unacceptable losses from U-BOATS and MINES.

Each navy had to try to bring the other to action, but the expected decisive fleet action in the North Sea did not materialize: Caution on both sides in the use of their surface forces led to long periods of inactivity. Inconclusive engagements at HELIGOLAND BIGHT, August 1914, and at the DOGGER BANK, January 1915, were followed by the Battle of JUTLAND, May 1916, the only occasion on which the main battle fleets fought each other. Although the Royal Navy was unable to achieve anything more than a draw at Jutland, the Germans realized that the High Seas Fleet would never be able to defeat its stronger opponent. Now they were more unwilling than ever to risk their battle fleet, which remained in port for much of the rest of the war.

The threat posed by the German surface fleet in other parts of the globe had receded much more quickly. Most German cruisers were sunk or captured during the first few months of the war, although some activity continued well into 1915. Admiral Maximilian von SPEE's East Asiatic Squadron represented a more serious threat. This threat materialized at the Battle of CORONEL, November 1914, when a British force under Sir Christopher CRADOCK was decimated. However, von Spee was neutralized shortly afterward at the Battle of the FALKLAND ISLANDS, December 1914, when he suffered severe losses. With Britain quickly dominating the world's seas, German merchant ships were forced to seek refuge in neutral ports, a factor that eventually contributed to severe shortages of supplies of food and raw materials in Germany.

Only in the Mediterranean was there a glimmer of hope for Germany. The British failure to intercept the German warships GOEBEN and Breslau as they moved east through the Mediterranean led directly to Turkey's entry into the war on the side of Germany and thus to a significant increase in the scope of naval and military operations. In response, Britain and France launched a badly planned naval assault on the DARDANELLES, February 1915, as the first stage of a plan to force Turkey out of the war. This assault failed completely, and the British were forced to mount a disastrous amphibious assault on the Gallipoli peninsula.

With its surface fleet tightly constrained from early in the war, Germany rapidly turned to the U-boat for salvation. It was to play a dominant role in German naval strategy from early in 1915, when Germany imposed an economic blockade on Britain, waging a three-year war against Allied merchant ships during the Battle of the ATLANTIC and elsewhere. At the beginning of the war the German navy had only 20 submarines available for service. An urgent construction program was introduced, and the number of operational units reached its peak in October 1917, when 140 boats were in service. The policy of torpedoing Allied merchant ships without warning was suspended more than once in response to American pressure following the sinking of the LUSITANIA, May 1915, and subsequent losses at the hands of the U-boat fleet.

However, despite the risk of direct American intervention, unrestricted U-boat warfare was reintroduced early in 1917. During the first half of the year, Allied shipping losses escalated dramatically and greatly exceeded the rate at which they could be replaced. In total, some six million tons of Allied shipping were sunk in 1917. Only when the British government belatedly agreed to introduce the CONVOY system in mid-1917 and took other countermeasures did the tide turn, averting a real danger that Great Britain would be starved out. The unsuccessful U-boat campaign also roused anti-German feelings in the United States and helped to bring the Americans into the war, thus providing the manpower needed to break the deadlock on land in 1918. The U-boat threat gradually diminished, although it remained sufficiently serious to justify the laying of new minefields on a large scale as well as the British raids on ZEEBRUGGE and Ostend in 1918.

With the U-boat war effectively over, the German navy could contribute little more to the war effort. Although the High Seas Fleet remained intact, it was weakened first by unrest and then, in October 1918, by open mutiny in response to the high command's plans for a final "death ride" into the North Sea, where a last battle with the Grand Fleet would take place. The mutiny marked the demise of the High Seas Fleet as a fighting force. At the end of the war all 160 German submarines in service were transferred to Britain. The Armistice also provided for the surrender of the High Seas Fleet to the Royal Navy on November 21, 1918 and its internment at SCAPA FLOW. There, on June 21, 1919 the entire fleet was scuttled—the final act of the wartime German navy, in protest at the terms of the Treaty of Versailles, which provided for the permanent transfer of the defeated fleet to the Allied powers.

Chronological List of Naval Events

1914

July 28	Austro-Hungarian declaration of war on Serbia; other powers soon become involved
August 4	The German warships *Goeben* and *Breslau* shell two Algerian ports
August 10	The *Goeben* and the *Breslau* escape through the Mediterranean to the Dardanelles and are handed over to Turkey
August 28	Battle of Heligoland Bight
November 1	Battle of Coronel
November 3	First German naval bombardment of the east coast of England
November 9	An Australian light cruiser destroys the German light cruiser EMDEN in the Cocoas Islands
December 8	Battle of the Falkland Islands

1915

January 24	Battle of the Dogger Bank
February	German U-boat campaign begins
February 19	The Anglo-French operation to force a passage through the Dardanelles begins
March 18	The British and French abandon the Dardanelles operation.
April 25	The Gallipoli landings begin
May 7	A U-boat sinks the British liner *Lusitania* without warning
September 18	Germany abandons its U-boat war following American protests over the sinking of the *Lusitania* and the *Arabic*

1916

February 23	Germany resumes unlimited U-boat warfare
May 10	Germany abandons U-boat attacks on merchant ships following further American protests (but later resumes them)
May 31	Battle of Jutland

1917

April 6	The United States enters the war
May 10	Britain belatedly introduces the convoy system in response to the continuing U-boat campaign

| *November 17* | Action off Heligoland Bight |

1918

January 20	The *Goeben* and the *Breslau* venture into the Aegean but the sortie ends in disaster
April 23	British raids on Zeebrugge and Ostend
October 29	Mutiny of the High Seas Fleet
November 11	World War I ends

1919

June 21	The Germans scuttle the High Seas Fleet at Scapa Flow

Paul Halpern, A *Naval History of World War I*, London, 1984; Richard Hough, *The Great War at Sea, 1914–18*, Oxford, 1983.

World War II
1939–45

*T*here are separate entries on the major naval theaters of the war: the Atlantic, the Mediterranean and the Pacific. A complete list of World War II entries may be found in the index. A full chronology for the war follows.

Chronological List of Naval Events

1939

September 1	Germany and the Soviet Union invade Poland
September 3	Britain and France declare war on Germany

The War in the Atlantic and Northern European Waters

1939

September 17	The British AIRCRAFT CARRIER *Courageous* is sunk by a German U-BOAT
October 14	A German U-boat sinks the British battleship ROYAL OAK at SCAPA FLOW
December 13	Battle of the RIVER PLATE

1940

April 9	Germany occupies Denmark and Norway
April 10	First Battle of NARVIK
April 13	Second Battle of NARVIK
April 15	British landings at Narvik and Trondheim
May 28–June 4	British evacuation of troops trapped at DUNKIRK
June 4–10	German fleet attacks the British evacuation fleet off Norway

July	Preparations for Operation Sea Lion, a German landing on the English coast, begin. By September it has been postponed indefinitely
October	German battle cruisers SCHARNHORST and GNEISENAU and heavy cruiser Hipper begin operations against Allied merchant shipping
October 17–20	CONVOY battle in the North Atlantic

1941

February 8–11	Convoy battle off Cape St. Vincent
May 18–27	The British fleet pursues and sinks the German battleship BISMARCK
December 14–23	Convoy battle off Portugal

1942

February 12	The CHANNEL DASH by the battle cruisers Scharnhorst and Gneisenau
July 2–13	CONVOY PQ-17 suffers heavy losses en route to the Soviet Union

1943

March 16–20	Battles of Atlantic Convoys HX229 and SC122, the largest of the war
April	Improved defensive measures for Allied convoys, introduced in the spring of 1943, turn the tide in the Battle of the Atlantic
December 26	Battle of the NORTH CAPE

1944

June 6	Allied landing in NORMANDY
August	German naval units begin to provide support for German ground forces on the Eastern Front

1945

May 8–9	War ends in Europe

The War in the Mediterranean

1940

July 3	Battle of Oran
July 9	Battle of CALABRIA (Punta Stilo)
July 19	Action off Cape Spada
September 23–25	Abortive British action at Dakar
November 11–12	British attack on TARANTO
November 27	Battle of Cape Teulada (Sardinia)

1941

January 10–11	"Excess" convoy leaves Gibraltar for Malta and Greece
February 9	British FORCE H bombards Genoa and Leghorn
March 28	Battle of CAPE MATAPAN
May 31	Evacuation of Crete
November 25	German U-Boat sinks the Barham, the first British battleship to be lost during World War II, off the coast of Cyrenaica
December 12	Action off CAPE BON
December 17	First Battle of SIRTE

1942

March 22	Second Battle of SIRTE
June 12–16	"Harpoon" and "Vigorous" convoys leave Gibraltar and Alexandria for Malta
August 10–15	"Pedestal" convoy travels from Gibraltar to Malta
November 8	Operation Torch—the Allied landings in northwest Africa—begins

1943

July 10	Allied landing on SICILY
September 9	Allied landing at SALERNO

1944

January 22	Allied landing at Anzio
August 15	Allied landing in the south of France

The War in the Pacific

1941

December 7	Japanese attack on PEARL HARBOR
December 10	The British battleship PRINCE OF WALES and the battle cruiser Repulse are sunk off Malaya by the Japanese
December 10–12	First Japanese amphibious landings on Luzon
December 17	Admiral Chester NIMITZ is appointed commander in chief of the U.S. Pacific Fleet

1942

February 1	Two U.S. Task Forces attack the Marshall Islands
February 19	Japanese carrier-based attack on Darwin, Australia
February 27	Battle of the JAVA SEA
February 28	Japanese landing in Bantam Bay, western Java
April 5	Japanese attack on Colombo Harbor, Ceylon

April 18	Aircraft from the carrier U.S.S. *Hornet* make first air attack on TOKYO
May 3–8	Battle of the CORAL SEA
May 5–8	British landings on Madagascar
June 3–7	Battle of MIDWAY
August 7	American landings on GUADALCANAL and Tulasi
August 8–9	Night action off SAVO ISLAND
August 23–25	Battle of the SOLOMON ISLANDS
October 11–12	Night action off CAPE ESPERANCE
October 26–27	Battle of the SANTA CRUZ ISLAND
November 12–13	First night battle off Guadalcanal
November 14–15	Second night battle off Guadalcanal
November 30–December 1	Night action off TASSAFARONGA

1943

March 26	Battle of the KOMANDORSKI ISLANDS
June 30	Landing on Rendova Island
July 5–6	Night action in the KULA GULF
July 12–13	Night action off KOLOMBANGARA
September 3	U.S. landings on Lae and Salamaua begin
November 2	Action in EMPRESS AUGUSTA BAY
November 19	U.S. landings on the Gilbert Islands

1944

January 29	U.S. carriers attack the Marshall Islands as landings begin
January 31	U.S. landing on Kwajalein
February 17–18	U.S. assault on the Japanese base on Truk Island
April 22	U.S. landing at Hollandia
June 15	U.S. landing on Saipan in the Marianas
June 19–20	Battle of the PHILIPPINE SEA
July 21	U.S. landing on Guam
September 21–22	U.S. Task Force 38 attacks Manila Harbor

October 10–16	Battle for Formosa
October 20	U.S. landing on Leyte
October 23–26	Battle of LEYTE GULF

1945

January 9	U.S. landing on Luzon
February 19	U.S. landing on IWO JIMA
April 1	U.S. landing on OKINAWA
April 6	Six-week KAMIKAZE offensive against the U.S. Fleet off Okinawa begins
July 18	U.S. carrier-based attacks on Japan begin
September 2	Pacific War ends

C. Barnett, *Engage the Enemy More Closely: The Royal Navy in the Second World War*, London, 1991; Richard Hough, *The Longest Battle. The War at Sea, 1939–45*, London, 1986; Stephen Howarth, ed., *Men of War. Great Naval Leaders of World War II*, London, 1992; S. E. Morison, *History of United States Naval Operations in World War II*, 15 vols., Boston, 1948–64; John Terraine, *Business in Great Waters: The U-boat Wars, 1916–45*, London, 1989.

WRNS

*T*he acronym of the Women's Royal Naval Service, a branch of the ROYAL NAVY from 1917 to 1990. Members of the WRNS have always been known as Wrens. The WRNS was formed in 1917 in order to help to meet the navy's recruitment needs during WORLD WAR I, 1914–18. Women were recruited to fill a variety of shore-based posts (mainly communications and administration) with the result that men were released for wartime service at sea. By 1918 some 5,000 women were employed in the WRNS. As soon as the wartime emergency was over the WRNS was disbanded; it was not reestablished until shortly before WORLD WAR II, 1939–45, began. Women have been employed in the Royal Navy ever since, although it was not until 1990 that their restriction to shore duties was lifted. Controversy initially surrounded the employment of women at sea, but it has now become an established feature of naval life in Britain. This major change was followed, in 1993, by the abolition of the WRNS as a separate organization and the full integration of women into a single naval service.

X-craft

British MIDGET SUBMARINES of WORLD WAR II, 1939–45. The X-craft first entered service with the Royal Navy in January 1943. They were designed to attack enemy warships in heavily defended anchorages that were beyond the range of land-based aircraft. With a limited range, they were towed close to the target and then proceeded under their own power. Their maximum speed when submerged was 5.5 knots. Operated by a crew of four, the X-craft had a displacement of 27 to 30 tons and a length of 51 feet 3 inches (15.6 m). Armament consisted of 2.2-ton Amatol explosive charges that were released under the target; they were detonated by a timing device. A diving chamber enabled a diver to leave the submarine to attach the devices to the hull of the enemy warship.

By April 1944, 12 X-craft had been built. They were involved in a number of successful operations, including, most notably, the attack on the German battleship TIRPITZ in September 1943 that caused severe damage to her machinery. However, the British paid a high price for this achievement; all six X-craft involved were lost. In another important action two midget submarines immobilized the Japanese cruiser TAKAO in Singapore harbor on July 31, 1945. As a result, she was out of action for the rest of the Pacific war. The surviving British midget submarines were scrapped at the end of the war.

Yalu River, Battle of the
September 17, 1894

A major Chinese setback during the SINO-JAPANESE WAR, 1894–95, that began, on September 16, 1894, with the departure of Admiral Ting Ju-ch'ang from Port Arthur. His squadron, consisting of ten warships, was ordered to escort troopships destined for the mouth of the Yalu River, some 200 miles (322 km) to the east. The Japanese army was making rapid progress in its march through Korea, and these Chinese reinforcements were ordered to try to halt their progress. On their return journey they met a Japanese squadron between the mouth of the Yalu and Haiyang Island. Commanded by Admiral Yuko Ito, the Japanese squadron consisted of four heavy cruisers and six other warships.

The engagement lasted most of the day but the Japanese, aided by their superior quick-firing guns, soon established their supremacy. During fierce fighting the Chinese lost five ships, although their IRONCLAD battleships *Ting Yuen* and *Chen Yuen* survived the battle. Admiral Ting was able to escape from the battle area during the night and return to Port Arthur, depriving Admiral Ito of the opportunity of renewing the engagement on the following day. He was well placed to do so because only one of his ships had sustained serious damage.

Yamamoto, Isoroku
1884–1943

*J*apanese naval commander who planned and directed the attack on PEARL HARBOR, December 1941, during WORLD WAR II, 1939–45. The son of a schoolmaster, Yamamoto was educated at the naval academy, Etajima, 1900–3. He served in a cruiser during the RUSSO-JAPANESE WAR, 1904–5, and was badly injured at the Battle of TSUSHIMA, May 27–28, 1905. Following his recovery, he became a specialist in gunnery. In 1914 he was adopted by the

wealthy Yamamoto family and took its surname. The navy sent him to Harvard University for two years, 1917–19, and soon after his return from the United States he developed a strong interest in NAVAL AVIATION. In 1923 he was appointed to the staff of the Japanese naval air training school and learned to fly. He became a leading advocate of naval airpower.

Following a period as naval attaché in the Japanese embassy in Washington, in 1930 Yamamoto was appointed commander of the First Air Fleet with the rank of rear admiral. Promoted to vice admiral in 1934, he became chief of the aviation department of the Japanese navy in 1935 and was vice minister of the navy, 1936–39. Yamamoto's view that Japan should avoid confronting the United States because of its potentially greater long-term strength and should not enter a formal alliance with the Axis powers won few converts. In 1939 he became commander in chief of the combined fleet, a post he held until his death. Faced with the prospect of war with the United States, he considered how the Japanese might gain an early advantage over their potentially stronger opponent. He planned a preemptive strike on the U.S. Pacific Fleet at PEARL HARBOR, which was launched on December 7, 1941 but was only a partial success.

The American carriers that had escaped destruction because of their absence at the time of the attack soon struck back: In April 1942 they were used to mount the first American air raid on Japan. In the Battle of the CORAL SEA, May 6–8, 1942, two American aircraft carriers led the task force that repulsed a Japanese thrust toward Australia. In response Yamamoto made plans to destroy the remnants of the U.S. Pacific Fleet by bringing it to battle during an operation to seize Midway and the Aleutians. (See ALEUTIANS CAMPAIGN). The outcome of the Battle of MIDWAY, June 4, 1942, was, however, radically different from Japanese intentions: It resulted in the destruction of the major part of Yamamoto's carrier force and marked the beginning of the decline in Japan's fortunes. Subsequent operations focused on the SOLOMON ISLANDS, where a naval

Admiral Isoroku Yamamoto: architect of the Japanese attack on Pearl Harbor, December 1941   *(Copyright © Imperial War Museum, London)*

inch (46-cm) guns—the largest ever mounted in a ship—which had a range of 27 miles (43.45 km) and could fire a broadside of nearly 29,000 pounds (13,154 kg). They were 865 feet (267 m) in length and were operated by a crew of 2,500 men. Both ships entered operational service with the JAPANESE NAVY in 1942, but neither engaged enemy ships during the war. A third member of the Yamato class, the *SHINANO*, was converted as an aircraft carrier while under construction.

Although these heavily armored super-battleships looked invulnerable to enemy attack, both were sunk by American carrier-borne aircraft. The *Yamato* was destroyed during the OKINAWA operations in April 1945 while taking part in a suicide attack without air support. She was hit by over 20 bombs and ten torpedoes. The *Musashi* was lost a few months earlier off Luzon during the Battle of LEYTE GULF in October 1944 when she was struck by an even larger number of aerial missiles. There is no doubt that their loss symbolized the destruction of Japanese naval power.

Russell Spurr, *A Glorious Way to Die: The Kamikaze Mission of the Battleship Yamato, April 1945*, London, 1982.

Yellow Sea, Battle of the

August 10, 1904

A major Japanese naval victory of the RUSSO-JAPANESE WAR, 1904–5. The battle of the Yellow Sea began as the Russian fleet, which had been blockaded at Port Arthur, Manchuria, broke out into the Yellow Sea on August 10. At the beginning of the month the Russians had started to come under shell fire from Japanese ground troops who were advancing through the Liaotang peninsula toward Port Arthur. The Russian fleet consisted of five battleships, four light cruisers and eight destroyers under the command of Admiral Vilgelm Vitgeft, who flew his flag in the *Tsessarevitch*. Its aim was to reach the safety of the Russian base at Vladivostok. Japanese naval forces, under the command of Admiral Heihachiro TOGO, were notified of the Russian departure by RADIO and moved to intercept the enemy fleet.

The two fleets came into contact at 12:30 P.M. During an initial engagement lasting some two hours, the Russians gained the upper hand and continued their withdrawal southeast through the Yellow Sea. Traveling on parallel courses, they made contact again at 5:30 P.M. to the north of the Shantung peninsula. Togo's flagship the *Mikasa* fared badly in the early exchanges, but the Russian flagship *Tsessarevitch* sustained major damage to her steering, which meant that she could not be controlled. At the same time the Russian commander Vitgeft and most of his senior staff were killed. The command passed to Prince Uktomsky, who ordered the fleet to return to Port Arthur. In the chaos that followed some Russian ships did manage to

air offensive was planned early in 1943, but Japanese plans were undermined in part because the Americans were able to read their naval signals. This ability led to Yamamoto's death on April 18, 1943—the signals relating to his movements by air were intercepted. He was shot down over the Solomons by American fighter aircraft based at Guadalcanal. Yamamoto's loss was a severe blow to Japanese morale and damaged the faltering Japanese strategy against the Allies. He had launched a brilliant campaign in the Pacific but was unable to sustain the momentum against the Americans, who exploited fully their interception of Japanese naval codes.

Hiroyuki Agawa, *The Reluctant Admiral: Yamamoto and the Imperial Navy*, New York, 1979.

Yamato

The Japanese warship *Yamato* and her sister ship *Musashi* were the largest BATTLESHIPS ever built, each having a displacement of 65,000 tons (78,200 tons under full load). Their main armament consisted of nine 18.1-

reach Port Arthur, where they were scuttled about six months later. Other Russian survivors escaped to neutral ports where they were interned. On August 14, in a further action—the Battle of Visan—in the Japan Sea, the Japanese clashed with the Russian Vladivostok squadron, which had intended to meet Admiral Vitgeft in the Straits of Korea but was unaware that he had already been defeated and killed. As a result of these battles, the Japanese navy secured command of the sea, and any further Russian naval challenge would require reinforcements from Europe. (See the Battle of TSUSHIMA.)

Yi Sung Sin

d. 1598

Korean admiral who designed and commanded the world's first armored warships. Yi also played a major role in the naval side of the Korean-Japanese War, 1592–98, and repelled two enemy invasions. In July 1592, as commander of Korean naval forces, he led an attack on the Japanese fleet as it crossed the Yellow Sea bringing troop transports in support of its army at Pyongyang. Yi used his fleet to great effect: Heavy enemy losses, including 59 warships and many of the troop transports, resulted. The Japanese fleet was rammed and boarded with archers in support. Yi was aided by the high quality of his fleet, which included two fast, low-decked GALLEYS, produced to his own design, that were partially armored and equipped with artillery. He was not employed at sea for some time afterward, but following a Japanese naval victory over Korea he was recalled to duty quickly. Yi was killed in a final battle with the Japanese at Chinhae Bay in November 1598. Some 200 enemy ships—nearly half the fleet—were lost as a result of this great Korean victory. The Japanese were forced to sue for peace and evacuate Korea.

Yorktown

The name of two American aircraft carriers that served in the Pacific during WORLD WAR II, 1939–45. The first *Yorktown*, which had a displacement of 19,900 tons, was launched in 1936 and completed in 1941. She had an overall length of 809 feet 6 inches (246.73 m) and a beam of 83 feet (25.2 m). Her armament included eight 5-inch (13-cm) antiaircraft guns; several 20-mm guns were added when the United States entered the war. Operated by a crew of 2,200, the *Yorktown* could accommodate 100 aircraft, and her armor protection had been improved compared with her predecessors. Her sister ships were the ENTERPRISE and the *Hornet*, and she gave her name to the entire class.

The *Yorktown* entered service with the U.S. Atlantic fleet but was quickly transferred to the Pacific after the Japanese attack on PEARL HARBOR, December 1941. The flagship of Vice Admiral Frank J. Fletcher, she was damaged at the Battle of the CORAL SEA, May 7–8, 1942, but was repaired in time for the Battle of MIDWAY, June 3–6, 1942. On June 4, 1942 she was attacked by Japanese aircraft who struck her with three bombs and two torpedoes. She survived these attacks but, two days later, before she could be salvaged, she was hit by two more torpedoes and finally sank the following day. The second *Yorktown* was an Essex-class aircraft carrier, completed in 1943, which served in the Pacific for the remainder of the war.

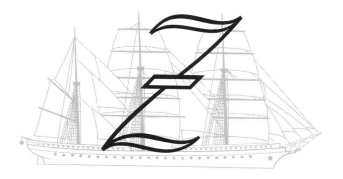

Zeebrugge Raid

April 23, 1918

Although German U-BOAT operations during WORLD WAR I, 1914–18, had been contained by 1918, they still posed a serious threat to Allied shipping, particularly in the English Channel. Many of the German submarines operating in this area were based at the Belgian seaports of Zeebrugge and Ostend. Both were connected by canal to the inland port of Bruges, where further U-boats and destroyers were accommodated. The British Admiralty had often considered the possibility of neutralizing these bases, but action was not authorized until Vice Admiral Sir Roger KEYES, commander of the Dover Patrol, developed a feasible plan for a blocking operation. Some 75 ships, under Keyes' command, took part in the raid, which began in the early hours of April 23, 1918.

A diversionary attack was mounted against the mile-

The British raid on Zeebrugge, 1918   *(Copyright © National Maritime Museum, Greenwich, London)*

411

long Zeebrugge mole, with some 200 marines being landed from the old cruiser *Vindictive*. They were to destroy German gun positions and blow up installations, but they immediately came under heavy German fire and were unable to achieve all of their objectives. The bridge connecting the mole to the shore was destroyed by an old submarine that had been packed with high explosive. At the same time three obsolete cruisers—the *Thetis*, *Intrepid* and *Iphigenia*—which had been filled with concrete, were moved into the inner harbor under heavy German fire. The *Thetis* did not reach the canal entrance and had to be scuttled prematurely after hitting an obstruction. The other two cruisers were sunk at the narrowest point, but they were not positioned correctly and failed to block the channel completely. As a result, U-boats and small destroyers still could use the canal to Bruges. The *Vindictive* and the other ships then withdrew, bringing this imaginative but high-risk operation to a close. There were nearly 200 British dead and a larger number wounded. The operation was noted for its examples of individual heroism, with as many as eight Victoria Crosses being awarded. The operation provided a much-needed boost to British morale even if it was, at best, no more than a partial success.

The raid on Ostend, which was mounted at the same time, was a complete failure, with the two BLOCKSHIPS being unable to reach the harbor entrance. Another attempt to close the canal at Ostend was made on May 9. It was also unsuccessful, with the blockships being grounded in thick fog.

Barrie Pitt, *Zeebrugge*, London, 1958.

Zeven Provincien

A famous Dutch SHIP OF THE LINE, launched at Delftshaven in 1665, named after the seven provinces forming the newly created state of the Netherlands. The *Zeven Provincien* was a swift and graceful three-decker with a displacement of 1,400 tons. She was similar to a GALLEON in basic design although her fore- and aftercastles were much lower than was normal. Some 203 feet (62 m) in length, she had a beam of more than 42 feet (13 m) and was operated by a crew of 743. Apart from the spritsail and the spritsail topsail, she had two square-rigged masts and one lateen-rigged mast. The shrouds of the three masts were fixed to chain-wales outside the ship's sides. The *Zeven Provincien* was armed with 30 42-pounders (19 kg), 30 24-pounders (11 kg) and 20 12-pounders (5.4 kg). Like other Dutch warships of the period, she carried her guns in only two tiers.

The *Zeven Provincien* served as the flagship of the Dutch commander in chief Admiral Michiel de RUYTER during the Second and Third ANGLO-DUTCH WARS and is closely associated with his struggle against the English. The Second Dutch War, 1665–67, was already under way as she entered service with the Dutch Navy. She was damaged during the FOUR DAYS' BATTLE, June 1666, but was shattered and dismasted at the Battle of ORFORDNESS in July. During the Third Dutch War, 1672–74, she operated against the combined fleets of England and France as de Ruyter successfully adopted a defensive strategy. The *Zeven Provincien* fought again during the War of the GRAND ALLIANCE, 1688–97, at the Battles of BARFLEUR and LA HOGUE, 1692, when the Dutch and English combined against the French. Her career finally came to an end in 1694 when she was broken up.

Zuikaku

*T*he AIRCRAFT CARRIER *Zuikaku* and her sister ship *Shokaku* formed the Japanese navy's Fifth Carrier Division, which served in the Pacific during WORLD WAR II, 1939–45. Entering service in 1941, they were the first Japanese carriers to be built without the restrictions previously imposed by international naval treaties. (See WASHINGTON CONFERENCE.) When they were laid down in 1939 they were the largest carriers under construction at that time. At the same time, they were similar in appearance and design to the *SORYU*, a first-generation Japanese carrier.

The *Zuikaku* was fitted with a flight deck that was 794 feet (242 m) in length; it was separate from the hull and was supported by pillars at the bow and stern. She was equipped with two catapults and three lifts. Her two hangar decks could accommodate 72 aircraft, including Mitsubishi Zero fighters. Two funnels to starboard were angled outward so that they were below the level of the flight deck. The *Zuikaku* had a displacement of 25,675 tons, and her four screws produced a fast maximum speed of some 34 knots.

The ships and aircraft of the Fifth Carrier Division played a supporting role during the attack on PEARL HARBOR in 1941 and were involved in subsequent carrier operations in the East Indies and the Indian Ocean. Later transferring to the Third Carrier Division, the *Zuikaku* finally was sunk by American aircraft during the Battle of LEYTE GULF, 1944. The *Shokaku* was also lost in 1944, during the Battle of the PHILIPPINE SEA.

Zumwalt, Elmo Russell, Jr.
1920–

*A*merican naval officer, Chief of Naval Operations during the VIETNAM WAR, 1964–75, and reformer of the U.S navy during the turbulent 1970s. Zumwalt was born on November 29, 1920 in San Francisco, California and graduated from the U.S. Naval Academy in June 1942 as part of the accelerated Class of 1943. Seeing duty at the GUADALCANAL landings in 1942 and in the ALEUTIANS in the spring of 1943, his service in the Pacific theater of

WORLD WAR II, 1939–45, continued with participation in the attacks at Saipan, Tinian, the Surigao Strait night action during the Battle of LEYTE GULF, as well as actions around the Philippines and Indonesia. During the KOREAN WAR, 1950–53, he was navigator of the battleship WIS-CONSIN.

Serving in important staff positions as well as commands at sea, he was promoted to the rank of captain in July 1961 and served on the staff of Paul Nitze, who was Assistant Secretary of Defense for International Affairs and then Secretary of the Navy during the early 1960s. In July 1965, at the age of 44, Zumwalt was promoted to rear admiral, the youngest American naval officer to reach flag rank. From September 1968 to the spring of 1970, he served as commander of U.S. Naval Forces in Vietnam as well as Chief of the Naval Advisory Group, overseeing the transfer of American riverine craft and logistical operations to the forces of South Vietnam. In July 1970, at the age of 49, he was appointed Chief of Naval Operations, the youngest ever to hold the office. As the navy's top officer, he introduced radical reforms in the service to curb racial disharmony and to raise the standards of living for enlisted personnel. Zumwalt retired in July 1974.

Norman Friedman, "Elmo Russell Zumwalt, Jr.", in *The Chiefs of Naval Operations*, ed. Robert W. Love, Jr., Annapolis, 1980.

SYNOPTIC INDEX

ADMINISTRATION AND ORGANIZATION

Admiralty
Agadir Crisis, 1911
Anglo-German Naval Agreement, 1935
Annapolis
Bounty
Brest
Charts and Maps
Cherbourg
Courts-Martial
Deptford
Devonport Dover
Flotilla
Gibraltar
Hague Convention, 1907
Hydrography
Impressment
Intelligence
Invergordon Mutiny, 1931
Kronstadt rebellion, 1921
Lend-Lease Agreement, 1941
L'Orient
Letter of Marque
Mutiny
Newport News, Virginia
Nore Mutiny
Panama Canal
Prize money
Rating of Ships
Recruitment
Scapa Flow
Spanish Main
Spithead
Squadron
United States Naval Academy
Washington Conference, 1921–22

BATTLES

American War of Independence, 1775–83
Cape St. Vincent, 1780
Chesapeake, March 1781
Chesapeake, September 1781
Cuddalore, 1783
Dogger Bank, 1781
Dominica, 1780
Dominica, 1782
Grenada, 1779
Lake Champlain, 1776
Martinique, 1781
Monte Christi, 1780
Negapatam, 1782
Porto Praya, 1781
Providien, 1782
Sadras, 1782
St. Kitts, 1782
St. Lucia, 1778
Trincomalee, 1782
Ushant, 1778
Ushant, 1781

American Civil War, 1861–65
Hampton Roads, 1862
Mobile Bay, 1864
New Orleans, 1862

Anglo-Dutch Wars, 1652–78
Augusta, 1676
Chatham, 1667
Dover, 1652
Dungeness, 1652
Elba, 1652
Four Days' Battle, 1666
Gabbard, 1653
Kentish Knock, 1652
Leghorn, 1653
Lowestoft, 1665
Orfordness, 1666
Plymouth, 1652
Portland, 1653
Porto Farina, 1655
Santa Cruz, 1657
Scheveningen, 1653
Schooneveldt, Battles of, 1673
Solebay, 1672
Texel, 1673

Anglo-Spanish War, 1587–1604
Azores, 1591
Cadiz, 1587
Spanish Armada, 1588

Austrian Succession, War of the, 1740–48
Cape Finisterre, 1747
Cape Finisterre, 1747
Havana, 1748
Negapatam, 1746
Toulon, 1744

Austro-Italian War, 1866
Lissa, 1866

Barbary Pirates, Operations against
Bugia, 1671

China War, Second, 1856–60
Fatshan Creek, 1857

Cold War
Bay of Pigs, 1961
Cuban missile crisis, 1962
Grenada invasion, 1984
Gulf of Sirte incident, 1981
Mayaguez

Crimean War, 1853–56
Sinope, 1853

Cyprus War, 1570–71
Lepanto, 1571

Eighty Years' War, 1568–1648
Downs, 1639

French Revolutionary and Napoleonic Wars, 1792–1815
Algeciras, 1801
Basque Roads, 1809
Belle Island, 1795
Camperdown, 1797
Cape Finisterre, 1805
Cape Ortegal, 1805
Cape St. Vincent, 1797
Copenhagen, First, 1801
Copenhagen, Second, 1807
Donegal, 1798
Glorious First of June, 1794
Gulf of Genoa, 1795
Hyères, 1795
Île de Groix, 1795
Lissa, 1811
Nile, 1798
San Domingo, 1806
Trafalgar, 1805
Walcheren Expedition, 1809

Grand Alliance, War of the, 1689–97
Bantry Bay, 1689
Barfleur, 1692
Beachy Head, 1690
La Hogue, 1692
Londonderry, relief of, 1689

Greek War of Independence, 1821–29
Navarino, 1827

India, Portuguese invasion of
Diu, 1509

Jenkins' Ear, War of, 1739–43
Porto Bello, 1739

Korean War, 1950–53
Inchon, 1950

Pacific, War of the, 1879–84
Iquique, 1879

Quadruple Alliance, War of the, 1718–20
Cape Passaro, 1718

Russo-Japanese War, 1904–5
Chemulpo, 1904
Dogger Bank, 1904
Japan Sea, 1904
Tsushima, 1905
Yellow Sea, 1904

Russo-Swedish War, 1788–90
Öland, 1789
Styrsudden, 1790
Svenskund, 1790
Viborg Bay, 1790

Russo-Turkish War, 1768–74
Tchesme, 1770

Seven Years' War, 1756–63
Cape François, 1757
Cuddalore, 1758
Île d'Aix, 1758
Lagos, 1759
Louisburg, capture of, 1758
Minorca, 1756
Negapatam, 1758
Pondicherry, 1759
Quebec, capture of, 1759
Quiberon Bay, 1759

Sino-Japanese War, 1894–95
Asan, 1894
Yalu River, 1894

Spanish-American War, 1898
Manila Bay, 1898
Santiago, 1898

Spanish Succession, War of the, 1701–14
Cartagena, 1708
Málaga, 1704
Marbella, 1705
Santa Marta, 1702
Vigo Bay, 1702

Swedish-Danish War, 1657–60
Sound, 1658

Swedish-Danish War, 1675–79
Jasmund, 1676
Kjoge Bight, 1677
Öland, 1676

Vietnam War, 1964–75
Tonkin Gulf Incident, 1964

War of 1812
Lake Champlain, 1814
Lake Erie, 1813

World War I, 1914–18
Atlantic, the, 1915–17
Coronel, 1914
Dardanelles, 1915
Dogger Bank, 1915
Falkland Islands, 1914
Heligoland Bight, 1914
Jutland, 1916
Zeebrugge, 1918

World War II, 1939–45
Atlantic and Mediterranean Theaters
Arctic Convoys, 1941–45
Atlantic, 1939–45
Barents Sea, 1942
Bismarck Sea, 1943
Calabria, 1940
Cape Bon, 1941
Cape Esperance, 1942
Cape Matapan, 1941
Cape St. George, 1943
Cape Spartivento, 1940
Channel Dash, 1942
Convoy PQ-17
Dieppe Raid, 1942
Duisburg Convoy, 1941
Dunkirk Evacuation, 1940
Malta Convoys
Mers-el-Kebir, 1940
Narvik, Battles of, 1940
Normandy landings, 1944
North Cape, 1943
River Plate, 1939
St.-Nazaire Raid, 1942
Salerno, 1943
Sicily landings, 1943
Sirte, First, 1941
Sirte, Second, 1942
Taranto, 1940

Pacific Theater
Aleutian Islands campaign, 1942–43
Ceylon, 1942
Coral Sea, 1942

Dutch East Indies campaign, 1942
Eastern Solomons, 1942
Empress Augusta Bay, 1943
Gilbert Islands, 1943
Guadalcanal, 1942
Iwo Jima, 1945
Java Sea, 1942
Kolombangara, 1943
Komandorski Islands, 1943
Kula Gulf, 1943
Leyte Gulf, 1944
Marshall Islands, 1944
Midway, 1942
Okinawa, invasion of, 1945
Pearl Harbor, 1941
Philippine Sea, 1944
Santa Cruz Islands, 1942
Savo Island, 1942
Solomon Islands, Battles of the, 1942–43
Sydney Harbour Raid, 1942
Tassafaronga, 1942
Tokyo raid, 1942
Vella Lavella, 1943
Vella Gulf, 1943

INDIVIDUAL SHIPS

Aircraft Carriers
Akagi
Argus
Ark Royal
Audacity
Eagle
Enterprise
Essex
Formidable
Forrestal
Furious
Graf Zeppelin
Hermes
Hiryu
Hiyo
Hosho
Illustrious
Independence
Indomitable
Kaga
Kiev
Langley
Lexington
Nimitz
Princeton
Ranger
Ryujo
Saratoga
Shinyo
Shoho
Taiho

Taiyo
Unryu
Wasp
Yorktown
Zuikaku

Armed Merchant Cruisers
Atlantis
Carmania
Greif
Jervis Bay
Rawalpindi
Wolf

Battle Cruisers
Alaska
Courageous
Derfflinger
Dunkerque
Gneisenau
Goeben
Hood
Indefatigable
Kongo
Lion
Moltke
Renown
Scharnhorst
Seydlitz
Tiger
Von Der Tann

Battleships
Admiral Graf Spee
Admiral Popov
Admiral Scheer
Agamemnon
Agincourt
Arizona
Arkansas
Bayern
Bismarck
Bouvet
Bretagne
Bulwark
Camperdown
Canopus
Colossus
Courbet
Dante Alighieri
Delaware
Deutschland
Dreadnought
Duilio
Duke of York
Fuso
Gangut
Inflexible
Invincible
Iowa

Tegetthoff, Baron Wilhelm von

Chile
Lynch, Patricio

China
Yi Sung Sin

Denmark
Sivertsen, Kurt
Skram, Peder
Tordenskjold, Peder
Trolle, Herluf

France
Bart, Jean
Boisot, Louis
Bougainville, Comte Louis
    Antoine
Bouvet, François
Brueys D'Aiguilliers, François
    Paul
Casabianca, Louis de
Chateau-Renault, François,
    Marquis de
Choiseul, Étienne
Clue Sabran, Marquis de la
Colbert, Jean-Baptiste
Conflans, Hubert de Brienne,
    Comte de
Darlan, Jean
Duquesne, Abraham
Duguay-Trouin, René
Estaing, Jean-Baptiste, Comte d'
Forbin, Claude de
Ganteaume, Comte Honoré
Grasse, Francois-Joseph,
    Comte de, Marquis de Tilly
Guichen, Luc-Urbain, Comte de
Hamelin, François
Kersaint, Armand, Comte de
La Bourdonnais, Bertrand,
    Comte de
La Galissonnière,
    Roland-Michel, Marquis de la
Suffren de Saint Tropez, Pierre de
Toulouse, Louis, Comte
Tourville, Anne-Hilarion de
    Contentin, Comte de
Villaret de Joyeuse, Louis
Villeneuve, Pierre, Comte de

Germany
Allemand, Zacharie
Arnauld de la Periere
Bachmann, Gustav
Canaris, Wilhelm
Capelle, Eduard von
Dönitz, Karl
Hipper, Franz Ritter von

Holtzendorff, Henning von
Ingenohl, Friedrich von
Kretschmer, Otto
Muller, Georg von
Prien, Gunther
Raeder, Erich
Reuter, Ludwig von
Scheer, Reinhard
Schepke, Joachim
Souchon, Wilhelm
Spee, Maximilian von
Tirpitz, Alfred von
Trotha, Adolf V

Great Britain
Allin, Sir Thomas
Anson, George, Lord
Arbuthnot, Marriot
Ayscue, Sir George
Bacon, Sir Reginald
Balchen, Sir John
Ball, Sir Alexander
Barrow, Sir James
Beatty, David, First Earl
Beaufort, Sir Francis
Belcher, Sir Edward
Benbow, John
Bentham, Sir Samuel
Beresford, Lord Charles
Berry, Sir Edward
Blackwood, Sir Henry
Blake, Robert
Blane, Sir Gilbert
Bligh, William
Borough, William
Boscawen, Edward
Brett, Sir Percy
Broke, Sir Philip
Byng, John
Byng, George, Viscount
    Torrington
Byron, John
Calder, Sir Robert
Carden, Sir Sackville
Carnegie, William, Earl of
    Northesk
Cartaret, Sir George
Cartaret, Philip
Chatfield, Alfred, First Baron
Churchill, Sir Winston
Cochrane, Thomas, Tenth Earl
    of Dundonald
Cockburn, Sir George
Codrington, Sir Edward
Collingwood, Cuthbert, First
    Baron Collingwood
Colomb, Philip
Cook, James
Cornwallis, Sir William
Cowan, Sir Walter

Crace, Sir John
Cradock, Sir Christopher
Crutchley, Sir Victor
Cunningham, Sir John
Cunningham, Andrew,
    Viscount
Dampier, William
Dance, Sir Nathaniel
Davis, John
Deane, Richard
Delavall, Sir Ralph
De Robeck, Sir John
Devereux, Robert, Earl of Essex
Digby, Sir Kenelm
Dilke, Sir Thomas
Douglas, Sir Charles
Drake, Sir Francis
Duckworth, Sir John
Duff, Robert
Duncan, Adam, First Viscount
Elphinstone, George, First
    Viscount
Evans, Edward, Baron
    Mountevans
Fisher, John, Baron Fisher
Forbes, Sir Charles
Fraser, Bruce, First Baron
Fremantle, Sir Thomas
Frobisher, Sir Martin
Gambier, James, Lord
Graves, Thomas
Greig, Samuel
Grenville, Sir Richard
Hall, Sir William
Hallowell, Sir Benjamin
Hardy, Sir Thomas
Harwood, Sir Henry
Hawke, Edward, First Baron
Hawkins, Sir John
Herbert, Arthur, First Earl of
    Torrington
Hervey, Augustus, Third Earl
    of Bristol
Hobart-Hampden, Augustus
    Charles (Hobart Pasha)
Holmes, Sir Robert
Hood, Samuel, Viscount Hood
Hood, Alexander, Viscount
    Bridport
Hopsonn, Sir Thomas
Horton, Sir Max
Hosier, Francis
Hoste, Sir William
Howard, Charles, Second Lord
    Howard of Effingham
Howe, Richard, Earl Howe
Hughes, Sir Edward
Jackson, Sir Henry
James II, Duke of York
Jellicoe, Sir John, First Earl

Jenkins, Robert
Jervis, John, First Earl St
    Vincent
Keats, Sir Richard
Kempenfelt, Richard
Keppel, Augustus, First
    Viscount
Keppel, Sir Henry
Keyes, Roger, First Baron
Knowles, Sir Charles
Lawson, Sir John
Leake, Sir John
Lestock, Richard
Lind, James
Lyons, Edmund, First Baron
Madden, Sir Charles
Mainwaring, Sir Henry
Mansell, Sir Robert
Mathews, Thomas
Middleton, Charles, First Lord
    Barham
Milne, Sir Archibald Berkeley
Monck, George, First Duke of
    Albemarle
Monson, Sir William
Montagu, Edward, First Earl of
    Sandwich
Montagu, John, Fourth Earl of
    Sandwich
Morgan, Sir Henry
Mountbatten, Louis, Prince
    Louis of Battenberg
Mountbatten, Louis, Earl
    Mountbatten of Burma
Myngs, Sir Christopher
Napier, Sir Charles
Narborough, Sir John
Nelson, Horatio, First Viscount
Noble, Sir Percy
Norris, Sir John
Orde, Sir John
Pakenham, Sir Thomas
Parker, Sir Hyde
Parker, Sir Peter
Parker, Richard
Parsons, Sir Charles
Pasco, John
Pellew, Sir Edward, Viscount
    Exmouth
Penn, Sir William
Pepys, Samuel
Pett, Peter
Phillip, Arthur
Phillips, Sir Tom
Popham, Sir Home Riggs
Pound, Sir Dudley
Price, David
Raleigh, Sir Walter
Ramsay, Sir Bertram Home
Rodney, George, First Baron

Rooke, Sir George
Rupert, Prince Palatine
Russell, Edward, Earl of Oxford
Saumarez, James, Lord de
Saunders, Sir Charles
Scott, Robert Falcon
Scott, Sir Percy
Shovell, Sir Clowdisley
Smith, Sir William Sydney
Somerville, Sir James
Spragge, Sir Edward
Strachan, Sir Richard
Sturdee, Sir Frederick
Sueter, Sir Murray
Thornycroft, Sir John
Tovey, John, First Baron
Troubridge, Sir Thomas
Troubridge, Sir Ernest
Tryon, Sir George
Tyrwhitt, Sir Reginald
Vernon, Edward
Vian, Sir Philip
Warren, Sir John
Watson, Charles
Wemyss, Rosslyn, First Baron
   Wester-Wemyss
William IV

Greece
Barbarossa
Kanaris, Constantine
Miaoulis, Andreas

Italy
Brin, Benedetto
Caracciolo, Prince Francesco
Doria, Andrea
Mocenigo, Pietro
Morosini, Francisco
Thaon di Revel, Paolo

Japan
Abe, Hiroaki
Arima, Masafumi
Fuchida, Mitsuo
Ito, Sejichi
Iwabuchi, Sanji
Koga, Mineichi
Kondo, Nobutake
Kurita, Takeo
Kusaka, Ryunosuke
Nagano, Osami
Nagumo, Chuichi
Onishi, Takijiro
Ozawa, Jisiburo
Takagi, Takeo
Tanaka, Raizo
Togo, Heihachiro
Toyoda, Soemu
Ugaki, Matome

Yamamoto, Isoroku

The Netherlands
Evertsen, Cornelis
Evertsen, Jan
Heemskerk, Jacob van
Heijn, Piet
Ruyter, Michiel Adriaanszoon de
Tromp, Cornelis Maartenszoon
Tromp, Maarten Harpertszoon
Wassenaer, Jacob van
Winter, Jan Willem de
Witt, Witte Corneliszoon de

Portugal
Albuquerque, Alfonso d'

Russia
Apraksin, Fyodor
Essen, Nikolai von
Gorshkov, Sergei
Kolchak, Aleksandr
Kuznetsov, Nikolai
Makarov, Stepan
Nakhimov, Paul
Peter the Great
Potemkin, Grigori, Prince
Rozhestvensky, Zinovi

Sweden
Charles XIII

Spain
Bazan, Alvaro de, Marquis of
   Santa Cruz
Cervera, Pascual
Juan of Austria, Don
Medina Sidonia, Don Alonso,
   Seventh Duke of
Menéndez de Avilés, Pedro

United States
Arnold, Benedict
Bainbridge, William
Bancroft, George
Barney, Joshua
Barron, James
Barry, John
Benson, William
Biddle, James
Biddle, Nicholas
Buchanan, Franklin
Burke, Arleigh
Bushnell, David
Byrd, Richard Evelyn, Jr.
Callaghan, Daniel
Chauncey, Isaac
Conyngham, Gustavus
Coontz, Robert E.

Cushing, William Barker
Dahlgren, John A.
Dale, Richard
Daniels, Josephus
Davis, Charles H.
Davis, Charles H., Jr.
Decatur, Stephen
Dewey, George
Du Pont, Samuel
Ericsson, John
Evans, Robley D.
Farragut, David
Fegen, Edward
Fiske, Bradley Allen
Fitch, Aubrey
Fletcher, Frank Friday
Fletcher, Frank Jack
Foote, Andrew Hull
Forrestal, James
Fox, Gustavus Vasa
Fulton, Robert
Ghormley, Robert Lee
Goodrich, Caspar F.
Halsey, William F., Jr.
Hart, Thomas C.
Hewitt, Henry
Hobson, Richmond P.
Holland, John P.
Hopkins, Esek
Hull, Isaac
Humphreys, Joshua
Ingersoll, Royal
Isherwood, Benjamin
Jones, Catesby ap Roger
Jones, John Paul
Joy, Charles Turner
Kimmel, Husband
King, Ernest
Kinkaid, Thomas
Kirk, Alan
Lawrence, James
Leahy, William
Lockwood, Charles
Luce, Stephen
McCalla, Bowman
MacDonough, Thomas
Mahan, Alfred
Maury, Matthew
Mayo, Henry
Melville, George
Mitscher, Mark
Moffett, William A.
Moorer, Thomas H.
Moreell, Ben
Nimitz, Chester
O'Kane, Richard H.
Peary, Robert
Perry, Matthew
Perry, Oliver
Porter, David

Porter, David Dixon
Pratt, William V.
Preble, Edward
Radford, Arthur W.
Reeves, Joseph M.
Rickover, Hyman
Riou, Edward
Rodgers, John, Jr.
Rodgers, John
Roosevelt, Franklin
Roosevelt, Theodore
Sampson, William
Schley, Winfield
Semmes, Raphael
Shepard, Alan
Sherman, Forrest
Shufeldt, Robert W.
Sigsbee, Charles D.
Sims, William
Sloat, John D.
Smalls, Robert
Sprauce, Raymond
Stark, Harold
Stewart, Charles
Stockton, Robert F.
Stoddert, Benjamin
Taylor, David W.
Taylor, Henry C.
Towers, John H.
Tracy, Benjamin
Truxton, Thomas
Turner, Richmond Kelly
Turner, Stansfield
Waddell, James I.
Wainwright, Richard
Welles, Gideon
Wickes, Lambert
Wilkes, Charles
Wilson, Henry
Winslow, John
Worden, John
Zumwalt, Elmo R., Jr.

NAVAL FORCES

Austro-Hungarian Navy
Buccaneers
Carrier Air Group
Confederate Navy
Corsair
Dutch Navy
Fleet Air Arm
Flotilla
Force Z
Force H
French Navy
German Navy
Grand Fleet
Great White Fleet
High Seas Fleet

Italian Navy
Japanese Navy
Marines
Privateer
Royal Naval Air Service
Royal Navy
Russian Navy
Sea Beggars
SEAL
Soviet Navy
Spanish Navy
Special Boat Squadron
Swedish Navy
United States Coast Guard
United States Navy
WAVES
WRNS

WARFARE

Amphibious Warfare
Antisubmarine warfare
Blockade
Broadside
Commerce Raiding
Convoy
Crossing the *T*
Fighting Instructions
Gunboat diplomacy
Mulberry Harbour
Naval aviation
Naval warfare
Piracy
Signaling
Wolf Pack

WARS AND OPERATIONS

American Civil War, 1861–65
American War of
    Independence, 1775–83
Anglo-Dutch Wars, 1652–54;
    1665–67; 1672–74
Austrian Succession, War of
    the, 1740–48
Cold War, 1972–73
Cold War, Naval aspects
Crimean War, 1853–56
Exploration and Discovery

Falklands War, 1982
French Revolutionary and
    Napoleonic Wars, 1792–1815
Grand Alliance, War of the,
    1689–97
Grenada invasion, 1983
Gulf War, 1990–1
Iran-Iraq War, 1980–88
Japan-Korea War, 1592–93
Jenkins' Ear, War of, 1739–43
Korean War, 1950–53
Opium Wars
Quasi-War, 1798–1800
Russo-Japanese War, 1904–5
Russo-Swedish War, 1788–90
Seven Years' War, 1756–63
Sino-Japanese War, 1894–95
Spanish-American War, 1898
Spanish Armada, 1588
Spanish Succession, War of
    the, 1701–14
Suez Crisis, 1956
Vietnam War, 1964–75
War of 1812
World War I, 1914–18
World War II, 1939–45

WARSHIP TYPES

Advice boat
Aircraft carrier
Amphibious vehicles
Armed merchant cruiser
Baltimore clipper
Battle cruiser
Battleship
Bireme
Blockship
Bomb vessel
Brig
Brigantine
Camship
Capital ship
Carrack
Catamaran
Chariot
Chasse-marée
Coastal motor boat
Cog

Corvette
Cruiser
Cutter
Defensively equipped merchant
    ships (DEMS)
Destroyer
East Indiaman
Fireship
Flagship
Fluyt
Frigate
Galeasse
Galeote
Galiot
Galleon
Galley
Guardship
Gundelow
High-charged ship
Hovercraft
Hulk
Hydrofoil
Ironclad
Kaiten
Ketch
Landing craft
Launch
Liberty ship
Low-charged ship
Macship
Midget submarine
Minelayer
Minesweeper
Monitor
Motor gunboat
Nef
Paddle steamer
Pinnace
Pocket-battleship
PT boat
Q-Ship
Ram
Razée
Round ship
Schnellboote
Shinyo
Ship of the line
Sloop
Submarine
Tinclad

Torpedo boat
Troopship
Urca
Warship design
X-Craft

WEAPONS AND
EQUIPMENT

Antiaircraft guns
Armor
ASDIC
Barbette
Camouflage
Cannon
Carcass
Carronade
Chain-shot
Cruise missile
Culverin
Cutlass
Dahlgren gun
Depth Charge
Director fire control system
Exocet missile
Floating battery
Guided missiles
Guns and gunnery
Hedgehog
Helicopter
Kamikaze
Long Lance torpedo
Mines
Murderer
Perier
Polaris
Poseidon
Radar
Radio
Robinet
Rocket
Sonar
Spar torpedo
Squid
Submarine-launched ballistic
    missile
Torpedo
Trident

INDEX

Page numbers in **boldface** indicate article titles. Those in *italics* indicate illustrations.

American officers 254, 380, 412–13
blockades 46, 390
hovercraft use 182
marines 238
mine use 390
patrol boat use 255
PT boat service 295
SEALs 331
Tonkin Gulf incident 369, 390
Vigo, Battle of (1805) 59
Vigo Bay, Battle of (1702) 75, 180–81, 311, 348, **390**
Villaret de Joyeuse, Louis Thomas 40, 143, 156, 187, **390–91**
Ville de Paris 161, 321
Villeneuve, Pierre Jean Pierre Baptiste Silvestre, Comte de 59, 64, 67, 144, 266, 269, 275, 373–74, **391**
Vincennes, U.S.S. 324, 351
Vindictive **391**, 412
Virginia see Merrimack
Virginius **391–92**
Viribus Unitis **392**
Vitgeft, Vilgelm 409, 410
Vittorio Veneto 64, 67, 229
Vixen 170
Vizcaya 323
Voltaire 56
Von Der Tann 35, 188, **392**
Voyage of the Beagle, The (Darwin) 38
Vrijheid 60, 401
VTOL *see* vertical takeoff and landing aircraft

W

Wachtfels see Wolf
Wachusett 242
Waddell, James I. **393**
Wager 57
Wagner, Charles 71
Wahoo 273
Wainwright, Richard **393**
Wake Island Relief Expedition (1941) 135
Walcheren expedition (1809) 143, 145, 352, **393–94**
Walker, F.W. 387
Wallis, Samuel 72, 111
Walpole, Robert 201
Walton, William 365
war, rules of conduct 167
warfare tactics *see* tactical warfare
War of 1812 (1812–15) 383, **394–95**
  battles
    Chesapeake engagement 53, 76, 221, 334
    Lake Champlain 219, 234, 395
    Lake Erie 220, 221, 284, 394, *394*
    blockades 394
    British impressments 188, 394
    commanding officers
      American 30, 33, 42, 75–76, 221,

234, 284, 289, 309, 351
    British 53
  frigates 145, 394
  guns and gunnery 71
  letters of marque 224
  privateering 33, 394
  ships 125, 127, 292, 303, 334
  Treaty of Ghent 395
  Washington, D.C., capture 79, 395
War of Independence *see* American War of Independence
War of Jenkins' Ear *see* Jenkins' Ear, War of
Warren, Sir John Borlase 112, 187, **395**
Warrior, H.M.S. (*Vernon III*) 22, 36, 156, 193, 339, 378, **395–96**
warship design **396–97**
  aircraft carrier 5, 136, 139, 396
  armor protection 22, 263, 306
  battle cruiser 227, 263
  battleship 35–36, 215, 396
  bireme 43, 150
  broadside ships 239
  bulge 1, 305, 306
  carrack 173–74, 396
  castle 80
  catamaran adaptations 72
  clinker-built boats 97
  coastal motor boats 78–79
  corvette 90
  dreadnought 115, 152, 263
  Ericsson's contributions 126, 252, 293
  Fiske's inventions 135
  frigate 145
  galeasse 148–49
  galleon 149, 263, 314, 396
  galley 150, 263, 396
  gunport 71, 263
  high-charged ships 70, 176, 238, 263, 396
  hovercraft 182
  hydrofoil 185
  ironclads 395–96
  low-charged ships 71, 231, 396
  nef 265
  paddle-wheel propulsion 8, 278, 282, 396
  Parsons's steam turbine 280, 293
  pocket-battleship 287, 397
  Princeton's machinery placement 293
  PT boats 294
  razée modifications 304
  round ships 265, 312
  screw propulsion 8, 79, 126, 243, 278, 293, 304
  shinyo boats 335
  snorkel tubes 354
  steam propulsion 8, 72, 79, 104, 107, 243, 278

Taylor's (David) contributions 364
Thornycroft's influence 366
urca 384
Washington Conference impact 5, 397
water tube boilers 62
see also submarine
warships *see* sailing ships; nuclear warships; submarine; warship design; *specific ships and types of warships*
Warspite, H.M.S. 58, 64, 94, 96, 261, 298, 321, **397**
Washington 20, 163, 272
Washington, George 12, 76, 219, 297
Washington Conference (1921–22) 5, **397**
Washington, D.C., capture (1814) 79, 395
Washington Naval Treaty (1922) 36, 90, 104, 198
Wasp, U.S.S. 123, 136, 335, **397–98**
Wassenaer, Jacob Van, Lord of Obdam 232, 343, **398**, 402
water tube boiler 62
Watson, Charles **398**
Watt, James 293
Wavell, Archibald 121
WAVES **398**
weapons and artillery
  armor protection 22, 263, 306
  atomic bomb 81, 208, 278
  bar-shot 73
  broadside 53
  carcass 69
  case-shot 73
  chain-shot 73
  Cold War buildup 81, 357, 384
  cutlass 97
  depth charge 104–5, 106
  explosive shell 263, 396
  fireship 133–34
  floating battery 137, 184
  grape-shot 73
  Hedgehog 105, 172, 342, 350–51
  mines 146, 247
  rams 150, 229, 263, 288, 302–3
  rockets 18, 308–9
  squids 18, 105, 342, 350–51
  see also guns and gunnery; missile; torpedo
weather line 141, 365
Weehawken 309
Weihaiwei, Battle of (1895) 339
Welles, Gideon 97, 141, **398–99**, 400
Wellesley, Arthur (Duke of Welllington) 88
Wellington, Duke of *see* Wellesley, Arthur
Wemyss, Rosslyn, Baron Wester Wemyss **399**

West, Benajmin 146
Westfalen 261
West Virginia 281
Whitehead, Robert 227, 349, 370
Whitworth, W. 261
whole cannon 62
Wickes, Lambert **399**
Wilhelm II, Emperor of Germany 234, 256
Wilhelm Heidkamp 261
Wilkes, Charles 374–75, **399–400**
Wilkes, John 399
Wilkes Expedition 399
Willaumez, Jean-Baptiste 34
William IV, King of England 400
William of Orange 31, 47, 56, 128, 160, 174, 314, 316, 376
William the Silent 331
Wilson, Henry Braid **400**
Wilson, Woodrow 24, 99, 136, 241
Windsor 323
Winslow, John Ancrum 400–1
Winter, Jan Willem de 60, 118, **401**
Wisconsin, U.S.S. 165, 191, 249, 267, **401**, 413
Witt, Witte Corneliszoon de 75, 118, 148, 209, 319, 328, 343, 377, **401–2**
Wolf 22, **402**
Wolfe, James 49, 297, 324, 333
Wolfe, Tom 334
wolf pack (U-boat formation) 24, 85, 113, 354, **402**
Wolseley, Garnet 42, 159
Wolverine 292
Women Accepted for Volunteer Emergency Service *see* WAVES
Women's Armed Service Integration Act of 1948 (U.S.) 398
Women's Royal Naval Service *see* WRNS
Woodward, John 131
Worden, John Lorimer **402**
World War I (1914–18) **402–4**
  amphibious operations 15, 198
  armed merchant cruisers 21–22, 70, 84, 161–62, 250–51, 402
  aviation role 262, 263, 313–14, 372, 380
  battle cruisers 35
  battles
    Atlantic 24, 83, 105, 231, 263, 384, 403
    Coronel 60, 89, 92, 93, 116, 131, 325–26, 349, 403, 404
    Dardanelles 36, 51, 62, 69, 100–101, 106, 134, 143, 189,

230, 236, 298, 313, 358, 360, 403, 404
    Dogger Bank 35, 39, 47, 75, 93, 106, 110–11, 152, 176, 189, 227, 251, 306, 333, 367, 380, 403, 404
    Falkland Islands 2, 35, 60, 62, 89, 93, 116, 131, 134, 189, 306, 325–26, 349, 352, 403, 404
    Gallipoli 15, 69, 78, *100*, 101, 106, 399, 403, 404
    Heligoland Bight 35, 39, 75, 93, 173, 181, 210, 227, 306, 380, 403, 404
    Jutland 4, 24, 35, 36, 39, 41, 75, 82, 93, 106, 107, 111, 152, 160, 169, 176, 177, 188, 190, 191, 193, 200, 204–5, 212, 215, 227, 251, 261, 276, 291, 298, 306, 315, 327–28, 333, 359, 367, 372, 377, 392, 397, 403, 404
    Zeebrugge raid 15, 29, 46–47, 210, 238, 391, 399, 403, 404, 411–12
  blockades 24, 39, 46, 152, 160, 170, 176, 200, 315, 403
  blockship use 46–47, 391, 412
  camouflage development 59
  commerce-raiding activities 22, 83, 250–51, 332
  convoys 24, 85, 152, 201, 263, 315, 338, 354, 403, 404
  Lusitania sinking 24, 232, 233, 403, 404
  marine units 238
  mine use 247, 263, 402
  submarines 1, 22, 24, 29, 83, 84, 105, 170, 181, 216, 257, 354–57, 370, 403, 404, 411–12
  tactical warfare changes 263
  Treaty of Versailles 17, 41, 153, 287, 397, 399, 403–4
  women in naval forces 398, 406
  see also Grand Fleet; High Seas Fleet; *participating nations*
World War II (1939–45) **404–6**
  aircraft carriers 5, 25, 60, 188–89, 224, 234–35, 263, 396
  amphibious operations 14–15
    Dieppe raid 15, 108–9, 238, 256, 303